MW00460683

# BONE HISTOLOGY

## An
## Anthropological Perspective

# BONE HISTOLOGY

## An
## Anthropological Perspective

*Edited by*

## Christian Crowder and Sam Stout

**CRC Press**
Taylor & Francis Group
Boca Raton   London   New York

CRC Press is an imprint of the
Taylor & Francis Group, an **informa** business

CRC Press
Taylor & Francis Group
6000 Broken Sound Parkway NW, Suite 300
Boca Raton, FL 33487-2742

© 2012 by Taylor & Francis Group, LLC
CRC Press is an imprint of Taylor & Francis Group, an Informa business

No claim to original U.S. Government works

Printed in the United States of America on acid-free paper
Version Date: 20110708

International Standard Book Number: 978-1-4398-6691-7 (Hardback)

This book contains information obtained from authentic and highly regarded sources. Reasonable efforts have been made to publish reliable data and information, but the author and publisher cannot assume responsibility for the validity of all materials or the consequences of their use. The authors and publishers have attempted to trace the copyright holders of all material reproduced in this publication and apologize to copyright holders if permission to publish in this form has not been obtained. If any copyright material has not been acknowledged please write and let us know so we may rectify in any future reprint.

Except as permitted under U.S. Copyright Law, no part of this book may be reprinted, reproduced, transmitted, or utilized in any form by any electronic, mechanical, or other means, now known or hereafter invented, including photocopying, microfilming, and recording, or in any information storage or retrieval system, without written permission from the publishers.

For permission to photocopy or use material electronically from this work, please access www.copyright.com (http://www.copyright.com/) or contact the Copyright Clearance Center, Inc. (CCC), 222 Rosewood Drive, Danvers, MA 01923, 978-750-8400. CCC is a not-for-profit organization that provides licenses and registration for a variety of users. For organizations that have been granted a photocopy license by the CCC, a separate system of payment has been arranged.

**Trademark Notice:** Product or corporate names may be trademarks or registered trademarks, and are used only for identification and explanation without intent to infringe.

**Visit the Taylor & Francis Web site at**
**http://www.taylorandfrancis.com**

**and the CRC Press Web site at**
**http://www.crcpress.com**

# Table of Contents

# Preface

*Bone Histology: An Anthropological Perspective* is a comprehensive look into the histological examination of hard tissues (bones and teeth). Because of their nature as hard tissues of the body, bones and teeth are of considerable importance for anthropological research. With the exception of forensic anthropology and the relatively rare cases of mummification, the physical remains of humans available to bioarchaeologists, paleopathologists, and paleontologists are limited to skeletal material. Fortunately, the same characteristics of hard tissues that lead to their persistence after death make them a storehouse of information about biological processes experienced during the life of the individual. Unlike for the soft tissues of the body, the activity of cells involved in growth and development, tissue maintenance, and adaptation of hard tissues are encoded in their microstructure. Our ability to extract biologically important information from hard tissues has greatly improved with the understanding of bone provided over the last 5 decades by the work of researchers such as Amprino, Currey, Enlow, Frost, Johnson, and Marotti, and for teeth the work of Dean, Reid, Boyde, Beynon, Bromage, and Shellis. We now understand that although bone serves an important metabolic function relating to mineral homeostasis, its primary function is biomechanical. This edited volume arose from discussions by the editors and colleagues over the years and encouragement gained during a Forensic Histology Workshop organized by the Department of Medical Education of the Armed Forces Institute of Pathology in July 2009. Through discussions at this workshop the authors fully appreciated the need for a comprehensive volume covering theoretical and applied aspects in histological analysis of skeletal tissue.

## Organization and Content

The first four chapters cover important aspects of the basic biology of hard tissues. Sam Stout and Christian Crowder provide an overview of bone remodeling and its importance for the interpretation of bone histomorphology. They discuss how bone microstructures should be considered in terms of how they relate to the bone remodeling process. In cortical bone, for example, the histomorphological features known as osteons or Haversian systems are products of the coordinated activity of bone resorbing and forming cells comprising basic multicellular units of bone remodeling. They focus attention on the relationship between histomorphology and the bone remodeling process, and emphasize that it is this relationship that underlies our ability to estimate age and infer bone remodeling activity from histomorphometry.

In Chapter 2, James Gosman explores our understanding of the biology underlying skeletal growth and development leading to adult skeletal morphology. His chapter presents an overview of the current knowledge of the fundamental process of longitudinal bone growth as it relates to histomorphology, regulatory systems, and ontogenetic changes in cortical and trabecular bone architecture. The chapter goes further by situating these concepts within a broader biocultural context, and discusses potential environmental and mechanobiological influences on skeletal growth and development that are especially important for skeletal biology in general, and physical and forensic anthropology in particular. The chapter underscores that the study of skeletal developmental variation from the anthropological and forensic perspective must adopt an integrative stance, which considers the broader scope of interrelated components that contribute to normal and abnormal skeletal growth and morphology.

Related, but distinct in a number of ways, to bone remodeling is the bone modeling process. Chapter 3 by Corey Maggiano defines bone modeling, distinguishes it from remodeling, and discusses the function of modeling in growth and mechanical adaptation from a microstructural perspective. This well-illustrated and innovative chapter concludes with a discussion of current methods employed to investigate how bones change in morphology, and envisions possible future directions.

Like bone, teeth are hard tissues of the body. As such they also preserve a record of their growth in their histological structures and are a valuable resource for skeletal analyses. In Chapter 4, Debbie Guatelli-Steinberg and Michaela Huffman discuss histological features of dental hard tissues and their utility in biological anthropology. Dental hard tissues preserve a record of their own growth in their histological structures, including enamel and dentine, in which incremental growth is reflected in growth lines, and long-period lines of demonstrated periodicity, and cementum, in which incremental growth produces alternating layers, and provide a basis for estimating chronological age at death. Since disruptions to growth leave their mark in dental hard tissues, they also can provide a record of birth and of physiological stress occurring in childhood, making it possible to identify physiologically stressful events experienced during the early years of life.

For those challenged with extremely fragmented remains, the question of whether the bone is of human origin is often critical. In many cases the extent of fragmentation precludes the use of macroscopic methods to differentiate human bone from nonhuman bone when diagnostic landmarks are not present. Histological analysis is a potential means to differentiate human from nonhuman bone. In Chapter 5, Dawn Mulhern and Douglas Ubelaker discuss the similarities and differences between human and nonhuman mammalian bone on a microscopic level. Illustrations of the typical histomorphology of a number of taxa are described and illustrated. The authors point out that although common bone microstructure is found throughout mammals, differences have been identified. These differences are primarily in the organization or size of structures, rather than unique kinds of structures. It is often possible, therefore, to differentiate nonhuman bone fragments using the pattern or the size of histological structures. The use of discriminant function analysis may permit the identification of an unknown fragment of bone with a reported level of certainty, which is especially important for forensic applications.

In Chapter 6, Margaret Streeter addresses histological age estimation with special emphasis on a new method that is applicable to subadult ribs. Patterns of histomorphological features, such as drifting osteons, woven bone, and lamellar drift, that reflect bone remodeling and modeling activity are used to define four phases covering an age range of less than 5 years to adult. Besides age estimation, this method shows promise for the study of skeletal development rates among populations. Because several book chapters have been devoted to the physiological basis for and the detailed description of histological methods of adult age estimation, Streeter focuses on a few of the more widely used methods.

The "new bone biology" concept recognizes the importance of the biomechanical function of bone. Chapters 7 and 8 discuss two important issues relating to this. In Chapter 7, John Skedros addresses the biomechanics of cortical bone. In addition to reviewing basic mechanical concepts, he describes how histomorphology can be used to interpret load history in the diaphyses of long bones when strain data are lacking or insufficient. Of particular interest to researchers and applied practitioners, such as forensic anthropologists, he introduces and discusses a worksheet/checklist of important considerations that facilitates the interpretation of load history in limb-bone diaphyses and ribs. Chapter 8, by Amanda Agnew and John Bolte, also deals with the biomechanics of bone but from the perspective of fracture risk. They note that, while risk of bone fracture has typically focused upon measures of bone quantity, the relationship between bone quality, and bone strength is important. Material properties of bone are discussed at several levels of organization, mineral and organic composition. The authors then discuss how type of bone, for example, woven, fibrolamellar, primary and secondary lamellar, and plexiform as well as the creation of fatigue damage in the form of microfractures produced during mechanical loading, affect bone quality. Findings from their ongoing research provide evidence that similar factors affect bone strength in human pediatric bone. Finally, of particular interest to anthropology and forensic science, they discuss the issue of bone fragility in past populations and how bone fracture patterns can help predict the loading context that caused a fracture.

When undertaking microstructural analysis of hard tissues in forensic, archaeological, paleontological, and paleopathological contexts the artifacts of taphonomic alteration must be recognized. Chapter 9 by Lynne Bell explores the subject of histotaphonomy, which is the analysis of taphonomy at the microstructural level. Although microbial alteration causes loss of information in archaeologically derived bone, the study of microbial bioerosion represents a tool for taphonomic reconstruction. She provides a brief history of histotaphonomy, reviews nomenclature associated with the field, and describes and provides examples of characteristic histotaphonomic changes to demonstrate how postmortem microstructural change can be used for taphonomic inquiry.

In Chapter 10, Michael Schultz discusses the application of light microscopy in paleopathology to classify pathological conditions. He explores the basis for reliable diagnosis, which consists of proper tissue selection and preparation to the interpretation of morphological structures in dry bone at the microlevel. He discusses a variety of pathological conditions with special emphasis on the diagnosis and differential diagnoses of a group of commonly seen inflammatory diseases in the archaeological record. Some principles of pathophysiology of the bony tissues are outlined and the morphological features seen at the microlevel characteristic for selected pathological conditions or even pathognomonic for special diseases are described and illustrated.

In Chapter 11, Susan Pfeiffer and Deborrah Pinto address the histological study of bone tissue of archaeological origin, focusing on research and methods based upon transmitted light microscopy. Whether determining if fragmentary remains are human, providing an age-at-death estimate, or evaluating skeletal health and disease, the authors demonstrate that the histological evaluation of bone provides useful information for bioarchaeological and paleopathological studies as well as modern forensic casework. They also note the important role that histological analysis can play in other types of analyses that require adequate preservation of bone tissue, such as assessing bone sample quality preliminary to ancient DNA or isotopic analyses. The authors make the important point that histological study of archaeologically derived material can contribute to research questions arising in forensic and biomedical fields. Given the potential for histological analysis in the broader scope of skeletal analysis, the authors propose that histology of normal cortical and cancellous human bone should be included in osteological training.

Access to collections of bone samples with known demographic information representing a diversity of populations is essential for hard tissue research, including the testing, improvement, and development of new methods. The next two chapters address this and describe two important resources. Chapter 12, authored by Brian Spatola, Franklin Damann, and Bruce Ragsdale, provide a history and description of the hard tissue collections maintained by the Anatomical Division of the National Museum of Health and Medicine (NMHM) at the Armed Forces Institute of Pathology. The NMHM's collection includes more than 10,000 glass slides of stained and undecalcified bone and joint specimens illustrating human growth and development, normal musculoskeletal anatomy, bone and joint pathology, tumor pathology, forensic bone histomorphometry, and comparative anatomy. This collection is available as part of the Anatomical Division's vast collection of anatomical and pathological specimens, which also includes more than 5600 dry bone skeletal specimens and 5500 formalin fixed soft tissue specimens dating back to the Civil War.

In Chapter 13, C. David Thomas and John Clement describe the Melbourne Femur Collection (MFC). This well-documented collection produced by researchers at the Melbourne Dental School (University of Melbourne, Australia) in collaboration with the Donor Tissue Bank of the Victorian Institute of Forensic Medicine currently contains approximately 500 samples of postmortem femoral bones as well as 90 surgical samples, such as femoral heads removed during hip replacements, making it one of the world's most complete and best documented archives of contemporary human bone tissue specimens. The history of the MFC and its future goals, including a discussion of ethical issues relating to obtaining biological samples are discussed. The chapter also includes examples of the range of potential research projects in which the MFC is applicable. The first describes the results of research into the relationship between histomorphological features of bone tissue from the femur midshaft, and the age at death. Their study is unique in terms of its methodology and sample size. It employed a semiautomated system that allowed the counting of Haversian canals from microradiographs made from sections of entire cross-sections of the femoral cortex. The second study illustrates the use of the collection as part of a biomedical study investigating a possible genetic marker of risk for developing osteoporosis in later life. These two chapters illustrate the importance of developing and maintaining hard tissue collections for scientific advancement.

The final two chapters of the book discuss technological aspects of hard tissue histology. Although forensic anthropologists employed in a medical examiner's office or crime laboratory typically have access to a standard histology department, other researchers and practitioners may not have access to these facilities. In Chapter 14, Helen Cho outlines practical issues and requirements for establishing a bone histology laboratory, including embedding, sectioning, mounting bone samples for histological analysis, and basic principles of light microscopy. Until relatively recently, methods of histomorphological analysis have provided only a two-dimensional perspective. Bone microstructure, however, exists in three dimensions. The final chapter, authored by David Cooper, David Thomas, and John Clement, provides an overview of conventional three-dimensional methodologies and describe recent developments in high-resolution imaging, such as the more powerful synchrotron x-ray sources, that offer the potential for greater detail for nondestructive histomorphological analyses in anthropological research.

This volume has assembled authors with extensive experience and expertise in various aspects of hard tissue histology. Its intended goal is to provide readers with an overview of the current state of research and potential applications in anthropology or any field that employs a histological approach to study hard tissues. This volume illustrates the degree to which histological analysis of hard tissue (bone and teeth) can contribute to the comprehensive understanding of skeletal biology. It is our hope that the contents provide a useful resource for students, researchers, and practitioners of anthropology and other fields related to skeletal biology.

# Editors

**Christian M. Crowder, PhD, D-ABFA**, received his BA from Texas A&M University, MA from the University of Texas at Arlington, and PhD from the University of Toronto. He is currently the Deputy Director of Forensic Anthropology for the Office of Chief Medical Examiner in New York City and a board certified forensic anthropologist. He is also an adjunct lecturer at Pace University, holds a faculty position at the New York University Medical Center and an affiliation with the NYU Anthropology Department. In his present position with the OCME, Crowder assists with anthropology casework in the five boroughs of New York City (Manhattan, Brooklyn, Queens, the Bronx, and Staten Island). He is also the site coordinator for the ongoing search and recovery of remains at the World Trade Center site. Prior to accepting the position in New York City, Crowder was a forensic anthropologist at the Joint POW/MIA Accounting Command–Central Identification Laboratory in Hawaii.

**Sam D. Stout** received his PhD in physical anthropology from Washington University in St. Louis in 1976, and is currently professor of anthropology in the Department of Anthropology at the Ohio State University, and professor emeritus of the University of Missouri Department of Anthropology. His research and teaching interests are in skeletal biology, particularly from a microscopic (histomorphological) perspective, and its applications in bioarchaeology and forensic anthropology. He is a fellow of the American Academy of Forensic Sciences.

# Contributors

**Amanda M. Agnew**
Department of Anthropology
and Division of Anatomy
The Ohio State University
Columbus, Ohio

**Lynne S. Bell**
Centre for Forensic Research
School of Criminology
Simon Fraser University
Burnaby, British Columbia, Canada

**John H. Bolte IV**
Department of Biomedical Infomatics
and Injury Biomechanics Research Laboratory
The Ohio State University
Columbus, Ohio

**Helen Cho**
Department of Anthropology
Davidson College
Davidson, North Carolina

**John G. Clement**
University of Melbourne
Melbourne, Australia

**David M. L. Cooper**
Department of Anatomy and Cell Biology
University of Saskatchewan
Saskatoon, Saskatchewan, Canada

**Franklin E. Damann**
National Museum of Health and Medicine
Armed Forces Institute of Pathology
Washington, DC

**James H. Gosman**
Department of Anthropology
The Ohio State University
Columbus, Ohio

**Debbie Guatelli-Steinberg**
Department of Anthropology
Department of Evolutionary Ecology and
    Organizational Biology
The Ohio State University
Columbus, Ohio

**Michaela Huffman**
Department of Anthropology
The Ohio State University
Columbus, Ohio

**Corey M. Maggiano**
Department of Anthropology
The Ohio State University
Columbus, Ohio

**Dawn M. Mulhern**
Department of Anthropology
Fort Lewis College
Durango, Colorado

**Susan Pfeiffer**
Department of Anthropology
University of Toronto
Toronto, Canada

**Deborrah Pinto**
Harris County Institute of Forensic Science
Houston, Texas

**Bruce D. Ragsdale**
Arizona State University
Tempe, Arizona
and Western Dermatopathology
San Luis Obispo, California

**Michael Schultz**
Department of Anatomy
University Medical School Göttingen
Göttingen, Germany

**John G. Skedros**
Bone and Joint Research Laboratory
Department of Veterans Affairs
SLC Health Care System
Salt Lake City, Utah

Department of Orthopaedics
University of Utah
Salt Lake City, Utah

**Brian F. Spatola**
National Museum of Health and Medicine
Armed Forces Institute of Pathology
Washington, DC

**Margaret Streeter**
Department of Anthropology
Boise State University
Boise, Idaho

**C. David L. Thomas**
University of Melbourne
Melbourne, Australia

**Douglas H. Ubelaker**
Department of Anthropology
National Museum of Natural History
Smithsonian Institution
Washington, DC

# Bone Remodeling, Histomorphology, and Histomorphometry

# 1

SAM STOUT
CHRISTIAN CROWDER

## Contents

## 1.1  Introduction

Skeletal analyses can be approached at several hierarchical levels, ranging from organ level macroscopic analyses of whole bones to the molecular level. Intermediate is the histological or tissue level, which Harold Frost (1986) described as the level of "skeletal intermediary organization," representing the collaborative activity of cells. Because of the mineralized structure of bone, the product of cellular activity is encrypted in its microscopic anatomy or histomorphology,[*] where it persists to be interpreted by the histomorphometrist. The first section of this chapter will discuss bone histomorphology as it relates to bone remodeling. Next, the chapter discusses aspects of histomorphometry and its role in evaluating bone at the histological level, followed by a discussion of methodological issues associated with applying histological techniques in anthropological research and forensic casework.

---

[*] The following three terms will be used throughout the chapter: Histology, the study of tissues, also called microscopal anatomy; histomorphology, the morphology of tissues; and histomorphometry, quantitative histology.

## 1.2    Bone Biology and Histomorphology

To interpret the biological information encrypted in the histomorphology of bone, a basic understanding of the biology underlying the creation of histomorphological structures is essential. Bone metabolism, whether for growth, adaptation, or homeostasis, involves two basic kinds of cells: (1) bone-forming osteoblasts and their derivatives, and (2) bone-resorbing osteoclasts. The normal activity of these cells is associated with two distinct physiological processes referred to as modeling and remodeling. Bone modeling is essentially restricted to the growing skeleton, where it works in concert with growth to adapt bones to their changing biomechanical environment by adjusting the amount and spatial distribution of bone tissue. Exceptions where modeling occurs in the adult skeleton are fracture repair and certain cases of mechanical loadings in pathological bone (Peck and Stout 2008). Bone remodeling is a lifelong process of bone turnover and is the predominant process in the adult skeleton responsible for its characteristic histomorphological features. Since this chapter will focus on adult bone histomorphology, with the exception of how modeling activity occurring in earlier life affects our interpretation of adult bone histomorphometry,[*] discussion will be limited to remodeling. For a more in-depth discussion regarding the biology of subadult bone and modeling, the reader is referred to chapters in this volume by James Gosman (Chapter 2), Corey Maggiano (Chapter 3), and Margaret Streeter (Chapter 6).

### 1.2.1    Bone Remodeling

Remodeling is the mechanism by which older bone is replaced by the coordinated (tethered) action of bone-resorbing osteoclasts and bone-forming osteoblasts, collectively referred to as a basic multicellular unit (BMU) of remodeling or simply bone remodeling units (BRU; Parfitt 1979). It is useful to describe the process in terms of three distinct phases: activation,[†] resorption, and formation. This sequence is sometimes denoted by the acronym ARF (Martin et al. 1998). The product of the ARF sequence is a basic structural unit (BSU) described histomorphologically as an osteon or Haversian system in cortical bone, or "hemi-osteon" in cancellous and endosteal bone. Histological age estimation in humans is possible because remodeling occurs throughout life and produces discrete, definable, and quantifiable microscopic features such as osteons[‡] (see Streeter in this volume). Bone remodeling occurs in all animals, but the appearance of osteons in cortical bone is not universal and when it does occur often shows a very weak age association due to species differences in non-age-related factors such as locomotion (biomechanics), life span, and endocrine functions (Burr 1992; Mulhern and Ubelaker 2003; Paine and Godfrey 1997; Przybeck 1985; Schaffler and Burr 1984; Schock et al. 1975; Schock et al. 1972; Singh et al.

---

[*] Histomorphometry refers to quantitative histology where histomophological features are described in terms of number per unit area or size (area) analogous to osteometry.

[†] Because the histological observation of a BMU in a cross-section of bone does not necessarily represent the actual birth of that BMU but rather the point at which the plane of section crosses a resorptive bay or cutting cone (Martin 1994; Parfitt 2005), the terms *initiation* (Peck and Woods 1988) and *origination* (Parfitt 2005) have been suggested.

[‡] Application to other animals is possible but problematic because of the highly variable expression of cortical remodeling in other species due to biomechanical and physiological differences (Schaffler and Burr 1984).

1974; Van Wagenen 1970). Discussion in this chapter is restricted to humans. For discussion of nonhuman bone histomorphology, see the chapter by Mulhern and Ubelaker in this volume.

Bone remodeling occurs on all bone envelopes (surfaces), including the endosteum and trabeculae. The histomorphological evidence for remodeling is most readily observed in cortical bone as the secondary osteon. For cancellous and endosteal bone surfaces, remodeling is associated with a sinus, referred to as a bone remodeling compartment (BRC), which is lined on its marrow side by flattened cells and on its osseous side by the bone surface (Hauge et al. 2001). Because BSUs in cortical bone (osteons) are relatively well defined in bone cross-sections, most of the histomorphometric methods typically employed in anthropological analyses are based upon intracortical remodeling.[*] Our discussion, therefore, will focus on cortical bone histomorphology and histomorphometry, particularly as it relates to the bone remodeling process and age estimation, which is the most common use of bone histology in anthropology. The accurate identification of histomorphological features that are traces of earlier remodeling events is crucial for histological age estimation. This requires an understanding of the remodeling process itself.

The bone remodeling process begins with the appearance of osteoclasts at the site of BMU initiation (activation) in response to systemic and biomechanical factors perceived by another cell of the osteoblast lineage, the osteocyte. These bone resorbing cells derive from hematopoietic stem cells within bone marrow that, under the influence of the cytokine colony stimulating factor (CSF)-1, proliferate and differentiate into osteoclast precursors that then enter the peripheral blood and arrive at the site of BMU initiation (Pettit et al. 2008). Teams of osteoclasts remove bone to create a cavity that is observable histomorphologically as a resorptive bay or cutting cone in cortical bone or a "hemicone" in cancellous bone (Parfitt 2005). In cortical bone the osteoclasts of the resorptive phase follow a trajectory related to the directions of mechanical strains, which for typical long bones this is longitudinal (van Oers 2008). Circulating osteoclast precursors express the receptor activator of NFκB, also called RANK. The binding of RANK ligand to this receptor is an important osteoclastogenic signal. Our understanding of how the production of osteoclasts and rate of bone resorption are regulated is described as a RANKL/RANK/OPG system wherein the production of osteoclasts is inhibited by the presence of another cytokine osteoprotegrin (OPG). It is interesting that all three of these regulators of remodeling cell activity are produced by cells of the osteoblast lineage, including stromal cells and bone lining cells (BLC). In cortical bone the cutting cone excavated by osteoclasts typically reaches a diameter of approximately 150 to 350 μm, which determines the cross-sectional size of the histomorphological feature (BSU or osteon) created by the BMU (van Oers et al. 2008). Reported rates at which cortical bone BMUs tunnel through bone is about 20 μm per day (Martin et al. 1998).

Following closely behind the osteoclasts is a growing capillary that nourishes and provides new osteoclast precursors to the advancing BMU. During a short reversal phase that occurs between the resorptive and formation phases a group of mononuclear cells line the resorptive bay. The exact function of these cells remains unclear. Evidence suggests that they smooth off the scalloped periphery of the resorptive bay in preparation for the deposition of a thin, wavy, mineral-deficient, sulfur-rich layer of matrix called a reversal line that

---

[*] For an illustration of the potential use of new technology for three-dimensional analysis of cortical bone, see the chapter by Cooper, Thomas, and Clement in this volume.

separates a BSU from surrounding interstitial lamellae (Everts et al. 2002; Robling et al. 2006). Recent evidence suggests that the bone lining cells, discussed later, play important roles in the transition between resorption and formation and the coupling of these processes during bone remodeling (Everts et al. 2002; Tang et al. 2009), and that the coupling of these two processes during bone remodeling results from the release of transforming growth factor (TGF)-beta1 during bone resorption. This polypeptide cytokine transforming growth factor causes the migration of osteoblast precursor cells, stromal, or mesenchymal stem cells, to the resorptive site of the forming BMU (Tang et al. 2009). Differentiation of these cells involves a 2- to 3-day multistage process (Martin et al. 1998).

Subsequent to the reversal phase of the remodeling BMU, which lasts approximately 9 days (Ott 2002), the osteoblasts begin to secrete the organic matrix of bone referred to as osteoid, which is composed of type I collagen and other noncollagenous proteins, proteoglycans, and water (Marks and Odgren 2002; Martin et al. 1998). Osteoid is mineralized through the deposition of calcium phosphate crystals. Because there is a lag time of about 10 days between osteoid deposition and mineralization (Martin et al. 1998), a layer of osteoid is found between the matrix depositing osteoblasts and mineralized bone. The area where mineralization begins is referred to as the mineralization front and it is at this location that in vivo labels of bone formation, such as tetracycline, are incorporated. The thickness of the intervening osteoid seam is normally about 7 μm (Pirok et al. 1966). Increased osteoid seam widths are observed in pathological conditions, such as osteomalacia, that are characterized by mineralization defects (Monier-Faugere et al. 1998). During mineralization crystals of calcium phosphate produced by osteoblasts are deposited within the osteoid matrix. The mineralization process is regulated by inorganic pyrophosphate, which inhibits abnormal calcification, and the levels of which are regulated by several other molecules, nucleotide pyrophosphatase phosphodiesterase 1 (NPP1) and ankylosis protein (ANK), which increase pyrophosphate levels, and nonspecific alkaline phosphatase (TNAP), which breaks down pyrophosphate. Another possible regulator of the bone mineralization process is a protein called osteopontin, levels of which are highly correlated with pyrophosphate levels (Johnson et al. 2006; NIAMS 2006).

Whereas osteoclasts undergo apoptosis after completing their resorptive task, osteoblasts have three potential fates. While some osteoblasts undergo apoptosis, some become trapped in the matrix that they are secreting to become the major bone cell, the osteocytes. Still others persist as the flat bone lining cells (BLC) that line bone surfaces. Both osteocytes and BLCs play important roles in bone metabolism in general and bone remodeling in particular.

After becoming embedded in bone matrix, osteocytes generate cytoplasmic processes that are contained within small spaces called canaliculi within the mineralized bone surrounding the cell that allow osteocytes to retain communication with surrounding cells, such as other osteocytes, osteoblasts, and bone lining cells. Osteocytes play a crucial role in bone maintenance. While they play a role in mineral homeostasis (Nijweide et al. 2002), it is now believed that their major role is biomechanical, sensing mechanical stains and initiation of microfracture repair resulting from mechanical loading (Parfitt 2005). Osteocytes continuously send signals that inhibit the activation of new remodeling BMUs, and it is the disruption of this signal after osteocyte apoptosis or microfracture that initiates activation of a new remodeling cycle (Martin 2000a).

Osteoblasts that do not become entombed in bone matrix to become osteocytes or undergo apoptosis remain on the surface of completed BMUs where they form a lining of flat cells called bone lining cells (BLCs; Martin et al. 1998). Evidence suggests that these "retired" osteoblasts are responsible for the activation of new BMUs in response to signals from osteocytes or hormones (Burr 2002; Martin 2000a).

Reported lengths for typical BMUs range from 4000 µm (Parfitt 2005) to 300 µm (Martin et al. 1998), the discrepancy probably being due to the difficulty in defining the longitudinal boundaries for individual BMUs. In cortical bone BMUs are observable histomorphologically as osteons (Figure 1.1). The terms *osteon* and *Haversian system* are synonymous; however, *secondary osteon* is commonly used to refer to these structures resulting from intracortical remodeling activity, distinguishing them from primary osteons that are similar in appearance. Primary osteons are not produced by remodeling but rather result from centripetal formation of bone lamellae around a central canal without preceding resorption of the ARF sequence that defines remodeling. Primary osteons usually occur near the endosteal surface where voids or spaces are filled in by osteoblasts during endosteal drift or trabecular compaction, although Carter and Beaupré (2001) also define primary osteons as structures produced when osteoblasts fill in large vascular canals formed in woven bone in rapidly growing animals. In the literature, non-Haversian canals are sometimes referred to by the term *primary osteon*, but these merely represent blood vessels that have become incorporated into the compact bone during radial bone growth (Figure 1.2).

Through the processes of bone remodeling it is possible for several types of secondary osteons to develop, such as type I osteons, type II (embedded) osteons, double-zonal osteons, and drifting osteons. Type I osteons are common secondary osteons and are typically the focus of most histological age estimation methods because of their accumulation with age. A less common secondary osteon is the type II or embedded osteon, which appears as a separate smaller osteon with its own reversal line set within a larger secondary osteon (Ericksen 1991). Their relationship to internal or external factors is unknown. Double-zonal osteons, another less common secondary osteon, demonstrate a hypercalcified ring

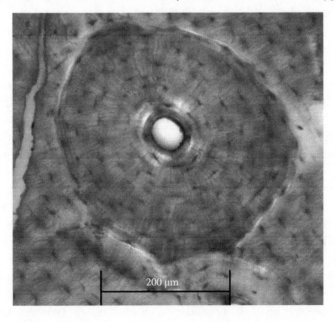

**Figure 1.1** Example of a secondary osteon or Haversian system.

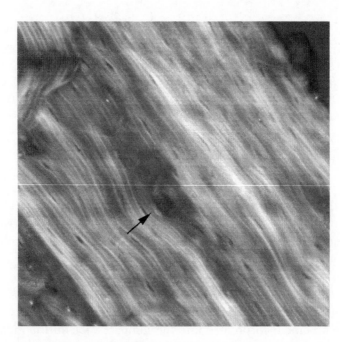

**Figure 1.2** Example of a primary vascular canal (arrow) in the periosteal cortex of a human femur. Primary vascular canals are vessels trapped in the lamellar bone during apposition. The lamellae appear to flow around the canal.

within their concentric lamellae (Robling and Stout 2000). It is believed that this represents an arrest line due to a disruption during the remodeling process, possibly caused by some type of stress (e.g., disease, nutritional). Drifting or waltzing osteons are defined as "Haversian systems in which there is continuous resorption on one side and continuous formation on the other" (Robling and Stout 1999:193). The resulting effect, when viewing a bone cross-section, is an osteon exhibiting a tail or whirlwind pattern (Figure 1.3). The tail indicates the direction of drift as it moved through the cortex. They are frequently seen in bones of children, especially during the first decade of life. Other researchers have noted that drifting osteons may be present at any decade of life (Crowder 2005; Epker and Frost 1965; Robling and Stout 1999).

The remodeling process is one of constant adjustment to retain bone integrity and homeostasis within the matrix. Bone formation takes roughly 10 times longer than bone resorption. This suggests that bone formation–resorption must be in perfect balance to retain bone integrity. A theoretical equilibrium ratio for bone remodeling proposed by Ortner and Putschar (1985) estimates that there would be 10 osteons in the formation stage for each resorption space (10:1) in normal bone. Deviations from this ratio may indicate possible pathological or nutritional conditions. Diet is an extrinsic variable that is believed to have a direct effect on the synthesis of the bone matrix (Garrow et al. 2000; Ortner 1975). A diet concentrated on one food type and lacking another may alter the equilibrium ratio. Early studies indicate that Eskimo populations demonstrated rapid bone loss in adulthood when compared to U.S. whites (Ericksen 1973; Thompson and Cowen 1984; Thompson and Gunness-Hey 1981). The disparities in the resorption rates were attributed to dietary differences between populations. Stout and Lueck (1995) compared cortical bone remodeling rates from three archaeological populations with those of a modern sample and determined that the earlier populations reached skeletal maturity at an older age. However, in a

**Figure 1.3** Image depicting drifting osteons from a rib cross-section.

study by Burr and colleagues (1990), there were no significant differences in bone loss with age between Pecos Indian archaeological remains and modern white populations. Pfeiffer and Lazenby (1994) stated that the discrepancies in age-related bone loss might be due to the fact that earlier (archaeological) populations died at younger ages or that "their diet or lifestyle facilitated effective bone maintenance" (p. 35). Abbott and colleagues (1996) report bone remodeling rates for Middle and Late Pleistocene human lower limb bones (Shanidar, Tabun) to be slower than rates reported for a more recent archeological sample from Pecos Pueblo, New Mexico, by Burr et al. (1990). However, recalculation of the data reported in Abbott and colleagues (1996) by Streeter et al. (2010) produced remodeling rates for the Pleistocene group that are similar to the values obtained in the more recent comparative sample. Whether bone remodeling rates differ significantly among populations and over time remains open to question. Insight into this question may be gained through an understanding of the theoretical aspects of bone remodeling.

## 1.2.2 Theory and the Origins of the "New Bone Biology"

Prior to the 19th century, bone architecture was often attributed to divine design or magic (Frost 1998a, 1998b). Researchers as far back as Galileo contemplated bone structure in the context of its mechanical environment (Martin et al. 1998). However, the idea was not popularized until Julius Wolff introduced a theory, known as Wolff's law, in 1892. Wolff's law states that bone's mechanical environment determines its final mass and trabecular architecture. While this theory is accepted as the foundation for functional adaptation of bone, Wolff's theory is based on a static mathematical relationship (Forwood and Turner 1995). Furthermore, Wolff never attempted to formulate this mathematical theory. Prior to Wolff, but within the same century, Bernard and Roux introduced two concepts of bone adaptation: the idea of physiologic homeostasis and the principle of bone functional adaptation based on the dynamic interaction between bone cells and the mechanical environment (Martin 2003a; Martin et al. 1998). The paradigm leading into the next century states that bone structure optimizes strength and that changes in structure are performed through bone cells in response to mechanical strain.

### 1.2.2.1 The Mechanostat

In the 1980s, orthopedic surgeon Harold M. Frost proposed a concept to explain the mechanism that controls bone mass during longitudinal bone growth, modeling, and BMU-based remodeling (Frost 1983, 1987a). Frost explained that a mechanical feedback system dubbed the mechanostat, which is based on the magnitude of strain resulting from an applied load, is responsible for controlling bone mass. Using a house thermostat as an analogy, the mechanism controlling bone mass would turn on in response to an error and off in its absence (Frost 1987a). Strain thresholds or set points called minimum effective strains (MES) activate or depress bone modeling and remodeling. The threshold strain ranges determine if, when, where, and how long biologic activity turns on or off (Frost 1998b). According to Frost, the MES set points may be altered by hormones and biochemical agents, hence fooling the mechanostat (Turner 1999). For more detailed discussion on biomechanical adaptation of bone see chapters by Maggiano, Agnew and Bolte, and Skedros in this volume.

During remodeling, strains above the threshold of the minimum effective strain for remodeling (MESr) will keep remodeling in conservation mode, retaining bone. When strains fall below the threshold, remodeling goes into disuse mode, removing bone permanently from the endosteal envelope (Frost 1997, 1998a). This can lead to osteopenia and, in severe cases, disuse osteoporosis. Mechanical loading can also affect remodeling (BMU activation rates) when strains are within the conservative mode. Repeated straining of bone will eventually create fatigue damage, producing microfractures in the bone (Frost 2000a). By mechanisms not fully understood, bone signals the BMU to remodel microdamaged areas (Frost 1997). Frost (1960) proposed that strain causes microcracks that disrupt the canalicular connection between bone cells within the matrix. This disruption provides the cells with the stimulus to initiate remodeling. If the strain increases to a level where microfractures are accumulating at a rate that the BMU cannot repair, gross bone failure will occur, resulting in fatigue fractures. For more on microfractures and fracture risk see Chapter 9 by Agnew and Bolte in this volume. The biological determinants of bone strength include baseline conditions that are found at birth (Frost 1999a). This indicates that genes may predetermine a skeletal element's baseline condition, while the mechanostat adds the functional adaptation.

### 1.2.2.2 The Utah Paradigm

In the mid-1990s, a series of Hard Tissue Workshops held at the University of Utah discussed the increasing discordance between the subfields of skeletal biology and lack of multidisciplinary approaches to skeletal research. From these workshops a new paradigm in skeletal physiology, dubbed the Utah paradigm, evolved (Frost 1998a). The Utah paradigm proposed a shift from the 1960 paradigm of skeletal physiology, which suggested that the bone effector cells determined bone health and disease under the control of nonmechanical agents to meet homeostatic needs (Frost 1998b, 2000b). The new paradigm explored the load-bearing skeletal elements at the organ, tissue, and cellular level focusing on the mechanical competence of bone (Frost 1999a, 1999b, 2000b). The mechanostat is the leading hypothesis in the Utah paradigm, in that it explains how load-bearing skeletal organs attain mechanical competence. This hypothesis does not explain the forces that control other skeletal elements, such as the cranial bones, which do not carry large biomechanical loads, implying that there are other factors involved. The Utah paradigm indicated that the driving force of load-bearing skeletal architecture and strength are mechanical factors, and that nonmechanical factors, such as hormones, vitamins, minerals, sex, and age, either hinder or help the process but do not replace it (Frost 1999b, 2000b). Growth hormones have the greatest effect on the mechanostat because they are directly associated with increasing muscle strength, body weight, and longitudinal bone growth (Frost 1998b). According the Utah paradigm of skeletal physiology, these nonmechanical agents do not dominate control of bone strength. Instead, control depends on the mechanical loads (Schoenau and Frost 2002).

In 2003, Frost published an update of the mechanostat hypothesis. It focused on postnatal bone mass and strength, how these variables adapt over time to the mechanical forces placed on them, and the application of the mechanostat to nonskeletal tissues. Although the mechanostat remains the leading theory describing factors controlling bone mass and strength, empirical data establishing a direct cause and effect relationship between muscle force and bone strength has not been established. Results of clinical experiments designed to test the mechanostat hypothesis indicate that bone development is driven by muscle development; however, it is not clear how much genetic factors, rather than mechanical factors, account for the correlation between bone and muscle mass (Parfitt 2004; Rauch et al. 2004).

### 1.2.2.3 *Osteocyte Inhibitor Theory*

Burr (2002) states that bone remodeling fulfills three goals: (1) maintenance of mineral homeostasis, (2) adaptation to bone's mechanical environment, and (3) repair of microdamage to insure mechanical integrity. Studies have shown that targeted remodeling occurs at sites associated with microcracks, indicating a cause-and-effect relationship (Burr and Martin 1993; Martin 2003a, 2003b). Frost's (1960) original proposal stated that microcracks disrupt canalicular connections between osteocytes, thus providing the stimulus to initiate remodeling. Burr (2002) describes a slightly different view, in which the osteocyte–canalicular system acts as an inhibitor of the osteoclastic activity.

According to the mechanostat, disuse activates remodeling and inhibits modeling, while overload inhibits remodeling and activates modeling. Martin (2000a, 2000b) states that the mechanostat limits itself to effects of strain on modeling and remodeling, and does not consider the removal of microdamage, caused by high strains, part of bone's mechanical adaptation. Martin (2000b, 2003a, 2003b) indicates that observations of bone in disuse and overload coincide with the idea that the osteocytes inhibit rather than stimulate remodeling.

Strain levels are necessary to nourish the osteocytes through interstitial fluid flow and lack of nutrition causes a disruption in the osteocyte network, producing a signal to switch bone into disuse mode (Martin 2003a, 2003b). When the osteocyte network is disrupted by osteocyte apoptosis, the constraining mechanism is released. This stimulates resorption activity. Osteocyte apoptosis has been correlated with regions of microdamage and new remodeling events (Burr 2002; Verborgt et al. 2000). Burr (2002) states that 70 percent of bone remodeling is nontargeted, leaving 30 percent that is damage initiated. The nontargeted or stochastic remodeling may be associated with metabolic purposes (Martin 2002). Unlike Frost's theory, the osteocyte inhibitor theory currently has little supporting evidence, so the current understanding of the relationship between stimulus and bone remodeling remains controversial because the relationship between causative and stochastic bone remodeling is not fully understood. It is likely that the osteocytes of osteons, like most cells, have a life span; and once the cell begins to fail in its normal functions or natural cell death occurs, remodeling is initiated. More recent studies have linked osteocyte apoptosis to bone resorption; however, the spatial and temporal relationships are still not fully characterized. Emerton et al. (2010) report that osteocyte apoptosis is necessary to initiate endocortical remodeling in the response to estrogen withdrawal in adult female mice. They observed that osteoclastic activity did not occur in the absence of osteocyte apoptosis. According to Bonewald and Johnson (2008), the study of osteocyte biology is becoming an intense area of research interest.

#### 1.2.2.4   The Principle of Cellular Accommodation Theory

The mechanostat theory remained relatively unchallenged until 1999 when Charles Turner presented a mathematical description of bone biology in which he coined the principle of cellular accommodation. Turner (1999) draws attention to the fact that the mechanostat theory does not explain why nonweight-bearing bones do not resorb away due to disuse remodeling. Furthermore, he states that the mechanostat theory does not conform to experimental observation. Although Frost postulates that the MES set points can be fooled by hormones, he does not explain how or why skeletal sites are regulated differently. The principle of cellular accommodation theory states that bone cells learn from their physical and biological environment and that they accommodate to the new environment. Therefore, the set points vary from site to site depending on the local strain. The set point in weight-bearing bones will be high, while the set point in nonweight-bearing bones will be much lower. Turner claims that Frost places biomechanics at the center of bone biology ignoring the fact that bone is "insensitive to mechanical loading in the absence of either parathyroid or growth hormones" (2000:186). This indicates that endocrine and paracrine agents do not have a secondary role but a primary role in bone formation. Further research indicates that bone cells not only learn from and accommodate to their environment, but they may retain a cellular memory of their previous loading environment (Turner et al. 2002). Turner's ideas and research may be a step toward a unified theory of bone remodeling considering loading history, cellular memory, and the role of hormonal/anabolic agents.

### 1.2.3   Bone Remodeling and Histological Age Estimation

When performing histological age estimation analyses, recall that they are based upon the accumulated evidence of bone remodeling. Discrete evidence of remodeling events in the past (osteons) is easily distinguished in the unstained section.* The key to accurately distinguishing secondary osteons (cortical BSUs) from other similar structures, such as primary osteons and vascular canals, is the presence of a well-defined reversal line, indicative of the resorptive and reversal phases of BMU creation. Osteons that lack an intact Haversian canal because of their partial resorption by subsequent remodeling activity can also be distinguished from interstitial primary lamellar bone by the presence of a reversal line, and the concentric nature of their lamellae and osteocytic lacunae. In practice, because of the effects of depth of field in light microscopy, reversal lines and lamellar patterns are more easily and reliably identified if the microscopist uses the fine focus to focus up and down when viewing sections (Figure 1.4). This procedure is well known by microscopists and provides some measure of dimensionality to microscopic structures. The lack of depth of

---

\* The material nature of bone makes the use of histochemistry (staining) usually unnecessary for histomorphological and histomorphometric analyses of the bone samples available for anthropological age estimation.

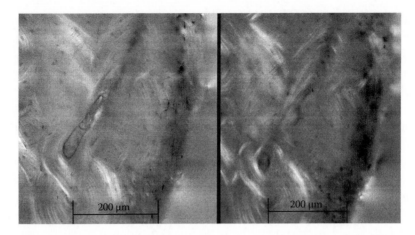

**Figure 1.4** Images taken at two focal planes. The left image shows either a Haversian canal branching event or an obliquely sectioned osteon producing an eccentric Haversian canal. The right image is slightly out of focus but shows that the microstructures in the previous focal plane represent a branching event. The area of interest now shows an intact osteon with a Haversian canal.

field for digitally captured images, therefore, can make the accurate differentiation of histomorphological features, such as reversal lines, difficult. This is why we recommend that analyses be performed directly through the microscope as well as from digital images.

Three important issues that should be considered when undertaking histological age estimations are mean tissue age (MTA), effective age of adult compacta, and osteon population density (OPD) asymptote. Cortical osteons and osteon fragments observed in a bone cross-section do not represent BMUs that have accumulated since birth but rather a later age characteristic of each bone called the effective age of adult compacta. Cortical drifts during growth remove some of the visible evidence of earlier BMU creations, osteons and their fragments, and the chronological age of an individual is usually greater than the actual age of a given area of bone tissue. Based upon data from the use of in vivo tissue-time labeling, the MTA and effective age for the birth of adult compacta for the middle third of the rib is estimated to be approximately 12.5 years (Wu et al. 1970). The years over which the BSUs observed in the cortex of the rib have accumulated can be estimated by chronological age minus 12.5 years. It is not appropriate, therefore, to apply most currently available histological age estimation formulas derived primarily from adult skeletons to subadults.

At the other end of the age scale, there is a problem as well. Some existing BSUs are partially removed by the creating of new BMUs to produce what are referred to as osteon fragments. Osteons and their fragments are the visible evidence of past remodeling activity and these are the major predicting variables used in most histological age estimation methods. However, the creation of a BMU can also completely remove an existing BSU. Although this is not a significant problem for bones from younger individuals that include significant amounts of unremodeled primary lamellar bone tissue, in older individuals the relative number of missing osteons (BSUs) increases eventually reaching an OPD asymptote. The OPD at which an asymptote is attained varies for different bones, depending upon factors such as remodeling activation rates, cortical diameter, and osteon size. Using data from Kerley (1965), Frost (1987b, 1987c) estimates an OPD asymptote for the midshaft femur to be about $50/mm^2$. Asymptote for the rib is reported to be reached at an OPD of about $30/mm^2$ (Stout and Paine 1994). Once asymptote is reached for OPD, visible evidence for BMU activation does not increase with age. This is a major problem for histological age estimation for elderly individuals. For example, OPD asymptote can occur as early as 50 years for the rib. Therefore, a histological age estimate of 50 years based upon an OPD of about 30/mm$^2$ can be only reported as an age 50 years or older. Taking advantage of other histomorphological features known to vary with age in addition to OPD may allow age estimation for elderly individuals. Stout and Streeter (2004, 2006) used osteon size and relative cortical area of the rib from a Mayan ruler to support a ninth decade of life age based upon inscriptions. Certain bones, such as the femur, are probably better for estimating age for older individuals because the OPD asymptotes occur at relatively older ages owing to their larger cortical areas. New age estimating methods that are more applicable to older individuals should be considered that employ combinations of bones and variables other than OPD should be explored. In order to quantify the amount, size, and shape of histological features, histomorphometric techniques are applied.

## 1.3   Bone Histomorphometry

Increasingly, skeletal biologists are employing histomorphometry in the analysis of both modern and ancient bone (Abbott et al. 1996; Ericksen 1976; Frost 1987b, 1987c; Kerley and Ubelaker 1978; Kimura 1992; Martin and Armelagos 1985; Mulhern and van Gerven 1997; Stout and Lueck 1995; Streeter et al. 2010). In short, histomorphometry is the quantification of microstructures in the skeletal tissue or their characteristics. Histomorphometric analysis of bone provides quantitative information, such as bone turnover (remodeling) and microarchitecture, which cannot be obtained from other approaches. Age-at-death estimation and the determination of human from nonhuman bone, in particular, have been widely used by anthropologists. As previously mentioned, histological age estimation is based on the observation of age-dependent change in the bone microstructure, most frequently the evidence of bone remodeling activity, the amount of unremodeled lamellar bone, and mean osteon size. Several book chapters have been devoted to the physiological basis for and the detailed description of histological age estimation methods (Crowder 2009; Robling and Stout 2008; Stout 1989; Stout and Paine 1992) and the determination of human versus nonhuman bone (Mulhern 2009). Therefore, the following will be limited to a general discussion of bone histomorphometry as it relates to anthropological analyses. Several chapters within this volume address quantitative methods and report data collected from numerous studies (see Streeter; Mulhern and Ubelaker; Cooper, Thomas, and Clement; and Guatelli-Steinberg and Huffman).

The quantification of bone turnover, microarchitecture, and static and dynamic cell activity is performed through measuring and counting of structures to characterize changes in bone histomorphology. Anthropology, as a discipline, is a relative newcomer in the quantification of bone structure and organization and, as result, analyses are often performed without full consideration of the underlying processes governing bone biology. To reliably evaluate bone at the histological level the analyst must interpret histomorphometric results in the context of bone biology. Anthropologists should also follow the standardization of nomenclature, symbols, and unit released by the American Society for Bone and Mineral Research (ASBMR) to assist in a universal understanding of bone histomorphometry and eliminate ambiguity in the reporting of data (Parfitt et al. 1987).

To ensure the proper application of any method utilizing histomorphometric techniques it is important to consult the methods from the original publication. The proper magnification, sampling area, and other specified procedures must be followed as prescribed for each method. Evaluating histological structures is a slow process and requires constant manipulation of the microscope's fine focus and light. Both polarized and nonpolarized light should be used to provide full resolution of structures during assessment. The application of automated techniques may be beneficial and reduce evaluation time; however, current technology may not allow for the complete dismissal of direct viewing through the microscope. This is illustrated in the study discussed in Chapter 13 by Thomas and Clement where they describe the results of research evaluating the relationship between histomorphological features of bone tissue and the age at death. Their study is unique in terms of its methodology and sample size. It employed a semiautomated system that allowed the counting of Haversian canals from microradiographs made from sections of entire cross-sections of the femoral cortex. While the results were less than promising, finding a poor association between Haversian canals and chronological age, the study provided valuable information relating to methodology, including sampling, sample size, and choice of variables.

### 1.3.1 Static Histomorphometry

Static histomorphometry allows for the quantification of histological structures being evaluated in a bone at a particular point in time. In most anthropological research and practical applications of bone histology methods (i.e., age estimation, human vs. nonhuman determination), static indices of bone microarchitecture are evaluated and calculated. Histological structures are manually or automatically measured through a variety of measurement or counting techniques. Typical variables (measurements) recorded include, but are not limited to, volume, length, perimeter, diameter, area, circularity, and osteon population density (osteon counts). As previously mentioned, the proper nomenclature should be followed when recording and reporting histological data. For example, the following is a list of commonly measured histological features for age estimation:

1. Total area of bone sampled (Sa.Ar.)—Amount of cortical bone. Sa.Ar. is expressed in square millimeters ($mm^2$), and can be determined either directly under the microscope using an appropriate eyepiece counting reticule or from digital images using image analysis software.
2. Number of intact osteons (N.On.)—Secondary osteons with at least 90 percent of their Haversian canal perimeters intact or unremodeled. Refer to Robling and Stout (2008) for an in-depth description of intact secondary osteons.
3. Number of fragmentary osteons (N.On.Fg.)—Secondary osteons in which 10 percent or more of the perimeters of their Haversian canals, if present, have been remodeled by subsequent generations of osteons. This variable also includes remnants of preexisting secondary osteons that no longer contain a Haversian canal. Refer to Robling and Stout (2008) for a more in-depth description of intact secondary osteons.
4. Osteon population density in #/mm2 (OPD)—This variable is the sum of N.On. and N.On.Fg. divided by Sa.Ar.
5. Relative cortical area (Ct.Ar./Tt.Ar.)—The relative amount of cortical bone in cross-sectional area of bone, or the ratio of cortical bone area (Ct.Ar.) to total area (Tt.Ar.) of a rib cross-section.

6. Mean osteonal cross-sectional area in mm² (On.Ar.)—The average area of bone contained within the cement lines of structurally complete osteons for each rib specimen. Osteons are considered structurally complete if their reversal lines were intact. Complete osteons with Haversian canals that deviated significantly from circular structures should be excluded. Mean area is calculated as the average cross-sectional area of 25 to 50 complete osteons per cross-section.

Several authors have used these variables and others to create algorithms to derive static indices of bone remodeling to be used for various purposes. Research by Stout and colleagues (1986, 1992, 1996) and Cho et al. (2002) have focused on developing equations to evaluate and predict age-related bone turnover in the rib. Frost (1987b,c) developed an algorithm to estimate the number of missing osteons that correspond to observed osteon populations densities (Stout and Paine 1994). The algorithm appeared promising to allow for more accurate age estimations when evaluating remodeling rates through static histomorphometry. Because new osteon creations eventually begin to remove all evidence of older turnover events, the algorithm allows for the estimation of the total number of osteon creations from the observed osteon population density of a cross-section. Frost provided a caveat, in that the lack of systematic studies to accurately determine the values for the variables within the algorithm, such as mean tissue age (MTA) and the fragment packing factor (k), limits its overall utility. Advances in dynamic histomorphometry will likely lead to a better understanding in how factors, such as biomechanics, affect the variables proposed by Frost. Dynamic histomorphometry, however, does not allow for the measure of bone remodeling rates averaged over the lifetime of an individual (Stout and Paine 1994) suggesting that a combination of static and dynamic research methods are needed to make advances in the field.

Basic static histomorphometry is typically performed through the preparation of undecalcified bone. Undecalcified[*] or decalcified bone samples may require special stains depending on the structures or processes that are being quantified. Traditionally used trichrome stains for paraffin-embedded tissue are not compatible with plastic-embedded bone (Villanueva and Mehr 1977); however, a number of stains are available for the histochemistry of plastic-embedded undecalcified bone (Anderson 1982). Various stains and staining techniques may be used to differentiate calcified bone from osteoid to allow the analyst to appreciate and measure the osteoid seam to quantify the amount of bone formation and resorption. Mineralized and unmineralized components of bone (i.e., osteoblasts, osteoclasts, and other cells) can easily be differentiated with the appropriate staining technique.[†] While evaluation of bone for age estimation or the determination of human versus nonhuman may not require any staining protocol, the analysis of, for example, a fracture callus using specific stains to estimate the timing of the injury will assist in quantifying the area of the mineralized callus, area of cartilaginous tissue within the callus, and the area or proportion of fibrotic tissue within the callus (Figures 1.5 and 1.6).

---

[*] Because the standard in most histology laboratories is to decalcify bone, the term undecalcified is often used rather than calcified bone.

[†] Histochemical staining is essentially limited to relatively fresh specimens, such as that acquired through biopsy or at autopsy. Bone cells and osteoid tissue is not preserved in archaeological or unfixed skeletal remains, making the use of histological staining unnecessary except for enhancing certain histomorphological features such as cement lines.

**Figure 1.5** Longitudinal section of the costochondral junction from an infant rib (hematoxylin and eosin [H&E] stain). The arrows denote fibrotic tissue and new bone development along the posterior aspect of the rib as the result of an antemortem costochondral fracture.

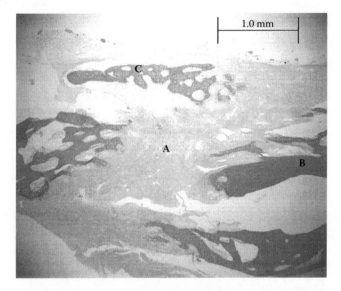

**Figure 1.6** Cross-section of an antemortem cranial fracture in an infant (H&E stain). (A) Fibrous tissue within the fracture gap, (B) primary lamellar bone, (C) new woven bone.

### 1.3.2 Dynamic Histomorphometry

Dynamic histomorphometry allows for the quantification of changes in cellular activity over time. To observe specific cellular responses, studies are performed in vitro or in vivo and the subject is exposed to various labeling techniques. One such procedure is to double-label bone with a fluorochrome, such as Tetracyclines, and measure histomorphometric parameters involved in bone turnover and bone mineralization over a specific period of time (Bassett et al. 1990; Frost 1969; Maggiano et al. 2006). The information obtained from static and dynamic histomorphometry provides useful information of bone turnover and other cellular responses in bone (Cho and Stout 2003; Cho et al. 2006; Pirok et al. 1966; Stout and Lueck 1995; Wu et al. 1970). Whereas dynamic histomorphometry reveals bone-remodeling rates occurring at the time that the tissue label was administered, static histomorphometry provides a measure of bone remodeling rates averaged over the age (effective age of adult compacta). Because static histomorphometry does not require the administration of an in vivo tissue time marker, it is most appropriate for anthropological research and can be used to estimate bone remodeling rates for unlabeled skeletal remains (Stout and Lueck 1995; Stout and Paine 1994; Wu et al. 1970). Although skeletal remains typically studied by anthropologists, including bioarchaeologists, forensic anthropologists, and paleontologists, are unlikely to contain intravital tissue labels, fortuitous evidence for labeling has been reported. For example, labeling was identified in skull fragments and used to support identification of the individual to whom they belonged (Stout and Ross 1991). Evidence of in vivo labeling of archaeological bone thought to have occurred through the consumption of stored grains infected with tetracycline-producing Streptomycetes has been reported (Bassett et al. 1990; Maggiano et al. 2003; Megan et al. 1989).

## 1.4   Reliability of Histological Analyses

Method reliability and validity is strongly emphasized in forensic anthropological research primarily because methods used in the forensic context must meet specific demands owing to the evidentiary nature of analytical results (Christensen and Crowder 2009; Crowder 2009). In the United States, the legal requirements for the evaluation of scientific evidence are set forth in *Daubert v. Merrell Dow Pharmaceuticals, Inc.*, 113 S.Ct. 2786 (1993). According to the *Daubert* criteria, a trial judge must determine if a method is adequately tested, subjected to peer review in a published journal, provided with potential error rates, and enjoys general acceptance within the relevant scientific community. Currently, methods of histological examination may not meet these standards. Very few large validation studies have been performed; thus error rates are unclear. Because of the guidelines established by the decisions in *Daubert v. Merrell Dow Pharmaceuticals, Inc.* (1993), *General Electric Co. v. Joiner* (1997), and *Kumho Tire Co. v. Carmichael* (1999), and in the wake of the National Academy of Sciences (NAS) report on the current state of the forensic sciences, methods used by forensic specialists may be more frequently challenged by the courts. Following the 1993 *Daubert* ruling and subsequent court rulings expanding the scope of the *Daubert* criteria, many forensic disciplines have determined that there is a need to critically reevaluate some of the techniques and methods used in their examinations, as well as the validity of the underlying scientific theories (Christensen and Crowder 2009). Methods with vague descriptions of samples, procedures, variables, or potential error rates should not be considered for use in the forensic setting. Thus, new methods or clarification of current methods are needed to improve scientific standards within the field. As previously mentioned, the ASBMR standardized the nomenclature for hard-tissue histologists (Parfitt et al. 1987) to relieve confusion and to reduce the semantic barriers that they must cross within the field; however, few researchers in anthropology have adhered to the protocol.

Crowder (2005) identified specific methodological issues in histological analyses and suggested protocols to improve histological methods (for the estimation of age at death) so that they may become a conventional tool for anthropological analysis and address the evidentiary standards. Recognizing and quantifying potential biases in histological analyses will support the development of best practices for histological analysis. Although various histological methods have been revised in the literature, the fundamental issues concerning the reliability and repeatability of these methods have not been fully addressed. The application of qualitative and quantitative bone histology as a preferred method in anthropological analyses has been hindered by researchers' uncertainty regarding the accuracy and reliability of the methods, as well as, an incomplete understanding in the literature of the biological processes behind intracortical bone remodeling. For example, while microscopic age changes are considered to be universal, the inconsistencies in reported accuracy of the methods when they are applied to individuals outside of the reference samples suggest that intrinsic and extrinsic biological factors, such as genetics and a wide range of suggested behaviors, have varying effects on bone microstructure. These issues can only be resolved through research designs that consider the dynamic nature of bone and evaluate results in the scope of skeletal biology.

## 1.5   Conclusions

The anthropological analyses of skeletal tissue should ideally employ a multilevel (e.g., gross [macroscopic] and microscopic) and multimodality (e.g., radiographs, CTs) approach. The inclusion of microscopic methods, especially histomorphometry can strengthen other analytical results and most important provide information that cannot be obtained from other methods. Most notably, in addition to age-at-death estimation, histomorphometry can provide insights into bone remodeling history that can be used to estimate remodeling rates creating what can be called "paleophysiology."

## References

Abbot S, Trinkaus E, Burr D (1996) Dynamic bone remodeling in later Pleistocene fossil hominids. Am J Phys Anthropol 99:585–601.

Anderson C (1982) Manual for the Examination of Bone. Boca Raton, FL: CRC Press, p. 116.

Bassett EM, Keith M, Armelagos G (1990) Tetracycline-labeled human bone from prehistoric Sudanese Nubia (A.D. 350). Science 209:1532–1534.

Bonewald LF, Johnson ML (2008). Osteocytes, mechanosensing and Wnt signaling. Bone 42(4):606–615.

Burr DB (1992) Estimated intracortical bone turnover in the femur of growing macaques: Implications for their use as models in skeletal pathology. Anat Rec 232:180–189.

Burr DB (2002) Targeted and nontargeted remodeling. Bone 30(1):2–4.

Burr DB, Ruff CB, Thompson DD (1990) Patterns of skeletal histologic change through time: Comparison of and archaic native American population with modern populations. Anat Rec 226:307–313.

Burr DB, Martin RB (1993) Calculating probability that microcracks initiate resorption spaces. J Biomech 26:613–616.

Carter DR, Beaupré G (2001) Skeletal Function and Form. Cambridge: Cambridge University Press.

Cho H, Stout SD, Madsen RW, Streeter MA (2002) Population-specific histological age-estimating method: A model for known African-American and European-American skeletal remains. J Forensic Sci 47(1):12–18.

Cho H, Stout S (2003) Bone remodeling and age-associated bone loss in the past: An histomorphometric analysis of the imperial Roman skeletal population of Isola Sacra. In: Agarwal SC, and Stout S, editors. Bone Loss and Osteoporosis: An Anthropological Perspective. New York: Kluwer Academic/Plenum, pp. 91–101.

Cho H, Stout S, Bishop T (2006) Cortical bone remodeling rates in a sample of African American and European American descent groups from the American Midwest: Comparisons of age and sex in ribs. Am J Phys Anthropol 130(2):214–226.

Christensen A, Crowder C (2009) Evidentiary standards for forensic anthropology. J Forensic Sci 54(6):1211–1216.

Crowder C (2005) Evaluating the use of quantitative bone histology to estimate adult age at death. Doctoral dissertation, University of Toronto, Ontario, Canada.

Crowder C (2009) Histological age estimation. In: Ubelaker DH, Blau S, editors. Handbook of Forensic Archaeology and Anthropology. Walnut Creek, CA: Left Coast Press, pp. 222–235.

*Daubert v. Merrell Dow Pharmaceuticals, Inc.*, 509 U.S. 579 (1993).

Emerton KB, Hu B, Woo AA, Sinofsky A, Hernandez C, Majeska RJ, Jepsen KJ, Schaffler MB (2010) Osteocyte apoptosis and control of bone resorption following ovariectomy in mice. Bone 46(3):577–583.

Epker BN, Frost HM (1965) The direction of transverse drift of activity forming osteons in the human rib cortex. J Bone Joint Surg 47a:1211–1215.

Ericksen MF (1973) Age-related bone remodeling in three aboriginal American populations. PhD dissertation, George Washington University, Washington DC.

Ericksen MF (1976) Cortical bone loss in three native American populations. Am J Phys Anthropol 45:443–452.

Ericksen MF (1991) Histological estimation of age at death using the anterior cortex of the femur. Am J Phys Anthropol 84:171–179.

Everts V, Delaissé JM, Korper W, Jansen DC, Tigchelaar-Gutter W, Saftig P, Beertsen W (2002) The bone lining cell: Its role in cleaning Howship's lacunae and initiating bone formation. J Bone Miner Res 17(1):77–90.

Forwood MR, Turner CH (1995) Skeletal adaptations to mechanical usage: Results from tibial loading studies in rats. Bone 17(4) Suppl:1975–2005.

Frost HM (1960) Presence of microscopic cracks in vivo in bone. Henry Ford Hosp Med Bull 8:25–35.

Frost HM (1969) Tetracycline based histological analysis of bone remodeling. Calcif Tissue Res 3:211–237.

Frost HM (1983) The skeletal intermediary organization. Metab Bone Dis Rel Res 4:281–290.

Frost HM (1986) Intermediary organization of the skeleton. Boca Raton, FL: CRC Press.

Frost HM (1987a) Bone "mass" and the "mechanostat": A proposal. Anat Rec 219:1–9.

Frost HM (1987b) Secondary osteon population densities: An algorithm for estimating missing osteons. Yrbk Phys Anthropol 30:239–254.

Frost HM (1987c) Secondary osteon populations: An algorithm for determining mean bone tissue age. Yrbk Phys Anthropol 30:221–238.

Frost HM (1997) Why do marathon runners have less bone than weight lifters? A vital-biomechanical view and explanation. Bone 20(3):183–189.

Frost HM (1998a) Changing concepts in skeletal physiology: Wolff's law, the mechanostat, and the "Utah paradigm." Am J Hum Biol 10:599–605.

Frost HM (1998b) From Wolff's law to the mechanostat: A new "face" of physiology. J Orthop Sci 3:282–286.

Frost HM (1999a) An approach to estimating bone and joint loads and muscle strength in living subjects and skeletal remains. Am J Hum Biol 11:437–455.

Frost HM (1999b) Why do bone strength and "mass" in aging adults become unresponsive to vigorous exercise? Insights of the Utah paradigm. J Bone Miner Metab 17:90–97.

Frost HM (2000a) Does bone design intend to minimize fatigue failures? A case for the affirmative. J Bone Miner Metab 18:278–282.

Frost HM (2000b) The Utah paradigm of skeletal physiology: An overview of its insights for bone, cartilage and collagenous tissue organs. J Bone Miner Metab 18:305–316.

Frost HM (2003) Bone's mechanostat: A 2003 update. Anat Rec Part A 275A:1081–1101.

Garrow JS, James WPT, Ralph A (2000) Human Nutrition and Dietetics, 10th edition. Edinburgh: Churchill Livingstone.

*General Electric Co. v. Joiner*, 522 US 136 (1997).

Hauge EM, Qvesel D, Eriksen EF, Mosekilde L, Melsen F (2001) Cancellous bone remodeling occurs in specialized compartments lined by cells expressing osteoblastic markers. J Bone Miner Res 16(9):1575–1582.

Johnson K, Goding J, Van Etten D, Sali A, Hu S-I, Farley D, Krug H, Hessle L, Millán JL, Terkeltaub R (2006) Linked deficiencies in extracellular PPi and Osteopontin mediate pathologic calcification associated with defective PC-1 and ANK expression. J Bone Miner Res 18(6):994–1004.

Kerley ER (1965) The microscopic determination of age in human bone. Am J Phys Anthropol 23:149–164.

Kerley ER, Ubelaker DH (1978) Revisions in the microscopic method of estimating age at death in human cortical bone. Am J Phys Anthropol 49:545–546.

Kimura K (1992) Estimation of age at death from second metacarpals. Z Morph Anthropol 79:169–181.

*Kumho Tire Co. v. Carmichael*, 526 U.S. 137 (1999).

Maggiano C, Dupras T, Schultz M, Biggerstaff J (2006) Spectral and photobleaching analysis using confocal laser scanning microscopy: A comparison of modern and archaeological bone fluorescence. Mol Cell Probes 20(3–4):154–162.

Maggiano C, Dupras TL, Biggerstaff J (2003) Ancient antibiotics: evidence for tetracycline in human and animal bone from kellis. In: Mills AJ, and Cope CA, editors. The Dakhleh Oasis Monograph. Oxford: Oxbow Books, pp. 331–344.

Marks SC, Odgren PR (2002) Structure and development of the skeleton. In: Bilezikian JP, Raisz LG, and Rodan GA, editors. Principles of Bone Biology. San Diego: Academic Press, pp. 3–16.

Martin DL, Armelagos GJ (1985) Skeletal remodeling and mineralization as indicators of health: An example from prehistoric Sudanese Nubia. J Hum Evol 14:527–537.

Martin RB (1994) On the histological measurement of osteonal BMU activation frequency. Bone 15:547–549.

Martin RB (2000a) Does osteocytes formation cause the nonlinear refilling of osteons? Bone 26(1):71–78.

Martin RB (2000b) Toward a unifying theory of bone remodeling. Bone 26(1):1–6.

Martin RB (2002) Is all cortical bone remodeling initiated by microdamage? Bone 30(1):8–13.

Martin RB (2003a) Functional adaptation and fragility of the skeleton. In Agarwald, SC and Stout, SD, editors. Bone Loss and Osteoporosis: An Anthropological Perspective. New York: Kluwer Academic/Plenum, pp. 121–136.

Martin RB (2003b) Fatigue damage, remodeling, and the minimization of skeletal weight. J Theor Biol 220:271–276.

Martin RB, Burr DB, Sharkey NA (1998) Skeletal Tissue Mechanics. New York: Springer-Verlag.

Megan C, El M, Anderson C (1989) Fluorochrome labelling in Roman period skeletons from Dakhleh Oasis, Egypt. Am J Phys Anthropol 80(2):137–143.

Monier-Faugere M, Langub MC, Malluche HH (1998) Bone biopsies: A modern approach. In: Avioli LV, Krane SM, editors. Metabolic Bone Diseases and Clinically Related Disorders, 3rd edition. San Diego: Academic Press, pp. 237–273.

Mulhern D (2009) Differentiating human from nonhuman skeletal remains. In: Ubelaker DH, Blau S, editors. Handbook of Forensic Archaeology and Anthropology. Walnut Creek, CA: Left Coast Press, pp. 222–235.

Mulhern DM, Van Gerven DP (1997) Patterns of femoral bone remodeling dynamics in a medieval Nubian population. Am J Phys Anthropol 104:133–146.

Mulhern D, Ubelaker DH (2003) Histologic examination of bone development in juvenile chimpanzees. Am J Phys Anthropol 122:127–133.

NIAMS (2006) Scientists Gain New Clues to Bone Mineralization. News and Events.

Nijweide PJ, Burger EH, Klein-Nulend J (2002) The osteocyte. In: Bilezikian JP, Raisz LG, Rodan GA, editors. Principles of Bone Biology, 2nd edition. San Diego: Academic Press, pp. 93–107.

Ortner DJ, Putschar WG (1985) Identification of Pathological Conditions in Human Skeletal Remains. Smithsonian Institution Press: Washington, DC.

Ortner DJ (1975) Aging effects on osteon remodeling. Calcif Tissue Res 18:27–36.

Ott SM (2002) Histomorphometric analysis of bone remodeling. In: Bilezikian JP, Raisz LG, Rodan GA, editors. Principles of Bone Biology. San Diego: Academic Press, pp. 303–319.

Paine R, Godfrey L (1997) The scaling of skeletal microanatomy in non-human primates. J Zool, Lond 241:803–821.

Parfitt A (1979) Quantum concept of bone remodeling and turnover: Implications for the pathogenesis of osteoporosis. Calcif Tissue Int 28:1–5.

Parfitt AM (2004) The attainment of peak bone mass: What is the relationship between muscle growth and bone growth? Bone 34:767–770.

Parfitt AM (2005) Targeted and nontargeted remodeling: Relationship to basic multicellular unit organization and progression. Bone 30(1):5–7.

Parfitt AM, Drezner MK, Glorieux FH, Kanis JH, Malluche H, Meunier PJ, Ott SM, Recker RR (1987) Bone histomorphometry: Standardization of nomenclature, symbols, and units. J Bone Miner Res 2:595–610.

Peck J, Stout S (2008) The effects of total hip arthroplasty on the structural and biomechanical properties of adult bone. Am J Phys Anthropol 138(2):221–230.

Peck W, Woods W (1988) The cells of bone. In: Riggs B, Melton LI, editors. Osteoporosis: Etiology, Diagnosis, and Management. New York: Raven, pp. 1–44.

Pettit AR, Chang MK, Hume DA (2008) Osteal macrophages: A new twist on coupling during bone dynamics. Bone 43:976–982.

Pfeiffer S, Lazenby R (1994) Low bone mass in past and present aboriginal populations. In: Draper HH, editor. Advances in Nutritional Research, Vol. 9. New York: Plenum Press, pp. 35–51.

Pirok DJ, Ramser JR, Takahashi H, Villanueva AR, Frost H (1966) Normal histological, tetracycline and dynamic parameters in human, mineralized bone sections. Henry Ford Hospital Medical Bulletin 14:195–218.

Przybeck T (1985) Histomorphology of the rib: Bone mass and cortical remodeling. In: Davies R, Leathers C, editors. Behavior and Pathology of Aging in Rhesus Monkeys. New York: Alan R. Liss, pp. 303–326.

Rauch F, Baily DA, Baxter-Jones A, Mirwald R, Faulkner R (2004) The "muscle-bone unit" during the pubertal growth spurt. Bone 34:771–775.

Robling AG, Castillo AB, Turner CH (2006) Biomechanical and molecular regulation of bone remodeling. Annu Rev Biomed Eng 8(1):455–498.

Robling AG, Stout SD (2008). Histomorphometry of human cortical bone: Applications to age estimation. In Katzenberg S, Saunders S, editors. Biological Anthropology of the Human Skeleton, 2nd edition. New York: Wiley-Liss.

Robling AR, Stout SD (1999) Morphology of the drifting osteon. Cells Tissue Organs 164:192–204.

Schaffler MB, Burr DB (1984) Primate cortical bone microstructure: Relationship to locomotion. Am J Phys Anthropol 65(2):191–197.

Schock C, Noyes F, Crouch M, Matthews C (1975) The effects of immobility on long bone remodelling in the rhesus monkey. Henry Ford Hosp Med J 23:107–115.

Schock C, Noyes F, Villaneuva A (1972) Measurement of Haversian bone remodelling by means of tetracycline labelling in the rib of rhesus monkeys. Henry Ford Hospital Medical Bulletin 20:131–144.

Schoenau E, Frost HM (2002) The "muscle-bone unit" in children and adolescents. Calcif Tissue Int 70:405–407.

Singh I, Tonna E, Grandel C (1974) A comparative histological study of mammalian bone. J Morphol 144:421–438.

Stout SD (1986) The use of bone histomorphometry in skeletal identification: The case of Francisco Pizarro. J Forensic Sci 31(1):296–300.

Stout SD (1989) Histomorphometric analysis of human skeletal remains. In Işcan MY, Kennedy KA, editors. Reconstruction of Life from the Skeleton. New York: Wiley-Liss, pp. 41–52.

Stout S, Streeter M (2006) Histomorphometric analysis of the cortical bone of the rib of Hanaab-Pakal. In: Tiesler V, and Cucina A, editors. Studying Janaab'Pakal and Recreating Maya Dynastic History. Tucson, AZ: University of Arizona Press.

Stout S, Streeter M (2004) Un Analisis Histomorfologico del Hueso Cortical de la Costilla de Janaab'Pakal. In: Tiesler V, Cucina A, editors. Janaab'Pakal De Palenque: Vida Y Muerte De Un Gobernanante Maya. Universidad National Automoma de Mexico, pp. 123–136.

Stout SD, Marcello AP, Perotti B (1996) Brief communication: A test and correction of the clavicle method of Stout and Paine for histological age estimation of skeletal remains. Am J Phys Anthropol 100:139–142.

Stout SD, Lueck R (1995) Bone remodeling rates and maturation in three archaeological skeletal populations. Am J Phys Anthropol 98:161–171.

Stout S, Paine R (1994) Bone remodeling rates: A test on an algorithm for estimating missing osteons. Am J Phys Anthropol 93:123–129.

Stout SD, Paine RR (1992) Brief communication: Histological age estimation using rib and clavicle. Am J Phys Anthropol 87:111–115.

Stout SD, Ross LM (1991) Bone fragments a body can make. J Forensic Sci 36(3):953–957.

Streeter M, Stout S, Trinkaus E, Burr D (2010) Brief communication: Bone remodeling rates in Pleistocene humans are not slower than the rates observed in modern populations: A reexamination of Abbott et al. (1996). Am J Phys Anthropol 141(2):315–318.

Tang Y, Wu X, Lei W, Pang L, Wan C, Shi Z, Zhao L, Nagy TR, Peng X, Hu J et al. (2009) TGF-beta1-induced migration of bone mesenchymal stem cells couples bone resorption with formation. Nat Med 15(7):757–765.

Thompson DD, Gunness-Hey M (1981) Bone mineral-osteon analysis of Yupik-Inupiaq skeletons. Am J Phys Anthropol 55:1–7.

Thompson DD, Cowen KS (1984) Age at death and bone biology of the Barrow mummies. Arctic Anthropol 21:83–88.

Turner CH (1999) Toward a mathematical description of bone biology: The principle of cellular accommodation. Calcif Tissue Int 65:466–481.

Turner CH (2000) Toward a mathematical description of bone biology: The principle of cellular accommodation. Calcif Tissue Int 67:185–187.

Turner CH, Robling AG, Duncan, RL, Burr, DB (2002) Do bone cells behave like a neuronal network? Calcif Tissue Int 70:435–442.

van Oers R (2008) A unified theory for osteonal and hemi-osteonal remodeling. Bone 42(2):250–259.

van Oers R, Ruimerman R, van Reitbergen B, Hilbers A, Huiskes R (2008) Relating osteon diameter to strain. Bone 43:476–482.

Van Wagenen G (1970) Menopause in a subhuman primate. Anat Rec 166:392.

Verborgt O, Gibson GJ, Schaffler MB (2000) Loss of osteocyte integrity in association with microdamage and bone remodeling after fatigue in vivo. J Bone Miner Res 15:60–67.

Villanueva AR, Mehr LA (1977) Modifications of the Goldner and Gomori one-step trichrome stains for plastic-embedded thin sections of bone. Am J Med Technol 43(6):536–538.

Wu K, Schubeck K, Frost H, Villanueva A (1970) Haversian bone formation rates determined by a new method in a mastadon and in human diabetes mellitus and osteoporosis. Calcif Tissue Res 6:204–219.

# Growth and Development
## Morphology, Mechanisms, and Abnormalities

2

JAMES H. GOSMAN

## Contents

## 2.1 Introduction

Forensic scientists analyze skeletal remains to make inferences about the individuals when living. These include assessments of age at death, cause and manner of death, ancestry, pathological conditions, health, trauma, skeletal biomechanics, and other aspects of behavioral interpretation. Essential to all these endeavors is an understanding of the biology underlying skeletal growth and development, and the journey to adult skeletal morphology. This pathway is characterized by complex, interactive, hierarchical biological systems, which are the subjects of intense research interest in many areas of concern: genetic influences, diet/nutrition, linear growth/stature, and bone functional adaptation. This chapter does not provide an exhaustive review of this vast topic nor embark into the familiar aging framework but rather presents a selective overview of the current knowledge of the fundamental process of longitudinal bone growth focusing on histomorphology, regulatory systems, and ontogenetic changes in cortical and trabecular bone architecture. These concepts are placed within a broader biocultural context, discussing important environmental

23

and mechanobiological influences on skeletal growth and development, and their implications for forensic anthropologists, researchers, and scientists.

## 2.2 Endochondral Ossification

### 2.2.1 General Process

Endochondral ossification is the foundation of linear growth of human long bones and is the procedure by which the skeletal cartilage anlagen are replaced by bone (Olsen et al. 2000). This process involves the formation of a cartilage primordium and growth plate, where chondrocytes initially undergo proliferation and a series of differentiation steps secreting a cartilage template that is eventually replaced by bone (Lai and Mitchell 2005). The anlagen elongate and expand in width by proliferation of chondrocytes and deposition of cartilage matrix. Chondrocytes undergo further maturation to hypertrophic chondrocytes (HC) and synthesize an extracellular matrix. Angiogenic factors secreted by hypertrophic chondrocytes induce angiogenesis from the perichondrium; osteoblasts, osteoclasts, and hematopoietic cells come with the blood vessels. The primary ossification center is thus formed.

Within the ossification center, the hypertrophic chondrocytic matrix is degraded, the hypertrophic chondrocytes undergo apoptosis, and osteoblasts replace the disappearing cartilage with trabecular bone. Bone marrow is also formed during this process. Simultaneously, osteoblasts in the perichondrium form a collar of compact bone around the diaphysis of the cartilage, locating the primary ossification center within a tube of bone. At one or both ends (epiphyses) of the cartilage, secondary ossification centers are formed, leaving a plate of cartilage (growth plate) between the epiphysis and diaphysis. Elongation of the long bone from the growth plate results from a coordinated sequence of chondrocyte proliferation, hypertrophy, and apoptosis. It is this choreographed process that creates the initial framework of trabecular bone and, thus in part, the foundation upon which the ontogenetic patterning and subsequent adult morphology rests. Concurrently, these processes are coordinated with growth in the epiphysis and radial periosteal appositional growth of the diaphysis (Olsen et al. 2000). Bone growth at the growth-plate cartilage or at an ossification center per se is insufficient to form the complex shapes of developing bones. This requires constant modeling and remodeling, which occurs within the bone tissue as well as in the endosteal, and periosteal bone envelopes in the form of bone deposition and resorption (Aiello and Dean 2002).

### 2.2.2 Morphological Features

Cartilage involved in endochondral ossification is found in both the growth plate (bounded by the epiphysis and metaphysis) and the articular-epiphyseal growth center. These are responsible for the extension of the primary and secondary centers of ossification (Mackie et al. 2008). This discussion will focus on the growth plate, which is organized into three morphologically distinctive zones, each with its own particular functional biology: the zones of resting (reserve), proliferative, and hypertrophic chondrocytes (Figure 2.1).

The resting zone is most distant from the ossification front and is the only zone that has a vascular supply, passing through the epiphysis and terminating at the upper end of

**Figure 2.1 (See color insert.)** Color photomicrograph of the specific structural features of the physis of the proximal aspect of the tibia of a four-week-old rabbit embryo. The epiphyseal bone is above, the physeal cartilage (growth plate) in purple, and the metaphyseal bone is below (blue). The physeal cartilage is composed of resting, proliferative (columnar), and hypertrophic zones (toluidine blue, ×60). (From Rivas R and Shapiro F, 2002, J Bone Joint Surg AM 84:85–100. Reproduced by permission, JBJS, Inc.)

the proliferative zone. The chondrocytes of this zone have cellular machinery indicative of protein synthesis (endoplasmic reticulum), but this low oxygen tension region exhibits little cellular proliferation or matrix production. The adjacent zone of proliferation is under the influence of systemic and local biochemical factors changing the round chondrocytes into flattened cells packed into multicellular clusters and arranged in columns. This zone merges into a transitional stage characterized by prehypertrophic chondrocytes, which in turn segues into the third zone composed of hypertrophic chondrocytes.

The hypertrophic chondrocytes have increased their volume five to ten times. They have an elevated content of glycolytic enzymes and are producing and secreting extracellular matrix, which in due course becomes mineralized. Chondrocyte proliferation and hypertrophy are responsible for elongation of the bone. In the middle portion of the hypertrophic zone the chondrocytes are releasing calcium, resulting in the zone of provisional calcification, which is characterized by vertical septa of the calcified matrix. Cell death of the hypertrophic chondrocytes ensues. The synthesis of type II collagen predominates and is an essential component for cartilage structural integrity and chondrocyte survival (Whyte 2006). Terminal chondrocyte hypertrophy is associated with a reduction in the synthesis of collagen type II and concomitant initiation of the secretion of collagen type X (van der Eerden et al. 2003). This later protein may be important in chondrocyte signaling networks (Leitinger and Kwan 2006).

The arrangement of the longitudinal bars of provisional calcification allows vascular ingrowth into the ossification front, delivering blood vessels, chondro/osteoclasts (multinucleate cartilage- and bone-resorbing cells), osteoblast precursors, and bone marrow cells. The chondro/osteoclasts remove the cartilage matrix and the osteoblasts use the remnants of the cartilage scaffold to lay down new bone matrix (osteoid), forming the primary spongiosa. The results of remodeling of this zone establish the region known as the secondary spongiosa. Trabecular bone produced at the growth plate is thought to contribute to metaphyseal and diaphyseal cortical bone (endosteal and Haversian) through a process of trabecular coalescence modified by modeling and remodeling (Cadet et al. 2003). This process is important to the longitudinal growth of cortical bone and provides a framework upon which intramembranous periosteal bone apposition/resorption operates, regulated in part, by the anatomically specific, local mechanical environment (Tanck et al. 2006), genetic patterning, regulatory framework, and hormonal status.

The shape of the long bone is likewise influenced by a genetically formed patterning regime, systemic and local biochemical signaling, and mechanical forces. This is likely to be both independent of and interrelated to linear growth and development (Lovejoy et al. 2003). Modeling is the process by which bone is actively removed in one location and added in another contributing to maintenance of shape during growth-related size change. Two associated growth plate structures are important in this regard: the perichondrial ring of Lacroix and the ossification groove of Ranvier. The perichondrial ring of Lacroix (1947) contains an extension of metaphyseal bone (bone bark) and collagen fibers, both of which provide stability to the growth plate. The ossification groove of Ranvier (Shapiro et al. 1977) is a wedge-shaped collection of cells on the periphery of the growth plate, which is thought to provide cartilage cells to the reserve and proliferative zones, and is instrumental in expanding the diameter of the growth plate.

## 2.2.3  Cellular Morphology

Growth cartilage chondrocyte ultrastructural studies have demonstrated two separate proliferative and hypertrophic cell types—"light" and "dark"—each with different cellular morphology and different patterns of cell death (Mackie et al. 2008; Wilsman et al. 1981). Currently no data are available for differentiating molecular processes. The light chondrocytes are rounded cells with minimal cytoplasmic processes extended into the extracellular matrix. They are characterized by sparse endoplasmic reticulum, a limited Golgi region, and a cell death process by disintegration within their cell membrane. The dark chondrocytes have an irregular shape with many dense cytoplasmic processes. They have a complex endoplasmic reticulum, a prominent Golgi apparatus, vesicles budding from the cell surface, and a cell death process by extrusion of cytoplasm into the extracellular space (Ahmed et al. 2007).

The chondrocyte cytoskeleton, which is thought to have a role in cell hypertrophy and the organization of growth cartilage, is an area of active research. The cytoskeleton is an interconnected network of microtubules, actin, and vimentin (intermediate filament family of proteins that support and anchor the position of organelles in the cytoplasmic matrix; Benjamin et al. 1994). This system in combination with the chondrocyte primary cilium are thought to interact with the extracellular matrix in regulating cell shape, intracellular signaling, and phenotype in regard to chondrocyte hypertrophy (Jensen et al. 2004). Defects in endochondral ossification have been noted in mouse strains with genetic alteration in chondrocyte primary cilium formation, resulting in neonatal dwarfism (McGlashan et al. 2007). The cytoskeleton is important in regard to mechanosensation/transduction functions. However, the exact role that the various components of the cytoskeleton play in the organization and changes of growth cartilage remains unclear at this time.

Mineralization of the matrix surrounding late hypertrophic chondrocytes (with hydroxyapatite) is an essential component of endochondral ossification. Cell membrane matrix vesicles are released by hypertrophic chondrocytes into the extracellular space, providing the nucleation site for mineralization (Kirsch et al. 1997; Mackie et al. 2008).

These vesicles contain an anatomically specific combination of various proteins including annexins (membrane-associated proteins that mediate the influx of calcium ions into the matrix vesicles), phosphate transporters, and phosphatases. The mineralization process is dependent on alkaline phosphatase, which is thought to remove extracellular pyrophosphate, an inhibitor of mineralization (Kirsch 2006). Recent studies have suggested that while mineralization is not essential for normal chondrocyte maturation, it is required for normal bone deposition on cartilage remnants. The bone volume fraction in the primary spongiosa is decreased in mice with reduced mineralization of growth cartilage matrix (Yamada et al. 2006).

### 2.2.4 Regulatory Framework

The complex, carefully coordinated sequence of perichondral development, angiogenesis, chondrocyte proliferation, and chondrocyte differentiation is required for the progression of endochondral bone formation and maintenance of normal childhood growth (Stevens and Williams 1999). Recent research is beginning to bring understanding to the fundamental regulatory processes for control of endochondral bone formation, which involves the interaction of systemic hormones, locally derived growth factors, and their effects on growth plate chondrocyte gene expression (Ballock and O'Keefe 2003). Studies have identified Indian hedgehog (Ihh) as a key coordinating molecule in these processes: stimulating growth plate chondrocyte proliferation, preventing chondrocyte hypertrophy, and regulating bone formation in the perichondrial collar and trabecular bone below the growth plate (Olsen et al. 2000). Parathyroid hormone-related peptide (PTHrP) is another important signaling molecule that is instrumental in regulating chondrocyte maturation and differentiation (Stevens and Williams 1999). Ihh and perichondrial PTHrP are essential components of a feedback loop that regulates cell differentiation and the relative proportions of proliferating and hypertrophic chondrocytes in growth plate (Kronenberg 2003). The Ihh portion of this feedback loop influences bone formation and the pool of proliferation chondrocytes by two known mechanisms: one independent of PTHrP and the other through PTHrP expression by cells in the periarticular perichondrium (Olsen et al. 2000). The second pathway relies on patched (Ptc)/smoothened (Smo) signaling. Patched is a transmembrane protein that is a molecular target suppressing the signal transduction in the absence of Ihh; smoothened is a receptor necessary for Ihh signaling to be activated (Figure 2.2).

Bone morphogenic proteins (BMPs) are members of the transforming growth factor-B superfamily. They have been demonstrated to play many roles in skeletal morphogenesis (van der Eerden et al. 2003). They are considered to be downstream mediators of Ihh signaling, a possible positive inducer of Ihh expression, and supportive of the proliferation of chondrocytes in growth cartilage (Mackie et al. 2008; Pathi et al. 1999). The Wnt family of proteins (named for the *wingless* gene originally identified in *Drosophila*) activate signaling pathways (beta-catenin and others) expressed in growth cartilage, which are vital for chondrocyte survival, proliferation, and hypertrophy. This is downstream from Ihh early in the proliferative zone but independent from Ihh later in this same zone (Mak et al. 2006). These factors and many other known, or as yet unknown, molecules are involved in the complex autoregulatory network of growth cartilage choreography (e.g., collagen X and vascular endothelial growth factor [VEGF]); the more important players and interactions are starting to be identified (reviewed by Mackie et al. 2008 and van der Eerden et al. 2003).

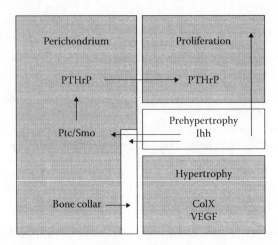

**Figure 2.2** Diagram showing how Indian hedgehog (Ihh) expressed by cells in the prehypertrophic zone of growth plate cartilage controls bone formation in the bone collar and proliferation of chondrocytes in the proliferative growth plate zone by both mechanisms independent of parathyroid hormone-related protein (PTHrP) as well as through stimulation of PTHrP synthesis by cells in the periarticular perichondrium. The latter functions by signaling through patched (Ptc)/smoothened (Smo) pathways. Increased signaling through the PTHrP receptor causes proliferation and maintenance of the pool of proliferative chondrocytes, and delay of chondrocyte hypertrophy (and associated expression of Ihh, collage X [ColX], and vascular endothelial growth factor [VEGF]). Decreased signaling has the opposite effect. (From Olsen B, Reginato A, and Wang W, 2000, Annu Rev Cell Dev Bi 16:191–220. Reproduced by permission, Annual Reviews.)

The major systemic hormones that regulate linear growth through endochondral bone formation during childhood include growth hormone (GH) and insulin-like growth factor-1 (IGF-1), thyroid hormone (T3), and glucocorticoids. The major contribution during adolescence comes from sex steroids. Recent research has demonstrated the importance of these hormones and locally derived proteins to the control of growth and their underlying molecular mechanisms (Stevens and Williams 1999; van der Eerden et al. 2003). The GH–IGF-1 signaling system is required for normal growth of the skeleton (Nilsson and Baron 2005). Targeted disruption studies have consistently demonstrated severe growth retardation and delayed bone development (Sims et al. 2000; Stevens and Williams 1999). GH stimulates chondrocyte proliferation and thus longitudinal growth through pathways both dependent and partly independent of IGF-1 (Yakar et al. 2002).

Childhood hypothyroidism results in a reversible but complete arrest of linear bone growth from the disorganization of epiphyseal growth plate chondrocytes and disrupted endochondral bone formation (Shao et al. 2006). These changes can be rescued by thyroid hormone replacement. Thyroid hormone and triiodothyronine (T3) are instrumental in the terminal differentiation of growth plate chondrocytes including cell hypertrophy, collagen type X expression, and alkaline phosphatase activity. Thyroid hormone receptors-$\alpha$ are responsible for the responses in growth cartilage, acting through the Wnt/beta-catenin signaling pathway (Wang et al. 2007).

Androgens and estrogens are crucial for peripubertal growth and skeletal maturation, and for the cessation of linear growth in adulthood as they induce epiphyseal growth plate fusion at the end of puberty. This process occurring in both males and females is under the control of estrogen's direct effects on estrogen receptors in growth cartilage (Grumbach

2000). Both sex steroids influence GH secretion, exert direct effects on the growth plate, and are important in the bone responsiveness to mechanical loading (see van der Eerden et al. 2003). The effects of glucocorticoids (GC) on bone growth include decreased bone volume and growth retardation, likely secondary to reduced chondrocyte proliferation (Smink et al. 2003) and increased hypertrophic chondrocyte apoptosis (Chrysis et al. 2003). Glucocorticoid receptors have been identified in hypertrophic chondrocytes of the human growth plate (Abu et al. 2000). Growth retardation related to GC is thought to be due to the direct effects from the GC receptor pathway as well as by perturbations in other growth-related pathways, such as modifications in the GH–IFG-1 mechanisms (Smink et al. 2003) and modulation of thyroid hormone activity (Miura et al. 2002).

## 2.3 Ontogenetic Changes in Cortical and Trabecular Architecture

### 2.3.1 Ontogenetic Patterns and Mechanical Loading

Endochondral ossification combined with periosteal appositional ossification establishes the initial bone shape upon which all subsequent biologically, genetically, and mechanically driven modeling/remodeling occurs. Bone morphogenesis from growth plate cartilage to the secondary spongiosa is thought to be highly conserved, quantitatively predictable, and very similar among mammalian species (Byers et al. 2000; Salle et al. 2002). Descriptive qualitative and quantitative histomorphometric data on the growth plate and associated metaphyseal region of long bones during human growth and development are well established in the scientific literature and demonstrate, in general, that trabecular bone mass (BV/TV) increases with age via an increase in trabecular thickness until skeletal maturity, while trabecular number decreases (Glorieux et al. 2000; Kneissel et al. 1997; Sontag 1994).

Recent studies of the ontogenetic patterning of human trabecular bone suggest a broad similarity in developmental processes, including modeling and remodeling, across various anatomical sites (humerus, femur, and tibia), while providing evidence suggesting a significant mechanical influence from initiation and maturation of human bipedal locomotion (Gosman 2007; Gosman and Ketcham 2009; Ryan and Krovitz 2006; Ryan et al. 2007). The bone volume fraction (BV/TV) values for all three bones start out very high in neonatal individuals, decline to a minimum in all three bones around one year of age, and then progressively increase again to adult levels through development. Most significantly for a locomotor signal in humans is the higher BV/TV in the lower limb than the upper limb. The trabecular thickness results also show a divergence between the humerus on the one hand, and the femur and tibia on the other. Trabecular thickness increases progressively with age in all three anatomical locations; trabeculae in the tibia and femur are consistently thicker than those in the humerus. The results indicate that the general patterns of change in trabecular number (decreases during ontogeny) and anisotropy (spatially specific) are similar across all three bones. Using finite element models to predict elastic properties of trabecular bone during development, Ryan and coworkers (2007) have demonstrated mechanically significant structural differences between the femur and humerus during development. The elastic properties of femoral trabecular bone increased at a much faster rate than those of the humerus after the acquisition of unassisted bipedal walking. These results match quite nicely with those of Ruff on the development of strength characteristics in the cortical bone of the humerus and femur in humans (Ruff 2003a, 2003b; Sumner and

Andriacchi 1996) as well as ontogenetic changes in femoral cross-sectional shape associated with the initiation of human gait (Wittman et al. 2009).

## 2.4   Environmental and Mechanobiological Influences

Skeletal growth and development processes and the resultant adult morphology are strongly influenced by environmental factors, especially perturbations early in life, diet and nutritional insufficiencies, and changes in physical activity. These provide continuity and change during life history through the processes of growth, modeling, remodeling, and skeletal adaptation. The current concepts of the biology of skeletal growth and development combined with a life course perspective sets the stage for further understanding of the prevalence, causes, and consequences of variation in human skeletal tissue—the core of forensic analyses and observations.

### 2.4.1   Early Onset–Later Disease: Maternal–Fetal Environment

Research over the past four decades has demonstrated that perturbations early in life "could have long-term, irreversible consequences" and "also that the insult must occur during a critical period of development to have maximal effect" (Gillman 2005:1848). Two essential critical periods are fetal development and adolescent growth and maturation (Cameron and Demerath 2002; Worthman and Kuzara 2005). First-generation studies on early origins of later disease concentrated on associations between birth weight and disease occurrence decades later (Barker 1998; Gluckman and Hanson 2004; Hales and Barker 2001). These researchers found relationships between low birth weight and later obesity, type 2 diabetes mellitus, and ischemic cardiovascular disease, proposing that this phenomenon was a consequence of the thrifty phenotype hypothesis (Hales and Barker 2001). This hypothesis identifies fetal adaptation to a deficient intrauterine environment as a general biological process associated with later-life disease. These early studies were criticized for having too narrow a focus and ignoring socioeconomic variables (Gillman 2002).

Current research is focused on a broad range of prenatal determinants on postnatal outcomes, including maternal diet, placental function and blood flow, and fetal metabolism (Gillman 2005; Schooling et al. 2008) as well as late consequences of variations in postnatal growth and development (Barker et al. 2005). Gluckman, Hanson, and others (2005) have proposed a scheme outlining a broader set of developmental and evolutionary strategies based on the capacity for a single genotype to produce different phenotypes in different environments. This form of developmental plasticity may be an adaptive response early in life with an effect later in life (Bateson, et al. 2004). These are termed *predictive adaptive responses* (PARs) in which the phenotype is not necessarily advantageous in the environment concurrent with or immediately following the inducing cue but is likely to be advantageous in an anticipated future environment (Gluckman et al. 2005). These human PARs may have become increasingly inappropriate in the recent human environmental circumstances (e.g., overnutrition and low physical activity levels), contributing to disease conditions in later life.

Recent research has taken on the quantitative study of human fetal bone development by histomorphometric (Salle et al. 2002) and microCT methods (Nuzzo et al. 2003). These techniques demonstrate an extremely rapid rate of trabecular bone metabolism, cell division, and modeling especially in the last trimester of fetal development, manifested by increasing bone volume fraction, trabecular thickness, brisk matrix mineralization, and increasing hydroxyapatite crystal size. There are data to suggest that environmental influences during early life (intrauterine) interact with the genome in establishing the functional level of a variety of metabolic processes involved in skeletal growth, including neonatal bone mass (Cooper et al. 2002; Javaid and Cooper 2002). After adjusting for gestational age, neonatal bone density is positively associated with birth weight, birth length, and placental weight. Maternal factors negatively associated with neonatal bone density are maternal smoking, maternal nutrition at 18 weeks gestation, and high maternal physical activity (Godfrey et al. 2001). Neonatal bone density has been demonstrated to be lower among winter births than among summer births. This is associated with winter month maternal vitamin D deficiency (Javaid and Cooper 2002; McGrath et al. 2005).

Mechanisms for the induction of fetal programming in regard to skeletal development are thought to include (1) a nutrient environment (in the most general sense) which may permanently alter gene expression important to the activity of metabolic enzymes or the responsiveness of various tissues within the growth plate to endocrine systems such as growth hormone/insulin-like growth factor I, as well as hypothalamic-pituitary-adrenal and gonadal hormones. Vitamin $D_3$ responsiveness is also likely to be a factor. The mechanisms are also thought to include (2) a nutrient environment, which may permanently reduce cell numbers in the growth plate. The high growth rates of the fetus are mostly the result of cell replication. Fewer cells equal a reduced capacity for growth. In addition, the slowing of whatever growth is occurring is considered to be a major adaptation to undernutrition (Cooper et al. 2002). Evidence is accumulating from human studies of the consequences of these various factors on intrauterine skeletal mineralization and neonatal bone density. The important element from a forensic perspective is that undernutrition and other adverse influences arising in fetal life can have a permanent effect on body structure. The intrauterine environment and early development are key variables in the study of variation in human remains, particularly when viewed from the broader context of differing environmental, cultural, and nutritional circumstances (Cardoso 2007; Rao and Apte 2009).

## 2.4.2   Diet/Nutrition

The nutritional environment is accommodating to skeletal development. That is, enough is good enough. There is no indication that an excess of nutrients will result in greater bone development (other than an indirect effect associated with increased body weight; Bass et al. 2005). The most significant effect of nutrition on bone development (trabecular and cortical) is when there is a state of deficiency of nutritional status. Nutritional status is the balance between nutrient-energy intake and nutrient-energy requirements. The immediate effect of malnutrition in children is reduced longitudinal growth. The longer term effect is bone loss due to increased endosteal resorption and trabecular thinning (Bass et al. 2005). Nutrient deficiencies documented to lead to skeletal growth disturbances, and for which the requirements are known, are energy, protein, calcium, iron, zinc, vitamin D, and vitamin A (Berti et al. 1998).

Nutrition influences skeletal development (linear growth and bone density) indirectly through hormone systems, namely, sex steroids, thyroid hormone, GH, and IGF-I. In terms of the trabecular and cortical bone envelopes, total energy, protein, and calcium are key nutrients. In animal models, protein and caloric restriction results in reduced linear growth, cortical thinning, and trabecular wasting. This is associated with a disruption in the sex steroid and GH–IGF axis inducing osteoblast resistance to IGF-1 in both the cortical and trabecular bone envelopes (Bourrin et al. 2000).

Human studies agree with the animal models, demonstrating that an energy deficit and protein deficiency both lead to an apparent reduction in bone formation and an increase in bone resorption (Cooke and Zanker 2004). In the growing skeleton, these result in retarded longitudinal growth, less trabecular bone accrual, and decreased trabecular bone density. The biochemical pathway by which energy and protein malnutrition influence bone growth and development is thought to be by suppressing IGF-I levels or the bone cells' sensitivity to IGF-I (Bourrin et al. 2000). This reduces bone formation. In addition to affecting the GH–IGF-I axis, these deficiencies, when severe, are also associated with imbalances in the sex steroid axis, namely, estrogen deficiency or resistance (Ammann et al. 2000). This increases bone resorption. A contributing factor, in the context of energy and protein deficiencies, may be reduced mechanical loading associated with reduced muscle mass, body weight, and physical inactivity (Bass et al. 2005).

Calcium is important to skeletal growth and tissue mineralization. It is commonly thought to be a key determinant for maximizing bone density during growth. Fortunately, bone density appears to be maintained across a broad range of dietary calcium intakes until a variable physiological threshold is reached. Reduced calcium intake has not been found to influence bone growth and development to the same degree as energy and protein malnutrition (Bass 2000). Calcium supplementation has been associated with increased bone density. However, a recent review of dietary calcium-intake-related studies suggests that the independent effect of calcium supplementation in children has not been verified (Lanou et al. 2005).

### 2.4.3   Bone Functional Adaptation

The life history interval, which encompasses the prepubertal to young-adult years, is the time period in which skeletal tissues are highly responsive to mechanical loads generated by physical activity. The assessments of levels of physical activity and workload, which are important issues in the anthropological research agenda, are fundamentally based on the mechanobiological concepts and regulatory signaling pathways previously discussed. Current methods for assessing physical activity levels from archaeological and forensic skeletal remains include relative cortical robusticity (Ruff et al. 1993), long bone diaphyseal geometry, enthesiopathies (Weiss 2003), degenerative joint disease (Klaus et al. 2009), histomorphometry (Stout and Leuck 1995), and changes in trabecular bone microarchitecture (Gosman and Ketcham 2009).

Daily cyclic loading of cortical and cancellous bone is produced by customary and habitual activities (walking, running, climbing, and carrying) applied consistently over a long period of time. Bone formation, resorption, and directionality are determined by the specifics of the daily stress stimulus. For example, changes in load magnitudes result in changes of bone density and thickness (Sundberg et al. 2001) and changes in load direction results in changes of architectural pattern (Carter and Beaupré 2001; Pontzer et al. 2006; Ruimerman et al. 2005). Age effects on bone structural adaptation are important considerations for accurate behavioral interpretations. There is age specificity in bone response to mechanical loading: qualitative and quantitative (Bertram and Swartz 1991). Age-related research has been primarily focused on cortical bone size and strength. Increased mechanical loading stimulates subperiosteal bone apposition and endosteal resorption prior to midadolescence and relatively greater endosteal apposition thereafter (Bass et al. 2002). The growth and development period generates constant shape changes requiring a highly active and responsive modeling/remodeling process; a process which moderates substantially after skeletal maturity (Pearson and Lieberman 2004). Diaphyseal cross-sectional strength and cancellous microarchitecture are responsive to mechanical loads, while bone length and articular size are less so (Lieberman et al. 2001; Ruff 2003b).

The interaction of mechanical loading, growth and development, and skeletal responsiveness accounts for skeletal adaptation into early adulthood (Turner and Robling 2003). Following this period, the skeletal response is greatly reduced; it does, however, continue over a longer time frame with the possibility of cumulative long-term effect (Ruff et al. 2006; Valdimarsson et al. 2005). Several very recent longitudinal studies of prepubertal and adolescent boys and girls have been published examining the relationship between physical activity and bone structural parameters in the femoral neck, femoral shaft, and tibia (Forwood et al. 2006; Kontulainen et al. 2005). These studies of bone functional adaptation indicate that physical activity and high-impact exercise intervention have a positive site-specific effect on cortical and cancellous bone strength parameters after controlling for biological maturity age and body size (Bass et al. 2002; Sundberg et al. 2001). Adult bone morphology represents retention of those structural features established during ontogeny modified by biological factors and functional adaptive changes accumulated during maturity.

Bone size, peak bone mass, and architecture (e.g., geometry) acquired during growth and development affect the consequences of loss of bone in later life. It is generally held that lifestyle in early life is important, and achieving adequate peak bone is protective of fragility fractures in the elderly (Heaney et al. 2000). Gafni and Baron (2007), however, call this into question, suggesting that bone mass accrual during the subadult years "will have only transient effects" and has little influence on the risk of developing osteoporosis later in life. In addition to bone mass, bone architecture and degree of mineralization are determining factors for bone strength. During growth and development, and to some extent during adult life, bones are capable of adaptation to patterns of physical activity by altering their geometry through modeling (Ruff et al. 2006). Bones arrive at adulthood with a mass and architecture determined in a large part by adaptation to mechanical and other conditions experienced during childhood and adolescence. Age associated bone loss is universal among human populations, past and present. The proximate causes of bone loss include physical activity, inadequate nutrition, or sex hormone deficiency. All bone loss is mediated directly or indirectly through remodeling disorders (Heaney 2003; Parfitt 2003): the severity and consequences can have a significant impact on mortality and morbidity.

## 2.5   Growth Abnormalities

Human growth (and eventual stature) is the process and sum of numerous interdependent factors including genetic influences, hormonal status, nutrition, health status, and psychosocial conditions. Disturbances of longitudinal bone growth in individuals are frequent and have diverse etiologies ranging from primary bone/cartilage conditions (chromosomal or genetic), secondary extraskeletal factors (hormonal; Drop et al. 2001; van der Eerden et al. 2003), and mechanobiological effects (Robling et al. 2006). On a populational basis, the preponderance of evidence points to environmental stress factors, nutrition, and infectious disease as significant actors in disturbances of ontogeny. Stress, as a biocultural concept, is central to the study of the health and well-being of past and living human populations. Stress is defined as physiological disruptions with consequences for the individual and populations studied. Goodman (1993) has advocated a processual model for stress based on the interaction of environmental conditions, cultural buffering (or lack of), and host resistance. Nutrition and disease are synergistic; poorly nourished children are more susceptible to infection (immunocompromised). Infection and disease further reduce the capacity of the body to absorb essential nutrients (Larsen 1997). If cultural systems are unable to completely buffer environmental stressors (nutrients, infection), the individual and population may express a biological response characterized by growth perturbations (growth rate, growth result). These concepts have been supported by numerous research studies; selected seminal and recent articles are discussed.

### 2.5.1 Growth Rate

Longitudinal growth in postnatal life is organized by at least three different endocrine regimes characterized by (1) high growth rate at birth rapidly decelerating to three years of age, (2) slow deceleration of growth velocity to puberty, (3) rapid change of growth to peak height velocity, and (4) subsequent growth cessation and growth plate fusion (see Veldhuis et al. 2006 for review). Growth rate is a real-time, sensitive indicator of health and well-being. Children raised in impoverished environments in developing countries are generally small for their age (Bogin 1999; Eveleth and Tanner 1990; Whitehall 2008). Crooks' (1994) study of school-age Mayan children in Belize documented a retarded growth pattern typical of undernutrition in comparison to reference populations. Bogin (1997, 1999) studied Guatemala City children, demonstrating that well-fed upper-class children are taller than poorly nourished lower-class children who have a markedly slower growth rate. The upper-class Guatemalan children are comparable to Europeans in growth rate. The cumulative difference in growth is marked for the period preceding adolescence. Bogin (1999) and Jantz and Jantz (1999) argue that the early years of childhood are the most environmentally sensitive. Secular changes are established early in childhood, with the greatest impact between ages of 6 months and 3 years. The adolescent growth spurt is thought to be under more genetic influence, thus more strongly expressed and less influenced by environmental factors (Bogin 1999). This is an important factor in cases of growth recovery after childhood undernutrition and illness (catch-up growth).

Industrialized countries in the 20th century have witnessed a secular trend in growth, primarily long bone length. Juveniles have been growing taller as a result of improved nutrition, sanitation, reduction in infectious diseases, and modern health care access. This trend has been reversed, however, in times of nutritional deprivation—wars, famines, and economic crises. The link between growth rate and environmental stress is well documented in numerous auxological studies throughout the developed and developing world, including the United Kingdom, Japan, Eastern Europe, Brazil, Mozambique, Sri Lanka, and India (Bielicki and Welon 1982; Gigante et al. 2009; Harris 1994; Matsumoto 1982; Padez et al. 2009; Schooling et al. 2008; Tanner et al. 1982; Webb et al. 2008).

## 2.5.2  Growth Faltering: Stunting

Growth faltering is the process of slowing down or cessation of growth in childhood. It may effect height (stunting) or body mass (wasting) acutely or over the long term. This discussion is focused on linear long bone growth (stunting) measured by height-for-age anthropometrics. Malnutrition, diarrhea disease, and parasitic infections are considered to be the leading causes of acute growth faltering in developing areas that have been well studied. King and Mascie-Taylor (2002), studying the nutritional status of children from Papua New Guinea, found that almost 70% of the children were stunted. They identified acute and chronic malnutrition in this largely traditional horticultural group as being a primary factor. Increased workload in male adolescent laborers has also been identified as a cause of faltering of linear growth in underdeveloped economic environments (Duyar and Ozener 2005).

Berti and colleagues' study of stunting in an Andean community (1998) concluded that "energy, protein, calcium deficiencies, and perhaps vitamin A deficiency, may be minor contributors to stunting and lack of catch-up growth, while zinc deficiency is likely a relatively larger contributor" (p. 237). They argue that these nutritional deficiencies alone may not be severe enough to lead to the severe, near-universal stunting observed in the study population. They suggest that the multiplicative effects of malnutrition, unhygienic environment, and disease (clinical or subclinical) leads to exaggerated levels of growth failure and stunting. The impact of these factors is especially severe early in life. This longitudinal study indicated that linear growth rates are depressed under 2 years of age and tend to stabilize thereafter.

The effects of disease on child growth have been documented over the past 25 years. Studies in a variety of settings of developing and low-income countries indicate that the presence of infectious disease significantly reduces child length and height gain (Martorell et al. 1979). Diarrhea diseases have been a major focus of interest; respiratory infections to a lesser degree. The scrutiny of diarrheal diseases and their relationship to growth retardation is based on their direct (and indirect) biological means of causing malnutrition. The direct effect is from malabsorption, small intestinal mucosal enteropathy (Campbell et al. 2002), and nutrient loss; the indirect effect is through reduced food intake because of diarrheal associated anorexia. Although the vicious cycles of diarrhea, infections, and malnutrition have long been recognized, the temporal aspects are only partially understood. The impact of diarrhea on short-term growth faltering has been widely demonstrated (Lima et al. 2000; Moffat 2003). Persistent diarrhea (>14 days), signaling growth shortfalls, is associated with numerous etiologic agents including *Cryptosporidium*, *Giardia*, enteric adenoviruses, and the enterotoxigenic *Escherichia coli*.

A growing body of research examining the impact of gastrointestinal parasites (protozoa and helminthes) on child nutritional status, health, and growth (Wilson et al. 1999) has demonstrated that infection with protozoan and helminthic parasites represents the most prevalent endemic medical condition in the world, and that these infections are associated with significant stunting and lower stature, weight, work capacity, and blood hemoglobin levels (Moffat 2003; Wilson et al. 1999).

## 2.5.3  Growth Failure: Stature

Growth suppression in childhood is related to attainment of adult height. There are significant variables, however. For example, growth in undernourished children may be prolonged for a year (or longer), closing the gap, but still resulting in short-stature adults. Various researchers have documented close ties between stress (poor nutrition, infectious disease, health), socioeconomic status, and stature (Li et al. 2007). Steckel (1995) used stature as an indication of economic circumstances and standard of living. He analyzed a wide range of recent populations concluding that terminal height is a product of nutritional adequacy and to a lesser extent, disease history. Steckel argues that stature is the outcome of nutritional intake minus demands (disease and work).

As discussed with childhood growth rate, stature trends upward with economic, nutritional, and health improvement; it decreases during times of economic hardship, nutritional deprivation, and deterioration in general health (Webb et al. 2008). Terminal height data from historical sources (military records, enslaved African Americans, and voter registrations) confirm temporal trends in stature linked to and varying with changing economic conditions, nutritional adequacy, and general health status—good times, taller; bad times, shorter. Short stature and small body size are associated with numerous maladaptive factors including increased disease, altered cognitive development, renal stunting, and decreased work capacity (Heys et al. 2009; Stinson 1992; Whitehall 2008). In addition, growth faltering and stunted stature are associated with higher morbidity and mortality based on increased susceptibility to the original environmental impoverishment. Crooks (1995) studied American children living in poverty, finding an increased prevalence of low stature, chronic illness, and lead poisoning. Poor health (and corresponding poor growth) was argued to be related to poverty by increased exposure to pathogens, living in risky situations, and reduced levels and quality of health care. Socioeconomic conditions, poor child health, and growth stunting may also be linked to chronic stimulation of the adrenal axis, as a stress response, acting through glucocorticoid receptor pathways (Flinn and England 1997; Smink et al. 2003).

### 2.5.4  Catch-Up Growth

Intrauterine growth retardation (IUGR) is diagnosed when the weight or length at birth is low for the infant's gestational age. Birth length is related more to the height the child attains in childhood or maturity; whereas birth weight is strongly related to neonatal mortality and morbidity (Cameron and Demerath 2002). Growth in supine length or height frequently remains retarded during the first two years of life; catch-up growth takes place at later ages. This catch-up phenomenon makes the relationship of birth length to mature height variable (Loesch et al. 1999). A proportion of children will catch up during childhood; some (20%) do not catch up at all. The possibility of catching up depends on the type or nature of the intrauterine experience, the type of damaging agent, its timing, and duration. Growth retardation of the fetus is associated with maternal constitution, health, and the quality of the maternal internal and external environments (Ulijaszek et al. 1998). Maternal preeclampsia is considered a main cause for intrauterine growth retardation. The immediate health consequences of IUGR include increased mortality and morbidity during the perinatal period from congenital malformations, pulmonary insufficiency, and infection. Longer term health consequences are mental and physical disabilities, and certain chronic diseases occurring later in life.

Children during the first year of life are especially vulnerable to environmental insults (malnutrition and infectious disease) because of their rapid growth rate. Diminution of their normal growth trajectory may have long-lasting consequences. The amount of catch-up growth achieved depends on duration and severity of the deprivation, and the degree of biological maturational delay. Accelerated growth rates may occur when deprived childhoods are moved into a more advantaged environment, resulting in a return to their stereotypical growth curve (centile position) and attained stature. Three alternative pathways exist: (1) prolongation of the maturation time table (1–2 years) at a slower growth rate, still resulting in the predicted stature; (2) increased growth rate at the expense of accelerated maturation, resulting in early puberty and short adult stature (Ulijaszek et al. 1998); or (3) irrevocable changes in the growth trajectory resulting in the absence of catch-up growth and a lower potential for final adult height (Cardoso and Garcia 2009). The variable outcomes for catch-up growth in height are contrasted to the predictable and reproducible catch up in weight for wasting (Ulijaszek et al. 1998).

Martorell and colleagues (1975) studied the growth increments in the height of stunted and nonstunted Guatemalan children (5–18 years of age), finding that the absolute gain in height did not decrease the deficit over this time span—no evidence of catch up. These researchers concluded that a period of malnutrition in the first years of life "locks in" a lower growth in height potential. Steckel's (1987) study of American slaves documents a contrasting outcome in the presence of environmental deprivation. The recorded heights of slaves (small by modern standards) underwent substantial catch up in height between age 15 and 17. It was during this time they received extra food (salt pork) while working in the fields. Poor prenatal care, early weaning, nutritionally poor and contaminated food supplements, and a heavy disease burden contributed to growth faltering during childhood, placing these slaves below the first or second centile of modern height standards. The improved diet when young adolescents entered the workforce resulted in recovery and catch-up growth producing adult statures in excess of the 25th centile.

In the absence of environmental deprivation and with no constraints on growth, human growth follows a relatively consistent pattern within and continuously parallel to the centile lines of their particular growth curve prior to adolescence. The effect of environmental stressors on growth as measured by a growth reference chart is to move the height-for-age centile downward (i.e., from the 50th to the 5th). Catch-up growth in height is a restoration of growth trajectory after cessation of a stressor. This pattern of growth that is more or less parallel to a particular centile has been traditionally considered an example of canalization as first described by Waddington (1957). This phenomenological concept as applied to growth is that the human growth pattern is genetically determined and target seeking (Cameron and Demerath 2002; Weedon et al. 2008). Waddington used the term *canalization* to describe the buffering of developmental processes against the influences of environmental perturbations (or mutations). He argued that developmental processes can (and often do) recover from major insults, to arrive at the same endpoint and produce a normal adult. He used the visual metaphor of a ball rolling down a grooved slope: the epigenetic landscape. The topography of the landscape represents genetic predetermination to follow particular developmental pathways (in this case the human growth pattern). The ball rolling down the landscape represents an individual's growth process. The pathways are represented by valleys that lead to discrete endpoints directed by the neuroendocrine-driven "sizo-stat" (Tanner 1978). The steepness of the valley sides represents the degrees of buffering against perturbations affecting the developmental process (Hallgrimsson et al. 2002).

Gafni and Baron (2000) have proposed an alternative mechanism to the sizo-stat theory, which is intrinsic to the biology of the growth plate. This model assumes that proliferative zone growth plate chondrocytes have a finite number of cell divisions ending in senescence. The authors suggest that growth retardation may reduce chondrocyte proliferation, leaving the cells less senescent. When growth resumes these less senescent cells have a greater proliferative potential than an unaffected growth plate, thus an increased growth rate (Nilsson and Baron 2004). This hypothesis has been supported by animal model data (Gafni et al. 2001). Its application as a process for human catch-up growth remains unclear (Emons et al. 2005; Wit and Boersma 2002).

## 2.6 Conclusion

Biocultural growth studies consistently demonstrate that there must be a major improvement in circumstances (nutrition, infection, and parasite load) for changes in growth faltering, catch-up, and attained stature to occur. Health and human skeletal growth represent a two-lane highway. The detrimental effects of the health burden of malnutrition, infectious disease, and parasite infestation on human growth parameters is well substantiated by the empirical data. The multifactorial and interdependent relationships between skeletal systems biology, pathogenic mechanisms, health, gene–nutrient interactions, and socioeconomic factors that influence longitudinal growth in humans continue to provide research challenges. The approach to the study of skeletal developmental variation including growth faltering and related processes from the anthropological and forensic perspective must embrace an integrative stance, which considers the entire spectrum of interrelated components that contribute to normal and abnormal skeletal growth and morphology.

## References

Abu E, Horner A, Kusec V, Triffitt J, and Compston J (2000) The localization of the functional gluco-corticoid receptor in human bone. J Clin Endocrinol Metab 85:883–889.

Ahmed Y, Tatarczuch L, Pagel C, Davies H, Mirams M, and Mackie E (2007) Physiological death of hypertrophic chondrocytes. Osteoarthr Cartilage 15:575–586.

Aiello L and Dean C (2002) An introduction to human evolutionary anatomy. London: Elsevier.

Ammann P, Bourrin S, Bonjour J, Meyer J, and Rizzoli R (2000) Protein undernutrition-induced bone loss is associated with decreased IGF-I levels and estrogen deficiency. J Bone Miner Res 15:683–690.

Ballock R and O'Keefe R (2003) The biology of the growth plate. J Bone Joint Surg AM 85:715–726.

Barker D (1998) Mothers, babies, and disease in later life, 2nd edition. New York: Churchill Livingstone.

Barker D, Osmond C, Forsen, T, Kajante E, and Eriksson J (2005) Trajectories of growth among children who have coronary events as adults. New Engl J Med 353:1802–1809.

Bass S (2000) The prepubertal years: A uniquely opportune stage of growth when the skeleton is most responsive to exercise? Sports Med 30:73–78.

Bass S, Saxon L, Daly RM, et al. (2002) The effect of mechanical loading on the size and shape of bone in pre-, peri-, and postpubertal girls: A study in tennis players. J Bone Minr Res 17:2274–2280.

Bass S, Eser P, and Daly R (2005) The effect of exercise and nutrition on the mechanostat. J Musculoskeletal Neuro Inter 5:239–254.

Bateson P, Barker D, et al. (2004) Developmental plasticity and human health. Nature 430:419–421.

Benjamin A, Archer C, and Ralphs J (1994) Cytoskeleton of cartilage cells. Microsc Res Technol 28:372–377.

Berti P, Leonard W, and Berti W (1998) Stunting in an Andean community: Prevalence and etiology. Am J Hum Biol 10:229–240.

Bertram J and Swartz S (1991) The "Law of Bone Transformation": A case of crying Wolff? Biol Rev 66:245–273.

Bielecki T and Welon Z (1982) Growth data as indicators of social inequalities: The case of Poland. Yearb Phys Anthropol 25:153–167.

Bogin B (1999) Patterns of human growth, 2nd edition. Cambridge: Cambridge University Press.

Bogin B and Loucky J (1997) Plasticity, political economy, and physical growth status of Guatemala Maya children living in the United States. Am J Phys Anthropol 102:17–32.

Bourrin S, Ammann P, Bonjour J, and Rizzoli R (2000) Dietary protein restriction lowers plasma insulin-like growth factor I (IGF-I), impairs cortical bone formation, and induces osteoblastic resistance to IGF-I in adult female rats. Endocrinology 141:3149–3155.

Byers S, Moore A, Byard R, and Fazzalari N (2000) Quantitative histomorphometric analysis of the human growth plate from birth to adolescence. Bone 27:495–501.

Cadet ER, Gafni RI, McCarthy EF, McCray DR, Bacher JD, Barnes KM, and Baron J (2003) Mechanisms responsible for longitudinal growth of the cortex: Coalescence of trabecular bone into cortical bone. J Bone Joint Surg Am 85(9):1739–1748.

Cameron N and Demerath E (2002) Critical periods in human growth and their relationship to diseases of aging. Yearb Phys Anthropol 45: 159–184.

Campbell D, Lunn P, and Elia M (2002) Age-related association of small intestinal mucosal enteropathy with nutritional status in rural Gambian children. Brit J Nutrition 88:499–505.

Cardoso H (2007) Environmental effects on skeletal versus dental development: using a documented subadult skeletal sample to test a basic assumption in human osteological research. Am J Phys Anthropol 132:223–233.

Cardoso H and Garcia S (2009) The not-so-dark ages: Ecology for human growth in medieval and early twentieth century Portugal as inferred from skeletal growth profiles. Am J Phys Anthropol 138:136–147.

Carter D and Beaupré G (2001) Skeletal function and form: Mechanobiology of skeletal development, aging, and regeneration. Cambridge: Cambridge University Press.

Chrysis D, Ritzen E, and Savendahl L (2003) Growth retardation induced by dexamethasone is associated with increased apoptosis of the growth plate chondrocytes. J Endocrinol 176:331–337.

Cooke C and Zanker C (2004) Energy balance, bone turnover, and skeletal health in physically active individuals. Med Sci Sport Exer 36:1372–1381.

Cooper C, Javaid M, Taylor P, et al. (2002) The fetal origins of osteoporotic fracture. Calcified Tissue Int 70:391–394.

Crooks D (1994) Growth status of school-age Mayan children in Belize, Central America. Am J Phys Anthropol 93:217–227.

Crooks D (1995) American children at risk: Poverty and its consequences for children's health, growth, and school achievement. Yearb Phys Anthropol 38:57–86.

Drop S, Greggio N, Cappa M, and Bernasconi S (2001) Current concepts in tall stature and overgrowth syndromes. J Pediatr Endocr Met 14:975–984.

Duyar I and Ozener B (2005) Growth and nutritional status of male adolescent laborers in Ankara, Turkey. Am J Phys Anthropol 128:693–698.

Emons J, Boersma B, Baron J, and Wit J (2005) Catch-up growth: testing the hypothesis of delayed growth plate senescence in humans. J Pediatr 147:843–846.

Eveleth P and Tanner J (1990) Worldwide variation in human growth. Cambridge: Cambridge University Press.

Flinn M and England B (1997) Social economics of childhood glucocorticoid stress response and health. Am J Phys Anthropol 102:33–53.

Forwood M, Baxter-Jones A, Beck T, et al. (2006) Physical activity and strength of the femoral neck during the adolescent growth spurt: A longitudinal analysis. Bone 38:576–583.

Gafni R and Baron J (2000) Catch-up growth: Possible mechanisms. Pediatr Nephrol 14:616–619.

Gafni R and Baron J (2007) Childhood bone mass acquisition and peak bone mass may not be important determinants of bone mass in late adulthood. Pediatrics 119(Suppl):S131.

Gafni R, Weise M, Robrecht D, Meyers J, Barnes K, De-Levi S, and Baron J (2001) Catch-up growth is associated with delayed senescence of the growth plate in rabbits. Pediatr Res 50:618.

Gigante D, Nazmi A, Lima R, Barros F, and Victora C (2009) Epidemiology of early and late growth in height, leg and trunk length: Findings from a birth cohort of Brazilian males. Eur J Clin Nutr 63:375–381.

Gillman M (2002) Epidemiological challenges in studying the fetal origins of adult chronic disease. Int J Epidemiol 31:294–299.

Gillman M (2005) Developmental origins of health and disease. New Engl J Med 353:1848–1850.

Glorieux F, Travers R, Taylor A, et al. (2000) Normative data for iliac bone histomorphometry in growing children. Bone 26:103–109.

Gluckman P and Hanson M (2004) Developmental origins of disease paradigm: a mechanistic and evolutionary perspective. Pediatr Res 56:311–317.

Gluckman P, Hanson M, and Spences H (2005) Predictive adaptive responses and human evolution. Trends Ecol Evol 20:527–533.

Godfrey K, Walker-Bone K, Robinson S, et al (2001) Neonatal bone mass: Influence of parental birthweight, maternal smoking, body composition, and activity during pregnancy. J Bone Miner Res 16:1694–1703.

Goodman A (1993) On the interpretation of health from skeletal remains. Curr Anthropol 34:281–288.

Gosman J (2007) Patterns in ontogeny of human trabecular bone from Sunwatch Village in the prehistoric Ohio Valley. Dissertation, Ohio State University, Columbus.

Gosman JH and Ketcham RA (2009) Patterns in ontogeny of human trabecular bone from SunWatch Village in the prehistoric Ohio Valley: General features of microarchitectural change. Am J Phys Anthropol 138:318–332.

Grumbach M (2000) Estrogen, bone, growth and sex: A sea change in conventional wisdom. J Pediatr Endocrinol Metab 13 Suppl 6:1439–1455.

Hales C and Barker D (2001) The thrifty phenotype hypothesis. Brit Med Bull 60:5–20.

Hallgrimsson B, Willmore K, and Hall B (2002) Canalization, developmental stability, and morphological integration in primate limbs. Yearb Phys Anthropol 45:131–158.

Harris B (1994) The height of schoolchildren in Britain, 1900-1950. In: Komlos J, editor. Stature, living standards, and economic development: Essays in anthropometric history. Chicago: University of Chicago Press, pp. 25–38.

Heaney R (2003) Is the paradigm shifting? Bone 33:457–465.

Heaney R, Abrams S, Dawson-Hughes B, Looker A, Marcus R, Matkovic V, and Weaver C (2000) Peak bone mass. Osteoporosis Int 11:985–1009.

Heys M, Schooling C, Jiang C, Adab P, Cheng K, Lam T, and Leunga G (2009) Childhood growth and adulthood cognition in a rapidly developing population. Epidemiology 20:91–99.

Jantz L and Jantz R (1999) Secular change in long bone length and proportion in the United States, 1800–1970. Am J Phys Anthropol 110:57.

Javaid M and Cooper C (2002) Prenatal and childhood influences on osteoporosis. Best Pract Res Cl En 16:349–367.

Jensen C, Poole C, McGlasham S, Marko S, Issa Z, Vujcich K, et al. (2004) Ultrastructural, tomographic and confocal imaging of the chondrocyte primary cilium in situ. Cell Biol Int 28:101–110.

King S and Mascie-Taylor C (2002) Nutritional status of children from Papua New Guinea: Associations with socioeconomic factors. Am J Hum Biol 14:659–668.

Kirsch T (2006) Determinants of pathological mineralization. Curr Opin Rheumatol 18:174.

Kirsch T, Nah H, Shapiro I, and Pacifici M (1997) Regulated production of mineralization-competent matrix vesicles in hypertrophic chondrocytes. J Cell Biol 139:1149–1160.

Klaus H, Larsen C, and Tam M (2009) Economic intensification and degenerative joint disease: Life and labor on the postcontact North Coast of Peru. Am J Phys Anthropol 139:204–221.

Kneissel M, Roschager P, Steiner W, et al. (1997) Cancellous bone structure in the growing and aging lumbar spine in a historic Nubian population. Calcified Tissue Int 61:95–100.

Kontulainen S, MacDonald H, Khan K, and McKay H (2005) Examining bone surfaces across puberty. J Bone Min Res 20:1202–1207.

Kronenberg H (2003) Developmental regulation of the growth plate. Nature 423:332–336.

Lacroix P (1947) Organizers and the growth of bone. J Bone Joint Surg Am 29:292–296.

Lai L and Mitchell J (2005) Indian hedgehog: Its roles and regulation in endochondral bone development. J Cell Biochem 96:1163–1173.

Lanou A, Berkow S, and Barnard N (2005) Calcium, dairy products, and bone health in children and young adults: A reevaluation of the evidence. Pediatrics 115:736–743.

Larsen C (1997) Bioarchaeology: Interpreting behavior from the human skeleton. Cambridge: Cambridge University Press.

Leitinger B and Kwan A (2006) The discoidin domain receptor DDR2 is a receptor for type X collagen. Matrix Biol 25:355–364.

Li L, Dangour A, and Power C (2007) Early life influences on adult leg and trunk length in the 1958 British birth cohort. Am J Hum Bio 19:836–843.

Lieberman D, Devlin M, and Pearson O (2001) Articular area responses to mechanical loading: Effects of exercise, age, and skeletal location. Am J Phys Anthropol 116:266–277.

Lima A, Moore S, Barboza M, et al. (2000) Persistent diarrhea signals a critical period of increased diarrhea burdens and nutritional shortfalls: A prospective cohort study among children in northwestern Brazil. J Infect Dis 181:1643–1651.

Loesch D, Huggins R, and Stokes K (1999) Relationship of birth weight and length with growth in height and body diameters from 5 years of age to maturity. Am J Hum Bio 11:772–776.

Lovejoy C, McCollum M, Reno P, and Rosenman B (2003) Developmental biology and human evolution. Annu Rev Anthropol 32:85–109.

Mackie E, Ahmed Y, Tatarczuch L, Chen K-S, and Mirams M (2008) Endochondral ossification: How cartilage is converted into bone in the developing skeleton. Int J Biochem Cell B 40:46–62.

Mak K, Chen M, Day T, Chuang P, and Yang Y (2006) Wnt/B-catenin signaling interacts differentially with Ihh signaling in controlling endochondral bone and synovial joint formation. Development 133:3695–3707.

Martorell R, Yarbrough C, Klein R, and Lechtig A (1979) Malnutrition, body size, and skeletal maturation: Interrelationships and implications for catch-up growth. Hum Biol 51:371–389.

Matsumoto K (1982) Secular acceleration of growth in height in Japanese and its social background. Ann Hum Biol 9:399–410.

McGlashan S, Haycraft R, Jensen C, Yoder B, and Poole C (2007) Articular cartilage and growth plate defects are associated with chondrocyte cytoskeletal abnormalities in Tg737 (orpk) mice lacking the primary cilia protein polaris. Matrix Biol 26:234–246.

McGrath J, Keeping D, Saha S, Chant D, Lieberman D, and O'Callaghan M (2005) Seasonal fluctuations in birth weight and neonatal limb length; does prenatal vitamin D influence neonatal size and shape. Early Hum Dev 81:609–618.

Miura M, Tanaka K, Komatsu Y, Suda M, Yasoda A, Sakuma Y, Ozasa A, and Nakao K (2002) Thyroid hormones promote chondrocyte differentiation in mouse ATDC5 cells and stimulate endochondral ossification in fetal mouse tibias through iodothyronine deiodinases in the growth plate. J Bone Miner Res 17:443–454.

Moffat T (2003) Diarrhea, respiratory infections, protozoan gastrointestinal parasites, and child growth in Kathmandu, Nepal. Am J Phys Anthropol 122:85–97.

Nilsson O and Baron J (2004) Fundamental limits on longitudinal bone growth: Growth plate senescence and epiphyseal fusion. Trends Endocrin Met 15:370–374.

Nilsson O and Baron J (2005) Impact of growth plate senescence on catch-up growth and epiphyseal fusion. Pediatr Nephrol 20:319–322.

Nuzzo S, Meneghini C, Braillon P, Mobilo S, and Peyrin F (2003) Microarchitectural and physical changes during fetal growth in human vertebral bone. J Bone Min Res 18:760–769.

Olsen B, Reginato A, and Wang W (2000) Bone development. Annu Rev Cell Dev Bi 16:191–220.

Padez C, Varela-Silva M, and Bogin B (2009) Height and relative leg length as indicators of the quality of the environment among Mozambican juveniles and adolescents. Am J Hum Bio 21:200–209.

Parfitt A (2003) New concepts of bone remodeling: A unified spatial and temporal model with physiologic and pathophysiologic implications. In: Agarwal S and Stout S, editors. Bone loss and osteoporosis: An anthropological perspective. New York: Kluwer Academic, pp. 3–17.

Pathi S, Rutenberg J, Johnson R, et al. (1999) Interaction of Ihh and BMP noggin signaling during cartilage differentiation. Dev Biol 209:239–253.

Pearson O and Lieberman D (2004) The aging of Wolff's "Law": Ontogeny and responses to mechanical loading in cortical bone. Yearb Phys Anthropol 47:63–99.

Pontzer H, Lieberman DE, Momin E, Devlin MJ, et al. (2006) Trabecular bone in the bird knee responds with high sensitivity to changes in load orientation. J Exp Biol 209:57–65.

Rao S and Apte P (2009) Social class-related gradient in the association of skeletal growth with blood pressure among adolescent boys in India. Public Health Nutr 21:1–7.

Rivas R and Shapiro F (2002) Structural stages in the development of the long bones and epiphyses: A study in the New Zealand white rabbit. J Bone Joint Surg AM 84:85–100.

Robling AG, Castillo AB, and Turner CH (2006) Biomechanical and molecular regulation of bone remodeling. Annu Rev Biomed Eng 8:455–498.

Ruff C (2003a) Growth in bone strength, body size, and muscle size in a juvenile longitudinal sample. Bone 33:317–329.

Ruff C (2003b) Ontogenetic adaptation to bipedalism: Age changes in femoral-to-humeral length and strength proportions in humans, with a comparison to baboons. J Hum Evol 45:317–349.

Ruff C, Trinkaus E, Walker A, and Larsen C (1993) Postcranial robusticity in *Homo*. I: Temporal trends and mechanical interpretation. Am J Phys Anthropol 91:21–53.

Ruff C, Holt B, and Trinkaus E (2006) Who's afraid of the big bad Wolff? "Wolff's Law" and bone functional adaptation. Am J Phys Anthropol 129:484–498.

Ruimerman R, Hilbers P, van Reitbergen B, and Huiskes R (2005) A theoretical framework for strain-related trabecular bone maintenance and adaptation. J Biomech 38:931–941.

Ryan TM and Krovitz GE (2006) Trabecular bone ontogeny in the human proximal femur. J Hum Evol 51:591–602.

Ryan TM, van Rietbergen B, and Krovitz G (2007) Mechanical adaptation of trabecular bone in the growing human femur and humerus. Am J Phys Anthropol 132:205.

Salle B, Rauch F, Travers R, Bouvier R, and Glorieux F (2002) Human fetal bone development: Histomorphometric evaluation of the proximal femoral metaphysis. Bone 30:823–828.

Schooling C, Jiang C, Heys M, Zhang X, Adab P, Cheng K, Lam T, and Leung G (2008) Are height and leg length universal markers of childhood conditions? The Guangzhou Biobank cohort study. J Epidemiol Commun H 62:607–614.

Shapiro F, Holtrop ME, and Glimcher MJ (1977) Organization and cellular biology of the perichondral ossification groove of Ranvier. J Bone Joint Surg Am 59:703–723.

Shao Y, Wang L, and Ballock R (2006) Thyroid hormone and the growth plate. Rev Endocr Metab Disord 7:265–271.

Sims N, Clement-Lacroix P, Ponte F, Bouali Y, Binart N, Moriggl R, Goffin V, Coschigano K, Gaillard-Kelly M, Kopchick J, et al. (2000) Bone homeostasis in growth hormone receptor-null mice is restored by IGF-I but independent of Stat5. J Clin Invest 106:1095–1103.

Smink J, Gresnigt M, Hamers N, Koedam J, Berger R, and van Buul-Offers S (2003) Short-term glucocorticoid treatment of prepubertal mice decreases growth and IGF-1 in the growth plate. J Endocrin 177:381–388.

Sontag W (1994) Age-dependent morphometric change in the lumbar vertebrae of male and female rats: Comparison with the femur. Bone 15:593–601.

Steckel R (1987) Growth depression and recovery: The remarkable case of American slaves. Ann Hum Bio 14:111–132.

Steckel R (1995) Stature and the standard of living. J Econ Lit 33:1903–1940.

Stevens S and Williams G (1999) Hormone regulation of chondrocyte differentiation and endochondral bone formation. Mol Cell Endocrinol 151:195–204.

Stinson S (1992) Nutritional Adaptation. Annu Rev Anthropol 21:143–170.

Stout S and Lueck R (1995) Bone remodeling rate and skeletal maturation in three archaeological skeletal populations. Am J Phys Anthropol 98:161–171.

Sumner D and Andriacchi, A (1996) Adaptation to differential loading: Comparison of growth-related changes in cross-sectional properties of the human femur and humerus. Bone 19:121–126.

Sundberg M, Gardsell P, Johnell O, Karlsson MK, et al. (2001) Peripubertal moderate exercise increases bone mass in boys but not in girls: A population-based intervention study. Osteoporosis Int 12:230–238.

Tanck E, Hannink G, Ruimerman R, Buma P, et al. (2006) Cortical bone development under the growth plate is regulated by mechanical load transfer. J Anat 208:73–79.

Tanner J (1978) Foetus into man. Cambridge, MA: Harvard University Press.

Tanner J, Hayashi T, Preece M, and Cameron N (1982) Increase in length of leg relative to trunk in Japanese children and adults from 1957 to 1977: Comparison with British and with Japanese Americans. Ann Hum Biol 9:411–423.

Turner C and Robling A (2003). Designing exercise regimens to increase bone strength. Exerc Sport Sci Rev 31:45–50.

Ulijaszek S, Johnston F, and Preece M, editors. (1998) The Cambridge encyclopedia of human growth and development. Cambridge: Cambridge University Press.

Valdimarsson O, Alborg H, Duppe H, et al. (2005) Reduced training is associated with increased loss of BMD. J Bone Min Res 20:906–912.

van der Eerden B, Karperien M, and Wit J (2003) Systemic and local regulation of the growth plate. Endocr Rev 24:782–801.

Veldhuis J, Roemmich J, Richmond E, and Bowers C (2006) Somatotropic and gonadotropic axes linkages in infancy, childhood, and the puberty-adult transition. Endocr Rev 27:101–140.

Waddington C (1957) The strategy of the genes: A discussion of some aspects of theoretical biology. New York: Macmillan.

Wang L, Shao Y, and Ballock R (2007) Thyroid hormone interacts with the Wnt/beta-catenin signaling pathway in the terminal differentiation of growth plate chondrocytes. J Bone Miner Res 22:1988–1995.

Webb E, Kuh D, Pajak A, Kubinova R, Malyutina S, and Bobak M (2008) Estimation of secular trends in adult height, and childhood socioeconomic circumstances in three Eastern European populations. Econ Hum Biol 6:228–236.

Weedon M, Lango H, Lindgren C, et al. (2008) Genome-wide association analysis identifies 20 loci that influence adult height. Nature Gen 40:575–583.

Weiss E (2003). Understanding muscle markers: Aggregation and construct validity. Am J Phys Anthropol 121:230–240.

Whitehall J (2008) Anthropometry and renal size of children suffering under sustained conflict in Sri Lanka. J Paediatr Child H 44:656–660.

Whyte M (2006) Chondrodystrophies and mucopolysaccharidoses. In: Favus M, editor. Primer on the metabolic bone diseases and disorders of mineral metabolism 6th edition. Washington, DC: American Society for Bone and Mineral Research, pp. 421–425.

Wilsman N, Farnum C, Hilley H, and Carlson C (1981) Ultrastructural evidence of a functional heterogeneity among physeal chondrocytes in growing swine. Am J Vet Res 42:1547–1553.

Wilson W, Dufour D, Staten L, et al. (1999) Gastrointestinal parasitic infection, anthropometrics, nutritional status, and physical work capacity in Columbian boys. Am J Hum Bio 11:763–771.

Wit J and Boersma B (2002) Catch-up growth: Definition, mechanisms, and models. J Pediatr Endocr Met 15:1229–1242.

Wittman A, Cowgill L, Pontzer H, and Ocobock C (2009) Waddling and toddling: Biomechanical effects of an immature gait. Am J Phys Anthropol 138(S48):19.

Worthman C, and Kuzara J (2005). Life history and the early origins of health differentials. Am J Hum Bio 17:95–112.

Yakar S, Rosen C, Beamer W, Ackert-Bicknell C, Wu Y, Liu J-L, Ooi G, Setser J, Frystyk J, Boisclair Y, et al. (2002) Circulating levels of IGF-1 directly regulate bone growth and density. J Clin Invest 110:771–781.

Yamada T, Kawano H, Koshizuka Y, Fukuda T, Yoshimura K, Kamekura S, Saito T, Ikeda T, Kawasaki Y, Azuma Y, et al. (2006) Carminerin contributes to chondrocyte calcification during endochondral ossification. Nature Med 12:665–670.

# Making the Mold
## A Microstructural Perspective on Bone Modeling during Growth and Mechanical Adaptation

COREY M. MAGGIANO

## Contents

## 3.1 Introduction

Endochondral ossification results in the extension of long bones. Intracortical remodeling maintains the constitutional integrity of existing bone tissue. What then accounts for growth and mechanical adaptation of intramembranous bones and diaphyses; the reduction of the metaphyses and compaction of trabecular voids during long bone extension; and the achievement of mature bone curvature, orientation, and robusticity?

A deceptively simple process, called bone modeling, accounts for all these changes. Typically defined in juxtaposition with intracortical remodeling, modeling is responsible for all formation and resorption initiated by the periosteal and endosteal membranes. In contrast, remodeling ensures the bone's material integrity is maintained by replacing old bone through resorption and subsequent formation at collections of cells called bone multicellular units (Frost 1973). Together these two processes ensure that, during skeletal maturation, bone achieves a delicate balance of adaptive architectural strength and efficiency of mass that is maintained as long as possible after maturation. Variation in relative bone size and shape informs much of skeletal inquiry, whether medical, forensic, or archaeological. Therefore, a detailed knowledge of bone modeling is required to understand basic processes underlying features of diagnostic, identificational, or inferential import.

Unfortunately, modeling activity is not easily conceptualized, in part because it is not easily measurable or even directly observable. Compact bone is an optically dense, dynamically adapting, mineral and organic tissue of remarkable structural and chemical complexity. We cannot watch bone histology as it changes and so are left to infer the process from resulting stratigraphic microarchitecture. In this regard observing modeling is even more challenging than other bone processes, which have relatively easily defined units of deposition or feature characterizations, as is the case for bone remodeling. Conceptualizing modeling accurately may be elusive, but it is necessary to truly understand bony changes at the microscopic scale.

A sometimes valuable thought experiment is to speed up a given process or occurrence until new observations or questions are revealed. Envision bone growth sped up; the lifetime of a femur could be viewed within a minute or two. Committing to a perspective like this can be revealing. We know now, bone is a dynamic tissue—not at all the static architecture once thought. So the solid state of bone becomes relatively unimportant from our high-speed perspective. Bone appears to ebb and flow constantly in three dimensions, permitting its consideration as a semisolid, rather like clay. From this perspective, anlage formation and endochondral ossification supply raw material for development, which is immediately molded and shaped. Looking closer, bone is added to its entire surface, during growth for example, but at other times, only to a specific region, affecting a change in diaphyseal shape or robusticity. If distinguishable, sites of activity would appear patch- or puddle-like, amorphous, forming in layers over the surface of a bone, expanding outward from epicenters of activation. Older or slower formations would be overlain by those faster or newer, each older at their epicenters than at their extremities. Other puddles or patches would reverse, or resorb, seemingly evaporating from the external margins toward deeper regions.

Some questions should leap to the foreground. What process accomplishes these bony changes? What determines the number of these phases of formation or resorption? How many of these "epicenters" of activity does it take to stimulate formation (or resorption) across large bone surfaces? How fast does the process occur and with what variability? Unfortunately, we cannot view bone growth from start to finish in minutes. Nor can we easily discern between separate osteogenic membrane activations, nor count them, nor measure their actual rate of formation or resorption rather than merely the rate at a particular transection. In fact these activations are nearly heuristic in comparison with observable units formed during remodeling, for example. A lack of measurable, histological units exacerbates difficulties involved in directly studying modeling processes, and the factors influencing them.

Thankfully, redoubled efforts of researchers interested in bone tissue have permitted significant gains in the understanding of bone modeling over the past 60 years. Bone morphological comparisons have been made between individuals and populations or subpopulations in various circumstances. Painstaking macrostructural observation has been made, detailing processes behind morphological change at larger scales. The cells responsible for these changes and their basic roles have been identified, including, osteoblasts, osteoclasts, osteocytes, and bone lining cells (BLCs). Boney response to physical stimuli has been tested and even inferred after death by using principles of beam mechanics to compare axes of major resistance to bending (Lanyon and Rubin 1984; Ruff and Hayes 1983a, 1983b). Polarized light analysis has been used to evidence microstructural variation in bone strength across the diaphyseal transverse cross-section (Ascenzi 1988; Takano et al. 1999; Goldman et al. 2003). Photochemical coincidence has also been harnessed to directly view the results of modeling bone apposition, even to measure its rate of trans-sectional formation in vivo, through fluorescent double-labeling techniques (Frost 1963; Rush et al. 1966; Taylor and Frost 1966). New technologies and methods are permitting ever increasing clarity in two- and three-dimensional bone microscopy (see Cooper and colleagues, this volume). So, despite challenges, researchers have revealed some secrets of bone's mold maker.

Of primary importance, they revealed what modeling can accomplish: (1) diametric diaphyseal growth and medullary centralization, (2) mechanical adaptation, (3) metaphyseal reduction, and (4) lamellar compaction. They also identified important physiological parameters affecting bone's capacity to morph via modeling, including the individual's age and mechanical loading history. Now we occupy a position on a precipice, overlooking a period of unprecedented insight and progress in understanding bone modeling and its functional application in fields focusing on skeletal biology.

The role of bone modeling during growth is complex. Not only must it negotiate the dominant demand for greater net formation than resorption, it must do so while permitting some regions to resorb completely to achieve functional morphology. Modeling also accounts for the eventual achievement of the bone's axis of orientation, its curvature or shape, and its overall thickness. All this is preformed by two membranes, the periosteum and the endosteum, which, for all their assumed similarity appear quite different histologically, function in different environments, are differently affected by mechanical and chemical stimuli; yet maintain a concerted effort, cooperating, even synergistically, in order to affect bony changes. This chapter defines, describes, and explains bone modeling microstructure and encourages perspectives both old and new that could permit advancement in hypothesis-driven analyses in skeletal biology, for forensic and bioarchaeological applications alike.

## 3.2   Defining Modeling

Despite the obvious importance of bone modeling as a biological process, there has been significant contention and confusion regarding the term's usage and even its basic definition. To develop a functional definition of *modeling*, we need to (1) differentiate modeling as a subprocess of general growth and development, (2) recognize that the process is similar in all bones, whether they are formed endochondrally or intramembranously, and (3) distinguish clearly between modeling and remodeling.

### 3.2.1   Growth and Modeling

An important defining characteristic of modeling is its complete conceptual distinction from other aspects of long bone development, growth, and fracture repair. Modeling can be differentiated from these processes, in that it accounts only for activity at the periosteal and endosteal membranes (here referred to collectively as PEM) rather than within the physis or callus (Frost 1973). Bone "growth" is a higher order and more general concept referring to overall increase in the size or mass of developing bone and transpires via two main processes: intramembranous and endochondral bone formation. A functional understanding of both processes recognizes that as a hard tissue, bone cannot grow via formation alone. Bone grown in such a manner would weigh too much to satisfy its structural and functional role in the mobile musculoskeletal system. In addition, unlike soft tissue, bone cannot be moved in relative tissue–space–time after it is formed. Therefore, growth necessitates alterations of the bone's shape through significant resorption in addition to net formation. Transpiring at the PEM, modeling satisfies much of this growth requirement. In general, it removes bone from the medullary surfaces and deposits bone diametrically, permitting an overall increase in bone size and local alterations, maintaining or adjusting bone shape during growth. The underlying mechanisms behind modeling are similar regardless of the bone type considered.

### 3.2.2   Intramembranous and Endochondral Bone Modeling

During the development of intramembranous bones, such as the scapula or skull, no cartilaginous precursor or "anlage" is necessary for primary bone formation (Martin et al. 1998), which takes place directly within or under mesenchymal condensations of differentiating osteoblasts attaching to primary trabecular spicules within the connective tissue itself (Fawcett 1994; Scheuer and Black 2000). The periosteum activates as the site of primary ossification immediately after its cellular condensation, differentiation, and maturation, thereby accounting for the continued growth of the bone (Fawcett 1994; Scheuer and Black 2000). This is also the site for adaptation due to loading histories through mechanosensation and localized formation and resorption. Endochondral bones form by a more complex, dual process. The bone is longitudinally extended via endochondral ossification at the metaphyseal plate but is augmented diametrically by intramembranous activity at the PEM (Martin et al. 1998; Scheuer and Black 2000). (Also, see Gosman, this volume, for more detailed discussions on bone development.) PEM activity is similar in both intramembranous and endochondral bone development, but growth and adaptation via long bone modeling primarily occurs diametrically, whereas flat bone modeling is seemingly more complex. Most modeling studies are biased in favor of long bones as elements of greater mobility and, therefore, interest. For the purposes of simplicity, the current discussion also addresses modeling from a long bone perspective, though it is important to remember involved modeling processes are transpiring on and within intramembranous bones as well.

### 3.2.3   Modeling and Remodeling

Once formed, bone tissue must be maintained. In some organisms (including humans), modeling's sister process, remodeling, accomplishes this function—one shaping, the other reconstituting. The two sister processes would seem easily separable. As Parfitt (1983) and

Jee and colleagues (2007) summarize, modeling and remodeling are separated by 6 or 11 (respectively) different defining traits, including speed of formation (modeling is faster) and microstrain activation (modeling requires approximately two times the strain to stimulate formation). Unfortunately, despite general differences, easy distinction on a case-by-basis is often elusive. Some considerable confusion exists regarding which process accounts for which bony changes. Primarily this is due to three main confounding issues: (1) unclear distinction between periosteal/endosteal osteogenic envelopes and those *formed* and functional during remodeling processes; (2) the unfortunate assumption that evidence of prior resorption indicates remodeling (equating resorption and remodeling on certain surfaces despite little or no evidence for bone multicellular unit formation); (3) the historic (and even modern) clinical use of the word *remodeling* as a general term to describe nearly all bony changes during growth, healing, or in response to various stimuli. Often this leads to *modeling* processes being labeled "periosteal or endosteal *remodeling*" (e.g., Frost 1964a, 1964b), necessitating caution in the interpretation of some early literature. By the 1970s, publications like Frost's (1973), attempted to clarify the distinction between these modeling and remodeling but the distinction has unfortunately remained unclear in some camps.

Distinction can be drawn between modeling and remodeling both functionally and structurally. Modeling accounts for changes in bone size, shape, and position (relative to other tissues) via primary, bone formation, and resorption at the PEM. It can result in dramatically larger volumes of deposited or resorbed bone tissue, sometimes encasing entire bone surfaces in sheet upon sheet of bone, or removing them altogether. In contrast, remodeling is the process of bone maintenance and repair, accomplished by bone multicellular units (BMUs), collections of osteoclasts and osteoblasts arranged in a particular structure. This multicellular unit penetrates existing primary bone via resorption at its leading end "or cutting cone" and concentrically and appositionally replacing it, from the void's periphery, inward, with new lamellar bone. Often these secondary lamellae close around an accompanying vessel and nerve system at their center, forming a vascular canal (Martin et al. 1998; Parfitt 2003). BMUs result in smaller bone structural units (BSUs), referred to as Haversian systems, or osteons (~200–350 µm) in intracortical tissue, and hemiosteons (60 µm) in cancellous tissue (Eriksen et al. 1994; Parfitt 1994, 2003). BMUs form in three sequential steps: activation (A), resorption (R), and formation (F) at a single two-dimensional location. It is more difficult to remember, however, that each BMU is simultaneously accomplishing both R and F in three dimensions (and potentially A as well, during branching events).

PEM activity and BMU activity are also distinguished by the degree of coupling between formative and resorptive processes. PEM activity requires no connection (in process or mechanism) between formation or resorption (Frost 1973; Martin et al. 1998; Robling et al. 2006). Therefore, according to convention, modeling could progress from A to F and subsequently reverse to R when necessary (or vice versa). This stands in stark contrast to BMU activity, which appears coupled with formation closely following resorption in both time and space (Martin et al. 1998; Parfitt 2000). Unfortunately, most observation of bone histologically is not in real time which can hide certain circumstances during development or disease. These circumstances challenge the closeness of BMU coupling, ensuring that formation lags behind resorption significantly, leading to large resorptive bays. This phenomenon is sometimes called "trabecularization" of compact tissue, an occurrence blurring the lines between compact, trabecular, and endocortical tissues and therefore between osteonal or hemiosteonal BSUs and those resulting from endosteal modeling events, necessitating caution in histological interpretation (see Section 3.4). For a more detailed discussion of the bone remodeling process or synergism between modeling and remodeling, also refer to the chapters in this volume by Stout and Crowder or Skedros, respectively.

In short, when referring to any process accomplished by the PEM rather than the BMU, the term *remodeling* can be abandoned in favor of *modeling*, even when formation follows previous resorption. In addition, great care should accompany the use of processual terminology, *periosteal* or *endosteal*; and positional terminology, *pericortical* or *endocortical*. Conflating these terms creates error and oversimplifies bony response, leaving important questions unasked. Confusion can also be averted here by using the acronym PEM to address the periosteal and endosteal membranes collectively; and by referring to bone tissue formed by these membranes by a cortical descriptor (i.e., pericortex or endocortex) when context permits (rather than only using these terms to refer to the current surfaces of the cortex, or as arbitrary "zones").

## 3.3  Modeling Form

### 3.3.1  Membrane Histology and Vascularization

The periosteal membrane (Figures 3.1 and 3.2) comprises an outer fibrous layer and an inner layer of osteogenic cells called the cambium, firmly adhered to the bone surface via Sharpey's fibers that extend deep into bone tissue (Tang and Chai 1986). A three-zone model has also been suggested by Squier and colleagues (1990), based on the functional separation of three zones: (1) an external region marked by mature fibroblasts and dense collagen fibers; (2) a region with increased vasculature, pericytes, and a more amorphous extracellular matrix; and finally, (3) tightly adhered to the bone itself, a thin osteogenic layer, packed with osteoprogenitor cells and osteoblasts.

**Figure 3.1 (See color insert.)** Juvenile periosteal tissue preserved by natural mummification (black solid arrow). The external bone surface was currently forming primary lamella at the time of death as evidenced by several partially enclosed primary vessel canals (white solid arrows). Thin-ground, undecalcified transection of the naturally mummified, archaeological, femoral mid-diaphysis, Dakhleh Oasis, Egypt. Micrograph taken with red quartz cross-polarized filter (hilfsobject). Scale bar indicates 50 μm.

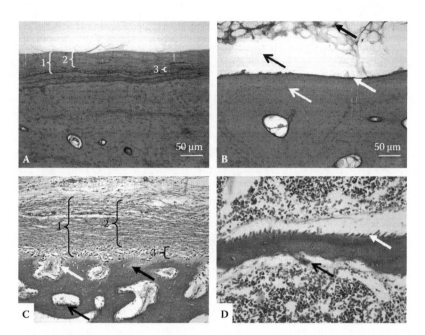

**Figure 3.2 (See color insert.)** (A) Mature periosteal membrane of the humerus (bracket 1), demonstrating clear distinction between the outer fibrous layer (bracket 2) and the smaller, darker osteogenic cellular layer (bracket 3). Note the most recent primary bone deposition has occurred in two thin phases (white arrow). (B) Mature endosteal membrane of the humerus (white arrow). Top margin shows marrow lipid tissue (black arrow) and marrow space (black lined arrow). Note a cement line between Haversian tissue (below white lined arrow) and the most recent endosteal primary formation phase (above white lined arrow). Parts A and B demonstrate a quiescent bone surface, as evidenced by the lack of unmineralized matrix. (C) Fetal (6-month gestation) metatarsal bone collar demonstrating cellular and tissue level changes associated with osteogenesis at the periosteum, including columnar osteoblasts (white arrow). Periosteal deposition of woven bone transpires via significant secretion of unmineralized matrix (osteoid) (black arrow). Note the targeted intracortical resorption at internal void surfaces facing the endosteum (bottom of image) as demonstrated by the position of osteoclasts (black lined arrow). (D) Endosteal formation in the same bone as part C via columnar osteoblasts on one side of a trabecular spicule, while the other side appears newly resorbed with one remaining osteoclast (black lined arrow) and Howships lacunae left behind as evidence. Also note the relatively clear space above and below formative or resorptive surfaces in this image, created by a "ceiling" of cells separating these surfaces from surrounding tissue matrix (See Section 3.4.4 for more information). All images are generated from paraffin embedded, decalcified, thin transections, stained with hematoxylin and eosin. Scale bar indicates 50 μm for parts A and B, taken at 100× magnification; part C was taken at 200× magnification; (D) at 400×. (Images courtesy of Lisa Lee.)

Fibroblasts and their excreted matrix, most dense in the easily discerned, external layer, lend the membrane its particular strength and exert surprising force on the bone itself via membrane insertion on the physis (Forriol and Shapiro 2005). Though the membrane does not completely enclose the epiphysis (Jee 2001), it resists 80% of the total force necessary to surgically remove the epiphysis (Forriol and Shapiro 2005). Pericytes in the second zone are less well understood but could be involved in osteogenesis, perhaps even in supplying osteoprogenitor cells (Diaz-Flores et al. 1992), as evidenced by their higher concentration in the more osteogenic periosteum and decreased presence in the endosteum (Brighton et al. 1992; Allen et al. 2004). The histomorphology of the osteogenic layer changes based on the activity of the constituent cells. In dormancy, these osteogenic cells are elongated; while in actively forming bone they adopt a more cuboidal shape, arranged as a simple stratified epithelium while secreting osteoid (uncalcified extracellular matrix; Ellender et al. 1988; Chow et al. 1998).

Reports are varied in their interpretation of similarities between the periosteum and endosteum. The periosteum and endosteum are histologically similar according to Shapiro (2002), but Hohmann and colleagues (1986) point out that the periosteum is densely inner-vated and contains lymphatic vessels. Still others emphasize their differences more strongly, labeling periosteal osteogenic tissue as fibroblast-like and in deep periosteal layers, whereas BLCs comprise the endosteum (Martin et al. 1998). It would seem that the periosteum is a more histologically complex membrane than the endosteum, whether currently depositing osteoid or not (Figure 3.2). Not only are the membranes distinct histologically, but their environments are completely different. The periosteum is constrained and interrupted by tendons, ligaments, and fibrocartilage, whereas the endosteum is awash with hematopoitic bone marrow (Jones et al. 1991). The periosteum accounts for the majority of blood flow to the bone and simultaneously achieves nearly all its venous drainage (Brookes 1971; Simpson 1985). Periosteal vessels create a complex network with fewer anastomoses in the diaphysis compared to the metaphysis (Crocker et al. 1970). On occasion, periosteal ves-sels can even affect a full cortical penetration to the medullary cavity (Reinelander 1972). In contrast, at least in the adult, the endosteum seems to penetrate bone tissue radially via Volkmann's canals, which connect Haversian systems laterally within the intracortex (Enlow 1962; Maggiano et al. in press).

The periosteum and endosteum are also differentially affected by mechanical and chemical stimuli. For example, the periosteum is well known for its capacity to induce formation in response to skeletal loading, particularly when supernormal loads are expe-rienced dynamically, separated by resting or recovery periods (Mosley et al. 1997; Mosley and Lanyon 1998, 2002; Robling et al. 2001). Carpenter and Carter (2008) have proposed a model in which pressures on periosteal surfaces, by adjacent muscles for example, can impede bone formation or induce bone resorption and affect bone cross-sectional shapes. Conversely, the endosteum has shown far reduced or nonexistent formative adaptation in response to mechanical loading (Meade et al. 1984; Jones et al. 1991; Gross et al. 2002; Lee et al. 2002; Srinivasan et al. 2002). Likewise, periosteal tissue is apparently more sen-sitive to pharmacological stimuli (Midura et al. 2003). Basic sex hormones affect each envelope differently. In general, periosteal formation is positively affected by androgens and negatively affected by estrogens (Turner et al. 1990). Alternately, endosteal estrogen stimulation generates bone formation during puberty (Martin 2003), which reverses with decreasing estrogen levels (Yao et al. 2000, 2001). Venken and colleagues (2006), however, call attention to the complexity of these pubescent bony changes, specifically in that bony response is not only hormone specific but also dose dependent. Even the general lifetime function of the two tissues are opposite according to some authors who regard formation as the net function of the periosteum and resorption as that of the endosteum (Epker et al. 1965; Stoker and Epker 1971). Despite these differences and despite their clear physical separation within bone tissues, the periosteum and endosteum are capable of extremely fine-tuned cooperation during growth and adaptation; without which, bone's composi-tional resilience and capacity for remodeling alone would insufficiently counter the loss of strength suffered by inappropriate morphology.

In the healthy, active individual, modeling is initiated and directed by a unique genetic and mechanical developmental history, accounting for most of what we recognize about a specific bone's morphology and function. This unique history is an important source of histomorphological variation and records itself stratigraphically within the microarchitecture of a bone.

### 3.3.2   Modeling Formation and Resorption

#### 3.3.2.1   Primary Bone Histology

In general, modeling formation at the PEM occurs either in rapid deposition of woven bone with less well-organized collagen content; or as more slowly forming, lamellar bone with more regularly organized collagen (Martin et al. 1998), though much can be gained from considering a continuum existing between the two (Martin et al. 1998). Giraud-Guille (1988) identified two types of alternating collagen fiber orientations in lamellar bone: orthogonal and helicoidal. Other researchers noticed that "pairs" of layers exist with either dense or loosely bundled collagen fibers (Marotti 1993). Regardless, most of this work has been limited to osteonal lamellar tissue. Whether important differences exist in the ultrastructure of primary and secondary lamellar bone collagen is unknown.

Individual lamellar sheets are fairly uniform in thickness at approximately 2–3 μm in cross-section (Ascenzi et al. 1982; Reid 1986) but of unknown dimensions along other axes. This is due to trade-offs between observable volumes and sufficient magnification and resolution. Unfortunately, only transections permit clear observation of PEM lamellae, rendering measurement in three-dimensions impossible. Light microscopy reveals their stratigraphy, however, detailing localized growth and adaptive processes at the histological scale. A single lamella (pl. lamellae) is a pair of layers (Martin et al. 1998) each with differing collagen orientation (typically one bright and one dark under polarized light; see Section 3.3.2.3; Johnson 1964), though on occasion the terminology is loose; *lamella* can refer to only one of the 2 μm sheets in the pair. Lamellae result from calcification of osteoid (average osteoid seam, 15 μm; Johnson 1964). Osteoid is layered upon existing mineralized bone surfaces by osteoblasts activated from preosteoblasts present and potentially resupplied within the PEM (Martin et al. 1998; Aubin 2001). Total calcification of an osteoid seam may take roughly 10 days and result in three lamellae (each with two 2.5 μm sheets; Johnson 1964). During their formation, lamellae encase some of the osteoblasts from the osteogenic membrane that produce them. These cells then adopt a new morphology, identifying them as osteocytes, locked in small oblong cavities, called lacunae (Martin and Burr 1989). Most often these lacunae are present within rather than between lamellae, specifically within those identified as "loosely" constructed by Marotti (1993). Extremely small cracklike fissures, or canaliculae (~500 nm in diameter) (Knothe Tate 2003), emanate from lacunae, connecting osteocytic processes to form the lacunar-canalicular system (LCS) through which osteocytic processes intercommunicate (Knothe Tate 2003; Taylor and Lee 2003; Figure 3.3).

The LCS is a complex network, or syncytium, acting as a means for transmission of chemical and mechanical signals, which, as part of compact bone's mechanotransduction system, are vital for healthy bone growth, maintenance, and adaptation (Donahue 2000; Knothe Tate 2003; Taylor and Lee 2003). Part of this system includes the BLCs covering most bone surfaces. Aubin (2001) outlines the complex cell lineages of the osteoprogenetors and describes the important role of BLCs in membrane activity. According to Martin

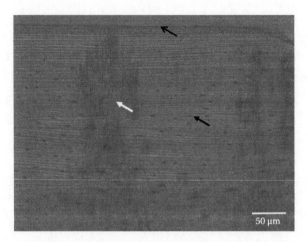

**Figure 3.3 (See color insert.)** Adult, primary endosteal lamellae with interspersed lacunae, once housing osteocytes entombed during active apposition. Endocortical surface is marked by the black lined arrow. Structure of the lacunar-canalicular system is emphasized by a diagenic effect which has slightly enlarged and darkened canaliculi radiating from some lacunae (white solid arrow). Outside these regions canaliculi are less visible. Thin-ground, undecalcified transection of archaeological, ulnar mid-diaphysis, Dakhleh Oasis, Egypt. Micrograph taken with red quartz cross-polarized filter (hilfsobject). Scale bar indicates 50 μm.

(2000), one of the potential roles for lining cells is protecting bone surfaces from a constant resorption signal, typically dampened in healthy, active tissue. To permit resorption these cells must somehow pull away from the bone's surface, exposing it to resorption, though this is one of many theories regarding bone mechanotransduction awaiting further study (Martin et al. 1998). Osteoclastic destruction transpires via mineral acidification and organic enzymatic digestion of the surface area enclosed by the cell's ruffled border (Väänänen et al. 2000), which limits the scale of resorption to small regions, leaving a "scalloped" surface due to Howship's lacunae (each typically <20 μm).

To discuss the microstructural variability induced by modeling activity, we must first become familiar with terminology used to identify PEM origin bone types. The terminology associated with primary lamellar bone architecture can be difficult to negotiate, especially when the human case is portrayed as usual or representative of vertebrate bone, in general. It most certainly is not. Human cortical bone, along with that of other primates, displays important differences from other animal bone, particularly in regions formed by the PEM during modeling. Locke (2004) encourages the use of the word *laminar* to define typical PEM apposition, rather than *lamellar*. First, referral to bone as *lamellar* does not separate primary and secondary bone formation (for example, both modeling [primary] and remodeling [secondary] apposition is lamellar). Second, human compact bone structure is not the norm. The vertebrate norm is often appositional sets of 4 to 20 lamellae, called laminae (Locke 2004) that are layered on top of one another and contain porous horizons formed by the regular entombment of vascular networks, at one time associated with the formative membrane (Locke 2004). Laminae display dramatic variability in their spatial relationships with one another, and in the degree or orientation of vessel incorporation within each layer. This leads to various additional tissue descriptors, including *plexiform* and *fibrolamellar*. Plexiform bone (Martin and Burr 1989) is similar to laminar bone except that it is less concentrically organized, repeatedly folding back on its self (Figure 3.4). Fibrolamellar tissue has more randomly distributed primary vascular voids, dominated by relatively interspersed primary osteons (Figure 3.5). Compare these to the even pace of appositional lamellar formation in a large reptile (Figure 3.6).

### 3.3.2.2 Primary Lamellae and Vessel Entrapment

Much of what distinguishes PEM primary tissue types depends on the organization of lamellar, vascular, and woven bone regions. Currey (2002) well-describes laminar, plexiform, and fibrolamellar bone from this perspective. In general, the formative layer is separated from the surface of the bone by struts of woven bone spanning a highly vascularized space upon which the newest layer is formed. Within these vascular voids, lamellar bone is laid down more slowly. Sometimes woven scaffolding can form so quickly that there are several tables of unfinished lamina upon one another and only deeper intracortical tissue displays more mature lamellar microstructure. To illustrate meaningful differences between these bone types, Currey (2002) cites a simple perspective outlined by Castanet and colleagues (1996), in which the relative speed of formation at the membrane determines structural

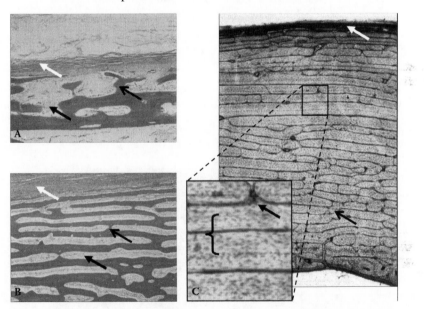

**Figure 3.4 (See color insert.)** (A) Periosteal woven bone deposition in the laminar fashion with plexiform vessel inclusion in the perinatal horse foal femur. White arrows in all images denote the periosteum; black arrows, the vascular void or canal; and black lined arrows mark bridging woven struts providing support for the newest of the forming external laminae. (B) In this young individual (same as part a) vessels are still within many layers of large unfilled voids prior to boney compaction. (C) Laminar bone exhibiting compacted plexiform structure in the 18-month-old Sinclair Minipig tibia. The white solid arrow denotes the most recent tables of bone forming under the periosteum but above the most recent vascular inclusions, whereas the black lined arrow marks tissue entrapping much older vascular networks, now deep within the cortex. Note that entombed vessels are dominantly circumferential but with short connections between generations of vascular sheath (black solid arrow in expansion). The black bracket indicates one full layer as described by Currey (2002), bordered by feint light lines of woven bone. Images A (100× magnification) and B (40× magnification) are microphotographs of paraffin embedded, decalcified thin-section treated with hematoxylin and eosin stain; image C is a 40× magnification microphotograph and digital zoom insert taken from an undecalcified thin-ground section containing visible, though feint, fluorochrome labeling. (Images courtesy of Steven Weisbrode.)

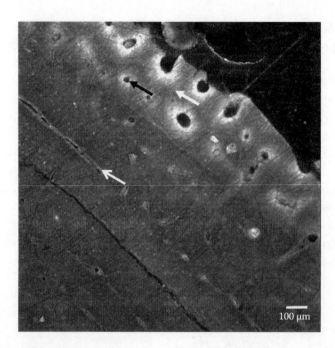

**Figure 3.5** Fibrolamellar bone tissue from the goat pericortex. Longitudinal primary vessel canals (black solid arrow) are surrounded by woven bone (white solid arrow), while internal compact structure appears more laminar, enclosing vessel networks (white lined arrow). Confocal laser scanning micrograph of archaeological bone fluorescence. Scale indicates 100 μm.

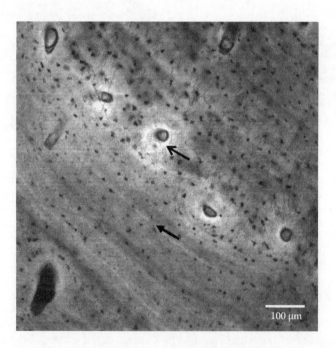

**Figure 3.6** Alligator pericortex demonstrating regular concentric lamellar apposition (black solid arrow) as well as the occasional inclusion of longitudinally oriented primary vascular canals, surrounded by highly mineralized woven bone (black lined arrow). Micrograph taken in white light transmission. Scale indicates 100 μm. (Image courtesy of Y. Castro, D. Vanmali, and T. Dupras.)

variance in the mallard duck: the fastest formation is accomplished by circumferential laminar formation, trapping nearly entire generations of vascular sheaths; and slower formation is accomplished by fibrolamellar or primary osteonal tissue, which captures vessels more rarely and particularly seems to favor longitudinal vessels.

This model would place much of human PEM bone in the slowest category of formation, one where vessel entrapment is even more uncommon. This is because human periosteal lamellar tissue typically traps few transverse vessels from the vascular sheath during osteogenesis and so cannot typically be referred to as laminar. Rapid growth periods in humans can demonstrate laminar-like sets of pericortical woven or lamellar bone separated by longitudinal primary vessel horizons locked within "generations" of lamellar apposition (Figure 3.7). However, even in the quickly growing infant human, laminar-like bone is typically limited to only one or two "layers" of the immature external periosteal cortex; this pattern exists rarely or briefly, and never reaches the volume seen in other species (measurable in centimeters on occasion).

When vessels do become entombed within human PEM bone, they are not trapped equally on both external and medullary surfaces. Periosteal vessels overlain by primary lamellar diaphyseal apposition are typically longitudinal and are often referred to as primary vascular canals, or "primary osteons" (Currey 2002); despite that they are completely unrelated to secondary osteons (or Haversian systems) formed by BMUs (Figures 3.8 and 3.9). In fact, for casual investigations, using this term often conflates two vastly different features in their vessel origin, formation, microstructural appearance, and physiological function. Primary osteons do not require resorption prior to enclosure and infilling (Currey 2002). Typically, primary osteons are sandwiched between lamellae that bend slightly

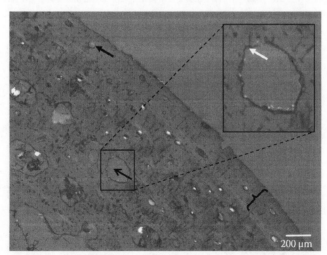

**Figure 3.7 (See color insert.)** Human infant pericortex demonstrating occasional inclusion of longitudinal vessels, as primary osteons (black solid arrow) as in fibrolamellar or primary osteonal bone. In this case there exists a single pseudo laminar layer within the forming (mostly woven) pericortex (black bracket). The black lined arrow denotes a resorption bay destined for expansion during endocortical resorption or infilling via BMU-based remodeling. The white arrow marks one of many Howships lacuna roughening the bay's perimeter, evidence that resorption was active antemortem. Thin-ground, undecalcified transection of archaeological, femoral mid-diaphysis, Dakhleh Oasis, Egypt. Micrograph taken with red quartz cross-polarized filter (hilfsobject). Scale bar indicates 200 μm.

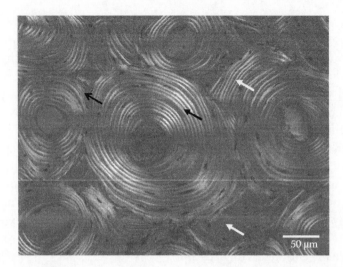

**Figure 3.8 (See color insert.)** Adult secondary osteons, or Haversian systems, with concentric lamellae and a central canal, which in life would house vessels and nerves. Note the similarity of lamellar structure between BMU tissue and PEM tissue (Figures 3.3 and 3.15) in both lamellar thickness and lacunar inclusion (here, a black solid arrow). The black lined arrow marks the central osteon's cement line (reversal line), the zone of maximum resorption during the resorptive phase of BMU activity. Subsequent formation progressed from this point toward the canal at the center. White solid arrows denote osteonal fragments from previous BMUs that passed through the region. No primary tissue is present in this field of view or in the larger region suggesting that the tissue can be classified as Haversian tissue and that the individual is likely mature or even of advancing age. Thin-ground, undecalcified transection of archaeological, humeral mid-diaphysis, Dakhleh Oasis, Egypt. Micrograph taken with red quartz cross-polarized filter (hilfsobject). Scale bar indicates 50 μm.

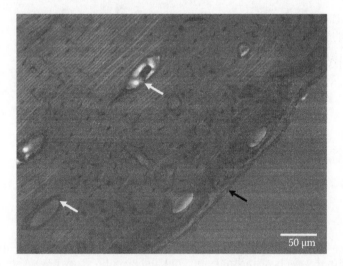

**Figure 3.9 (See color insert.)** Primary osteons, or primary vascular canals, from a juvenile (white solid arrows), have no lamellae or cement line of their own. Instead, they are entrapped by successive lamellar apposition at the periosteum. The black solid arrow denotes the bone surface most recently applied by the periosteum, continuing to inhume several other longitudinal primary vessels. Thin-ground, undecalcified transection of archaeological, humeral mid-diaphysis, Dakhleh Oasis, Egypt. Mid-diaphyseal micrograph taken with red quartz cross-polarized filter (hilfsobject). Scale bar indicates 50 μm.

under and over them, but contain few or no lamellae of their own (Bright and Elmore 1968; Chamay 1970; Currey 2002). Primary vascular canals can also be seen in completely woven tissue as well. In contrast, endosteal bone rarely traps vasculature in the same way as the periosteum; instead, Volkmann's canals extend during growth to maintain the connection between the endosteal vascular network and deeper tissue, leaving a characteristic radial orientation to these lateral canals (Figure 3.10). This has been observed in the rhesus tibia (Enlow 1962) as well as the human femur (Maggiano et al. in press), but could be expected as a normal trait of primary endosteal deposition. More research is necessary to investigate the local effects of this differential vascularization between the peri- and endocortex.

Having considered human bone modeling microstructure in reference to that of other animals we come to a conclusion of necessity: human bone biologists should maintain reference to human PEM bone tissue as *primary lamellar,* but should qualify by the membrane of origin when possible (i.e., periosteal lamellae, or pericortex), rather than simply *lamellar* or *laminar.* This is because (1) without delineating between primary and secondary lamellae we run the risk of confusing modeling and remodeling processes and resulting bone tissue, and (2) it is rare to find apparent, 4–20 lamellar sets by which we would

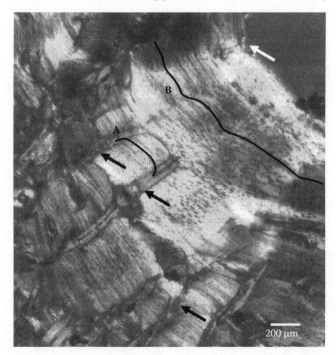

**Figure 3.10 (See color insert.)** Dense primary endosteal lamellae, comprising nearly a fourth of the total cross-sectional area, have failed to entrap a single longitudinal vessel from the endosteal surface (white arrow). Instead, lamellae formed under endosteal vasculature, pushing it away, filling the spaces between transverse Volkmann's canals (black solid arrows mark examples). These vessels extended to maintain connectivity to the intercortical Haversian network (out of view to the lower left). (A) As bone is laid between transverse vessels its lamellae "pillow" slightly, perhaps due to slower rates of calcification adjacent to the pulsating vessels. (B) This effect can be easily seen in lamellae merely adjacent to transverse vessels, even when these vessels are not within the plane of sectioning. Thin-ground, undecalcified transection of archaeological, humeral mid-diaphysis, Xcambó, Mexico. Micrograph taken with red quartz cross-polarized filter (Hilfsobject). Scale bar indicates 200 µm. (Image courtesy of I. Maggiano.)

otherwise define adult, PEM-origin human bone as laminar by Locke's (2004) definition (or fibrolamellar, or plexiform for that matter). Several recent works have been dedicated to the quantification and qualification of histological variance among species, including Hillier and Bell (2007) and Martiniaková and coworkers (2009), and can be referenced for more detailed information on species identification of fragmentary remains. Also, for further discussion of histomorphological differences between human and nonhuman bone, see Mulhern and Ubelaker in this volume.

### 3.3.2.3  *Modeling Microstructure*

Unlike the BMU, PEM primary lamellar formation occurs independently of resorption. This is not to say that resorption cannot occur on the same surface as immediate subsequent formation (or vice versa), just that previous resorption is not a requirement for formation. The rate of human periosteal apposition has only been measured in a few studies. Balena and colleagues (1992) report, periosteal formation rates reached an upper value of 4 μm/year as measured in transilial bone biopsies from pre- and postmenopausal women (Parfitt 2002). In later investigations of the ilium (Parfitt et al. 2000) it was found that the net periosteal apposition rate was 0.581 on the external periosteum, compared to an "inferred" net endocortical apposition rate of 0.154 μm/day on the inner endosteum. They report that this amounts to a total mean periosteal mineral apposition rate of 1.04 μm/day in children 2–20 years old (Parfitt et al. 2000). It is typically argued that the general formation rate for modeling is faster than remodeling (2–10 μm/day compared to 0.3–1.0 μm/day, respectively; as shown in a table from Jee et al. 2007 providing data collected from Parfitt 1983 and Jee 2001). However, one should take caution in interpreting numerical comparisons that can at times report rates of apposition by a single layer of osteoblasts with rates of growth contributed by multiple layers of osteoblasts, as would be the case in measuring total diametric (PEM) changes in general, or even "single" membrane locations undergoing rapid plexiform growth in non-human animals—both examples where surface topography permits several teams of osteoblasts to contribute to growth along the same axis simultaneously.

Martin and colleagues (1998) provide an interesting discussion on modeling growth rates and their alteration with physical exertion by discussing four-point bending experiments of Forwood and Turner (1994; Turner et al. 1994). These authors found that in the rat, periosteal woven bone deposition in response to mechanical strain seemed to be all or nothing while periosteal and endosteal lamellar deposition were both dependent on strain magnitude (Forwood and Turner 1994; Turner et al. 1994). Martin and colleagues (1998) suggest this contributes a quantum-like aspect to modeling due to histological and functional limitations of periosteal and endosteal histology.

In addition to changing rates of formation, modeling activity affects variable magnitudes of bone volume. When the membrane is fully engaged in formation, lamellae can span nearly the entire PEM; generating *circumferential lamellae*. This leads to the familiar histological landscape of a long bone transverse cross-section (especially in preadolescents or young adults): PEM lamellae sandwiching more highly remodeled bone occupying the intercortex (Enlow 1962; Figure 3.11). Garn (1972) found that the period during and immediately after the adolescent growth spurt was marked by endosteal formation continuing sometimes into the fourth decade of life, especially in males. After primary modeling is accomplished and skeletal maturation is complete, the periosteum may remain slightly active while endosteal bone formation ceases altogether (Lazenby 1990; Ruff et al. 2006). Primary pericortex becomes more rapidly remodeled than endosteal tissue (Kerley 1965;

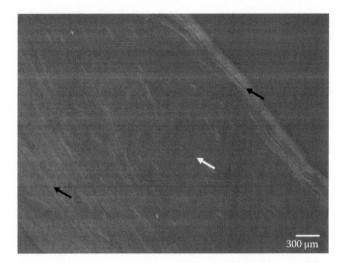

**Figure 3.11 (See color insert.)** The traditionally described histological landscape of young compact bone. Primary lamellar bone (black solid arrows) formed by the periosteum (lower left) and endosteum (upper right). White solid arrow marks remodeled Haversian tissue formed by BMU activity. This remodeling transpired in the older intercortical primary tissue and has now turned over a large area, replacing primary osteons with secondary, and increasing the general porosity of the region. Thin-ground, undecalcified transection of archaeological, humeral mid-diaphysis, Dakhleh Oasis, Egypt. Micrograph taken with red quartz cross-polarized filter (hilfsobject). Scale bar indicates 300 μm.

Martin and Armelagos 1979) due to increased transference of stress along the outside of bending bones (Pauwels 1965; Ruff and Hayes 1983a; Kimura and Amtmann 1984; Van Buskirk 1989; Heller et al. 2001), and potentially due to the increased tensile strength of primary compared to secondary bone (Vincentelli and Grigorov 1985). This can result in significant areas of unremodeled primary endosteal lamellae, even in individuals approaching the estimated fifth decade of life (Maggiano et al. in press). After this age it becomes more likely that continued remodeling or age-associated endocortical resorption could remove all remnants of primary endosteal tissue (Maggiano et al. in press).

Not all periosteal or endosteal modeling is achieved by full membrane formation or resorption. Modeling can also occur in smaller more amorphous or regional domains of varying cortical depths as observed in transverse cross-sections. Consecutive and concentric lamellae that are at least partially uninterrupted are modeling BSUs and are referred to here as *phases*, borrowed from geology and archaeology's term for a specific frame of stratigraphic deposition. In 1973, Frost used formation or resorption "packets" as a general descriptor for the same phenomenon. Frost (1964b) recommends the term *foci* for sites of initial modeling apposition or resorption, a term also used here. A phase or focus can be modified by the descriptor "formation" or "resorption" when necessary. Unfortunately, the same limitations discussed previously with regard to lamellar quantification, apply to modeling phases. Current techniques suffer an inability to follow either lamellae or their phases, to terminal ends in three dimensions. Features microscopic in one axis and macroscopic in another, locked within hard tissue, pose a great challenge for quantification. However, polarization microscopy is a useful aid in viewing lamellar stratigraphy.

Polarized-light microscopy takes advantage of bone's ability to refract light at multiple indices. This property, called birefringence, creates an image in which white incident light is brightened, darkened, or colored (with filters) depending on changes in the orientation (Bromage et al. 2003) or density (Marotti 1993) of collagen bundles within lamellae (Boyde and Riggs 1990). Polarized light greatly emphasizes lamellar orientation and facilitates the observation of fine changes in lamellar microstructure, undetectable with white light microscopy. Especially visible are changes in lamellar orientation, either with or without disruptions to the lamellar structure. These changes are often unreported or tersely discussed in literature, where circumferential lamellae are treated generally as if they are contiguous and concentric, which is not the case.

Variation in lamellar orientation holds valuable stratigraphic information regarding growth and adaptation processes or stimuli. For example, if the newest lamellae (adjacent to the bone surface) are concentric with a membrane of origin, that membrane was either (1) currently forming lamellar bone at the time of death or extraction, or (2) it had paused after formation with little or no subsequent membrane activity. Alternately, lamellar phases can be cross-cut by those more newly formed. If a PEM phase is currently resorbing, lamellae can bear telltale evidence of osteoclastic activity (such as Howships lacunae) and can appear cross-cut at some oblique angle. Microscopic evidence of this process can persist long after its occurrence, especially when subsequent formation phases entomb cross-cut lamellae, typically marked by the presence of a cement line (Figure 3.12). A cement line is a region characterized by a localized disruption of typical lamellar microstructure, sometimes preserving Howships lacunae under high magnification, similar to the peripheral margin of a secondary osteon or hemiosteon. Other lines are smoother, with no resorptive evidence and are called arrest lines. Presumably modeling cement lines would demonstrate some of the same interesting attributes as their remodeling cousins, including increased mineral composition, unique mechanical properties, and biomechanical importance as described by Skedros and colleagues (2005).

Other times no evidence of lamellar disruption is apparent, yet lamellae from one phase appear cross-cut by a previous or subsequent phase at a different region of the prior bone surface. This common but often unreported occurrence results in inconsistent circumferential lamellae due to complex modeling phase interactions. Partially interrupted phases are more difficult to interpret due to the reduced visibility of the transition between consecutive uninterrupted apposition and lamellar arrest lines (Figure 3.13), compared with more obvious arrest lines in osteons (refer to Figure 3.12). There are also forensic or bioarchaeological implications for understanding the histomorphology of primary modeling arrest lines compared to uninterrupted lamellar apposition, particularly if it were found that they were diagnostic for certain mechanical or pathological circumstances. Complex interactions between phases of primary lamellar apposition are especially easy to observe in larger areas of deposition as seen in the endocortex of young adults in both the rhesus monkey (Enlow 1962) and human (Maggiano et al. in press).

Interpretation of some lamellar structures is aided by remembering that at one time they were not solid, they existed as puddles of osteoid. For example, radially oriented vessels often introduce a pillowing of primary lamellae between them. This effect, when severe and along the periosteal surface has been implicated in advanced treponemal and leperous periostitis; the structures themselves being referred to as *polsters*, meaning literally "cushions" in German (Schultz 2001, this volume). Manifesting in a much less severe fashion, it can also be seen in typical endosteal primary lamellar regions, as in Figure 3.10. It has long been well known that static and pulsatile strains can inhibit bone formation or even induce resorption of bone tissue (Du Boulay 1956; Feik et al.

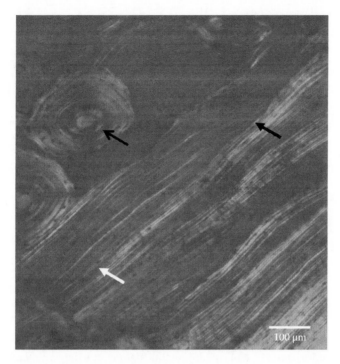

**Figure 3.12 (See color insert.)** Endosteal primary lamella now occupying an intracortical position adjacent to several Haversian systems. These particular primary lamellae are laid in several formative phases. The white arrow marks consecutive, uninterrupted formation of the major phase, while the black arrow marks a cement line cutting across previous lamellae of the same major phase, splitting this local region into two separate minor formation phases due to a single, slight resorption focus. This presents stratigraphic evidence of a single phase of formation continuing in one region while at another, reversal occurs followed by formation, directing drift in a specific net direction. Subsequent phases to the bottom right of the image also bear evidence of targeted modeling resorption in the form of roughened cement lines that cross-cut previous lamellae. Also note the presence of an arrest line in a secondary osteon (black lined arrow) for comparison with cement lines demonstrating resorptive evidence. Thin-ground, undecalcified transection of archaeological, humeral mid-diaphysis, Dakhleh Oasis, Egypt. Micrograph taken with red quartz cross-polarized filter (hilfsobject). Scale bar indicates 100 μm.

1987). Therefore, one potential cause for transverse lamellar orientation effects near vessels is the pressure applied by the vessel or even through direct pulsation of the vessel, which could hypothetically slow calcification through osteoid perturbation. This later possibility remains intuitive but unexplored, particularly in modern histomorphometry. Further experimentation on these issues could also weigh in on other debates such as how digital and vessel impressions are left on bone surfaces and why secondary osteon infilling slows as it approaches completion. Originally reported by Jee and Arnold (1954), the decline in formation rate during osteon closure has been further verified experimentally (Marshall et al. 1959; Manson and Waters 1965) and supported theoretically by Martin (2001). For a more detailed treatment of quasi-static and pulsatile effects on bone formation and resorption, see Carpenter and Carter (2008). For a summary of other hypotheses and mathematical models explaining rate of infilling during remodeling, see Martin and coauthors (1998) and Martin (2000), respectively.

Interpreting modeling histology in regions like this also requires conceptualizing a changing surface area of activity on the PEM. Theoretically a given formation phase focus

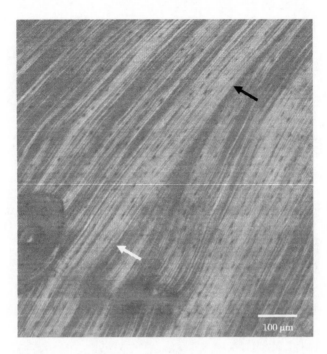

**Figure 3.13 (See color insert.)** Endosteal lamellae demonstrating complex phase activity. The white solid arrow marks continued uninterrupted formation through the entire field of view. Conversely, the black solid arrow denotes a modeling arrest line. Though subtle in appearance, the effect is significant, marking a pause in phase formation in the upper right region while formation continues for hundreds of micrometers (past the lower field of view boundary). Thin-ground, undecalcified transection of archaeological, humeral mid-diaphysis, Dakhleh Oasis, Egypt. Micrograph taken with red quartz cross-polarized filter (hilfsobject). Scale bar indicates 100 μm.

is comprised of initially activated osteoblasts on the PEM bone surface. Changes in the osteogenic signal responsible for this activation could cause the active region (and therefore the associated phase of resorption or formation) to expand or contract in surface area. This occurrence should be visible in the bone's primary microstructure. For example, increasing a phase's surface area of formation should result in unique lamellar organization relative to others that are decreasing (Figure 3.14). In addition, there exists the potential for "migrating" surface areas of formation in which lamellar sheets are apposed in a stepwise fashion, changing the foci for the phase with each team or region of newly activated osteoblasts. The transverse section of a migrating formation surface could, theoretically, be confused for changing surface areas of formation if the lamellar migration was strong and its direction was perpendicular to the plane of sectioning. In practical consideration, however, conditions responsible for changing the surface area of an active formation phase seem far more likely than those necessitating its migration. Changes in a phase's surface area of formation are likely related to changes in the formation signal and should depend on the context of the phase's focus, including the scale and topography of the original area of formation. It is also important to remember that Howship's lacunae could provide evidence for the same circumstance during resorption, positively or negatively affecting resorptive phase surface area as it progresses over time as well. However, without subsequent formation, this phenomenon is not viewable stratigraphically. As a conceptual example of how complex

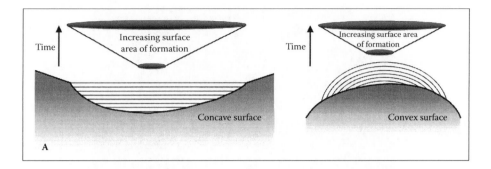

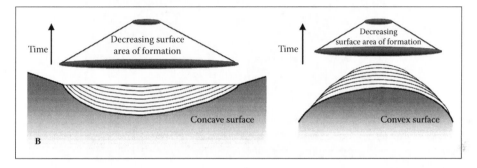

**Figure 3.14** Two theoretically distinct lamellar phase microstructures depending on changing surface areas of formation over time, represented schematically. (A) A concave surface, viewed in transverse cross-section, is filled in. Each successive layer is larger in surface area than the last, requiring the activation of more and more previously dormant osteogenic cells from the membrane (top left). On a convex surface the same event produces a different lamellar stratigraphy (top right). (B) A concave surface, in which each successive layer's area is, instead, smaller than the last, where fewer and fewer cells are actively forming bone (bottom left). On a convex surface the same event produces a different lamellar architecture (bottom right). These changes in surface area accompany meaningful changes in some aspect of the formation signal that initiates or directs modeling activity. The size of the formation phase or its local microtopography could also be a factor influencing surface areas of formation. The prevalence or biological significance of this type of microstructural variation is untested, but could theoretically offer information on changes in signal strength, dispersion, or direction due to whole-bone or micro-topographic biomechanical loading.

localized changes like this can be, consider the migrating and changing surface area active during osteonal drifting as described by Robling and Stout (1999).

To further illustrate some interesting occurrences achievable by multiple foci of PEM activity, imagine an endocortical region in which a remnant of trabecular structure separates two membrane regions where formation is necessary. Two separate formation phases could occur on either side of the interposing structure (Figure 3.15). Subsequent phases not only pack on more endosteal lamellae but also ensure that intracortical remodeling could eventually both obscure the circumstance originally separating these phases, and with continued significant formation, rejoin them. In other circumstances, formations are small and numerous, with evidence for prior resorption (Figure 3.16). Especially at these smaller scales (<300 μm), distinguishing between modeling events and hemiosteons, well-described by Parfitt (2003), could prove challenging (Jee et al. 2007). In order to understand the role of the hemiosteon, we typically focus on trabecular tissue, the investigation of endosteal modeling phases during growth could contribute to our understanding of the complex circumstances created by spongy tissue (see Section 3.4.4 for more detail).

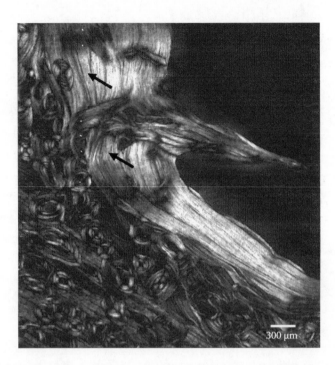

**Figure 3.15** The black solid arrows mark two different sets of modeling foci separated by an irregular trabecular spicule (potentially a remnant from an earlier growth period). If formation continued past this interruption these two foci could merge if timed correctly or the slower of the two would abut the faster. Thin-ground, undecalcified transection of archaeological, humeral mid-diaphysis, Dakhleh Oasis, Egypt. Merged cross-polarized micrograph. Comprising images taken when primary lamellae were at 45° to normal x, y stage orientation. Scale bar indicates 300 μm.

**Figure 3.16 (See color insert.)** A series of endocortical modeling formation phases present as adjustments to a much larger phase (past the lower field of view boundary). The white solid arrow marks the most recent phase, whereas the white lined arrows mark overlain fragments, indicating prior resorption took place before the final phase was formed. These phases are small enough to permit confusion with hemiosteons, although the latter are typically only reported in trabecular bone. Black solid arrow denotes medullary surface. Thin-ground, undecalcified transection of archaeological, humeral mid-diaphysis, Dakhleh Oasis, Egypt. Micrograph taken with red quartz cross-polarized filter (hilfsobject). Scale bar indicates 50 μm.

Together, these microstructural circumstances explain why a typical volume of circumferential lamellae can be constructed of noncircumferential phases of apposition interacting in a complex context that reveals the history of growth and adaptation in the region. More research is necessary to access the implications of these observations fully. For example, reversal lines could indicate meaningful changes in adaptive response, and significant arrests in phase formation could indicate the severity of a malnutrition or disease event, interrupting growth.

## 3.4 Modeling Function

### 3.4.1 Growth

In order to envision how small-scale changes in lamellar orientation, apposition, and resorption account for modeling during growth and adaptation, we need to expand our perspective, considering the concerted efforts of both surface membranes simultaneously. Over an individual's lifetime, the function of bony envelopes is sometimes oversimplified. Growth typically requires periosteal expansion and endosteal resorption (Epker et al. 1965; Stoker and Epker 1971). However, modeling cannot be this simple if the goal is to affect complex morphological change in an adaptive context. For example, according to Garn (1970), more than 25% of an individual's total cortical thickness will be accounted for by the narrowing of the medullary cavity via endosteal bone deposition. Without concerted local modeling activity bones would be unable to alter their curvature or orientation with respect to other elements. In addition, longitudinal extension would fail to form an effective compact diaphysis; instead metaphyses would grow unaltered volumes of trabecular tissue. To account for necessary shape change during growth, the relative rates of formation and resorption activity must be altered from region to region along both the periosteum and endosteum.

### 3.4.2 Drift

One of the easiest modeling processes to envision involves the uneven distribution of bone on different sides of the diaphysis. For example, Enlow (1962) notes that in order to achieve the adult morphology of the rhesus tibia, lateral periosteal formation is accompanied by medial resorption. During this process, the bone actually moves in anatomical space–time so dramatically that its adult position is far removed from its immature position (Figure 3.17). Conceivably, modeling drift alone (with no turnover from remodeling) could account for a bone that microscopically contains almost entirely new bone tissue, the immature tissue having been resorbed by one or several envelopes. This phenomenon, in part, accounts for the fact that mean bone tissue age is significantly younger than chronological age (Wu et al. 1970). Enlow (1962) called the general process *osseous drift*, whereas Frost's term, *modeling drift*, has been preferred in the literature (Epker and Frost 1965; Frost 1973, 2001; Jee and Frost 1992).

Modeling drift at the periosteum alone cannot account for adult long bone morphology, because the described pattern would yield an eccentric medullary cavity. Therefore, periosteal formation and resorption are often mirrored in process on the endosteum. That is, during lateral diaphyseal drift, the endosteum must apply new bone lamellae to

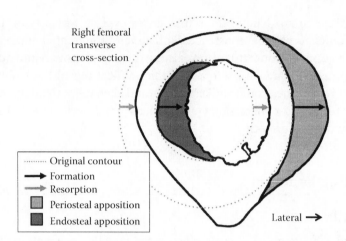

**Figure 3.17** Schematic of a right femoral transverse cross-section demonstrating significant net linear drift. Lateral periosteal apposition is accompanied by medial endosteal apposition, shifting the bone laterally relative to its original position. Resorption transpires on the medial periosteal and lateral endosteal surfaces, maintaining the centralized position of the medullary cavity. Endosteal lamellae (dark gray) have relatively few secondary osteons in comparison to periosteal lamellae (light gray), which are more mechanically strained and could remodel more quickly (see text for details). Adapted from Maggiano IS, Maggiano C, Tiesler Blos V et al., A distinct region of microarchitectural variation in femoral compact bone: histomorphology of the endosteal lamellar pocket. (Int J Osteoarch, in press.)

the medial surface while resorbing those on the lateral surface. For example, the net ventral drift noted in the rib also requires pleural endosteal formation and ventral endosteal resorption. Only in this way can the medullary cavity maintain its central position within the drifting diaphyses. Exactly how this resorption is accomplished is not clearly understood. Close observation of the resorbing endocortex indicates, not only active endosteal modeling resorption by the presence of Howship's lacunae, but also dramatic resorption occurring in large intracortical resorption bays.

Modeling drift has been observed in several other bones important for histological analysis. Rubin (1964) described resorption on some ribs' pleural periosteum, opposed by formation on the cutaneous surface, an observation commented and elaborated upon in other works (Epker and Frost 1965; Streeter and Stout 2003). Ribs in older age demonstrated more equalized formation and resorption (Epker and Frost 1965). Balena and colleagues (1992) also found no evidence for net periosteal formation or drift at all, for that matter, in their examination of the *adult* transilium. Subsequent and detailed investigations of the illium quantitatively measured drift using histomorphometry to measure the independent contributions to *external* periosteal formation and endosteal resorption, and *internal* periosteal resorption and endosteal formation (Parfitt et al. 2000). The adult histomorphological patterns that indicate drift have also been observed at the femoral (Maggiano et al. in press), humeral, and ulnar mid-diaphysis (Maggiano unpublished results), but await further study.

Conceptually, there are two types of long bone drift, although only one has been reported in the literature. The first is linear drift that shifts the bone's position (or a portion thereof) in any net direction well summarized by a straight line. Typically, linear drift at the diaphysis will be evident in a more or less transverse orientation to the longitudinal axis of a long bone. Intramembranous bones, however, could conceivably drift linearly along any major or minor axes. Linear drift is the drift type most commonly referred to in the literature (Enlow 1962; Epker and Frost 1965; Frost 1973; Mosley et al. 1997; Streeter and Stout 2003) and could result in diaphyseal curvature or the reorientation of the bone with respect to the larger skeletal system. Unfortunately, due to previously discussed limitations, few drift studies have yet to observe and record human drift directions such that changes in shape or orientation could be quantified or compared.

The second type of drift, here referred to as *curvilinear drift*, can be visualized in the transverse cross-section as stepwise alteration in the direction of drift at one or both surface envelopes, through the complex manipulation of primary PEM phases. This can be accomplished via changes in the size, shape, or relative location of their surfaces of formation, for example. This type of drift could also be formed by several large linear drifts that are at significant angles to one another, lending the impression that drift direction is curvilinear. It is important to remember that drift could be strong enough on occasion to completely alter the position of a bone in cross-sectional tissue–space–time. In these circumstances, most of the endocortical, and intracortical regions could be composed of periosteal lamellae; likewise on the opposite side of the diaphysis, the pericortex and intracortex could contain dominantly endosteal lamellae. It is unknown how often and in which bone elements this severe drift occurs, but this is another reason caution should be employed when referencing primary lamellar tissue by region or membrane origin (i.e., referring to the outer third of the cortex as the "pericortex" could be misleading in cases of significant drift, where some included primary tissue on a given side is potentially endosteal in membrane origin).

Modeling drift is both incredibly important and understudied. For example, we might expect that because the mid-diaphysis is the site for maximum load-induced deformation (Biewener 1992), and because bone is mechanically responsive, that the diaphysis should demonstrate the most dramatic evidence of modeling drift by mechanical adaptation. However, the same shape or orientation for a long bone can be formed by several different means (Figure 3.18). A curved diaphysis could be formed by drift occurring in each end of the diaphysis, only at the mid-diaphysis, or in all these regions simultaneously. We have yet to identify the net drift directions of most skeletal elements and have few data on drift variability per element, across or between populations. Without these data, we discuss bone curvature or shape but have relatively no idea how it came to be. The theory of modeling drift also implies adjacent tissues could be far more separated by age at formation than previously realized. For example, endosteal tissue formed during the adolescent growth spurt could abut Haversian tissue laid down within the sixth decade of life (Maggiano et al. in press). It is in this microstructural environment that we attempt to estimate age or measure stable isotopic ratios. Some studies have recognized this limitation. The concept of tissue age at formation is a subtle extension of the modeling drift concept and accounts for the fact that adjacent bony tissues could be years apart in formation. This occurrence must be factored into equations used to estimate age in the rib, for example (Wu et al. 1970). Unfortunately, the average tissue age at formation is unreported for other elements (Robling and Stout 2003).

### 3.4.3 Metaphyseal Reduction and Medullary Extension

In addition to drift, modeling processes account for the shaping of bone during its elongation at the growth plate (Figure 3.19b, white checkering). This occurs, in part, via metaphyseal reduction: Frost's (1973) "necking down" or "metaphyseal drift system" where periosteal resorption reduces and smoothes the diameter of metaphyseal tissue destined for eventual inclusion in the diaphysis (Enlow 1962; Jee and Frost 1992; Rauch et al. 2001).

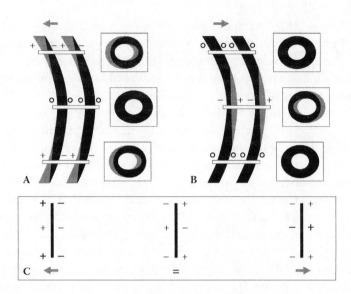

**Figure 3.18** Schematic representing curvature achievement during long bone modeling. Large and small plusses and minuses indicate varying magnitudes of modeling formation and resorption, respectively. Arrows indicate the direction of net drift. (A) This schematic, curved diaphysis results from a modeling drift to the left at regions distant from the mid-shaft. (B) A net right drift can result in the exact same curvature when only the mid-shaft is undergoing modeling activity (upper right). Transverse cross-sections at each region demonstrate how the positioning and orientation of primary lamellae can reveal which occurrence accounts for the curve. (C) At least three other meaningfully different circumstances could model a previously straight long bone into the same curved shape. Curvature could be gained during net drift of the entire diaphysis (bottom left and right), or could be balanced with no net drift whatsoever (bottom center).

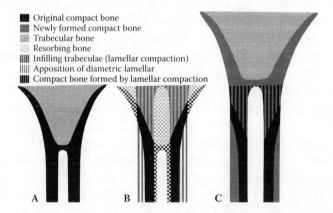

**Figure 3.19** (A) Schematic of immature cortical (black) and trabecular (gray) regions destined for modeling alteration during long bone extension. (B) Bone is resorbed at the metaphyseal periphery and within the medullary cavity, affecting both compact and trabecular tissue alike (white checkering). New compact tissue must also be constructed, both within trabecular voids during lamellar compaction, and at the periosteum via diametric apposition (gray bars). (C) Even in the adult there remains evidence of these changes as the bone extends in length through endochondral ossification (black). (Adapted from Enlow D (1962) A study of the postnatal growth and remodeling of bone, Am J Anat 110:79–101.)

In this fashion, the growing metaphysis undergoes periosteal resorption almost immediately following the formation necessary to stabilize the new tissue forming at the widening physis (Enlow 1962). Slowly, as the bone elongates, the flared diameter reduces to that of the diaphysis. Only the cessation of longitudinal extension "freezes" the metaphyseal morphology, precluding continued large-scale resorption at the metaphyseal surface. The resulting adult morphology is then free of course to alter through mechanically adaptive modeling, albeit with a reduced sensitivity to mechanical change in adulthood as reviewed by Ruff and colleagues (2006). Though metaphysical reduction was well described by Enlow (1962) almost 50 years ago, very little work has been done quantifying or describing the process in a detailed fashion. This is potentially due to a serious limitation of bone biology. Namely, that absent bone is much more difficult to measure than newly formed bone. It would be particularly interesting to uncover the stimuli for periosteal reversal to resorption during this time period. During growth, the periosteal membrane is intenely sensitive to formation signaling due to systemic demands for growth and the local demands of mechanical strain. How does this particular region avoid the stimuli for continuous diametric growth required at the mid-diaphysis, for example?

The same limitation affects our understanding of a similar, often ignored process: medullary extension, where the cavity expands and elongates, ensuring optimum strength–weight ratios for the growing bone. This involves the resorption of trabecular tissue longitudinally and compact tissue diametrically (Enlow 1962; Garn 1970). Medullary expansion at the cost of compact tissue employs both endosteal surface resorption *and* large intracortical resorption bays to permit an increase in resorptive surface area. These cavities, typically positioned on the inner third of the cortex, are popularly connected with age-associated bone loss but are present in abundance during periods of growth (Figure 3.20) or within part of the inner-cortex during linear diaphyseal drift, (for example, to the right of the

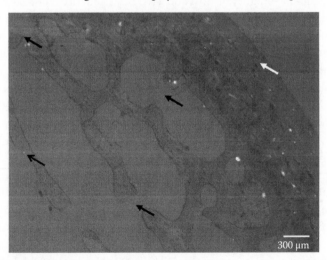

**Figure 3.20 (See color insert.)** Infant cortical woven expansion at the periosteum (white solid arrow) is countered by dramatic endocortical resorption (marked by Howship's lacunae roughening bone surfaces) both at the endosteal margin (black lined arrow) and in expanding, large, resorption bays (black solid arrows). Black solid arrows also denote loss of several "trabecularized" cortical connections. Thin-ground, undecalcified transection of archaeological, femoral mid-diaphysis, Dakhleh Oasis, Egypt. Micrograph taken with red quartz cross-polarized filter (hilfsobject). Scale bar indicates 300 μm.

medullary cavity in Figure 3.17). In this fashion, resorption could speed up exponentially as multiple teams of osteoclasts at different positions simultaneously contribute to resorption along desired axes. In trabecular (or fully trabecularized) tissue, however, this rate of resorption can drop due to a decrease of total surface area from loss of connectivity (Esrund et al. 1995). How much tissue is removed at the endosteal membrane itself versus, through proliferation (Parfitt 1988) and expansion (Han et al. 1997; Parfitt 2003) of resorptive bays, is unknown and should be more closely assessed. Without more investigation into this particular occurrence, we are left to attribute trabecularization via large resorptive bays to either, (1) *BMU decoupling* (some might argue merely "formation lag," but lag over this time and space calls the effectiveness of coupling into question); or (2) *intracortical modeling resorption* (a term neither used in the literature nor likely to be well accepted). Indeed the synergy between modeling and remodeling process is astounding (and confounding). But this is not the only example of well-orchestrated, complex manipulation of both sister processes simultaneously.

### 3.4.4   Lamellar Compaction

The process Enlow (1962) termed *lamellar compaction* (Figure 3.19b, light and dark gray stripes) is the reverse of compact bone trabecularization, involving the in-filling of previous voids to form compact tissue. Just as bone once compact must become spongy, spongy bone must become compact if regional demands of growth are to be met. Lamellar compaction is also rarely researched from a modern perspective, in general (an important exception is Parfitt et al. 2000), but especially in long bones. It is much easier to observe in the "flat bones" and the rib because these elements maintain some number of medullary trabeculae throughout life, most of which are formed by prior external periosteal growth and subsequent expansion of resorptive bays (Parfitt et al. 2000). The process is often overlooked in long bones. However, compaction also occurs during their extension, in bone–space which was once trabecular but during maturation must become compact. Why this process happens is suggested through experimental and computerized modeling data examined in an interesting work contributed by Tanck and colleagues in 2006, which argues the lamellar compaction near the spongy cortex transpires via mechanical adaptation phenomena. Therefore, it is possible that lamellar compaction is actually a secondary effect of longitudinal growth.

The microscopic structure of compacted trabecular voids is difficult to interpret. In cross-section, Enlow describes this tissue's lamellae as more disrupted and "whorled" (Enlow 1962). This is likely due to the morphological complexity of trabecular voids compared to the relative simplicity of peri- and endocortex surfaces and the ordered formation taking place in intracortical BMUs. As long as quiescent BLCs along trabecular void surfaces, like those of the endosteum, maintain their reactivation and osteogenic capacity, Enlow's lamellar compaction provides a rapid and direct means of transforming trabecular space into compact tissue via modeling. This potential is suggested by direct observation in animal studies that show "uncoupled" formation due to mechanical loading (Chow et al. 1998) or intermittent parathyroid hormone treatment (Dobnig 1995) via reactivation of quiescent BLCs, necessitating similar studies on BLCs of endosteal compartments during growth. However, trabecular voids could also be filled by hemi-osteonal remodeling, if remodeling formation can outpace resorption—a phenomenon reported or discussed often (Jee and Frost 1992; Martin et al. 1998; Parfitt 2000, 2003; Frost 2003). The basic understanding of hemi-osteonal remodeling in trabeculae is augmented by histological observations suggesting that the BLC layer of the surface remains intact as a "ceiling" above osteoclastic resorption and subsequent osteoblastic formation transpiring underneath (Hauge et al. 2001). Exactly where the defining line between modeling and remodeling lies indeed whether there is a line is significantly unclear in this specific case.

Could the formative membrane give us a clue? How different, for these purposes, is the BLC layer of trabecular void from that of the endosteum of the medullary void? Basic histology suggests they are similar, aside from the concentration and type of hematopoitic tissue within the void space. Regardless of any histological similarities, however, trabecular struts should experience dramatically different local surface area mechanics (Ensrud et al. 1995; Szulc and Seeman 2009) where these conditions could be optimal for the activation of BMU activity to avoid instigating loss of trabecular connectivity via standard osteonal remodeling (Parfitt 2003). But the continuation or movement of the BMU could still be a problem within this environment. Conversely, during growth, the endosteal membrane allows direct local or general bone formation and resorption (not necessarily in that order), potentially permitting greater growth and adaptive plasticity without requiring the activation and mobile manipulation of more numerous BMUs. Might not these same benefits be preferable in trabecular tissue also, particularly when the goal is complete infilling of some trabecular voids during elongation of long bones? Might not resorptive modeling phases also necessitate compartmentalization via a BLC "ceiling" as well? For example, these compartments are visible on both the forming and resorbing sides of the bone shown in Figure 3.2D during fetal development when we would expect modeling to be at its most active. What about in the adult where modeling activity is dampened? More quantitative histological investigation is necessary to compare localized modeling apposition and hemiosteonal apposition and reveal their formative circumstances.

For example, how (or if) trabecular modeling and hemiosteonal remodeling could be differentiated histologically is a question raised by Jee et al. (2007). They answer in the affirmative by supporting Frost's (1988a, 1988b, 1989) usage of the term *minimodeling* to differentiate packets (here, phases) of bone formation on trabecular surfaces with no evidence of prior resorption due to the presence of smooth cement lines, or arrest lines (Jee et al. 2007). However, if one considers primary lamellar structure in compact bone, the argument that smooth cement lines equate with modeling, and rough with remodeling, is not apparent at all. As shown previously in Section 3.3.2.3, even a single massive phase of modeling formation may have small regions that appear to have divided into separate resorption phases. In compact tissue, this is most common in endosteal deposition where phases deposited during drift are (1) decidedly noncircumferential, and (2) can abut other bone structures at their terminal ends (like old trabecular spicules). If the encounter angle between the new and old tissue were acute enough to threaten structural integrity, for example, the area could necessitate localized resorption to rectify the awkward topography. After all, with good architectural reason, growing bone seems to abhor sharp angles.

Modeling is a wonderfully complex process. Jee and colleagues (2007) call attention to this fact, even in trabecular space, by recognizing some packets of trabecular minimodeling represent "mixed remodeling–minimodeling" as described by Ma et al. (2006). The same effect, albeit on a larger scale, is reported here as a normal phenomenon of primary lamellar modeling apposition over large expanses of endocortical tissue, as shown in Figure 3.12. More research is necessary before we can easily discern between modeling and remodeling within small, geometrically complex trabecular voids. For now, it is useful to consider that the speed of formation necessary in these voids during growth and development could demand the particular advantages of modeling processes, rather than slower remodeling with "overfilling" (Salle et al. 2002). In these contexts it is also important to remain cautious of all-or-nothing interpretations of rough cement lines and smooth arrest lines, or even of modeling and remodeling processes themselves.

Regardless of how trabecular spaces are filled, conceptually they must be filled, lest metaphyseal reduction expose spongy bone on the surface of the metaphysis. Of course, after compaction, this tissue exists at a relatively low volume for a short period of time during growth and so could be challenging to study. It could be quickly remodeled or even lost to endosteal resorption during subsequent phases of growth (which is probably more likely). Its brief existence does not imply nonimportance, however. What circumstances could cause in-filling in these trabecular spaces though they exist adjacent to similar tissue marked for near simultaneous destruction during medullary elongation and expansion? How is this process related to that of metaphyseal reduction? Answers could be useful in helping us to understand how trabecular struts could be reinforced to combat oseopenia connected with increased fracture risk in advancing age.

### 3.4.5   Functional Adaptation

For over half a century, skeletal biologists have been reinventing their perspective on bone biology, adding to their observations regarding cell type and function a more complete consideration of bone strength. Now we emphasize bone's ability to sense its normal and supernormal loading and adjust, constitutionally and morphologically, to withstand them. In this new paradigm, sometimes called the Utah paradigm (Frost 2001), modeling and remodeling occur in direct response to mechanical loading, and growth is necessary but not sufficient to account for bone features or their change over time (for further discussion, see Stout and Crowder in this volume). This perspective has carried us far, from an incomplete, overfocus on cellular activity and mineral homeostasis, to a more complete understanding of bone as a dynamic tissue, responsive to mechanical strain. The realization that modeling and remodeling can be affected by loading history approaches communal epiphany. But reservation is required in its employment, lest a new form of oversimplification, mechanical determinism, takes over, obscuring other primary influences on bone.

#### 3.4.5.1   The Primacy Question

Modeling processes illustrate the perfect point for discussion. How do we separate what portion of bone modeling is adaptive and what portion is developmental? Ideally whatever bone can accomplish with no mechanical stimuli we can call development or growth. Whatever growth alone cannot account for requires mechanical stimulation.

Frost (2001) used a car analogy to represent the components of bone activity and their employment. Presented here is a reconfiguration of this illustrative analogy. To envision the role of growth and mechanical adaptation, we can compare two extreme points of view. In one, a driver would depress the gas pedal and speed off in a straight line until unfortunately smashing into the first impeding object of sufficient mass. A second driver of another mind seats himself and steers the wheel vigorously, shifting gears, engaging the parking break, and activating the turn indicators, all while parked serenely in his driveway. Insisting on the dominance of either adaptational or developmental processes in bone biology is like forcing one of these extremes upon a hapless driver.

Debate between prime forces typically inhibits a holistic understanding of important concepts like bone strength, form, or function. However, when the goal is to uncover and identify the mechanisms behind bone form and function, this separation must be made despite challenges. By the previous analogy, despite insisting that a functional car be both controllable and mobile, some specialists should know: a gas pedal does one job, and a steering wheel the other.

For example, if we had to choose the "prime effector" for bone modeling we should probably choose growth. Whether bone adapts to mechanical loading is, by definition, secondary to whether the bone exists—secondary, but of immense importance. Evidence for this perspective can be found in Wong and colleagues' (1993) finding that even without fetal movements required for normal development, the primary bone collar still forms around the diaphysis early in development. Yet, sufficient evidence has also been collected to argue that fetal movements are vital for the achievement of functional morphology (Rodríguez et al. 1988; Hall and Herring 1990). In a particularly well-phrased argument for why we should not view bony change solely through biomechanical eyes, Turner (2000) points to works that demonstrated the insensitivity of bone to mechanical adaptation when either growth hormones (Forwood et al. 2000) or parathyroid (Chow et al. 1998) are unavailable. He also reminds us that the positive osteogenic effects of prostaglandin E2 (Akamine et al. 1992) and PTH (Ma et al. 1995) are completely independent of physical loading. To put it another way, *that* modeling occurs is attributed to growth and development; *how* it occurs is attributed in large part to mechanical (and other epigenetic) factors.

Attempting to directly measure the differential effects of growth and mechanical adaptation on modeling is challenging. One way to do that is to uncover the genetic sources of modeling variation. Hansen and colleagues (2009) recently attempted to do just that by measuring the heritability of femoral cross-sectional geometry in baboons. They found that genetic effects accounted for only about 15% to 23% of cross-sectional geometric phenotypical variance. Likewise, Volkman's (2004) research group determined that genetics accounted for 2.9% to 15.4% of the variance observed for mechanical traits they measured in the rat femur (most of which remained significant after standardization by body mass). Robling and Turner (2002) point out that mechosensation is not without its own genetic component. For comparison, however, approximately 75% of human height is estimated to be heritable (Beunen et al. 2000; Ulijaszek 2001; Silventoinen 2003; Liu et al. 2006), providing yet another reason to investigate modeling processes on their own merit, distinct from the process of long bone elongation.

### 3.4.5.2 *The Mechanical Environment*

The most critical determinants of a long bone's mechanical rigidity are strength relative to size, cross-sectional shape, and composition (density and mineral content; Martin and Burr 1989; Biewener 1992; Sone et al. 2006; Goldman et al. 2007). Bone tissue has the ability to adapt all three determinants to physical loading conditions. This has been demonstrated frequently through experimentation (Woo et al. 1981; Matsuda et al. 1986; Rubin et al. 1995; Mosley and Lanyon 1998) and in recent studies on athletes (Jones et al. 1977; Ashizawa et al. 1999; Judex et al. 1999; Bass et al. 2002; Kontulainen et al. 2002). Structural adaptation is accomplished through a negative feedback system, which adds, resorbs, or replaces material, maintaining mechanical integrity (Frost 1964a, 1988c; Turner 1999; Skerry 2006). Although this phenomenological system, often called the mechanostat, predominantly focuses on localized mechanical strain, systemic factors are also influential, including genes, hormones, nutrition, and even climate (Frost 1987; Turner 1999; Pearson and Lieberman 2004). Recent evidence even suggests that the brain may also have a direct role to play in apportioning response to functional adaptation (Rubin and Rubin 2008).

The importance of mechanical adaptation for proper bone modeling is hard to overestimate and is only now being fully realized. Computerized modeling of mechanical factors in femoral bone growth and development has demonstrated evidence that bones are in some ways "self-designing" structures (Carter et al. 1996). In addition to the vital role even fetal muscular contraction provides, we also know that the onset of bipedal locomotion in early child development affects bone morphology and development in many ways (Haapasalo et al. 2000; Gosman and Ketcham 2009). In general, limbs that experience mechanical loading respond by changing bone shape and size. Limbs that have lost or never attained mobility, due to disorder or pathological condition, demonstrate highly predictable bone malformation or deformation (Schoenau and Frost 2002). Since mechanical demands influence modeling, we can expect modeling activity to continue after longitudinal growth cessation at around 20 years of age, despite well-known decreases in mechanosensitivity of bone after maturation. This is precisely the observation of Garn's (1972) radiological study, showing endocortical formation continuing into the fourth decade of life. Corroboration was provided by Sumner and Andriacchi (1996) who reported diametric growth continued into the third decade during their assessment of cross-sectional properties of the humerus and femur. The potential cause for such a phenomenon is that muscular strength increases well into the third decade (Parker et al. 1990), and the skeletal system must adjust accordingly.

Some nonhuman animal studies have investigated the mechanical effects of muscle activity on bone more directly by removing a necessary muscular or skeletal element surgically, or labeling bone with fluorescent markers for response observation. Epker and Frost (1965) related the work of Avis (1961) and Washburn (1947), studies in which the removal of certain muscles inhibits the formation of the mandibular angle and coronoid process, respectively. Mosley and fellow researchers (1997) have demonstrated that the ulnae of growing rats responds dramatically to physical loading by increasing the overall diameter of apposition, whereas active controls demonstrated only normal lateral modeling drift. More specifically, they found that at lower strains, overall bone formation decreased, rather than increased. Adaptive response was, instead, accomplished by a change in long bone shape via straightening of the diaphysis. At higher strains, total bone modeling increased, both by increased lateral drift apposition and reversal to formation on opposing envelope surfaces as well, affecting a general diametric increase in total cortical area. Similar studies on rat ulnae by Robling and colleagues (2001) showed that even brief static loads could stunt modeling apposition as well as longitudinal growth, and that this effect is proportional to the magnitude of loading. They also found a positive bone growth effect from applied dynamic loading (Robling et al. 2001). To summarize the net findings of similar research, it seems that bone formation is stimulated by specific activity circumstances. Dynamic, supernormal strains, with higher strain rates interspersed by periods of recovery, are more osteogenic than static, lower strain, low strain rate during sustained activity (Mosely et al. 1997; Burr 2002; Fluckey et al. 2002). For more information see summaries of functional adaptation experiments provided by Currey (2002), and Ruff and colleagues (2006), or reviews covering classic experimentation on the subject (Nilsson and Westlin 1971; Jones et al. 1977).

It is important to remember, however, that "primary" influence of muscle activity is not the only mechanical influence on modeling process. Body mass and height, or the length of the bone in question can have their own effects in addition to differential physical activity

(Robling and Stout 2003). Some theorists have argued that periosteal formation on occasion can be caused mechanically by increased loads due to endosteal bone loss (Lazenby 1990; Beck et al. 2001; Carpenter and Carter 2008). The "secondary" mechanical environment can account for the unique morphology of the tibia as well. Carpenter and Carter (2008) showed that static loading from the muscle bellies surrounding the tibia could account, in large part, for its triangular cross-section. Similar static (or hydrodynamic) loading of the extraperiosteal environment likely accounts for the vessel or digital impressions visible on bony surfaces. For all these reasons the mechanical effect on modeling is both significant and complex, and requires a detailed understanding of the primary and secondary effects of the local mechanical environment.

## 3.5 Variation

Microstructural changes due to modeling variation depend on the species and bone element observed, as well as the individual's sex, age, and physical activity. We must also consider the effects of differential access to nutrition and exposure to pathological circumstance. Therefore, it is unsurprising that high levels of microstructural variability can be seen within a cross-section, between cross-sections, and among individuals and populations. A thorough review of variability in bone growth and adaptation, especially the effects of nutrition and disease, is beyond the scope of the current discussion, which seeks only to provide a general overview of major contributors to modeling variation. How this variation plays out on the microstructure of modeling phenomena is comparably unknown.

Some generalities can be made however. The primary contributor to modeling variation is age. No male will ever look so different from a female that their age becomes an unimportant contributor to modeling processes, regardless of their respective levels of health and activity, or their population of origin. If more bone exists at the periosteum of a male than a female, the difference is unimportant if nothing is known regarding their relative age. Fortunately, we rarely have zero relative-age information. But this is much more important than merely stating that the volume of bone affected by modeling is time dependent. Skeletal age can be quite different from chronological age, and certain ages affect modeling changes more dramatically than others. In addition, we can expect the interaction contribution of age to be stronger than those of other sources of variation. For example, the strength of a sex-effect on modeling depends on age. Even more telling, the strength of an interaction effect between sex and skeletal element variation is also age dependent. Add to this the significance of differences in tissue age at formation and stratigraphy between even immediately adjacent microstructures, and age- and time-associated stratigraphy quickly become the most important considerations for interpreting modeling changes in bone.

The sex of an individual also has both primary and secondary effects on modeling processes. It affects hormone stimuli and growth timing, and the total muscle volume by which physical strain is exerted on bone. But sex can also affect access to food, the frequency and type of physical exertion, and exposure to disease, from one population to another, limiting potential growth and adaptive response through modeling. Several researchers have found significant differences between populations in skeletal sexual dimorphism in general (Burr et al. 1990; Cho et al. 2006) and specifically regarding various cross-sectional measures related to modeling processes (Martin and Atkinson 1977; Ruff and Hayes 1983a; Feik et al. 2000; Maggiano et al. 2008).

Although ethnic variance is difficult to separate into genetic (ancestry) and epigenetic effects, bone mass also varies significantly between populations (Heaney 1995)—a phenomenon that has also been reported in cross-sectional geometric data collected on the post-Classic Maya and medieval Germans (Maggiano et al. 2008). There is no reason to expect that this sexual or populational variation (especially when collected from diaphyseal cross-sectional geometrics) should be absent from data collected on modeling microstructure. But how this dimorphism occurs could be variable and is relatively unexplored via histomorphology.

To complicate matters more thoroughly, all these effects can be specific to the element, affecting individual bones differently or even causing variation between sections taken from the same element (Chan et al. 2007). Attempting to discern between these effects on bone modeling microstructure can be extremely challenging. Attention to experimental design must be meticulous, controlling for as many of these variables as possible, when experimentation is possible, that is.

## 3.6   Current and Future Directives

For reasons already discussed, it is much easier to investigate resulting bone morphology than it is to understand how that morphology was achieved. Currently, there exists three main techniques for viewing modeling processes: (1) polarized light microscopy, (2) fluorescent labeling histomorphometrics, and (3) cross-sectional geometrics. Each of these techniques has contributed to our current understanding of bone modeling and could be used in conjuncture with novel methods to reveal even more meaningful data in the future.

The first, polarization microscopy, has become quite valuable for observing modeling formative and resorptive processes in bone, as previously discussed. The added contrast provided by birefringence eases the observation of lamellar structure, reversal, arrest, and active resorption (Schultz 2001). Modifications of this type of microscopy using a red quartz filter (hilfsobject) falsely color lamellae of differing orientation warm or cool hues (as shown in many figures here), emphasizing lamellar orientation all the more clearly (45° angle = highest birefringence): yellow-red tones are given to lamellae oriented from the lower left to the upper right, whereas green-blue tones tint upper left to lower right facing lamellae (Schultz 2001). Other researchers have found significant correlations between the birefringent properties of lamellar tissue and local mechanical strength properties (Bromage et al. 2003; Goldman et al. 2007; Skedros et al. 2011), which indicate polarization microscopy's usefulness, not only for interpretation, but for quantitative analysis as well.

The second method, fluorescent labeling (Frost 1963; Mosely and Lanyon 1998; Robling et al. 2001), is capable of directly measuring bone apposition histologically, both in rate and area (or volume), and typically employs fluorescent bone labels, like tetracycline or calcein. These fluorochromes adhere to bone surfaces and are trapped there only during formation, providing a bright label in the bone tissue for subsequent fluorescent microscopic analyses. Typically nonhuman test groups are given a dose of fluorochrome before and after some treatment or stimulus. The measured difference between these labels, when combined with the known times of administration, yields bone formation rates and permits histomorphological measurement of microstructure. The technique works because bone apposition is stratigraphic and therefore records its own process within its microstructure. It is more difficult to measure the morphology or rate of resorption because the bone records no visible history of bone lost and the technique is invasive and destructive. Chemical tracer techniques that measure resorption provide aggregate data rather than data regarding specific bones or microsites. For now, the only visual information we can retrieve on resorption is in observing decreased total cortical area in comparison with controls. Unfortunately, this is a comparatively poor proxy for actually viewing tissue as it is resorbed.

Third, cross-sectional geometrics applies the principles of beam theory to long bone diaphyses (Ruff and Hayes 1983a, 1983b), primarily to reconstruct the mechanical loading history of the element based on the shape and size of the mid-diaphysis. This technique is particularly useful for bioarchaeological applications and typically applies computer-aided cross-sectional analyses to calculate the bone's mechanical resistance to compression, torsion, and bending along various axes (Nagurka and Hayes 1980). Initially, cross-sectional analyses concentrated on changes in physical activity patterns during the transition between subsistence strategies (Ruff and Hayes 1983a, 1983b; Ruff et al. 1984; Bridges 1989) and between modern humans and other ancient hominids (Trinkaus 1976; Ruff et al. 1993; Trinkaus and Churchill 1999). Several more recent studies have investigated activity effects on skeletal structure between or within population samples (Holt 2003; Weiss 2003; Stock and Pfeiffer 2004; Rhodes and Knüsel 2005; Sládek et al. 2006; Wescott 2006; Maggiano et al. 2008). The particular strength of this technique is that it addresses the contribution of bone diaphyseal shape in addition to total cortical area, providing a better measure of bone function and potential growth. Unfortunately, it does not provide information on the modeling history of the element specific enough to reconstruct how the current form was achieved. This is because it is not often used in conjunction with thin-ground sectioning and microscopy (for important exceptions, see Lazenby 1986; Walker et al. 1994; Burr et al. 1990; and Robling and Stout 2003, however these latter studies focused mostly on porosity or remodeling rates and physical activity). For more discussion of bone biomechanics and cross-sectional geometry, see chapters by Skedros, and Agnew and Bolte in this volume.

Histological examinations of thin-ground bone sections have been successfully applied to many forensic and bioarchaeological topics, including biological age estimation (Kerley 1965; Thompson 1979; Stout and Paine 1992; Robling and Stout 2000; Cho et al. 2002), bone remodeling rate analysis (Burr et al. 1990; Stout and Lueck 1995; Abbott et al. 1996; Cho and Stout 2003; Robling and Stout 2003), disease diagnoses (Schultz 1993, 2001), taxonomic identification (Schultz 1999; Hillier and Bell 2007), and taphonomy (Stout 1978; Schultz 1997). The histological study of bone growth and functional adaptation must sometimes homogenize compact bone structure across a section or remove factors introducing variation. For this reason microscopic studies sometimes focus on remodeling processes due to the relative ease of quantifying osteons. However, periosteal and endosteal lamellar bone structure can also provide useful information regarding bone growth and mechanical adaptation. If applications for histological modeling processes have been rare in bioarchaeology or forensics, for example, it could be due to a lack of distinct features for quantification. This leaves a gap between our knowledge of bone macro- and micromorphology that inhibits the development of new theoretical approaches. More work is necessary to identify meaningful units that can aid in measuring modeling processes.

Future research could simultaneously employ these well-established techniques to gather histological data along important mechanical axes. In addition, new techniques could push past the current limitations regarding the measurement or observation of modeling phenomena. Novel polarized light microphotography, for example, can emphasize modeling lamellae while ensuring that Haversian tissue remains dim in comparison

(Figure 3.21; Maggiano et al. 2009b). This method could be used to facilitate quantitative area measurement and qualitative histomorphological assessment of modeling activity apparent in thin-ground sections. Automated image analysis can also be employed, once sufficient contrast is achieved between modeling and Haversian lamellae in order to quantify and compare remnants of modeling drifts, for example, between elements, individuals, or populations (Maggiano et al. 2009b). Some success has been achieved in quantifying predictably distinct remnants of endosteal drift as a meta-feature, referred to collectively as the endosteal lamellar pocket (ELP; Maggiano et al. 2008, 2009b, in print). Further analysis of the ELP could reveal new relationships between modeling drift and age, sex, and physical activity. These techniques could very well offer new means to test what are now increasingly old questions regarding bone modeling formation and adaptation and resulting structures.

Three-dimensional confocal laser scanning fluorescence microscopy (CLSM) could also provide a new perspective for future modeling studies. Typically, bone is considered too dense for meaningful investigation using this technique but several researchers have recently identified CLSM as useful for undecalcified bone microscopy, even when only using bones' natural autofluorescence rather than labeling (Maggiano et al. 2003, 2006, 2009a). This form of microscopy removes out of focus light and can be employed on side-by-side screens comparing structures illuminated by fluorescence and polarized light simultaneously. CLSM can only illuminate relatively small depths of bone (typically less than 100 µm; Maggiano et al. 2009a), but consecutive sectioning techniques could be developed by which fluorescent labels marking modeling activations could be followed for

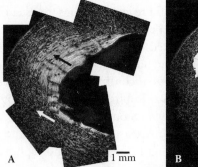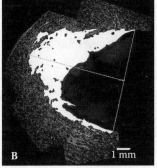

**Figure 3.21** (A) Potential merged micrograph technique using cross-polarization to emphasize endosteal lamellae. Each image was taken of endosteal lamellae when they were at 45° orientation and therefore at brightest birefringence in polarized light. This method ensures primary lamellae remain bright by removing darkening artifacts from cross-polarization interference. Haversian tissue retains this artifact, keeping it relatively dark in comparison (white solid arrow). Nearly the entire cortex on the left side is endosteal in origin, indicating strong linear drift. Several features common to this endocortical region include hemicircumferential lamellar orientation, reduced osteonal presence, and radially oriented Volkmann's canals. Together, they can be considered a "meta-feature," referred to as the endosteal lamellar pocket (ELP; black solid arrow in A, white mask in B), currently under evaluation as a quantitative indicator of modeling processes (Maggiano et al. in press). (B) The ELP is automatically recognized via computerized image analysis using pixel intensity and region of interest size thresholding to create a quantifiable indicator of endosteal drift (white mask; Maggiano et al. 2009b). Thin-ground, undecalcified transection of archaeological, humeral mid-diaphysis, Dakhleh Oasis, Egypt. Merged cross-polarized micrograph. Comprising images taken when primary lamellae were at 45° to normal x, y stage orientation. Scale bar indicates 1 mm.

larger distances through the peri- or endocortex. The viewing depth of CLSM systems has been largely untested on stained, decalcified bone sections. When combined with novel fluorescent labeling techniques, this technology could offer significant benefits for understanding three-dimensional bone histology despite the loss of information from the absent mineral component. In addition, specialized versions of confocal microscopes using fiber optics and miniaturized objectives permit in vivo three-dimensional observations of cellular activity and have already been used to observe neuronal activity in the living brain (Fukada et al. 2006). What potential exists for this technique within living bone analyses is yet unexplored.

Bone modeling accounts for a large portion of achieved bone mass and morphology over the lifetime of an individual. Unfortunately, it remains relatively poorly understood on a microstructural scale. New lines of research like those suggested here are meant to focus on some of the unknown aspects of human modeling processes to understand the form and function of skeletal tissue in general, as well as illuminate specific aspects of skeletal biology for applied efforts in medicine, forensics, and archaeology.

## Acknowledgments

I thank my wife and colleague Isabel Maggiano for her well-timed and discerning contributive, critical, and supportive assistance. Sincere thanks goes to S. Stout and C. Crowder and other authors contributing to this edited volume. S. Stout and A. Agnew were particularly instrumental in fine-tuning the perspective of this chapter. Research contributing directly to the current work results from cooperative efforts between the Department of Anthropology, The Ohio State University (OSU), Columbus, Ohio, and the following institutions, coauthors, and contributors: Department of Biology, University of Hildesheim, Germany (I. Maggiano, H. Kierdorf, S. Flohr); the Anatomy Center, University of Göttingen, Göttingen, Germany (M. Schultz); the Facultad de Ciencias Antropológicas of the Universidad Autonóma de Yucatán, Mérida, Mexico (V. Tiesler); the Anthropology and Biology Departments, University of Central Florida (UCF), Orlando, Florida (T. Dupras); and the Center for Environmental Biotechnology, University of Tennessee, Knoxville, Tennessee (J. Biggerstaff). Many of the pristine archaeological samples showcased here are the results of tireless archaeological efforts of the Dakhleh Oasis Project (A. J. Mills, C. A. Hope, and E. Molto, T. Dupras) with the permissions of the Egyptian Supreme Council of Antiquities, but in particular, T. Dupras's support has been unwavering, invaluable, and inspiring. Thin-ground sectioning and imaging for many of these samples were preformed at the University of Göttingen thanks to the collaborative efforts of M. Schultz, his research group, and M. Brandt. Many others should be thanked for their support, including G. Vercellotti, M. Streeter, and J. Skedros who are all greatly appreciated for their passion for science, comments, and conversation. Direct contributors of images used in this work are L. Lee (College of Medicine, Division of Anatomy, OSU); Y. Castro, D. Vanmali, and T. Dupras (Department of Anthropology, UCF); S. Weisbrode (Department of Veterinary Biosciences, OSU), and I. Maggiano (sample from excavations directed by Thelma Sierra Sosa from the Instituto Nacional de Antropología e Historia, Mexico). Thank you all for your time and contributions.

# References

Abbott S, Trinkaus E, Burr D (1996) Dynamic bone remodeling in later Pleistocene fossil homininds. Am J Phys Anthrop 99:585–601.

Akamine T, Jee WS, Ke HZ, Li XJ, Lin BY (1992) Prostaglandin E2 prevents bone loss and adds extra bone to immobilized distal femoral metaphysis in female rats. Bone 13:11–22.

Allen MR, Hock JM, Burr DB (2004) Periosteum: biology, regulation, and response to osteoporosis therapies. Bone 35:1003–1012.

Ascenzi A (1988) The micromechanics versus the macromechanics of cortical bone—a comprehensive presentation. J Biomed Eng 110:358–363.

Ascenzi A, Benvenuti A, Bonucci E (1982) The tensile properties of single osteonic lamellae: technical problems and preliminary results. J Biomech 15:29–37.

Ashizawa N, Nonaka K, Michikami S et al (1999) Tomographical description of tennis-loaded radius: reciprocal relation between bone size and volumetric BMD. J Appl Physiol 86:1347–1351.

Aubin JE (2001) Regulation of osteoblast formation and function. Rev Endocr Metab Disord 2:81–94.

Avis V (1961) The significance of the angle of the mandible: an experimental and comparative study. Am J Phys Anthrop 1:55–63.

Balena R, Shih M, Parfitt AM (1992) Bone resorption and formation on the periosteal envelope of the ilium: a histomorphometric study in healthy women. J Bone Miner Res 7:1475–1482.

Bass S, Saxon L, Daly R et al. (2002) The effect of mechanical loading on the size and shape of bone in pre-, peri-, and postpubertal girls: a study in tennis players. J Bone Miner Res 17:2274–2280.

Beck TJ, Stone KL, Oreskovic TL et al. (2001) Effects of current and discontinued estrogen replacement therapy on hip structural geometry: the study of osteoporotic fractures. J Bone Miner Res 16:2103–2110.

Beunen G, Thomis M, Maes HH et al. (2000) Genetic variance of adolescent growth in stature. Ann Hum Biol 27(2):173–186.

Biewener A (1992) Biomechanics—structures and systems. Oxford University Press, Oxford.

Boyde A, Riggs CM (1990) The quantitative study of the orientation of collagen in compact bone slices. Bone 11:35–39.

Bridges P (1989) Changes in activities with the shift to agriculture in the southeastern United States. Curr Anthropol 30:385–394.

Bright RW, Elmore SM (1968) Physical properties of epiphyseal plate cartilage. Surg Forum 19:463–465.

Brighton CT, Lorich DG, Kupcha R et al. (1992) The pericyte as a possible osteoblast progenitor cell. Clin Orthop 275:287–299.

Bromage TG, Goldman HM, McFarlin SC, et al. (2003) Circularly polarized light standards for investigations of collagen fiber orientation in bone. Anat Rec 274B:157–168.

Brookes M (1971) The blood supply of bone. Butterworths, London, 7–22.

Burr DB (2002) Targeted and nontargeted remodeling. Bone 30:2–4.

Burr D, Ruff C, Thompson D (1990) Patterns of skeletal histologic change through time: comparison of an archaic native population with modern populations. Anat Rec 226:307–313.

Carpenter RD, Carter DR (2008) The mechanobiological effects of periosteal surface loads. Biomech Model Mechanobiol 7(3):227–242.

Carter DR, Van der Meulen MCH, Beaupré GS (1996) Mechanical factors in bone growth and development. Bone 18(1, Suppl 1):5–10.

Castanet J, Grandin A, Abourachid A, De Ricqles A (1996) Expression de la dynamique de croissance dans la structure de l'os p!eriostique chez Anas platyrhyncos. Comptes rendus de l'Academie de Sciences Paris. Sciences de la vie 319:301–308.

Chamay A (1970) Mechanical and morphological aspects of experimental overload and fatigue in bone. J Biomech 3:263–270.

Chan AH, Crowder CM, Rogers TL (2007) Variation in cortical bone histology within the human femur and its impact on estimating age at death. Am J Phys Anthropol 132:80–88.

Cho H, Stout S (2003) Bone remodeling and age-associated bone loss in the past: an histomorpho-
metric analysis of the Imperial Roman skeletal population of Isola Sacra. In: Agarwal S and
Stout S (eds) Bone loss and osteoporosis: an anthropological perspective. Kluwer Academic/
Plenum Publishers, New York.

Cho H, Stout S, Madsen R et al. (2002) Population-specific histological age-estimating method:
a model for known African-American and European-American skeletal remains. J For Scie
47:12–18.

Cho H, Stout S, Bishop T (2006) Cortical bone remodeling rates in a sample of African American
and European American descent groups from the American midwest: comparisons of age and
sex in ribs. Am J Phys Anthrop 130:214–226.

Chow JW, Fox S, Jagger CJ, Chambers TJ (1998) Role for parathyroid hormone in mechanical responsiveness of rat bone. Am J Physiol 274:E146–154.

Chow JW, Wilson AJ, Chambers TJ et al (1998) Mechanical loading stimulates bone formation by
reactivation of BLCs in 13-week-old rats. J Bone Min Res 13(11):1760–1767.

Crocker DJ, Murad TM, Geer JC (1970) Role of the pericyte in wound healing: an ultrastructural
study. Exp Mol Pathol 13:51–65.

Currey JD (2002) Bones: structure and mechanics. Princeton University Press, Princeton, NJ.

Diaz-Flores L, Gutierrez R, Lopez-Alonso A et al. (1992) Pericytes as a supplement source of osteoblasts in periosteal osteogenesis. Clin Orthop 275:280–286.

Dobnig H (1995) Evidence that the intermittent treatment with parathyroidhormone increases bone
formation in adult rats by activation of bone lining cells. Endocrin 136:3632–3639.

Donahue H (2000) Gap junctions and biophysical regulation of bone cell differentiation. Bone
26(5):417–422.

Du Boulay G (1956) The significance of digital impressions in children's skulls. Acta Radiol 46:
112–122.

Ellender G, Feik SA, Carach BJ (1988) Periosteal structure and development in a rat caudal vertebra.
J Anat 158:173–187.

Enlow D (1962) A study of the postnatal growth and remodeling of bone. Am J Anat 110:79–101.

Ensrud K, Palermo L, Black D, et al. (1995) Hip and calcaneal bone loss increase with advancing age:
longitudinal results form the study of osteoporotic fractures. J Bone Miner Res 10:1778–1787.

Epker BN, Frost HM (1965) A histological study of remodeling at the periosteal, Haversian canal,
cortical endosteal, and trabecular endosteal surfaces in human rib. Anat Rec 152:129–135.

Epker BN, Kelin M, Frost HM (1965) Magnitude and location of cortical bone loss in human rib with
aging. Clin Orthop 41:198–203.

Eriksen EF, Axelrod DW, and Melsen F (1994) Bone histomorphometry. Raven Press, New York.

Fawcett DW (1994) Bloom and Fawcett: a textbook of histology, 12th edn. Chapman and Hall, New
York.

Feik SA, Storey E, Ellender G (1987) Stress induced periosteal changes. Br J Exp Pathol 68:803–813.

Feik SA, Bruns R, Clement J (2000) Regional variations in cortical modeling in the femoral midshaft: sex and age differences. Am J Phys Anthrop 112:191–205.

Fluckey JD, Dupont-Versteegden E, Montague DC, et al. (2002) A rat resistance exercise regimen
attenuates losses of musculoskeletal mass during hindlimb suspension. Acta Physiol Scand
174:293–300.

Forriol F, Shapiro F (2005) Bone development: interaction of molecular components and biophysical
forces. Clin Orthop Relat Res 432:14–33.

Forwood MR, Li L, Kelly WL, Bennett MB (2000) Growth hormone is permissive for skeletal adaptation to mechanical loading (unpublished).

Forwood MR, Turner CH (1994) The response of rat tibiae to incremental bouts of mechanical loading: a quantum concept for bone formation. Bone 15(6):603–609.

Frost H (1963) Measurement of human bone formation by means of tetracycline labeling. Can J
Biochem Physiol 41:31–42.

Frost H (1964a) Dynamics of bone remodeling. In: Frost HM (ed), Bone biodynamics. Little, Brown, and Co, Boston.

Frost H (1964b) The laws of bone structure. Thomas, Springfield, IL.

Frost H (1987) Bone "mass" and the "mechanostat": a proposal. Anat Rec 219:1–9.

Frost H (1973) Bonemodeling and skeletal modeling errors. Orthopaedic Lectures Volume IV. Charles C. Thomas, Springfield, IL.

Frost H (1988a) Structural adaptations to mechanical usage: a proposed "three-way rule" for bone modeling. Part I. Vet Comp Orthop Traumatol 1:7–17.

Frost H (1988b) Structural adaptations to mechanical usage: a proposed "three-way rule" for bone modeling. Part II. Vet Comp Orthop Traumatol 2:80–85.

Frost H (1988c) Vital biomechanics: proposed general concepts for skeletal adaptations to mechanical usage. Calc Tiss Int 42:145–156.

Frost H (1989) Mechanical usage, bone mass, bone fragility. A brief overview. In: Kleerekoper M, Krane SM (eds) Clinical disorders in bone and mineral metabolism. Mary Ann Liebert, New York.

Frost H (2001) From Wolff's law to the Utah paradigm: insights about bone physiology and its clinical applications. Anat Rec 262:398–419.

Frost H (2003) On changing views about age-related bone loss. In: Agarwal SC, Stout SD (eds) Bone loss and osteoporosis: an anthropological perspective. Kluwer Academic/Plenum, New York.

Fukada Y, Kawano Y, Tanikawa Y, et al. (2006) In vivo imaging of the dendritic arbors of layer V pyramidal cells in the cerebral cortex using a laser scanning microscope with a stick-type objective lens. Neurosci Lett 400:53–57.

Garn S (1970) The earlier gain and later loss of cortical bone. Thomas, Springfield, IL.

Garn S (1972) The course of bone gain and the phases of bone loss. Orthop Clin North Am 3:503–509.

Giraud-Guille MM (1988) Twisted plywood architecture of collagen fibrils in human compact bone osteons. Calcif Tissue Int 42:167–180.

Goldman H, Bromage T, Thomas C et al. (2003) Preferred collagen fiber orientation in the human mid-shaft femur. Anat Rec 272A:434–445.

Goldman H, Cooper D, McFarlin S, et al. (2007) Two and three dimensional analysis of cortical bone microstructure from the human juvenile mid-shaft femur. Am J Phys Anthrop 44(Suppl):117.

Gosman JH, Ketcham RA (2009) Patterns in ontogeny of human trabecular bone from SunWatch Village in the Prehistoric Ohio Valley: general features of microarchitectural change. Am J Phys Anthrop 138(3):318–332.

Gross TS, Srinivasan S, Liu CC et al. (2002) Non-invasive loading of the murine tibia: an in vivo model for the study of mechanotransduction. J Bone Min Res 17:493–501.

Haapasalo H, Kontulainen S, Sievanen H et al. (2000) Exercise-induced bone gain is due to enlargement in bone size without a change in volumetric bone density: a peripheral quantitative computed tomography study of the upper arms of male tennis players. Bone 27:351–357.

Hall BK, Herring SW (1990) Paralysis and growth of the musculoskeletal system in the embryonic chick. J Morph 206:45–66.

Han ZH, Palnitkar S, Rao DS, et al. (1997) Effects of ethnicity and age or menopause on the remodeling and turnover of iliac bone: implications for mechanisms of bone loss. J Bone Miner Res 12:498–508.

Hansen HL, Bredbenner TL, Nicolella DP et al. (2009) Cross-sectional geometry of the femoral midshaft in baboons is heritable. Bone 45:892–897.

Hauge EM, Qvesel D, Erikson EF, Moselkilde L, Melsen F (2001) Cancellous bone remodeling occurs in specialized compartments lined by cells expressing osteoblastic markers. J Bone Miner Res 16:1575–1582.

Heaney R (1995) Bone mass, the mechanostat, and ethnic differences. J Clin Endocrinol Metab 80:2289–2290.

Heller M, Bergmann G, Deuretzbacher G et al (2001) Musculo-skeletal loading conditions at the hip during walking and stair climbing. J Biomech 34:883–893.

Hillier M, Bell L (2007) Differentiating human bone from animal bone: a review of histological methods. J For Scie 52:249–263.

Hohmann EL, Elde RP, Rysavy JA et al. (1986) Innervation of periosteum and bone by sympathetic vasoactive intestinal peptide-containing nerve fibers. Science 232:868–870.

Holt B (2003) Mobility in Upper Paleolithic and Mesolithic Europe: evidence from the lower limb. Am J Phys Anthropol 122:200–215.

Jee WS (2001) Integrated bone tissue physiology: anatomy and physiology. In: Cowin S (ed), Bone mechanics handbook. CRC Press, Boca Raton, FL.

Jee WS, Arnold JS (1954) Rate of individual Haversian system formation. Anat Rec 118:315.

Jee WS, Frost H (1992) Skeletal adaptations during growth. Triangle 31:77–88.

Jee WS, Tian XY, Setterberg RB (2007) Cancellous bone minimodeling-based formation: a Frost, Takahashi legacy. J Musculoskelet Neuronal Interact 7:232–239.

Johnson LC (1964) Morphologic analysis in pathology: the kinetics of disease and general biology of bone. In: Frost HM (ed), Bone biodynamics. Little, Brown, and Co Boston.

Jones HH, Priest JD, Hayes WC et al. (1977) Humeral hypertrophy in response to exercise. J Bone Joint Surg 59(2):204–208.

Jones DB, Nolte H, Scholubbers JG et al. (1991) Biochemical signal transduction of mechanical stain in osteoblast-like cells. Biomater 12:101–110.

Judex S, Whiting W, Zernicke R (1999) Exercise-induced bone adaptation: considerations for designing an osteogenically effective exercise program. Int J Ind Ergonom 24:235–238.

Kerley ER (1965) The microscopic determination of age in human bone. Am J Phys Anthropol 23:149–164.

Kimura T, Amtmann E (1984) Distribution of mechanical robustness in the human femoral shaft. J Biomech 17:41–46.

Knothe Tate ML (2003) "Whither flows the fluid in bone?" An osteocyte's perspective. J Biomech 36:1409–1424.

Kontulainen S, Sievanen H, Kannus P et al. (2002) Effect of long-term impact-loading on mass, size, and estimated strength of humerus and radius of female racquet sports players: a peripheral quantitative computed tomography study between young and old starters and controls. J Bone Min Res 17:2281–2289.

Lanyon and Rubin (1984) Static versus dynamic loads as an influence on bone remodelling. J Biomech 17(12):897–905.

Lazenby RA (1986) Porosity-geometry interaction in the conservation of bone strength. J Biomech 19:257–258.

Lazenby RA (1990) Continuing periosteal apposition. I. Documentation, hypotheses, and interpretation. Am J Phys Anthropol 82:478–484.

Lee KC, Maxwell A, Lanyon LE (2002) Validation of a technique for studying functional adaptation of the mouse ulna in response to mechanical loading. Bone 31:407–412.

Liu Y, Xiao P, Guo Y, et al. (2006) Genetic linkage of human height is confirmed to 9q22 and Xq24. Hum Genet 119:295–304.

Locke M (2004) Structure of long bones in mammals. J Morph 262:546–565.

Ma Y, Jee WSS, Chen Y, Gasser J, Ke HZ, Li XJ, Kimmel DB (1995) Partial maintenance of extra cancellous bone mass by antiresorptive agents after discontinuation of human parathyroid hormone (1–38) in right hindlimb immobilized rats. J Bone Miner Res 10:1726–1734.

Ma YF, Zeng Q, Donley DW, Ste-Marie L, Gallagher JC, Dalky GP, Marcus R, Eriksen EF (2006) Teriparatide increases bone formation in modeling and remodeling osteons and enhances IGF-II immunoreactivity in postmenopausal women with osteoporosis. J Bone Miner Res 21:855–864.

Maggiano C, Dupras T, Biggerstaff J (2003) Ancient antibiotics: evidence for tetracycline in human and animal bone from Kellis. In: Mills AJ and Hope CA (eds) The Dakhleh Oasis Monograph, Vol, 3. Oxbow Books, Oxford, 331–344.

Maggiano C, Dupras T, Schultz M, Biggerstaff J (2006) Spectral and photobleaching analysis using confocal laser scanning microscopy: a comparison of modern and archaeological bone florescence. Molecular and Cellular Probes 20(3-4):154–162.

Maggiano C, Dupras T, Schultz M, et al. (2009a) Confocal laser scanning microscopy: a flexible tool for polarized light and three-dimensional fluorescence imaging of archaeological compact bone histology. J Arch Sci 36:2392–2401.

Maggiano C, Maggiano IS, Stout S (2009b) Quantitative histomorphometric evaluation of the endosteal lamellar pocket: comparing digital and point-count methods for the measurement of modeling drift remnants in the long bones of adult. Am J Phys Anthrop (Suppl.) 44:181.

Maggiano IS, Maggiano C, Tiesler Blos V et al. (in press) A distinct region of microarchitectural variation in femoral compact bone: histomorphology of the endosteal lamellar pocket. Int J Osteoarch.

Maggiano IS, Schultz M, Kierdorf H et al. (2008) Cross-sectional analysis of long bones, occupational activities and long-distance trade of the Classic Maya from Xcambó—archaeological and osteological evidence. Am J Phys Anthrop 136(4):470–477.

Manson JD, Waters NE (1965) Observations on the rate of maturation of the cat osteon. J Anat 99:539–549.

Marotti G (1993) A new theory of bone lamellation. Calcif Tiss Int 53(Suppl 1):S47–S56.

Marshall JH, Jowsey J, Rowland RE (1959) Microscopic metabolism of calcium in bone IV. Ca45 deposition and growth rate in canine osteons. Radiat Res 10:243–257.

Martin, R.B. 2000. Does osteocyte formation cause the nonlinear refilling of osteons? Bone 26(1):71–78.

Martin RB (2001) Is all cortical bone remodeling initiated by microdamage? Bone 30:8–13.

Martin DL, Armelagos GJ (1979) Morphometrics of compact bone: an example from Sudanese Nubia. Am J Phys Anthrop 51:571–578.

Martin RB (2003) Functional adaptation and fragility of the skeleton. In: Agarwal SC, Stout SD (eds) Bone loss and osteoporosis: an anthropological perspective. Kluwer Academics/Plenum Publishers, New York.

Martin RB, Burr DB, and Sharkey NA (1998) Skeletal tissue mechanics. Springer, New York.

Martin RB, Atkinson P (1977) Age and sex-related changes in the structure and strength of the femoral shaft. J Biomech 10:223–231.

Martin RB, Burr DB (1989) Structure, function and adaptation of compact bone. Raven Press, New York.

Martiniaková M, Omelka R, Grosskopf B et al. (2009) Histological analysis of compact bone tissue in adult laboratory rats. Slovak J Anim Sci 42(Suppl 1):56–59.

Matsuda J, Zernicke R, Vailas A et al. (1986) Structural and mechanical adaptation of immature bone to strenuous exercise. J Appl Physiol 60:2028–2034.

Meade JB, Cowin SC, Klawitter JJ et al (1984) Bone remodeling due to continuously applied loads. Calci Tiss Int 36(Suppl 1):S25–S30.

Midura RJ, Su X, Morcuende JA et al. (2003) Parathyroid hormone rapidly stimulates hyaluronan synthesis by periosteal osteoblasts in the tibial diaphysis of the growing rat. J Biol Chem 278:51462–51468.

Mosley JR, Lanyon LE (1998) Strain rate as a controlling influence on adaptive modeling in response to dynamic loading of the ulna in growing male rats. Bone 23(4):313–318.

Mosley JR, Lanyon LE (2002) Growth rate rather than gender determines the size of the adaptive response of the growing skeleton to mechanical strain. Bone 30(1):314–319.

Mosley JR, March BM, Lynch J et al (1997) Strain magnitude related changes in whole bone architecture in growing rats. Bone 20(3):191–198.

Nagurka M, Hayes W (1980) An interactive graphics package for calculating cross-sectional properties of complex shapes. J Biomech 13:59–64.

Nilsson BE, Westlin NE (1971) Bone density in athletes. Clin Orthop Relat Res 77:179–182.

Parfitt AM (1983) The physiologic and clinical significance of bone histomorphometric data. In: Recker RR (ed) Bone histomorphometry: techniques and interpretation. CRC Press, Boca Raton, FL.

Parfitt AM (1988) Bone remodeling: Relationship to the amount and structure of bone and the pathogenesis and prevention of fractures. In Riggs BL, Melton LJ (eds) Osteoporosis–etiology, diagnosis and management. Raven Press, New York, 45–94.

Parfitt AM (1994) Osteonal and hemi-osteonal remodeling: the spatial and temporal framework for signal traffic in adult human bone. J Cell Biochem 55:273–286.

Parfitt AM (2000) The mechanism of coupling: a role for the vasculature. Bone 26:319–323.

Parfitt AM (2002) Parathyroid hormone and periosteal bone expansion. J Bone Miner Res 17:1741–1743.

Parfitt AM (2003) New concepts of bone remodeling: a unified spatial and temporal model with physiologic and pathophysiologic implications. In: Agarwal S, Stout S (eds) Bone loss and osteo-porosis: an anthropological perspective, Kluwer Academic/Plenum Publishers, New York.

Parfitt AM, Travers R, Rauch F, et al. (2000) Structural and cellular changes during bone growth in healthy children. Bone 27:487–494.

Parker DF, Round JM, Sacco P et al. (1990) A cross-sectional survey of upper and lower limb strength in boys and girls during childhood and adolescence. Ann Hum Bio 17:199–211.

Pauwels F (1965) Gesammelte Abhandlungen zur funktionellen Anatomie. Springer, Berlin.

Pearson O, Lieberman D (2004) The aging of Wolff's law: ontogeny and responses to mechanical loading in cortical response. Yearbk Phys Anthropol 47:63–99.

Rauch F, Neu C, Manz F et al. (2001) The development of metaphyseal cortex-implications for distal radius fractures during growth. J Bone Miner Res 16:1547–1555.

Reid SA (1986) A study of lamellar organization in juvenile and adult human bone. Anat Embr 174:329–338.

Reinelander FW (1972) Circulation in bone. Biochemistry and physiology of bone, Vol. II. Academic Press, New York.

Rhodes J, Knüsel C (2005) Activity-related skeletal change in medieval humeri: cross-sectional and architectural alterations. Am J Phys Anthropol 128:536–546.

Robling AD, Stout SD (1999) Morphology of the drifting osteon. Cell Tiss Org 164:192–204.

Robling A, Stout S (2000) Histomorphometry of human cortical bone: applications to age estimation. In: Katzenberg M, Saunders S (eds) Biological anthropology of the human skeleton. Wiley-Liss, New York.

Robling A, Stout S (2003) Histomorphology, geometry, and mechanical loading in past populations. In: Agarwal S, Stout S (eds) Bone loss and osteoporosis: an anthropological perspective, Kluwer Academic/Plenum, New York.

Robling AG, Turner CH (2002) Mechanotransduction in bone: genetic effects on mechanosensitivity in mice. Bone 31(5):562–569.

Robling AD, Duijvelaar KM, Geevers JV et al. (2001) Modulation of appositional and longitudinal bone growth in the rat ulna by applied static and dynamic force. Bone 29(2):105–113.

Robling AD, Castillo AB, Turner CH (2006) Biomechanical and molecular regulation of bone remod-eling. Annu Rev Biomed Eng 8:466–498.

Rodríguez JI, Garcia-Alix A, Palacios J et al. (1988) Changes in long bones due to fetal immobility caused by neuromuscular disease. J Bone Joint Surg 70A:1052–1060.

Rubin P (1964) Dynamic classification of bone dysplasias. Yearbook Medical Publishers, Chicago.

Rubin C, Gross T, McLeod K et al. (1995) Morphologic stages in lamellar bone formation stimulated by a potent mechanical stimulus. J Bone Miner Res 10:488–495.

Rubin J, Rubin C (2008) Functional adaptation to loading of a single bone is neuronally regulated and involves multiple bones. J Bone Min Res 23(9):1369–1371.

Ruff C, Hayes W (1983a) Cross-sectional geometry of Pecos Pueblo femora and tibiae—a biomechan-ical investigation: I. Method and general patterns of variation. Am J Phys Anth 60:359–381.

Ruff C, Hayes W (1983b) Cross-sectional geometry of Pecos Pueblo femora and tibiae—a biome-chanical investigation. II. Sex, age and side differences. Am J Phys Anthropol 60:383–400.

Ruff C, Holt B, Trinkaus E (2006) Who's afraid of the big bad Wolff?: Wolff's law and bone functional adaptation. Am J Phys Anth129:484–498.

Ruff C, Larsen C, Hayes W (1984) Structural changes in the femur with the transition to agriculture on the Georgia coast. Am J Phys Anthropol 64:125–136.

Ruff C, Trinkaus E, Walker A et al. (1993) Postcranial robusticity in Homo. I. Temporal trends and mechanical interpretation. Am J Phys Anthropol 91:21–53.

Rush T, Pirok D, Frost H (1966) "Fractional labeling": the fraction of actively forming osteons that take tetracycline labels in normal human bone. Henry Ford Hosp Med Bull 14:255–263.

Salle BL, Rauch F, Travers R, et al. (2002) Human fetal bone development: histomorphometric evaluation of the proximal femoral metaphysis. Bone 30:823–828.

Scheuer L and Black S (2000) Developmental juvenile osteology. Academic Press, San Diego.

Schoenau E, Frost HM (2002) The "Muscle-Bone-Unit" in children and adolescents. Calcif Tiss Int 70:405–407.

Schultz M (1993) Spuren unspezifischer Entzündungen an prähistorischen und historischen Schädeln. Ein Beitrag zur Paläopathologie. In: Kaufmann B (ed) Anthropologische Beiträge 4 A und 4 B. Anthropologisches Forschungsinstitut Aesch und Anthropologische Gesellschaft Basel, Aesch und Basel, 1–84.

Schultz M (1997) Microscopic investigation of excavated skeletal remains: a contribution to paleo-pathology and forensic medicine. In: Haglund W, Sorg M (eds) Forensic taphonomy: the post-mortem fate of human remains. CRC Press, Boca Raton, FL, 201–222.

Schultz M (1999) Microscopic investigation in fossil hominoidea: a clue to taxonomy, functional anatomy, and the history of diseases. Anat Rec 157:225–232.

Schultz M (2001) Paleopathology of bone: a new approach to the study of ancient diseases. Am J Phys Anthrop 44:106–147.

Shapiro F (2002) Pediatric orthopedic deformities. Basic science, diagnosis, and treatment. Elsevier, San Diego.

Silventoinen K (2003) Determinations of variation in adult body height. J Biosoc Sci 35:263–285.

Simpson AH (1985) The blood supply of periosteum. J Anat 140:697–770.

Skedros JG, Holmes JL, Vajda EG, and Bloebaum RD (2005) Cementlines of secondary osteons in human bone are not mineral-deficient: new data in a historical perspective. The Anat Rec Part A 286A:781–803.

Skedros JG, Kiser CJ, Mendenhall SD (2011) A weighted osteon morphotype score outperforms regional osteon percent prevalence calculations for interpreting cortical bone adaptation. Am J of Phys Anthrop 144:41–50.

Skerry T (2006) One mechanostat or many? Modifications of the site-specific response of bone to mechanical loading by nature and nurture. J Muculoskel Neurolog Inter 6:122–127.

Sládek V, Berner M, Sailer R (2006) Mobility in central European Late Eneolithic and Early Bronze Age: femoral cross-sectional geometry. Am J Phys Anthropol 130:320–332.

Sone T, Imai Y, Joo Y et al. (2006) Side-to-side differences in cortical bone mineral density or tibiae in young male athletes. Bone 38:708–713.

Squier CA, Ghoneim S, Kremenak CR (1990) Ultrastructure of the periosteum from membrane bone. J Anat 171:233–239.

Srinivasan S, Weimer DA, Agans SC et al. (2002) Low magnitude mechanical loading becomes osteo-genic when rest is inserted between each load cycle. J Bone Miner Res 17:1613–1620.

Stout S (1978) Histological structure and its preservation in ancient bone. Curr Anthrop 19:601–604.

Stout S, Lueck R (1995) Bone remodeling rates and maturation in three archaeological skeletal populations. Am J Phys Anthrop 98:161–171.

Stout S, Paine R (1992) Brief communication: histological age estimation using rib and clavicle. Am J Phys Anthrop 87:111–115.

Stock J, Pfeiffer S (2004) Long bone robusticity and subsistence behaviour among later Stone Age foragers of the forest and fynbos biomes of South Africa. J Archaeol Sci 31:999–1013.

Stoker NG, Epker BN (1971) Age changes in endosteal bone remodeling and balance in the rabbit. J Dent Res 50:1570–1574.

Streeter M, Stout S (2003) The histomorphometry of the subadult rib: age-associated changes in bone mass and the creation of peak bone mass. In: Agarwal S, Stout S (eds) Bone loss and osteoporosis: an anthropological perspective, Kluwer Academic/Plenum, New York.

Sumner DR, Andriacchi TP (1996) Adaptation to differential loading: comparison of growth-related changes in cross-sectional properties of the human femur and humerus. Bone 19(2):121–126.

Szulc P, Seeman E (2009) Thinking inside and outside the envelopes of bone: dedicated to PDD. Osteoporos Int 20(8):1281–1288.

Takano Y, Turner CH, Owan I, et al. (1999) Elastic anisotropy and collagen orientation of osteonal bone are dependent on the mechanical strain distribution. J Orthop Res 17:59–66.

Tanck E, Hannik G, Ruimerman R, et al. (2006) Cortical bone development under the growth plate is regulated by mechanical load transfer. J Anat 208:73–79.

Tang X, Chai B (1986) Ultrastructural investigation of osteogenic cells. Chinese Med J 99:950–956.

Taylor T, Frost H (1966) The existence of a zone of finite thickness during tetracycline labeling of bone. Henry Ford Hosp Med Bull 14:397–403.

Taylor D, Lee TC (2003) Microdamage and mechanical behaviour: predicting failure and remodelling in compact bone. J Anat 203:203–211.

Thompson D (1979) The core technique in the determination of age at death in skeletons. J For Sci 24:902–915.

Trinkaus E (1976) The evolution of the hominid femoral diaphysis during the Upper Pleistocene in Europe and the near East. Z Morphol Anthropol 67:291–319.

Trinkaus E, Churchill S (1999) Diaphyseal cross-sectional geometry of near eastern Middle Palaeolithic humans: the humerus. J Archaeol Sci 26:173–184.

Turner C (1999) Toward a mathematical description of bone biology: the principle of cellular accommodation. Calc Tiss Int 65:466–471.

Turner C (2000) Letter to the Editor, Reply: Toward a mathematical description of bone biology: the principle of cellular accommodation. Calc Tiss Int 67:184–187.

Turner CH, Forwood MR, Rho JY, Yoshikawa T (1994) Mechanical loading thresholds for lamellar and woven bone formation. J Bone Miner Res 9:87–97.

Turner RT, Wakley GK, Hannon KS (1990) Differential effects of androgens on cortical bone histomorphometry in gonadectomized male and female rats. J Orthop Res 8:612–617.

Ulijaszek SJ (2001) Secular trends in growth: the narrowing of ethnic differences in stature. Brit Nutr Foundation Bull 26:43–51.

Väänänen HK, Zhao H, Mulari M, Halleen JM (2000) The cell biology of osteoclast function. J Cell Sci 113:377–381.

Van Buskirk W (1989) Elementary stress analysis of the femur and tibia. In: Cowin S (ed) Bone mechanics. CRC Press, Boca Raton, FL.

Venken K, De Gendt K, Boonen S et al. (2006) Relative impact of androgen and estrogen receptor activation in the effects of androgens on trabecular and cortical bone in growing male mice: a study in the androgen receptor knockout mouse model. J Bone Min Res 21:576–585.

Vincentilli R, Grigorov M (1985) The effect of Haversian remodeling on the tensile properties of human cortical bone. J Biomech 18:201–207.

Volkman SK, Galecki AT, Burke DT et al. (2004) Quantitative trait loci that modulate femoral mechanical properties in a genetically heterogeneous mouse population. J Bone Min Res 19(9):1497–1505.

Walker RA, Lovejoy CO, Meindl RS (1994) Histomorphological and geometric properties of human femoral cortex in individuals over 50: implications for histomorphological determination of age-at-death. Am J Hum Bio 6:659–667.

Washburn SL (1947) The relation of the temporal muscle to the form of the skull. Anat Rec 99:239–248.

Weiss E (2003) Effects of rowing on humeral strength. Am J Phys Anthropol 121:293–302.

Wescott D (2006) Effects of mobility on femur midshaft external shape and robusticity. Am J Phys Anthropol 130:201–213.

Wong M, Germiller J, Bonadio J et al. (1993) Neuromuscular atrophy alters collagen gene expression, pattern formation, and mechanical integrity of the chick embryo long bone. Prog Clin Biol Res 383B:587–597.

Woo S, Kuei S, Amiel D et al. (1981) The effect of prolonged physical training on the properties of long bone: a study of Wolff's law. J Bone Joint Surg 63:780–787.

Wu K, Schubeck K, Frost H et al. (1970) Haversian bone formation rates determined by a new method in a mastodon, and in human diabetes mellitus and osteoporosis. Calcif Tiss Res 6:204–219.

Yao W, Jee WSS, Chen JL et al. (2000) Making rats rise to erect bipedal stance for feeding partially prevented orchidectomy-induced bone loss and added bone to intact rats. J Bone Min Res 15:1158–1168.

Yao W, Jee WSS, Chen JL et al. (2001) A novel method to "exercise" rats: making rats rise to erect bipedal stance for feeding-raised cage model. J Musculoskelet Neuronal Interact 1:241–247.

# Histological Features of Dental Hard Tissues and Their Utility in Forensic Anthropology

# 4

DEBBIE GUATELLI-STEINBERG
MICHAELA HUFFMAN

## Contents

## 4.1 Introduction

Because of their hardness, teeth are the most likely remains of an individual to endure through time. It is fortunate that teeth, which may be the only remains a forensic anthropologist or paleoanthropologist has to work with, preserve a wealth of information about the individuals of whom they were once a part. Teeth retain a record of their own growth in their hard tissues: the enamel, dentine, and cementum (Figure 4.1). In paleoanthropology, analysis of dental hard tissue growth has yielded major insights into the evolution of hominin growth patterns and life history (for a review see Dean, 2006). Disruptions in the growth of dental hard tissues have also revealed information about the experience of physiological stress in our hominin ancestors and relatives (reviewed in Guatelli-Steinberg, 2008). In forensic contexts, histological examination of the growth record preserved in dental hard tissues provides a means to reconstruct or estimate age at death (Hillson, 1996) to determine whether an infant survived after birth (Whittaker and Richards, 1978) and to identify periods of disturbed growth (Skinner and Anderson, 1991; Teivens et al., 1996).

These paleoanthropological and forensic uses are founded on two aspects of dental hard tissues: the histological features associated with their growth and the histological changes they undergo with age. The primary objective of this chapter is therefore to provide a basic introduction to dental hard tissue growth processes and age-related changes as they are manifested histologically. The secondary objective of this chapter is to discuss how this knowledge can be used in forensic settings. The purpose is to provide an overview of such uses; detailed explanations of methodology can be found in the primary literature cited here.

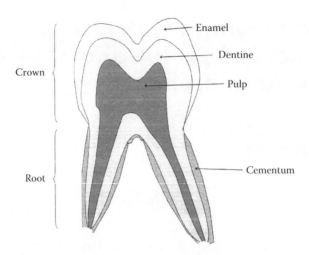

**Figure 4.1** Diagram of tooth longitudinal section showing the hard tissues (enamel, dentine, and cementum) as well as pulp. (Modified from Guatelli-Steinberg, D (2010) Growing planes: incremental growth in the teeth of human ancestors. In: Larsen CS (ed) A Companion to Biological Anthropology. Wiley-Blackwell, Malden, MA.)

## 4.2   Enamel Growth Processes and Associated Histological Features

Although teeth themselves are hard, their hardest component is enamel, the whitish outer covering of dental crowns that comes into direct contact with food. Ninety-six percent of mature enamel is mineral, composed of hydroxyapatite (Ten Cate, 1994). No cells are contained within mature enamel such that once formed, enamel cannot regrow in the way that bone can (Ten Cate, 1994). Incremental growth layers in enamel, loosely analogous to tree rings (but representing much shorter periods of time), can be preserved for millennia. Because enamel (in different teeth) forms throughout the prenatal through late childhood periods (Hillson, 1996), incremental markings in enamel chronicle its growth during the early years of life.

Enamel begins to form at the cusp tip of a crown. In response to the first-formed dentine, *ameloblasts* (enamel-forming cells) secrete an organic matrix of proteins which serves to "accept" mineral (Ten Cate, 1994). Ameloblasts continue to differentiate from epithelial cells sequentially along the presumptive enamel–dentine junction (EDJ). As they become functional, ameloblasts migrate away from the EDJ and toward what will eventually become the enamel surface. In this first or secretory stage of enamel formation, enamel reaches a state of 30% mineralization (Ten Cate, 1994). After ameloblasts have formed the full thickness of the enamel, they undergo morphological changes associated with the maturation stage of enamel formation, cycling between removing water and the organic components of the matrix and introducing additional mineral. Enamel reaches its fully mineralized state at the end of this stage (Ten Cate, 1994), and the ameloblasts undergo programmed cell death (apoptosis; Nanci, 2007).

The rhythmic, incremental pattern of enamel growth is revealed in its microstructural details. Aside from a small portion of the first and last-formed enamel, the enamel formed by each ameloblast attains a rodlike structure, called an enamel rod (e.g., Ten Cate, 1994) or enamel prism (e.g., Dean, 1987; Figures 4.2 and 4.3). Enamel rods reflect the path of the ameloblasts that formed them (Risnes, 1986). The diameters of the enamel rods appear

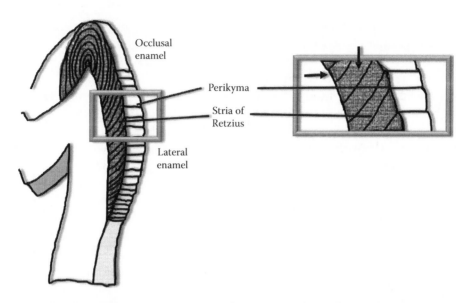

**Figure 4.2** Diagram of longitudinal section of tooth crown showing incremental growth structures. In inset at right, horizontal arrow indicates orientation of enamel rods (prisms) and downward pointing arrow indicates orientation of cross-striations. (Diagram adapted from Ten Cate AR (1994) Oral Histology: Development, Structure, and Function, 4th ed. Mosby, St. Louis.)

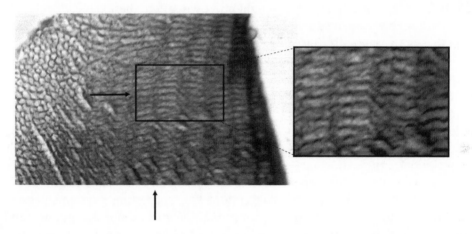

**Figure 4.3** Thin section of enamel. Left portion of image is demineralized enamel, while right portion shows enamel rods during secretory phase of amelogeneis; horizontal arrow shows orientation of rods and vertical arrow points to a stria of Retzius. Inset shows enlargement of rods on which faint cross-striations are visible perpendicular to length of rod. (Image courtesy of Donald J. Reid.)

to expand and constrict rhythmically along their length when viewed under a scanning electron microscope (SEM; Dean, 1987). Areas of expansion are also called varicosities. The microscopic appearance of these *varicosities* and *constrictions* along the enamel rod is analogous to the appearance of a line of toothpaste when squeezed from a tube. Varicosities and constrictions are thought to represent cyclic rhythms in ameloblast secretion (Boyde, 1989). Fine lines known as *cross-striations*, visible in ground sections with a light microscope or polarizing light microscope, are associated with varicosities (Dean, 1987), and are spaced regularly (every 4 microns) along the enamel rod (Hillson, 2005). As Dean (1987) points out, the terms *varicosities* and *cross-striations* have been used interchangeably, as they are both manifestations of incremental growth along the enamel rod and are coincident with each other. In most recent literature, the term *cross-striations* is preferred, and therefore will be used from this point forward.

Experimental studies in the 1930s and 1940s on a variety of mammals indicated that cross-striations form according to a circadian rhythm (see Dean, 1987, for a review). Bromage (1991) produced experimental verification of this rhythm (in *Macaca nemistrina*) by counting cross-striations between enamel markings that had been produced by injecting animals with fluorescent dyes at known intervals. Boyde (1979) offered an explanation for the daily formation of cross-striations and their association with prism varicosities. He suggested that over the course of a 24-hour period, the rate of enamel secretion would vary, causing the prisms to enlarge and contract with a daily rhythm. Furthermore, daily variation in the metabolic activity of ameloblasts would alter the local concentration of $CO_2$ and therefore the amount of carbonate incorporated into enamel. This explanation is consistent with changes that have been observed in mineral density at cross-striations giving them their characteristic refractive properties when viewed under a light microscope (Boyde, 1979).

Cross-striations are also referred to as short-period increments to differentiate them from a second kind of incremental growth present in enamel, represented by long-period increments (Dean, 2000). When an individual has died before crown formation is complete, it is possible to use these increments to estimate age at death, as described in Section 4.3.

When viewed under a transmitted light microscope, long-period increments appear as course dark lines traversing a series of enamel rods. Hillson (2005) suggests that the dark appearance of these lines is caused by light scattering, possibly brought about by changes in crystal size or orientation. In confocal or SEM images, prism continuity appears to be disrupted along these lines (Hillson, 2005). More commonly, these long-period increments are called *brown striae of Retzius* (Hillson, 2005), or more simply *striae of Retzius* (Figures 4.2 and 4.3).

Striae of Retzius are actually a series of growth layers in a three-dimensional tooth, which form when all ameloblasts along the enamel-forming front simultaneously slow their secretion of the enamel matrix (Dean, 1987). An important point is that this simultaneous slowing of secretory ameloblasts occurs at regular intervals throughout all of the teeth of an individual (Dean, 1987; Fitzgerald, 1998), suggesting a systemic, although as yet unknown, physiological cause. To determine this interval one counts the number of cross-striations that lie between adjacent striae of Retzius. The number of cross-striations represents the periodicity, in days, of the striae. In humans, the average periodicity is 8 or 9 days, ranging from a minimum of 6 to a maximum of 12 days for any one individual (Dean and Reid, 2001; Reid and Dean, 2006).

In a tooth's cuspal or occlusal enamel, striae of Retzius cover each other in a series of domes, and so are not visible from the tooth's surface (Figure 4.2). Thus, in cuspal enamel, striae of Retzius are called "hidden" or "buried" increments. However, on the sides of a tooth, in a tooth's lateral enamel, the striae of Retzius emerge onto the surface of enamel as *perikymata* (plural; perikyma, singular; Figure 4.2). The name is derived from the Greek root (kyma) for wave, owing to the wavelike "crests" and "troughs" perikymata exhibit (Hillson, 1996). As long as they haven't been worn or eroded away, perikymata can, with the aid of a stereomicroscope (reflected light), be directly observed and counted on dental remains. Because perikymata are simply surface manifestations of the striae of Retzius, it follows that the periodicity of an individuals' striae is exactly the same as the periodicity

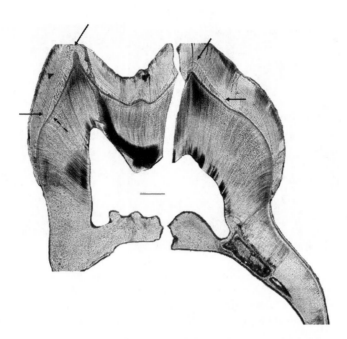

**Figure 4.4** Longitudinal section of deciduous molar: solid arrows point to neonatal line as it courses through the enamel; dashed arrow points to the matching neonatal line in the dentine. (Image courtesy of Donald J. Reid.)

of his or her perikymata. By counting all of the perikymata from the cusp of the tooth to its cervix (the "bottom" of the tooth), and considering a range of possible periodicities, an estimated range for the time a tooth's lateral enamel took to form can be calculated. Using perikymata to estimate lateral enamel formation time is useful when it is not possible to section dental remains.

As discussed later, knowing the periodicity of an individual's striae of Retzius is a critical component of histological estimations of age at death. Of equal importance are two other prominent kinds of enamel microstructures: the *neonatal line* and *accentuated striae*, the latter of which are sometimes called *Wilson bands* (Rose et al., 1978). The neonatal line is a prominent stria that occurs in the enamel of teeth forming at birth—the deciduous teeth and permanent first molars (Hillson, 1996; Figure 4.4). This relatively broad and well-defined stria may result from decreases in the concentration of plasma calcium after birth (Nóren, 1984) as the enamel in the neonatal line is hypomineralized (Smith and Avishai, 2005). Alternatively, the neonatal line may be the consequence of disturbances to ameloblast secretion brought about by the birth process (Whittaker and Richards, 1978). In estimating age at death, the neonatal line provides the starting point for counting incremental growth lines in enamel, and it has other applications to forensics as well (see Section 4.3).

Finally, accentuated striae are prominent striae that may be coincident with or fall between the incremental striae of Retzius. As their name implies, accentuated striae appear darker and thicker than incremental striae of Retzius when viewed with a light microscope (Figure 4.5). These prominent lines often appear to be associated with hypoplastic defects present at the enamel surface (Goodman and Rose, 1990). Hypoplastic defects, deficiencies of enamel thickness that develop as the enamel is forming, are usually caused by nutritional deficiencies or febrile disease (Ten Cate, 1994). These associations suggest that accentuated striae also form in response to systemic growth disturbances. Further support for

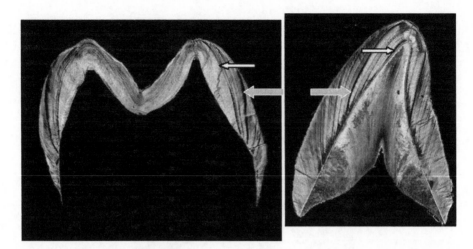

**Figure 4.5** Longitudinal sections of first permanent molar (left) and canine (right). White arrows point to a pair of matching accentuated striae that formed in response to the same disruptive event in both teeth. Gray arrows point to a second pair of matching accentuated striae representing a second disruptive event occurring later in time than the first. (Image courtesy of Rebecca Ferrell.)

this suggestion is found in the work of Teivens and colleagues (1996), in which the locations of accentuated striae corresponded to the ages at which diseases had been documented in the medical histories of seven infants. Accentuated striae play a key role in studies of tooth growth because they mark the enamel-forming front in all teeth forming at the time of the growth disturbance. It is therefore possible to use sequences of accentuated striae to match the crown growth chronologies of different teeth (e.g., Boyde, 1963, 1990; Dean and Beynon, 1991; Reid et al., 1998) and in so doing, as explained next, to reconstruct age-at-death.

## 4.3    Enamel Histology and Forensic Applications

If a child died when his or her teeth were forming, radiographic standards (e.g., Demirjian et al., 1973) can be used to assess his or her dental age—the age at which individuals in a reference sample attained similar stages of dental development. However, dental age is, of course, not necessarily the same as an individual's chronological age. The histological structures of enamel described earlier make it possible to estimate an individual's chronological age at death, provided that the tooth crowns themselves had not yet finished forming when the individual died.

Boyde (1963, 1990) was the first to use histological structures in enamel to estimate age at death. He identified a neonatal line in the cusp of a first permanent molar and matched the pattern of accentuated striae in the molar with that of the first incisor, which had just completed its formation when the individual died. By matching the sequence of accentuated striae in the molar to that of the incisor, Boyde was able to count cross-striations from the first formed enamel at the molar's neonatal line to the last formed enamel in the incisor, arriving at 1,692 cross-striations, or an age at death of 1,692 days. Since Boyde's pioneering work, others have used this same method on known-age material. Antoine and coworkers (1999), for example, counted cross-striations from the neonatal line to the last-formed enamel in a child whose remains were excavated from the crypt of Christ Church in Spitalfields, England. The age at death for this individual was recorded on the coffin plate as 3 years and 4 months. The age at death estimate of Antoine and colleagues (1999) was very close to this, at 3 years and a little over 3 months.

Cross-striations are often difficult to count continuously in enamel sections (Hillson, 2005). They are particularly difficult to count in cuspal enamel, where the enamel prisms weave in and out of the plane of section in what is known as *decussating* or *gnarled* enamel (Hillson, 2005). One method used in these cases is to measure the spacing of cross-striations (where they are visible in the cuspal enamel) and apply it to the length of prisms in the cuspal enamel (multiplying by a correction factor to allow for prism decussation; Dean 1998; Reid et al., 1998). To determine lateral enamel formation time, it is not necessary to be able to see each cross-striation, as the more easily visible striae of Retzius can be counted and multiplied by their periodicity (Hillson, 2005).

When teeth cannot be sectioned, counts of perikymata on enamel surfaces can provide a means to estimate age at death in children whose enamel had not yet completely formed at the time of death. Doing so requires the substitution of averages for the age at which a tooth began to mineralize, the length of time taken for the "hidden" or cuspal enamel to form, and the periodicity of an individual's perikymata (e.g., Bromage and Dean, 1985). It is clear that using an average periodicity of 9 days would not work well if applied to an individual whose periodicity was actually 6 or 12 days. Nevertheless, Stringer and coworkers (1990) used this method to obtain age estimates that closely approximated known ages at death in several archeological specimens.

While the foregoing discussion highlights the use of histological structures in enamel to assess age at death, there are other useful applications of these features in forensic contexts. To discern the neonatal line in a tooth section using a light microscope, it is necessary that an infant survived for at least 7 to 10 days so that the neonatal line can be observed between enamel that formed before and after birth (Smith and Avishai, 2005; Whittaker and Richards, 1978). Thus, the absence of a neonatal line in an infant's dental remains indicates that the infant was either stillborn or did not survive long after birth. Under an SEM, it is possible to see a difference in the appearance and orientation of the enamel prisms across the neonatal line itself (Whittaker and Richards, 1978). When imaged in this way, the "sharply defined" prenatal side of the line can be differentiated from the "more diffuse" neonatal part of the line (Whittaker and Richards, 1978). SEM imaging, therefore, makes it possible to determine whether an infant survived even for a short period after birth. Interestingly, the actual widths of neonatal lines appear to be affected by the nature of the birth. Eli and others (1989) found that neonatal lines were wider than normal in infants born in difficult (operative) deliveries but thinner than normal in infants born by Caesarean section.

The presence or absence of accentuated striae in infant teeth may be relevant to forensic cases in which a child is suspected to have died of sudden infant death syndrome (SIDS). Teivens and colleagues (1996) compared histological sections of enamel from the teeth of infants who had died of SIDS with those of infants who had died from known chronic or acute diseases. Those who had died of SIDS had few accentuated striae, whereas those dying of chronic or acute diseases had more. Although the authors certainly do not claim that the presence of accentuated striae rules out a diagnosis of SIDS, they suggest that the absence of accentuated striae in a child suspected to have died of SIDS would lend support to the diagnosis.

Skinner and Anderson (1991) explored the use of accentuated striae in identifying the remains of young children. These authors point out that it is often difficult to identify the dental remains of young children because they lack identifying dental work. Skinner and Anderson (1991) examined accentuated striae in the dental remains of a Canadian child whose dental age at death (using radiographic charts) was 5.6 ± 0.75 years. The authors found a good match between the timing of the accentuated striae and the timing of physiologically stressful episodes (e.g., periods of illness or significant weight loss requiring hospitalization) documented in the medical records of a Canadian child who had been lost in the woods when he was 5 years and 7 months old. Although the match between the timing of accentuated striae and known stress events may not be sufficient evidence to identify dental remains in this or other cases, it does provide information of potential forensic relevance.

## 4.4   Dentine: Histological Structures Associated with Growth and Age

Dentine is the yellowish hard tissue that underlies the enamel in the crown and forms the bulk of the hard tissue of the root. It is less mineralized than enamel, consisting of 70% mineral (primarily hydroxyapatite), 20% organic material (especially collagen), and 10% water (Ten Cate, 1994). The composition of dentine gives it an elastic quality that protects the hard and brittle overlying enamel from fracturing under masticatory stress (Ten Cate, 1994).

Dentine is the first mineralized tissue to be produced during crown formation. As mentioned, its presence stimulates the differentiation of ameloblasts from precursor cells in the enamel epithelium. However, prior to this event, the precursor cells in the enamel epithelium induced the differentiation of *odontoblasts*, the cells that form dentine (Ten Cate, 1994). Thus, there has been *reciprocal induction* of dental tissues (Ten Cate, 1994). This process of reciprocal induction begins at the cusp tip and extends down the length of the enamel–dentine junction, such that the formation of dentine always precedes the formation of enamel (Hillson, 2005). In the root, cells of *Hertwig's epithelial root sheath* stimulate the differentiation of odontoblasts.

Ondontoblasts form dentine as they move away from the enamel–dentine junction (and root surface) toward the pulp, the soft tissue at the center of the tooth. As they travel toward the pulp, odontoblasts leave behind long processes within structures known as *dentine tubules* (Figure 4.6; Hillson, 2005; Ten Cate, 1994). These processes remain for the life span of the tissue, as do the dentine tubules, the latter of which provide a permanent record of the paths traveled by odontoblasts. These paths are S-shaped in the crown, but straighter in the root, and they traverse the entire thickness of the dentine (Ten Cate, 1994). Dentine formed outside of the tubules is called *intertubular* dentine, whereas that which forms inside the tubules is known as *intratubular* dentine (Ten Cate, 1994). Odontoblasts form intertubular dentine by first secreting an organic matrix (*predentine*) and then secreting matrix vesicles, which contain hydroxyapatite crystallites (Ten Cate, 1994). These vesicles serve as foci of crystallization. Intratubular dentine formation occurs somewhat differently and results in dentine, which is 40% more mineralized than intertubular dentine (Ten Cate, 1994).

Like enamel, the growth of dentine is incremental. Indeed, there are daily, or short-period lines in dentine called *lines of von Ebner* (Dean, 2000). There are long-period lines in dentine as well, known as *Andresen lines,* which have the same periodicity as the striae

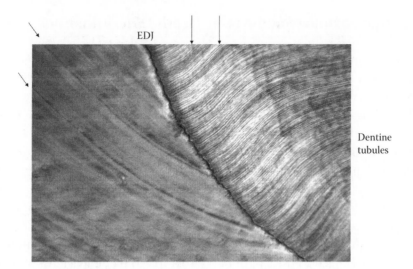

**Figure 4.6** Thin section of enamel (left) and dentine (right), separated by the EDJ. The oblique arrows point to accentuated striae in the enamel, while the downward pointing arrows point to contour lines of Owen in the dentine. Note how the accentuated striae and the contour lines of Owen are slightly offset where they "meet" at the EDJ owing to the fact that dentine formation precedes enamel formation. (Image courtesy of Donald J. Reid.)

of Retzius within an individual and are therefore likely to result from a common physiological growth rhythm (Dean, 2000). In addition, *contour lines of Owen*, prominent lines parallel or coincident with Andresen lines in dentine, appear to be caused by the same disruptions responsible for the formation of accentuated striae (Hillson, 2005; Figure 4.6). Accentuated striae, marking the enamel-forming front at the time of disruptions, and contour lines of Owen, marking the dentine-forming front at these same points in time can be seen to "meet" at the EDJ (e.g., Macho et al., 1996; Figure 4.6). The accentuated striae are shifted just incisally to their corresponding contour lines owing to the fact that enamel formation lags slightly behind dentine formation (Hillson, 2005). A particularly marked countour line of Owen corresponds with the neonatal line in enamel and is also referred to as a neonatal line (Ten Cate, 1994; see Figure 4.4).

Dentine produced during the formation of the crown and root is called *primary dentine* (Ten Cate, 1994). However, in contrast with enamel, dentine continues to be produced after the tooth has formed. There is continued deposition of dentine in both the crown and root at the border of the dentine and pulp. This *secondary dentine* is produced along the perimeter of the pulp chamber and root canal, reducing their volume as individuals age (Ten Cate, 1994). Note that secondary dentine is different from *reparative*, or *tertiary* dentine, which is produced by odontoblasts in response to destructive stimuli, such as caries (Ten Cate, 1994). Intratubular dentine is also produced in response to caries, occluding the tubules and preventing further infection (Arnold et al., 2001). As one ages, intratubular dentine continues to be produced, reducing the diameter of the tubule lumen, and often completely filling the tubule (Ten Cate, 1994). The complete mineralization of the tubules causes the dentine to become translucent or *sclerotic* (Ten Cate, 1994). As explained next, these changes form the basis for dentine-based age estimation techniques.

## 4.5   Dentine Histology and Age-at-Death Determinations

Although the neonatal line, Andresen lines, and contour lines of Owen can be used in the same manner as their enamel homologues to estimate age at death from dental crowns, it is not always possible to see the daily increments in dentine clearly (Dean and Scandrett, 1996). Thus, Hillson (2005) recommends that cross-striations in enamel be used to "calibrate" these lines in dentine.

Growth lines in dentine are especially useful in age estimation when the dental remains of an individual include teeth that have completed crown formation but have not yet completed root growth. In such cases, although it is difficult to count Andresen lines in dentine, it is possible to use the orientation of Andresen lines or contour lines of Owen in root dentine together with the average daily rate of dentine formation to calculate rates of root extension (see Dean and Vesey, 2008, for an explanation of this method). Root extension rates can then be applied to the length of the root to estimate the length of time the root took to form (e.g., Macchiarelli et al., 2006). That time can be added to the age at crown completion (calculated using the methods described for enamel) to obtain the individual's age at death.

If an individual died after all root formation was complete, there are other aspects of dentine histology that can be used to estimate age at death from his or her dental remains. The percentage of the pulp chamber filled in by secondary dentine can be measured (Gustafson, 1950). However, Hillson (2005:253) points out that when this is done only "modest correlations with known age are achieved, and other methods of age determination seem to be better in humans."

A more promising use of dentine in estimating age at death in individuals whose dentition has already formed is through the measurement of sclerotic dentine. Although the amount of sclerotic dentine in the crown has no correlation with age, the amount of sclerotic dentine in the root is strongly age related (Hillson 1996). Root dentine sclerosis first appears in the late teen ages, beginning at the apex of the root and moving up the root toward the crown (Hillson 1996, 2005). As mentioned, sclerotic dentine is transparent, and although it can be most clearly seen in tooth sections, it can also be seen in whole roots by placing a shining bright light behind them (Hillson, 2005).

Bang and Ramm (1970) measured the length of sclerotic areas in 926 teeth extracted from 265 individuals of known age. They found reasonably high correlations between age at extraction and root transparency. Based on this finding, these researchers developed a set of regression equations to estimate age, which they then tested on 24 individuals. Their results suggested that their equations had a predictive accuracy of ±5 years up until the age of 60, after which the method greatly underestimated age.

Other researchers have improved on Bang and Ramm's study. Making serial sections of roots, Vasiliadis et al. (1983a, 1983b) determined the proportion of root volume composed of sclerotic dentine. This method had even greater predictive accuracy than that of Bang and Ram (1970) in that actual age differed from predicted ages by ±3.5 years. However, as Hillson notes (2005), their sample consisted primarily of individuals who were 50 years of age or younger. Despite this drawback, Hillson (2005:254) concludes that "these results are better than most alternative aging methods for adult humans."

## 4.6   Cementum: Histological Features

Cementum covers the roots of teeth, and is "cemented" to the dentine of the roots (Ten Cate, 1994). It provides a surface for the attachment of the periodontal ligament (PDL), which anchors the tooth in its socket (Hillson, 2005). Collagen fibers (extrinsic fibers) of the PDL are embedded within the cementum, connecting the PDL to the root (Ten Cate, 1994). Cementum is similar in composition to bone, consisting of 70% mineral, 21% collagen, and 1% additional organic material (Hillson, 2005). The collagen consists not only of the extrinsic fibers of the PDL, but also of smaller, intrinsic, fibers produced by the cells which form cementum (Hillson, 2005).

The formation of cementum is accomplished by *cementoblasts*, which differentiate from precursor cells in response to the deposition of root dentine. Cementoblasts deposit an organic matrix around the extrinsic (PDL) fibers and mineralization then follows in a fashion similar to that of dentine (see earlier; Ten Cate, 1994). Cementum can be considered to form in two phases. The first phase involves the deposition of *primary cementum*, which covers approximately two-thirds of the root closest to the crown and is formed as the tooth erupts (Ten Cate, 1994). The primary cementum is acellular (Ten Cate, 1994). In the second phase, cementum is deposited more rapidly, and the cementoblasts become embedded within the cementum, occupying spaces or *lacunae* (Hillson, 2005). The "entrapped" cementoblasts are referred to as *cementocytes* (Hillson, 2005; Ten Cate, 1994), and their presence renders secondary cementum a cellular tissue. Secondary cementum is deposited after the tooth has erupted and surrounds the apical two-thirds of the root (Ten Cate, 1994). Cementocytes continue to produce cementum throughout one's lifetime, a fact that makes cementum of use in aging techniques. It is important to note that cementum may be deposited in abnormally large quantities as a response to root inflammation or as a consequence of extreme tooth wear (Hillson, 2005). In such cases, the cementum at the root apex becomes abnormally thick, in a condition known as *hypercementosis*.

In histological sections of secondary cementum, it is possible to see alternating bands of light and dark layers (also called *contour lines of Salter*), which seem to be the result of faster versus slower periods of cementum deposition (Hillson, 2005; Figure 4.7). As Hillson (2005) explains, rapidly formed cementum tends to incorporate more cementocyte lacunae, more intrinsic collagen fibers, more extrinsic collagen fibers, and is also less well mineralized. With its higher content of collagen fibers and cementum lacunae, the faster forming cementum tends to scatter light, making it appear under a microscope as dark in transmitted light and bright in reflected light (Hillson, 2005). More slowly formed cementum contains fewer of these light-scattering elements, causing it to appear bright under transmitted light and dark under reflected light. Under an SEM (in back-scatter mode), the layers of the less heavily mineralized fast-forming cementum appear dark, while the more heavily mineralized slow-forming cementum layers are bright (Hillson, 2005). The banding pattern in an individual's cementum therefore tracks variation in the rate at which cementum deposition has occurred. This phenomenon serves as the foundation for aging techniques based on cementum layering.

Cement layers              Dentine

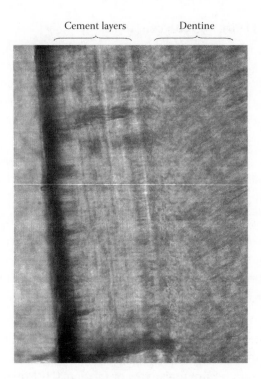

**Figure 4.7** Light and dark bands running the length of the image are layers of cementum under polarized light. (Image by Michaela Huffman.)

## 4.7    Cementum Histology and Age-at-Death Estimation

In marine as well as land mammals, variation in the rate at which cementum is produced varies according to a yearly growth cycle. (For a thorough review, which also covers studies of yearly cycles of dentine deposition in marine mammals, see Hillson, 2005.) Many studies have linked periods of rapid cementum deposition with seasons of more abundant resources and thus faster growth (Hillson, 2005). For example, Mitchell (1963, 1967), used reflected light microscopy to examine cementum layers in red deer (*Cervus elaphus*) for which the season of death was known. In deer killed during the winter months (January through March), the outermost layer of cementum was dark, indicating slower growth. In deer killed between May and December, the outermost layer was bright, indicating faster growth. Assuming that a pair of dark and light layers represented one year, these authors arrived at age-at-death estimates that were very close to the known ages at which these deer were killed. Although not all studies have yielded results as clear as this one, the counting of cementum layers is "now widely recognized as a technique for age and season of death estimation in mammals for wildlife management purposes" (Hillson 2005:245).

The discovery that there are yearly cycles of cementum deposition in nonhuman mammals has suggested that the same might be true of humans. In applying this technique to humans, the number of paired light–dark bands is counted and added to an estimated age for the tooth's eruption, which is assumed to be the time at which the first layer of secondary cementum is deposited. Thus, inherent in this method is a level of uncertainty associated with applying an average eruption age to the eruption age of a particular individual's tooth. A theoretical concern with this technique that it is not clear that cementum layers actually represent yearly growth cycles in humans, as they do in other mammals.

Stott and coworkers (1982) were the first to apply these techniques to humans. Adding ages of eruption to counts of cementum layers of the teeth removed from three human cadavers, these researchers obtained age-at-death estimates that were close to actual ages at death. Such promising results were not obtained by Miller and others (1988) in their larger study of 100 extracted teeth, titled "Failure of Use of Cemental Annulations in Teeth to Determine the Age of Humans." More recently, Wittwer-Backofen and colleagues (2004), using a sample size of 363 extracted teeth, obtained highly accurate age estimations. However, because only images suitable for counting cementum layers were used to test the method, the high accuracy reported in this study (±2.5 years) was probably artificially elevated. In a subsequent study Wittwer-Backofen and others (2008) assessed the utility of this method in teeth from an archaeological sample. In this study, high interobserver variability in counting cementum layers was found along with little consistency in age estimates.

The results of accuracy tests of the cementum layering method are therefore mixed. Besides the issues already mentioned, the use of estimates for age at eruption and the question of whether cementum layers in humans are really produced in yearly cycles, there are other problems that probably contribute to these variable results. First, interobserver reliability is poor (Huffman, 2008; Roksandic et al., 2009; Witter-Backofen et al., 2008). Second, diagenic changes can make cementum annulations difficult to see (Roksandic et al., 2009). Third, cementum is not deposited evenly over the root. Related to this fact, Huffman (2010) found that depending on the region of the root where cementum layers are counted, multiple ages can be calculated. Finally, hypercementosis can artificially inflate age estimates (Jackes, 2009). At present then, age-at-death estimates based on cementum layers in humans are not secure. Future work is needed to determine the periodicity of cementum layers in humans as well as to address the numerous methodological issues currently associated with this technique.

In addition to cementum layers, there is a repeating surface structure in roots, completely unrelated to cementum layers, which may prove useful in age estimation. These structures on the surface of the cementum are called *periradicular bands* (Figure 4.8), and they superficially appear to be continuations along the root of the perikymata in the crown. However, periradicular bands have not been clearly shown to be external manifestations of Andresen lines in the way that perikymata have been demonstrated to be external manifestations of striae of Retzius in enamel. Even so, Smith and coworkers (2007) suggest that periradicular bands do have the same periodicity as perikymata, based on their counts of an equivalent number of Andresen lines and periradicular bands between two reference points in a root.

On the other hand, Dean and Smith (2009) counted the number of perikymata and the number of periradicular bands between two hypoplastic events recorded, respectively, in the crown and root of two different teeth of WT 15000, the Narikotome boy. Although the hypoplastic grooves represent the same two events in both the crown and root, these researchers counted 15 perikymata between the hypoplastic grooves in the crown but only 10 periradicular bands between the hypoplastic grooves in the root. The different counts suggest that either perikymata and periradicular bands may not be marking equivalent intervals of time, or if they are, that periradicular bands are less consistently expressed on the surface of cementum than perikymata are expressed on the surface of enamel.

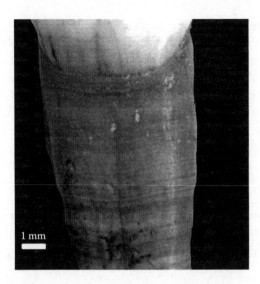

**Figure 4.8** Dark bands encircling tooth root are periradicular bands in a Neanderthal tooth. (Photo by Debbie Guatelli-Steinberg, modified from Guatelli-Steinberg D [2009] Evol Anthropol 18:9–20.)

Moreover, in his analysis of periradicular bands in OH 16 (Homo habilis), Dean notes that there is little modern material in which periradicular bands are as clearly visible as they are in this fossil specimen. Thus, at present, additional work needs to be done to determine whether periradicular bands in the root can be used to evaluate age at death in the way that perikymata in the crown can be and to what extent periradicular bands can be observed on modern human tooth roots.

## 4.8   Conclusions

The fact that dental hard tissues contain within them their own growth record makes them as potentially useful in forensic contexts as they have proven to be in the field of paleoanthropology. Their most obvious use lies in assessing age at death. For individuals whose crowns had not completely formed at the time of death, counts of enamel growth increments, either in histological sections or at the enamel surface, yield estimates that are very close to actual ages at death (Antoine et al., 1999; Stringer et al., 1990). For individuals who died before root growth was completed, it is possible to use incremental markings in dentine to determine the amount of time the existing portion of the root took to form. Root formation time can be added to the age at which crown completion occurred to obtain an age-at-death estimate. Whether periradicular bands in the cementum of the root can also be used in this way requires further analysis.

For individuals whose roots have completely formed, the most accurate aging method to date appears to be that of Vasiliadis et al. (1983a, 1983b), based on original work by Bang and Ramm (1970), which relies on measuring the volume of sclerotic or transparent dentine in the root. The use of cementum layers in aging has received much attention, especially in recent literature, but there are a number of methodological as well as theoretical issues currently associated with this method.

Many years ago, Gustafson (1950) proposed a model that employed several age-related changes in teeth (including those of the dental hard tissues) as variables in regression equations to predict age at death. These variables were dental attrition, periodontosis (gingival recession), secondary dentine, cementum apposition, root resorption, and root dentine sclerosis. His results suggested that the method was highly predictive of actual age (±3.63 years). However, additional work demonstrated that there were statistical problems with Gustafson's study and its degree of error was revised to ±7.03 years (Maples and Rice, 1979). Gustafson's method therefore performs less well than that of Vasiliadis and colleagues (1983a, 1983b) or Bang and Ramm (1970). Thus, for individuals whose roots have completed formation, the most accurate histological dental aging technique developed thus far relies on the measurement of root dentine sclerosis.

The use of the neonatal line and of accentuated striae in forensic contexts is an exciting area. While the absence of the neonatal line in an infant's dental remains suggest that he or she was either stillborn or lived for only a very short time after death, there may be other potential uses involving measurement of neonatal line thickness. Based on the work of Eli and coworkers, (1989), it would be interesting to know if ranges of neonatal line thickness associated with different kinds of birth might be reliably used to determine if dental remains belonged to an infant who had been born by Caesarean section. Given that accentuated striae form in response to physiological stress, it should be possible to determine the timing of growth disruptions in the dental remains of children who have died from neglect or abuse. It is interesting that Teivens and colleagues (1996) found few accentuated striae in the teeth of infants who had died of SIDS. Thus, there is clearly room for innovative uses of dental histology in forensic contexts.

## Acknowledgments

We thank Donald J. Reid for his comments on the manuscript as well as for the use of several images. We also thank Rebecca Ferrell for granting them permission to include her images in this chapter. Finally, we express our gratitude to Christian Crowder and Sam Stout for the invitation to contribute to this volume.

## References

Antoine D, Dean C, Hillson S (1999) The periodicity of incremental structures in dental enamel based on the developing dentition of post-Medieval known-age children. In: Mayhall JT, Heikinnen T (eds) Dental Morphology. Oulu University Press, Oulu.

Arnold WH, Konopka S, Gaengler P (2001) Qualitative and quantitative assessment of intratubular dentine formation in human natural carious lesions. Calcif Tissue Int 69:268–273.

Bang G, Ramm E (1970) Determination of age in humans from root dentine transparency. Acta Odontol Scand 28:3–35.

Boyde A (1963) Estimation of age at death of young human skeletal remains from incremental lines in dental enamel. London: Third International Meeting in Forensic Immunology, Medicine, Pathology, and Toxicology: Plenary Session 11A.

Boyde A (1979) Carbonate concentration, crystal centres, core dissolution, caries, cross striations, circadian rhythms, and compositional contrast in the SEM. J Dent Res (special issue) 58:981–983.

Boyde A (1989) Enamel. In: Berkovitz BKB, Boyde A, Frank RM, Höhling HJ, Moxham BJ, Nalbandian J, Tonge CH (eds) Teeth: Handbook of Microscopic Anatomy. Springer, New York.

Boyde A (1990) Developmental interpretations of dental microstructure. In: DeRousseaus CJ (ed) Primate Life History and Evolution: Monographs in Primatology, 14th vol. Wiley-Liss, New York.

Bromage T G (1991) Enamel incremental periodicity in the pig-tailed macaque: a polychrome fluorescent labeling study of dental hard tissues. Am J Phys Anthropol, 86:205–214.

Bromage T G, Dean MC (1985) Re-evaluation of age at death of immature fossil hominids. Nature 317:525–527.

Dean MC (1987) Growth layers and incremental markings in hard tissues; a review of the literature and some preliminary observations about enamel structure in *Paranthropus boisei.* J Hum Evol 16:157–172.

Dean MC (1998) A comparative study of cross striation spacing in cuspal enamel and of four methods of estimating the time taken to grow molar cuspal enamel in *Pan*, *Pongo* and *Homo.* J Hum Evol 35:449–462.

Dean MC (2000) Incremental markings in enamel and dentine: what they can tell us about the way teeth grow. In: Teaford M, Meredith MS, Ferguson M (eds) Development, Function, and Evolution of Teeth. Cambridge University Press, Cambridge.

Dean MC (2006) Tooth microstructure tracks the pace of human life-history evolution. Proc R Soc B 273:2799–2808.

Dean MC, Beynon AD (1991) Histological reconstruction of crown formation times and initial root formation times in a modern human child. Am J Phys Anthropol 86:215–228.

Dean MC, Reid DJ (2001) Anterior tooth formation in Australopithecus and Paranthropus. In: Brook A (ed) Dental Morphology. Sheffield Academic Press, Sheffield.

Dean MC, Scandrett AE (1996) The relation between long-period incremental markings in dentine and daily cross-striations in enamel in human teeth. Arch Oral Biol 41:233–241.

Dean MC, Smith BH (2009) Growth and development of the Nariokotome youth, KNM-WT 15000. In: Grine FE, Fleagle JG, Leaky RE (eds) Vertebrate Paleobiology and Paleoanthropology Series: The First Humans—Origin and Early Evolution of the Genus *Homo*, 4th part. Springer, Netherlands.

Dean MC, Vesey P (2008) Preliminary observations on increasing root length during the eruptive phase of tooth development in modern humans and great apes. J Hum Evol 54:258–271.

Demirjian A, Godstein H, Tanner JM (1973) A new system of dental age assessment. Hum Biol 45:211–227.

Eli I, Sarnat H, Talmi E (1989) Effects of the birth process on the neonatal line in the primary tooth enamel. Pediatr Dent 11:220–223.

Fitzgerald CM (1998) Do enamel microstructures have regular time dependency? Conclusions from the literature and a large scale study. J Hum Evol 35:371–386.

Goodman AH, Rose JC (1990) Assessment of systemic physiological perturbations from dental enamel hypoplasias and associated histological structures. Yearb Phys Anthropol 33:59–110.

Guatelli-Steinberg D (2008) Using perikymata to estimate the duration of growth disruptions in fossil hominin teeth. In: Irish J, Nelson G (eds) Dental Anthropology: Applications and Methods. Cambridge University Press, Cambridge.

Guatelli-Steinberg D (2009) Recent studies of dental development in Neandertals: implications for Neanderthal life histories. Evol Anthropol 18:9–20.

Guatelli-Steinberg, D (2010) Growing planes: incremental growth in the teeth of human ancestors. In: Larsen CS (ed) A Companion to Biological Anthropology. Wiley-Blackwell, Malden, MA.

Gustafson G (1950) Age determinations on teeth. J Am Dent Ass 41:45–54.

Hillson S (1996) Dental Anthropology. Cambridge University Press, Cambridge.

Hillson S (2005) Teeth. Cambridge University Press, Cambridge.

Huffman M (2010) Analysis of cementum layers in archaeological material. Dent Anthropol 23:67–73.

Jackes M (2009) Teeth and the past in Portugal and the Mesolithic-Neolithic transition. In: Koppe T, Smith BH, Meyer G, Brook A, Alt KW (eds) Frontiers of Oral Biology: Comparative Dental Morphology. 14th International Symposium on Dental Morphology, 13th vol.

Macchiarelli R, Bondioli L, Debéhath A, Mazurier A, Tournepiche J-F, Birch W, Dean, C (2006) How Neandertal molar teeth grew. Nature 444:748–751.

Macho GA, Reid DJ, Leakey MG, Jablonski H, Beynon AD (1996) Climatic effects on dental development of Theropithecus oswaldi from Koobi Fora and Olorgesailie. J Hum Evol 30:57–70.

Maples WR, Rice PM (1979) Some difficulties in the Gustafson dental age estimations. J Forensic Sci 24:168–172.

Miller CS, Dove SB, Cottone JA (1988) Failure of use of cemental annulations in teeth to determine the age of humans. J Forensic Sci 33:137–143.

Mitchell B (1963) Determination of age in Scottish red deer from growth layers in dental cementum. Nature 198:350–351.

Mitchell B (1967) Growth layers in dental cementum for determining the age of red deer (Cervus elaphus). J Anim Ecol 36:279–293.

Nanci A (2007) Ten Cate's Oral Histology, 7th ed. Elsevier Science, Amsterdam.

Nóren JG (1984) Microscopic study of enamel defects in deciduous teeth of infants of diabetic mothers. Acta Odontol Scand 42:153–156.

Reid DJ, Dean MC (2006) Variation in modern human enamel formation times. J Hum Evol 50:329–346.

Reid DJ, Beynon AD, Ramirez-Rozzi FV (1998) Histological reconstruction of dental development in four individuals from a medieval site in Picardie, France. J Hum Evol 35:463–477.

Roksandic M, Vlak D, Schillaci MA, Voicu D (July 2009) Technical Note: Applicability of tooth cementum annulation to an archaeological population. Am J Phys Anthropol (early view).

Rose JC, Armelagos GJ, Lallo JW (1978) Histological enamel indicator of childhood stress in prehistoric skeletal samples. Am J Phys Anthropol 49:511–516.

Skinner M, Anderson GS (1991) Individualization and enamel histology: a case report in forensic anthropology. J For Sci 36:939–948.

Smith P, Avishai G (2005) The use of dental criteria for estimating postnatal survival in skeletal remains of infants. J Arc Sci 32:83–89.

Smith TM, Toussaint M, Reid DJ, Olejniczak AJ, and Hublin JJ (2007) Rapid dental development in a Middle Paleolithic Belgian Neanderthal. Proc Natl Acad Sci 104:20220–20225.

Stott GG, Sis RF, Levy BM (1982) Cementum annulations as an age criterion in forensic dentistry. J Dent Res 61:814–817.

Stringer CB, Dean MC, Martin RD (1990) A comparative study of cranial and dental development within a recent British sample and among Neandertals. In: De Rousseau CJ (ed) Primate life history and evolution. Wiley-Liss, New York.

Teivens A, Mörnstad H, Norén JG (1996) Enamel incremental lines as recorders for disease in infancy and their relation to the diagnosis of SIDS. For Sci Intl 81:175–183.

Ten Cate AR (1994) Oral Histology: Development, Structure, and Function, 4th ed. Mosby, St. Louis.

Vasiliadis L, Darling AE, Levers BGH (1983a) The amount and distribution of sclerotic human root dentine. Arch Oral Biol 28:645–649.

Vasiliadis L, Darling AE, Levers BGH (1983b) The histology of sclerotic human root dentine. Arch Oral Biol 28:693–700.

Whittaker DK, Richards D (1978) Scanning electron microscopy of the neonatal line in human enamel. Archs Oral Biol 23:45–50.

Wittwer-Backofen U, Gampe J, Vaupel JW (2004) Tooth cementum annulation for age estimation: results from a large known-age validation study. Am J Phys Anthropol 123:119–129.

Wittwer-Backofen U, Buckberry J, Czarnetzki A, Doppler S, Grupe G, Hota G, Kemkes A, Larsen CS, Prince D, Wahl JJ, Fabig A, Weise S (2008) Basics in paleodemography: a comparison of age indicators applied to the early medieval skeletal sample of Lauchheim. Am J Phys Anthropol 137:384–396.

# Differentiating Human from Nonhuman Bone Microstructure

# 5

DAWN M. MULHERN
DOUGLAS H. UBELAKER

## Contents

## 5.1 Introduction

How and why does human bone differ from the bone of other animals on a microstructural level? Humans have differences in growth patterns, nutritional requirements, and mechanical strain compared to other animals, and this is reflected in bone microstructure. Identifying the qualitative and quantitative similarities and differences between human and nonhuman bone on a microscopic level is potentially important for studies in growth and development, evolution, and biomechanics, but also has practical applications in forensic anthropology for identifying the origin of bone that has undergone taphonomic alterations causing difficulties with gross analysis (e.g., fragmentation, burning, cortical erosion, etc.). In a medicolegal investigation, a quick identification of bone as nonhuman (and not forensically significant) ultimately saves time and resources. A large body of literature addresses these questions and there have been recent attempts to compile the available data for more practical application (Hillier and Bell 2007).

The purpose of this chapter is to discuss the microscopic differences between human bone and the bone of other mammals, since this is the most likely area for confusion regarding species identification. The chapter begins with a review of the basic features of mammalian bone microstructure, followed by a discussion of general microscopic differences in mammalian bone, including specific qualitative and quantitative differences in human and nonhuman bone microstructure. The chapter concludes with several recent studies that use discriminant function analysis to distinguish human and nonhuman bone.

## 5.2   Basic Bone Microstructure

Foote (1916) observed that differences in bone tissue among taxa are due to differences in the relative amounts of three bone types: lamellar, laminar, and Haversian. This early study implicated that pattern identification was particularly important for distinguishing human and nonhuman bone. Over the years, great strides have been made in understanding the biological processes that govern bone development and organization at the histological level. In more recent years, the use of image software and other technology has allowed more precise investigation of microscopic structures and the most recent data suggest that detectable variability may be present among species in bone organization as well as the size and shape of individual structures (Cattaneo et al. 1999; Martiniaková et al. 2006). Therefore, an approach to bone differentiation among species that combines qualitative and quantitative methods is desirable.

To differentiate bone type and organization, it is important to clearly define the basic bone microstructures. Within the literature, certain latitude exists in describing bone microstructure resulting in conflicting or conflated terms. Bone is classified according to factors such as vascular arrangement, the type of bone tissue, and the overall organization. Mammals may exhibit woven bone, lamellar bone, or a combination of woven and lamellar bone, known as fibrolamellar bone. Woven bone, which is laid down quickly and haphazardly at a rate of at least 4 μm per day, is a type of primary bone found in fetal bone, during fracture repair, as well as in some pathological conditions, such as neoplasms and infections (Ortner 2003).

Lamellar bone consists of thin layers of lamellae successively laid down. In each lamella, the closely packed collagen fibers are mutually parallel, but the direction changes from one lamella to the next. Lamellar bone has a more organized structure and is laid down more slowly than woven bone, at a rate of less than 1 μm per day. Lamellar bone includes primary bone, which is laid down de novo on an existing bone surface, such as circumferential lamellar or laminar bone, as well as secondary bone, which replaces existing bone. Haversian systems, or secondary osteons, are the product of bone remodeling by osteoclasts and osteoblasts, where a cylindrical cavity is excavated and then filled in with concentric lamellae, leaving a vascular (Haversian) canal in the center. With few exceptions, most vertebrates other than birds and mammals do not show much Haversian remodeling (Currey 2002). The amount of remodeling that takes place is related to bone size, as small birds and mammals exhibit little or no secondary remodeling, but large birds (like ostriches) and larger mammals (perissodactyls, artiodactyls, carnivores, and primates) experience moderate to extensive remodeling. In artiodactyls, Haversian bone is often concentrated in areas corresponding to muscle insertions (Currey 2002; Skedros 2003).

Fibrolamellar bone is primary bone that is characterized by alternating sheets of lamellar and woven bone. Because of its organization, fibrolamellar bone offers much more surface area compared to primary or secondary bone upon which bone can be formed. The type of fibrolamellar bone present may be related to demands of growth rate and mechanical strain. For example, bone with radially oriented vascular cavities may achieve the fastest growth due to more efficient, continuous production of bone struts by the periosteum, but at the cost of reduced mechanical resistance (de Margerie et al. 2004). Fibrolamellar bone can be laid down more quickly than lamellar bone because it is made of woven bone scaffolding and is therefore found in mammals with bones that grow quickly in diameter such as dinosaurs; birds; and fast-growing mammals, such as artiodactyls, but mechanically it is probably inferior to lamellar bone (Currey 2002).

The primary vascular canals of fibrolamellar bone may be further described by their orientation (Enlow and Brown 1956), also referred to as *laminarity* (Skedros and Hunt 2004). Laminarity is the relative proportion of the vascular area represented by circularly orientated primary vascular canals. The terms *plexiform bone* or *laminar bone* are commonly substituted for *fibrolamellar bone* but should perhaps be used only to describe certain forms of fibrolamellar bone. For example, laminar fibrolamellar bone is characterized by lamellae arranged in circumferential layers (de Margerie et al. 2004 after de Riqlès 1975). This type of bone is found in ectotherms that periodically cease and resume growth due to metabolic changes, such as during hibernation (Currey 2002). The bricklike structure commonly identified as plexiform bone occurs when the vascular plexuses contained within lamellar bone is sandwiched by nonlamellar bone (Martin and Burr 1989). This is the type of structure commonly associated with nonhuman mammals.

## 5.3   The Human Growth Pattern

In fetal and neonate humans, fibrolamellar bone is laid down first, but is then replaced by primary and secondary lamellar bone through the process of modeling and remodeling (see chapters by Stout and Crowder, Maggiano, and Streeter in this volume). Although remodeling in some anatomical areas (e.g., endosteal and trabecular surfaces) may involve formation of additional lamellar bone, most remodeling, especially with the bone cortex, involves formation of Haversian bone. During times of rapid development in humans (infancy, early childhood, and during the adolescent growth spurt), fibrolamellar bone with a regular, geometric structure may be present, but it does not exhibit the bricklike plexiform structure seen in nonhuman bone (Pfeiffer 1996).

In a study of 150 human fetal tibiae ranging from the 6th to the 9th intrauterine month, Baltadjiev (1995) found that secondary remodeling was present but rare. Burton et al. (1989) reported the presence of remodeling in fetal and neonatal bone. These researchers found secondary bone remodeling in the long bones and ribs as early as the 24th week. Out of four fetal skeletons, three exhibited secondary osteons, including one individual with a single secondary osteon in the radius, one individual with 26 secondary osteons (13 in the ulna, 3 in the radius, 5 in the tibia, and 5 in the seventh rib), and one individual with 58 secondary osteons (12 in the humerus, 5 in the ulna, 20 in the radius, 4 in the femur, 10 in the fibula, 6 in the 6th rib, and 1 in the tenth rib). A neonate exhibited 179 secondary osteons (11 in the humerus, 1 in the ulna, 6 in the radius, 14 in the femur, 13 in the tibia, 8 in the fibula, 10 in the clavicle, and 116 distributed among the first through fifth and seventh through eleventh ribs), with many more particularly in the ribs compared to the fetal specimens.

After initial rapid growth during the fetal period, circumferential lamellae are laid down more slowly around the outside of a bone shaft (Kerley 1965). In a study of 126 bone sections including femora, tibiae, and fibulae, Kerley (1965) found that the percentage of circumferential lamellar bone and number of primary canals (including primary osteons) were both high during childhood but decreased with age. Conversely, the number of secondary osteons was low during childhood and increased with age. Rauch and colleagues (2007) observed microscopic changes in the iliac crest in 56 individuals between 1.5 and 22.9 years and found that while the balance between bone formation and resorption was constant, the activation frequency of remodeling was higher in younger children. Also, secondary osteon and Haversian canal dimensions and number per unit area did not change with age. Although age-related changes in secondary osteon density have been well documented in adulthood (Currey 1964; Kerley 1965; Singh and Gunberg 1970, Frost 1987a, 1987b), this pattern may not be apparent in subadult bone due to the removal of some secondary bone during growth and modeling. In a study of 326 ribs, Pirok and colleagues (1966) found an overall decrease in the bone appositional rate from 10 through 70-plus years, as well as a steep decrease in the creation of new secondary osteons from about 10 years through the early 30s, followed by a slight increase through the mid-70s.

Overall, the human pattern in fetal bone is fibrolamellar, followed by more formation of circumferential lamellae and primary lamellar bone (including primary osteons) during childhood (Cuijpers 2009). Bone remodeling apparently begins in the fetal skeleton, although evidence of some secondary bone will be removed during childhood through cortical drift. During adulthood, secondary osteons continue to accumulate so that in older adults, entire cortices may be packed with intact and fragmentary secondary osteons.

## 5.4   Qualitative Differences in Mammalian Bone

Enlow and Brown (1958) and Foote (1916) describe qualitative differences in bone histology among mammals. In general, these descriptions indicate that Infraclass Metatheria (marsupials) and orders Monotremata, Insectivora, Chiroptera, Edentata, and Rodentia are the least like human bone in that they generally lack secondary Haversian bone. Specifically, monotremes and marsupials have primary vascular tissue with absent or undifferentiated Haversian bone. Singh and colleagues (1974) reported primary longitudinal canals combined with areas of nonvascular bone in the inner and outer layers of the compacta in the opossum. Insectivores and bats are unique among mammals in having poorly developed primary tissue or nonvascular tissue. Edentates are characterized by mostly primary reticular bone with some areas of longitudinal vessels. Rodent bone is generally either reticular or primary vascular, but limited secondary Haversian tissue may be present. Martiniaková and colleagues (2006) found only nonvascular bone tissue in the femoral diaphysis of 15 rats. Singh and colleagues (1974) observed mostly primary longitudinal canals in the long bones of 10 rats, but occasional secondary osteons were present.

The mammalian orders Cetacea, Sirenia, Proboscidae, Xenarthra, Lagomorpha, Perissodactyla, Artiodactyla, Carnivora, and Primates all exhibit Haversian bone, although the extent of the Haversian tissue and size of structures varies among taxa. More detailed data for orders Lagomorpha, Perissodactyla, Artiodactyla, Carnivora, and Primates can be found in the available literature, so the microscopic features of these taxa are discussed in this chapter.

### 5.4.1  Order Lagomorpha

Order Lagomorpha, may exhibit Haversian bone, particularly in the ribs and skull (Enlow and Brown 1958). Martiniaková and colleagues (2006) observed a sample of 15 rabbit femora and found that the dominant feature was primary vascular longitudinal bone. The rabbits lacked plexiform bone but exhibited irregular or dense Haversian bone in the middle portion of the compacta. The cortical thickness of rabbit bone, along with the extensive presence of primary vascular longitudinal bone would likely exclude adult human bone in many cases, but perhaps not human subadult bone. The presence of secondary osteons in rabbits adds further uncertainty when attempting to distinguish by pattern only, but secondary osteons and Haversian canals in rabbits are much smaller than those found in humans, as will be discussed in the next section.

### 5.4.2  Order Perissodactyla

Enlow and Brown (1958) indicate that the basic pattern in horses (order Perissodactyla) is reticular, sometimes approaching a plexiform pattern. Haversian bone ranges from isolated secondary osteons to dense areas of Haversian bone.

Foote (1916) provided descriptions and illustrations of a horse femur and the femora of several mules. The horse femur exhibited rings of Haversian systems alternating with bands of lamellar bone. The mules have some Haversian bone, particularly in the posterior aspects of the cross sections, but most of the bone is fibrolamellar.

Stover and colleagues (1992) studied the microscopic structure of the dorsal cortex of the third metacarpal in 30 thoroughbred horses and found that horses younger than 6 months of age had rows of primary osteons, radially oriented vascular canals connected to some of the Haversian canals, and no remodeling of primary bone. From 1 to 2 years, resorption spaces and incompletely filled secondary osteons were common. Horses older than 3 years had numerous secondary osteons and fewer resorption spaces and forming osteons. Horses older than 5 years exhibited large, irregular resorption spaces. Mori and colleagues (2003) found a similar pattern in the tibiae of young foals, with a fibrolamellar bone structure characterized by rows of primary osteons. Georgia and Albu (1988) found that Haversian canal density increased in the endosteal layer of the femoral cortex in young horses compared to the middle and periosteal layers of bone.

While it is conceivable that a fragment of horse bone could be comprised entirely of Haversian bone, these studies indicate that horse bone is likely to exhibit a fibrolamellar structure, characterized by a reticular or plexiform pattern, or osteon banding, thereby showing clear differences from human bone (Cuijpers 2006).

### 5.4.3  Order Artiodactyla

The general pattern of bone microstructure found in artiodactyls is that of plexiform bone in the outer layers of the compacta (isolated secondary osteons may be found in older areas) and dense Haversian bone in the middle and endosteal layers (Enlow and Brown 1958; Martiniaková et al. 2006). As with horses, it is possible that a bone fragment could be comprised entirely of Haversian bone (particularly rib) but commonly will exhibit a fibrolamellar pattern as well as Haversian bone. In many cases, it should be possible to differentiate artiodactyl bone from human bone based on pattern.

Enlow and Brown (1958) describe cow ribs that exhibit dense Haversian bone throughout the cortex. Mori and colleagues (2005) studied the tibial microstructure of four calves and found that the newborn calf exhibited exclusively fibrolamellar bone structure. Calves 6 months and 1 year had scattered secondary osteons, but the bone mostly retained a plexiform structure. Martiniaková and colleagues (2006) found that 15 cow femora were characterized by primary vascular plexiform bone with some dense Haversian tissue in the middle portions of the compacta. An important distinguishing feature of the cow bone in this study (compared to rabbits, sheep, pigs, and humans) was the presence of nonvascular bone tissue along the anterior and posterior endosteal borders as well as the lateral periosteal border.

Enlow and Brown (1958) found that a sheep's rib showed a basically plexiform structure with limited secondary bone replacement. Mori and colleagues (2005) found that the tibia of two sheep 6 months old and younger did not have any secondary osteons, but a 1-year-old sheep showed some secondary osteon development in the middle layers of the cortex. In a study that included 15 sheep femora, Martiniaková et al. (2006) found that a distinguishing feature (compared to rabbits, cows, pigs, and humans) was the presence of "irregular" Haversian bone, characterized by scattered, isolated, and few Haversian systems, particularly along the anteriolateral periosteal border. Foote (1916) illustrates a sheep femur that shows mostly plexiform structure, but also a crescent of osteonal bone along the anterior, lateral, and posterior aspects of the inner compacta. Mulhern and Ubelaker (2001) observed a basically plexiform structure in nine subadult sheep. One of these sheep also exhibited linear bands of primary osteons in the endosteal layer of the cortex. Rajtová and colleagues (1995) observed the humerus, radius, metacarpus, femur, tibia, and metatarsus of ten 3-year-old sheep and found dense Haversian bone in the bones of the forelimb as well as the metatarsus. The shape of the osteons ranged from round to oval to irregular in all of these bones.

Enlow and Brown (1958) indicate that a goat rib is characterized by dense Haversian bone. Rajtová et al. (1995) observed the humerus, radius, metacarpus, femur, tibia and metatarsus of ten 3- to 4-year-old goats and reported dense Haversian bone in the distal limb elements (metacarpus and metatarsus). The shape of the secondary osteons was variously described as round, oval, irregularly round and irregular.

Enlow and Brown (1958) found dense Haversian bone throughout the rib cortex of a peccary, but plexiform structure in the rib of a domestic hog. Foote (1916) illustrated the femora of a domestic pig and a wild boar, both with a similar microstructural pattern, including a mostly plexiform structure, but with two clusters of secondary osteons in the lateroposterior and medioposterior aspects of the bone that extend across the entire cortex and separated by a section of plexiform bone. Mori and colleagues (2005) found more secondary osteons throughout the cortex of a 6-month-old pig compared to young calves and sheep, but relatively few secondary osteons in the outer cortex. Martiniaková and colleagues (2006) found that the femora of 15 pigs had mostly plexiform bone, with some dense Haversian tissue in the middle of the compacta. They found that the pig was different from rabbits, sheep, cows, and humans in that it had numerous resorption spaces between secondary osteons, particularly in the anteriomedial cortex. Mulhern and Ubelaker (2001) observed a basically plexiform structure in the femora of six miniature swine. Four swine also exhibited linear bands of mostly primary osteons in the endosteal layer of the cortex. The miniature swine exhibited resorption spaces and occasional secondary osteons within the linear bands of primary osteons, suggesting that secondary bone formation may initially follow the primary osteon bands.

Based on samples of five to six bones for each species, Morris (2007) reported that plexiform bone is universally found in deer and pig femora and is commonly found in deer and pig humeri. Based on Morris's sample, it is uncommonly found in deer ribs and not found at all in pig ribs. In the same sample, she also found the presence of osteon banding in two-thirds of the deer femora, one-third of the deer humeri, and half of the pig femora; it was absent in pig humeri and ribs.

Skedros and colleagues (2003) observed the humerus, radius, principle metacarpal, medial proximal phalanx, and left sixth rib from 11 mule deer. The basic pattern of the metacarpal, radius and humerus is plexiform in structure. Secondary osteons were distributed over 30% or less of the mid-diaphyseal cortices. Foote (1916) described and illustrated the femoral microstructure of a mule deer as well as a reindeer, which are almost entirely made up of plexiform bone, with a few Haversian systems in the posterior aspect of the bone. An elk femur also exhibits mostly plexiform bone, but this is occasionally interrupted by round or oval secondary osteons throughout the cortex.

### 5.4.4 Order Carnivora

Carnivores commonly exhibit dense Haversian bone, with a general pattern in long bones of primary bone (either plexiform or primary osteons arranged in bands) toward the outer layers of the compacta and more dense Haversian bone toward the endosteal layers. However, bones can also have secondary replacement throughout the cortex, potentially making them impossible to distinguish from human bone by pattern alone. Compared to perissodactyls and artiodactyls, carnivore bones are more likely to be confused with human bone based on pattern.

The mandibles of the bear, raccoon, mink, badger, dog, wolf, cat, and fox show Haversian bone replacement, but still retain a reticular or radial pattern. Dog and bear ribs are almost completely Haversian, whereas the long bones of the bear and dog exhibit plexiform structure in the outer layers, with scattered secondary osteons, but the inner layers of the compacta are characterized by dense Haversian bone (Enlow and Brown 1958).

In some contrast to this, Foote (1916) illustrated the femur of one bear, which is mostly plexiform, with only a small cluster of secondary osteons in the posterior cortex. The eight dog femora illustrated by Foote vary somewhat, with some exhibiting a significant amount of plexiform bone, but all with at least some Haversian development that is particularly concentrated in the posterior cortex (three of the dog bones have osteons around the entire cortex, concentrated in the middle part of the compacta). A gray fox showed a similar pattern to the dogs, with Haversian bone in the middle part of the cortex, surrounded by a plexiform structure.

Diaz and Rajtová (1975) reported that a dog tibia exhibited few primary osteons but many densely packed secondary osteons with a regular, round shape throughout the cortex. Georgia and Albu (1988) describe a pattern of longitudinal canals arranged in parallel rows in the periosteal layers of five young dog diaphyses, with greater density of canals toward the endosteal layers of the compacta.

Morris (2007) found plexiform bone in four out of six dog femora, but plexiform bone was absent in six dog humeri and ribs. Osteon banding was absent in all femora, humeri, and ribs in this study.

The ribs and long bones of the cat exhibit inner and outer circumferential lamellae, with Haversian bone replacement particularly in the middle of the compacta (Enlow and Brown 1958). This is consistent with an illustration of a cat femur as well as a lynx femur by Foote (1916). A mountain lion femur shows secondary osteon replacement throughout most of the cortex, with circumferential lamellae along parts of the periosteal and endosteal edges (Foote 1916). Diaz and Rajtová (1975) found that the domesticated cat had rows of primary osteons in the outer layers, occasionally interrupted by large Haversian systems; the rest of the cortex was made up of large, irregularly shaped secondary osteons. Like the domestic cat, the wildcat also exhibited secondary osteons throughout much of the cortex, but in contrast, only had isolated primary osteons in the outer layers and the shape of the secondary osteons was generally round. An illustration of a wildcat femur by Foote (1916) showed a crescent of secondary osteons in the middle of the anterior, medial, and posterior cortex, with primary osteons throughout the rest of the cortex.

The long bones of the skunk also exhibit numerous secondary osteons in the middle layers of the compacta, with primary canals in the outer layers. The epiphyses of the skunk also have Haversian bone replacement of primary tissues, but a reticular or radial pattern is present (Enlow and Brown 1958). A skunk femur illustrated by Foote (1916) shows scattered, irregularly shaped Haversian systems. Longitudinal primary canals and no secondary replacement characterize the mongoose femur.

According to Enlow and Brown (1958), the long bones of the mink have a reticular pattern and the rib exhibits scattered primary longitudinal canals and scattered secondary osteons. A mink femur illustrated by Foote (1916) shows a crescent of secondary osteons in the outer layers of the compacta extending posteriorly from the anteriomedial to the anteriolateral aspect of the bone; the rest of the bone exhibits a lamellar structure. Diaz and Rajtová (1975) described scattered primary osteons in the outer layers of the mink femoral compacta and secondary osteons with irregular sizes and shapes in the endosteal layers.

Diaz and Rajtová (1975) indicate that the martin has primary osteons in the outer layers, including rows in the lateral diaphysis and scattered osteons in the medial diaphysis. Secondary osteons of variable size are present, particularly in the medial aspect.

Hidaka and colleagues (1998) observed the humeri, radii, femora, and tibiae of 20 adult raccoon dogs and found secondary osteons that were uniformly round in shape in all bones.

Hidaka and colleagues (1998) described the microstructure of the humeri, radii, femora, and tibiae of 11 adult badgers, which showed elliptic secondary osteons. The femur of a badger illustrated by Foote (1916) shows mostly plexiform structure with a band of secondary osteons in the anterior and lateral aspects of the compacta.

An otter femur illustrated by Foote (1916) is almost completely filled with secondary osteons.

### 5.4.5  Order Primates

Enlow and Brown (1958) describe the overall pattern of primate bone as lamellated with longitudinal primary canals that may be replaced over time by Haversian systems. They also indicate that the density of primary canals determines the eventual density of secondary osteons. In some areas of the bone, multiple generations of secondary osteons may be present. In addition to humans, dense Haversian bone has been reported in rhesus monkeys (Przybeck 1985), spider monkeys (Foote 1916; Schaffler and Burr 1984), orangutans (Foote 1916), and chimpanzees (Schaffler and Burr 1984; Mulhern and Ubelaker 2009).

Foote (1916) described and illustrated the femoral microstructure of a ruffed lemur and ring-tailed lemur. The ruffed lemur exhibited primary osteons in the outer cortex, but also a ring of secondary osteons in the middle and inner cortex. The ring-tailed lemur showed a very unusual structure, with a "mesh" of bone along the anterior, medial, and posterior aspects of the periosteal border; a ring of secondary osteons in the inner cortex; and many irregular spaces throughout the cortex.

The golden galago and Demidoff's galago exhibit a combination of primary longitudinal bone, scattered secondary osteons, reticular, and nonvascular bone (Singh et al. 1974). Foote (1916) provides an illustration of a tamarin femur, which shows a ring of secondary osteonal bone between an outer an inner layer of circumferential lamellar bone. A spider monkey femur was characterized by Haversian bone throughout most of the cortex, with lamellar bone along the periosteal and endosteal borders (Foote 1916). This is consistent with a study by Schaffler and Burr (1984) that reported a high percentage of secondary osteonal bone in two spider monkeys and suspensory primates generally compared to arboreal and terrestrial quadrupeds.

The long bones of the spot-nosed monkey and baboon exhibited mostly primary longitudinal canals and a few secondary osteons (Singh et al. 1974). This observation is consistent with the illustration provided by Foote (1916) of a baboon as well as a mandrill.

Like the old world monkeys, the long bones of the white-handed gibbon also showed mostly primary longitudinal canals and only a few secondary osteons (Singh et al. 1974). A gibbon femur illustrated by Foote (1916) shows lamellar bone with many canals in the outer and middle cortex, and a ring of Haversian bone in the inner cortex.

Illustrations of three great ape femora by Foote (1916) show some differences. In the orangutan, secondary osteonal bone is present throughout most of the cortex, with some lamellar bone along the periosteal and endosteal borders. The gorilla bone is more than half lamellar, with longitudinal canals and a ring of Haversian bone in the inner cortex (although in the posterior aspect, secondary osteons are present the entire width of the compacta). Like the gorilla femur, the chimpanzee femur is more than half lamellar with primary canals. A ring of secondary osteons fills the inner layers, particularly in the posterior and anteriolateral aspects of the bone.

When attempting to identify the origin of an unknown fragment of bone based upon qualitative histomorphology, the presence of plexiform bone (Figure 5.1), which can be found in perissodactyls, artiodactyls, and carnivores, is a reliable indicator of bone with a nonhuman origin. Osteon banding, or multiple, linear rows of primary or secondary osteons is more common in nonhuman bone than human bone. Although human bone may show a limited linear pattern involving a few secondary osteons, the presence of multiple rows with numerous, usually primary osteons (Figure 5.2a,b) is a good indicator of nonhuman bone (Mulhern and Ubelaker 2001). It should be noted that Pfeiffer (1996) identified linearly organized primary osteons in human subadult ribs that were associated with periods of rapid growth including infancy (four individuals between 0 and 2 years), mid-childhood (one 7-year-old), and adolescence (two 16-year old individuals), and suggested that this may represent woven bone that is transitioning to lamellar bone. If scattered or densely packed secondary osteons are present (Figure 5.3) and plexiform bone and osteon banding are absent, human bone cannot be ruled out based on pattern alone.

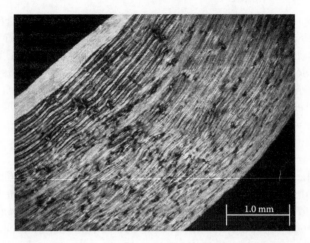

**Figure 5.1** Example of plexiform bone in a deer femoral cross-section at 40× magnification. (Photograph courtesy of Christian Crowder and Victoria Dominguez.)

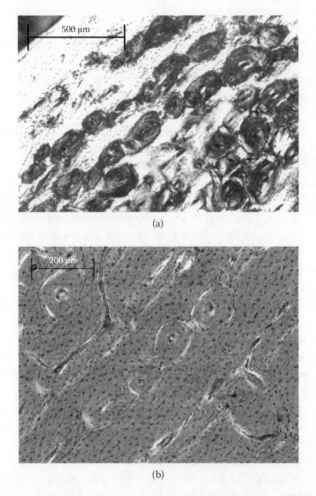

**Figure 5.2** (a) Example of secondary osteon banding in a dog femur at 100× magnification. (b) Example of secondary osteon banding in a pig femur at 200× magnification. (Photographs courtesy of Christian Crowder and Victoria Dominguez.)

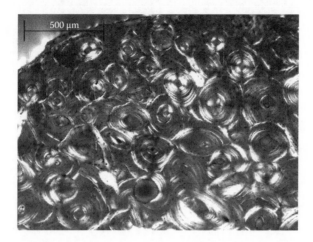

**Figure 5.3** Example of human Haversian bone at 100× magnification. (Photo courtesy of Christian Crowder.)

## 5.5 Quantitative Differences in Mammalian Bone

Quantitative variables include counts of structures, such as secondary osteon density, as well as size of structures, such as Haversian canal or secondary osteon diameter, perimeter, or area. Another promising area of research is secondary osteon shape, or circularity, with more regular, circular osteons reported in nonhuman bone compared to human bone (Tersigni 2008).

Quantitative differences between human and nonhuman bone are potentially important for differentiation, but comparisons among many of the published studies are problematic owing to small sample sizes as well as variation in the chronological age of the specimens, the specific bone evaluated from the specimen and the spatial location within the bone that was evaluated. Nevertheless, several recent studies have had some success in applying discriminant function analysis to distinguishing human and nonhuman bone, particularly using dimensions of Haversian canal size (Cattaneo et al. 1999; Urbanová and Novotny 2005; Martiniaková et al. 2006).

As a general rule, secondary osteon density is not useful for distinguishing human and nonhuman bone because of the wide range of variability dependent on chronological age, location within the bone, and so forth. If secondary osteons are present and plexiform bone is absent, it is usually not possible to confirm or rule out the presence of human bone based on secondary osteon density alone. However, secondary osteon density was an important factor used by Owsley and colleagues (1985) in a case differentiating deer bone from human bone. A murder suspect claimed that several small bone fragments in his truck were from a deer. These fragments were compared to bone from the murder victim and a deer, with the result that secondary osteon density (as well as Haversian canal size) was consistent with other bones from the murder victim and not consistent with deer bone. The key in this case is that the secondary osteon density was compared with a specific individual and not with the possible range for human bone.

Tables 5.1 to 5.6 provide Haversian canal and secondary osteon dimensions reported for numerous mammalian species, including humans. Many of the older studies may only include diameters, but more recent studies report areas as well. No attempt was made to

**Table 5.1  Means and Standard Deviations for Haversian Canal and Osteon Dimensions in Human Bone**

| Study | Sample | Bone | N[1] | Min, Max Haversian Canal Diameter (μm) | Haversian Canal Perimeter (μm) | Haversian Canal Area (μm²) | Osteon Diameter (μm) | Osteon Perimeter (μm) | Osteon Area (μm²) |
|---|---|---|---|---|---|---|---|---|---|
| Jowsey 1966 | Human adult | Femur | 26 | — | 173 (45) | — | 223 (50) | — | — |
| Currey 1964 | Human adult | Femur | 19 | 77.4 (20.6) | — | — | 199.9 (27.5) | — | — |
| Martiniaková et al. 2006 | Human | Femur | 15 | 32.26 (7.23)–59.99 (21.59) | 127.09 (35.84) | 2164.15 (1096.98) | 90.20 (19.19)–263.76 (60.08) | 550.85 (102.48) | 37762.06 (12860.20) |
| Evans 1976 | Human adult male | Femur, tibia, fibula | 17 | — | — | — | — | — | 30000[2] 40000[3] |
| Pfeiffer 1998 | Human adult (Cape Town) | Ribs | 30 | — | — | 1886 (3119) | — | — | 28442 (16606) |
| Cho et al. 2002 | Human adult (African-American) | Rib | 69 | — | — | — | — | — | 36000 (8310) |
| Cho et al. 2002 | Human adult (European-American) | Rib | 34 | — | — | — | — | — | 39000 (5830) |
| Qiu et al. 2003 | Human | Rib | 9 | — | 165 (54) | 2000 (1000) | — | — | 44000 (18000) |

| | | | | | | | | | |
|---|---|---|---|---|---|---|---|---|---|
| Stout and Lueck 1995 | Human adult | Rib | 45 | — | — | — | — | — | 40000 (6710) |
| Pirok et al. 1966 | Human adult | Clavicle | 15 | 64 (12) | — | — | 255 (52) | — | — |
| Pirok et al. 1966 | Human adult | Humerus | 4 | 72 (23) | — | — | 282 (70) | — | — |
| Burr et al. 1990 | Human adult male (ancient Native American) | Femur | 28 | — | 161.03 (25.13) | 2267 (904) | — | 668.10 (91.62) | 34345 (9765) |
| Burr et al. 1990 | Human adult female (ancient Native American) | Femur | 23 | — | 167.84 (25.87) | 2404 (821) | — | 733.26 (82.99) | 40778 (8918) |
| Pfeiffer et al. 2006 | Human adult (18th cent London) | Femur | 20 | — | — | 3665 (3901) | — | — | 44533 (22443) |
| Pfeiffer et al. 2006 | Human adult (18th cent London) | Rib | 19 | — | — | 1377 (879) | — | — | 31142 (12622) |
| Mulhern 2000 | Human adult (ancient Nubian) | Rib | 80 | — | — | 1100 (170) | — | — | 36000 (894) |
| Mulhern and Van Gerven 1997 | Human adult (ancient Nubian) | Femur | 45 | — | — | 2100 (656) | — | — | 38000 (6557) |

[1] Represents number of specimens, not number of structures.
[2] Mean for younger male age group (femur, tibia, and fibula combined).
[3] Mean for older male age group (femur, tibia, and fibula combined).

convert diameters to areas so as not to introduce additional error. As shown in Table 5.1, the average Haversian canal area reported for humans ranges from 1100 µm² for the ribs of ancient Nubians (Mulhern 2000) to 2404 µm² for the femur of prehistoric Native Americans (Burr et al. 1990), with modern groups falling in between this range. Average osteon area ranges from 28,442 µm² in the long bones of modern South Africans (Pfeiffer 1998) to 44,533 µm² in the femora of adults from 18th century London (Pfeiffer et al. 2006).

Overall, Haversian canal size is the most consistent distinguishing feature between human and nonhuman bone, with smaller Haversian canals in nonhuman taxa. Secondary osteon areas are either smaller than those found in humans or overlap with secondary osteon sizes in humans. Mean Haversian canal size and secondary osteon size are never larger in nonhuman taxa compared to humans. The following specific comparisons are based on average values reported in the literature for human and nonhuman bone.

### 5.5.1   Order Lagomorpha

As shown in Table 5.2, three studies have reported Haversian canal and secondary osteon dimensions in rabbits (Jowsey 1966; Martiniaková et al. 2003, 2006). Invariably, dimensions are much smaller in rabbits than values reported for human bone (Table 5.1) and therefore should be readily distinguished when differentiating from human bone.

### 5.5.2   Order Perissodactyla

Data on microstructural variables for horses are somewhat inconsistent, with average secondary osteon size on the low end of the human range in studies by Dittman (2003) and Martin and colleagues (1996), but well below the human range in a study by Owsley and colleagues (1992; Tables 5.1 and 5.3). Haversian canal size is at the small end of the human range in studies by Albu et al. (1990), Dittman (2003), and Martin et al. (1996), but still within the low end of the human range in the study by Owsley et al. (1992). A study by Urbanová and Novotny (2005) reported values for Haversian canal size and secondary osteon size that are well within the range observed in humans. Small sample sizes and bone sampled may contribute to these differences. Overall, there is no clear difference in secondary osteon or Haversian canal size between horses and humans when all of these studies are considered together. It may not be possible to distinguish horse and human bone by the size of structures except in cases where secondary osteon or Haversian canal size is clearly below the range observed in humans.

### 5.5.3   Order Artiodactyla

In some cases, a fragment of bone from an artiodactyl may be comprised entirely of Haversian bone. Microstructural measurements for order Artiodactyla are shown in Table 5.4. Five studies reporting microstructural variables for cows show some variability, with data from Dittman (2003) showing secondary osteon and Haversian canal dimensions much smaller than humans, but data from Martiniaková and colleagues (2006), Urbanová and Novotny (2005), and Albu and colleagues (1990) providing average values that are within the human range. Jowsey (1966) reported an average secondary osteon diameter for cows that is consistent with that of Martiniaková and colleagues (2006), but a Haversian canal perimeter that is much larger than those reported for the other

**Table 5.2 Means and Standard Deviations for Haversian Canal and Osteon Dimensions in Order Lagomorpha**

| Study | Sample | Bone | N[1] | Min, Max Haversian Canal Diameter (µm) | Haversian Canal Perimeter (µm) | Haversian Canal Area (µm²) | Osteon Diameter (µm) | Osteon Perimeter (µm) | Osteon Area (µm²) |
|---|---|---|---|---|---|---|---|---|---|
| Jowsey 1966 | Rabbit | Femur | 6 | — | 36 (12) | — | 72 (14) | — | — |
| Martiniaková et al. 2003 | Rabbit | Femur | 10 | 8.66 (2.95)– 26.31 (12.09) | 53.96 (20.23) | 367.48 (229.79) | 41.05 (12.34)– 129.05 (29.74) | 261.96 (50.68) | 8339.98 (3255.10) |
| Martiniaková et al. 2006 | Rabbit | Femur | 15 | 8.96 (2.99)– 26.85 (11.97) | 55.23 (19.74) | 384.01 (227.45) | 41.81 (12.98)– 130.81 (29.28) | 265.96 (51.58) | 8631.22 (3455.78) |

[1] Represents number of specimens, not number of structures.

**Table 5.3 Means and Standard Deviations for Haversian Canal and Osteon Dimensions in Order Perissodactyla**

| Study | Sample | Bone | N[1] | Min, Max Haversian Canal Diameter (µm) | Haversian Canal Perimeter (µm) | Haversian Canal Area (µm²) | Osteon Diameter (µm) | Osteon Perimeter (µm) | Osteon Area (µm²) |
|---|---|---|---|---|---|---|---|---|---|
| Albu et al. 1990 | Horse (young) | Femur | 5 | 36.21–58.78 | — | — | — | — | — |
| Urbanová and Novotny 2005 | Horse | Femur, tibia | ? | 29.37 (0.76)– 45.12 (1.17) | 128.93 (3.10) | 1213.83 (69.53) | 224.69 (183.74)– 238.50 (5.17) | 700.80 (15.02) | 35506.87 (1602.37) |
| Owsley et al. 1992 | Horse | Metacarpal | 6 | — | — | 1300 (200) | — | — | 15900 (2280) |
| Dittman 2003 | Horse | Metacarpal or radius | 5 | 26.94 (3.20)– 33.66 (4.03) | 100.25 (12.09) | 786.66 (200.43) | 158.2 (14.03)– 205.75 (18.42) | 619.61 (54.12) | 27294.34 (4781.25) |
| Martin et al. 1996 | Horse | Metacarpal | 24 | 31.3 (4.0) | — | — | 172 (19) | — | — |

[1] Represents number of specimens, not number of structures.

**Table 5.4 Means and Standard Deviations for Haversian Canal and Osteon Dimensions in Order Artiodactyla**

| Study | Sample | Bone | N[1] | Min, Max Haversian Canal Diameter (µm) | Haversian Canal Perimeter (µm) | Haversian Canal Area (µm²) | Osteon Diameter (µm) | Osteon Perimeter (µm) | Osteon Area (µm²) |
|---|---|---|---|---|---|---|---|---|---|
| Albu et al. 1990 | Bovine | Femur | 5 | 39.81–70.94 | – | – | – | – | – |
| Jowsey 1966 | Cow (adult) | Femur | 4 | – | 213 (47) | – | 250 (40) | – | – |
| Dittman 2003 | Cow | Metacarpal or radius | 4 | 18.41 (1.85)–23.55 (2.79) | 69.45 (8.02) | 368.11 (87.67) | 121.72 (6.72)–157.51 (10.32) | 474.25 (27.96) | 15601.12 (1799.29) |
| Urbanová and Novotny 2005 | Cow | Femur, tibia | ? | 30.99 (1.16)–42.56 (1.38) | 123.41 (4.01) | 1176.37 (79.35) | 181.49 (5.65)–238.46 (8.07) | 698.71 (22.86) | 36067.23 (2951.58) |
| Martiniaková et al. 2006 | Cow | Femur | 15 | 15.58 (4.32)–48.76 (15.59) | 99.72 (26.49) | 1224.71 (653.33) | 76.22 (14.63)–269.63 (69.15) | 533.61 (107.31) | 32664.97 (11110.13) |
| Dittman 2003 | Sheep | Metacarpal or radius | 4 | 19.22 (2.69)–25.35 (1.75) | 101.3 (7.24) | 396.53 (83.5) | 86.45 (28.83)–130.72 (33.79) | 372.89 (106.65) | 10568.11 (5436.51) |
| Martiniaková et al. 2006 | Sheep | Femur | 15 | 11.46 (3.07)–33.63 (8.65) | 69.60 (14.12) | 609.23 (234.15) | 65.11 (17.31)–206.27 (66.87) | 419.82 (94.62) | 21034.67 (8425.89) |
| Ratjová et al. 1995 | Sheep | Various | 10–12 | 15–70 | – | – | 55–320 | – | – |
| Urbanová and Novotny 2005 | Sheep | Femur, tibia | ? | 18.36 (0.60)–31.76 (1.14) | 88.55 (2.97) | 574.13 (38.44) | 123.79 (2.42)–169.66 (3.50) | 486.09 (9.28) | 16457.60 (599.95) |
| Ratjová et al. 1995 | Goat | Various | 10 | 18–120 | – | – | 78–360 | – | – |
| Dittman 2003 | Goat | Metacarpal or radius | 5 | 14.45 (2.88)–18.75 (3.25) | 55.11 (10.18) | 233.44 (102.33) | 123.92(15.04)–176.85 (14.48) | 513.76 (43.64) | 17880.68 (3310.18) |
| Dittman 2003 | Pig | Metacarpal or radius | 2 | 17.54 (2.29)–21.54 (3.09) | 65.01 (8.75) | 325.53 (96.56) | 114.91 (8.88)–142.51 (4.95) | 436.90 (19.66) | 13701.48 (593.29) |

| Source | Animal | Bone | N | | | | | | |
|---|---|---|---|---|---|---|---|---|---|
| Martiniaková et al. 2006 | Pig | Femur | 15 | 15.61 (5.18)–40.60 (14.55) | 87.40 (25.04) | 1015.21 (539.63) | 83.15 (17.24)–211.07 (55.42) | 459.27 (97.53) | 28031.80 (10004.39) |
| Albu et al. 1990 | Pig | Femur | 5 | 28.73–39.85 | — | — | — | — | — |
| Urbanová and Novotny 2005 | Pig | Femur, tibia | ? | 26.23 (1.39)–36.18 (1.37) | 106.03 (4.28) | 826.45 (66.88) | 180.72 (9.88)–232.26 (11.95) | 681.48 (34.49) | 33118.87 (3239.81) |
| Morris 2007 | Pig | Rib | 5 | — | — | 602 (469) | — | — | 11300 (570) |
| Morris 2007 | Pig | Femur | 6 | — | — | 645 (341) | — | — | 13900 (650) |
| Morris 2007 | Pig | Humerus | 4 | — | — | 775 (560) | — | — | 25100 (166) |
| Urbanová and Novotny 2005 | Wild pig | Femur, tibia | ? | 23.36 (0.92)–32.36 (1.24) | 95.02 (3.35) | 672.01 (47.99) | 162.56 (5.92)–207.78 (8.23) | 610.24 (22.76) | 27168.05 (1907.80) |
| Urbanová and Novotny 2005 | Red deer | Femur, tibia | ? | 17.80 (0.58)–24.97 (0.74) | 73.75 (2.08) | 409.35 (22.26) | 85.01 (2.10)–110.11 (2.75) | 321.99 (7.72) | 7410.84 (357.90) |
| Urbanová and Novotny 2005 | European roe deer | Femur, tibia | ? | 15.13 (0.63)–23.72 (0.92) | 69.34 (2.38) | 327.58 (23.08) | 100.96 (2.51)–127.72 (3.37) | 514.30 (13.09) | 9900.04 (455.86) |
| Owsley et al. 1985 | Deer | Humerus | 1 | 31–250 (mean = 71) | — | — | — | — | — |
| Morris 2007 | Deer | Rib | 6 | — | — | 245 (164) | — | — | 11300 (590) |
| Morris 2007 | Deer | Femur | 6 | — | — | 387 (205) | — | — | 13900 (650) |
| Morris 2007 | Deer | Humerus | 5 | — | — | 401 (186) | — | — | 14700 (600) |

[1] Represents number of specimens, not number of structures.

cows and any other animal, including humans. Again, these studies have relatively small sample sizes and sampled different bones. As with the horse, it may be possible in some cases to distinguish cow bone with small secondary osteon and Haversian canal sizes from human bone.

Four studies provide data for sheep (Ratjová et al. 1995; Dittman 2003; Urbanová and Novotny 2005; Martiniaková et al. 2006). In the studies by Dittman (2003), Urbanová and Novotny (2005), and Martiniaková and colleagues (2006), average Haversian canal size and osteon size are smaller than average values reported for humans. However, it should be noted that there are fairly large differences among the values for secondary osteon size reported by the three studies, with Dittman and colleagues (2003) reporting the smallest average area (10568.11 ± 5436.51) and Martiniaková and colleagues (2006) reporting the largest average area (21034.67 ± 8425.89). The ranges for Haversian canal and secondary osteon dimensions reported by Ratjová and colleagues (1995) for humerus, radius, meta-carpus, femur, tibia, and metatarsus overlap with humans, but these values represent the overall range, with no means or standard deviations provided, whereas most diameters are reported as an average minimum with a standard deviation and average maximum with a standard deviation.

Among the different sheep bones studied by Ratjová and colleagues (1995), the ranges for secondary osteon and Haversian canal dimensions were fairly consistent, with the only exceptions that the humerus had Haversian canal diameters at the smaller end of the range (not greater than 38 μm), and the tibia and metatarsus lacked secondary osteon diameters in the lower end of the range (below 110 μm). Based on the available data, it should be possible to distinguish sheep bone from human bone based on the presence of smaller second-ary osteons and Haversian canals in sheep.

According to a study by Dittman (2003), goats have smaller Haversian canals and sec-ondary osteons than humans. However, Ratjová and colleagues (1995) found secondary osteon and Haversian canal diameters that overlap in size with those found in humans, although there was a pattern of smaller secondary osteon and Haversian canal sizes in the metacarpus and metatarsus compared to the humerus, radius, femur, and tibia. Again, in some cases, it may be possible to distinguish goat and human bone if secondary osteons and Haversian canals are clearly smaller than those found in humans.

Pigs have smaller Haversian canal sizes than humans but have secondary osteon sizes that may overlap with humans (Albu et al. 1990; Dittman 2003; Urbanová and Novotny 2005; Martiniaková et al. 2006; Morris 2007). Based on these studies, it appears that pigs may exhibit some variability in osteon size throughout the skeleton, with larger dimen-sions in the femur and humerus (Urbanová and Novotny 2005; Martiniakovà et al. 2006; Morris 2007) compared to ribs (Morris 2007) or radius/metacarpal (Dittman 2003). Based on these studies, Haversian canal size is a better distinguishing feature than secondary osteon size when comparing pigs and humans.

Three studies provide metric data for deer. Haversian canal diameter for one deer humerus reported by Owsley and colleagues (1985) has values that overlap with those in the human range. Urbanová and Novotny (2005) found average secondary osteon sizes and Haversian canal sizes for red deer and European roe deer (sample size unknown) that are well below averages reported for human bone. Morris (2007) also found osteon and Haversian canal sizes for deer (including six ribs, six femora, and five humeri) that are much smaller than values reported for human bone.

## 5.5.4 Order Carnivora

Haversian canal and secondary osteon dimensions for order Carnivora are illustrated in Table 5.5. Research quantifying the microstructure of carnivore bone is scarce, which is unfortunate, since carnivore bone is probably more likely to be confused with human bone based on a pattern than perissodactyl and artiodactyl bone. The general pattern from these studies suggests that carnivores have smaller Haversian canal sizes and osteon sizes compared to humans. In the studies discussed next, secondary osteon and Haversian canal sizes in bears, Haversian canal and secondary osteon sizes in cats, and osteon sizes in the mink and martin are all smaller than those observed in humans. Dogs may sometimes have secondary osteon dimensions that overlap with humans.

Until recently, no studies have quantified the microstructure of bear bone. In a preliminary study, Hulsey et al. (2009) reported Haversian canal and secondary osteon areas that are smaller than humans in bear metacarpals and metatarsals (*n* = 4). Haversian canal area was a stronger distinguishing feature than secondary osteon area between bears and humans.

In dogs, average Haversian canal diameters reported by Georgia and colleagues (1982) overlap with the smaller end of the human range, although Jowsey (1966) found Haversian canals in dogs that were clearly smaller than average canals in humans. Secondary osteon diameters overlap with those found in humans according to studies by Jowsey (1966) and Diaz and Ratjová (1975). Urbanová and Novotny (2005) and Morris (2007) reported average Haversian canal areas and secondary osteon areas that are well below the averages reported for humans. Perhaps more than other nonhuman species mentioned here, dogs may have considerable variability in body size based on breed. Most studies do not report the breed of dog sampled, so the effect of body size on secondary osteon dimensions is unknown. Sample size is unknown for the Urbanová and Novotny (2005) study, but the others have very small samples, ranging from only one to six individuals.

Jowsey (1966) reported secondary osteon and Haversian canal sizes in six cats that fall below the average sizes observed in humans. A study by Diaz and Ratjová (1975) including one domestic cat and one wild cat also reported secondary osteon sizes smaller than those found in humans. Finally, Diaz and Ratjová 1975 found that a mink and martin both had secondary osteon diameters smaller than those observed in humans.

## 5.5.5 Order Primates

Reported values for secondary osteon and Haversian canal size in nonhuman primates are shown in Table 5.6. Rhesus monkeys have Haversian canal and secondary osteon diameters within the range of humans based on a small study by Jowsey (1966; *n* = 2). Havill (2004) measured the Haversian canal and secondary osteon dimension of 75 macaques and found that Haversian canal area is within the human range, whereas mean secondary osteon area is below the averages reported for humans. Gibbons show similar Haversian canal and secondary osteon dimensions to macaques, with Haversian canal areas at the low end of the human range and secondary osteon areas below the average secondary osteon areas reported in humans (Dittman 2003). The great apes exhibit secondary osteon and Haversian canal dimensions within the range of humans (Dittman 2003; Mulhern and Ubelaker 2009).

**Table 5.5   Means and Standard Deviations for Haversian Canal and Osteon Dimensions in Order Carnivora**

| Study | Sample | Bone | N[1] | Min, Max Haversian Canal Diameter (μm) | Haversian Canal Perimeter (μm) | Haversian Canal Area (μm²) | Osteon Diameter (μm) | Osteon Perimeter (μm) | Osteon Area (μm²) |
|---|---|---|---|---|---|---|---|---|---|
| Hulsey et al. 2009 | Bear | Metacarpal, metatarsal | 4 | 29 | — | 580 | 183 | — | 21421 |
| Jowsey 1966 | Dog | Femur | 4 | — | 85 (37) | — | 154 (38) | — | — |
| Diaz & Ratjová 1975 | Dog | Tibia | 1 | — | — | — | 100–200 | — | — |
| Georgia et al. 1982 | Dog | Femur | 5 | 26.3–69.09 | — | — | — | — | — |
| Urbanová and Novotny 2005 | Dog | Femur, tibia | ? | 21.11 (0.40)–34.42 (0.68) | 98.23 (1.79) | 694.37 (26.03) | 117.15 (1.74)–151.59 (2.35) | 444.74 (6.48) | 14034.94 (141.11) |
| Morris 2007 | Dog | Rib | 6 | — | — | 392 (259) | — | — | 10300 (540) |
| Morris 2007 | Dog | Femur | 6 | — | — | 432 (314) | — | — | 15600 (670) |
| Morris 2007 | Dog | Humerus | 6 | — | — | 314 (227) | — | — | 14900 (740) |
| Jowsey 1966 | Cat | Femur | 6 | — | 102 (36) | — | 163 (60) | — | — |
| Diaz & Ratjová 1975 | Cat | Tibia | 1 | — | — | — | 110–155 | — | — |
| Diaz & Ratjová 1975 | Wild cat | Tibia | 1 | — | — | — | 90–175 | — | — |
| Diaz & Ratjová 1975 | Mink | Tibia | 1 | — | — | — | 65–90 | — | — |
| Diaz & Ratjová 1975 | Martin | Tibia | 1 | — | — | — | 86–165 | — | — |

[1] Represents number of specimens, not number of structures.

**Table 5.6  Means and Standard Deviations for Haversian Canal and Osteon Dimensions in Nonhuman Primates**

| Study | Sample | Bone | N[1] | Min, Max Haversian Canal Diameter (μm) | Haversian Canal Perimeter (μm) | Haversian Canal Area (μm²) | Osteon Diameter (μm) | Osteon Perimeter (μm) | Osteon Area (μm²) |
|---|---|---|---|---|---|---|---|---|---|
| Jowsey 1966 | Rhesus monkey | Femur | 2 | — | 167 (46) | — | 216 (52) | — | — |
| Havill 2004 | Macaque | Femur | 75 | — | — | 1486.39 (502.66) | — | — | 23765.02 (5479.19) |
| Dittman 2003 | Gibbon | Metacarpal or radius | 5 | 33.4 (3.71)– 45.4 (3.94) | 132.7 (12.67) | 1256.1 (254.97) | 139.1 (14.12)– 203.4 (12.10) | 597.20 (44.60) | 23471.0 (4367.31) |
| Mulhern & Ubelaker 2009 | Juvenile chimpanzee | Humerus | 8 | — | — | 1300 (300) | — | — | 33000 (5000) |
| Mulhern & Ubelaker 2009 | Juvenile chimpanzee | Femur | 12 | — | — | 1600 (500) | — | — | 33000 (600) |
| Dittman 2003 | Chimpanzee | Metacarpal or radius | 5 | 36.1 (2.90)– 49.8 (4.60) | 143.1 (13.06) | 1547.5 (347.56) | 150.8 (9.89)– 215.6 (27.24) | 633.3 (70.35) | 27858.0 (4855.76) |
| Dittman 2003 | Gorilla | Metacarpal or radius | 3 | 47.4 (9.08)– 59.9 (6.24) | 176.8 (20.04) | 2356.2 (619.10) | 186.2 (4.50)– 251.0 (17.50) | 746.0 (29.50) | 38018.0 (1809.35) |
| Dittman 2003 | Orangutan | Metacarpal or radius | 4 | 43.0 (5.54)– 54.5 (5.96) | 164.2 (16.41) | 1992.5 (490.01) | 177.5 (3.88)– 236.7 (12.34) | 719.3 (30.53) | 34640.5 (3447.9) |

[1] Represents number of specimens, not number of structures.

## 5.6   Discriminant Function Analysis

Several studies have attempted to use discriminant function analysis to distinguish human and nonhuman bone. Cattaneo and colleagues (1999) developed a canonical discriminant function based on the area, and minimum and maximum diameter of the Haversian canal. The predicted correct classification was 79.3% and in an initial test of long bones from 21 human and nonhuman samples, all were correctly classified as human or nonhuman. In a follow-up study, the accuracy of the equation was tested on juvenile and flat bones (Cattaneo et al. 2009). Both long and flat bones were correctly identified 100% of the time for quail, chicken, and cat; long bones were correctly identified 100% of the time for turkey and cat (long bones tested only). Incorrect classification occurred 1.3% of the time for pig flat and long bones, 1.9% of the time for wolf, and 4.7% of the time for cow, which all are considerably better than the predicted correct classification rate. Results for human bone samples were not as promising, however. Human adult long bones were incorrectly classified in 30% of cases, human adult flat bones were incorrectly classified in 71.8% of cases, subadult flat bones in 60% of cases, subadult long bones in 56.1% of cases, human newborn flat bones in 68% of cases, and human newborn long bones in 93.3% of cases. This study emphasizes the importance of understanding the variability among different bone types and ages.

Urbanová and Novotny (2005) developed two series of equations based on the best discriminating factors between human and nonhuman bone, with the first series including number of osteons per square millimeter, maximum secondary osteon diameter, and Haversian canal area, and the second series also incorporating midshaft femoral cortical thickness. These equations were developed from a sample of 53 human femora and tibiae (number of individuals was not reported) and bones from 10 nonhuman taxa. The paper does not report sample sizes for each nonhuman taxon. The first equation predicted correct classification in 94% of cases and the second equation predicted correct classification in 100% of cases.

Martiniaková and colleagues (2006) developed classification functions for the identification of five different species, including human, pig, cow, sheep, and rabbit, using Haversian canal area, perimeter, and maximum and minimum Haversian canal diameter, as well as secondary osteon area, perimeter, and minimum and maximum diameters, with cross-validated correct classification rates of 76.1%. The human femora used for this study were obtained from adult male Slovak cadavers. This study differs from the previous two in providing specific classification functions for all five species analyzed.

Discriminant function analysis holds promise as a potential method for distinguishing human and nonhuman bone. This type of quantitative approach is preferred in a forensic context, but further studies are needed to better understand various aspects of bone biology, such as factors that influence the size and shape of osteons, and the allometric relationship between bone macrostructure and microstructure.

## 5.7   Conclusion

Distinguishing human and nonhuman bone on a microscopic level is not always possible, but the pattern or size of structures can sometimes be used to rule out human origin. Specifically, the presence of plexiform bone is indicative of nonhuman bone as are small secondary osteons and Haversian canals. Osteon banding is usually indicative of nonhuman bone, but linearly arranged primary osteons may be present in humans during periods of rapid growth. Qualitative and quantitative observations should be combined when assessing the origin of an unknown fragment. Recent studies using discriminant function analysis indicate that statistical methods based on multiple metric factors may be useful for distinguishing human and nonhuman bone in a fragmentary or burned context. Burned bone may be problematic, however, as Nelson (1992) found that burning caused significant shrinkage of histological structures in human femoral bone.

In forensic casework, the identification of bone fragments using histological methodology is limited by the lack of information regarding what bone or part of a bone is represented. Usually if the fragment is of sufficient size to indicate what bone or part of bone is present, identification can be accomplished through morphological assessment. In the absence of this information, the analyst must consider the possibility that the fragment might originate from any area of the skeleton consistent with its morphological indicators.

Recognizing the limitations of using quantitative data for distinguishing human and nonhuman bone is particularly important. The quantitative data available for comparative analysis (Tables 5.1 to 5.6) are limited, with many studies based on very small sample sizes. In addition, age influences osteon density in mammals and the ages of the mammals used in histological studies are not always provided. Quantitative studies may not always be comparable as the result of differences in measurements. (Also, improvements in technology mean that more recent studies probably provide more accurate measurements than older studies.) Finally, the factors influencing the size and shape of osteons are not well understood. Clearly more research is needed on variation throughout the skeleton before more exact interpretations can be made.

# References

Albu I, Georgia R, Georoceneau M (1990) The canal system in the diaphyseal compacta of the femur in some mammals. Anatomischer Anzeiger 170(3-4):181–187.

Baltadjiev G (1995) Micromorphometric characteristics of osteons in compact bone of growing tibiae of human fetuses. Acta Anat 154:181–185.

Burr DB, Ruff CB, Thompson DD (1990) Patterns of skeletal histologic change through time: comparison of an Archaic Native American population with modern populations. Anat Rec 226:307–313.

Burton P, Nyssen-Behets C, Dhem A (1989) Haversian remodeling in human fetus. Acta Anat 135:171–175.

Cattaneo C, DiMartino S, Scali S, Craig OE, Grandi M, Sokol RJ (1999) Determining the human origin of fragments of burnt bone: a comparative study of histological, immunological and DNA techniques. Forensic Sci Int 102:181–191.

Cattaneo C, Porta D, Gibelli D, Gamba C (2009) Histological determination of the human origin of bone fragments. J Forensic Sci 54(3):531–533.

Cho H, Stout S, Madsen RW, Streeter MA (2002) Population-specific histological age-estimating method: a model for known African-American and European-American skeletal remains. J Forensic Sci 47(1):12–18.

Cuijpers, AGFM (2006) Histological identification of bone fragments in archaeology: telling humans apart from horses and cattle. Int J Osteoarchaeology 16:465–480.

Cuijpers, AGFM (2009) Distinguishing between the bone fragments of medium-sized mammals and children: a histological identification method for archaeology. Anthropo Anz 67(2):181–203.

Currey JD (1964) Some effects of ageing in human Haversian systems. J Anat 98(1):69–75.

Currey JD (2002) Bones: structure and mechanics. Princeton University Press, Princeton, NJ.

de Margerie E, Robin J-P, Verrier D, Cubo J, Groscolas R, Castanet J (2004) Relationship between bone microstructure and growth rate: a fluorescent labeling study in the king penguin chick (*Aptenodytes patagonicus*). J Exp Biol 207:869–879.

de Riqlès A (1975) Recherches paléohistologiques sur les os longs des Tétrapodes. VII: Sur la classification, la signification fonctionnelle et l'histoire des tissues osseux des Tétrapodes. Premiére partie: structures. Ann Paléont (Vertébrés) 55:1–52.

Diaz CMC, Rajtová V (1975) Comparative study of lamellar bone in some Carnivora. Folia Morphologica 23(3):221–229.

Dittman K (2003) Histomorphometrische untersuchung der knochenmikrostructur von primaten and haustieren mit dem ziel der speziesdentifikaton unter berücksichtingung von domestikationseffekten. Anthrop Anz 61(2):175–188.

Enlow DH, Brown SO (1956) A comparative histological study of fossil and recent bone tissues, part I. Tex J Sci 7(4):405–443.

Enlow DH, Brown SO (1958) A comparative histological study of fossil and recent bone tissues, part III. Tex J Sci 10(2):187–230.

Evans FG (1976) Mechanical properties and histology of cortical bone from younger and older men. Anat Rec 185:1–12.

Foote JS (1916) A contribution to the comparative histology of the femur. Smithsonian Contributions to Knowledge 35(3).

Frost HM (1987a) Secondary osteon populations: an algorithm for determining mean bone tissue age. Yrbk Phys Anthropol 30:221–238.

Frost HM (1987b) Secondary osteon population densities: an algorithm for estimating the missing osteons. Yrbk Phys Anthorpol 30:239–254.

Georgia R, Albu I (1988) The Haversian canal network in the femoral compact bone in some vertebrates. Morphologie et Embryologie (Bucur). 34(3):155–159.

Georgia R, Albu I, Sicoe M, Georoceanu M (1982) Comparative aspects of the density and diameter of Haversian canals in the diaphyseal compact bone of man and dog. Morphologie et Embryologie (Bucur). 28(1):11–14.

Havill LM (2004) Osteon remodeling dynamics in *Macaca mulatta*: normal variation with regard to age, sex and skeletal maturity. Calc Tis Int 74:95–102.

Hidaka S, Matsumoto M, Ohsako S, Toyoshima Y, Nishinakagawa H (1998) A histometrical study on the long bones of raccoon dogs, *Nyctereutes procyonoides* and badgers, *Meles meles*. J Vet Med Sci 60(3):323–326.

Hillier ML, Bell LS (2007) Differentiating Human bone from animal bone: a review of histological methods. J Forensic Sci 52(2):249–261.

Hulsey BI, Klippel WE, Jantz LM (2009) Metacarpal and metatarsal histology of humans and black bears. Abstract. Proceedings of the American Academy of Forensic Sciences. 2009 Annual Meeting, Denver CO. 15:303.

Jowsey J (1966) Studies of Haversian systems in man and some animals. J Anat 100(4):857–864.

Kerley ER (1965) The microscopic determination of age in human bone. Am J Phys Anthropol 23:149–164.

Martin BR, Burr DB (1989) Structure, function, and adaptation of compact bone. Raven Press, New York, NY.

Martin RB, Gibson VA, Stover SM, Gibeling JC, Griffin LV (1996) Osteonal structure in the equine third metacarpus. Bone 19(2):165–171.

Martiniaková M, Grosskopf, B, Omelka R, Vondráková M, Bauerová M (2006) Differences among species in compact bone tissue microstructure of mammalian skeleton: use of a discriminant function analysis for species identification. J Forensic Sci 51(6):1235–1239.

Martiniaková M, Vondráková M, Fabiš M (2003) Investigation of the microscopic structure of rabbit compact bone tissue. Scripta Medica 76(4):215–220.

Mori R, Tetsuo K, Soeta S, Sato J, Kakino J, Hamato S, Takaki H, Naito Y (2005) Preliminary study of histological comparison on the growth patterns of long-bone cortex in young calf, pig, and sheep. J Vet Med Sci 67(12):1223–1229.

Morris ZH (2007) Quantitative and spatial analysis of the microscopic bone structures of deer (Odocoileus virginianus), dog (Canis familiaris), and pig (Sus scrofa domesticus). M.A. thesis. Louisiana State University and Agricultural and Mechanical College. Baton Rouge, LA.

Mulhern DM (2000) Rib remodeling in a skeletal population from Kulubnarti, Nubia. Am J Phys Anthropol 111:519–530.

Mulhern DM, Ubelaker DH (2001) Differences in osteon banding between human and nonhuman bone. J Forensic Sci 46(2):220–222.

Mulhern DM, Ubelaker DH (2009) Bone microstructure in juvenile chimpanzees. Am J Phys Anthropol 140(2):368–375.

Mulhern DM, Van Gerven DP (1997) Patterns of femoral bone remodeling dynamics in a Medieval Nubian population. Am J Phys Anthropol 104:133–146.

Nelson R (1992) A microscopic comparison of fresh and burned bone. J Forensic Sci 37(4):1055–1060.

Ortner DJ (2003) Identification of pathological conditions in human skeletal remains, 2nd ed. Academic Press, San Diego, CA.

Owsley DW, Mires AM, Keith MS (1985) Case involving differentiation of deer and human bone fragments. J Forensic Sci 30(2):572–578.

Owsley DW, Roberts DE, Manning EM (1992) Field recovery and analysis of horse skeletal remains. J Forensic Sci 37(1):163–175.

Pfeiffer S (1996) Cortical bone histology in juveniles. Microscopic examinations of bioarchaeological remains: keeping a close eye on ancient tissues. In G Grupe and J Peters, eds., Documenta Archaeobiologiae Band 4, Veriag Marie Leidorf GmbH, Rahden/Westf.

Pfeiffer S (1998) Variability in osteon size in recent human populations. Am J Phys Anthropol 106:219–227.

Pfeiffer S, Crowder C, Harrington L, Brown M (2006) Secondary osteon and Haversian canal dimensions as behavioral indicators. Am J Phys Anthropol 131:460–468.

Pirok DJ, Ramser JR, Takahashi H, Villanueva AR, Frost HM (1966) Normal histological, tetracycline and dynamic perameters in human, mineralized bone sections. Henry Ford Hosp Med Bull 14:195–218.

Przybeck TR (1985) Histomorphology of the rib: bone mass and cortical remodeling. In RT Davis and CW Leathers (eds) Behavior and pathology of aging in rhesus monkeys. Alan R. Liss, New York.

Qiu S, Fyhrie DP, Palnitkar S, Rao DS (2003) Histomorphometric assessment of Haversian canal and osteocyte lacunae in different-sized osteons in human rib. Anat Rec 272A:520–525.

Rajtová V, Briancin J, Kokardová M (1995) Lamellar bone structure in small ruminants. Folia Veterinaria 39:59–64.

Rauch F, Travers R, Glorieux FH (2007) Intracortical remodeling during human bone development—a histomorphometric study. Bone 40:274–280.

Schaffler MB, Burr DB (1984) Primate cortical bone microstructure: relationship to locomotion. Am J Phys Anthropol. 65:191–197.

Singh IJ, Gunberg DL (1970) Estimation of age at death in human males from quantitative histology of bone fragments. Am J Phys Anthropol 33:373–382.

Singh IJ, Tonna EA, Gandel CP (1974) A comparative histological study of mammalian bone. J Morphol 144:421–438.

Skedros JG, Hunt KJ (2004) Does the degree of laminarity correlate with site-specific differences in collegen fibre orientation in primary bone? An evaluation in the turkey ulna diaphysis. J Anat 205:121–134.

Skedros JG, Sybrowsky CL, Parry TR, Bloebaum RD (2003) Regional differences in cortical bone organization and microdamage prevalence in Rocky Mountain mule deer. Anat Rec 274A:837–850.

Stout SD, Lueck R (1995) Bone remodeling rates and skeletal maturation in three archaeological skeletal populations. Am J Phys Anthropol 98:161–171.

Stover SM, Pool RR, Martin RB, Morgan JP (1992) Histological features of the dorsal cortex of the third metacarpal bone mid-diaphysis during postnatal growth in thoroughbred horses. J Anat 181:455–469.

Tersigni MTA (2008) Osteon area and circularity: A method for the assessment for human and non-human fragmentary remains. Abstract. Proceedings of the American Academy of Forensic Sciences. 2009 Annual Meeting, Washington DC, 14:375.

Urbanová P, Novotny V (2005) Distinguishing between human and non-human bones: histometric method for forensic anthropology. Anthropologie 43(1):77–85.

# Histological Age-at-Death Estimation

MARGARET STREETER

## Contents

## 6.1  Introduction

Increasingly, bone biologists are employing histomorphometry in the analysis of both modern (Frost, 1987; Kimura, 1992; Skedros et al., 2005; Skedros and Baucom, 2007; Han et al., 2009; Britz et al., 2009) and ancient human bone (Ericksen, 1976; Thompson and Trinkaus, 1981; Martin and Armelagos, 1985; Stout and Lueck, 1995; Abbott et al., 1996; Streeter et al., 2010). Histological age at death estimation, in particular, has been widely used (Kerley and Ubelaker, 1978; Stout and Paine, 1992; Cho et al., 2002). Early in the 20th century Balthazard (1911) demonstrated the potential for histological age estimation when he published his analysis of the correlation between age and mean osteon diameter in the midshaft tibia. However, more than 50 years passed before the potential for age estimation based on the bone microstructure was fully realized. Several book chapters have been devoted to the physiological basis for and the detailed description of histological aging methods (Stout, 1989, 1992; Robling and Stout, 2000) with the most recent and comprehensive treatment of this topic addressed by Robling and Stout (2008) and Crowder (2009). Therefore, the following will be limited to a brief discussion of the more widely used methods of histomorphometric age assessment in adult bone followed by a detailed description of the first histological age estimating method developed for use in the subadult skeleton (Streeter, 2005).

## 6.2   Histological Age Estimation in Adult Bones

The histological determination of age in human cortical bone is based on the observation of age-dependent change in the bone microstructure, most frequently employed is the evidence of bone remodeling activity. This remodeling activity is typically characterized through the evaluation of osteon population density (OPD), the number of primary vascular canals, the amount of unremodeled lamellar bone, the percent remodeled bone, and the average size of secondary osteons or Haversian canals. For a detailed discussion of bone growth, modeling, and remodeling see chapters by Gosman, Maggiano, and Stout and Crowder in this volume. Quantification of these and other microanatomical structures in a variety of bone sampling sites has been used to generate a number of formulas for estimating age at death (Robling and Stout, 2008). Histological age estimation is particularly applicable in the instance of burned or very fragmentary skeletons, where morphology is altered to the extent that it is not useful for age estimation based on gross morphological methods. Because most age predicting methods are bone specific, the exact methodology used to histologically estimate age is often dictated by the particular skeletal element that is available for study. To address the need for aging methods that use a variety of skeletal elements and also in an effort to identify the skeletal element and sampling site with the greatest age associated change in bone microstructure, a large number of histological aging methods have been developed (Ahlqvist and Damsten, 1969; Singh and Gunberg, 1970; Rother et al., 1978; Thompson, 1979; Hauser et al., 1980; Fangwu, 1983; Thompson and Galvin, 1983; Cera and Drusini, 1985; Uytterschaut, 1985, 1993; Samson and Branigan, 1987; Druisini and Businaro, 1990; Narasaki, 1990; Ericksen, 1991; Stout and Paine, 1992; Kimura, 1992; Yoshino et al., 1994; Cool et al., 1995; Watanabe et al., 1998; Cho et al., 2002; Han et al., 2009; Martrille et al., 2009). Bone remodeling, which is the basis for these histological aging methods, is known to be influenced by factors such as skeletal element, age, sex, physical activity, ancestry, and nutritional and health status (Takahashi and Frost, 1966a, 1966b; Ericksen, 1976; Stout and Simmons, 1979; Burr et al., 1990; Jee and Frost, 1992; Kimura, 1992; Stout and Lueck, 1995; Cho et al., 2002; Agarwal et al., 2004; Paine and Brenton, 2006; Chan et al., 2007; Crowder and Rosella, 2007). Furthermore, variations associated with sampling sites and methods employed in the evaluation of bone remodeling must be considered (Chan et al., 2007; Crowder and Rosella, 2007). Therefore, the greatest reliability will be obtained when methods are adhered to and the demographics of the population used to develop the predicting equation are similar to those of the sample to be aged.

### 6.2.1   Age Estimation Methods in Long Bones

The majority of methods developed for histological aging have utilized long bones (femora, tibiae, humeri, fibulae, ulnae, and metacarpals), but methods have also been proposed that use the bones of the axial skeleton (ribs and clavicle) and the skull. Not until the publication of the method developed by Kerley (1965) did histomorphological methods of age estimation become practical. Kerley's method is applicable to complete midshaft cross-sections from the femur, tibia, or fibula. Intact and fragmentary osteons, unremodeled lamellar bone, and the number of primary vascular canals are quantified in four microscopic fields at a magnification of 100×. In this method these features are quantified in one circular field adjacent to the periosteum located in each quadrant of the cortex (anterior, posterior, medial, and lateral). The values obtained are totaled and inserted into the appropriate formula (e.g., for whole osteon number, fragmentary osteon number).

A revision of the Kerley (1965) method by Kerley and Ubelaker (1978) includes modified age predicting formulas and introduces a method to account for differences in field size between microscopes. It is important to note that the proper magnification, sampling area, and definition of histomorphological features must be followed as prescribed for each method. To ensure the proper application of any age estimation method it is important to consult the original publication (Chan et al., 2007; Crowder, 2009). The original Kerley method is an exception, and the more recent revised procedure by Kerley and Ubelaker (1978) and should be consulted.

Concerned about the invasive and destructive nature of histological aging methods that require complete cross-sections of bone and recognizing a need for a procedure that utilizes a smaller sample, techniques have been proposed that require only a small bone sample (Singh and Gunberg, 1970; Thompson, 1979; Thompson and Galvin, 1983; Narasaki, 1990; Ericksen, 1991; Han et al., 2009). Therefore, Thompson (1979) developed a sampling method using a small core (0.4 cm) removed from the midshaft. He generated a series of stepwise linear regression formulas applicable to the bones of both upper and lower extremities (humerus, ulna, femur, and tibia). Thompson's (1979) method has the advantage of providing multiple formulas that incorporate 19 variables including the number of secondary osteons, mean osteon size, and cortical thickness in various combinations. In this method, four adjacent periosteal fields are read on the midshaft core. Formulas are selected based on the combination of variables available and the status of the bone or individual (skeletal element, male/female, right/left, and pathological/nonpathological). The inclusion of a number of formulas with multiple variables for numerous long bones increases the likelihood that fragmentary bones or those affected by diagenesis could be employed in age estimation.

When tested on a forensic sample of varied ancestry Thompson's (1979) formula for age estimation in the tibia proved to be inaccurate in individuals less than 55 years old. Therefore, Thompson and Galvin (1983) proposed a new age regression formula specific to the tibia using a core taken from the medial midshaft. They reported that osteon number alone quantified in three adjacent periosteal fields was more accurate at estimating age in the tibia than including additional variables. Therefore, the revised regression formula uses only osteon numbers.

## 6.2.2 Age Estimation Methods in Other Bones

Age estimation methods have been developed for sampling sites other than the long bones (Singh and Gunberg, 1970; Druisini and Businaro, 1990; Stout and Paine, 1992; Cool et al., 1995; Cho et al., 2002). The Stout and Paine (1992) regression formula was the first method developed for use on the rib and clavicle.[*] Intact and fragmentary osteons are quantified over the entire cortical surface. Osteon population density (OPD) is determined and inserted into the regression formulas provided for rib or clavicle to estimate age. There are several advantages to using these two bones for histological age estimation. The reluctance of curators to allow sampling is a major obstacle to the application of histomorphological techniques applied to archaeological or fossil bone. The sampling process for the rib and clavicle is preferrable since it does not require the destruction of a major long bone such as

---

[*] The first predictive equation for the sixth rib was introduced in a case study by Sam Stout (1986).

the tibia or femur (Stout and Paine, 1992). Also, ribs represent the nonaxial skeleton and provide an alternative sampling site when long bones are not available. Ribs may also be less subject to non-age-related bone remodeling than the weight-bearing long bones of the leg and thus reflect more systemic influences on the remodeling history of the individual. Another beneficial feature of this method is the practicality of counting the entire cross-section of the bone. The area of the rib is relatively small compared to larger bones such as the femur or tibia. Sampling the entire cortex reduces sampling error caused by spatial variance of microstructures resulting in a more accurate estimate of osteon population density.

Questions have been raised about the applicability of regression formulas to skeletal remains from different populations (Ubelaker, 1977; Richman et al., 1979; Thompson and Gunnes-Hey, 1981). Studies have indicated that bone remodeling rates and, consequently, age-estimation based on remodeling formulas, differ between populations (Cho et al., 2002). The concerns about the reliability of aging formulas developed on one population and applied to another population prompted Cho et al. (2002) to develop population-specific formulas. The variables used by Cho and colleagues (2002) included OPD, mean osteon area, the ratio of cortical area to total subperiosteal area (relative cortical area), and a population specific (indicator) variable. OPD is determined, as described in the Stout and Paine (1992) method, across the entire rib cortical surface and inserted into the appropriate population specific regression formula. A sample of ribs of known African American and European American ancestry was used to generate the formulas. The sample included modern African American and European Americans from the Midwest United States. This method also provides a formula for use when ancestry is unknown and for use on incomplete rib cross-sections.

## 6.3   Histology of the Subadult Rib

The microanatomy of the subadult rib cortex differs from the densely remodeled cortex seen in the adult rib (Landeros and Frost, 1966). In the subadult, evidence of the ongoing processes of growth and modeling dominate. Remodeling begins prenatally (Burton et al., 1989; Baltadjiev, 1995), but due to the influence of modeling drift it is less evident until the second half of the first decade, and there is a poor correlation between age and osteon counts until late in the second decade (Streeter, 2005; Streeter and Stout, 2006). Little research has focused on the cortical bone of the immature skeleton. Studies on subadult bone histology have described fetal compact bone (Burton et al., 1989; Glorieux et al., 1991) or analyzed the trabecular bone of normal and pathological individuals (Baltadjiev, 1999; Jones et al., 1999; Glorieux et al., 2000; Salle et al., 2002). But the few studies that have included subadult cortical bone have been composed primarily of adults with relatively small samples of immature individuals that were grouped by decades (Sedlin et al., 1963a, 1963b; Sedlin, 1964; Epker and Frost, 1965a, 1965b; Takahashi and Frost, 1965a, 1965b). These broad categories tend to obscure developmental patterns associated with stages of growth that could be used to histologically estimate age.

To expand our understanding of normal patterns of development and to identify changes that could be employed in the age estimation of subadults, the analysis of a modern sample of known age subadults was conducted (Streeter, 2005). Cortical bone cross-sections of 72 subadult ribs (45 males and 27 females) from individuals ranging in age between 2 and 21 years (mean age of 14.1 years) were collected at autopsy on traumatic deaths. Fifty of the rib samples were reported to be from individuals of European ancestry, 14 of African ancestry, 3 of Asian ancestry, and 3 were recorded as mixed or unknown ancestry. The results of this study, described next, provide a detailed histomorphological record of the transition of the human rib cortex from very young individuals through early childhood and the accelerated development of adolescence on into the characteristic and more familiar morphology of approaching adulthood. The description of the developing rib cortex is followed by the phase descriptions that are employed for age estimation.

### 6.3.1 Growth and Modeling in the Subadult Rib

Skeletal growth is the process through which bones attain their adult proportions by increase in size and change in shape (Bogin, 1999). Modeling works with growth to shape bones through deposition by osteoblasts on some surfaces while bone resorption by osteoclasts takes place on other surfaces (Jaworski, 1984; Frost, 1985). Ribs are initially formed of woven bone (Figure 6.1), which is replaced by primary lamellar bone (Figure 6.2) on the

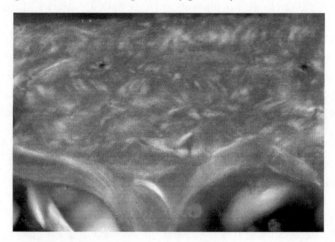

**Figure 6.1** Woven bone (100× polarized).

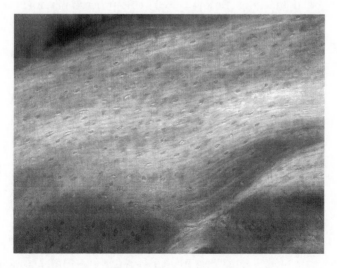

**Figure 6.2** Unremodeled primary lamellar bone (100× polarized).

periosteal and endosteal surfaces through modeling drift, the mechanism for controlling the spatial distribution of bone in response to physiological and biomechanical stimuli (Enlow, 1968; Frost, 1985). Several important studies have examined cortical rib growth and how cross-sectional area measurements of the rib change with age (Sedlin et al., 1963a, 1963b; Sedlin, 1964; Takahashi and Frost, 1965a, 1965b; Epker and Frost, 1966; Takahashi and Frost, 1966; Martin 1991; Zachetta et al., 1995). The total area of the rib cross-section (the area located within the periosteum) increases through bone formation at the periosteum. The cortical area (bone located within the periosteum, total area minus the marrow cavity) increases throughout the second decade after which it begins to decline as a consequence of slowed periosteal expansion and an increased rate of marrow cavity expansion. In early life, the percent cortical bone, the relative amount of cortical area to total area, is in balance but in the third decade of life the rate of marrow cavity expansion becomes greater than the appositional deposition at the periosteum leading to a thinner cortex (lower percent cortical bone) by the fifth decade (Sedlin et al., 1963b; Sedlin, 1964; Takahashi and Frost, 1965b).

Studies of the rib cortical morphology have revealed patterns of age-related change (Sedlin et al., 1963b; Epker and Frost, 1965a, 1965b; Takahashi and Frost, 1965b; Takahashi and Frost, 1966). Cortical area measures reflect growth and modeling that occurs primarily during skeletal development. During growth of the rib cage, modeling drifts coordinate periosteal and endosteal resorption and formation on different surfaces to expand and move the entire cortex in the direction of the cutaneous surface and away from the pleural surface (Frost, 1963; Epker and Frost, 1966; Landeros and Frost, 1966). Through this modeling drift, older bone is being resorbed on the pleural-periosteal and the cutaneous-endosteal rib surfaces, while new bone is formed on the pleural-endosteal and cutaneous-periosteal surfaces (Landeros and Frost, 1966). The cutaneous-periosteal surface is almost exclusively a smooth formation front while the pleural-periosteal surface exhibits the scalloped Howship's lacunae indicative of a resorption surface (Epker and Frost, 1966). New cortical bone is created through this formation drift (Jee and Frost, 1992). Evidence of this drift can be seen as trabecular bone that was once located in the marrow cavity but subsequently has become incorporated into the cortex (Figure 6.3) by the deposition of lamellar bone on trabecular margins (Enlow, 1968). This process is known as corticalization

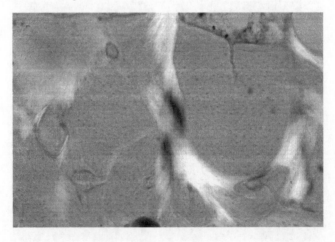

**Figure 6.3** Trabeculae incorporated into the cutaneous cortex through modeling drift (100× polarized).

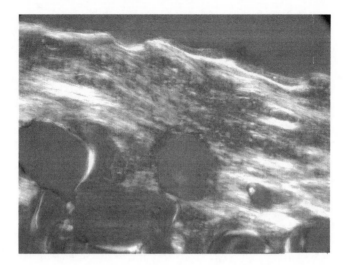

**Figure 6.4** Trabecularization of cortical bone in cutaneous cortex (100× polarized).

(of trabecular bone; Parfitt, 1988). What could be thought of as the opposite process also occurs in subadult ribs during growth-associated modeling. Cancellization or trabecularization of the cortex takes place when modeling drift removes bone from the endosteal surface and the osteons near the marrow cavity are partially resorbed (perforation of the Haversian canal) which ultimately transforms the osteonal bone of the cortex into cancellous bone, trabeculae (Enlow, 1968). This cancellization is observed in subadult ribs on the cutaneous-endosteal surface (Figure 6.4).

The following summarizes the age-related changes in the histomorphology of subadult ribs. In the rib of the very young (less than 2 years old), the cortex has a rather featureless appearance consisting primarily of woven bone. With increasing age, the woven bone is gradually replaced with primary lamellar bone, through the interaction of growth and modeling (Enlow, 1963). This primary lamellar bone is deposited as circumferential lamellar bone that is layered parallel to the periosteal surface and in circumscribed areas on endosteal surface (see Chapter 3 by Maggiano in this volume; Martin et al., 1998).

The layers of primary lamellae are often disrupted by small primary vascular canals, blood vessels that were originally located on the surfaces of the rib but have subsequently been incorporated into the cortex (Figure 6.5) as consecutive layers of lamellae were deposited around them during growth and modeling (Enlow, 1963; Martin et al., 1998). Although primary vascular canals may be surrounded by a small number of concentric lamellae, they do not possess a cement line and are non-Haversian in origin and demonstrate no age-associated pattern of occurrence (Streeter, 2005).

## 6.3.2 Remodeling in the Subadult Rib

Remodeling is the process of continuous bone renewal of discrete packets of bone that begins in utero (Burton et al., 1989) and persists throughout life (Frost, 1963). The primary lamellar bone that is the main component of the growing skeleton is gradually replaced with secondary lamellar bone through the formation of secondary osteons (Figure 6.6; see Stout and Crowder in this volume). In contrast to the condition observed in adult bones, Haversian systems in the form of intact and fragmentary type 1 osteons are less common

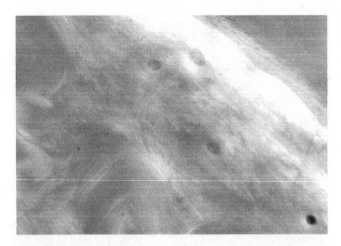

**Figure 6.5** Primary vascular canals near the periosteum of the cutaneous cortex (100× polarized).

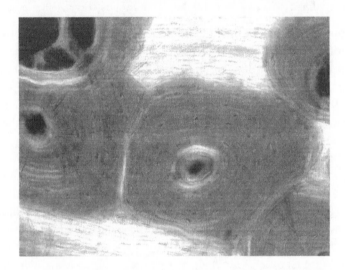

**Figure 6.6** Type I (secondary) osteon (100× polarized).

in the immature skeleton (Martin, 1991) until the end of the second decade (Streeter, 2005). A form of the Haversian system called a drifting osteon (Figure 6.7) that is typically rare in adult bone is the most common osteon type produced in the bones of subadults (Lacroix, 1971; Burton et al., 1989; Robling and Stout, 1999).

All of the aforementioned histological aging methods have focused on the remodeling that occurs after skeletal maturity. Resorption of cortical bone through modeling drift removes evidence of early remodeling, producing an overall low osteon density (Frost, 1985). As a result, there is a poor correlation between age and osteon accumulations in subadults making histological aging methods based on osteon counts problematic (Streeter, 2005). However, other age-associated histomorphological patterns that reflect growth and modeling are observable in the subadult rib cortex. Streeter (2005) describes four distinct developmental phases (Table 6.1) that can be used to obtain an estimated age range for unknown subadult ribs.

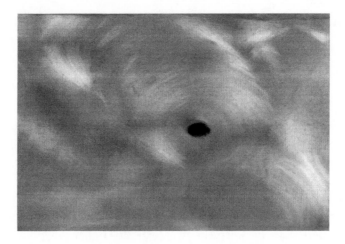

**Figure 6.7** Drifting osteon (100× polarized).

**Table 6.1   Summary of Rib Phases**

| Primary Lamellar Bone | Remodeling | Woven Bone | Cutaneous Cortex | Pleural Cortex |
|---|---|---|---|---|
| **Phase I: Less than 5 Years** | | | | |
| Rare, small areas on pleural endosteal and cutaneous periosteal surfaces initially | Rare | Most of both cortices | Thinner, mostly woven bone, many primary vascular canals | Thicker, some woven bone, primary lamellae initially form endosteally |
| **Phase II: 5–9 Years** | | | | |
| Primarily on pleural cortex | Large drifting osteons on pleural cortex originating at periosteum | Some areas on cutaneous cortex, rare woven bone on pleural cortex | Thinner, mostly intracortical woven bone with many primary vascular canals | Thicker, largely primary lamellar bone, few drifting osteons many Volkmann's canals |
| **Phase III: 10–17 Years** | | | | |
| Both cortices intracortically and often on cutaneous periosteal surface | Drifting osteons on both cortices | Thin rind on cutaneous periosteal surface | Thinner, mostly lamellar bone with some remodeling, periosteal woven bone, and large resorptive bays (drifting osteons) | Thicker, denser remodeling still some areas of primary lamellar bone |
| **Phase IV: 18–21 Years** | | | | |
| Isolated areas on both cortices intracortically | Both cortices, fewer drifting osteons more type I osteons | None or rare | Thinner, dense remodeling, osteons 3 to 4 rows deep, rarely primary lamellar bone periosteally | Thicker, dense remodeling, osteons 3 to 5 rows deep, occasional areas of primary lamellar bone intracortically |

## 6.4    Histological Age Estimation in Subadult Ribs

The histological estimation of age in the subadult rib utilizes a cross-section taken from the middle third of the fifth, sixth, or seventh rib. The thin sections are cut and polished to a thickness of approximately 80 μm and prepared using standard histological methods (Stout and Paine, 1992). This subadult aging method was developed using a light microscope that was fitted with a pair of 10× widefield oculars and 4×, 10×, and 20× objectives, but any magnifications that ensure accurate identification of the histological features in question are suitable. A polarizer is necessary to detect woven bone.

Initial scanning of the rib cortex at a low magnification (e.g., 2× or 4×) facilitates the identification of the thicker pleural cortex, and the thinner and more porous cutaneous cortex. The location of the costal grove on the inferior surface of the pleural cortex can also be used to differentiate between the two cortices. Higher power objectives should be used as needed for identification of histological structures such as primary vascular canals, Volkmann's canals, and secondary osteons.

### 6.4.1    Four Developmental Phases of the Subadult Rib Cortex

Also see Table 6.1.

#### 6.4.1.1    Phase I (Less than 5 Years of Age)

The developing rib cortex is initially composed of woven bone. The margins of the marrow cavity are indistinct at first but the medullary space becomes more clearly defined and the trabeculae of the marrow cavity become distinct from the cortex in the later years of this phase (Figure 6.8). Modeling drift is discernible as the deposition of circumferential lamellar bone gradually replaces the woven bone. This transition occurs first on the pleural endosteal and later on the cutaneous periosteal cortex. Osteoclastic resorption is evident as the scalloped surfaces (Howship's lacunae) along the pleural periosteal and the cutaneous endosteal margins (Figure 6.8). The cutaneous cortex is primarily comprised of woven

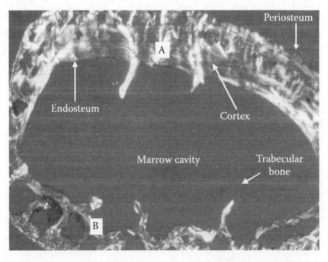

**Figure 6.8** Phase I. Woven bone in the rib of a 3-year-old (20× polarized). (A) Pleural cortex. (B) Cutaneous cortex.

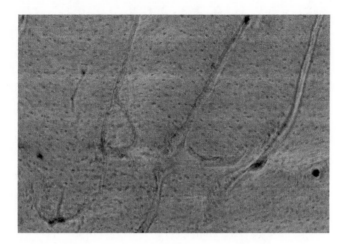

**Figure 6.9** Volkmann's canals in the pleural cortex (200× polarized).

bone, whereas the pleural cortex is distinguished by the appearance of primary lamellar bone that contains many Volkmann's canals (Figure 6.9).

### 6.4.1.2 Phase II (5 to 9 Years of Age)

The defining feature of phase II is the evidence of intracortical remodeling in the form of drifting osteons (Robling and Stout, 1999), a unique characteristic of the subadult cortex. These drifting osteons form first in the primary lamellar bone near the periosteal surface of the pleural cortex (Figure 6.10). They are often aligned in parallel rows drifting on a trajectory from the periosteum toward the endosteum. Many of these drifting osteons are incompletely formed with active bone deposition observable on one side ("the tail") of the wide, eccentrically oriented, vascular canal. and resorption is indicated by the presence of

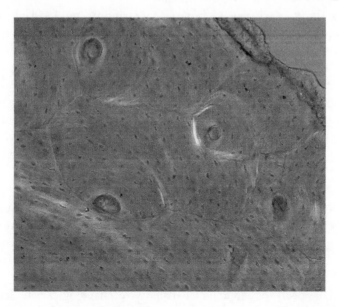

**Figure 6.10** Phase II. Drifting osteons at the periosteal surface of the pleural cortex in the rib of an 7-year-old (100× polarized).

**Figure 6.11** Phase II. Several drifting osteons originating at periosteum and drifting in parallel toward the endosteum in the rib of a 9-year-old (100× polarized).

the scalloped Howship's lacunae on the opposite side of the canal perimeter (Figure 6.11). In the last three phases differences in the thickness of the two cortices are marked. The pleural cortex is often two to three times the width of the thinner cutaneous cortex. As in the previous phase, a large number of Volkmann's canals are evident throughout the pleural cortex (Figure 6.9). Focusing in and out reveals that many of the Volkmann's canals link osteons to the periosteal and endosteal surfaces. Cortical drift is evident in the resorption (scalloped surface) on the pleural-periosteal and cutaneous-endosteal surfaces, whereas formation (smooth surface) occurs on the pleural-endosteal and cutaneous-periosteal surfaces. Scattered patches of natal woven bone may still be observed intracortically especially on the cutaneous cortex.

### 6.4.1.3   Phase III (10 to 17 Years of Age)

On both cortices, the primary lamellar bone is increasingly remodeled with drifting osteons often two or more rows deep (Figure 6.12). In contrast to the pleural cortex, the cutaneous cortex is typically very porous in appearance produced by the presence of large resorptive bays. Inspection at high magnification reveals the characteristic simultaneous resorption and formation fronts of very large drifting osteons (Figure 6.13). The most characteristic feature of this phase is the thin rind of primary lamellar or woven bone that forms along the cutaneous-periosteal surface (Figure 6.12). This unremodeled bone is often interspersed with primary vascular canals, a reflection of the accelerated cortical modeling typical of the increase in the growth rate associated with this age range (adolescent growth spurt).

### 6.4.1.4   Phase IV (18 to 21 Years of Age)

In the later years of the second decade, the two rib cortices attain a more adult morphology with typical secondary (type I) osteons becoming more common (Figure 6.14). The accumulation of Haversian systems has reached a density three or more rows thick resulting in the creation of osteon fragments. Volkmann's canals may still be seen on unremodeled areas of the pleural cortex but primary vascular canals are rare.

This method has been applied to bones from two archaeological sites: a medieval Polish sample (Agnew et al., 2007) and a Peruvian Late Intermediate Period (AD 1000–1300) sample (Bradbury et al., 2009). In the Polish rib sample, the developmental sequence that was

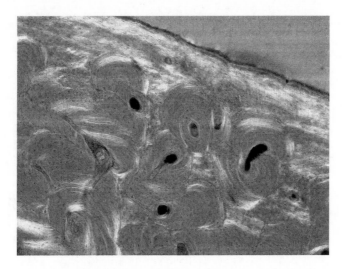

**Figure 6.12** Phase III. Multiple rows of drifting osteons on cutaneous cortex of a 15-year-old (100× polarized).

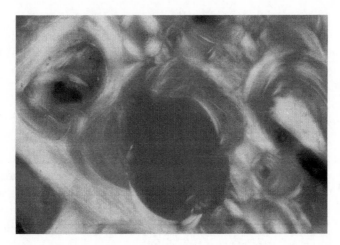

**Figure 6.13** Phase III. Large drifting osteons that break through and result in trabecularization of the cutaneous cortex of a 10-year-old (100× polarized).

described in the modern sample was observed, but it did not correlate well with the age estimates based on skeletal gross morphology (Agnew et al., 2007). The Peruvian sample was placed into broad age categories (under or over 10 years of age) and most of the ribs in the Peruvian sample demonstrated the same developmental sequence as the modern sample. There are several possible explanations for the failure of the qualitative histological method to agree with the age estimation based on skeletal morphology. The method was developed on a modern sample of mostly European Americans ancestry. Differences between populations based on genetic, physiological, and nutritional or health status could account for the differences in the timing of developmental stages. Those Peruvian ribs that varied from the systematic pattern seen in both the modern sample and the majority of Peruvian ribs displayed a very different histomorphology (remodeling in different areas of the cortex as well as different patterns of modeling drift) suggesting the presence of some factor such as those mentioned earlier. While the pattern of developmental phases observed

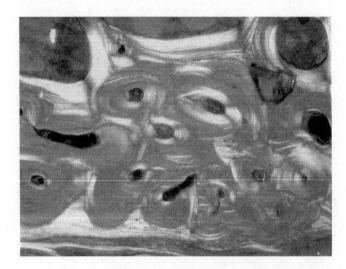

**Figure 6.14** Phase IV. Pleural cortex of a 21-year-old with multiple rows of type I osteons (100× polarized).

in the modern subadult ribs has been noted in the two archaeological samples, the reliability of this method has yet to be determined. A modern sample of subadult ribs of known age that could be tested independently to determine the accuracy of the subadult rib aging method is needed.

## 6.5   Conclusion

A number of methods for histological age estimation have been developed over the past five decades. These methods are primarily based on an age-associated increase in histomorphological evidence for intracortical bone remodeling. Because of the effects of growth and modeling, these methods are not applicable to the skeletal remains of subadults. However, like remodeling, growth and drift leave behind histomorphological evidence that can be employed to arrive at age estimates for subadults.

## References

Abbott S, Trinkaus E, and Burr DB (1996) Dynamic bone remodeling in later Pleistocene fossil hominids. Am J Phys Anthropol 99:585–601.

Agarwal SC, Dumitriu M, Tomlinson GA, and Grynpas MD (2004) Medieval trabecular bone architecture: the influence of age, sex and lifestyle. Am J Phys Anthropol 124:33–44.

Agnew A, Streeter M, and Stout SD (2007) Histomorphological aging of subadult: a test of Streeter's method on a medieval archaeological population. Am J Phys Anthropol Suppl 44:61.

Ahlqvist J, and Damsten O (1969) A modification of Kerley's method for the microscopic determination of age in human bone. J Forensic Sci 14:205–212.

Baltadjiev G (1999) Micromorphometric characteristics of osteons in compact bone of growing tibia of human fetuses. Acta Anat 154:181–185.

Balthazard L (1911) Les canaux de Haver de l'os humain aux different ages. Ann Hyg Pub Med. Leg 15:144–152.

Bogin B (1999) Patterns of human growth, 2nd ed. Cambridge: Cambridge University Press.

Bradbury C, Streeter M, and Buikstra J (2009) Growth and development in a Peruvian archaeological sample. Am J Phys Anthropol Suppl 48:96.

Britz HM, Thomas CD, Clement JG, and Cooper DM (2009) The relation of femoral osteon geometry to age, sex, height and weight. Bone 45(1):77–83.

Burr DB, Ruff CB, and Thompson DD (1990) Patterns of skeletal histological change through time: comparison of an archaic Native American population with modern populations. Anat Rec 226:307–313.

Burton P, Nyssen-Behets C, and Dhem A (1989) Haversian bone remodeling in human fetus. Acta Anat 135:171–175.

Cera F, and Drusini A (1985) Analisi critica e sperimentale dei metodi di detrminazione dell'eta attraverso le microstructure ossee. Quaderni di Anatomia Partica XLI:105–121.

Chan AHW, Crowder CM, and Rogers TL (2007) Variation in cortical bone histology within the human femur and its impact on estimation age at death. Am J Phys Anthropol 132:80–88.

Cho H, Stout SD, Madsen RW, and Streeter MA (2002) Population-specific histological age estimating method: a model for known African-American and European American skeletal remains. J Forensic Sci 47:12–18.

Cool SM, Hendrikz JK, and Wood WB (1995) Microscopic age changes in human occipital bone. J Forensic Sci 40:789–796.

Crowder CM (2009) Histological age estimation. In: Blau S and Ubelaker DH, editors. Handbook of forensic anthropology and archaeology. Walnut Creek, CA: Left Coast Press.

Crowder CM and Rosella L (2007) Assessment of intra-and intercostal variation in rib histomorphometry: its impact on evidentiary examination. J Forensic Sci 52(2):271–276.

Drusini A, and Businaro F (1990) Skeletal age determination by mandibular histomorphometry. Inter J Anthropol 5:235–243.

Enlow DH (1963) Principles of bone remodeling. Springfield, IL: CC Thomas.

Enlow DH (1968) The human face: an account of the postnatal growth and development of the craniofacial skeleton. New York: Harper and Row.

Epker BN, and Frost HM (1965a) The direction of transverse drift of actively forming osteons in human rib cortex. J Bone Jt Surg 47A:1211–1215.

Epker BN, and Frost HM (1965b) Correlation of bone resorption and formation with the physical behavior of loaded bone. J Dental Res 44:33–42.

Epker BN, and Frost HM (1966) Biomechanical control of bone growth and development: a histological and tetracycline study. J Dent Res 45:364–371.

Ericksen MF (1976) Cortical bone loss with age in three Native American populations. Am J Phys Anthropol 45:443–452.

Ericksen MF (1991) Histological estimation of age at death using the anterior cortex of the femur. Am J Phys Anthropol 84:171–179.

Fangwu Z (1983) Preliminary study on determination of bone age by microscopic method. Acta Anthropol Sinica II:142–151.

Frost HM (1963) Dynamics of bone remodeling. In: Frost HM, editor. Bone biodynamics. Springfield, IL: CC Thomas.

Frost HM (1985) Secondary osteon populations: an algorithm for determining mean bone tissue age. Yrbk Phys Anthropol 30:221–238.

Frost HM (1987) The "New Bone": some anthropological potentials. Yrbk Phys Anthropol 28:211–226.

Glorieux FH, Salle BL, Travers R, and Audra PH (1991) Dynamic histomorphometric evaluation of human fetal bone formation. Bone 12(6):377–381.

Glorieux FH, Travers R, Taylor A, Bowen JR, Rauch F, Norman M, and Parfitt AM (2000) Normative data for iliac bone histomorphometry in growing children. Bone 26:103–109.

Han SH, Kim SH, Ahn YW, Huh GY, Kwak DS, Park DK, Lee UY, and Kim YS (2009) Microscopic age estimation from the anterior cortex of the femur in Korean adults. J Forensic Sci 54:519–522.

Hauser R, Barres D, Durigon M, and Derbert L (1980) Identification parl'histomorphometrie du femur et du tibia. Acta Me. Legalis et Scoialis 30:91–97.

Jaworski ZFG (1984) Lamellar bone turnover systems and its effector organ. Calcif Tissue Int 36:S46–S55.

Jee WSS, and Frost HM (1992) Skeletal adaptations during growth. Triangle 31:77–88.

Jones SJ, Glorieux FH, Travers R, and Boyde A (1999) The microscopic structure of bone in normal children and patients with osteogenesis imperfecta: a survey using backscattered electron imaging. Calcif Tissue Int 64:8–17.

Kerley ER (1965) The microscopic determination of age in human bone. Am J Phys Anthropol 23:149–164.

Kerley ER, and Ubelaker DH (1978) Revision in the microscopic method of estimating age at death in human cortical bone. Am J Phys Anthropol 49:545–546.

Kimura K (1992) Estimation of age at death from second metacarpals. Z Morph Anthropol 79:169–181.

Lacroix P (1971) The internal remodeling of bone. In Bourne GH. Editors. The biochemistry and physiology of bones. New York: Academic Press.

Landeros O, and Frost HM (1966) Comparison of amounts of remodeling activity in opposite cortices of rib in children and adults. J Dent Res 45(1):152–158.

Martin BR (1991) On the significance of remodeling space and activation rate changes in bone remodeling. Bone 12:391–400.

Martin BR, Burr DB, and Sharkey NA (1998) Skeletal tissue mechanics. New York: Springer.

Martin D, and Armelagos G (1985) Skeletal remodeling and mineralization as indicators of health: an example from prehistoric Sudanese Nubia. J Human Evol 14:527–537.

Martrille L, Irinopoulou T, Bruneval P, Baccino E, and Fornes P (2009) Age at death estimation in adults by coputer-assisted histomorphometry of decalcified femur cortex. J Forensic Sci 54(6):1231–1237.

Narasaki S (1990) Estimation of age at death by femoral osteon remodeling: application of Thompson's core technique to modern Japanese. J Anthropol Soc Nippon 98:29–38.

Paine RR, and Brenton BP (2006) Dietary health does affect histological age assessment: an evaluation of the Stout and Paine (1992) age estimation equation using secondary osteons from the rib. J Forensic Sci 51:489–492.

Parfitt AM (1988) Bone remodeling: relationship to the amount and structure of bone, and the pathogenesis and prevention of fractures. In: Riggs BL, Melton LJ, editors. Osteoporosis: Etiology, diagnosis and management. New York: Raven.

Pfeiffer S, and Zehr MK (1996) A morphological and histological study of the human humerus from Border Cave. J Human Evol 31:49–59.

Richman EA, Ortner DJ, and Shulter-Ellis FP (1979) Differences in intracortical bone remodeling in three aboriginal American populations: possible dietary factors. Calcif Tissue Int 28:209–214.

Robling AG, and Stout SD (1999) Morphology of the drifting osteon. Cells Tissues Org 164:192–204.

Robling AG, and Stout SD (2000) Methods of determining age at death using bone microstructure. In: Katzenberg MA, Saunders S, editors. Biological anthropology of the human skeleton, 1st ed. New York: Wiley-Liss.

Robling AG, and Stout SD (2008) Histomorphometry of human cortical bone: applications to age estimation. In: Katzenberg MA, Saunders SR, editors. Biological anthropology of the human skeleton, 2nd ed. New York: Wiley-Liss.

Rother VP, Kruger G, Mechlitt J, and Hunger H (1978) Histomorphometrische sowie regressions- und factor-analytische untersuchungen von alternsveranderungen deshumerus. Anat Anz 144:346–365.

Salle BL, Rauch F, Travers R, Bouvier R, and Glorieux FH (2002) Human fetal bone development: histomorphometric evaluation of the proximal femoral metaphysis. Bone 30(6):823–828.

Samson E, and Branigan K (1987) A new method of estimating age at death from fragmentary and weathered bone. In: Garland AN, Janaway RC, editors. Death, decay and reconstruction: approaches to archaeology and forensic sciences. Manchester, UK: Manchester University Press.

Sedlin ED (1964) The ratio of cortical area to total cross-section area in rib diaphysis: a quantitative index of osteoporosis. Cl Orthop 36:161–168.

Sedlin ED, Frost HM, and Villanueva BS (1963b) Variations in cross-section area of rib cortex with age. J Geront 18:9–13.

Sedlin ED, Frost HM, and Villanueva BS (1963a) Age changes in resorption in human rib cortex. J Gerontol 18:345–349.

Singh IJ, and Gunberg DL (1970) Estimation of age at death in human males from quantitative histology of bone fragments. Am J Phys Anthropol 33:373–382.

Skedros JG, and Baucom SL (2007) Mathematical analysis of trabecular "trajectories" in apparent trajectorial structures; the unfortunate historical emphasis on the human proximal femur. J Theoretical Biology 244:15–45.

Skedros JG, Holmes JL, Vajda EG, and Bloebaum RD (2005) Cement lines of secondary osteons in human bone are not mineral-deficient: new data in a historical perspective. Anat Rec A Discov Mol Cell Evol Biol 286:781–803.

Stout SD (1986) The use of bone histomorphometry in skeletal identification: the case of Francisco Pizarro, J Forensic Sci 31(1):296–300.

Stout SD (1989) Histomorphometric analysis of human skeletal remains. In: Kennedy KK, Iscan MY, editors. Reconstruction of life from the skeleton. New York: Liss.

Stout SD (1992) Methods of determining age at death using bone microstructure. In: Sanders SR, Katzenberg MA. editors. Skeletal biology of past peoples: research methods. New York: Wiley-Liss.

Stout SD, and Lueck R (1995) Bone remodeling rates and skeletal maturation in three archaeological skeletal populations. Am J Phys Anthropol 98:161–171.

Stout SD, and Paine RR (1992) Histological age estimation using rib and clavicle. Am J Phys Anthropol 87:111–115.

Stout SD, and Simmons DJ (1979) Use of histology in ancient bone research. Yrbk Phys Anthropol 44:263–270.

Streeter M (2005) Histomorphometric characteristics of the subadult rib cortex: normal patterns of dynamic bone modeling and remodeling during growth and development. Dissertation, University of Missouri, Columbia.

Streeter M (2010). A four-stage method of age at death estimation for use in the subadult rib cortex. J Forensic Sci 55(4):1019–1024.

Streeter M, Stout SD, Trinkaus E, and Burr DB (2010) Bone remodeling rates in Pleistocene humans are not slower than the rates observed in modern populations: a reexamination of Abbott et al. (1996). Am J Phys Anthropol 141(2):315–318.

Takahashi H, and Frost HM (1965a) A tetracycline-based evaluation of the relative prevalence and incidence of formation of secondary osteons in human cortical bone. Can J Physio Pharm 43:783–791.

Takahashi H, and Frost HM (1965b) Correlation between body habitus and cross-sectional area of ribs. J Physiol Pharm 43:773–781.

Takahashi H, and Frost HM (1966) Age and sex related changes in the amount of cortex in normal human ribs. Acta Orthop Scand 37:122–130.

Thompson DD (1979) The core technique in the determination of age at death in skeletons. J Forensic Sci 24(4):902–915.

Thompson DD, and Galvin CA (1983) Determination of age at death by tibial osteon remodeling in an autopsy series. Forensic Sci Int 22:203–211.

Thompson DD, and Gunnes-Hey M (1981) Bone mineral-osteon analysis of Yupik-Inupiaq skeletons. Am J Phys Anthropol 55:1–7.

Thompson DD, and Trinkaus E (1981) Age determination for the Shanidar 3 Neandertal. Sci 212:575–577.

Ubelaker DH (1977) Problems of the microscopic determination of age at death. Paper presented at the Annual meeting of the American Academy of Forensic Sciences, San Diego, CA.

Uytterschaut HT (1985) Determination of skeletal age by histological methods. Z Morphol Anthropol 75:331–340.

Watanabe Y, Konishi M, Shimada M, Ohara H, and Iwamoto S (1998) Estimation of age from the femur of Japanese cadavers. Forensic Sci Int 98:55–65.

Yoshino M, Imaizuni K, Miyasaka S, and Seta S (1994) Histological estimation of age at death using microradiographs of humeral compact bone. Forensic Sci Int 64:191–198.

Zachetta JR, Plotkin H, and Alverez Figueira ML (1995) Bone mass in children: normative values for the 2–20-year-old population. Bone 16(4 Suppl):393S–399S.

# Interpreting Load History in Limb-Bone Diaphyses
## Important Considerations and Their Biomechanical Foundations

7

JOHN G. SKEDROS

## Contents

Scientists don't set out to make discoveries; they set out to uncover stories.

—**L. Fisher,** *How to Dunk a Doughnut: The Science of Everyday Life* **(p. 4, 2002)**

## 7.1   Introduction

This chapter addresses concepts in the biomechanics of cortical bone that are essential for those who desire to uncover "stories" in bone morphology. This is a common theme of anthropological studies, especially in the appendicular skeleton where structural and material characteristics are often used to interpret the load history of a bone or bone region.* In this chapter, discussion of various mechanical concepts and parameters, including stress, strain, elastic modulus (stiffness), strength, energy absorption (toughness), primarily appears in Section 7.2. Readers who are less familiar with these terms and concepts can consider reading the biomechanics tutorial by Turner and Burr (1993) or find similar information in textbooks that consider bone biomechanics (Cowin 2001; Currey 2002; Martin et al. 1998). Readers who are already familiar with these terms and concepts could move on to the subsequent sections that address the other main theme of this chapter: using structural or material characteristics (e.g., regional histological variations) to interpret load history of appendicular bones when strain data are lacking or insufficient.

---

* The complete record of forces imposed on a bone over a period of time is called the *load history* of the bone (Carter and Beaupré 2001). The functional adaptation of a bone to its load history is best explained or understood by considering the strains and stresses that are created by the applied loads.

## 7.1.1 Considerations for Interpreting the Functional Adaptation of Bone

Before delving into the section on bone biomechanics, the six considerations that are deemed the most important for interpreting functional adaptations in diaphyses of limb bones and ribs are listed next. These considerations, therefore, focus on cortical bone and they are discussed in detail after the biomechanics section.

The comprehensive list of considerations in Table 7.1 is designed to serve as a worksheet/checklist that facilitates comparisons to be drawn between bones of different species or between different bones of the same animal. This approach is also helpful for determining if differences in histomorphology (nanostructure/microstructure) between regions within the same bone are adaptive (e.g., see the multidomain load hypothesis in Section 7.7.7). All investigators and students of bone adaptation, including those with focused interests in forensic and physical

**Table 7.1 Worksheet/Checklist of Important Considerations for Interpreting Adaptation in the Appendicular Skeleton**

Examination of Bone Diaphyses of Similar Volume (Left of Rib) and Small Volumes (Right of Rib), and Different Species

| Considerations | Human Femur | Human Tibia | Horse Radius | Sheep Radius | Goat Radius | Deer Calcaneus | Alligator Femur | Human Rib | Turkey Ulna | Rat Femur | Rat Ulna | Pigeon Humerus |
|---|---|---|---|---|---|---|---|---|---|---|---|---|
| **Animal Size/Mass Category** (*mammalian* locomotor behavior; skeletal form/scaling issues) | | | | | | | | | | | | |
| Mammal: Large (1–300 kg) | X | X | X | X | X | X | X | X | X | | | |
| Medium (0.1–1 kg) | | | | | | | | | | | | X |
| Small (0.001–0.1 kg) | | | | | | | | | | X | X | |
| Reptile | | | | | | | X | | | | | |
| Bird | | | | | | | | | | | | X |
| Other | | | | | | | | | | | | |
| (See Biewener, 1990) | | | | | | | | | | | | |
| **Bone Volume/Size** (stressed volume effect) | | | | | | | | | | | | |
| "Large" (larger than "small") | X | X | X | X | X | X | X | | | | | |
| "Small" | | | | | | | | | ? | X | X | X |
| **Skeletal Division**‡ | | | | | | | | | | | | |
| Appendicular | X | X | X | X | X | X | X | | X | X | X | X |
| Axial | | | | | | | | X | | | | |
| **Skeletal Location** (proximal vs. distal) (regional functional morphology; e.g., humerus vs. metacarpal; see Figure 7.13) | | | | | | | | | | | | |
| Proximal location | X | | | | | | X | | | | | |
| Intermediate or distal location | | I | I | I | I | D | | | I | X | I | X |
| Other location or issue | | | | | | | | X | | | | |
| **Muscle, Ligament, Tendon "Protection"/Influences** | | | | | | | | | | | | |
| High | X | | | | | | X | | | X | | X |
| Medium | | X | X | X | X | | | X | X | | X | |
| Low (mostly surrounding tendons) | | | | | | X | | | | | | |

*(continued)*

**Table 7.1 (continued)   Worksheet/Checklist of Important Considerations for Interpreting Adaptation in the Appendicular Skeleton**

Examination of Bone Diaphyses of Similar Volume (Left of Rib) and Small Volumes (Right of Rib), and Different Species

| Considerations | Human Femur | Human Tibia | Horse Radius | Sheep Radius | Goat Radius | Deer Calcaneus | Alligator Femur | Human Rib | Turkey Ulna | Rat Femur | Rat Ulna | Pigeon Humerus |
|---|---|---|---|---|---|---|---|---|---|---|---|---|
| **Within Bone Level** (includes cortical vs. cancellous issues) | | | | | | | | | | | | |
| Epiphyseal/metaphyseal | | | | | | | X | | | | | |
| Diaphyseal | X | X | X | X | X | X | X | NA | X | X | X | X |
| **In Vivo Strain Environment** | | | | | | | | | | | | |
| Well characterized | | | X | X | X | | | | X | | | X |
| Fair/poorly characterized | X | X | | | | | X | | | X | | |
| No data | | | | | | | | X | | | X | |
| **Load Complexity Category** (see Figures 7.21 and 7.22) | | | | | | | | | | | | |
| High = reduced load predictability | | | | | | | | | | | | |
| High | X | X | | | | | | | | ? | | X |
| Intermediate B | X | X | X | X | X | | X | | X | X | | |
| Intermediate A | | | X | X | X | | ? | | X | | X | |
| Low | | | | | | X | ? | | | | | |
| Low = increased load predictability | | | | | | | | | | | | |
| **Volitional Changes in Habitual Load Complexity** (e.g., human exercise) | | | | | | | | | | | | |
| Yes, No, Possibly (P) | Y | Y | P | N | N | N | N | N | N | N | N | N |
| **Maturation-Related Changes in Habitual Load Complexity** | | | | | | | | | | | | |
| Yes, No, Possibly (P) | N | P | N | N | N | N | N | N | Y | N | N | N |
| **Bone Selected for:** (based primarily on K values from bird and mammal data; Currey and Alexander, 1985)[†] | | | | | | | | | | | | |
| Yield strength | | | | | | | | | | | | |
| Fatigue strength | | | | | | | | | | | | |
| Ultimate strength | | | | | | | | | | | | |
| Impact strength | | | | | | | | | | | | |
| Stiffness | | | | | | | | | | | | |
| Other | | | | | | | | | | | | |
| **Importance of Toughness or Energy Absorption** | | | | | | | | | | | | |
| High | X | X | X | X | X | X | | | | | | |
| Intermediate | | | | | | | | | | | | |
| Low | | | | | | | X | X | X | X | X | X |
| **Cortical Envelope**[a] | | | | | | | | | | | | |
| Circumferential lamellar bone | | | | | | | | | | | | |
| Periosteal derived; Pericortex | | | | | | | | | | | | |
| Middle | | | | | | | | | | | | |
| Endosteal derived; Endocortex | | | | | | | | | | | | |
| All envelopes | | | | | | | | | | | | |

**Table 7.1 (continued)    Worksheet/Checklist of Important Considerations for Interpreting Adaptation in the Appendicular Skeleton**

Examination of Bone Diaphyses of Similar Volume (Left of Rib) and Small Volumes (Right of Rib), and Different Species

| Considerations | Human Femur | Human Tibia | Horse Radius | Sheep Radius | Goat Radius | Deer Calcaneus | Alligator Femur | Human Rib | Turkey Ulna | Rat Femur | Rat Ulna | Pigeon Humerus |
|---|---|---|---|---|---|---|---|---|---|---|---|---|
| **Anticipated Histology** | | | | | | | | | | | | |
| Fibrolamellar/Plexiform or other Primary | | | | | | | X | | X | X | X | X |
| < 25% Osteonal | | | | | | | X | | X | | | |
| > 25% Osteonal | X | X | X | X | X | X | | X | | | | |
| Other Histology | | | | | | | | | | | | |
| **Metabolism-Mediated Remodeling** | | | | | | | | | | | | |
| High | | | | | | | | X | | | | |
| Intermediate | | | | | | | | | | | | |
| Low | X | X | X | X | X | X | X | | X | X | X | X |
| **Sexual Dimorphism; Race/Ethnicity** | | | | | | | | | | | | |
| Yes, No, Possibly (P) | P | P | N | N | N | N | N | P | N | N | N | N |
| **Growth Rate, Bone/Region** | | | | | | | | | | | | |
| High | | | | | | | | | | | | |
| Medium | | | X | X | X | X | | X | X | X | X | X |
| Low | X | X | | | | X | X | X | | X | X | |
| **Phase of Ontogeny**[b] | | | | | | | | | | | | |
| Attainment | | | | | | | | | | | | |
| Maintenance | X | X | X | X | X | X | X | X | X | X | X | X |
| Senescence | | | | | | | | | | | | |
| **Aging/Senescence Effects**[c] | | | | | | | | | | | | |
| Strong | | | | | | | | | | | | |
| Medium | X | X | | | | | | X | | | | |
| Weak | | | X | X | X | | X | | X | X | X | X |
| Possibly | | | | | | X | X | | | | | |
| None | | | | | | | | | | | | |

(See Figure 7.10) applies to Phase of Ontogeny.

(See Pearson & Lieberman, 2004)

[‡] Cranial-facial, vertebral, and sternum adaptations are not considered here.

[†] K values (top of second page) are measures of robusticity; they are not marked above because they had not all been determined.

[a] = See Chapter 3 for discussion of the "PEM" (periosteal and endosteal membranes).

[b] = Non-elderly adults are in the maintenance phase.

[c] = These are marked here as if some humans had relatively advanced age (e.g., 65–75 years). (see Zebaze et al. 2010)

[NA]= Not applicable.

[?] = Unclear or unknown.

anthropology, will benefit from applying these considerations in situations where load history or provenance of the bone or bone region are in question. This approach also enhances the general understanding of bone adaptation for individuals who are involved in deciphering the skeletal location, load history, and related stories of fragmentary bone specimens.

1. The stressed volume effect—The stressed volume effect (or *volume effect*) is that larger structures are more prone to failure than small structures. Consequently, a larger bone is more prone to fatigue failure than a smaller bone. As discussed later, this could help explain why an osteon-based repair mechanism evolved in some species. When interpreting load history it is important to decide if the volume effect is applicable. This consideration emphasizes that *rules of adaptation* or *rules of construction/development* differ between bones where secondary osteons* form (because the tissue volume is sufficiently high) versus bones where secondary osteons are lacking (because the tissue volume is sufficiently low; hence an osteon-level mechanism for repairing microdamage or renewing bone is not needed). Stated differently, low-volume bones do not remodel, and this is why it can be problematic when comparing their adaptability to high-volume bones that do remodel. (Remodeling refers to secondary osteon formation; see the Appendix for definitions.)

2. The modeling–remodeling distinction—This distinction emphasizes that there is a *division of labor* in the ultimate mechanical goals of modeling and remodeling, where modeling is the process that governs the achievement of structural requirements, primarily stiffness and strength. By contrast, remodeling is the process that governs the achievement of material (i.e., tissue) requirements, primarily toughness and fatigue resistance. When interpreting load history using a bone's structural and material characteristics, it is important to consider the modeling–remodeling distinction and think through its implications.

3. The shear resistance–priority hypothesis—Situations where the shear resistance–priority hypothesis is at play must be detected: Are the stark disparities in the mechanical properties of bone in tension, compression, and shear likely important? Does shear or tension have "priority" in mediating adaptations in the bone or bone region that is being examined? This consideration emphasizes that in many cases regional variations in a bone's histological organization are adaptations that preferentially accommodate one of these strain modes (Figures 7.1 and 7.2).† For example, these variations are typically present in generally exclusive regions in a bone loaded in habitual bending but are absent in torsion.

* All osteons referred to in this chapter are secondary osteons (Haversian systems), which are formed by the activation–resorption–formation sequence that defines the remodeling process.

† The three strain "modes" are tension (lengthened), compression (shortened), and shear. The highest strain "magnitudes" are usually in compression (Lieberman et al. 2004). Among various stimuli, available data suggests that strain is the mechanical parameter most directly involved in causally mediating bone adaptations (Ehrlich and Lanyon 2002; Lanyon 1987; Rubin and Lanyon 1984b). Mechanical strain is the change in length of a loaded structure as a percentage of its initial (unloaded) length. (Note: Shear strain is not a change in length but a change in angle.) This dimensionless ratio is a measure of material or tissue deformation. In vivo strain data from a variety of animals suggests that physiological strains are generally between 200 and 3,000 microstrain (i.e., between 0.02 percent and 0.30 percent change in length) in compression (Biewener et al. 1983a, 1983b; Rubin and Lanyon 1985). The upper limit may be only 1,500 microstrain in tension (Fritton et al. 2000). For an isotropic material loaded axially, stress and strain are related by Hooke's law, which says that they are proportional to one another.

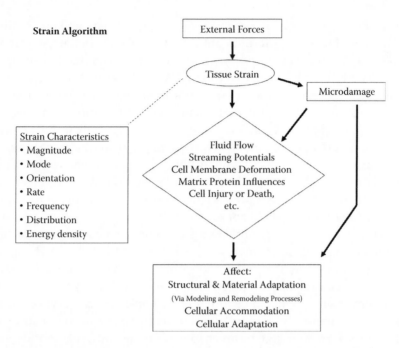

**Figure 7.1** Proposed bone stimulus–response algorithm. This figure demonstrates that tissue strain may not be as proximate in influencing bone adaptation as are, for example, fluid-flow dynamics and other biomechanical or biochemical stimuli. Cellular accommodation refers to the ability of bone cells to adjust to their physical and biochemical environment. Note that the various mechanisms listed in the central diamond have been proposed as candidate processes mediating bone remodeling (Currey 2002; Ehrlich and Lanyon 2002).

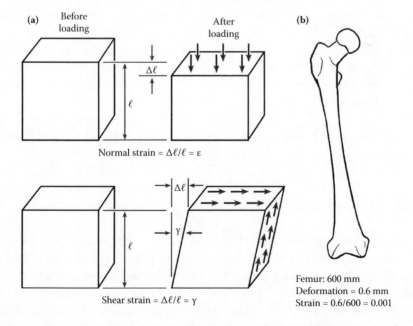

**Figure 7.2** Strain (deformation) is defined as the change in length (Δl) divided by the original length (l). As strain is a ratio, it has no units. (a) At top this is shown in compression stress, and at bottom in shear stress; (b) femur strained at 1000 microstrain (0.001), which is 0.1% deformation.

4. The mechanical relevance of osteons, osteon morphotypes, and predominant collagen fiber orientation—Determine if there are variations in the regional distribution of secondary osteon *morphotypes*, which can be seen best in thin sections of bone viewed in circularly polarized light. When in vivo strain data are lacking or insufficient, the distribution of osteon morphotypes may be the most reliable characteristic for distinguishing a torsion load history from a bending load history. Osteon morphotypes can help to differentially "toughen" (i.e., enhance the capacity to absorb energy) a bone's cortices for regional differences in prevalent/predominant strain modes. Osteon morphotypes are distinguished by differences in their lamellar/collagen organization and orientation. When osteons are few or absent, predominant collagen fiber orientation can still be a highly reliable characteristic for interpreting load history in many bones.

5. The load-complexity categories—Designate the load-complexity category for the bone or bone region of interest. This helps clarify why some bones or bone regions are more likely than others to exhibit regional variations in nanostructural/microstructural adaptation. Failure to recognize this issue can lead to inadequate comparisons. Habitual bending (low-complexity category) versus habitual torsion (high-complexity category) are at the extremes of the four load-complexity categories that are described in this chapter. Consequently, this consideration also helps clarify why nanostructural/microstructural variations are useful for interpreting load history in some bones that are habitually bent but not in bones that are habitually loaded in torsion.

6. Influences of skeletal immaturity, differential growth rates, and precocial versus altricial ambulation—Detect cases where skeletal immaturity or differential growth rates might be present and could confound interpretations of bone adaptation. This consideration emphasizes that the appositional rate of bone growth can produce histological variations even within the same bone, and these variations might not be mechanically adaptive. In other words, investigators must detect and distinguish situations where there could be little functional relevance in the morphologic correlates of *programmed osteogenesis* when compared to those that are truly attributable to load history.

Keep these six considerations in mind as you examine the following overview of basic biomechanical concepts.

## 7.2   Basic Biomechanical Concepts

*The structural versus material distinction.* A sound understanding of basic mechanical concepts is necessary for accurately assessing many of the issues that must be considered (Table 7.1) when interpreting a bone's load history through the examination of its structural and material characteristics. For most studies of limb-bone adaptation, the following mechanical parameters are the most important to thoroughly understand: stiffness, strength, toughness, and fatigue resistance. These parameters are usually considered in terms of material properties, but to some degree can describe how well the whole bone can bear loads, which is measured via structural strength tests. As argued later in consideration 2 (Section 7.4, "The Modeling–Remodeling Distinction"), the structural versus material distinction is important for the purposes of this chapter, especially because a bone's structural requirements may have little to do with regional variations in its material/compositional requirements. In fact, as argued later, regional material variations (e.g., patterns of predominant collagen fiber orientation and osteon morphotypes) are relatively more useful than structural characteristics (e.g., a bone's cross-sectional shape or variations in its cortical thickness) for interpreting the load history of a bone region.

### 7.2.1 Structural Properties of Bone

Much of the following paragraph is paraphrased from van der Meulen et al. (2001). In their study, these investigators generally more strongly ascribe to the idea of structural/material synergism/compensation than the view that is conveyed in this chapter.

What is a whole-bone structural test and what does it measure? Different types of loads, such as bending or torsion, can be applied to whole bones in vitro to determine the structure's stiffness and failure load (structural strength). The structural stiffness is a measure of the resistance to deformation under the applied load, and the structural strength is the load required to cause the whole bone to fail. These data are represented in a *load–deformation curve* (which contrasts with the stress–strain curve of a material test). These two whole-bone measurements are structural properties and are influenced by both the material from which the structure is composed (the tissue material properties, see later) as well as how and where that material is distributed (the geometric form of the tissue). Therefore, both material and geometric properties are required to assess the structural integrity of a long bone, and neither material nor geometry alone is sufficient to predict the structural failure load. Currently, there is no substitute for a mechanical test to measure whole-bone structural behavior; no alternative parameter has been identified that is fully indicative of strength and can serve as a surrogate measure.

*Measures of diaphyseal shape and robusticity: Moments and axes of inertia.* Structural properties include features of a bone's cross-sectional shape and robusticity (i.e., the amount and distribution of cortical area with respect to the total cross-sectional area; Table 7.2). This includes the second moment of area, or inertia (I) as many also call it. The second moment of inertia helps describe the mechanical consequences of cross-sectional shape and mass distribution of a cross-section from a tubular structure such as the diaphysis of a long limb bone. Tubular structures have a larger moment of inertia both in bending and torsion than cylindrical structures with the same amount of mass (Figure 7.3). The second moment of inertia is determined by integrating small units of area ($\delta A$) across the bone's cross-section with respect to distances from its centroid: $I = \int(y^2 \, \delta A)$. This is essentially a measure of how the material is distributed about a given axis.

The axes of the second moment of inertia are measured in directions, which are typically considered in terms of (1) the anatomical orientation of the cross-section (e.g., anterior-posterior Iy; medial-lateral Ix), and (2) the maximum or major (Imax or Imaj) and the minimum or minor (Imin) principal axes across which the distributions of mass are greatest and least, respectively (Figure 7.4). Consequently, across the Imax and Imin axes are, respectively, the directions of greatest and least bending resistance (rigidity). The polar moment of the inertia (J) is proportional to the tubular structure's torsional rigidity, which is estimated by summing the magnitudes of Imin and Imax (or other orthogonal moments; e.g., Iy + Ix).

In the analysis of a bone's cross-sectional cortical geometry, the sum of Imax and Imin (or Iy + Ix), therefore reflects bone robusticity where increases in robusticity are typically

**Table 7.2   Biomechanically Important Structural and Material Characteristics in Diaphyseal Bone Hierarchical Organization**[a]

1. Structural Characteristics

- Bone length
- Diaphyseal curvature
- Cross-sectional shape and robusticity (e.g., moments and axes of area [inertia])
- Average and regional cortical thickness variations

2. Material Characteristics

- Mineral content (% ash)
- Microstructure

    Secondary osteon population density and fractional area (On.N/T.Ar, On.Ar/T.Ar)
    Secondary osteon cross-sectional area, shape, and orientation
    Predominant collagen fiber orientation (CFO), collagen density
    Collagen fiber orientation heterogeneity (CFO-het)
    Secondary osteon morphotypes (e.g., bright, alternating, parallel-fibered, hooped)
    Lamellar organization (lamellation) of various osteon morphotypes
    Mineral heterogeneity (e.g., relatively highly mineralized interstitial bone, young osteons, etc.)
    Porosity (e.g., Haversian canals, primary vascular canals)
    Variations in primary histologic organization (e.g., laminar vs. reticular vascular patterns in fibrolamellar/plexiform bone)
    Osteocyte population density, osteocyte lacunae-canalicular geometries

- Nanostructure

    Types and densities of collagen molecular cross-links
    Mineral crystallite orientation, size, and heterogeneity
    Spatial distribution of noncollagenous proteins (e.g., osteopontin and osteocalcin)
    Nature of bonding of proteins (including collagen) with mineral crystallites

*Source:* Barth HD, Launey ME, Macdowell AA, Ager JW, 3rd, and Ritchie RO, 2010, Bone 46(6):1475–1485.
*Note:* See Chapter 3 for further discussion of these terms: *laminar, plexiform, fibrolamellar*. Further discussion and description of nanostructural versus microstructural characteristics of bone can be found in Barth et al. (2010).
[a] Cancellous (trabecular) bone is not considered here.

seen as greater percentages of cortical area with respect to the area of the entire cross-section. More specifically, the ratio of the principal cross-sectional moments (e.g., Imax/Imin) reflects the degree of ellipiticality or oblongation of the bone's cross-sectional shape, whereas Iy/Ix reflects differences in its anterior-posterior/medial-lateral rigidity. Studies by Carlson and co-workers (Carlson 2005; Carlson and Judex 2007) provide good examples of how these measures of robusticity and ellipiticality are defined and used in anthropological studies that are aimed at deciphering load history. The units of these robusticity measures are to the fourth power, and is why small changes in a bone's outer diameter can have large effects on its bending and torsional rigidities (Figure 7.3).

A good way to introduce the basic concepts of the axes and directions of the cross-sectional moments of inertia is to consider the analogy of a 2-by-4 wood plank commonly used in building homes. When considering the plank's rectangular cross-section it is clear that it would be most difficult to bend it in the direction of the long dimension of the rectangle and easier to bend it along the short dimension. Hence, the direction of greatest bending resistance (see "DGBR" in Figure 7.5) is along (in the direction of) the longer dimension and least along the narrower dimension. The problem with the nomenclature in terms of the "axes" of the moments of inertia is this: the minor or minimum axis (Imin) is along the long dimension of the rectangle and the major or maximum axis (Imax) is

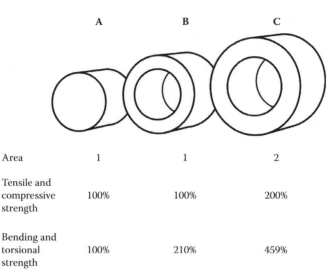

**Figure 7.3** Examples of the influence of cross-sectional geometry on the structural strength of three circular bars. Although bars A and B have the same area (1 square unit), bar B has a greater moment of inertia because it has a hollow interior and greater outer diameter. Bar C has twice the mass (or area in the cross-section; 2 square units) and therefore a much greater moment of inertia. Note that the cross-sectional areas of the bars are directly proportional to their tensile and compressive strengths. By contrast, because the moment of inertia is to the fourth power, the bending and torsional strengths become exponentially greater from bar A to C.

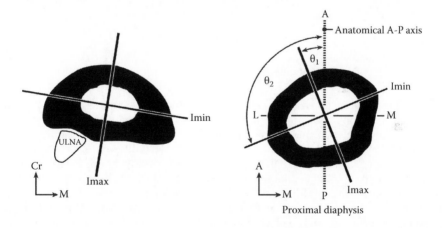

**Figure 7.4** (a) Transverse cross-section at mid-diaphysis of a goat radius (Main 2007) showing the Imin and Imax axes. (b) Transverse cross-section of an adult chimpanzee proximal femoral diaphysis showing the Imin and Imax axes. Also shown are the angles that these axes deviate from the anterior-posterior (AP) axis. Cr = cranial, M = medial, A = anterior, L = lateral, P = posterior.

along the narrower dimension. If this nomenclature seems contradictory, then be aware that what is being referred to here are the "axes" of bending rigidity not the "directions" of the applied bending. Consider, for example, the axis of Imax, which is along the narrower direction of the wood plank's cross-section. What this means is that the greatest bending rigidity occurs when the direction of bending is across (i.e., perpendicular to) the Imax axis, and bending rigidity is least when the direction of bending is across (i.e., perpendicular to) the Imin axis. These definitions can be confusing in the anthropological literature

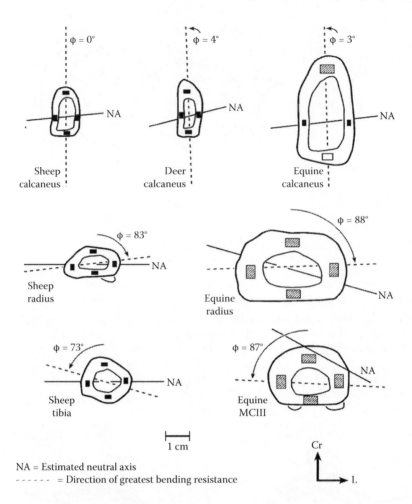

**Figure 7.5** Representative drawings of cross-sections of tension/compression bones (simple load-complexity category; top), and more complexly loaded bones (middle and bottom). The phi (Φ) angles are the acute angles formed by the direction of greatest bending resistance (DGBR) (-----) and the sagittal plane (vertical orientation in each drawing; DGBR is co-linear with axis of Imin, and 90° to axis of Imax). Small rectangles within the cortices are locations where nanostructural/microstructural analyses were conducted in our previous study (Skedros et al. 2009) and are the locations of the images shown in Figure 7.18. In this chapter anterior and posterior, respectively, are used as surrogates for the anatomical locations of the opposing sagittal-plane cortices in the calcanei (dorsal and plantar) and radii (cranial and caudal). Cr = cranial = anterior; L = lateral.

because some prominent investigators have adhered to them (e.g., Demes 2007), whereas others have not (e.g., Ruff and Hayes 1983). In the latter example, Ruff and Hayes (1983) take "major axis" to mean the principal axis in the direction of greatest bending rigidity, not the axis *across* which bending rigidity is greatest.

### 7.2.2 Material Properties of Bone

At the most basic level, bone is a composite of type 1 collagen and mineral (typically a carbonated hydroxyapatite), and this composite is enriched with noncollagenous proteins that also have important biochemical and biomechanical functions. Important mechanical and biophysical interactions of the collagen-mineral composite for elastic and plastic

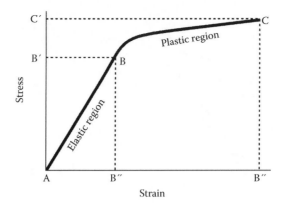

**Figure 7.6** A typical stress–strain curve obtained from a material test in tension (pulled). Beyond the yield point (B) is where permanent deformation of the specimen occurs. Yield stress (B′) is the load per unit area sustained by the specimen at the yield point, and yield strain (B″) is the amount of deformation withstood by the specimen before plastic deformation occurred. The strain at any point in the elastic region of the curve is proportional to the stress at that point. Therefore, the slope of the elastic region (A–B) is the material stiffness or elastic modulus; increased steepness of the A–B slope represents increased stiffness. The ultimate failure point (C) is the point beyond which failure of the specimen occurred. Ultimate stress (C′) and strain (C″) are shown. The area A–B–B″ is the elastic energy absorbed; the area B″–B–C–C″ is the plastic energy absorbed. Total energy absorbed is a sum of elastic and plastic energy. Brittle materials have shorter B–C regions than more ductile materials (longer B–C regions).

behaviors are described by Burstein et al. (1975), Skedros et al. (2006c), and Gupta and Zioupas (2008). Bone material properties are the tissue-level mechanical properties that describe the constituent material and are independent of the size and shape of the bone. These material properties are determined by machining precise samples from the bone of interest and testing them in a particular loading mode. With respect to material properties, it is important for all students of bone adaptation to memorize all features of a typical stress–strain curve, which shows the results of a material test (Figure 7.6).

The material properties are influenced by compositional measures such as mineral content (ash fraction), predominant collagen fiber orientation (CFO), and osteon population densities. This material heterogeneity and its directionality (e.g., preferred orientation of osteons or collagen fibers) contribute to the material anisotropy of bone (Figure 7.7). Bone tissue is also viscoelastic—it has stress–strain characteristics that are dependent upon the applied strain rate. In other words, a specimen of bone tissue that is exposed to very rapid loading will absorb more energy than a specimen that is loaded more slowly. Therefore, bone tissue is both anisotropic and viscoelastic. Because of these characteristics one must specify the strain rate and the direction of applied loading when discussing bone material behavior.

As noted, mechanical behaviors defined by stress and strain deal with material properties; the corollaries for structural properties are load and deformation, respectively. Stiffness and strength are the chief properties of a bone whether it is considered as a structure or as a material. The modulus of elasticity shows the stiffness of the bone material. Yield stress (strength at initial failure) and strain (see definition in the second footnote on page 158) determine how much energy can be absorbed before irreversible changes take place in the material. Ultimate stress is the strength at final failure.

Post-yield stress and strain determine mainly how much energy can be absorbed after yielding but before the material fractures (Figure 7.8). Irreversible changes occur at the

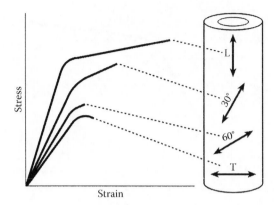

**Figure 7.7** Influence of tissue anisotropy on stress–strain curves using specimens obtained from a human femoral diaphysis and tested in tension (pulled). L = longitudinal (tested along the long axis of the bone); T = transverse (tested transverse to the long axis of the bone). The other tested directions are 30° and 60° to the long axis of the bone.

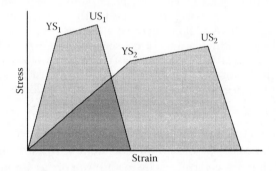

**Figure 7.8** Two stress–strain curves obtained from specimens with significantly different histocomposition. The more compliant material (at right) requires more energy to break it. Energy absorption is proportional to the area under each curve; hence the less compliant material (at left) absorbs less energy than the more compliant material even though it has higher yield stress (YS) and ultimate stress (US).

yield point and are caused by accumulating microdamage. The total area under the stress–strain curve is equivalent to the work that must be done per unit volume of the bone specimen before it breaks. For the purposes of this chapter, this "work" can be considered as being equivalent to energy absorption or toughness. All of these terms refer to the amount of energy required to fracture a material; the more overall energy consumed before failure, the tougher the material (Zioupos and Currey 1998; see Appendix). The total area under the stress–strain curve can be divided into two portions: pre-yield energy absorption (elastic energy) and post-yield energy absorption (plastic energy; Figure 7.6). As described later, regional CFO variations typically correlate more strongly with energy absorption than with stiffness (elastic modulus) or strength (Skedros et al. 2006a). Fracture mechanical properties show the extent to which bone is resistant to crack initiation and to crack travel (which are different things and governed by somewhat different features). Crack travel resistance is indicated by post-yield stress and strain.

In addition to stiffness, strength, and toughness, fatigue resistance is one of the four most important mechanical parameters that must be considered when interpreting the load history and adaptation of a bone or bone region. Fatigue failure is when a structure is loaded repeatedly and breaks at a lower load than would cause it to fail if it were loaded only once. Fatigue resistance is when fatigue failure is prolonged or avoided altogether. Nearly all the material characteristics of bone that are listed in Table 7.2 have some bearing on a bone's fatigue behavior. For detailed discussion of fatigue behavior, failure, and resistance in bone, readers are referred to Currey's book (2002).

### 7.2.3   Using the Stress–Strain Curve for Considering Mechanisms of Bone Adaptation Produced by Remodeling-Induced Affects on CFO, Osteon Morphotypes, and Osteon Population Densities

This final section is an exercise that considers how primary modifications for pre-yield (elastic) behavior can secondarily have beneficial consequences for post-yield behavior. This exercise helps to clarify why regional patterns of CFO and osteon morphotypes have cardinal importance for interpreting load history.

Consider this question: How does a bone achieve enhancements to its post-yield material properties when it would seem that natural selection would be at work in the pre-yield portion of the stress–strain curve (where bone tissue usually exists with regard to prefracture deformation throughout the course of an animal's life)? Another way to think about this is to ask: How can material adjustments that appear to be aimed at enhancing behavior in the pre-yield portion of the stress–strain curve also improve post-yield behavior? (See Figure 7.9a.) Can this be accomplished through quasi-independent natural selection for pre-yield versus post-yield behavior, or is post-yield behavior simply a consequence of the inherent material properties of bone (which seems to be the case in deer antler where secondary osteons are scarce; Krauss et al. 2009)?

Three important facts that help to answer these questions are: (1) remodeling can be activated by bone microdamage that naturally occurs in the pre-yield phase (Reilly 2000; tough materials allow some microdamage formation as long as these microdamage entities do not propagate much), (2) remodeling can probably be activated by strains that are greatly amplified at the osteocyte level but may not have caused classical microdamage (e.g., microcracks), and (3) osteonal interfacial debonding (e.g., at the cement line) can be a good thing because it allows for the dissipation of energy, which helps to avoid ultimate failure (Bigley et al. 2006; Hiller et al. 2003; Reilly et al. 1997; Figure 7.9b). Adaptations that enhance the bone tissue performance that are triggered by microdamage (an "extragenetic" factor, Figure 7.10) and are most readily subject to natural selection, can include the formation of strain-mode-specific osteon morphotypes or modeling-mediated adjustments in bone nanostructure/microstructure (e.g., interfaces and bonding characteristics associated with patterns of predominant CFO, or patterns of vascular anatomy and their associated histological interfaces). This is discussed further in Section 7.8. These can be thought of as *primary adaptations*, namely, those that are primarily aimed at enhancing pre-yield behavior. These primary adaptations can have beneficial (perhaps serendipitous) effects for post-yield behavior. In turn, even though the plastic phase is not often experienced, the possibility that strains would become high enough to enter this phase must be anticipated (or pre-adapted) so that failure is not rapidly catastrophic. From this perspective, it is plausible that the differences in tension osteon morphotypes (e.g., the degree of the completeness of the peripheral bright "hoop"; Figures 7.11 and 7.12) could help enhance beneficial debonding when post-yield strains are experienced. By contrast, the majority of the wall of tension osteon morphotypes (i.e., the longitudinal

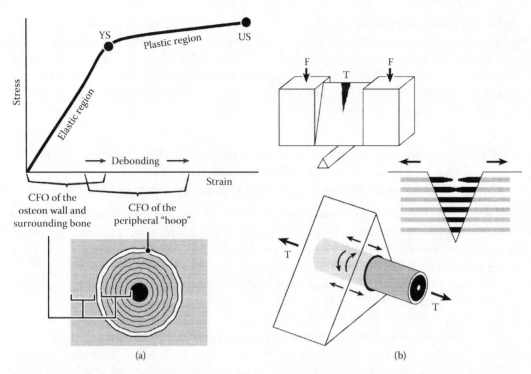

**Figure 7.9** (a) Stress–strain curve of a tension test that shows the hypothesis that the longitudinal collagen that forms the majority of the wall in tension osteons helps to satisfy the material requirements of the bone-mineral composite for elastic behavior by curbing excessive strains in order to avoid irreversible damage. The oblique-to-transverse collagen fiber orientation (CFO) of the peripheral lamellae (hoops) of these osteons (see Figures 7.11 and 7.12) allow for debonding at the cement line in a quasi-controlled fashion as the yield point (YS) is approached, and this can continue beyond this point into the initial portion of the plastic region (between YS and US). This "beneficial" debonding dissipates energy that helps to avoid reaching the US point where fracture then occurs. This depiction is based on data and observations described by Bigley et al. (2006), Martin et al. (1998), and Williams et al. (2010). (b) Three drawings depicting an energy absorption (toughness) test in tension (T) of a machined specimen (at top) loaded at each end with a force (F). Energy is absorbed as the osteons debond, pullout, and bridge the forming crack (middle drawing). Osteon morphotypes (see Section 7.6) that appear to be adapted to accommodate habitual tension and resist tension overload have a peripheral lamella with highly oblique/transverse collagen (hoop) that probably also absorbs energy by resisting shear stresses (curved lines in lower drawing) during debonding and pull out. (Adapted from Martin et al. 1998, figure 5.14, p. 203.)

collagen fibers) accommodates the requirements for pre-yield behavior, which is where the usual loading occurs (Figure 7.9). Osteon size might also play a role in this context (Bigley et al. 2006; Hiller et al. 2003), and could be linked to osteon morphotype (e.g., larger osteons having brighter and more complete peripheral hoops). This coupled pre-yield–post-yield adaptation hypothesis is currently under investigation in order to better understand how a bone's nanostructural and microstructural properties contribute to its toughness across the pre-yield–post-yield transition (Williams et al. 2010).

The biomechanical concepts highlighted by this exercise provide the factual basis for the focus of the remainder of this chapter: how and why osteon morphotypes and predominant CFO are often the most important of many characteristics that must be assessed when interpreting the load history of the bone or bone region.

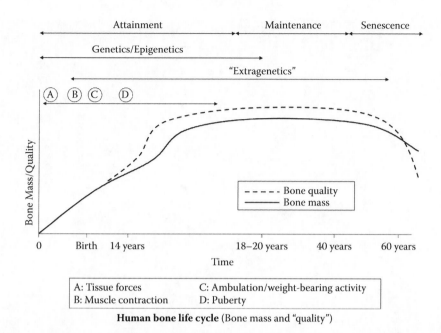

**Human bone life cycle** (Bone mass and "quality")

**Figure 7.10** This stylized depiction of ontogenetic changes in bone mass and "quality" (e.g., bone tissue mechanical properties) in humans and is adapted from several sources (Biewener and Bertram 1993; Carter and Beaupré 2001; Kassem et al. 1996). This figure helps to conceptualize the putative shifts in the temporal importance of genetic, epigenetic, and extragenetic influences, especially with respect to varying histocompositional characteristics within or between bones. In this context, for example, the regional material variations that emerge in the tension and compression cortices during mid-to-late phases of growth of horse radii (Riggs et al. 1993a) and sheep calcanei (Figure 7.25) may serve to enhance the toughness and fatigue resistance for these habitual nonuniform strain environments. From the prenatal phase and well into the attainment phase, the adaptive growth response of cartilage, or chondral modeling (not discussed in this chapter), has a profound influence on the growth and form of limb bones, especially at their epiphyses where articulations are formed with adjacent bones (Hammond et al. 2010). Shown is also the second bone mass growth spurt that occurs in humans, which has not been demonstrated in any other amniote.

## 7.3    Consideration 1: The Stressed Volume Effect

The stressed volume effect helps distinguish fundamental differences in the adaptability of bones from small versus large animals. The volume effect also helps explain why some bones do not form osteons. Material science teaches the crux of the volume effect: larger structures are more prone to failure than small structures. An explanation for this difference is that failures are initiated at flaws in the material of a structure, and larger volumes are more likely to contain a significant flaw (Martin 2003a). In applying this concept to the comparison of a large-volume versus a small-volume bone made of the same material, Taylor (2000) argues that the larger bone is more prone to fatigue failure than the smaller bone. In this situation, natural selection would favor a mechanism for reducing and repairing the higher probability of flaws in large-volume bones. This seems to be the most compelling and parsimonious explanation for the existence of secondary osteons and why they often do not form (i.e., are not readily used to renew small packets of tissue) in the

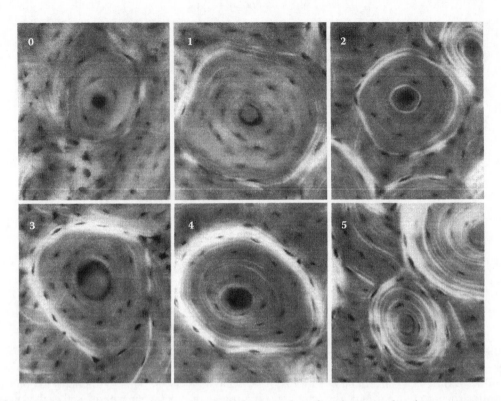

**Figure 7.11** The 6-point scoring scheme with examples of each osteon birefringence pattern (osteon morphotype). These images are reproduced from the original study of Martin et al. (1996a). The numerical values of each of the six morphotypes are used to calculate the osteon morphotype score (MTS) of entire microscopic images that contain many osteons (Skedros et al. 2009). Four of the six numerical scores shown include consideration of the completeness and birefringence strength (brightness) of the peripheral ring "O" or hoop: 0 = category N, a dark osteon with no birefringent lamellae; 1 = category OWI, a combination of OI and OW; 2 = category OW, similar to O but the birefringent ring is weak (W); 3 = category OI, similar to O but the birefringent peripheral ring is incomplete (I); 4 = category O osteon with dark interior and strongly birefringent peripheral lamellae; 5 = category D, birefringent lamellae are distributed throughout the wall of the osteon (distributed osteon group). This group includes bright osteons (less frequent) and alternating osteons (more frequent). (Images are reproduced from Martin et al. (1996a) with permission of Elsevier Science, Inc.)

usual physiological/biomechanical circumstances in small animals (e.g., small mammals like mice and rats, and many birds).

This next point is not intuitive; the volume effect also implies that bones in larger animals cannot withstand as much stress in daily use as bones in smaller animals.* Hence, a bone from a large animal would be comparatively weaker, with the stress concentrator effect of osteocyte lacunae also contributing disproportionately. Taylor (2000) suggests

---

* Although a general effect of body mass on osteon population density, percent area, and/or other osteonal morphological characteristics has also been postulated (Britz et al. 2009; Paine and Godfrey 1997), this is not as well supported as the stressed volume effect. In fact, studies where it has been suggested that osteon size or osteocyte population density exhibit scaling relationships with body mass (perhaps in proportion to basal metabolic rate) appear to have been confounded by various issues, including considering trabecular and cortical bone types in the same analysis and erroneously reporting osteons as being large and commonly present in small mammals that were used in the analyses (e.g., rats) (see discussions in Skedros et al. (Skedros et al. 2005a; Skedros et al. 2004).

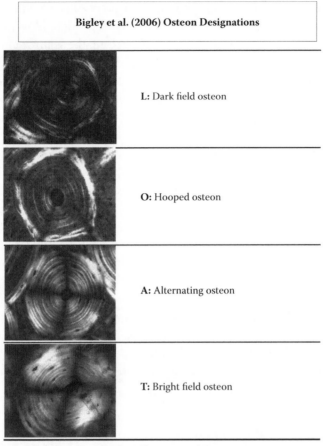

Bigley et al. (2006) Osteon Designations

L: Dark field osteon

O: Hooped osteon

A: Alternating osteon

T: Bright field osteon

A and T fall into the "distributed" category of Figure 7.11.

**Figure 7.12** Examples of the osteon morphotypes that were analyzed in push-out tests by Bigley et al. (2006). (Images are courtesy of Lanny Griffin.)

that this paradox is resolved in larger animals by enhancing the bone material through histological modifications. Fatigue-related requirements are therefore important for understanding the biomechanical bases of variations in histomorphological characteristics (e.g., osteon population densities, osteon morphotypes, predominant CFO, and types of primary bone) between the different stressed volumes of bones of small and large animals. In some cases this interpretation may also help to explain why significant histological (e.g., osteon population density) and compositional (e.g., mineral content = ash fraction) differences occur within or between bones of the same limb (e.g., between thin/thick cortices or gracile/robust bones; Skedros et al. 2003c, 2004; Tommasini et al. 2005). Although, experimental studies have confirmed the basic premise of the volume effect (Bigley et al. 2007, 2008), some caution must be exercised when drawing comparisons between species that exhibit differences in histology (at least in younger animals). This is because these differences might reflect substantial dissimilarity in bone appositional growth rates, perhaps for precocial versus altricial ambulation (see consideration 6, Section 7.8).

*Why consider the stressed volume effect in an anthropology text?* This concept is the first consideration because a question that all enthusiasts of bone adaptation eventually ponder is: Why do secondary osteons form in some bones but not in others? What then follows is typically a discussion of the relative importance of osteonal remodeling in terms of microdamage repair versus metabolism (e.g., making calcium available for metabolic demands such as dietary stress and lactation). Therefore, the volume effect helps in forming a phylogenetic-, ontogenetic-, and biomechanical-based framework for explaining why the capacity for osteon-based tissue renewal never, or nearly never, forms in some bones.

The volume effect also helps provide the intellectual framework for identifying the constraints inherent in comparing or extrapolating adaptations and adaptability between osteonal bones (typically larger) and nonosteonal bones (typically smaller). For example, it helps to avoid the assumption that modeling and remodeling rules generally apply to all bones of vertebrates (see definitions of modeling and remodeling in the Appendix). For example, there may be little value in attempting to extrapolate the adaptability of a rat ulna to a human tibia (Tami et al. 2003). This is especially true in terms of many morphological characteristics because relatively small volume bones are constrained in their potential for histological adaptation. In contrast to the large-volume human tibia (Ebacher et al. 2007), the modeling process of the rat ulna is sufficient for affecting all mechanical adaptations for physiological and supraphysiological loading. If a bone does not exhibit even modest osteon formation, then this could invalidate comparisons of its modeling-mediated adaptations to a bone that models and remodels. For example, compare and contrast the studies of small-volume bones by Schneider et al. (2007), Tami et al. (2003), Carlson and Judex (2007), Kumar et al. (2010), Pinto et al. (2010), and Wallace et al. (2010) in terms of how they (or you might) consider or extrapolate their results in the perspective of functional adaptation of hominid limb bones.

### 7.3.1  Exceptions to the Rule and the Human Bias

Caution must be exercised when considering the volume effect in some cases because there are examples in larger animals that have greater remodeling in their smaller-volume bones. For example, human metacarpals have been shown to be highly remodeled (Coutelier 1976; Koltze 1951). Figure 7.13 also shows that the smallest bone in the deer forelimb skeleton is the most highly remodeled (this observation led to the inclusion of the proximal versus distal bone consideration in Table 7.1). These examples show that unresolved species-related or other less-than-simple biomechanical issues are at play (Drapeau and Streeter 2006; Lieberman et al. 2003; Skedros et al. 2003c).

What also makes it difficult to apply the volume effect in some comparative cases is what can be called the dual influences of the human bias and the altricial/precocial growth or ambulation distinction. The human bias is the common idea that osteonal bone must somehow be better because it is prevalent in humans, even at a relatively young age. But this view must be reconciled with the predominance of primary bone (fibrolamellar/plexiform) that works quite well in many other mammals, especially earlier in their growth. To avoid the pitfalls of these biases, it is useful to determine if the growth, ambulation, or other ambulation-related activity (e.g., flight in birds) of the bone or limb are altricial or precocial (see Section 7.8 for more discussion). Table 7.1 lists some additional issues (e.g., body mass and skeletal scaling relationships) that can help one remember that there are other potentially important considerations when comparing small-volume bones to large-volume bones.

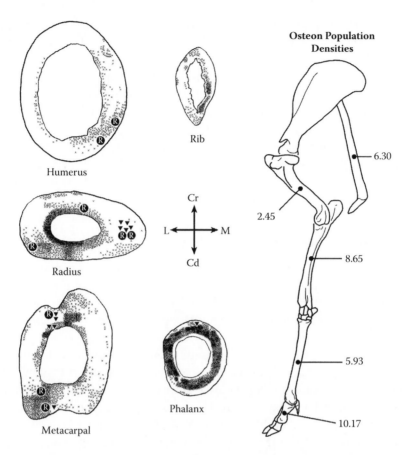

**Figure 7.13** At left are transverse sections of the mid-diaphyses of the forelimb bones from one of the mature mule deer examined by Skedros et al. (2003c). X = secondary osteons, R = resorption spaces, and triangles (▼) = newly forming osteons. Secondary osteons typically occupy approximately 30% or less of the mid-diaphyseal cortex of the principal metacarpal, radius, and humerus. At right is the side view of the forelimb skeleton of an adult Rocky Mountain mule deer showing the averaged values of osteon population densities (no./mm²) at mid-diaphysis from 11 adult animals.

## 7.4   Consideration 2: The Modeling–Remodeling Distinction

When present, modeling and remodeling* are the two processes by which a bone's functional morphology emerges during normal development. By adding or removing bone from periosteal and endosteal surfaces, modeling is the process that adjusts structural

---

* As defined in the Appendix, remodeling refers to the activation–resorption–formation (A–R–F) sequence of the basic multicellular unit (BMU) that forms either a secondary osteon (Haversian system) within cortical bone or hemiosteon on surfaces such as trabecular struts in cancellous bone. Some skeletal biologists still prefer to use the term remodeling as a catch-all phrase that refers more generally to both modeling and remodeling. An example of this can be found in the work of Donald H. Enlow and his collaborators. This more general use of remodeling is also common parlance among orthopaedic surgeons. It is of historical interest that Harold Frost, the champion of the modeling–remodeling nomenclature used here, was an orthopaedic surgeon but he could not convince the vast majority of his colleagues to adopt his definitions.

characteristics including diaphyseal curvature, cortical thickness, and cross-sectional shape. By contrast, remodeling is the process that modifies material organization of the bone through the actions of secondary osteons.

Remodeling-mediated material (tissue level) modifications can occur differently (i.e., produce differences in histomorphology) between discrete cortical regions of the same cross-section (e.g., between the opposing tension and compression cortices of a habitually bent bone). These remodeling-mediated modifications can include porosity (produced from the introduction of central Haversian canals), osteon density and size, predominant CFO and osteon morphotypes (see Section 7.6), and bulk and tissue mineral content (because active remodeling introduces porosity and reduces mean tissue age by producing relatively higher percentages of younger osteons, which are incompletely mineralized).

### 7.4.1  Determining the Ontogenetic Phase

In which ontogenetic phase is the bone: attainment, maintenance, or senescence (aged)? Before delving further into the modeling–remodeling distinction, it is important to review terms that are used to describe phases of a bone's ontogeny so that possible genetic, epigenetic, and extragenetic influences on bone modeling and remodeling can be more precisely considered and discussed.

There is an evolving neology for the traditional use, and present polysemy, of the terms *genetic* and *epigenetic*. For this reason it is wise to avoid using the more conventional dichotomous terms *intrinsic* (i.e., genetic) versus *extrinsic* (i.e., epigenetic) influences in skeletal development and adaptation. This is because the concept of extrinsic factors must be expanded to include nonheritable *extragenetic* stimuli (see later). This relatively new usage (Skedros et al. 2007a) differs from the conventional use of genetic and epigenetic when considering bone adaptation (e.g., see Pearson and Lieberman 2004). Extragenetic (environmental) influences that affect bone adaptation include microdamage events and strains that exceed hypothesized thresholds (Skedros et al. 2001; Figure 7.14). These influences or stimuli are not heritable (in contrast to genetic and epigenetic influences). It is suggested that extragenetic factors can have important influences on bone's structural and material organization by activating or modifying bone modeling and remodeling processes. However, it is important to consider that while extragenetic stimuli may not be heritable, they do act on genetic and cellular machinery that is heritable.

Figure 7.10 is a diagrammatic depiction of presumed temporal influences of genetic, epigenetic, and extragenetic factors throughout the attainment, maintenance (from skeletal maturity to nonelderly adult), and senescence phases of skeletal ontogeny. In addition to considering how a bone's morphology (Table 7.2) might be influenced by one or more of these factors, it is also important to simultaneously know which phase of ontogeny it is in, or if it is in a transition zone between phases. For example, this is especially important in cases where there could be important aging effects on bone microstructure. Furthermore, modeling activities can be relatively difficult or impossible to evoke—but remodeling activities are not—when the animal is well into, and beyond, the maintenance phase.

### 7.4.2  Modeling–Remodeling Synergism/Compensation

Many investigators have suggested that strong correlations between the outcomes of modeling (e.g., adjustments in cortical thickness or moments of inertia) and remodeling

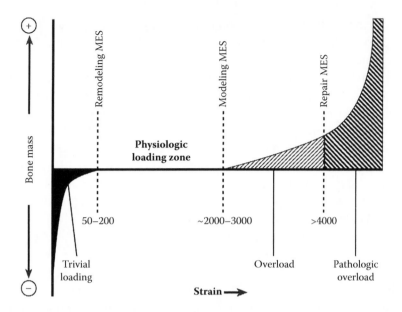

**Figure 7.14** The four mechanical usage windows or zones, according to the Mechanostat hypothesis as popularized by Harold Frost. This figure emphasizes that there are differences between thresholds for modeling and remodeling activities. Below the minimum effective strain of remodeling (MESr) (low or "trivial" loading zone), strains are low and bone remodeling is *activated*. Above the remodeling MESr but below the modeling MESm (the physiologic loading zone), remodeling activity is relatively *repressed*, and is also under the influence of hormonal and metabolic influences. [This physiologic loading zone is analogous to the "lazy" zone described by Carter et al. (1996) and "dead" zone described by Huiskes et al. (1992; see Burr 1992).] Above the modeling MESm, lamellar bone is gained through increased modeling. Above the repair MESp (pathologic overload zone), new woven bone is added rapidly to bone surfaces; this is neither modeling nor remodeling, but probably represents a repair reaction. There are data suggesting that a site-specific customary strain stimulus exists for each site within the skeleton (even within the same diaphysis), and it is that combination of different strain parameters to which the modeling and remodeling processes are directed (Skerry 2006).

(e.g., increased porosity or osteon density; reduced mineral content) reflect their synergism/compensation in affecting local or whole-bone performance (Beck et al. 2000; Burr et al. 1990; Lazenby 1986; Tommasini et al. 2005; Ural and Vashishth 2006; van der Meulen et al. 2001). For simplicity, compensation is considered here to be a form of synergism. However, synergism/compensation between modeling and remodeling in cortical bone is not well supported. (This does not refer to metaphyseal/epiphyseal regions where overall structural strength might be achieved by synergism/compensation in the relative amounts of cortical and cancellous bone mass.) For example, in a study of osteon population density and cortical thickness in the distal aspect of the mid-third diaphyses of 27 adult human tibiae (age range: 21–87), Ural and Vashishth (2006) showed that these parameters were negatively correlated. This led to their statement that "the change in bone microstructure and geometry interact with each other at certain sites and determine the overall mechanical properties and bone fracture" (p. 1497). Ural and Vashishth, however, did not find a similar relationship between osteon density and cortical thickness in the proximal aspect of the mid-third diaphysis of the same tibiae. They suggested that these site-specific differences are associated with differences in strain magnitudes and distributions in addition to regional differences in muscle attachments. These suggestions invoke two important considerations that potentially point to what distinguishes the load histories of these nearby regions: (1) the load-complexity category (see Section 7.7), and (2) the degree of local muscle, tendon, ligament protection/influence (Table 7.1).

Another example of putative modeling–remodeling (structural–material) synergism/compensation has been suggested by Drapeau and Streeter (2006) in their study of cross-sectional geometry and osteon population densities in the mid-diaphyseal locations of 18 matched pairs of adult human tibiae and femora (age range: 18–50 years). In the tibiae, they found significant correlations between osteon population densities and axes of cross-sectional moments of inertia (Imax, Imin; defined in Section 7.2). The authors were puzzled by the absence of a similar relationship in the femoral diaphyses. As discussed further later, the basis of this expectation is further confounded by the fact that these bones are in different load-complexity categories.

Lazenby (1986) also felt that structural–material synergism/compensation was detected in a sample of 13 adult human femora (age range: 50–96; one bone from an 80-year-old individual was omitted from the statistical analysis). Lazenby reported a significant inverse relationship between the magnitude of the axes of the cross-sectional moment of inertia and porosity, with the presumed common objective of adjusting the bone's bending rigidity. In other words, greater porosity was found in the direction of maximum bending resistance indicating that "weaker" material properties from greater porosity were coupled with "stronger" bending resistance from cortical bone geometry. In addition, the porosity difference along the Imax and Imin axes appeared to decline as the geometrical difference between Imax and Imin declined, indicating that the porosity became more evenly distributed as the bone's cross-section and distribution of mass became more circular/symmetrical ($r = -0.56$; $p = 0.05$). In addition to the fact that this relationship has not been independently corroborated (e.g., Drapeau and Streeter 2006), this study appears to be subject to insufficient statistical power. This is due to the small sample size and selection bias because, as noted, 1 of the 13 femora was excluded due to greater porosity along its Imax when the other 12 had greater porosity along their Imin. When all 13 femora are included, there is no correlation between the rigidity ratio and the porosity ratio ($r = -0.06$, $p > 0.8$); thus demonstrating no relationship between porosity distribution and cortical bone distribution as defined by Imax and Imin—rejecting the hypothesis of synergism/compensation between modeling and remodeling.

Putative examples of modeling–remodeling synergism expressed in terms of "regional" safety factors in diaphyseal cortices have also been refuted. For adequate structural performance a bone must have adequate safety factors. A bone's safety factor refers to the ratio of yield stress (or strain) to peak physiological stress (or strain), and represents a means of quantifying how strong the bone is in relation to how strong it needs to be to avoid fracture (safety factor = yield or ultimate stress/peak physiological stress).

Safety factors, when considered in skeletal biomechanics, usually refer to an entire bone (Biewener 1993; Rubin and Lanyon 1982). The idea of regional safety factors (i.e., those from a distinct cortical location within the same transverse cross-section) has also been considered in studies of the goals of bone adaptation (Lanyon et al. 1979; Riggs et al. 1993b; Skedros et al. 1994a). Indeed, in these studies it was hypothesized that a major objective of correlated structural and material characteristics (e.g., inverse relationship of cortical thickness and mineralization) in limb-bone diaphyses exhibited by some bones is the achievement of uniform regional safety factors between discrete cortical locations (e.g., between anterior and posterior cortices at mid-diaphysis). This hypothesis is a poignant example of putative synergism between the modeling and remodeling processes.

As attractive as the hypothesis of unifying regional safety factors between discrete cortical locations may seem, this synergism has not been supported in studies of equine third metacarpals (Skedros et al. 2003a). Readers who seek more in-depth understanding of this topic are referred to this study. These results provide the impetus for challenging the idea of close synergism/compensation between structure (modeling) and material (remodeling). It is possible that some form of synergism/compensation might exist if safety factors are defined in terms of energy absorption or fatigue resistance (Joo et al. 2007). Studies that explore this possibility are needed.

### 7.4.3 The Division of Labor

In view of these refutations and inconsistencies, it can be argued that many examples of structural/material associations that have been shown in limb-bone diaphyses are circumstantial, bearing little relevance in the context of highly coupled functional adaptation. Additionally, existing knowledge of the capacity for intercellular communication in bone suggests that it is not sufficient for achieving the high level of coordination between modeling and remodeling that would be required to accomplish synergism/compensation in an entire diaphysis or across the breadth of a diaphysis. (This would be especially true with advancing age as osteocytic functions become senescent.) Even in youth, this idea is consistent with data reported by Tommasini et al. (2007), where sexual dimorphism was found to affect tibial size and shape but not tissue-level (remodeling parameters) mechanical properties in a sample of 14 young human tibiae (36.9 ± 8.1 years). However, a rigid refutation of this idea is not wise because structural/material synergism/compensation might be at work to some extent in cases where size–shape relationships occur in a broader size range of individuals of the same species (e.g., Tommasini et al. 2005), or in cases of precocial versus altricial limb development or ambulation (e.g., artiodactyls, musk oxen, jackrabbits, and seagulls; Carrier 1983; Carrier and Leon 1990; Currey and Pond 1989; Heinrich et al. 1999).

Results from several of our investigations have also provided us with a basis for arguing that the ultimate goals of modeling and remodeling processes are so distinct, they work as if there is a division of labor in achieving the goals of bone adaptation (Figure 7.15). In this argument, modeling is aimed at influencing whole-bone structural performance; whole-bone structural performance typically means the overall strength and stiffness of the bone when end loads are imparted to it. It is relatively easy to achieve this whole-bone goal by adjusting cortical thickness or bone shape (e.g., curvature or cross-sectional dimensions) as long as the material is suitable. In fact, if variable adjustments in strain between regions of the same cross-section are signals that reflect the attainment of adapted morphology (Kumar et al. 2010), then small adjustments in cortical thickness or cross-sectional shape can readily achieve this in large-volume, as in small-volume bones. Achieving this goal by regional material adjustments via remodeling is not as efficient or effective. For example, it would not be energetically efficient to modify local strains via osteon-mediated reductions in mineralization and increases in porosity (by increasing the density of osteon central canals). During the attainment of a bone's adapted morphology (when periosteal/endosteal bone apposition/resorption is still possible; Figure 7.10), regional adjustments in local strains could be achieved more readily and efficiently by minor adjustments in

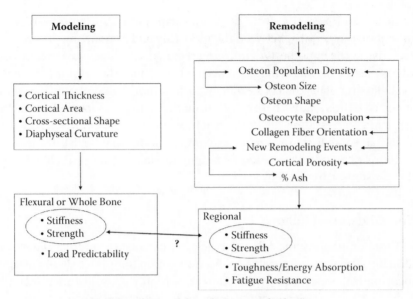

**Modeling & Remodeling: "A Divison of Labor"**
? = It is unclear whether regional remodeling-related variations
significantly affect local stiffness and strength in natural conditions.

**Figure 7.15** A structural versus material division of labor is suggested, respectively, between modeling and remodeling processes in the development and adaptation of a limb bone. In this context, modeling processes seem sufficient for achieving requisite stiffness, strength, and load predictability in a whole bone or discrete region (e.g., in the middle portion of the diaphysis, or between anterior cortex versus posterior cortex of this region; Bertram and Biewener 1988; Skedros et al. 1996). Remodeling processes influence regional material properties primarily in the context of toughness and fatigue resistance. Interrelationships among the material characteristics are shown with arrows and in the context of biomechanically relevant adaptation. The question mark (?) indicates that it is controversial whether necessary adjustments in regional stiffness and strength in a bone diaphysis are actually achieved by the remodeling process in natural conditions since these adjustments can be satisfied by the modeling process during growth.

cortical thickness by the modeling process (Goodship et al. 1979; Lanyon et al. 1982). This is an example of the modeling–remodeling division of labor depicted in Figure 7.15.

If there is a division of labor between modeling and remodeling, then what are the specific labors of the remodeling process? To answer this it must be noted that the main mechanical properties that a bone must have, whether it is viewed as a structure or a material, are stiffness, strength, toughness, and fatigue resistance (see Section 7.2 and the Appendix for definitions). When regional variations in these properties are needed within the same bone (e.g., to accommodate potential strain-mode-related microdamage accumulation in bending), adequate stiffness and strength can be achieved by modeling. In contrast, local adjustments in toughness and fatigue resistance, if achieved by modeling, would likely result in an overbuilt bone lacking efficiency and safety (e.g., its mass could become too great to move it efficiently and microdamage accumulation could become highly problematic, reducing the fracture threshold; Martin 2003b). Consequently, when regional material adjustments are needed they can be achieved by remodeling because this is the most efficient way to affect toughness and fatigue resistance, especially in local regions (e.g., between opposing cortices of the same cross-section).

Failure to recognize the modeling–remodeling distinction explains why investigators have been perplexed when they failed to detect expected developmental/functional adaptation in limb diaphyses in adults that experience significant differences in loading. For example, consider the results of studies by Carlson and co-workers (2006; 2008) where attempts were made to find relationships between diaphyseal shape (e.g., principal moments of inertia) and locomotor behaviors along with other nonbehavioral factors in femora and humeri of free-ranging chimpanzees and other primates. The failure to detect a relationship in this solely structural context caused the authors to conclude that "diaphyseal shape may be unresponsive to mechanical demands of these [six] specific locomotor modes" (Carlson et al. 2006:394). This supports the caution by Demes et al. (2001:264) "against broad behavioral conclusions derived from long bone cross-sectional shape." The modeling–remodeling division of labor helps explain why the capacity to change diaphyseal shape is so constrained in adults, and it reminds us that modeling is relatively difficult to evoke in the skeletons of adults, but remodeling is not (Lieberman et al. 2003). The search for structural/geometric adaptation is often futile in an adult bone because the capacity to evoke adaptation via modeling is very unlikely or no longer possible—a bone's shape appears to be highly constrained genetically or developmentally (Hansen et al. 2009; Wallace et al. 2010) unless unusual circumstances occur (e.g., increased robusticity of the racket arm when an avid tennis player is skeletally immature; Bertram and Swartz 1991; Haapasalo et al. 2000). A poignant example of developmental constraint in the emergence of diaphyseal morphology—and hence the futility of using geometric.cross-sectional morphological characteristics as a means for identifying intergroup differences in load history in some cases (even across a growth range in some bones)—is displayed by data reported by Morimoto et al. (2011) in femora of immature-to-adult wild and captive chimpanzees. In contrast, remodeling parameters, such as changes in the presence and distributions of osteon morphotypes (see consideration 4, Section 7.6), would be expected to have the capacity and plasticity to adapt the bone tissue in the femoral diaphyses for many of the different locomotor behaviors that were considered by Carlson and coworkers (2006, 2008) and Morimoto and coworkers (2011).

## 7.5   Consideration 3: The Shear Resistance-Priority Hypothesis

Mechanical data that support the basic premise for stating this hypothesis are diagrammatically represented in Figure 7.16 for cortical bone, cancellous bone, and cartilage. As shown, there are three strain modes: shear, tension, and compression. In all cases, shear strains are most deleterious, with tension being a close second in most cases (Burstein et al. 1972; Hiller et al. 2003; Reilly and Currey 2000; Skedros and Baucom 2007; Taylor et al. 2003; Turner et al. 2001). For this reason, this hypothesis could also be called the shear/tension resistance-priority hypothesis.

Nonuniform strain distributions in cortical bone, whether produced by bending or combined bending and torsion, are an essential consequence of a bone's function (Figure 7.17). A load history of habitual bending provides a good example for clarifying this point. Bending is not only a loading regime that is phylogenetically/ontogenetically highly conserved in the diaphyses of many appendicular bones (Rubin and Lanyon 1984a), but bending also produces the majority (>70%) of longitudinal strains occurring during peak loading of controlled in vivo activity (Biewener and Bertram 1993; Biewener et al.

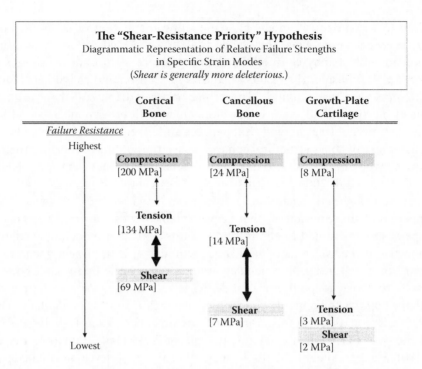

**Figure 7.16** Diagrammatic representation of the shear-resistance priority hypothesis. This shows that cortical and cancellous bone types are disproportionately weaker in shear than in tension or compression (increased vertical separation in the diagram). Although the disparity in cartilage is less marked, this tissue has poor tensile and shear strengths. This suggests that tension and shear are important in driving the ontogenetic adaptation of these tissue types. Values for this figure were obtained from these sources: cortical bone: Cowin (1989) for human bone; values for bovine bone include compression 197MPa, tension 130 MPa, and shear 70 MPa; cancellous bone: Estimated from Keaveny et al. (2001) for bovine bone using strength anisotropy ratios (longitudinal ÷ transverse strength) and bone volume fractions between 0.3 and 0.5; cartilage: the compression value is estimated from human articular cartilage (Yamada 1970). The values for tension and shear are from bovine tibia growth plates (Williams et al. 1999, 2001).

1986).* Consequently, the strain modes produced by this load regime must be accommodated. If they are not accommodated, then they will pose a significant dilemma because the "tension" and "shear" regions will be more prone to microdamage accumulation than

---

* In their review article, Ruff et al. (2006) emphasize that in vivo strain data available for most bones that have been studied generally consist of a few average cyclic strain parameters that are extracted from a short period of recordings while the animal performs a very restricted task. This could be construed to mean that the concept of habitual load history used in this chapter is excessively simplified, supporting the view that a much more complete record of strain history is required to relate bone biology and morphology to strain. But it is also important to realize that experimental studies have shown that very few loading cycles are sufficient for maintaining bone mass (Rubin et al. 1995, 1996a). This might suggest that even brief amounts of loading are sufficient to produce regional strain-mode-related remodeling variations between regions of the same cross-section of a limb bone diaphysis. Consequently, a "habitual" load history that produces regional variations in CFO/osteon morphotypes could, on a daily basis, be relatively brief (especially when considering the potentially deleterious consequences of shear and tension). Prospective experimental studies are needed to better define habitual load histories for specific bones and circumstances (e.g., Adams et al. 1997; Fritton et al. 2000) and how or when they are sufficient to produce differences in local histomorphology.

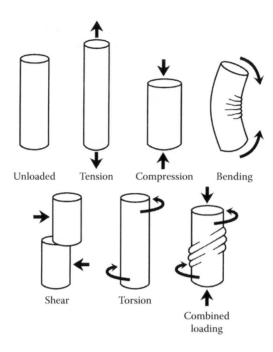

**Figure 7.17** Various idealized load conditions that can be imparted to a bone or bone region. Although shear would also exist in a bone subject to bending (mostly toward the neutral axis), it is more prevalent/predominant and diffusely distributed in torsion.

the "compression" regions. How then, does a bone accommodate these regional disparities in the propensity to fail? As argued in consideration 2 (Section 7.4), this cannot be adequately accomplished by the modeling process (unless the bone's volume is sufficiently small such that microdamage formation is unlikely even when these strain-mode disparities exist). Microstructural accommodation for regional strain-mode disparities must then be accomplished by a repair mechanism—the remodeling process. In the following section is a description of one solution for the regional prevalence of tension and shear in generally exclusive regions—the formation of corresponding strain-mode-specific osteon morphotypes (e.g., a longitudinal/hooped osteon for habitual tension, and a distributed/bright osteon for compression).

If, however, a bone is loaded primarily in torsion, then regional variations in nanostructural/microstructural adaptations for strain modes do not occur. This is because in habitual torsion, there are no significant regional disparities in strain modes. The prevalent/predominant mode in torsion is shear; by the adult stage, the adaptation for this mode is seen as relative uniformity in matrix organization (e.g., CFO patterns that are relatively more uniform across the entire bone cross-section; Skedros and Hunt 2004; Skedros et al. 2009). It must be emphasized that this discussion focuses on strain mode. There have been cases where relative uniformity in CFO across a bone's mid-diaphysis has been observed even though there are locally increased concentrations of osteons in one cortical region of the cross-section. For example, this has been observed in the anterior cortex of the highly torsion-loaded sheep tibiae (Skedros et al. 2009); these locally increased osteon densities were attributed to the relatively high strain magnitudes in this complexly loaded region. There are notable examples in other bones where strain magnitude and CFO are not correlated (Mason et al. 1995; Skedros et al. 1996).

## 7.6    Consideration 4: The Mechanical Relevance of Osteons, Secondary Osteon Morphotypes, and Predominant Collagen Fiber Orientation

### 7.6.1    The Many Potentially Modifiable Characteristics of Osteons

Besides their role in elaborating calcium for metabolic demands, secondary osteons (Haversian systems) can affect biomechanical adaptation through various modifications in one or more of the following characteristics (Table 7.2; Currey 2002; Davison et al. 2006; Skedros et al. 2005b; Skedros et al. 2006b; Skedros et al. 2007b; Skedros et al. 2006c; Skedros et al. 2006d):

1. Orientation
2. Anastomoses and furcations
3. Cross-sectional shape
4. Cross-sectional size
5. Population density (producing lamellar and cement line interfaces)
6. Predominant collagen fiber orientation (CFO) and/or collagen packing density
7. Osteon morphotypes
8. Mineral crystallite orientation, size, and/or heterogeneity
9. Microscopic heterogeneity in mineralization (e.g., young and old osteons)
10. Collagen cross-links
11. Regional concentrations of noncollagenous proteins (e.g., osteopontin)
12. Population density of living osteocytes and the associated vascular supply

Because, as discussed later, items 6 and 7 are the most important characteristics for differentially adapting bone tissue for bending versus torsion they are also most important for interpreting load history in limb-bone diaphyses when in vivo strain data are lacking or insufficient.

### 7.6.2    Habitual Loads Often Require Histomorphological Adaptation

When interpreting load history, it is important to consider the likelihood that the loading of most limb bones is sufficiently "habitual" to require regional histomorphological adaptations (see footnote on page 180). These might be seen as regional variations in predominant CFO or in the prevalence of specific osteon morphotypes. This is because bone tissue must be organized in a way that allows for some microcrack and microdamage formation while simultaneously restricting their propagation. Mechanisms by which a bone's histological organization enables this seemingly paradoxical situation are considered in Figure 7.9 and are explained further later.

In early experimental studies, Currey (1975) and Carter et al. (1976) showed that primary bone is stronger and more fatigue-resistant than the more extensively remodeled bone. They attributed these results to the presence of secondary osteons, which reduce mineral content by increasing porosity and reducing mean tissue age, which in turn, creates an inherently weaker structure by increasing cement line and lamellar interfaces. For nearly two decades, these results puzzled many bone investigators because they showed that prevalent osteonal bone, as seen in humans (the "human bias," Section 7.3.1), is mechanically inferior to the fibrolamellar/plexiform bone that is prevalent in artiodactyls. But it was eventually recognized that the interfaces, microscopic mineralization variations, CFO, and lamellar patterns/heterogeneity introduced by osteons enhanced the tissue's capacity to attenuate microcrack propagation (Ciarelli et al. 2009; Martin and Burr 1989; Reilly and Currey 1999; Reilly et al. 1997; Yeni and Norman 2000). This appears to be most typically correlated with the higher density of cement lines provided by an increased population density of osteons (Gibson et al. 2006; Liu et al. 2000; O'Brien et al. 2005). Additional beneficial consequences of osteons include the toughness provided by the formation of osteon morphotypes (see later) and the repopulation of tissue with viable osteocytes (Figure 7.15).

*The aim of adaptation is to accommodate not resist habitual and beneficial strains, at least up to a point.* Although the best way to avoid fatigue failure may be to decrease microcrack incidence, Martin et al. (1998) argued that bone that is highly resistant to microdamage initiation will be inefficient at controlling microcrack propagation. The trade-off for highly stressed, fatigue-prone bone, therefore, may be efficient repair and a decrease in propagation, rather than prevention of microcrack initiation (Reilly et al. 1997). Studies have suggested that secondary osteonal bone is rather poor at minimizing microcrack formation, but rather good at attenuating the distance and rate of microcrack propagation (Burr et al. 1988; Martin et al. 1998; Reilly and Currey 1999; Reilly et al. 1997; Taylor 1997). From this perspective it is important to reconcile the contrary teaching of conventional wisdom that the overall goal of adaptation is to resist excessive bone stresses and strain. This conventional view tends to suggest that microdamage formation should be avoided altogether. An overbuilt bone then results, and the consequence could be increased microdamage anyway (as argued in Section 7.4.3 and in terms of the volume effect). As noted, recent empirical data do not support the conventional view. Therefore, it is best to consider adaptation as accommodating the safe range of strains engendered by habitual loading (Bertram and Biewener 1988)—this is especially important when considering the benefits described later for regional variations in osteon morphotypes and predominant CFO.

The capacity of bone to accommodate or resist microdamage formation/propagation through microstructural/nanostructural modifications is called toughening. One of the most important, but nonspecific, toughening mechanisms includes the introduction of microstructural interfaces such as cement lines of secondary osteons (Gibson et al. 2006; Skedros et al. 2005b; Ural and Vashishth 2005). Another important and specific, toughening mechanism has been revealed in studies that have examined thin sections of bone using polarized light. In these studies, specific osteon morphotypes have been identified, and their increased regional prevalence can differentially toughen bone for its mechanical disparities in tension, compression, and shear (Figure 7.18; Bigley et al. 2006; Hiller et al. 2003; Skedros et al., 2009, 2011). Examples of how osteon morphotypes influence bone failure from the material level to the structural level of the whole bone are described by Ebacher et al. (2007) in their in vitro study of human tibia fractures.

### 7.6.3 Predominant Collagen Fiber Orientation (CFO)

Predominant CFO is strongly strain-mode specific, and regional CFO patterns are often produced by the regional prevalence of specific osteon morphotypes. In order to quantify these relationships, osteon morphotype scoring, first introduced by Martin and co-workers (1996a), has become a useful method for discerning mechanically relevant variations in the

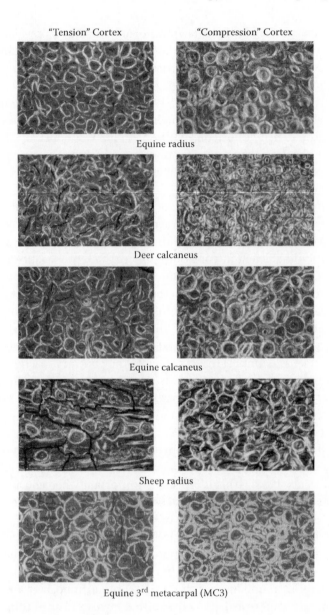

"Tension" Cortex          "Compression" Cortex

Equine radius

Deer calcaneus

Equine calcaneus

Sheep radius

Equine 3$^{rd}$ metacarpal (MC3)

**Figure 7.18** Representative circularly polarized light (CPL) images of bone from tension cortices (at left) and compression cortices (at right) of several nonhuman species (from Skedros et al. 2009; see Figure 7.5 for image locations). The width of each image is 1.52 mm. The specimens were embedded in polymethyl methacrylate in an unstained and fully calcified state, and ultramilled to 100 microns thickness. All images were taken under the same illumination and 50× magnification.

regional distributions of secondary osteons when viewed under circularly polarized light (CPL; Skedros et al. 2011).

In a microscopic analysis using CPL and thin plane-parallel transverse sections, the seminal study by Martin et al. (1996a) described six phenotypic variants of the secondary osteons in the diaphyseal cortices of adult equine third metacarpals. In addition to identifying these six variants (osteon morphotypes), they introduced a numerical method for scoring regional variations in their distribution. Under CPL these osteon morphotypes are distinguished by variations in birefringent (brightness) patterns that are attributed to their lamellar collagen organization/orientation. These range from (1) hoop osteons, containing a bright peripheral ring of highly oblique-to-transverse collagen fibers that surround longitudinal fibers, which appear darker in CPL, to (2) distributed osteons with highly oblique-to-transverse collagen patterns distributed across the entire osteon wall, which appears bright in CPL (Figure 7.11). Martin and co-workers' scoring scheme, which can be expressed as an osteon morphotype score (MTS), represents a significant advance in interpreting bone adaptation because the regional prevalence of these osteon morphotypes appears to be common, having been observed in various bones of diverse species (Beraudi et al. 2010; Currey 2002; McFarlin et al. 2008; Riggs et al. 1993a; Skedros et al. 1996, 2009, 2011; Vincentelli 1978; Warshaw 2007).

As shown in Figure 7.11, we modified the osteon MTS method of Martin et al. (1996a) as a means for more accurately interpreting relationships of morphotypes with specific load environments (Skedros et al. 2009, 2011). In bones that receive habitual bending, studies using CPL images have shown osteon morphotypes with relatively greater amounts of transverse collagen (bright gray levels) distributed in the osteon wall represent adaptation for prevalent compression, while osteon morphotypes with more longitudinal collagen (dark) represent adaptation for prevalent tension (Figures 7.18 and 7.19; Riggs et al. 1993a, 1993b; Skedros et al. 2004, 2006a, 2007a). Consequently, these differences help identify

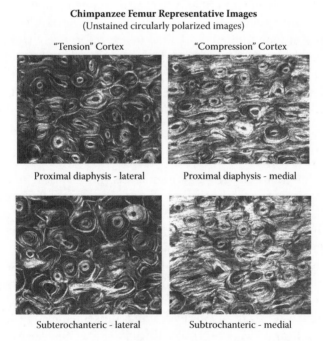

**Chimpanzee Femur Representative Images**
(Unstained circularly polarized images)

"Tension" Cortex                    "Compression" Cortex

Proximal diaphysis - lateral        Proximal diaphysis - medial

Subterochanteric - lateral          Subtrochanteric - medial

**Figure 7.19** Representative circularly polarized-light images taken from the proximal diaphyseal cross-sections of an adult chimpanzee femur. At left, are images from the lateral tension cortex that shows generally darker osteons, which are quantified as lower osteon morphotype scores using our scoring scheme (e.g., values lower than 5 in Figure 7.11). At right, are images from the medial compression cortex that shows generally brighter osteons, which are quantified as higher osteon morphotype scores using our scoring scheme (e.g., 5 in Figure 7.11). The width of each image is 1.4 mm. The specimens were embedded in polymethyl methacrylate in an unstained and fully calcified state, and ultramilled to 100 microns thickness. All images were obtained under the same illumination and magnification.

habitual bending because morphotypes found in tension-loaded regions differ significantly from those in compression-loaded regions. Osteons that appear to be hybrids of those in tension and compression regions tend to predominate in the neutral axis regions, probably representing adaptations for prevalent/predominant shear. In contrast to bending, bones or bone regions loaded in prevalent/predominant torsion do not exhibit regional variations in osteon morphotypes—regional variations in osteon morphotypes are not expected here because the uniform bone matrix organization is believed to represent *the* adaptation for the diffusely distributed shear stresses that are produced in this loading mode.

### 7.6.4   Early Observations and Studies of Osteon Morphotypes

The genesis of studies showing differential mechanical properties of osteon morphotypes can be traced to those of Ascenzi and Bonucci (1967, 1968). These investigators elucidated a correlation between the mechanical properties of individual secondary osteons and the birefringence patterns that they identified: predominantly bright, predominantly dark, or alternating bright and dark lamellae. They observed that the dark osteons had greater strength in tension than those having bright or alternating lamellae. Following the interpretation of lamellar structure postulated by von Ebner (1887) and Gebhardt (1906), osteons with alternating lamellae, as seen when viewed between crossed polarizers, were assumed to have plies in which the collagen fibers alternated between longitudinal and transverse directions (Figure 7.20). Osteons appearing entirely bright or dark were assumed to have mostly transversely or longitudinally oriented fibers, respectively (Bromage et al. 2003). (See Marotti 1996; Turner and Burr 1997; Yamamoto et al. 2000; and Ascenzi and co-workers 2003, 2006, for discussions regarding alternative explanations that have been considered, but are not as well supported, for the physical bases of these differences in lamellar birefringence.) A brief review of observations of osteon morphotypes in polarized light reported from the 1930s through the 1980s can be found in Skedros et al. (1996).

#### 7.6.4.1   *Strength Enhancement versus Toughening*

Conventional wisdom that strength enhancement is the goal of regionally predominant CFO and specific osteon morphotypes has been trumped by more recent data showing that toughening is the aim. The earlier conventional paradigm stemmed from studies of the relationship between CFO and mechanical properties of macroscopic cortical bone specimens without respect to regional habitual loads. In the contexts of nonspecific or unspecified load histories, studies of cortical bone anisotropy using plane-polarized light (see Bromage et al. 2003 for discussion of how this differs from circularly polarized light) have shown that predominant CFO is correlated with strength or failure strain of tested specimens (Ascenzi 1988; Evans 1958; Evans and Vincentelli 1974; Reilly and Burstein 1974, 1975; Vincentelli and Evans 1971). Martin and Ishida (1989) also quantified birefringence with plane-polarized light and reported that longitudinal CFO was an important predictor of tensile strength in bovine cortical bone. Martin and Boardman (1993) found similar results for the bending strength and elastic modulus of bovine cortical bone. Using four-point bending to test cortical beams cut from equine radial diaphyses, and both CPL and plane-polarized light analyses of tested specimens, Martin et al. (1996b) showed that longitudinally oriented collagen correlated with greater modulus and monotonic strength. In sum, these data reflect conventional wisdom that the in vivo role for variations in predominant CFO is primarily for affecting strength-related material properties.

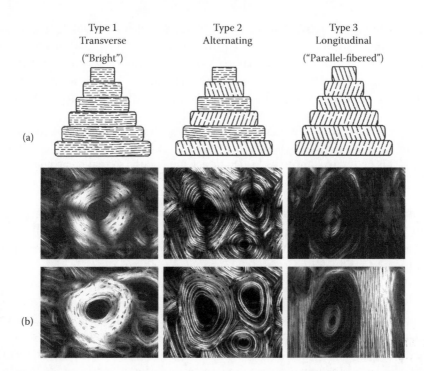

**Figure 7.20** Examples of three osteon morphotypes in linear (top microscopic images) (a) and circularly polarized light (bottom images; the dark cross-shaped extinction patterns are absent) (b). The illustrations at the top of this figure are diagrammatic depictions of the predominant collagen fiber orientation (CFO) patterns that result in the presence or absence of the bire-fringence patterns seen in the lamellae of the osteons in the microscopic images. The osteon images are from Bromage et al. (2003), and the layout of the figure is based both on Bromage et al. (2003), and Ascenzi and Bonucci (1968). These investigators ascribe to the view that the birefringence (gray-level) variations, seen for example in the alternating osteon, are primarily based on lamellar variations in predominant CFO. Other investigators have argued that varia-tions in collagen fiber density account for the gray-level variations in the alternating osteons (Marotti 1996); this view is not well supported by experimental data and also appears to be influenced by limitations of specimen preparation techniques (Yamamoto et al. 2000). (Images are courtesy of Timothy Bromage.)

By contrast, this conventional paradigm is challenged by more recent studies that have used strain-mode-specific loading (i.e., compression testing of bone habitually loaded in compression, and tension testing of bone habitually loaded in tension). These studies have shown that predominant CFO more strongly influences regional material toughness (energy absorption). For example, in a study of mid-diaphyseal cortical specimens of mature equine third metacarpals, we have examined the relative contributions of multiple material characteristics (CFO, porosity, ash fraction, osteon population density, percent osteon area, and individual osteon cross-sectional area) in strain-mode-specific testing (Skedros et al. 2006a). In tension testing (dumbbell specimens), CFO was one of the top three characteris-tics in explaining variability in yield stress, ultimate stress, plastic energy absorption, and total energy absorption. In compression testing (cube specimens), CFO was among the top three characteristics in explaining yield energy absorption, plastic energy absorption, and total energy absorption. These results add to a growing body of experimental data that reveal an important role for predominant CFO, collagen content, and intermolecular col-lagen cross-links in affecting energy absorption (a measure of toughness; Banse et al. 2002;

Burr 2002; Nyman et al. 2007; Skedros et al. 2006d; Wang et al. 1998). In a study of strain-mode-specific mechanical testing of an equine radius (12-year-old Thoroughbred), Reilly and Currey (1999) showed that the patterns of microdamage formed, and the mode of failure of specimens from the anterior tension and posterior compression cortices, suggest that each cortex was adapted to its respective habitual loading mode (p. 551):

> bone can be adapted to be better at resisting the growth of one type of microcrack (either tension or compression) but that this then causes it to be bad at resisting the other type. Therefore, it is better for bone to be loaded in one mode only, so that it can adapt histologically to that mode.

In comparison to these studies addressing the mechanical importance of regional variations in averaged CFO values, there are only two studies that specifically evaluate the mechanical consequences of differences in the distributions of specific osteon morphotypes. In the first study, Hiller et al. (2003) showed that variations in the distributions of distributed (i.e., bright and alternating) and hooped osteons (Figure 7.11) in dorsal (anterior), medial, and lateral cortices of equine third metacarpals can affect regional fatigue life and toughness by differentially dissipating energy (via osteonal pullout; Figure 7.9). In mechanical testing studies of equine third metacarpals, we have also implied that regional variations in the prevalence of these various osteon morphotypes produce the regional differences in CFO that strongly influenced energy absorption in strain-mode-specific testing (Skedros et al. 2006a).

In the second study, Bigley et al. (2006) advanced the mechanical push-out methods pioneered by Ascenzi and coworkers, and reported important details of the mechanical properties of individual osteons in isolation and with consideration of their surrounding matrix histomorphology. Using the diaphysis of the third metacarpal of an adult thoroughbred horse and observations in both polarized light and scanning electron microscopy, their experimental study revealed clear differences in interfacial strength (at cement line and interlamellar interfaces) associated with variations in CFO that typify the four osteon morphotypes that they evaluated (Figure 7.12). In their push-out tests, interfacial failure was typically observed at the cement line interface or within the osteon wall (i.e., interlamellar interface). For alternating osteons the cement line is weaker (12.4 MPa) than the interlamellar interface (33.3 MPa, $p = 0.04$). By contrast, the cement line is stronger for the bright osteon (47.1 MPa) than the interlamellar interface (33.4 MPa, $p = 0.04$). Overall, bright osteons had the highest interfacial debonding strength (40.3 MPa), and dark osteons had the lowest strength (22.8 MPa; $p < 0.05$). In terms of maximum interfacial shear stress, the bright osteons also had highest stress (82.6 MPa), the dark osteons had the least (63.6 MPa; $p < 0.05$), and alternating and hooped osteons had intermediate values (76.3 MPa and 71.0 MPa, respectively). Their linear regression analyses also suggest that there may be a relationship between the amount of oblique-to-transverse collagen fibers (compression-adapted collagen in the osteon wall) and these important mechanical properties, independent of the presence of alternating rings. The histomorphology of the surrounding matrix also profoundly influenced the shear strength of the osteons. For example, as the fractions of bright, dark, and hooped osteons increased, the debonding shear strength increased, whereas when alternating osteons increased, the shear debond strength decreased. In view of these mechanical test results, it is clear that osteon MTSs that are based in mechanical and morphological contexts should distinguish bright from alternating osteons in addition to distinguishing hooped from nonhooped osteons (Skedros et al. 2011). In summary, these studies show the mechanical importance of osteon morphotypes.

### 7.6.4.2 When Strain Data Are Lacking, What Is the Most Reliable Structural or Material Characteristic for Interpreting Load History in Limb Bones?

Table 7.2 lists the main structural and material characteristics to utilize in load history analysis. Among these, consider that the data that are addressed in the preceding sections support the conclusions that predominant CFO and osteon morphotypes are the strongest characteristics for interpreting load history—much stronger than mineral content, osteon and osteocyte population densities, and osteon size. In nearly all bones that have been studied, osteon morphotypes produce regional variations in CFO (Beckstrom et al. 2010; Mason et al. 1995; Skedros and Hunt 2004; Skedros and Kuo 1999; Skedros et al. 1996, 2004, 2007a, 2009, 2011). Refer to these papers for data that support CFO as the most important characteristic in this context. There might be a role for mineral crystallite orientation for interpreting load history in cases where preferred alignment of the mineral component (i.e., the extrafibrillar mineral) of the collagen-mineral composite might be dissociated from the predominant CFO (Skedros et al. 2006c). But techniques required for the less destructive analysis of mineral orientation as an indicator of predominant load direction are not readily available (Espinoza Orías et al. 2009). Consequently, preparing bone specimens for the analysis of patterns in predominant CFO using circularly polarized light is probably the single most important technical step for interpreting the load history of most bones, even if they do not exhibit osteonal remodeling (Boyde and Riggs, 1990; Skedros et al., 1996; Skedros and Hunt, 2004).

Some readers may have selected variations in osteon population density as the strongest characteristic for interpreting load history. In fact, osteon population densities and other osteon morphologic characteristics (e.g., size, shape, etc.) receive great attention in anthropological studies that are aimed at distinguishing species or deciphering the load history of limb bones and ribs (Abbott et al. 1996; Burr et al. 1990; Martiniaková et al. 2006; Mulhern and Ubelaker 2009; Pfeiffer et al. 2006; Robling and Stout 2003; Schaffler et al. 1985; Urbanová and Novotný 2005). In contrast to empirical studies showing strong correlations of CFO with strain-related parameters of load history (Skedros et al. 2006c; Takano et al. 1999), these studies typically show much weaker correlations of osteon populations and other osteon characteristics (e.g., size and shape) with load history and other related biomechanical issues. Consequently, these osteon parameters are a distant second to the distribution of osteon morphotypes and regional patterns of predominant CFO. Nevertheless, osteon densities in bone must be considered in most cases because they tend to be concentrated, although not always (Gibson et al. 2006; Mason et al. 1995; Skedros et al. 2009), in the more highly strained regions (compression cortices) of bones that are loaded in habitual bending.

In a study of 87 (1 outlier) modern human femoral mid-diaphyseal specimens (45 male, 43 female; 17–97 years; 12,690 osteons), Britz et al. (2009) found a weak inverse relationship between osteon size and body weight (9%–10% variance explained, $p < 0.01$)—a relation that was superimposed on the more dominant pattern of decreasing osteon size with age (18%–28% of variance explained, $p < 0.001$). Although there was no evidence that this relationship was related to strain magnitude, a prior study reported smaller osteons in the femora and tibiae of late Pleistocene adult hominids that was interpreted as reflecting increased strains produced by increased strenuous activity (Abbott et al. 1996). This idea is supported by the analytical study by van Oers et al. (2008) that showed an inverse relationship between osteon size and strain magnitude in compression (smaller osteons in higher compression). These investigators felt that this relationship mirrored data reported in the literature, especially noting our studies showing smaller osteons in the compression cortices (where strains are highest) of the habitually bent calcanei of adult deer, sheep, elk, and horses (Skedros et al. 1994b, 1997). However, this relationship has not been shown in other bones where an association with spatial high-low strain magnitude distributions and osteon size should have been obvious (Mason et al., 1995; Skedros et al., 2009). Additionally, a mathematical error was detected in the Abbott et al. (1996) study mentioned earlier and a re-examination of their data by Streeter et al. (2010) found that the osteon population densities were not higher and the osteons are not smaller for the presumably more strenuously loaded Pleistocene hominid limb bones. From these perspectives, osteon size is unreliable for interpreting load history. Although there is evidence that osteon size tends to increase toward the endosteum (Britz et al. 2009), inconsistency in this relationship suggests that, when present, it might be an effect of proximity to the marrow and not a consequence of low strain (Skedros et al. 1997, 2001).

Differences in the distributions of osteocyte densities also caught our attention because of the possibility that this characteristic might strongly correlate with load history, especially in distinguishing bending from torsion. We postulated this relationship because it seemed reasonable that bone tissue could somehow perceive regional nonuniformities in the strain environment (e.g., strain modes and magnitudes). In other words, this "perception" would require the presence of a cellular network that communicates across broad regions of a bone (e.g., up and down a diaphysis or across an entire diaphyseal cross-section). For this to work, the most likely resident cells with this function would be osteocytes because they (1) are the most numerous bone cells, (2) exhibit modified inter-cellular gap junctions and, hence, cell-to-cell molecular and electrical transmission, and (3) form gap junctions with bone lining cells that reside on the porous surfaces where osteoclast migration or activation commences for modeling and remodeling processes (Marotti 1996; Martin et al. 1998; Skedros et al. 2005a). Experimental data show that apoptotic osteocytes, caused by microdamage-induced injury that can occur naturally, trigger the remodeling process (i.e., apoptotic osteocytes attract osteoclasts; Verborgt et al. 2000; Cardosa et al. 2009). In these perspectives it seemed reasonable to hypothesize that regional differences in osteocyte densities would be present and would reflect differences in the sensitivity of the cellular network for monitoring and ensuring a normal range of strains in a habitual load environment. However, correlations of osteocyte population density with strain history (modes and magnitudes) and marrow proximity have not been shown in bones where these relationships should be obvious (Skedros 2005; Skedros et al. 2005a). These results further support the conclusion that predominant CFO is the strongest characteristic for predicting load history in these contexts.

### 7.6.4.3 *Exceptions to the Rule and Important Caveats*
As expected in biological studies, there are always exceptions to the rule. For example, although strain-mode-related variations in the patterns of CFO can be present in bones where remodeling does not occur (Mason et al. 1995; Skedros and Hunt 2004), there can be circumstances of growth and cases in some bones that poorly remodel where it is difficult or impossible to use this characteristic for deciphering load history. In this perspective, it is important to point out exceptional cases or situations where predominant CFO can be misleading. We have shown the lack of expected strain-mode-specific (tension vs. compression) CFO patterns in Rhesus macaque ulnae and chicken tarsometatarsals

even though they are considered to be habitually bent bones (Demes et al. 2001; Judex et al. 1997b; Skedros et al. 2003b). In the case of the macaque ulnae, the histology in the tension and compression regions did not show significant differences in CFO and appeared to be comprised of fairly recently deposited laminar bone without much remodeling. By contrast, the lack of expected regional tension versus compression CFO patterns in the chicken tarsometatarsi evades a similarly straightforward maturation-related explanation (these bones did show localized osteon remodeling). Thus it may be difficult, or impossible, to discern load history in terms of "expected" histomorphological correlates of functional adaptation in some bones that are growing, have recently stopped growing, or are from species that do not exhibit much remodeling (Skedros et al. 2004, 2007a). Examples of this might also be reflected in the seemingly patchy or irregular distribution of several primary histological types shown by McFarlin et al. (2008) in various primate limb bones spanning a range from immature to adult. But this does not necessarily mean an absence of correlation between these types of primary histology and their overall or regional predominant nonosteon CFO, which the authors did not measure. In turn, many of the bones in their study are also in the high-load-complexity category where regional CFO variations (whether from the primary or secondary bone) would not be expected (see Section 7.7).

In summary, these examples show that regional strain-mode-related variations in predominant CFO and associated osteon morphotypes, although they seem highly reliable for distinguishing habitual bending from torsion in many cases, fall short of being 100% sensitive and 100% specific in this context. This emphasizes an important practical point—investigators must always examine many structural and material characteristics when attempting to interpret the load history of a bone or bone region when in vivo strain data are lacking or insufficient. Perhaps histocompositional characteristics that have been scarcely studied could help in these exceptional cases (e.g., distributions of types and amounts of collagen molecular cross-links or noncollagenous proteins).

## 7.7  Consideration 5: Load-Complexity Categories: Bending, Intermediate A, Intermediate B, and Torsion

The general theme of this section is that regional variations in predominant CFO coupled with in vivo strain data suggest that habitual loading of a bone or bone region can be best understood in the context of one of four load-complexity categories (Figure 7.21). To understand the rationale for the criteria used to create the four load-complexity categories, it is useful to start by distinguishing the load histories that are at the extremes: simple bending (least complex) to torsion combined with bending and compression (most complex). Another way to think about these extremes is that there is greater load predictability in simple bending and less load predictability in complex torsion and bending. Figure 7.22 shows examples of diaphyseal regions of some bones that can be placed in one of the four load-complexity categories. These four categories are based on the three general/habitual load categories that have been described by Currey (1984), which represent a spectrum from relatively simple to complex loading, respectively: (a) short cantilever (e.g., sheep, deer, and equine calcanei), (b) curved column (e.g., equine and sheep radii), and (c) straight or quasi-curved column (e.g., equine third metacarpals and sheep tibiae). As shown in Figure 7.21, the four load-complexity categories are based on typical ranges of neutral axis rotation; where the neutral axis rotates the most there is prevalent/predominant torsion (the highest load-complexity category). In

Bone Histology: An Anthropological Perspective

| Habitual Load Complexity Categories Based on N.A. Rotation Criterion[a] (Unless indicated, diaphyseal regions are considered.) |
|---|

| Complexity Category | Examples (Based on N.A. rotation during middle portion of the stance phase.) |
|---|---|
| **Low** (N.A.: <10° rotation) (Tension and compression minimally overlap; Shear is localized near N.A.) | **1. Artiodactyl and perissodactyl calcanei** (Lanyon, 1974; Su et al., 1999) **2. Potoroo calcaneus** (Biewener et al., 1996) **3. Chicken metatarsus** (Judex et al., 1997; Skedros et al., 2003)[b] |
| **Intermediate A** (N.A.: 10°–20° rotation) | **4. Dog, sheep and horse radii** (Carter et al., 1980; Coleman et al., 2002) **5. Macaque ulna** (Demes et al., 1998; Skedros et al., 2003) |
| **Intermediate B** (N.A.: 20°–40° rotation) | **6. Sheep metatarsal** (Lieberman et al., 2004) **7. Chimpanzee femoral neck** (Kalmey and Lovejoy, 2002; Skedros et al., 2008) **8. Immature turkey ulna** (Skedros and Hunt, 2004)[b,c] **9. Horse third metacarpal** (Gross et al., 1992; Skedros et al., 1996) **10. Human tibia** (Lanyon et al., 1975; Burr et al., 1996; Milgrom et al., 2000; Peterman et al., 2001) **11. Human femur proximal diaphysis** (Skedros et al., 1999) |
| **High** (N.A.: >40° rotation) (Tension and compression overlap extensively; Shear is relatively more diffusely distributed across the cortex when compared to other categories.) | **12. Goat radius** (Main and Biewener, 2004; Main, 2007; Moreno et al., 2008) **13. Mature turkey ulna** (Rubin and Lanyon, 1985; Skedros and Hunt, 2004)[b,c] **14. Horse third metacarpal** (Skedros et al., 2006) **15. Human tibia (in some athletes)** (Lanyon et al., 1975; Burr et al., 1996; Milgrom et al., 2000; Peterman et al., 2001) **16. Human femur mid-diaphysis** (Cristofolini et al., 1996; Goldman et al., 2003; Drapeau and Streeter, 2006) **17. Sheep tibia** (Lanyon and Bourn, 1979; Lieberman et al., 2004) **18. Pigeon humerus** (Biewener and Dial, 1995) **19. Chimpanzee femoral neck** (Kalmey and Lovejoy 2002; Skedros et al., 2008) **20. Human femoral neck** (Pidaparti and Turner, 1997; Skedros et al., 1999; Skedros and Baucom, 2007) **21. Free-flying bat humerus** (Swartz et al., 1992) **22. Chicken femur** (Carrano and Biewener, 1999; Skedros, 2002) **23. Alligator femur** (Blob and Biewener, 1999; Lee, 2004) **24. Greyhound femur** (Szivek et al., 1992) |

**Figure 7.21** The four load-complexity categories. Studies that either support segregating these bones or bone regions into these categories or support the comments in the footnote of this table are listed here (Biewener 1990; Biewener et al. 1996; Burr et al. 1996; Carter et al. 1980; Coleman et al. 2002; Currey and Alexander 1985; Demes et al. 1998; Gross et al. 1992; Kalmey and Lovejoy 2002; Lanyon 1974; Lanyon et al. 1975; Lieberman et al. 2004; Main 2007; Main and Biewener 2004; Milgrom et al. 2000; Moreno et al. 2008; Pearson and Lieberman 2004;

turn, they help to conceptualize and simplify the characteristic loading patterns of diaphyseal regions where a focus on structural characteristics can be misleading. Additional studies are needed to develop more rigorous, and empirically tested, criteria for distinguishing these categories (see Moreno et al. 2008). Examples showing how to use these load-complexity categories appear in Sections 7.7.6 and 7.7.7.

## 7.7.1 Bending vs. Torsion

Becoming proficient at differentiating general features of bone morphology (from a bone's shape and girth to its microstructure/nanostructure) in habitual bending versus habitual torsion, will help to increase your awareness of the strengths and weaknesses of using histological organization to infer the load history of a bone or bone region. The assertion that predominant bending or torsion are the most representative load histories of bone diaphyses, with most other load regimes being somewhere along the continuum between these, is supported by in vivo strain measurements from bones of various mammalian and avian species that typically demonstrate these load regimes as being most prevalent during peak loading of controlled ambulation (de Margerie et al. 2005; Lanyon and Bourn 1979; Lieberman et al. 2003). In fact, bending is the load regime that is most highly conserved in many appendicular long bone diaphyses (Rubin and Lanyon 1984a), and bending also produces the majority (>70%) of longitudinal strains occurring during peak loading of controlled in vivo activity (Biewener and Bertram 1993; Biewener et al. 1986; see footnote on page 180). The bending versus torsion distinction is also clinically relevant and is related

---

Peterman et al. 2001; Rubin et al. 1996b; Rubin and Lanyon 1985; Ruff et al. 2006; Skedros et al. 1996, 2003b, 2004, 2008; Skedros and Hunt 2004; Su et al. 1999; Turner 1998).

[a] The criterion for designating these categories is the magnitude of the rotation of neutral axis (N.A.) during middle portion of stance phase. As shown by the double-headed arrows, this criterion can place some bone regions or closely related bones in different habitual load-complexity categories; for example: (1) sheep and goat radii, (2) human proximal femoral diaphysis and mid-diaphysis, and (3) immature and mature turkey ulnae. In some cases the bone can be placed into a different category if there are differences in habitual load complexity as a result of physical activity (e.g., increased torsion in human tibiae of individuals who regularly participate in twisting/turning sports). This possibility is usually seen in primates; more specifically, is almost always secondary to human volition (e.g., sports training) or human intervention (e.g., horse or greyhound dog racing).

From the low to the high complexity categories there is an increased prevalence of shear/torsion and decreased prevalence of strains produced by axial loads. The "Intermediate B" category includes bones wherein some typical functional loading (e.g., changes in gait) cause moderate, but typically predictable, shifts in the neutral axis. The magnitudes of these shifts are greater than those that occur, for example, in canine and horse radii ("Intermediate A") during controlled locomotion.

Creation of these categories is also supported by data showing that bone modeling/remodeling responses can differ between cortical regions that experience a relatively larger percentage of axial strain (e.g., "low" complexity category) vs. shear strain (e.g., "high" complexity category) (Rubin et al., 1996b; Turner, 1998).

Divisions between these categories, although are useful for the purposes of this chapter, should be considered provisional since they eventually will be more rigorously defined and likely revised as new data become available (e.g., see Ruff et al., 2006; Moreno et al., 2008).

[b] As noted in the text, predominant CFO variations in avian bones (and some mammals and/or growing bones of many species) can be significantly confounded by differences in local rates of bone growth.

[c] Studies of CFO in immature and mature turkeys have revealed a "tension/compression" pattern only in ulnae of *immature* animals. It has been hypothesized that the absence of this pattern in *mature* animals is a consequence of increased torsional loading in adults (Skedros and Hunt, 2004).

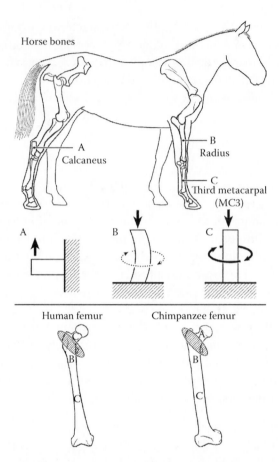

**Figure 7.22** At top are lateral-to-medial views of the right forelimb and hindlimb skeletons of an adult horse showing a spectrum from simple loading to complex loading, respectively: calcaneus (A), radius (B), and third metacarpal (MC3) (C). The drawings are simplified renditions of each bone type, showing: (A) the calcaneus as a cantilevered beam, (B) the radius as a curved beam with longitudinal loading; the curvature accentuates bending. Torsion (dotted line) is also present but is less than the torsion in the MC3 (solid circular line in C), and (C) the MC3 with off-axis longitudinal loading producing bending and torsion, the latter being greater than in the other two bones. Several studies reporting in vivo strain data were used to create these drawings (Biewener et al. 1983a, 1983b; Gross et al. 1992; Lanyon 1974; Rubin and Lanyon 1982; Schneider et al. 1982; Turner et al. 1975). At bottom are the hypothesized multidomains for a human femur (left; also see Figure 7.24) and chimpanzee femur (right); the letters within the femora correspond to the basic load conditions in the horse bones. The intertrochanteric regions of these bones (indicated by ellipses with oblique lines) are transition zones between the neck and proximal diaphyseal domains. In accordance with predominant CFO data (Beckstrom et al. 2010; Skedros et al. 1999), these drawings show the speculation that the chimpanzee femoral neck (also more robust and elliptical in cross-sectional shape) receives more prevalent/predominant bending than the human femoral neck.

to regional patterns of predominant CFO and distributions of osteon morphotypes. For example, as noted in Chapter 8 of this book (by Agnew and Bolte), bone failure at the material level directly influences structural failure of the whole bone, and this is especially true in bending- and torsion-related fracture (Ebacher et al. 2007).

  *When you think of bending, think of roughly discrete regions of tension, compression, and shear.* Bending creates a neutral axis, which is a region where longitudinal strains (i.e., along the long axis of the bone) drop to zero in materials that are ideal (isotropic, uniform, and continuous). In other words, the neutral axis is the location (or a zone in typical bones because the neutral axis is never stationary) where there is a transition from longitudinal tension to compression. In the neutral axis regions, however, shear strains become large because the maximum strains are obliquely oriented with respect to the long axis of the bone. Although longitudinal strains drop toward zero in neutral axis regions, strain gradients and fluid flux increase—these parameters influence nutrient delivery (Judex et al. 1997b). Bending, therefore, creates a dilemma because the mechanical properties, including fracture and microdamage mechanics, of cortical bone differ in tension, compression, and shear (mechanical properties of bone in tension and shear are worse than compression; Section 7.5, Figure 7.16). Differential histological modifications are necessary in order to more optimally resist or accommodate the formation of fatigue microdamage in these common nonuniform, potentially deleterious, strain environments that are engendered by habitual bending (Akkus et al. 2003; Reilly et al. 1997). To reduce its tendency to fracture in regions where physiologic loading produces a degradation of mechanical integrity, regional variations in bone nanostructure (e.g., CFO and collagen molecular cross-links) and microstructure (e.g., osteon morphotypes, osteon density, osteon percent area, and osteon diameter) can modify matrix mechanical properties (e.g., strength, fatigue resistance, and energy absorbed to failure) (Carter et al. 1976; Corondan and Haworth 1986; Diab and Vashishth 2007; Evans 1976; Evans and Bang 1966, 1967; Evans and Vincentelli 1974; Hiller et al. 2003; Moyle et al. 1978; Simkin and Robin 1974; Skedros et al. 2006a; Vincentelli and Grigorov 1985; Yeni et al. 1997).

*When you think of torsion think of diffusely distributed shear.* In contrast to habitual bending, if a bone is loaded primarily in torsion, regional variations in nanostructural and microstructural adaptations (Table 7.2) would not be expected as there are typically no significant temporal or spatial disparities in strain modes. As noted earlier, the prevalent mode in torsion is shear, and the general or diffuse distribution of this strain mode does not warrant regional histological adaptation (Skedros and Hunt 2004).

### 7.7.2 Solutions in Engineered Structures: The Single I-Beam versus Multiple I-Beam Analogy

When contrasting adaptations for bending and torsion, it is helpful to consider, from an engineering context where the material is not living, what common structural solutions could readily accommodate each of these load regimes. An engineering solution for a structure that must accommodate unidirectional bending is an I-beam (Figure 7.23a). The most I-beam-like bones that we have studied are sheep and deer calcanei.* When bending is unpredictable, occurring in multiple directions, a shifting neutral axis must be accommodated to avoid catastrophic failure. In bones, such loading is typically the result of a relatively complex load history that is often characterized by prevalent/predominant torsion. A structural solution for this loading might be an array of radially arranged I-beams;

---

* Bones that resemble I-beams more closely such as the mandibular ramus of a wolf are very uncommon, perhaps because this design would preclude the various benefits of a marrow cavity and its contents for most animals. But in the case of manatees it is clear that tubular morphology is not an absolute constraint of long bone design. In these animals the marrow cavities of the limb bones and ribs are essentially absent; they are filled with bone for buoyancy dynamics. In manatees, the primary site of hematopoiesis is in the vertebral bodies.

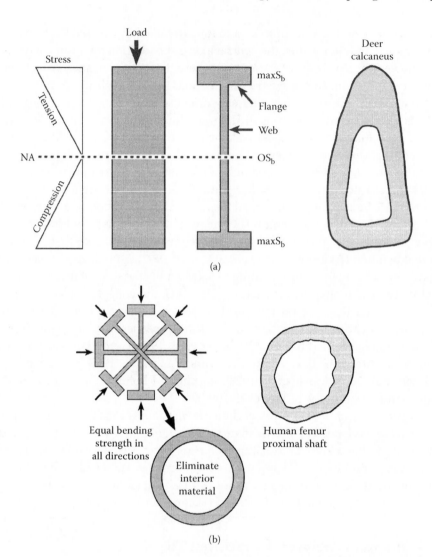

**Figure 7.23** (a) A simple structural solution for unidirectional loading is an I-beam. The neutral axis (NA) is where the longitudinal strains fall to zero, which is in the central portion of a rectangular beam (middle) and the I-beam. The I-beam exhibits an economy of material where the maximum beam stresses ($S_b$) are in the flanges; these longitudinal stresses are nearly zero at the center of the web ($OS_b$). The section at the far right is from a mule deer calcaneus. (b) Analogy of torsion/multidirectional loading being accommodated by multiple intersecting I-beams, which is most efficiently accommodated by making the structure tubular (annular cross-section). The section at the far right is a transverse section from a human proximal femoral diaphysis. Even though this section is quasi-circular, variations in predominant CFO that correspond to habitual medial-lateral bending have been reported (Skedros et al. 1999). Consequently, a section with this shape does not necessarily rule out the presence of habitual bending.

however, the intersections of the I-beams that result (Figure 7.23b) are not efficient because the material toward the center is not needed. What then emerges is an annulus. Bone biomechanics teaches that prevalent torsion (e.g., often more typical toward the mid-diaphysis of some bones) is associated with an annular cross-sectional shape—in limb diaphyses this morphology suggests the presence of a broadly shifting neutral axis (Biewener 2003; Lieberman et al. 2004). In turn, a history of torsional loading would produce prevalent and more diffusely distributed shear stresses. This contrasts with the more localized shear stress in neutral axes of bones that are loaded in habitual bending.

### 7.7.3 Cross-Sectional Shape and Cortical Thickness Can Lead One Astray When Interpreting Load History

Because bone, a living tissue, does not adhere to the rules of structural engineering, cross-sectional shape and cortical thickness cannot be relied on for interpreting load history. For example, Figure 7.5 shows bones in several of the load-complexity categories where the cross-sectional shapes and cortical thicknesses do not consistently reflect the direction of greatest bending resistance. The direction of the greatest bending resistance of sheep and deer calcanei is in the direction of bending whereas it is approximately 90° to the direction of bending in the radii of horses and sheep. Additionally the thickest cortices in these calcanei are on the compression side of the bones (i.e., the upper cortices of those shown in Figure 7.5), whereas equine and sheep radii have more similar thicknesses of the compression and tension cortices. Additional discussion of the unreliability potentially incurred by using axes of cross-sectional moments of inertia to interpret bending distributions and neutral axis locations can be found in Lieberman et al. (2004), Demes (2007), and Ruff et al. (2006).

Even when a bone's cross-section is quasi-circular it is possible to be led astray when interpreting load history because this shape could, for example, lead to the conclusion that there is insufficient bending to evoke microstructural/nanostructural adaptation. An example of this has been shown in the equine third metacarpal, which, although roughly circular, can still have variations in CFO that reflect habitual bending (Skedros et al. 1996, 2006a). Additional examples are the quasi-circular sections of proximal human and chimpanzee femoral diaphyses that also show patterns of CFO that are consistent with a medial–lateral compression–tension strain distribution of habitual bending (Figure 7.23b; Beckstrom et al. 2010; Skedros et al. 1999, 2011). These data again emphasize that investigators must attempt to quantify a myriad of material characteristics when interpreting a bone's load history from its morphological characteristics, even when the bone's cross-sectional shape is quasi-circular.

### 7.7.4 The Value of Bending: Predictability, Fluid Flow, Nutrient Delivery, and Beneficial Signals

If bending creates the dilemma of regionally prevalent, but potentially deleterious, shear and tension (Section 7.5), then why is bending such a common load history? In turn, does this load regime have some less obvious or fundamental biological value even though strain-mode-specific nanostructural/microstructural toughening accommodates the tension/shear/compression strain distribution of bending (Section 7.6)? There appears to be a link between load predictability and the answers to these questions as discussed later.

Investigators who have written about the value of bending point out examples of how a bone's asymmetric cross-sectional shape or longitudinal curvature might be designed to allow bending to occur while controlling its magnitude (Bertram and Biewener 1988). This load predictability is structurally beneficial because the bone can differentially adapt its histology for spatially and temporally predictable nonuniform strain mode/magnitude distributions (Reilly and Currey 1999). Load predictability is also beneficial because it is linked to a predictably nonuniform strain distribution that in turn ensures predictability in the fluid-flow dynamics that are essential for nutrient delivery to bone cells (Ehrlich and Lanyon 2002; Judex et al. 1997b; Skedros et al. 1996). Predictable bending might also produce spatial–temporal epigenetic and extragenetic strain-related signals (e.g., electrical potentials) that are vital in the development and maintenance of some bones (Bertram and Biewener 1988; Burger et al. 2003; Carter et al. 1981; Francillon-Vieillot et al. 1990; Ganey and Odgen 1998; Judex et al. 1997a; Lee et al. 2002; Rubin et al. 1996a; Skedros et al. 1996, 2007a).

### 7.7.5   Changes in Strain Distribution Caused by Changes in Load Predictability Can Lead to Stress Fractures: Example in Thoroughbred Horses

In contrast to load predictability, load unpredictability would not allow for microstructural toughening via osteonal remodeling; in some cases this could lead to catastrophic failure. A poignant example of this is the explanation for why the majority of stress fractures in the equine third metacarpals occur in the dorsal-lateral cortex. Nunamaker (2001) has suggested that the shift from prevalent tension in the dorsal cortex during race training at lower speeds to compression at higher racing speeds may provide an explanation for these fractures in thoroughbred horses. He suggests that tension-related adaptations produced by remodeling and modeling activities[*] would not be expected to accommodate compression strains produced at greater speeds: "It seems obvious that bone that models and remodels for tensile forces on the dorsal aspect of MCIII [third metacarpal] will be poorly adapted for the large compressive strains that are seen during racing" (Nunamaker, 2001:213). In turn, when the tension-adapted dorsal cortex receives more prevalent, high-magnitude compression strains microcrack formation is enhanced. This probability is supported by Reilly and Currey (2000), who showed that microdamage formed in compression is highly detrimental to tensile mechanical properties. In tension versus compression, microdamage not only occurs at different thresholds (more readily forms in tension), but can exhibit different morphologic characteristics (e.g., length, shape, and orientation; Boyce et al. 1998; George and Vashishth 2005; Joo et al. 2004; Muir et al. 1999; Reilly and Currey 1999; Reilly et al. 1997).

In third metacarpals from horses that run at high speeds, the probability that microdamage formation might also occur at different strain thresholds for different regions might be especially important for understanding the material organization in the dorsal-lateral region (e.g., increased prevalence of tension- and shear-adapted osteon morphotypes) since it experiences a greater range of strain by being loaded in tension and compression when compared to the palmar-medial and dorsal-medial cortices (Skedros et al. 1996, 2006a, 2009). The prevalence of shear strains, which can be more deleterious to mechanical properties than tensile strains (Figure 7.16), probably increases in the vicinity of the dorsal-lateral cortex during racing because the neutral axis (where shear strains tend to be greatest) traverses this region at these speeds. In view of these possibilities, an equine third metacarpal that is sufficiently exposed to subracing speeds would be expected

---

[*] In addition to remodeling-mediated adaptation, adaptive modeling-mediated adjustments in the cross-section shape of the third metacarpals can occur in racing thoroughbreds. This is possible in racing thoroughbreds because they are skeletally immature (Nunamaker et al. 1989); hence, they still have the capacity to activate subperiosteal/subendosteal bone growth.

to become adapted primarily to tension and shear in the dorsal/lateral cortices. However, if higher speeds are acutely and more consistently sustained, the dorsal/lateral cortices of the third metacarpal may be exposed to high-magnitude compression for which it has not nanostructurally/microstructurally adapted. Could the idea of an activity-induced shifting neutral axis also help to better explain the occurrence of stress fractures in human military recruits or in human femoral neck fragility fractures (Mayhew et al. 2005)?

### 7.7.6   Between-Bone Examples of Using the Load-Complexity Categories

Following are three examples of how the load-complexity categories can be applied as one of the many considerations shown in Table 7.1.

*Example 1: The load-complexity categories help to minimize confusion in some comparisons.* In a sample of 18 adult human femora and tibiae (age range: 18–50), Drapeau and Streeter (2006) examined relationships between cross-sectional geometric properties (modeling-related parameters) with osteon population densities (OPD) and percent areas of osteon bone (remodeling-related parameters). The histomorphometric analyses were performed in the anterior, posterior, medial, and lateral cortices at the mid-diaphysis. They sought to determine if there were statistically significant differences in these osteon parameters along the geometric anterior-posterior (AP) and medial-lateral (ML) axes (i.e., axes of the cross-sectional moments of area). Statistical significance was found only in the tibiae: (1) in the more circular femur, OPD and percent of remodeled bone in the AP and ML axes were not significantly different, and (2) in the tibia, OPD was 25% greater ($p < 0.003$) in the AP axis than in the ML axis, and the percent of remodeled bone was 35% greater ($p < 0.001$). The authors seemed perplexed by these findings; they could not be reconciled within the conventional paradigm of modeling–remodeling synergism/compensation (Section 7.4.2). In fact, they also noted the unexpected lack of strain-mode-related regional CFO patterns in mid-diaphyseal human femora in the study of Goldman et al. (2003; discussed later). The problem is, in part, that no regional variations in these remodeling parameters would be expected in the mid-diaphyseal femur because this region is in the high load-complexity category compared to the human tibial mid-diaphysis, which is in the intermediate B category for most individuals (the mid-diaphyseal tibia might be highly torsionally loaded in individuals that participate regularly in twisting and turning sports; one of the double arrows in Figure 7.21). Therefore, when viewed in terms of the histological organization of bones in the different load-complexity categories, the relatively more uniform microstructure/nanostructure described by Drapeau and Streeter (2006) and Goldman et al. (2003) is expected in the human mid-diaphyseal femur.

*Example 2.* Bone locations subject to highly complex load history should have little, or no, strain-mode/magnitude influences on their regional histology. In their microscopic study of human femoral mid-diaphyses ($n = 87$, 17–97 years), Britz et al. (2009) found an inverse relationship between body weight and osteon size. Although the causal basis of this relationship could not be determined, the potential influence of the habitual loading of this region should be considered in addition to the effects of aging and other biomechanical/metabolic issues. Because the mid-diaphysis of the human femur is complexly loaded (combined compression, bending, and torsion; Figures 7.17 and 7.21) there should be little regional differences in osteon characteristics (e.g., population density, size, and cross-sectional shape) attributable to differences in strain modes/magnitudes between various cortical regions (e.g., anterior vs. posterior; medial vs. lateral). Although these investigators did not conduct this regional analysis on their data, influences of regional strain modes or magnitudes would not be expected because of the more diffusely distributed shear stresses that are produced in a habitually torsion-loaded location. Consequently, barring untoward aging effects, the mid-diaphyseal human femur is a good choice for the analysis of potential relationships between osteonal characteristics and general mechanical-related parameters (e.g., body weight) without incurring the confounding influences of habitual/local nonuniform strain variations. By contrast, if the more simply loaded tibial mid-diaphysis had been examined, then the potential influences of body weight could have been more difficult to detect because of the potent/superimposed influence of the locally prevalent/predominant tension and compression stresses in the anterior and posterior cortices, respectively. This is because, in contrast to the mid-diaphyseal femur, the mid-diaphyseal tibia is typically in the intermediate B load-complexity category where bending produces these quasi-habitual tension and compression regions (Peterman et al. 2001) and the distinctive osteon morphotypes that would be expected in these regions (Vincentelli 1978).

*Example 3: Using the worksheet/checklist can help reduce confusion when comparing ribs to limb bones.* Pfeiffer and colleagues (2006) attempted to elucidate biomechanically distinctive patterns of variability in osteon and Haversian canal sizes between ribs and femora, focusing on a sample from a population that was very physically active throughout its life span versus others that were not—individuals, respectively, were from the later stone age (LSA) versus those from historic samples (Spitalfields and St. Thomas, p. 466). Expected differences were based on the presumptions that (1) ribs experience "regular biomechanical stimuli of respiration" and have "more persistently active medullary tissue than the femur, and the rib must undergo proportionally more modeling and remodeling during growth," and (2) femora experience "highly variable volitional behavior" requiring them "to respond to a wider range of mechanical loading environments, from disuse to extreme loading." These investigators also state that one of their "original hypotheses regarding the determinants of On.Ar [osteon area] was that smaller osteons would be created in more strongly built bones, as tension and compression stimulated more osteogenic activity" (p. 466).

Their findings lead to the conclusion that "the patterning of osteon size does not appear to be linked to physical activity or to different rates of metabolic activity within the skeleton, at least not in a straightforward way" (p. 460). This conclusion is appropriate in view of their contradictory and inconsistent findings: (1) ribs On.Ar (osteon area) are, in general, significantly smaller than in femora; (2) although femora and ribs from the same skeleton normally show femoral On.Ar larger than rib On.Ar (37 of 44 individuals with paired femora and ribs), the sample that is likely to have been the most physically active (LSA) shows On.Ar values that are not consistently smallest—indeed, in LSA ribs On.Ar is the largest in absolute terms when compared to the other less active populations; (3) although mean femoral values of On.Ar are more diverse than rib On.Ar values, within-sample coefficients of variation are similar; and (4) Haversian canal areas were highly variable, and did not reflect expected anatomical site (femur vs. rib), age, sex, or population effects.

One of the problems in drawing comparisons between ribs and femora is that ribs are difficult to place into one of the load-complexity categories because in vivo and adequate in vitro strain data are lacking. But if human ribs have a quasi-habitual neutral axis (intermediate A complexity category), then the lateral cortex would receive prevalent/predominant tension and the medial (pleural) cortex would receive compression. If this strain-mode distribution actually exists and is habitual in human ribs, then histomorphological analysis should be conducted accordingly (e.g., regional distributions and overall prevalence of osteon morphotypes and predominant CFO should be quantified). As argued above earlier, osteon population density, osteon size, and porosity are not strong correlates of habitual bending. But a habitual neutral axis location in human ribs seems unlikely when compared to the relatively elongated cross-sectional morphologies of ribs where substantial bending is clearly present; for example, in ribs of jackrabbits where thoracic loading during running imparts bending that is much more severe than would be anticipated in human ribs even during running (Simons 1999; Dennis Bramble, personal communication). Consequently, in terms of mechanical/stress-related structural/material adaptation (especially in terms of histomorphological characteristics), is the rib versus femur comparison in humans fundamentally flawed? This is very likely unless the constraints and limitations of this comparison can be recognized and reconciled. Readers who are interested in this issue are referred to Table 7.1 to see if they agree with how human ribs were designated in each of the considerations. Perhaps the most intriguing consideration in this context is how to reconcile the appendicular versus axial skeleton distinction inherent in rib versus limb-bone comparisons; further discussion of this issue is beyond the scope of this chapter.

### 7.7.7 The Multidomain Load Hypothesis: A Within-Bone Example of Using the Load-Complexity Categories

Evidence of different load-complexity categories or domains within the same bone lead to the development of the multidomain load hypothesis. As illustrated in Figure 7.22 (top), we have applied the concept of distinct load-complexity domains to help make sense of differences in structural and material (histomorphological) characteristics, and their potential interactions, between different bones in the same animal (Skedros et al. 2009). Figure 7.22 (bottom) and Figure 7.24 show how to apply these categories to the hypothesized presence of different load domains within human and chimpanzee femora. In these examples, we argue that the greater and lesser trochanters (the intertrochanteric region) in each bone is a transition zone between one proximal and two distal load domains (Skedros and Baucom 2007).

In the human femur, the proximal domain—the femoral neck—is habitually loaded in net compression by the gluteus medius/minimus and in torsion by the actions of other muscles, body weight, and variable joint reaction forces (Lovejoy 1988; Skedros and Baucom 2007). (The femoral head could also be considered a separate domain, but this possibility is not addressed further here.) By contrast, it has been argued that the upper portion of the distal domain—the proximal metaphyseal-diaphyseal region—is customarily loaded in bending and torsion (but with relatively less torsion than seen in the mid-neck and mid-diaphysis, discussed later), which is restrained to some extent by the iliotibial band (Skedros and Baucom 2007). Although the iliotibial band might reduce lateral pitching of the trunk in humans, in vivo strain data obtained during walking at peak loading of stance phase reveal that net tension is still present on the lateral aspect of the proximal metaphysis-diaphysis in the human femur (Aamodt et al. 1997). This is the most important experimental support for considering the human proximal femoral diaphysis as a habitual lateral-medial tension–compression environment (Skedros and Baucom 2007). Quantitative data showing clear patterns of CFO in the subtrochanteric region and proximal diaphysis of adult human femora are consistent with this interpretation (Skedros et al. 1999).

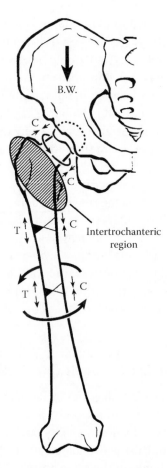

**Figure 7.24** Habitual loading of a modern human femur showing the multidomain load hypothesis. Torsion is depicted by the curved lines. B.W. = body weight. In the lower portion of Figure 7.22 are drawings that contrast the hypothesized habitual loadings of the femoral neck domains between chimpanzee and human femora.

*The mid-diaphyseal load domain of the human femur.* The mid-diaphyseal load domain extends from the proximal (subtrochanteric) domain to the distal third of the diaphysis where the strain distribution again changes (Duda et al. 1998). Several studies of CFO patterns in the mid-diaphysis of the human femur have attempted to detect the expected history of habitual medial-to-lateral bending (Goldman et al. 2003; Portigliatti Barbos et al. 1984, 1987). This hypothesized load history is based on the idea that the habitual medial-lateral (compression) to anterior-lateral (tension) bending seen in the proximal diaphysis would be transmitted distally and would be of sufficient intensity or duration to evoke similar regional strain-mode-specific CFO patterns at the mid-diaphysis. However, these studies failed to detect evidence of this load history. Why are these mid-diaphyseal data so different from the proximal diaphyseal data?

Although the strain environment at the mid-diaphyseal femur has, to my knowledge, never been measured experimentally in vivo, in vitro strain measurements on femora loaded in simulated single-legged stance contradict the idea of a habitual medial-lateral bending moment at the mid-diaphysis. Results of in vitro strain gauge studies of femora loaded in simulated single-legged stance show both a reduction in the magnitude of the medial-to-lateral bending moment at mid-diaphysis (the bending moment is substantially greater in the subtrochanteric area) and increased interspecimen variability of the strain distribution at mid-diaphysis (Cristofolini et al. 1996; Oh and Harris 1978).

Consequently, the relatively complex load environment of the femoral mid-diaphysis (where torsion > bending) might explain why expected tension/compression (lateral/ medial) CFO differences are typically absent there, but are present in the proximal diaphysis and subtrochanteric regions (where bending > torsion) (Beckstrom et al. 2010; Skedros et al. 1999, 2011). Hence, the load complexity changes along the femoral diaphysis—from less complex/variable at the proximal diaphysis to more complex/variable at the mid-diaphysis. An explanation for the relatively uniform CFO in adult human mid-diaphyseal femora is similar to that stated earlier—bone regions that receive varying amounts of torsion and bending would not be expected to produce clear regional patterns of predominant CFO and possibly also osteon-related characteristics.

The hypothesized differences in load history from the proximal femoral diaphysis (bending > torsion) to the mid-diaphysis (torsion > bending) in humans are also consistent with the CFO data reported in chimpanzee femora (Beckstrom et al. 2010; Skedros et al. 2011). This explanation, based on changes in habitual load-complexity, for the dissimilar histological findings between mid- and proximal-diaphyseal chimpanzee femora is also consistent with that offered in a previous study of equine third metacarpals from our laboratory (Skedros et al. 2006a)—nonstereotypical and complex load histories that produce significant amounts of torsion would not be expected to produce clear regional patterns of CFO-based histological organization (Skedros and Hunt 2004). Additional support for proximal-distal changes in habitual load complexity within a bone's diaphysis, and how this could be mediated by strain-related and site-specific differences in thresholds for modeling and remodeling activities, can be found in Hsieh et al. (2001), Skerry (2006), and Espinoza Orías et al. (2009).

It has also been suggested that the relatively circular cross-sectional shape of the human femoral mid-diaphysis reflects cross-sectional morphology expected in a loading environment characterized by prevalent torsion (and the increased variability of the neutral axis location produced by such loading; Carter and Spengler 1982; Ruff 1981; Wainwright et al. 1982). But a quasi-circular shape is also typical in the proximal diaphysis where the bending moment is the greatest in the entire femur. Again, this reinforces the idea that cross-sectional shape can be misleading when interpreting load history. These data again support the assertion that patterns of predominant CFO and osteon morphotypes are strong predictors of load history because they help distinguish bending from torsion.

## 7.8   Consideration 6: Skeletal Immaturity, Differential Growth Rates, and Precocial versus Altricial Ambulation

### 7.8.1   Cortical Modeling Drifts

Functional adaptations in the composition and histological organization of a bone can be difficult to interpret during the phase when it is undergoing extensive growth-related modeling. When growth-related modeling causes the bone to change cross-sectional shape or curvature, it is considered to be undergoing *cortical drift*. In most of the examples of bone adaptation used in this chapter it has been assumed that cortical drift, even if fairly recent, is not an important confounding variable when interpreting load history. The modeling process is considered further in Chapter 3 by Maggiano.

### 7.8.2  The Lack of Secondary Osteons

The lack of osteons in a fragmentary bone specimen could have several explanations, including (1) the fragment is from a species that does not readily form osteons, (2) the bone fragment is from a young animal that forms osteons later in development, and (3) the bone fragment is from a bone that has large areas of primary (nonosteonal) tissue, but osteons can form and can be in high concentrations in some locations but absent or few in others (Figure 7.13). These cases can be hard to resolve when attempting to decipher skeletal or species provenance, and load history. Investigators must search for as much bone material as possible; finding unfused growth plates can be very helpful when faced with these dilemmas.

### 7.8.3  Bone Histology in Precocial versus Altricial Growth

Appendicular bones of some larger animals function well even though their osteonal remodeling is relatively sparse while other bones of the same limb skeleton are highly remodeled with secondary osteons. An example of this is shown in Figure 7.13, which is from my study of the forelimb bones of mature mule deer (Skedros et al. 2003c). Bones that must grow fast for precocial ambulation, such as in limb skeletons of artiodactyls (e.g., sheep, cows, deer) and horses, often have primary bone (e.g., fibrolamellar or plexiform) earlier in their growth (Figure 7.25). As Currey (2003) has pointed out, the primary bone histology of these species is sufficiently strong in longitudinal loading but is relatively weak across the grain. In many cases, osteons eventually form in these bones, probably reflecting the repair of microdamage that forms during normal use. By contrast, primates exhibit altricial ambulation and thus have appendicular bones that grow more slowly. For reasons that are unclear and do not necessarily appear attributable to slow growth, the relatively rapid onset of remodeling is more likely found in this situation. When compared to fibrolamellar/plexiform bone, osteonal bone has comparatively less disparity in strength when loaded in longitudinal and transverse directions. The volume affect (Section 7.3) appears to have little relevance in the context of the altricial–precocial distinction.

### 7.8.4  Amprino's Rule

The idea that primary bone microstructure may reflect bone formation rate was suggested by Amprino (1947) and is a general finding that has been reported by Currey (2002), Stover et al. (1992), and others (de Ricqlès et al. 1991; Mori et al. 2003). This relationship has been demonstrated experimentally in mallard duck limb bones by Castanet et al. (1996) and de Margerie (2002). de Margerie et al. (2004) advanced these studies by examining growth rates and associated bone tissue types (laminar, longitudinal, reticular, or radial fibrolamellar) in transverse sections in growing king penguin limb bones (i.e., humerus, radius, femur, tibiotarsus). They showed that the highest growth rates were associated with radial microarchitecture of fibrolamellar bone, where vascular cavities in the woven network are aligned radially. Additionally, there seems to be a greater tendency for the microstructure of slower growing bone to be aligned in the longitudinal direction, especially if growth is greater in that direction. For example, Petrtýl et al. (1996) speculate that the longitudinal

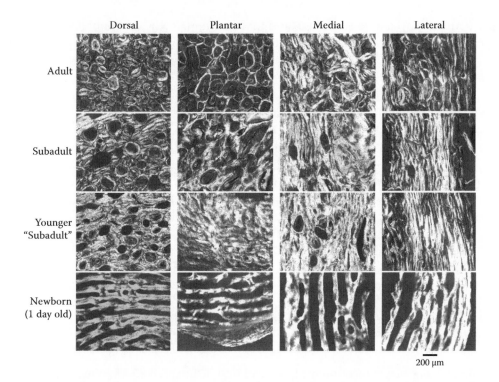

|  | Dorsal | Plantar | Medial | Lateral |

**Figure 7.25** Circularly polarized light images showing growth-related changes in sheep cal-canei. The images are from a transverse section of the proximal aspect of calcanei of four animals spanning a range from 1-day-old newborn to adult. In the 6- to 8-month-old subadults, alternating and bright osteon morphotypes begin to appear in the anterior (dorsal) compression cortex. Hoop/parallel-fibered osteons (i.e., their osteon walls have more longitudinal collagen than alternating and bright osteons) also begin to appear in subadult bones and are prevalent in the posterior (plantar) tension cortices of the adult bones. Hoop refers to the highly transverse (circumferential) collagen at the osteon periphery (see Figure 7.11). Note also that the second-ary osteons in the anterior compression cortex are smaller than those in the posterior tension cortex; secondary osteons are absent in the posterior cortex of the younger subadult shown here. In all images, anterior is toward the top edge of the image and lateral is toward the right edge of the image.

orientation of the canals in the primary bone tissue of the human femoral diaphysis is a consequence of longitudinal shifting of the periosteum against the bone surface. Similar interpretations have been suggested for the longitudinal primary vascular canals in the slow-growing long bones of alligators (Lee 2004).

When considering potential evidence of bone adaptation in the three-dimensional vascular patterns of bone it is important to ask whether the vessels are within primary bone or secondary bone. This important distinction, which distinguishes unremodeled from remodeled bone, is not yet reliable in microlevel computerized tomographic images because the current state of this technology does not provide sufficient resolution (Cooper et al. 2006; Pazzaglia et al. 2010; also see Chapter 15 by Cooper et al.). Nevertheless, when considering vascular architecture in primary bone this possibility should be considered: preferred vascular orientation in bone may simply be a product of programmed develop-ment expressed as different rates of osteogenesis within and between skeletal elements. Alternatively, the regional microstructural lamellar anisotropy (i.e., predominant CFO) of the bone matrix that surrounds the vessels can be independent of rates of osteogenesis. This matrix anisotropy can be enhanced, and may be dramatically different, between regions exposed to different mechanical loads during matrix formation. As noted, prevalent/predominant strain characteristics that appear to be most clearly linked with the production of these variations include specific strain modes (i.e., tension, compression, and shear). In this case, it is the adaptability of CFO, not the vascular orientation, that is relatively more important in producing the apparent CFO differences. Prospective experimental studies, although limited, support an important causal role for strain mode in this context (Boskey et al. 1999; Puustjarvi et al. 1999; Takano et al. 1999). In this interpretation, predominant CFO may be more strongly influenced by load history, which contrasts with situations where three-dimensional arrangement of vessels (e.g., preferred orientations) may be more strongly influenced by the rate of osteogenesis. The point here is that in some cases osteogenesis can result in bone histology that could fool investigators into thinking that they have detected accommodations/adaptations to load history. Again, this issue is typically a consideration in cases where osteon formation is scarce or absent; more examples and discussion on this topic can be found in Skedros and Hunt (2004), Schneider et al. (2007), and Pazzaglia et al. (2007).

## 7.9 Conclusions

The load history of a bone or bone region can best be interpreted when using a systematic approach that includes an assessment of numerous considerations, including those shown in Table 7.1. Among these considerations, the following six were selected for discussion in this chapter: (1) the stressed volume effect; (2) the modeling–remodeling distinction; (3) the shear resistance-priority hypothesis; (4) mechanical relevance of osteons, osteon morphotypes, and predominant collagen fiber orientation; (5) load-complexity categories; and (6) influences of skeletal immaturity, differential growth rates, and precocial versus altricial ambulation. A sound understanding of basic biomechanical concepts is necessary for accurately assessing many of the issues that must be considered when interpreting a bone's load history through the examination of its morphology in terms of specific structural and material characteristics. Among this myriad of characteristics, regional variations in predominant collagen fiber orientation—often produced by the increased prevalence of specific osteon morphotypes—appear to be the strongest characteristic for distinguishing torsion from bending, which are common load histories in limb-bone diaphyses. The application of the worksheet/checklist approach presented in Table 7.1 also facilitates comparisons between appendicular bones and ribs, as well as between regions of the same bone.

## Appendix: Definitions

**Adaptation:** Adaptation in cortical bone commonly refers to either: (1) changes in bone structure or material organization in response to loading conditions outside a normal physiologic stress/strain range, distribution, duration, and so forth (Martin and Burr 1989; Schaffler et al. 1985); or (2) the presence of regional differences in structural or material organization that are strongly influenced by normal functional stimuli occurring during normal development within or between bones (Bertram and Swartz 1991; Martin and Burr 1989; Riggs et al. 1993a). In this chapter the use of the term *adaptation* is not meant to imply an evolutionary adaptation within a species, but rather a specific adaptation within the lifetime of an individual. In other words, "adaptations" are considered to be biomechanically relevant regional variations and temporal changes in cortical bone structural and material organization that are produced by the modeling and remodeling processes during normal skeletal development. In addition to being mediated by genetic and epigenetic influences, which are heritable, these processes can be influenced by nonheritable (extragenetic) stimuli such as regional variations in microdamage incidence.

This chapter primarily deals with identifying correlations between structure, material, function, and load history. These correlations might be produced by (1) adaptation via natural selection and (2) accommodation via epigenetic events. We have suggested that the nonuniform strain distribution experienced in the early development of most limb bones is proximate to the historical origin (i.e., mechanistic/causal) of the structure-function relationship (Skedros et al. 2007a). Therefore, the word *adaptation* in this context is deemed appropriate sensu stricto. Although the word *accommodation* is also used in this chapter, some readers might argue that this is inappropriate because in most cases where it is used there has been no attempt to see how affecting the epigenetic signals that influence bone development would change structure or material (like Starck and Chinsamy 2002).

**Anisotropy:** This refers to a material with a grain whose properties or technical constants are different when measured in different directions, most having some degree of symmetry to their internal structure. Bone is anisotropic, but examples of limited anisotropy can also be found in bone (orthotropic and transversely isotropic; Currey 2002; Martin et al. 1998). If the properties are the same in different directions, then the material is isotropic.

**Fatigue resistance:** Fatigue resistance is when fatigue failure is prolonged or avoided altogether. Fatigue failure is when a structure is loaded repeatedly and breaks at a load that would not cause it to fail if it were loaded only once. Fatigue behavior, failure, and resistance are complex topics that would require several textbook chapters to adequately address; readers are referred to Currey's book (2002) for a detailed discussion.

**Modeling:** Modeling activities affect the formation and resorption of secondary or nonsecondary bone (e.g., primary bone, and trabecular bone in some cases) on periosteal or endosteal surfaces. They are detected as changes or differences in a bone's curvature, cross-sectional shape and regional cortical thickness. Consequently, modeling is a concept describing a combination of nonproximate, though coordinated, resorption and formation drifts whose net result is, typically, to change the distribution of bone. Such drifts are called macro-modeling in cortical bone and mini-modeling in cancellous bone. The re-alignment of trabecular tracts along the lines of stress would be a consequence of mini-modeling.

**Remodeling:** Remodeling activities affect the replacement of intracortical bone; this is achieved through the activation of basic multicellular units (BMUs = osteoclasts and osteoblasts) that create secondary osteons (Haversian systems) in cortical bone and secondary osteons or hemiosteons in trabecular bone (Jee et al. 1991; Parfitt et al. 1996).

**Toughness:** Toughness refers to the amount of energy required to fracture a material; the more the overall amount of energy consumed, the tougher the material (Zioupos and Currey 1998). Tough materials resist damage propagation but do not necessarily resist damage formation. Toughness tests typically involve propagating a crack in a controlled direction through a specimen machined into a specific shape for this test. Toughness measurements obtained from these formal toughness tests are different from the toughness that is often informally used to describe the energy absorbed by a specimen during a more conventional failure test. In this case, energy absorption is measured as the area under the stress–strain curve (Turner and Burr 1993), which is an indirect measure of propagation toughness (Vashishth 2004).

# References

Aamodt A, Lund-Larsen J, Eine J, Andersen E, Benum P, and Schnell Husby O. 1997. *In vivo* measurements show tensile axial strain in the proximal lateral aspect of the human femur. J Ortho Res 15(6):927–931.

Abbott S, Trinkaus E, and Burr DB. 1996. Dynamic bone remodeling in later Pleistocene fossil hominids. Am J Phys Anthropol 99:585–601.

Adams DJ, Spirt AA, Brown TD, Fritton SP, Rubin CT, and Brand RA. 1997. Testing the daily stress stimulus theory of bone adaptation with natural and experimentally controlled strain histories. J Biomech 30(7):671–678.

Akkus O, Knott DF, Jepsen KJ, Davy DT, and Rimnac CM. 2003. Relationship between damage accumulation and mechanical property degradation in cortical bone: Microcrack orientation is important. J Biomed Mater Res 65A(4):482–488.

Amprino R. 1947. La structure du tissu osseux envisagée comme expression de différences dans la vitesse de l'accroissement. Arch Biol 58:315–330.

Ascenzi A. 1988. The micromechanics versus the macromechanics of cortical bone—a comprehensive presentation. J Biomech Eng 110(4):357–363.

Ascenzi A, and Bonucci E. 1967. The tensile properties of single osteons. Anat Rec 158(4):375–386.

Ascenzi A, and Bonucci E. 1968. The compressive properties of single osteons. Anat Rec 161(3):377–391.

Ascenzi MG, Ascenzi A, Benvenuti A, Burghammer M, Panzavolta S, and Bigi A. 2003. Structural differences between "dark" and "bright" isolated human osteonic lamellae. J Struct Biol 141(1):22–33.

Ascenzi MG, and Lomovtsev A. 2006. Collagen orientation patterns in human secondary osteons, quantified in the radial direction by confocal microscopy. J Struct Biol 153(1):14–30.

Banse X, Sims TJ, and Bailey AJ. 2002. Mechanical properties of adult vertebral cancellous bone: correlation with collagen intermolecular cross-links. J Bone Miner Res 17(9):1621–1628.

Barth HD, Launey ME, Macdowell AA, Ager JW, 3rd, and Ritchie RO. 2010. On the effect of X-ray irradiation on the deformation and fracture behavior of human cortical bone. Bone 46(6):1475–1485.

Beck TJ, Looker AC, Ruff CB, Sievanen H, and Wahner HW. 2000. Structural trends in the aging femoral neck and proximal shaft: analysis of the Third National Health and Nutrition Examination Survey dual-energy x-ray absorptiometry data. J Bone Miner Res 15(12):2297–2304.

Beckstrom A, Skedros J, Kiser C, and Keenan K. 2010. Predominant collagen fiber orientation data support the multi-domain load hypothesis in the chimpanzee femur. Am J Phys Anthropol Suppl 50:63.

Beraudi A, Stea S, Bordini B, Baleani M, and Viceconti M. 2010. Osteon classification in human fibular shaft by circularly polarized light. Cells Tissues Organs 191(3):260–268.

Bertram JEA, and Swartz SM. 1991. The "law of bone transformation": a case of crying Wolff? Biol Rev Camb Philos Soc 66(3):245–273.

Bertram JEA, and Biewener AA. 1988. Bone curvature: sacrificing strength for load predictability? J Theor Biol 131:75–92.

Biewener AA. 1990. Biomechanics of mammalian terrestrial locomotion. Science 250(4984): 1097–1103.

Biewener AA. 1993. Safety factors in bone strength. Calcif Tissue Int 53(Suppl 1):S68–S74.

Biewener AA. 2003. Animal locomotion. New York: Oxford University Press Inc.

Biewener AA, and Bertram JEA. 1993. Mechanical loading and bone growth *in vivo*. In: Hall BK, editor. Bone, vol. 7, Bone Growth–B. Boca Raton, FL: CRC Press, 1–36.

Biewener AA and Dial KP. 1995. *In vivo* strain in the humerus of pigeons (*Columba livia*) during flight. J Morphol 225:61–67.

Biewener AA, Fazzalari NL, Konieczynski DD, and Baudinette RV. 1996. Adaptive changes in trabecular architecture in relation to functional strain patterns and disuse. Bone 19(1):1–8.

Biewener AA, Swartz SM, and Bertram JEA. 1986. Bone modeling during growth: dynamic strain equilibrium in the chick tibiotarsus. Calcif Tissue Int 39:390–395.

Biewener AA, Thomason J, Goodship A, and Lanyon LE. 1983a. Bone stress in the horse forelimb during locomotion at different gaits: a comparison of two experimental methods. J Biomech 16:565–576.

Biewener AA, Thomason J, and Lanyon LE. 1983b. Mechanics of locomotion and jumping in the forelimb of the horse (*Equus*): in vivo stress developed in the radius and metacarpus. J Zool Lond(201):67–82.

Bigley RF, Gibeling JC, Stover SM, Hazelwood SJ, Fyhrie DP, and Martin RB. 2007. Volume effects on fatigue life of equine cortical bone. J Biomech 40(16):3548–3554.

Bigley RF, Gibeling JC, Stover SM, Hazelwood SJ, Fyhrie DP, and Martin RB. 2008. Volume effects on yield strength of equine cortical bone. J Mech Behav Biomed Mater 1(4):295–302.

Bigley RF, Griffin LV, Christensen L, and Vandenbosch R. 2006. Osteonal interfacial strength and histomorphometry of equine cortical bone. J Biomech 39:1629–1640.

Blob RW, Biewener AA. 1999. *In vivo* locomotor strain in the hindlimb bones of *Alligator mississippiensis* and *Iguana iguana*: implications for the evolution of limb bone safety factor and non-sprawling limb posture. J Exp Biol 202 (Pt 9):1023–1046.

Boskey AL, Wright TM, and Blank RD. 1999. Collagen and bone strength. J Bone Miner Res 14:330–335.

Boyce TM, Fyhrie DP, Glotkowski MC, Radin EL, and Schaffler MB. 1998. Damage type and strain mode associations in human compact bone bending fatigue. J Orthop Res 16:322–329.

Boyde A, and Riggs CM. 1990. The quantitative study of the orientation of collagen in compact bone slices. Bone 11:35–39.

Britz HM, Thomas CD, Clement JG, and Cooper DM. 2009. The relation of femoral osteon geometry to age, sex, height and weight. Bone 45(1):77–83.

Bromage TG, Goldman HM, McFarlin SC, Warshaw J, Boyde A, and Riggs CM. 2003. Circularly polarized light standards for investigations of collagen fiber orientation in bone. Anat Rec 274B(1):157–168.

Burger E, Klein-Nulend J, and Smit T. 2003. Strain-derived canalicular fluid flow regulates osteoclast activity in a remodelling osteon—a proposal. J Biomech 36(10):1453–1459.

Burr DB. 1992. Orthopedic principles of skeletal growth, modeling and remodeling. In: Carlson DS, and Goldstein SA, editors. Bone biodynamics in orthodontic and orthopedic treatment. Ann Arbor, MI: University of Michigan, 15–50.

Burr DB. 2002. The contribution of the organic matrix to bone's material properties. Bone 31(1):8–11.

Burr DB, Milgrom C, Fyhrie D, Forwood M, Nyska M, Finestone A, Hoshaw S, Saiag E, and Simkin A. 1996. In vivo measurement of human tibial strains during vigorous activity. Bone 18(5):405–410.

Burr DB, Ruff CB, and Thompson DD. 1990. Patterns of skeletal histologic change through time: comparison of an archaic native American population with modern populations. The Anat Rec 226:307–313.

Burr DB, Schaffler MB, and Frederickson RG. 1988. Composition of the cement line and its possible mechanical role as a local interface in human compact bone. J Biomech 21:939–945.

Burr DB, Turner CH, Naick P, Forwood MR, Ambrosius W, Hasan MS, and Pidaparti R. 1998. Does microdamage accumulation affect the mechanical properties of bone? J Biomech 31:337–347.

Burstein AH, Currey JD, Frankel VH, and Reilly DT. 1972. The ultimate properties of bone tissue: effects of yielding. J Biomech 5:35–44.

Burstein AH, Zika JM, Heiple KG, and Klein L. 1975. Contribution of collagen and mineral to the elastic-plastic properties of bone. J Bone Joint Surg Am 57(7):956–961.

Cardoso L, Herman BC, Verborgt O, Laudier D, Majeska RJ, and Schaffler MB. 2009. Osteocyte apoptosis controls activation of intracortical resorption in response to bone fatigue. J Bone Miner Res 24(4):597–605.

Carlson KJ. 2005. Investigating the form-function interface in African apes: relationships between principal moments of area and positional behaviors in femoral and humeral diaphyses. Am J Phys Anthropol 127(3):312–334.

Carlson KJ, Doran-Sheehy DM, Hunt KD, Nishida T, Yamanaka A, and Boesch C. 2006. Locomotor behavior and long bone morphology in individual free-ranging chimpanzees. J Hum Evol 50:394–404.

Carlson KJ, and Judex S. 2007. Increased non-linear locomotion alters diaphyseal bone shape. J Exp Biol 210(Pt 17):3117–3125.

Carlson KJ, Sumner DR, Morbeck ME, Nishida T, Yamanaka A, and Boesch C. 2008. Role of non-behavioral factors in adjusting long bone diaphyseal structure in free-ranging pan troglodytes. Int J Primatol 29(6):1401–1420.

Carrano MT and Biewener AA. 1999. Experimental alteration of limb posture in the chicken (*Gallus gallus*) and its bearing on the use of birds as analogs for dinosaur locomotion. J Morphol 240:237–249.

Carrier DR. 1983. Postnatal ontogeny of the musculo-skeletal system in the black-tailed jack rabbit (*Lepus californicus*). J Zool Lond 201:27–55.

Carrier DR, and Leon LR. 1990. Skeletal growth and function in the California gull (*Larus californicus*). J Zool Lond 222:375–389.

Carter DH, and Beaupré GS. 2001. Skeletal function and form. Mechanobiology of skeletal development, aging, and regeneration. Cambridge, UK: University of Cambridge.

Carter DR, Caler WE, Spengler DM, and Frankel VH. 1981. Fatigue behavior of adult cortical bone: the influence of mean strain and strain range. Acta Orthop Scand 52:481–490.

Carter DR, Hayes WC, and Schurman DJ. 1976. Fatigue life of compact bone-II. Effects of microstructure and density. J Biomech 9:211–218.

Carter DR, Smith DJ, Spengler DM, Daly CH, and Frankel VH. 1980. Measurements and analysis of *in* vivo bone strains on the canine radius and ulna. J Biomech 13:27–38.

Carter DR, and Spengler DM. 1982. Biomechanics of fracture. In: Sumner-Smith G, editor. Bone in clinical orthopaedics: a study in comparative osteology. Philadelphia, PA: W.B. Saunders Co., pp. 305–334.

Carter DR, van der Meulen MCH, and Beaupré GS. 1996. Mechanical factors in bone growth and development. Bone 18(Suppl):5S–10S.

Castanet J, Grandin A, Abourachid A, and de Ricqlès A. 1996. [Expression of growth dynamic in the structure of the periosteal bone in the mallard, *Anas platyrhynchos*]. C R Acad Sci III 319(4):301–308.

Ciarelli TE, Tjhia C, Rao DS, Qiu S, Parfitt AM, and Fyhrie DP. 2009. Trabecular packet-level lamellar density patterns differ by fracture status and bone formation rate in white females. Bone 45(5):903–908.

Coleman JC, Hart RT, Owan I, Takano Y, and Burr DB. 2002. Characterization of dynamic three-dimensional strain fields in the canine radius. J Biomech 35(12):1677–1683.

Cooper D, Thomason C, Clement J, and Hallgrimsson B. 2006. Three-dimensional microcomputed tomography imaging of basic multicellular unit-related resorption spaces in human cortical bone. Anat Rec A Discov Mol Cell Evol Biol 288(7):806–816.

Corondan G, and Haworth WL. 1986. A fractographic study of human long bone. J Biomech 19(3):207–218.

Coutelier L. 1976. Le remaniement interne de l'os compact chez l'enfent (The internal remodeling of compact bone in children). Bulletin de l' association des anatomistes (Bull Assoc Anat) 60(168):95–110.

Cowin SC. 1989. The mechanical properties of cortical bone tissue. In: Cowin SC, editor. Bone mechanics. Boca Raton, FL: CRC Press, pp. 97–127.

Cowin SC. 2001. Mechanics of materials. Boca Raton, FL: CRC Press.

Cristofolini L, Viceconti M, Cappello A, and Toni A. 1996. Mechanical validation of whole bone composite femur models. J Biomech 29(4):525–535.

Currey JD. 1975. The effects of strain rate, reconstruction, and mineral content on some mechanical properties of bovine bone. J Biomech 8:81–86.

Currey JD. 1984. Can strains give adequate information for adaptive bone remodeling? Calcif Tissue Int 36:S118–S122.

Currey JD. 2002. Bones: Structure and Mechanics. Princeton, NJ: Princeton University Press.

Currey JD. 2003. The many adaptations of bone. J Biomech 36(10):1487–1495.

Currey JD, and Alexander RM. 1985. The thickness of the walls of tubular bones. J Zool Lond 206:453–468.

Currey JD, and Pond CM. 1989. Mechanical properties of very young bone in the axis deer (*Axis axis*) and humans. J Zool Lond 218:59–67.

Davison KS, Siminoski K, Adachi JD, Hanley DA, Goltzman D, Hodsman AB, Josse R, Kaiser S, Olszynski WP, Papaioannou A et al. 2006. Bone strength: the whole is greater than the sum of its parts. Semin Arthritis Rheum 36(1):22–31.

de Margerie E. 2002. Laminar bone as an adaptation to torsional loads in flapping flight. J Anat 201:521–526.

de Margerie E, Robin JP, Verrier D, Cubo J, Groscolas R, and Castanet J. 2004. Assessing a relationship between bone microstructure and growth rate: a fluorescent labelling study in the king penguin chick (*Aptenodytes patagonicus*). J Exp Biol 207(Pt 5):869–879.

de Margerie E, Sanchez S, Cubo J, and Castanet J. 2005. Torsional resistance as a principal component of the structural design of long bones: comparative multivariate evidence in birds. Anat Rec A Discov Mol Cell Evol Biol 282(1):49–66.

de Ricqlès A, Meunier FJ, Castanet L, and Francillon-Vieillot H. 1991. Comparative microstructure of bone. In: Hall BK, editor. Bone Vol. 3, Bone Matrix and Bone Specific Products. Boca Raton, FL: CRC Press, pp. 1–78.

Demes B. 2007. In vivo bone strain and bone functional adaptation. Am J Phys Anthropol 133(1):717–722.

Demes B, Qin YX, Stern JT, Jr., Larson SG, and Rubin CT. 2001. Patterns of strain in the macaque tibia during functional activity. Am J Phys Anthropol 116(4):257–265.

Demes B, Stern JT, Jr., Hausman MR, Larson SG, McLeod KJ, and Rubin CT. 1998. Patterns of strain in the macaque ulna during functional activity. Am J Phys Anthropol 106(1):87–100.

Diab T, and Vashishth D. 2007. Morphology, localization and accumulation of in vivo microdamage in human cortical bone. Bone 40(3):612–618.

Drapeau MS, and Streeter MA. 2006. Modeling and remodeling responses to normal loading in the human lower limb. Am J Phys Anthropol 129(3):403–409.

Duda GN, Heller M, Albinger J, Schulz O, Schneider E, and Claes L 1998. Influence of muscle forces on femoral strain distribution. J Biomech 31:841–846.

Ebacher V, Tang C, McKay H, Oxland TR, Guy P, and Wang R. 2007. Strain redistribution and cracking behavior of human bone during bending. Bone 40(5):1265–1275.

Ehrlich PJ, and Lanyon LE. 2002. Mechanical strain and bone cell function: a review. Osteoporos Int 13(9):688–700.

Espinoza Orias AA, Deuerling JM, Landrigan MD, Renaud JE, and Roeder RK. 2009. Anatomic variation in the elastic anisotropy of cortical bone tissue in the human femur. J Mech Behav Biomed Mater 2(3):255–263.

Evans FG. 1958. Relations between the microscopic structure and tensile strength of human bone. Acta Anat (Basel) 35(4):285–301.

Evans FG. 1976. Mechanical properties and histology of cortical bone from younger and older men. Anatomical Record 185:1–12.

Evans FG, and Bang S. 1966. Physical and histological differences between human fibular and femoral compact bone. In: Evans FG, editor. Studies on the anatomy and function of bone and joints. New York: Springer, pp. 142–155.

Evans FG, and Bang S. 1967. Differences and relationships between the physical properties and the microscopic structure of human femoral, tibial and fibular cortical bone. Am J Anat 120:79–88.

Evans FG, and Vincentelli R. 1974. Relations of the compressive properties of human cortical bone to histological structure and calcification. J Biomech 7(1):1–10.

Fisher L. 2002. How to dunk a doughnut: the science of everyday life. London: Weidenfeld and Nicholson.

Francillon-Vieillot H, de Buffrénil V, Castanet J, Géraudie J, Meunier F, Sire J, Zylberberg L, and de Ricqlès A. 1990. Microstructure and mineralization of vertebrate skeletal tissues. In: JG Carter, editor. Skeletal biomineralization: patterns, processes and evolutionary trends. New York: Van Nostrand Reinhold, pp. 471–530.

Fritton SP, McLeod KJ, and Rubin CT. 2000. Quantifying the strain history of bone: spatial uniformity and self-similarity of low-magnitude strains. J Biomech 33(3):317–325.

Ganey TM, and Odgen JA. 1998. Pre- and post-natal development of the hip. In: Callaghan JJ, Rosenbery AG, and Rubash HE, editors. The adult hip. Philadelphia: Lippincott-Raven, pp. 39–55.

Gebhardt W. 1906. Über funktionell wichtige anordnungsweisen der feineren und görberen bauelemente des wirbeltierknochens. II. Spezieller teil. Der bau der Haversschen lamellensysteme und seine funktionelle bedeutung. Arch Entw Mech Org 20:187–322.

George WT, and Vashishth D. 2005. Damage mechanisms and failure modes of cortical bone under components of physiological loading. J Orthop Res 23(5):1047–1053.

Gibson VA, Stover SM, Gibeling JC, Hazelwood SJ, and Martin RB. 2006. Osteonal effects on elastic modulus and fatigue life in equine bone. J Biomech 39(2):21–225.

Goldman HM, Bromage TG, Thomas CD, and Clement JG. 2003. Preferred collagen fiber orientation in the human mid-shaft femur. Anat Rec 272A(1):434–445.

Goodship AE, Lanyon LE, and McFie H. 1979. Functional adaptation of bone to increased stress. An experimental study. J Bone Joint Surg Am 61(4):539–546.

Gross TS, McLeod KJ, and Rubin CT. 1992. Characterizing bone strain distribution in vivo using three triple rosette strain gauges. J Biomech 25:1081–1087.

Gupta HS, and Zioupos P. 2008. Fracture of bone tissue: The "hows" and the "whys." Med Eng Phys 30(10):1209–1226.

Haapasalo H, Kontulainen S, Sievanen H, Kannus P, Jarvinen M, and Vuori I. 2000. Exercise-induced bone gain is due to enlargement in bone size without a change in volumetric bone density: a peripheral quantitative computed tomography study of the upper arms of male tennis players. Bone 27(3):351–357.

Hammond AS, Ning J, Ward CV, and Ravosa MJ. 2010. Mammalian limb loading and chondral modeling during ontogeny. Anat Rec (Hoboken) 293(4):658–670.

Hansen HL, Bredbenner TL, Nicolella DP, Mahaney MC, and Havill LM. 2009. Cross-sectional geometry of the femoral midshaft in baboons is heritable. Bone 45(5):892–897.

Heinrich RE, Ruff CB, and Adamczewski JZ. 1999. Ontogenetic changes in mineralization and bone geometry in the femur of muskoxen (*Ovibos moschatus*). J Zool Lond 247:215–223.

Hiller LP, Stover SM, Gibson VA, Gibeling JC, Prater CS, Hazelwood SJ, Yeh OC, and Martin RB. 2003. Osteon pullout in the equine third metacarpal bone: Effects of *ex vivo* fatigue. J Orthop Res 21(3):481–488.

Hsieh Y-F, Robling AG, Ambrosius WT, Burr DB, and Turner CH. 2001. Mechanical loading of diaphyseal bone in vivo: the strain threshold for an osteogenic response varies with location. J Bone Min Res 16(12):2291–2297.

Huiskes R, Weinans H, and van Rietbergen B. 1992. The relationship between stress shielding and bone resorption around total hip stems and the effects of flexible materials. Clin Orthop 274:124–134.

Jee WSS, Li XJ, and Ke HZ. 1991. The skeletal adaptation to mechanical usage in the rat. Cells and Materials 1:131–142.

Joo W, Jepsen KJ, and Davy DT. 2004. Complex cross-modal effects of damage on cortical bone properties. Trans Orthop Res Soc 29:515.

Joo W, Jepsen KJ, and Davy DT. 2007. The effect of recovery time and test conditions on viscoelastic measures of tensile damage in cortical bone. J Biomech 40(12):2731–2737.

Judex S, Gross TS, Bray RC, and Zernicke RF. 1997a. Adaptation of bone to physiological stimuli. J Biomech 30:421–429.

Judex S, Gross TS, and Zernicke RF. 1997b. Strain gradients correlate with sites of exercise-induced bone-forming surfaces in adult skeleton. J Bone Miner Res 12:1737–1745.

Kalmey JK, and Lovejoy CO. 2002. Collagen fiber orientation in the femoral necks of apes and humans: do their histological structures reflect differences in locomotor loading? Bone 31:327–332.

Kassem M, Melton LJ, and Riggs BL. 1996. The Type I Type II mode for involutional osteoporosis. In: Marcus R, Feldman D, and Kelsay J, editors. Osteoporosis. New York: Academic Press, 691–702.

Keaveny TM, Morgan EF, Niebur GL, and Yeh OC. 2001. Biomechanics of trabecular bone. Annu Rev Biomed Eng 3:307–333.

Koltze H. 1951. Studie zur äusseren Form der Osteone. Zeitschrift fuer Anatomie und Entwicklungsgeschichte 115:585–596.

Krauss S, Fratzl P, Seto J, Currey JD, Estevez JA, Funari SS, and Gupta HS. 2009. Inhomogeneous fibril stretching in antler starts after macroscopic yielding: indication for a nanoscale toughening mechanism. Bone 44(6):1105–1110.

Kumar NC, Dantzig JA, Jasiuk IM, Robling AG, and Turner CH. 2010. Numerical modeling of long bone adaptation due to mechanical loading: correlation with experiments. Ann Biomed Eng 38:594–604.

Lanyon LE. 1974. Experimental support for the trajectorial theory of bone structure. J Bone Joint Surg 56B:160–166.

Lanyon LE. 1987. Functional strain in bone tissue as an objective, and controlling stimulus for adaptive bone remodelling. J Biomech 20:1083–1093.

Lanyon LE, and Bourn S. 1979. The influence of mechanical function on the development and remodeling of the tibia: an experimental study in sheep. J Bone Joint Surg 61-A:263–273.

Lanyon LE, Goodship AE, Pye CJ, and MacFie JH. 1982. Mechanically adaptive bone remodeling. J Biomech 15(3):141–154.

Lanyon LE, Hampson WG, Goodship AE, and Shah JS. 1975. Bone deformation recorded in vivo from strain gauges attached to the human tibial shaft. Acta Orthop Scand 46(2):256–268.

Lanyon LE, Magee PT, and Baggott DG. 1979. The relationship of functional stress and strain to the processes of bone remodeling: an experimental study on the sheep radius. J Biomech 12:593–600.

Lazenby R. 1986. Porosity-geometry interaction in the conversation of bone strength. J Biomech 19(3):257–258.

Lee AH. 2004. Histological organization and its relationship to function in the femur of *Alligator mississippiensis*. J Anat 204(3):197–207.

Lee TC, Staines A, and Taylor D. 2002. Bone adaptation to load: microdamage as a stimulus for bone remodelling. J Anat 201(6):437–446.

Lieberman DE, Pearson OM, Polk JD, Demes B, and Crompton AW. 2003. Optimization of bone growth and remodeling in response to loading in tapered mammalian limbs. J Exp Biol 206:3125–3138.

Lieberman DE, Polk JD, and Demes B. 2004. Predicting long bone loading from cross-sectional geometry. Am J Phys Anthropol 123:156–171.

Liu D, Wagner HD, and Weiner S. 2000. Bending and fracture of compact circumferential and osteonal lamellar bone of the baboon tibia. J Mater Sci Mater Med 11(1):49–60.

Lovejoy CO. 1988. Evolution of human walking. Sci Am 259(5):118–125.

Main RP. 2007. Ontogenetic relationships between in vivo strain environment, bone histomorphometry and growth in the goat radius. J Anat 210(3):272–293.

Main RP, and Biewener AA. 2004. Ontogenetic patterns of limb loading, in vivo bone strains and growth in the goat radius. J Exp Biol 207(Pt 15):2577–2588.

Marotti G. 1996. The structure of bone tissues and the cellular control of their deposition. Ital J Anat Embryol 101:25–79.

Martin RB. 2003a. Fatigue microdamage as an essential element of bone mechanics and biology. Calcif Tissue Int 73:101–107.

Martin RB. 2003b. Fatigue damage, remodeling, and the minimization of skeletal weight. J Theor Biol 220(2):271–276.

Martin RB, and Boardman DL. 1993. The effects of collagen fiber orientation, porosity, density, and mineralization on bovine cortical bone bending properties. J Biomech 26:1047–1054.

Martin RB, and Burr DB. 1989. Structure, function and adaptation of compact bone. New York: Raven Press.

Martin RB, Burr DB, and Sharkey NA. 1998. Skeletal tissue mechanics. New York: Springer-Verlag.

Martin RB, Gibson VA, Stover SM, Gibeling JC, and Griffin LV. 1996a. Osteonal structure in the equine third metacarpus. Bone 19(2):165–171.

Martin RB, and Ishida J. 1989. The relative effects of collagen fiber orientation, porosity, density, and mineralization on bone strength. J Biomech 22(5):419–426.

Martin RB, Mathews PV, Lau ST, Gibson VA, and Stover SM. 1996b. Collagen fiber organization is related to mechanical properties and remodeling in equine bone. A comparison of two methods. J Biomech 29:1515–1521.

Martiniaková M, Grosskopf B, Omelka R, Vondraková M, and Bauerová M. 2006. Differences among species in compact bone tissue microstructure of mammalian skeleton: use of a discriminant function analysis for species identification. J Forensic Sci 51(6):1235–1239.

Mason MW, Skedros JG, and Bloebaum RD. 1995. Evidence of strain-mode-related cortical adaptation in the diaphysis of the horse radius. Bone 17(3):229–237.

Mayhew PM, Thomas CD, Clement JG, Loveridge N, Beck TJ, Bonfield W, Burgoyne CJ, and Reeve J. 2005. Relation between age, femoral neck cortical stability, and hip fracture risk. Lancet 366(9480):129–135.

McFarlin SC, Terranova CJ, Zihlman AL, Enlow DH, and Bromage TG. 2008. Regional variability in secondary remodeling within long bone cortices of catarrhine primates: the influence of bone growth history. J Anat 213(3):308–324.

Milgrom C, Finestone A, Simkin A, Ekenman I, Mendelson S, Millgram M, Nyska M, Larsson E, and Burr D. 2000. In-vivo strain measurements to evaluate the strengthening potential of exercises on the tibial bone. J Bone Joint Surg Br 82(4):591–594.

Moreno CA, Main RP, and Biewener AA. 2008. Variability in forelimb bone strains during non-steady locomotor activities in goats. J Exp Biol 211(Pt 7):1148–1162.

Mori R, Kodaka T, Sano T, Yamagishi N, Asari M, and Naito Y. 2003. Comparative histology of the laminar bone between young calves and foals. Cells Tissues Organs 175(1):43–50.

Morimoto N, Ponce de Leon MS, and Zollikofer CPE. 2011. Exploring femoral diaphyswal shape variation in wild and captive chimpanzees by means of morphometric mapping: a test of Wolff's law. Anat Rec 294:589–609.

Moyle DD, Welborn JW, 3rd, and Cooke FW. 1978. Work to fracture of canine femoral bone. J Biomech 11(10-12):435–440.

Muir P, Johnson KA, and Ruaux-Mason CP. 1999. In vivo matrix microdamage in a naturally occurring canine fatigue fracture. Bone 25(5):571–576.

Mulhern DM, and Ubelaker DH. 2009. Bone microstructure in juvenile chimpanzees. Am J Phys Anthropol 140(2):368–375.

Nunamaker D. 2001. Bucked shins in horses. In: Burr DB, and Milgrom C, editors. Musculoskeletal fatigue and stress fractures. Boca Raton, FL: CRC Press, pp. 203–219.

Nunamaker DM, Butterweck DM, and Provost MT. 1989. Some geometric properties of the third metacarpal bone: a comparison between the thoroughbred and standardbred racehorse. J Biomech 22(2):129–134.

Nyman JS, Roy A, Tyler JH, Acuna RL, Gayle HJ, and Wang X. 2007. Age-related factors affecting the postyield energy dissipation of human cortical bone. J Orthop Res 25(5):646–655.

O'Brien F, Taylor D, and Lee, CT. 2005. The effect of bone microstructure on the initiation and growth of microcracks. J Orthop Res 23(2):475–480.

Oh I, and Harris WH. 1978. Proximal strain distribution in the loaded femur. An in vitro comparison of the distributions in the intact femur and after insertion of different hip-replacement femoral components. J Bone Joint Surg Am 60(1):75–85.

Paine RR, and Godfrey LR. 1997. The scaling of skeletal microanatomy in non-human primates. J Zool Lond 241:803–821.

Parfitt AM, Mundy GR, Roodman GD, Hughes DE, and Boyce BF. 1996. A new model for the regulation of bone resorption, with particular reference to the effects of bisphosphonates. J Bone Miner Res 11:150–159.

Pazzaglia UE, Bonaspetti G, Rodella LF, Ranchetti F, and Azzola F. 2007. Design, morphometry and development of the secondary osteonal system in the femoral shaft of the rabbit. J Anat 211(3):303–312.

Pazzaglia UE, Zarattini G, Giacomini D, Rodella L, Menti AM, and Feltrin G. 2010. Morphometric analysis of the canal system of cortical bone: an experimental study in the rabbit femur carried out with standard histology and micro-CT. Anat Histol Embryol 39(1):17–26.

Pearson OM, and Lieberman DE. 2004. The aging of Wolff's law: ontogeny and responses to mechanical loading in cortical bone. Yrbk Phys Anthro 47:63–99.

Peterman MM, Hamel AJ, Cavanagh PR, Piazza SJ, and Sharkey NA. 2001. In vitro modeling of human tibial strains during exercise in micro-gravity. J Biomech 34(5):693–698.

Petrtýl M, Hert J, and Fiala P. 1996. Spatial organization of Haversian bone in man. J Biomech 29:161–169.

Pfeiffer S, Crowder C, Harrington L, and Brown M. 2006. Secondary osteons and haversian canal dimensions as behavioral indicators. Am J Phys Anthropol 131:460–468.

Pidaparti RMV, and Turner CH. 1997. Cancellous bone architecture: advantages of nonorthogonal trabecular alignment under multidirectional loading. J Biomech 30:979–983.

Pinto M, Jepsen KJ, Terranova CJ, and Buffenstein R. 2010. Lack of sexual dimorphism in femora of the eusocial and hypogonadic naked mole-rat: a novel animal model for the study of delayed puberty on the skeletal system. Bone 46(1):112–120.

Portigliatti Barbos M, Bianco P, Ascenzi A, and Boyde A. 1984. Collagen orientation in compact bone: II. Distribution of lamellae in the whole of the human femoral shaft with reference to its mechanical properties. Metab Bone Dis and Relat Res 5:309–315.

Portigliatti Barbos M, Carando S, Ascenzi A, and Boyde A. 1987. On the structural symmetry of human femurs. Bone 8:165–169.

Puustjärvi K, Nieminen J, Rasanen T, Hyttinen M, Helminen HJ, Kroger H, Huuskonen J, Alhava E, and Kovanen V. 1999. Do more highly organized collagen fibrils increase bone mechanical strength in loss of mineral density after one-year running training? J Bone Miner Res 14:321–329.

Reilly DT, and Burstein AH. 1974. The mechanical properties of cortical bone. J Bone Joint Surg 56-A:1001–1022.

Reilly DT, and Burstein AH. 1975. The elastic and ultimate properties of compact bone tissue. J Biomech 8:393–405.

Reilly GC. 2000. Observations of microdamage around osteocyte lacunae in bone. J Biomech 33:1131–1134.

Reilly GC, and Currey JD. 1999. The development of microcracking and failure in bone depends on the loading mode to which it is adapted. J Exp Biol 202:543–552.

Reilly GC, and Currey JD. 2000. The effects of damage and microcracking on the impact strength of bone. J Biomech 33:337–343.

Reilly GC, Currey JD, and Goodship AE. 1997. Exercise of young thoroughbred horses increases impact strength of the third metacarpal bone. J Orthop Res 15:862–868.

Riggs CM, Lanyon LE, and Boyde A. 1993a. Functional associations between collagen fibre orientation and locomotor strain direction in cortical bone of the equine radius. Anat Embryol 187:231–238.

Riggs CM, Vaughan LE, Boyde A, and Lanyon LE. 1993b. Mechanical implications of collagen fibre orientation in cortical bone of the equine radius. Anat Embryol 187:239–248.

Robling AG, and Stout SD. 2003. Histomorphology, geometry, and mechanical loading in past populations. In: Agarwal SC, and Stout SD, editors. Bone loss and osteoporosis: an anthropological perspective. New York: Kluwer Academic/Plenum, pp. 189–205.

Rubin CT, Fritton S, Sun YQ, and McLeod KJ. 1996a. Biomechanical parameters which stimulate bone formation: The ugly duckling of the skeletal growth factors. In: Davidovitch Z, and Norton LA, editors. Biological mechanisms of tooth movement and craniofacial adaptation. Boston: Harvard Society for the Advancement of Orthodontics, pp. 51–59.

Rubin CT, Gross TS, McLeod KJ, and Bain SD. 1995. Morphologic stages in lamellar bone formation stimulated by a potent mechanical stimulus. J Bone Miner Res 10:488–495.

Rubin CT, Gross TS, Qin Y, Fritton SP, Guilak F, and McLeod KJ. 1996b. Differentiation of the bone-tissue remodeling response to axial and torsional loading in the turkey ulna. J Bone Joint Surg 78A(10):1523–1533.

Rubin CT, and Lanyon LE. 1982. Limb mechanics as a function of speed and gait: a study of functional strains in the radius and tibia of horse and dog. J Exp Biol 101:187–211.

Rubin CT, and Lanyon LE. 1984a. Dynamic strain similarity in vertebrates; an alternative to allometric limb bone scaling. J Theor Biol 107(2):321–327.

Rubin CT, and Lanyon LE. 1984b. Regulation of bone formation by applied dynamic loads. J Bone Joint Surg Am 66(3):397–402.

Rubin CT, and Lanyon LE. 1985. Regulation of bone mass by mechanical strain magnitude. Calcif Tissue Int 37:411–417.

Ruff C, Holt B, and Trinkaus E. 2006. Who's afraid of the big bad Wolff?: "Wolff's law" and bone functional adaptation. Am J Phys Anthropol 129(4):484–498.

Ruff CB. 1981. Structural changes in the lower limb bones with aging at Pecos Pueblo. Philadelphia, PA: University of Pennsylvania.

Ruff CB, and Hayes WC. 1983. Cross-sectional geometry of Pecos Pueblo femora and tibiae—A biomechanical investigation: I. Method and general patterns of variation. Am J Phys Anthropol 60:359–381.

Schaffler MB, Burr DB, Jungers WL, and Ruff CB. 1985. Structural and mechanical indicators of limb specialization in primates. Folia Primatol Basel(45):61–75.

Schneider P, Stauber M, Voide R, Stampanoni M, Donahue LR, and Muller R. 2007. Ultrastructural properties in cortical bone vary greatly in two inbred strains of mice as assessed by synchrotron light based micro- and nano-CT. J Bone Miner Res 22(10):1557–1570.

Schneider RK, Milne DW, Gabel AA, Groom JJ, and Bramlage LR. 1982. Multidirectional in vivo strain analysis of the equine radius and tibia during dynamic loading with and without a cast. Am J Vet Res 43(9):1541–1550.

Simkin A, and Robin G. 1974. Fracture formation in differing collagen fiber pattern of compact bone. J Biomech 7(2):183–188.

Simons RS. 1999. Running, breathing and visceral motion in the domestic rabbit (Oryctolagus cuniculus): testing visceral displacement hypotheses. J Exp Biol 202(Pt 5):563–577.

Skedros JG. 2002. Use of predominant collagen fiber orientation for interpreting cortical bone loading history: bending vs. torsion. J Bone Miner Res 17:S307.

Skedros JG. 2005. Osteocyte lacuna population densities in sheep, elk and horse calcanei. Cells Tissues Organs 181(1):23–37.

Skedros JG, and Baucom SL. 2007. Mathematical analysis of trabecular "trajectories" in apparent trajectorial structures: the unfortunate historical emphasis on the human proximal femur. J Theor Biol 244(1):15–45.

Skedros JG, Beckstrom AB, Kiser CJ, and Bloebaum RD. 2008. The importance of bipedality/bending in mediating morphological adaptation in the chimpanzee femoral neck might be overstated. Am J Phys Anthropol Suppl 46:195.

Skedros JG, Bloebaum RD, Mason MW, and Bramble DM. 1994a. Analysis of a tension/compression skeletal system: Possible strain-specific differences in the hierarchical organization of bone. Anat Rec 239:396–404.

Skedros JG, Dayton MR, Sybrowsky CL, Bloebaum RD, and Bachus K. 2006a. The influence of collagen fiber orientation and other histocompositional characteristics on the mechanical properties of equine cortical bone. J Exp Biol 209:3025–3042.

Skedros JG, Dayton MR, Sybrowsky CL, Bloebaum RD, and Bachus KN. 2003a. Are uniform regional safety factors an objective of adaptive modeling/remodeling in cortical bone? J Exp Biol 206(Pt 14):2431–2439.

Skedros JG, Demes B, and Judex S. 2003b. Limitations in the use of predominant collagen fiber orientation for inferring loading history in cortical bone. Am J Phys Anthropol Suppl 36:193.

Skedros JG, Grunander TR, and Hamrick MW. 2005a. Spatial distribution of osteocyte lacunae in equine radii and third metacarpals: considerations for cellular communication, microdamage detection and metabolism. Cells Tissues Organs 180(4):215–236.

Skedros JG, Holmes JL, Vajda EG, and Bloebaum RD. 2005b. Cement lines of secondary osteons in human bone are not mineral-deficient: new data in a historical perspective. Anat Rec A Discov Mol Cell Evol Biol 286(1):781–803.

Skedros J, Hughes P, Nelson K, and Winet H. 1999. Collagen fiber orientation in the proximal femur: challenging Wolff's tension/compression interpretation. J Bone Miner Res 14(Suppl 1):S441.

Skedros JG, and Hunt KJ. 2004. Does the degree of laminarity mediate site-specific differences in collagen fiber orientation in primary bone? An evaluation in the turkey ulna diaphysis. J Anat 205(2):121–134.

Skedros JG, Hunt KJ, and Bloebaum RD. 2004. Relationships of loading history and structural and material characteristics of bone: development of the mule deer calcaneus. J Morphol 259:281–307.

Skedros JG, Kiser CJ, Keenan KE, and Thomas SC. 2011. Analysis of osteon morphotype scoring schemes for interpreting load history: evaluation in the chimpanzee femur. J Anat 218:480–499.

Skedros JG, Kiser CJ, and Mendenhall SD. 2011. A weighted osteon morphotype score out-performs regional osteon percent prevalence calculations for interpreting cortical bone adaptation. Am J Phys Anthropol 144:41–50.

Skedros JG, and Kuo TY. 1999. Ontogenetic changes in regional collagen fiber orientation suggest a role for variant strain stimuli in cortical bone construction. J Bone Miner Res 14(Suppl 1):S441.

Skedros JG, Mason MW, and Bloebaum RD. 1994b. Differences in osteonal micromorphology between tensile and compressive cortices of a bending skeletal system: indications of potential strain-specific differences in bone microstructure. Anat Rec 239(4):405–413.

Skedros JG, Mason MW, and Bloebaum RD. 2001. Modeling and remodeling in a developing artiodactyl calcaneus: a model for evaluating Frost's mechanostat hypothesis and its corollaries. Anat Rec 263:167–185.

Skedros JG, Mason MW, Nelson MC, and Bloebaum RD. 1996. Evidence of structural and material adaptation to specific strain features in cortical bone. Anat Rec 246(1):47–63.

Skedros JG, Mendenhall SD, Anderson WE, Gubler KE, Hoopes JV, and Sorenson SM. 2006b. Osteon phenotypic morphotypes: a new characteristic for interpreting bone quality in cortical bone. 52nd Annual Meeting of the Orthopaedic Research Society, 31:1600.

Skedros JG, Mendenhall SD, Kiser CJ, and Winet H. 2009. Interpreting cortical bone adaptation and load history by quantifying osteon morphotypes in circularly polarized light images. Bone 44(3):392–403.

Skedros JG, Sorenson SM, Hunt KJ, and Holyoak JD. 2007a. Ontogenetic structural and material variations in ovine calcanei: a model for interpreting bone adaptation. Anat Rec 290(3):284–300.

Skedros JG, Sorenson SM, and Jenson NH. 2007b. Are distributions of secondary osteon variants useful for interpreting load history in mammalian bones? Cells Tissues Organs 185(4):285–307.

Skedros JG, Sorenson SM, Takano Y, and Turner CH. 2006c. Dissociation of mineral and collagen orientations may differentially adapt compact bone for regional loading environments: Results from acoustic velocity measurements in deer calcanei. Bone 39:143–151.

Skedros JG, Su SC, and Bloebaum RD. 1997. Biomechanical implications of mineral content and microstructural variations in cortical bone of horse, elk, and sheep calcanei. Anat Rec 249(3):297–316.

Skedros JG, Sybrowsky CL, Bloebaum RD, Bachus KN, and Wang X. 2006d. The relative influence of collagen crosslinks on the mechanical properties of equine cortical bone. In: Transactions of the 52nd Annual Meeting of the Orthopaedic Research Society, 1581.

Skedros JG, Sybrowsky CL, Parry TR, and Bloebaum RD. 2003c. Regional differences in cortical bone organization and microdamage prevalence in Rocky Mountain mule deer. Anat Rec 274A(1):837–850.

Skerry TM. 2006. One mechanostat or many? Modifications of the site-specific response of bone to mechanical loading by nature and nurture. J Musculoskelet Neuronal Interact 6(2):122–127.

Starck JM, and Chinsamy A. 2002. Bone microstructure and developmental plasticity in birds and other dinosaurs. J Morphol 254(3):232–246.

Stover SM, Pool RR, Martin RB, and Morgan JP. 1992. Histological features of the dorsal cortex of the third metacarpal bone mid-diaphysis during postnatal growth in thoroughbred horses. J Anat 181:455–469.

Streeter M, Stout S, Trinkaus E, and Burr D. 2010. Brief communication: Bone remodeling rates in Pleistocene humans are not slower than the rates observed in modern populations: a reexamination of Abbott et al. (1996). Am J Phys Anthropol 141(2):315–318.

Su SC, Skedros JG, Bachus KN, and Bloebaum RD. 1999. Loading conditions and cortical bone construction of an artiodactyl calcaneus. J Exp Biol 202(Pt 22):3239–3254.

Swartz SM, Bennett MB, and Carrier DR. 1992. Wing bone stresses in free flying bats and the evolution of skeletal design for flight. Nature 359:726–729.

Szivek JA, Johnson EM, Magee FP. 1992. *In vivo* strain analysis of the greyhound femoral diaphysis. J Invest Surg 5:91–108.

Takano Y, Turner CH, Owan I, Martin RB, Lau ST, Forwood MR, and Burr DB. 1999. Elastic anisotropy and collagen orientation of osteonal bone are dependent on the mechanical strain distribution. J Orthop Res 17:59–66.

Tami AE, Nasser P, Schaffler MB, and Knothe Tate ML. 2003. Noninvasive fatigue fracture model of the rat ulna. J Orthop Res 21(6):1018–1024.

Taylor D. 1997. Bone maintenance and remodeling: A control system based on fatigue damage. J Orthop Res 15(4):601–606.

Taylor D. 2000. Scaling effects in the fatigue strength of bones from different animals. J Theor Biol 206:299–306.

Taylor D, O'Reilly P, Vallet L, and Lee TC. 2003. The fatigue strength of compact bone in torsion. J Biomech 36(8):1103–1109.

Tommasini SM, Nasser P, and Jepsen KJ. 2007. Sexual dimorphism affects tibia size and shape but not tissue-level mechanical properties. Bone 40(2):498–505.

Tommasini SM, Nasser P, Schaffler MB, and Jepsen KJ. 2005. Relationship between bone morphology and bone quality in male tibias: implications for stress fracture risk. J Bone Miner Res 20(8):1372–1380.

Turner AS, Mills EJ, and Gabel AA. 1975. In vivo measurement of bone strain in the horse. Am J Vet Res 36(11):1573–1579.

Turner CH. 1998. Three rules for bone adaptation to mechanical stimuli. Bone 23(5):399–407.

Turner CH, and Burr DB. 1993. Basic biomechanical measurements of bone: a tutorial. Bone 14:595–608.

Turner CH, and Burr DB. 1997. Orientation of collagen in osteonal bone. Calcif Tissue Int 60(1):90.

Turner CH, Wang T, and Burr DB. 2001. Shear strength and fatigue properties of human cortical bone determined from pure shear tests. Calcif Tissue Int 69:373–378.

Ural A, and Vashishth D. 2005. Cohesive finite element modeling of age-related toughness loss in human cortical bone. J Biomech 39(16):2982.

Ural A, and Vashishth D. 2006. Interactions between microstructural and geometrical adaptation in human cortical bone. J Orthop Res 24(7):1489–1498.

Urbanová P, and Novotný V. 2005. Distinguishing between human and non-human bones: histometric method for forensic anthropology. Anthropologie XLIII:77–85.

van der Meulen MC, Jepsen KJ, and Mikic B. 2001. Understanding bone strength: size isn't everything. Bone 29:101–104.

van Oers RF, Ruimerman R, Tanck E, Hilbers PA, and Huiskes R. 2008. A unified theory for osteonal and hemi-osteonal remodeling. Bone 42:250–259.

Vashishth D. 2004. Rising crack-growth-resistance behavior in cortical bone: implications for toughness measurements. J Biomech 37(6):943–946.

Verborgt O, Gibson GJ, and Schaffler MB. 2000. Loss of osteocyte integrity in association with microdamage and bone remodeling after fatigue in vivo. J Bone Min Res 15(1):60–67.

Vincentelli R. 1978. Relation between collagen fiber orientation and age of osteon formation in human tibial compact bone. Acta Anat (Basel) 100(1):120–128.

Vincentelli R, and Evans FG. 1971. Relations among mechanical properties, collagen fibers, and calcification in adult human cortical bone. J Biomech 4(3):193–201.

Vincentelli R, and Grigorov M. 1985. The effect of Haversian remodeling on the tensile properties of human cortical bone. J Biomech 18:201–207.

van Oers RF, Ruimerman R, Tanck E, Hilbers PA, Huiskers R. 2008. A unified theory for osteonal and hemiosteonal remodeling. Bone 42:250–259.

von Ebner V. 1887. Über den feineren bau der skeletteile der kalkschwamme usw. Wiener Stizber 95:213–236.

Wainwright SA, Biggs WD, Currey JD, and Gosline JM. 1982. Elements of structural systems. Mechanical design in organisms. Princeton, NJ: Princeton University Press, pp. 254–258.

Wallace IJ, Middleton KM, Lublinsky S, Kelly SA, Judex S, Garland T, Jr., and Demes B. 2010. Functional significance of genetic variation underlying limb bone diaphyseal structure. Am J Phys Anthropol 143:21–30.

Wang XD, Masilamani NS, Mabrey JD, Alder ME, and Agrawal CM. 1998. Changes in the fracture toughness of bone may not be reflected in its mineral density, porosity, and tensile properties. Bone 23(1):67–72.

Warshaw J. 2007. Primate bone microstructural variability: relationships to life history, mechanical adaptation and phylogeny [Doctor of Philosophy, dissertation]. The City University of New York, New York.

Williams JL, Do PD, Eick JD, and Schmidt TL. 2001. Tensile properties of the physis vary with anatomic location, thickness, strain rate and age. J Orthop Res 19(6):1043–1048.

Williams JL, Vani JN, Eick JD, Petersen EC, and Schmidt TL. 1999. Shear strength of the physis varies with anatomic location and is a function of modulus, inclination, and thickness. J Orthop Res 17(2):214–222.

Williams T, Jardine C, Keenan K, Skedros J, and Kiser C. 2010. Secondary osteon cross-sectional size and morphotype score are independent in limb bones subject to habitual bending or torsion. Am J Phys Anthropol Suppl 50:245.

Yamada H. 1970. Strength of biological materials. Baltimore: Williams and Wilkins Co., pp. 23–30.

Yamamoto T, Domon T, Takahashi S, Islam N, and Suzuki R. 2000. Twisted plywood structure of an alternating lamellar pattern in cellular cementum of human teeth. Anat Embryol (Berl) 202(1):25–30.

Yeni YN, Brown CU, Wang Z, and Norman TL. 1997. The influence of bone morphology on fracture toughness of the human femur and tibia. Bone 21:453–459.

Yeni YN, and Norman TL. 2000. Calculation of porosity and osteonal cement line effects on the effective fracture toughness of cortical bone in longitudinal crack growth. J Biomed Mater Res 51:504–509.

Zebaze RM, Ghasem-Zadeh A, Bohte A, Luliano-Burns S, Mirams M, Price RI, Mackie EJ, Seeman E. 2010. Intracortical remodelling and porosity in the distal radius and post-mortem femurs of women: a cross-sectional study. Lancet 375(9727):1729–1736.

Zioupos P, and Currey JD. 1998. Changes in the stiffness, strength, and toughness of human cortical bone with age. Bone 22:57–66.

# Bone Fracture
## Biomechanics and Risk

# 8

AMANDA M. AGNEW
JOHN H. BOLTE IV

## Contents

## 8.1   Introduction

Understanding bone fracture mechanisms is essential for studies in skeletal biology. The implications of this knowledge can be applied across numerous disciplines including but not limited to, bioarchaeology, forensic anthropology, paleopathology, paleoanthropology, injury biomechanics, and clinical orthopedics. Insight into how and why bone fractures occur can reveal valuable information about health and disease, trauma, and behavior in both modern and past human populations. Additionally, by considering fracture etiology and behavior, researchers may be able to place fractures into a broader context (e.g., reconstructing the series of events in a forensic case) and apply the knowledge to better prevent future fractures (e.g., osteoporosis research). This chapter intends to present an overview of possible direct biological contributors to bone fragility and fracture.

### 8.1.1   Classifying Fracture Context

The interaction between biology and environment is paramount in studies focused on health and fracture risk. Traumatic fractures are heavily influenced by nonbiological external forces contributing to risk and are often classified as either accidental or intentional. In some cases it may be possible to determine the difference based on fracture types and distribution. Accidental trauma includes, but is not limited to, falls, car accidents, and sports injuries. Injury biomechanics is a field of study devoted to understanding the response of the human body to various loading conditions and to classifying both soft and hard tissue injuries. By analyzing injury mechanisms, automobile safety features such as seatbelts and airbags are designed and constantly improved. Such an example highlights the value of applying knowledge of fracture mechanisms.

It is important to recall that while biology and environment have a close relationship in determining bone health and fracture risk, additional external factors such as behavior have the potential to put someone at an even greater risk for fracture. Unfortunately, external factors may include intentional violence, which can often lead to traumatic fractures requiring evaluation in a forensics context. In such cases it is necessary to first establish the timing of bone injury (i.e., antemortem, perimortem, or postmortem). Whereas antemortem fractures may help in the identification process and are important to establish whether a history of trauma exists, perimortem fractures are most pertinent in criminal cases. The types and distribution of perimortem fractures throughout a skeleton can provide crucial information about the context of a crime. In addition, characteristics of a bone wound can implicate a specific type of weapon (Humphrey and Hutchinson 2001), important information in an investigation. For example, blunt force trauma can be differentiated from sharp force trauma and ballistics trauma by examination of the direction of beveling (Hart 2005). In some cases, fracture analysis can assist in the determination of manner and cause of death. A common example is that of the fractured hyoid bone, often indicating death by strangulation (Ubelaker 1992). For a thorough review of fracture types and their presentation in dry bone, see Aufderheide and Rodriguez-Martin (1998), Galloway (1999), Kimmerle and Baraybar (2008), and Ortner (2003).

Nontraumatic fractures (e.g., stress fractures) often result from repetitive loading and not a single dynamic loading event. These types of fractures result more from biological than environmental causes. While a traumatic event is an obvious cause of fracture, bone failure can result from much simpler scenarios. For example, in osteopenic individuals, muscle contraction (Warden et al. 2002) and even coughing (De Maeseneer et al. 2000) have been shown to play a role in rib fracture development. A specific example is the high incidence of femoral neck (hip) fractures in osteoporotic persons. This is often explained as someone "fell and broke their hip," when it is possible that these events were reversed and the individual broke their hip upon the impact of taking a step, which in turn actually caused them to fall. A thinning cortex and loss of trabecular bone and connectivity are primarily responsible for hip fracture vulnerability (Blain et al. 2008). Additionally, geometric changes of the femoral neck may be partly responsible for the reported increased fracture risk in modern populations (Sievänen et al. 2007), and explain why so few osteoporotic fractures are identified in past populations.

In certain situations, the environment can directly and rapidly affect bone biology and response to loading. Astronauts who have spent considerable time in zero-gravity conditions or individuals who are bedridden for prolonged periods of time are both at an increased risk for fracture since bone loss can be extreme. For a review of how the skeleton responds when in an unloaded state, see Oganov (2003).

For the purpose of this chapter, only potential *biological* contributors to increased fracture risk will be emphasized. Additionally, cortical bone will remain the focus of the following discussion. The role of trabecular bone should not be de-emphasized in discussing fracture risk, but has been covered extensively in the literature and is generally outside the scope of this chapter.

## 8.2   Biology of Fracture Risk

### 8.2.1   Adaptation

The skeletons of large mammals epitomize evolutionary compromise. It is essential to have a structural framework that is strong yet of limited mass to facilitate quick movement. Remodeling allows the skeleton to maintain a minimal size while extending its fatigue life (Martin 2003), and its role in understanding bone strength will be discussed later in this chapter. However, modeling influences bone behavior by allowing bone to change size and shape in response to loads. (For a discussion of modeling and remodeling processes, see chapters by Maggiano, and Stout and Crowder in this volume.) Skeletal robusticity is the direct result of applied loads throughout life. Interestingly, the need for strong bones may be diminishing in a modern and technologically advanced world in which people increasingly rely on cultural mechanisms of adaptation. The biological response for such a phenomenon would be decreased skeletal mass, and this is precisely what Ruff (2000) has shown with documentation of decreased cortical area through time. According to Ruff (2006), the human skeleton (and that of its direct ancestors) is becoming less robust, and relative bone strength has decreased 15% from 2 million to 5,000 years ago. With a continued decrease in cortical area, in the last 5,000 years an additional 15% of bone strength has been lost (Ruff 2006).

Bones are adapted to withstand loads (Parfitt 2002) and fracture is the mechanical failure of this adaptive mechanism. Currey (2003b) argues this does not necessarily mean that the *purpose* of bone is simply to resist fracture. In fact, certain sites throughout the human skeleton are poorly adapted to fracture resistance (e.g., femoral neck), and some individuals are at a greater risk of fracture than others. Increasing age has been shown to be a risk factor for fracture based on multiple biological variables concerning bone composition (Zioupos and Currey 1998), and despite a heavy clinical emphasis on bone mass, it is not solely responsible for determining fragility (Heaney 2003). Many elderly individuals suffer from bone loss, yet some are more susceptible to fractures than others. Osteoporosis, defined by severely low bone mass with associated risk of resulting fracture, has become a common and worldwide health problem. The World Health Organization (WHO) defines osteoporosis based on bone mineral density (BMD) values. Regardless of this value, however, for any given bone mass, fracture risk still increases with age (Hui et al. 1988). In addition, individuals with previous fractures (even those with a higher bone mass) are more likely to sustain subsequent fractures than someone with a lower bone mass who had never experienced a fracture (Kanis et al. 2004; Sornay-Rendu et al. 2005). This suggests there are additional factors to consider as contributors to a propensity for fracture.

### 8.2.2   Beyond Bone Mass

Past research has put an overwhelming emphasis on utilizing the *quantity* of bone as a predictor for fracture risk. For example, BMD is often used as a surrogate for bone mass and is routinely measured by dual-energy x-ray absorptiometry (DXA) and quantitative computed tomography (QCT) to assess fracture risk. BMD is commonly relied upon in clinical practice (Miller et al. 2005) because of evidence that low BMD is associated with increased fracture risk (Jergas and Gluer 1997). A relationship between BMD and bone mechanical properties has been established (Bousson et al. 2006; Ebbesen et al. 1999; Lochmmuller et al. 2002; Mallory 2001; Martin et al. 2004). However, the effectiveness of BMD in identifying fracture risk is debated because of potentially confounding factors, such as bone size and strength, skeletal site, body composition, age, sex, and interpretation errors (Bolotin 2007; Cvijetic and Korsic 2004; Foley et al. 2009; Gafni and Baron 2004; Genant and Jiang 2006; Hogler et al. 2003; Leslie et al. 2007; Pors Nielsen 2000; Stone et al. 2003; Wren et al. 2000). Additionally, although changes in bone quantity and mineralization may not always be reflected in BMD outputs, both affect BMD values and can heavily influence bone's response to loading (Boivin and Meunier 2003; Burr 2006).

Bone strength appears to be more dependent on geometry than BMD values alone (Genant and Jiang 2006; Kok et al. 1995). Bone geometry, since highly dependent on cross-sectional area and distribution around a neutral axis, is critical in fracture resistance. Numerous studies have established a relationship between bone geometry and behavior, strength, and fracture risk (Augat et al. 1996; Bagi et al. 2006; Bousson, et al. 2006). For example, mechanical testing of ribs by Kemper and colleagues (2007) has confirmed that variations in the structural response of bone are closely related to variations in cross-sectional geometry while material properties are maintained. The biomechanical analysis of cross-sectional geometry is fairly common in bioarchaeological investigations as well, especially applied to the femur. The implications of such research can lead to suggestions about physical activity levels, mobility, nutrition, and so forth, in past populations. Ruff (2008) provides a useful review of such applications. A review of how loading history affects geometry is explained by Skedros (this volume), and Robling and Stout (2003) present an interesting example of interpreting loading history based on cross-sectional geometry and histomorphometry in an archaeological population.

Although the precedent set by reliance on bone mass is undoubtedly crucial in characterizing bone strength, the role of bone quality has been somewhat neglected and has only more recently been recognized as a major contributor in the assessment of fracture (Recker and Barger-Lux 2004). Hernandez (2008) relays the importance of examining numerous factors (e.g., remodeling), all relative to bone mass, in determining mechanical response and fracture.

The bone quality framework, proposed by Felsenberg and Boonen (2005), incorporates both structural properties, which are influenced by bone quantity but not restricted to only size (e.g., geometry, architecture, porosity, etc.) and material properties (e.g., mineral and collagen composition). The objective of this chapter is to emphasize that bone quality is as important as bone quantity in determining fragility and fracture risk (Heaney 1993), and should not be exempt from investigation into patterns of bone behavior. Although bone fragility is most often attributed to decreasing bone mass and increasing age (see Rosen et al. 1999), it is necessary to explore additional variables (some of which are outlined in this chapter) as contributors. Even more recent paleopathological studies of bone loss are incorporating questions concerning bone quality (Agarwal et al. 2004; Agarwal and Grynpas 1996; Grynpas 2003). The role of bone quality in defining a bone's mechanical behavior is complex and warrants further research as it is yet still incompletely understood.

Because the biology of fracture risk is dependent on bone fragility (Turner 2002), it is necessary to understand the link between fragility and different mechanical properties. (The term *fragility* is loosely used here to describe a state in which a low resistance to fracture is experienced.) However, the relationship between bone strength and propensity for fracture is not simple (Currey 2001). Frost (2002) describes the major determinants of bone strength: (1) the material properties of bone tissue, (2) the amount of accumulated microdamage in a bone, and (3) the amount of bone present (bone mass) as well as its distribution (geometry). The ability of a bone to resist fracture is dependent on these factors, which are reviewed here, with an emphasis on those that are relatively underrepresented in the literature (i.e., determinants 1 and 2).

### 8.2.3   Mechanical Properties

Researchers perform numerous mechanical tests (representing loading in tension, compression, shear, and torsion) in an attempt to document and compare properties of bone through its life span. In most materials, when a force is applied that exceeds the strength of that material, failure results. Since bone is constantly changing in composition and is extremely variable, it is necessary to analyze additional properties to characterize bone's resistance to fracture (Felsenberg and Boonen 2005). Mechanical properties can be divided into extrinsic (structural) properties and intrinsic (material) properties.

Extrinsic mechanical properties of bone are influenced by bone size and can depend upon both intrinsic material properties and bone geometry. Extrinsic properties include ultimate force, stiffness, hardness, brittleness, and work. These properties are demonstrated on a force versus displacement curve from a typical tensile test (Figure 8.1). Ultimate force is how much load bone material can support prior to failure. Although this maximum load is important, it is also critical that bone be stiff enough to withstand various loading conditions (Currey 2002), however stiffness is not necessarily a direct measurement of propensity for fracture or fragility (Turner 2002; Turner and Burr 1993). Stiffness, k, is related to a bone's ability to resist plastic deformation and is calculated as the slope of the elastic portion of the force-displacement curve prior to reaching the yield point. The yield point,

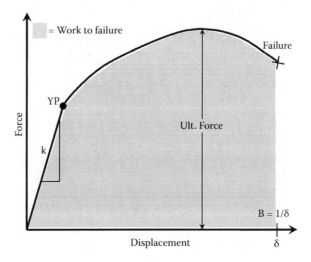

**Figure 8.1** Force versus displacement curve for a typical tensile test. (Created by J. Bolte.)

YP, is the point at which the material exits its elastic phase and begins to deform plastically. For example, hardness relates to a bone's resistance to plastic deformation. Brittleness, B, is calculated as the inverse of displacement at time of failure. Compared with many other materials bone is considered brittle because it typically fractures before plastic deformation is reached and absorbs little energy. As is typical for brittle materials, bone is strong in compression but weak in tension (Currey 2002). Finally, work (energy) to fracture is calculated as the area under the force–displacement curve until failure (shown in gray in Figure 8.1).

Intrinsic properties of bone are the core material properties that are needed to better understand material composition and are not influenced by size or distribution of bone as extrinsic properties are. Intrinsic properties are based on a stress–strain curve (Figure 8.2) calculated from mechanically testing samples of the material. Common intrinsic properties include Young's modulus, yield stress and strain, ultimate stress and strain, and toughness. For example, in a tensile test Young's modulus, E, is a measure of the elasticity of the bone material calculated from the slope of the stress–strain curve. Yield stress is the amount of stress at which bone begins to deform plastically (the elastic limit), shown as YP in Figure 8.2. Ultimate strength is the point of maximum stress and is achieved as the material undergoes gross deformation before ultimate failure. Finally, toughness is a measure of bone's ability to absorb energy and resist fracture, determined by calculating the area under the stress–strain curve up to failure, shown in gray in Figure 8.2. The following discussion will reference many of the mechanical properties outlined here.

### 8.2.3.1 Determinants of Material Properties in Bone

Bone's hierarchical microstructure influences its material properties and mechanical response (Currey 2002). When defining material properties it is commonly assumed the material is homogenous, but this is far from true for many biological tissues. The material properties of bone are determined by the quantity and arrangement of its organic (collagen) and mineral components, which are constantly changing with age. Both the organic and mineral components of bone provide unique contributions to its response to loading, but it is difficult to assess their individual roles (Burr 2002a). The mineral content of bone

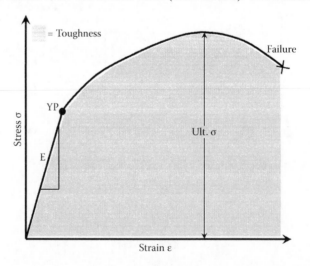

**Figure 8.2** Stress versus strain curve for a typical tensile test. (Created by J. Bolte.)

assists in defining strength and stiffness (Currey et al. 1996b), while the organic content contributes more to its toughness (Zioupos 2001b). Their combination allows bone to have unique and variable properties.

**8.2.3.1.1** Mineral    It is widely accepted that variations in mineralization affect the mechanical properties of bone (Martin et al. 1998). Increasing mineralization with age has been shown to be responsible for an associated increase in Young's modulus (Currey et al. 1996a), stiffness, and strength (Follet et al. 2004); however, excessive mineralization will cause bone to become brittle (Zioupos et al. 2000).

Remodeling activity directly affects the arrangement and progression of mineralization, which in turn affects the direction-dependent mechanical properties of bone (Wagner and Weiner 1992). Newly remodeled bone is less mineralized than older existing bone tissue, and a decrease in bone turnover, as can occur with age, can result in relatively hypermineralized bone. (For a more detailed discussion of the bone remodeling process, see the chapter by Stout and Crowder in this volume.) A study evaluating the micromechanical properties of bone and utilizing nanoindentation (a technique that measures "microhardness") found recently generated secondary osteons to be considerably less hard than older osteons in femora (Huja et al. 2006). Unfortunately, it is difficult to relate microhardness values to true intrinsic properties of bone, although a correlation has been shown to occur with Young's modulus (Boivin et al. 2008). It would be beneficial if future research could address this disconnect.

**8.2.3.1.2** Collagen    Individual collagen fibers composing lamellar bone are said to be anisotropic (behave differently according to the direction of applied force); however, the arrangement and orientation of collagen fibers in lamellar bone as a composite material result in a marked increase in isotropy (decreased direction dependency). Therefore, collagen orientation plays an important role in how lamellar bone responds to applied loads (Ziv et al. 1996). For example, longitudinally oriented collagen fibers are shown to relate to increased bone strength, but not necessarily fatigue life (Martin et al. 1996). To extend this concept further, collagen fiber orientation determines osteon morphotypes as defined by birefringence patterns in polarized light, suggesting osteon types have different mechanical properties, possibly related to strain history (Skedros this volume; Skedros et al. 2009).

Collagen degradation can have an adverse affect on mechanical properties (Wynnyckyj et al. 2009) and increase bone fragility (Paschalis et al. 2004). Specifically, a decrease in bone toughness has been observed as collagen is degraded (Currey 2003a; Wang et al. 2002). It has even been suggested that a major role of remodeling is not only to prevent hypermineralization or microcrack accumulation (both of which can have negative mechanical effects), but also to maintain the integrity of the collagen network and thereby increase work to fracture (Burr 2008). See Viguet-Carrin and colleagues (2006) for a more thorough review of collagen's influence on bone's mechanical properties.

**8.2.3.1.3** Affect of Bone Type    Bone strength is partially dependent on the types of bone present in cross-section (Frost 2001). Woven, fibrolamellar, primary and secondary lamellar, and plexiform are examples of bone types. (For a review of their different forms and functions, see chapters in this volume by Maggiano, Stout and Crowder, and Mulhern and Ubelaker.) One study was successfully able to isolate bone types and found primary lamellar bone to be harder than secondary lamellar bone (Liu et al. 2000). The unique presence of primary lamellar bone in the growing skeleton makes it a rational target to assess the role that different bone types play in defining cortical bone strength. Mechanical properties vary between primary and secondary lamellar bone (Currey 2002), and past studies on animal and adult human bones have suggested that secondary osteon accumulations are associated with reduced bone strength (Liu et al. 2000; Vincentelli and Grigorov 1985) despite their positive role in extending the fatigue life of bone. Recent ongoing research by the authors provides evidence that human pediatric bone may reveal a more complex relationship.

Human pediatric rib sections were subjected to quasi-static (2.5 mm/min) 3-point bend tests and analyzed histomorphometrically near the location of failure. Initial results suggest that strength parameters are more closely related to bone geometry than bone composition. However, a significant relationship ($p < 0.001$) was found between Young's modulus and the percent area of secondary lamellar (osteonal) bone in cross-section, as distinct from primary bone (including woven, fibrolamellar, and primary lamellar; Figure 8.3). Interestingly, this is a positive relationship; however, further testing and analysis is necessary before any interpretation of these data can be offered. The lack of a significant relationship between percent area of porosity and Young's modulus may provide evidence that variation in mineralization or collagen arrangement, which may vary with bone type (in addition to geometry) could play a more critical role in determining fracture behavior of pediatric bone. Future emphasis should be placed on mechanical testing of immature human bone under different loading conditions to better understand fracture mechanics and the influence of bone biology during development.

Bone type can also determine fracture behavior. Liu et al. (2000) found that post-failure, primary lamellar bone tends to break cleanly, whereas lamellar bone containing osteon accumulations remains attached, providing an additional adaptive explanation for secondary lamellar bone function. Lynn and Fairgrieve (2009) found lamellar bone separation to be typical for fracture surfaces under dynamic loading conditions. They also found that osteon pullout is more likely to occur in fleshed than unfleshed bone, providing useful

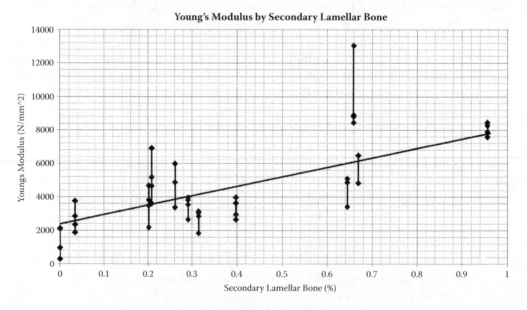

**Figure 8.3** Plot showing significant positive relationship between Young's modulus and relative secondary lamellar bone area from mechanical testing of pediatric ribs. A univariate mixed model was used to create the mean estimate line. (Created by A. Agnew.)

information for understanding fracture conditions. Osteon pullout, an interesting adaptive process that debonds the osteon at its interface, allows for the fatigue life and toughness of the bone to be extended. Osteon pullout has been shown to be affected by load type and vary by location, but this phenomenon's affect on bone integrity requires further investigation (Hiller et al. 2003).

### 8.2.4  Microdamage and Remodeling

While collagen and mineral characteristics both contribute to the material properties of bone tissue, bone matrix quality is also affected by microdamage accumulation (Burr 2006). Normal physiological loading environments can cause microdamage (also referred to as microcracks or microfractures) to occur within bone (O'Brien et al. 2005). An example of microcracks can be seen in Figure 8.4. Microdamage, in the form of fatigue fractures, is initiated in regions of high strain during cyclic loading (Danova et al. 2003). Bone undergoing such repeated strains, which may actually be much lower than the strain necessary to cause the failure seen in a single loading event (Currey 2002), is more likely to experience microfractures. As cyclic loading increases and the number of microfractures increase, a progressive loss of strength can be observed as microcracks grow and coalesce forming macrocracks. Therefore, bone failure at the material level directly influences structural failure of the whole bone (Ebacher et al. 2007). If microcracks accumulate, mechanical properties of the bone are altered (Sobelman et al. 2004) as is evident by a loss of stiffness (Burr et al. 1998; Yeni and Fyhrie 2002), toughness (Mashiba et al. 2001), and bone strength (Burr et al. 1997; Nagaraja et al. 2005), as well as a decrease in resistance to fracture (Danova, et al. 2003) and increased fragility (Burr et al. 1998).

Although an association has been established between microdamage and bone strength, remodeling may play a larger role in this relationship than previously acknowledged (Allen and Burr 2008). The presence of fatigue damage demands a physiological response in the form of bone turnover (Muir et al. 2007). The goal of this *targeted* remodeling is to prevent microdamage accumulation in an attempt to maintain total bone strength (Burr 2002b) and increase bone's fatigue life (Burr 1993; Martin 2003; Verborgt et al. 2000). There are two possible scenarios in which microdamage accumulates in bone: (1) damage is initiated

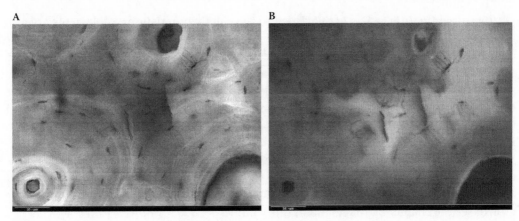

**Figure 8.4 (See color insert.)** Linear microcracks observed in human rib sections stained with basic fuchsin at 40× objective magnification under (A) bright field transmitted light compared to (B) epiflourescent reflected light. (Images by A. Agnew.)

too quickly for remodeling to efficiently repair it (possibly a dynamic loading event), or (2) the remodeling process is deficient and cannot repair it (Taylor 1997).

If remodeling is suppressed, the resulting hypermineralized bone allows considerable microdamage accumulation (Wasserman et al. 2005). This increase in microdamage can be of the magnitude of five- to sixfold (Mashiba et al. 2000). Other effects of suppressed remodeling include increased brittleness and decreased impact strength (Currey 2002). If remodeling becomes overactive, the resulting greater number of resorptive bays that remain partially unfilled predisposes bone to further microdamage (Seeman and Delmas 2006). A positive feedback control system is thus responsible for regulating bone turnover in this scenario. Remodeling serves to remove damage, but an accumulation of remodeling related porosity can reduce bone strength and stiffness, causing more microdamage to accumulate and trigger more targeted remodeling with continued loading (Robling et al. 2006). Heaney (2003) argues that remodeling is the major determinant of skeletal fragility in spite of the positive role it plays in repairing microdamage.

### 8.2.4.1 *Cortical Porosity*

Changes in the morphology and number of secondary osteons as well as the amount of porosity reflect the degree of remodeling activity in bone. With increasing age a negative balance in remodeling is reached as bone resorption exceeds bone formation creating increased porosity (Thomas et al. 2005). Since remodeling rates can vary between sexes (Cho et al. 2006), the effects of differences in porosity may be partially to blame for sex-differentiated fragility (Ghasem-Zadeh et al. 2009). The accumulation of microdamage also varies between sexes. It tends to increase at a faster rate in females (Norman and Wang 1997), putting them at an increased risk of fracture at any age.

Cortical porosity has been shown to affect Young's modulus (Zioupos 2001b) and toughness (Yeni et al. 1997), and likely provides a stress concentration for microcracks initiation (Voide et al. 2009). Bending strength and resistance to fracture is mainly dependent on bone's compressive strength, which seems to be most sensitive to cortical porosity and secondary osteon size (Ebacher et al. 2007). The role that cortical porosity plays in defining bone loss and failure may be underestimated (Zebaze et al. 2009) and deserves the attention of future studies as new technologies are utilized (see Cooper et al. 2007 and Cooper in this volume).

Increased fracture risk is not confined to the elderly population. Adolescents are also at great risk for fracture (especially of the forearm) during their growth spurt despite bone mass reaching its peak during this period. Muscle mass accumulates greatly during the adolescent growth spurt as well and is a major force in determining bone mass and strength. However, if the increase in muscle mass exceeds that of bone mass creating a disconnect between growth of these two elements, the risk for fracture increases (Frost and Schonau 2000). Increased fracture risk in growing bone can also be attributed to an increase in basic multicellular unit (BMU) activation resulting in excessive cortical porosity (Parfitt 1994). Additionally, fractures sustained in growing bone and associated low peak bone mass reveal a persistent fragility causing deleterious effects with age (Clark et al. 2006; Cooper et al; 2006, Ferrari et al. 2006). For further discussion of modeling during growth see the chapter by Maggiano in this volume.

The osteocyte network is responsible for detection of microfractures and initiating repair through remodeling (Frost 2003; Hazenberg et al. 2006). However, if excessive microcracks sever bone cell communication via canaliculi, it becomes difficult for remodeling to occur (O'Brien et al. 2005). Impaired osteocyte function may even be associated with remodeling-related bone fragility (Mullender et al. 2005). Increased microcrack accumulation in areas with fewer osteocytic lacunae provides evidence for an association between the two features (Qiu et al. 2005; Vashishth et al. 2000). Voide et al. (2009) found that osteocytic lacunae may be responsible for directing microcracks but not initiating them. For a review of the role of osteocytes and other bone cells in response to loading, refer to Ehrlich and Lanyon (2002) and Noble and Reeve (2000).

Bones can begin to fatigue quickly based on strain magnitudes during cyclic loading (Schaffler and Jepsen 2000), although it is not entirely clear at what point fatigue-induced microdamage affects bone strength. Microdamage has been shown to appear in the elastic region before yield in a typical force-deflection curve (Reilly and Currey 1999, 2000), supporting earlier work suggesting microcracks may even initiate yielding in bone (Zioupos and Currey 1994). Similarly, Tang and Vashishth (2007) found that microdamage occurred under applied strains before any stiffness was lost. However, Burr and colleagues (1995, 1998) suggest that the mechanical integrity of loaded bone can be compromised before microdamage appears (most notably after 15% of stiffness is lost). Therefore, damage may occur at different stages of fatigue and depend on loading conditions (Schaffler and Jepsen 2000). This complex relationship should be further explored, with an emphasis on comparing dynamic and cyclic loading patterns in different skeletal elements.

### 8.2.4.2  Bone's Defense

Bone tissue appears to have a few defense mechanisms to avoid failure. The formation of small microcracks themselves may be an effective line of defense. It has been proposed that initiation and propagation of microcracks may provide a toughening mechanism in loaded bone to dissipate energy efficiently (Mullins et al. 2007; Vashishth et al. 2003). See Nalla (2005) for further perspectives on cracking and fracture toughness. Type and direction of loading influences microdamage morphology to best defend against fracture (Akkus et al. 2000; Reilly and Currey 1999; Wasserman et al. 2008). Consequently, the distribution and type of microfractures can aid in classification of gross fracture type in certain instances (Schultz 2003). Three-dimensional techniques that are available to visualize complex microdamage may provide evidence that distinct damage morphologies do not exist as previously thought (Voide et al. 2009).

In spite of bone's defense attempts, fragility is accentuated as a result of microfractures accumulating increasingly with age (Zioupos and Currey 1998). Aging bone becomes more fragile and brittle, losing the ability to absorb excessive energy. Therefore, the quantity of microcracks that bone can tolerate without failure decreases with age (Zioupos 2001a), as does bone toughness (Ritchie et al. 2006). The morphology of damage is age-dependent as young bone develops more diffuse damage (as opposed to linear microcracks), which allows it to better dissipate energy and resist catastrophic fracture (Diab et al. 2006; Diab and Vashishth 2007). Microfractures are thus a major contributor to age-related bone fragility, which may partially depend on changing material properties of bone with age (Frank et al. 2002).

Osteon morphology can affect the fracture resistance of cortical bone (Yeni et al. 1997), perhaps offering another mechanism of defense. A greater number of small osteons (rather than fewer large osteons) may be beneficial to help prevent gross fracture, since cement lines inhibit microcrack propagation and absorb energy (O'Brien et al. 2005). In this way, increased remodeling extends the fatigue life of bone (Gibson et al. 2006). This is consistent with recent research showing that the formation of smaller osteons is associated with areas undergoing higher strains (van Oers et al. 2008). However, cement lines can also be a source of weakness as they become less able to absorb energy in aging bone (Yeni and Norman 2000). Bone is also able to initiate and compartmentalize microdamage throughout the cortex relative to where different stresses are applied to best prevent catastrophic fracture (Diab and Vashishth 2005). However, there are limits to this defense as it has been shown that even a slight change in loading conditions can cause proliferation of microcracks beyond their usual limits (Wang and Niebur 2006). On a broader scale, a decreased fatigue life resulting from "mixed-mode" loading activities provides a greater susceptibility to fracture (George and Vashishth 2006).

## 8.3 Discussion

### 8.3.1 Bone Quantity in the Past

The role of bone quantity should not be neglected in the pursuit of information about fragility in present and past populations. Bone loss (and by extension risk of fracture) in past populations can reveal valuable information about the health and lifestyle of those people. Osteoporosis and bone loss have been addressed in many archaeological populations, successfully providing insight into trends in population specific pathogenesis and disease processes (see Mays 1999). Agarwal (2008) and Agarwal and Stout (2003) provide perspectives on bone loss and its affect on health in past populations. Brickley and Ives (2008) also offer a comprehensive review of metabolic bone disease in bioarchaeology.

DXA has been utilized successfully on archaeological bone specimens to assess age-related bone loss (Mays et al. 2006), bone growth and related stress (McEwen et al. 2005), and age- and sex-related patterns of bone health (Agarwal and Grynpas 2009). For example, in ancient Egyptians, low BMD in male workers versus high BMD in male officials may reveal nutritional effects of a lower status, and low BMD in female officials and high BMD in female workers may reveal a sedentary lifestyle for female officials (Zaki et al. 2009). An interesting risk factor for low BMD and associated fracture risk is the late onset of puberty (Kindblom et al. 2006). This has implications when studying past populations since pubertal onset is inconsistently environmentally sensitive based on nutrition and other lifestyle factors, and is influenced by differential growth rates and life expectancies seen in populations spread geographically and diachronically (Eveleth and Tanner 1990; Lewis 2007). For a useful interpretation of BMD in subadult populations, see Binkley et al. (2008).

### 8.3.2 Fracture Patterns

Bone fracture patterns can help predict the loading context that caused failure since mechanical properties of bones vary according to mode and direction of loading (e.g., bone is stronger in compression than in shear; Martin et al. 1998). Utilizing experimental, rather than solely theoretical, approaches to understanding fracture patterns is suggested. For example, significant variation in human rib response (i.e., type of fracture) but consistency in location of fracture under controlled loading conditions (Daegling et al. 2008) supports other work showing the location of rib fractures can often discern the direction of impact (Love and Symes 2004). Detailed examination of a fracture can provide crucial information regarding the loading event during life to assist in determining cause and manner of death. For example, parry fractures of the distal ulna are often classified as defense wounds and can provoke a criminal investigation. Of significant interest to forensic anthropologists, location and type of fractures in infants and children may provide evidence for injury mechanism and determine if abuse should be considered (Lewis 2007). Even the histological appearance of fracture surfaces can be useful in determining forensic context (Lynn and Fairgrieve 2009).

### 8.3.3 Conclusions

As research in skeleton biology progresses, it is crucial to examine multiple contributors to fracture risk and embrace the role that bone quality, in addition to bone quantity, plays in determining bone strength. To improve understanding of fracture risk, material and geometric properties (Siu et al. 2003) as well as histomorphometric properties of bone should all be considered. As this chapter reveals, the analysis of bone behavior traverses many disciplines and is truly multidimensional. Individuals from many backgrounds (e.g., those studying past population's biology and behavior, injury prevention in traffic accidents or a clinical setting, forensic investigation, etc.) all benefit from increased knowledge on the interaction of bone biology and fracture.

Methods for the description and analysis of skeletal trauma have been extensively summarized (see Lovell 2008). However, it is vitally important to study how and why skeletal trauma occurs as well. By examining the biological mechanisms involved in fracture risk and how fractures are initiated, researchers can make sounder interpretations of fracture cause and context in past and present populations as well as in future prevention.

# References

Agarwal SC (2008) Light and broken bones: Examining and interpreting bone loss and osteoporosis in past populations. In: Katzenberg MA, Saunders SR, editors. Biological anthropology of the human skeleton. John Wiley & Sons, Hoboken, NJ.

Agarwal SC, Dumitriu M, Tomlinson GA et al (2004) Medieval trabecular bone architecture: The influence of age, sex, and lifestyle. Am J Phys Anthropol 124:33–44.

Agarwal SC, Grynpas M (1996) Bone quantity and quality in past populations. Anat Rec 246:423–432.

Agarwal SC, Grynpas M (2009) Measuring and interpreting age-related loss of vertebral bone mineral density in a medieval population. Am J Phys Anthropol 139:244–252.

Agarwal SC, Stout SD (2003) Bone loss and osteoporosis: An anthropological perspective. Kluwer Academic/Plenum, New York.

Akkus O, Jepsen KJ, Rimnac CM (2000) Microstructural aspects of the fracture process in human cortical bone. J Mater Sci 35:6065–6074.

Allen MR, Burr DB (2008) Skeletal microdamage: Less about biomechanics and more about remodeling. Clinical Rev Bone Miner Metab 6:24–30.

Aufderheide A, Rodriguez-Martin C (1998) The Cambridge encyclopedia of human paleopathology. Cambridge University Press, Cambridge.

Augat P, Reeb H, Claes L (1996) Prediction of fracture load at different skeletal sites by geometric properties of the cortical shell. J Bone Miner Res 11:1356–1363.

Bagi CM, Hanson N, Andresen C et al. (2006) The use of micro-CT to evaluate cortical bone geom-
    etry and strength in nude rats: Correlation with mechanical testing, PQCT and DXA. Bone
    38:136–144.
Binkley TL, Berry R, Specker BL (2008) Methods for measurement of pediatric bone. Rev Endocrine
    Metab Disorders 9:95–106.
Blain H, Chavassieux P, Portero-Muzy N et al. (2008) Cortical and trabecular bone distribution in
    the femoral neck in osteoporosis and osteoarthritis. Bone 43:862–868.
Boivin G, Bala Y, Doublier A et al. (2008) The role of mineralization and organic matrix in the micro-
    hardness of bone tissue from controls and osteoporotic patients. Bone 43:532–538.
Boivin G, Meunier PJ (2003) The mineralization of bone tissue: A forgotten dimension in osteopo-
    rosis research. Osteoporosis Int 14:19–24.
Bolotin HH (2007) DXA in vivo BMD methodology: An erroneous and misleading research and
    clinical gauge of bone mineral status, bone fragility, and bone remodelling. Bone 41:138–154.
Bousson V, Le Bras A, Roqueplan F et al. (2006) Volumetric quantitative computed tomography
    of the proximal femur: Relationships linking geometric and densitometric variables to bone
    strength. Role for compact bone. Osteoporosis Int 17:855–864.
Brickley M, Ives R (2008) The bioarchaeology of metabolic bone disease. Elsevier, New York.
Burr DB (1993) Remodeling and the repair of fatigue damage. Calcified Tissue Int 53(Suppl
    1):S75–S81.
Burr DB (2002a) The contribution of the organic matrix to bone's material properties. Bone
    31:8–11.
Burr DB (2002b) Targeted and nontargeted remodeling. Bone 30:2–4.
Burr DB (2006) Biomechanics: Preclinical and clinical. Clin Rev Bone Miner Metab 4:155–166.
Burr DB (2008) Bone quality and fractures: Influence of remodeling on structural and material prop-
    erties. Bone 43:S20.
Burr DB, Forwood MR, Fyhrie DP et al (1997) Bone microdamage and skeletal fragility in osteo-
    porotic and stress fractures. J Bone Miner Res 12:6–15.
Burr DB, Turner C, Naick P et al. (1995) Does microdamage accumulation affect the mechanical
    properties of bone? Transac Orthopaedic Res Soc 20:127.
Burr DB, Turner CH, Naick P et al. (1998) Does microdamage accumulation affect the mechanical
    properties of bone? J Biomech 31:337–345.
Cho H, Stout S, Bishop T (2006) Cortical bone remodeling rates in a sample of African American
    and European American descent groups from the American Midwest: Comparisons of age and
    sex in ribs. Am J Phys Anthropol 130:214–226.
Clark EM, Ness AR, Bishop NJ et al. (2006) Association between bone mass and fractures in chil-
    dren: A prospective cohort study. J Bone Miner Res 21:1489–1495.
Cooper C, Westlake S, Harvey N et al. (2006) Developmental origins of osteoporotic fracture.
    Osteoporosis Int 17:337–347.
Cooper DML, Thomas CDL, Clement JG et al (2007) Age-dependent change in the 3d structure of
    cortical porosity at the human femoral midshaft. Bone 40:957–965.
Currey J (2003a) Role of collagen and other organics in the mechanical properties of bone.
    Osteoporosis Int 14:S29–S36.
Currey JD (2001) Bone strength: What are we trying to measure? Calcified Tissue Int 68:205–210.
Currey JD (2002) Bones: Structure and mechanics. Princeton University Press, Princeton, NJ.
Currey JD (2003b) How well are bones designed to resist fracture? J Bone Miner Res 18:591–598.
Currey JD, Brear K, Zioupos P (1996a) The effect of porosity and mineral content on the young's
    modulus of elasticity of compact bone. J Biomech 21:131–139.
Currey JD, Brear K, Zioupos P (1996b) The effects of ageing and changes in mineral content in
    degrading the toughness of human femora. J Biomech 29:257–260.
Cvijetic S, Korsic M (2004) Apparent bone mineral density estimated from DXA in healthy men and
    women. Osteoporosis Int 15:295–300.

Daegling DJ, Warren MW, Hotzman JL et al. (2008) Structural analysis of human rib fracture and implications for forensic interpretation. J Foren Sci 53:1301–1307.

Danova NA, Colopy SA, Radtke CL et al. (2003) Degradation of bone structural properties by accumulation and coalescence of microcracks. Bone 33:197–205.

De Maeseneer M, De Mey J, Debaere C et al. (2000) Rib fractures induced by coughing: An unusual cause of acute chest pain. Am J Emerg Med 18:194–197.

Diab T, Condon KW, Burr DB et al. (2006) Age-related change in the damage morphology of human cortical bone and its role in bone fragility. Bone 38:427–431.

Diab T, Vashishth D (2005) Effects of damage morphology on cortical bone fragility. Bone 37:96–102.

Diab T, Vashishth D (2007) Morphology, localization and accumulation of in vivo microdamage in human cortical bone. Bone 40:612–618.

Ebacher V, Tang C, McKay H et al. (2007) Strain redistribution and cracking behavior of human bone during bending. Bone 40:1265–1275.

Ebbesen EN, Thomsen JS, Beck-Nielsen H et al. (1999) Lumbar vertebral body compressive strength evaluated by dual-energy x-ray absorptiometry, quantitative computed tomography, and ashing. Bone 25:713–724.

Ehrlich P, Lanyon L (2002) Mechanical strain and bone cell function: A review. Osteoporosis Int 13:688–700.

Eveleth PB, Tanner J (1990) Worldwide variation in human growth. Cambridge University Press, Cambridge.

Felsenberg D, Boonen S (2005) The bone quality framework: Determinants of bone strength and their interrelationships, and implications for osteoporosis management. Clin Ther 27:1–11.

Ferrari SL, Chevalley T, Bonjour J-P et al. (2006) Childhood fractures are associated with decreased bone mass gain during puberty: An early marker of persistent bone fragility? J Bone Miner Res 21:501–507.

Foley S, Quinn S, Jones G (2009) Tracking of bone mass from childhood to adolescence and factors that predict deviation from tracking. Bone 44:752–757.

Follet H, Boivin G, Rumelhart C et al. (2004) The degree of mineralization is a determinant of bone strength: A study on human calcanei. Bone 34:783–789.

Frank JD, Ryan M, Kalscheur VL et al. (2002) Aging and accumulation of microdamage in canine bone. Bone 30:201–206.

Frost HM (2001) From Wolff's law to the Utah paradigm: Insights about bone physiology and its clinical applications. Anat Rec 262:398–419.

Frost HM (2002) Emerging views about "Osteoporosis," bone health, strength, fragility, and their determinants J Bone Mine Metab 20:319–325.

Frost HM (2003) Bone's mechanostat: A 2003 update. Anat Rec 275A:1081–1101.

Frost HM, Schonau E (2000) The "Muscle-bone" Unit in children and adolescents: A 2000 overview. JPEM 13:571–590.

Gafni RI, Baron J (2004) Overdiagnosis of osteoporosis in children due to misinterpretation of dual-energy x-ray absorptiometry (dexa). J Pediatr 144:253–257.

Galloway A, editor. (1999) Broken bones: Anthropological analysis of blunt force trauma. CC Thomas, Springfield, IL.

Genant HK, Jiang JY (2006) Imaging assessment of bone quality in osteoporosis. Clin Rev Bone Miner Metab 4:213–224.

George WT, Vashishth D (2006) Susceptibility of aging human bone to mixed-mode fracture increases bone fragility. Bone 38:105–111.

Ghasem-Zadeh A, Zebazea R, Iuliano-Burns S et al. (2009) Sexual dimorphism in bone fragility is partly due to the differing intracortical remodelling and porosity. Bone 44:S76–S77.

Gibson VA, Stover SM, Gibeling JC et al. (2006) Osteonal effects on elastic modulus and fatigue life in equine bone. J Biomech 39:217–225.

Grynpas MD (2003) The role of bone quality on bone loss and bone fragility. In: Agarwal S, Stout SD, editors. Bone loss and osteoporosis: An anthropological perspective. Kluwer Academic/ Plenum, New York.

Hart GO (2005) Fracture pattern interpretation in the skull: Differentiating blunt force from ballistics trauma using concentric fractures. J Foren Sci 50:1276-1281.

Hazenberg JG, Freeley M, Foran E et al. (2006) Microdamage: A cell transducing mechanism based on ruptured osteocyte processes. Journal of Biomechanics 39:2096-2103.

Heaney RP (1993) Is there a role for bone quality in fragility fractures? Calcified Tissue Int 53 (Suppl 1):3-6.

Heaney RP (2003) Is the paradigm shifting? Bone 33:457-465.

Hernandez CJ (2008) How can bone turnover modify bone strength independent of bone mass? Bone 42:1014-1020.

Hiller LP, Stover SM, Gibson VA et al. (2003) Osteon pullout in the equine third metacarpal bone: Effects of ex vivo fatigue. J Orthopaedic Res 21:481-488.

Hogler W, Briody J, Woodhead HJ et al. (2003) Importance of lean mass in the interpretation of total body densitometry in children and adolescents. J Pediatr 143:81-88.

Hui S, Slemenda C, Johnston C (1988) Age and bone mass as predictors of fracture in a prospective study. J Clin Invest 81:1804-1809.

Huja SS, Beck FM, Thurman DT (2006) Indentation properties of young and old osteons. Calcified Tissue Int 78:392-397.

Humphrey JH, Hutchinson DL (2001) Macroscopic characteristics of hacking trauma. J Foren Sci 46:228-233.

Jergas M, Gluer CC (1997) Assessment of fracture risk by bone density measurements. Semin Nucl Med 27:261-275.

Kanis JA, Johnell O, De Laet C et al. (2004) A meta-analysis of previous fracture and subsequent fracture risk. Bone 35:375-382.

Kemper A, McNally C, Pullins C et al. (2007) The biomechanics of human ribs: Material and structural properties from dynamic tension and bending tests. Stapp Car Crash J 51:1-39.

Kimmerle EH, Baraybar JP (2008) Skeletal trauma: Identification of injuries resulting from human rights abuse and armed conflict. CRC Press, Boca Raton, FL.

Kindblom JM, Lorentzon M, Norjavaara E et al. (2006) Pubertal timing predicts previous fractures and BMD in young adult men: The good study. J Bone Miner Res 21:790-795.

Kok WL, Stromsoe K, Hoiseth A et al. (1995) Bending strength of the femur in relation to non-invasive bone mineral assessment. J Biomech 28:857-861.

Leslie WD, Tsang JF, Caetano PA et al. (2007) Number of osteoporotic sites and fracture risk assessment: A cohort study from the manitoba bone density program. J Bone Miner Res 22:476-483.

Lewis ME (2007) The bioarchaeology of children: Perspectives from biological and forensic anthropology. Cambridge University Press, Cambridge.

Liu D, Wagner HD, Weiner S (2000) Bending and fracture of compact circumferential and osteonal lamellar bone of the baboon tibia. J Mater Sci: Mater Med 11:49-60.

Lochmmuller EM, Burklein D, Kuhn V et al. (2002) Mechanical strength of the thoracolumbar spine in the elderly: Prediction from in situ dual-energy x-ray absorptiometry, quantitative computed tomography (QCT), upper and lower limb peripheral QCT, and quantitative ultrasound. Bone 31:77-84.

Love JC, Symes SA (2004) Understanding rib fracture patterns: Incomplete and buckle fractures. J Foren Sci 49:1153-1158.

Lovell NC (2008) Analysis and interpretation of skeletal trauma. In: Katzenberg MA, Saunders SR, editors. Biological anthropology of the human skeleton, 2nd edition. John Wiley & Sons, Hoboken, NJ.

Lynn KS, Fairgrieve SI (2009) Microscopic indicators of axe and hatchet trauma in fleshed and defleshed mammalian long bones. J Foren Sci 54:793-797.

Mallory A (2001) The relationship between the material properties of femoral cortical bone and bone density. Biomedical Engineering, University of Southern California. p. 102.

Martin DE, Severns AE, Kabo JM (2004) Determination of mechanical stiffness of bone by PQCT measurements: Correlation with non-destructive mechanical four-point bending test data. J Biomech 37:1289–1293.

Martin R (2003) Fatigue damage, remodeling, and the minimization of skeletal weight. J Theo Bio 220:271–276.

Martin RB, Burr D, Sharkey N (1998) Skeletal tissue mechanics. Springer, New York.

Martin RB, Lau ST, Mathews PV et al. (1996) Collagen fiber organization is related to mechanical properties and remodeling in equine bone: A comparison of two methods. J Biomech 29:1515–1521.

Mashiba T, Hirano T, Turner CH et al. (2000) Suppressed bone turnover by bisphosphonates increases microdamage accumulation and reduces some biomechanical properties in dog rib. J Bone Miner Res 15:613–620.

Mashiba T, Turner CH, Hirano T et al. (2001) Effects of suppressed bone turnover by bisphosphonates on microdamage accumulation and biomechanical properties in clinically relevant skeletal sites in beagles. Bone 28:524–531.

Mays S, Turner-Walker G, Syversen U (2006) Osteoporosis in a population from medieval Norway. Am J Phys Anthropol 131:343–351.

Mays SA (1999) Osteoporosis in earlier human populations. J Clin Densitometry 2:71–78.

McEwen J, Mays S, Blake G (2005) The relationship of bone mineral density and other growth parameters to stress indicators in a medieval juvenile population. Int J Osteoarchaeology 15:155–163.

Miller PD, Hochberg MC, Wehren LE et al. (2005) How useful are measures of BMD and bone turnover? Curr Med Res Opin 21:545–554.

Muir P, Sample S, Barrett J et al. (2007) Effect of fatigue loading and associated matrix microdamage on bone blood flow and interstitial fluid flow. Bone 40:948–956.

Mullender MG, Tan SD, Vico L et al. (2005) Differences in osteocyte density and bone histomorphometry between men and women and between healthy and osteoporotic subjects. Calcified Tissue Int 77:291–296.

Mullins LP, Bruzzi MS, McHugh PE (2007) Measurement of the microstructural fracture toughness of cortical bone using indentation fracture. J Biomech 40:3285–3288.

Nagaraja S, Couse TL, Guldberg RE (2005) Trabecular bone microdamage and microstructural stresses under uniaxial compression. J Biomech 38:707–716.

Nalla RK, Stölken JS, Kinney JH et al. (2005) Fracture in human cortical bone: Local fracture criteria and toughening mechanisms. J Biomech 38:1517–1525.

Noble BS, Reeve J (2000) Osteocyte function, osteocyte death and bone fracture resistance. Molec Cell Endocrinol 159:7–13.

Norman TL, Wang Z (1997) Microdamage of human cortical bone: Incidence and morphology in long bones. Bone 20:375–379.

O'Brien FJ, Hardiman DA, Hazenberg JG et al (2005) The behaviour of microcracks in compact bone. European J Morphol 42:71–79.

Oganov VS (2003) Physiological factors responsible for the development of osteopenia under conditions of mechanical unloading. Hum Physiol 29:539–547.

Ortner D (2003) Identification of pathological conditions in human skeletal remains. Academic Press, New York.

Parfitt AM (1994) The two faces of growth: Benefits and risks to bone integrity. Osteoporosis Int 4:382–398.

Parfitt AM (2002) Targeted and nontargeted bone remodeling: Relationship to basic multicellular unit origination and progression. Bone 30:5–7.

Paschalis EP, Shane E, Lyritis G et al (2004) Bone fragility and collagen cross-links. J Bone Miner Res 19:2000–2004.

Pors Nielsen S (2000) The fallacy of BMD: A critical review of the diagnostic use of dual x-ray absorp-
    tiometry. Clin Rheumatol 19:174–183.

Qiu S, Sudhaker R, Fyhrie D et al. (2005) The morphological association between microcracks and
    osteocyte lacunae in human cortical bone. Bone 37:10–15.

Recker R, Barger-Lux MJ (2004) The elusive concept of bone quality. Curr Osteoporosis Rep
    2:97–100.

Reilly D, Currey JD (1999) The development of microcracking and failure in bone depends on the
    loading mode to which it is adapted. J Exp Biol 202:543–552.

Reilly GC, Currey JD (2000) The effects of damage and microcracking on the impact strength of
    bone. J Biomech 33:337–343.

Ritchie RO, Nalla RK, Kruzic JJ et al. (2006) Fracture and ageing in bone: Toughness and structural
    characterization. Strain 42:225–232.

Robling AG, Castillo AB, Turner CH (2006) Biomechanical and molecular regulation of bone remod-
    eling. Ann Rev Biomed Eng 8:455–498.

Robling AG, Stout S (2003) Histomorphology, geometry, and mechanical loading in past popula-
    tions. In: Agarwal SC, Stout S, editors. Bone loss and osteoporosis: An anthropological per-
    spective. Kluwer Academic/Plenum, New York.

Rosen CJ, Glowacki J, Bilezikian J, editors (1999) The aging skeleton. Academic Press, New York.

Ruff C (2000) Biomechanical analyses of archaeological human skeletons. In: Katzenberg M, Saunders
    S, editors. Biological anthropology of the human skeleton. Wiley-Liss, New York.

Ruff C (2006) Gracilization of the modern human skeleton: The latent strength in our slender bones
    teaches lessons about human lives, current and past. Amer Scient 94:508–514.

Ruff C (2008) Biomechanical analyses of archaeological human skeletons. In: Katzenberg MA,
    Saunders SR, editors. Biological anthropology of the human skeleton, 2nd edition. John Wiley
    & Sons, Hoboken, NJ.

Schaffler MB, Jepsen KJ (2000) Fatigue and repair in bone. Int J Fatigue 22:839–846.

Schultz M (2003) Light microscope analysis in skeletal paleopathology. In: Ortner D, editor.
    Identification of pathological conditions in human skeletal remains. Academic Press, San
    Diego.

Seeman E, Delmas P (2006) Mechanisms of disease: Bone quality—the material and structural basis
    of bone strength and fragility. N Engl J Med 354:2250–2261.

Sievänen H, Józsa L, Pap I et al (2007) Fragile external phenotype of modern human proximal femur
    in comparison with medieval bone. J Bone Miner Res 22:537–543.

Siu WS, Qin L, Leung KS (2003) PQCT bone strength index may serve as a better predictor than
    bone mineral density for long bone breaking strength. J Bone Miner Metab 21:316–322.

Skedros JG, Mendenhall SD, Kiser CJ et al. (2009) Interpreting cortical bone adaptation and
    load history by quantifying osteon morphotypes in circularly polarized light images. Bone
    44:392–403.

Sobelman OS, Gibeling JC, Stover SM et al. (2004) Do microcracks decrease or increase fatigue resis-
    tance in cortical bone? J Biomech 37:1295–1303.

Sornay-Rendu E, Munoz F, Garnero P et al. (2005) Identification of osteopenic women at high risk
    of fracture: The Ofely study. J Bone Miner Res 20:1813–1819.

Stone KL, Seeley DG, Lui L-Y et al. (2003) BMD at multiple sites and risk of fracture of multiple types:
    Long-term results from the study of osteoporotic fractures. J Bone Miner Res 18:1947–1954.

Tang SY, Vashishth D (2007) A non-invasive in vitro technique for the three-dimensional quantifica-
    tion of microdamage in trabecular bone. Bone 40:1259–1264.

Taylor D (1997) Bone maintenance and remodeling: A control system based on fatigue damage.
    Journal of Orthopaedic Res 15:601–606.

Thomas CDL, Feik SA, Clement JG (2005) Regional variation of intracortical porosity in the mid-
    shaft of the human femur: Age and sex differences. J Anat 206:115–125.

Turner CH (2002) Biomechanics of bone: Determinants of skeletal fragility and bone quality.
    Osteoporosis Int 13:97–104.

Turner CH, Burr DB (1993) Basic biomechanical measurements of bone: A tutorial. Bone (New York) 14:595.

Ubelaker D (1992) Hyoid fracture and strangulation. J Foren Sci 37:1216–1222.

van Oers RFM, Ruimerman R, van Rietbergen B et al (2008) Relating osteon diameter to strain. Bone 43:476–482.

Vashishth D, Tanner KE, Bonfield W (2003) Experimental validation of a microcracking-based toughening mechanism for cortical bone. Journal of Biomechanics 36:121–124.

Vashishth D, Verborgt O, Divine G et al (2000) Decline in osteocyte lacunar density in human cortical bone is associated with accumulation of microcracks with age. Bone 26:375–380.

Verborgt O, Gibson G, Schaffler M (2000) Loss of osteocyte integrity in association with microdamage and bone remodeling after fatigue in vivo. J Bone Miner Res 15:60–67.

Viguet-Carrin S, Garnero P, Delmas PD (2006) The role of collagen in bone strength. Osteoporosis Int 17:319–336.

Vincentelli R, Grigorov M (1985) The effect of Haversian remodeling on the tensile properties of human cortical bone. J Biomech 18:201–207.

Voide R, Schneider P, Stauber M et al. (2009) Time-lapsed assessment of microcrack initiation and propogation in murine cortical bone at submicrometer resolution. Bone 45:164–173.

Wagner HD, Weiner S (1992) On the relationship between the microstructure of bone and its mechanical stiffness. J Biomech 25:1311–1320.

Wang X, Niebur GL (2006) Microdamage propagation in trabecular bone due to changes in loading mode. J Biomech 39:781–790.

Wang X, Shen X, Li X et al. (2002) Age-related changes in the collagen network and toughness of bone. Bone 31:1–7.

Warden SJ, Gutschlag FR, Wajswelner H et al. (2002) Aetiology of rib stress fractures in rowers. Sports Med 32:819–836.

Wasserman N, Brydges B, Searles S et al. (2008) *In vivo* linear microcracks of human femoral cortical bone remain parallel to osteons during aging. Bone 43:856–861.

Wasserman N, Yerramshetty J, Akkus O (2005) Microcracks colocalize within highly mineralized regions of cortical bone tissue. Eur J Morphol 42:43–51.

Wren TAL, Yerby SA, Beaupré GS et al. (2000) Interpretation of calcaneus dual-energy x-ray absorptiometry measurements in the assessment of osteopenia and fracture risk. J Bone Miner Res 15:1573–1578.

Wynnyckyj C, Omelon S, Savage K et al. (2009) A new tool to assess the mechanical properties of bone due to collagen degradation. Bone 44:840–848.

Yeni YN, Brown CU, Wang Z et al. (1997) The influence of bone morphology on fracture toughness of the human femur and tibia. Bone 21:453–459.

Yeni YN, Fyhrie DP (2002) Fatigue damage-fracture mechanics interaction in cortical bone. Bone 30:509–514.

Yeni YN, Norman TL (2000) Calculation of porosity and osteonal cement line effects on the effective fracture toughness of cortical bone in longitudinal crack growth. J Biomed Mater Res 51:504–509.

Zaki ME, Hussien FH, Banna E et al. (2009) Osteoporosis among ancient Egyptians. International Journal of Osteoarchaeology 19:78–89.

Zebaze R, Ghasem-Zadeh A, Bohte A et al. (2009) Age-related bone loss: The effect of neglecting intracortical porosity. Bone 44:S117–S118.

Zioupos P (2001a) Accumulation of in-vivo fatigue microdamage and its relation to biomechanical properties in ageing human cortical bone. J Microsc 201:270–278.

Zioupos P (2001b) Ageing human bone: Factors affecting its biomechanical properties and the role of collagen. J Biomater Appl 15:187–229.

Zioupos P, Currey J (1998) Changes in the stiffness, strength, and toughness of human cortical bone with age. Bone 20:57–66.

Zioupos P, Currey J, Casinos A (2000) Exploring the effects of hypermineralisation in bone tissue by using an extreme biological example. Connect Tissue Res 41:229–248.

Zioupos P, Currey JD (1994) The extent of microcracking and the morphology of microcracks in damaged bone. J Mater Sci 29:978–986.

Ziv V, Wagner HD, Weiner S (1996) Microstructure-microhardness relations in parallel-fibered and lamellar bone. Bone 18:417–428.

**Figure 2.1** Color photomicrograph of the specific structural features of the physis of the proximal aspect of the tibia of a four-week-old rabbit embryo. The epiphyseal bone is above, the physeal cartilage (growth plate) in purple, and the metaphyseal bone is below (blue). The physeal cartilage is composed of resting, proliferative (columnar), and hypertrophic zones (toluidine blue, ×60). (From Rivas R and Shapiro F, 2002, J Bone Joint Surg AM 84:85–100. Reproduced by permission, JBJS, Inc.)

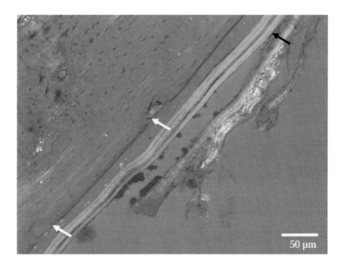

**Figure 3.1** Juvenile periosteal tissue preserved by natural mummification (black solid arrow). The external bone surface was currently forming primary lamella at the time of death as evidenced by several partially enclosed primary vessel canals (white solid arrows). Thin-ground, undecalcified transection of the naturally mummified, archaeological, femoral mid-diaphysis, Dakhleh Oasis, Egypt. Micrograph taken with red quartz cross-polarized filter (hilfsobject). Scale bar indicates 50 μm.

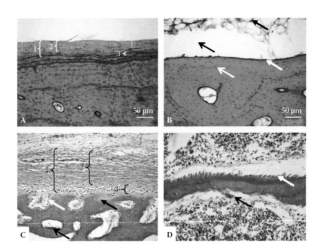

**Figure 3.2** (A) Mature periosteal membrane of the humerus (bracket 1), demonstrating clear distinction between the outer fibrous layer (bracket 2) and the smaller, darker osteogenic cellular layer (bracket 3). Note the most recent primary bone deposition has occurred in two thin phases (white arrow). (B) Mature endosteal membrane of the humerus (white arrow). Top margin shows marrow lipid tissue (black arrow) and marrow space (black lined arrow). Note a cement line between Haversian tissue (below white lined arrow) and the most recent endosteal primary formation phase (above white lined arrow). Parts A and B demonstrate a quiescent bone surface, as evidenced by the lack of unmineralized matrix. (C) Fetal (6-month gestation) metatarsal bone collar demonstrating cellular and tissue level changes associated with osteogenesis at the periosteum, including columnar osteoblasts (white arrow). Periosteal deposition of woven bone transpires via significant secretion of unmineralized matrix (osteoid) (black arrow). Note the targeted intracortical resorption at internal void surfaces facing the endosteum (bottom of image) as demonstrated by the position of osteoclasts (black lined arrow). (D) Endosteal formation in the same bone as part C via columnar osteoblasts on one side of a trabecular spicule, while the other side appears newly resorbed with one remaining osteoclast (black lined arrow) and Howships lacunae left behind as evidence. Also note the relatively clear space above and below formative or resorptive surfaces in this image, created by a "ceiling" of cells separating these surfaces from surrounding tissue matrix (See Section 3.4.4 for more information). All images are generated from paraffin embedded, decalcified, thin transections, stained with hematoxylin and eosin. Scale bar indicates 50 μm for parts A and B, taken at 100× magnification; part C was taken at 200× magnification; (D) at 400×. (Images courtesy of Lisa Lee.)

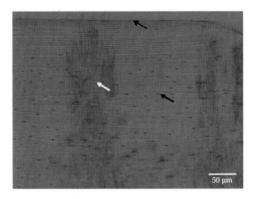

**Figure 3.3** Adult, primary endosteal lamellae with interspersed lacunae, once housing osteocytes entombed during active apposition. Endocortical surface is marked by the black lined arrow. Structure of the lacunar-canalicular system is emphasized by a diagenic effect which has slightly enlarged and darkened canaliculi radiating from some lacunae (white solid arrow). Outside these regions canaliculi are less visible. Thin-ground, undecalcified transection of archaeological, ulnar mid-diaphysis, Dakhleh Oasis, Egypt. Micrograph taken with red quartz cross-polarized filter (hilfsobject). Scale bar indicates 50 μm.

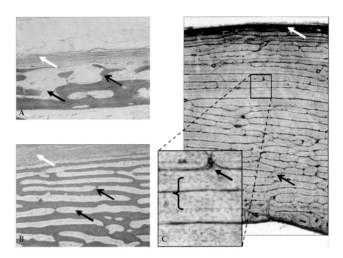

**Figure 3.4** (A) Periosteal woven bone deposition in the laminar fashion with plexiform vessel inclusion in the perinatal horse foal femur. White arrows in all images denote the periosteum; black arrows, the vascular void or canal; and black lined arrows mark bridging woven struts providing support for the newest of the forming external laminae. (B) In this young individual (same as part a) vessels are still within many layers of large unfilled voids prior to boney compaction. (C) Laminar bone exhibiting compacted plexiform structure in the 18-month-old Sinclair Minipig tibia. The white solid arrow denotes the most recent tables of bone forming under the periosteum but above the most recent vascular inclusions, whereas the black lined arrow marks tissue entrapping much older vascular networks, now deep within the cortex. Note that entombed vessels are dominantly circumferential but with short connections between generations of vascular sheath (black solid arrow in expansion). The black bracket indicates one full layer as described by Currey (2002), bordered by feint light lines of woven bone. Images A (100× magnification) and B (40× magnification) are microphotographs of paraffin embedded, decalcified thin-section treated with hematoxylin and eosin stain; image C is a 40× magnification microphotograph and digital zoom insert taken from an undecalcified thin-ground section containing visible, though feint, fluorochrome labeling. (Images courtesy of Steven Weisbrode.)

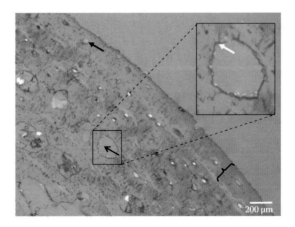

**Figure 3.7** Human infant pericortex demonstrating occasional inclusion of longitudinal vessels, as primary osteons (black arrow) as in fibrolamellar or primary osteonal bone. In this case there exists a single pseudo laminar layer within the forming (mostly woven) pericortex (black bracket). The black solid lined arrow denotes a resorption bay destined for expansion during endocortical resorption or infilling via BMU-based remodeling. The white arrow marks one of many Howships lacuna roughening the bay's perimeter, evidence that resorption was active antemortem. Thin-ground, undecalcified transection of archaeological, femoral mid-diaphysis, Dakhleh Oasis, Egypt. Micrograph taken with red quartz cross-polarized filter (hilfsobject). Scale bar indicates 200 μm.

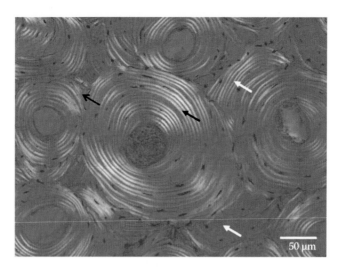

**Figure 3.8** Adult secondary osteons, or Haversian systems, with concentric lamellae and a central canal, which in life would house vessels and nerves. Note the similarity of lamellar structure between BMU tissue and PEM tissue (Figures 3.3 and 3.15) in both lamellar thickness and lacunar inclusion (here, a black solid arrow). The black lined arrow marks the central osteon's cement line (reversal line), the zone of maximum resorption during the resorptive phase of BMU activity. Subsequent formation progressed from this point toward the canal at the center. White solid arrows denote osteonal fragments from previous BMUs that passed through the region. No primary tissue is present in this field of view or in the larger region suggesting that the tissue can be classified as Haversian tissue and that the individual is likely mature or even of advancing age. Thin-ground, undecalcified transection of archaeological, humeral mid-diaphysis, Dakhleh Oasis, Egypt. Micrograph taken with red quartz cross-polarized filter (hilfsobject). Scale bar indicates 50 μm.

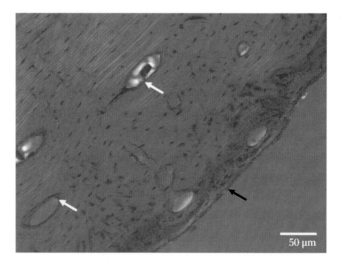

**Figure 3.9** Primary osteons, or primary vascular canals, from a juvenile (white solid arrows), have no lamellae or cement line of their own. Instead, they are entrapped by successive lamellar apposition at the periosteum. The black solid arrow denotes the bone surface most recently applied by the periosteum, continuing to inhume several other longitudinal primary vessels. Thin-ground, undecalcified transection of archaeological, humeral mid-diaphysis, Dakhleh Oasis, Egypt. Mid-diaphyseal micrograph taken with red quartz cross-polarized filter (hilfsobject). Scale bar indicates 50 μm.

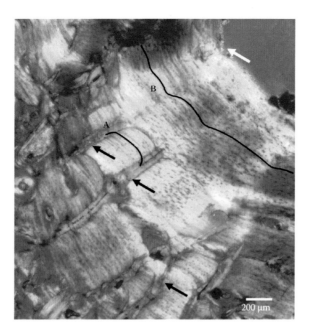

**Figure 3.10** Dense primary endosteal lamellae, comprising nearly a fourth of the total cross-sectional area, have failed to entrap a single longitudinal vessel from the endosteal surface (white arrow). Instead, lamellae formed under endosteal vasculature, pushing it away, filling the spaces between transverse Volkmann's canals (black solid arrows mark examples). These vessels extended to maintain connectivity to the intercortical Haversian network (out of view to the lower left). (A) As bone is laid between transverse vessels its lamellae "pillow" slightly, perhaps due to slower rates of calcification adjacent to the pulsating vessels. (B) This effect can be easily seen in lamellae merely adjacent to transverse vessels, even when these vessels are not within the plane of sectioning. Thin-ground, undecalcified transection of archaeological, humeral mid-diaphysis, Xcambó, Mexico. Micrograph taken with red quartz cross-polarized filter (Hilfsobject). Scale bar indicates 200 μm. (Image courtesy of I. Maggiano.)

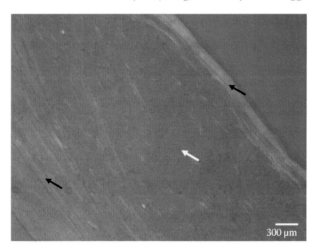

**Figure 3.11** The traditionally described histological landscape of young compact bone. Primary lamellar bone (black solid arrows) formed by the periosteum (lower left) and endosteum (upper right). White solid arrow marks remodeled Haversian tissue formed by BMU activity. This remodeling transpired in the older intercortical primary tissue and has now turned over a large area, replacing primary osteons with secondary, and increasing the general porosity of the region. Thin-ground, undecalcified transection of archaeological, humeral mid-diaphysis, Dakhleh Oasis, Egypt. Micrograph taken with red quartz cross-polarized filter (hilfsobject). Scale bar indicates 300 μm.

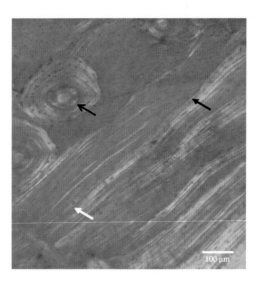

**Figure 3.12** Endosteal primary lamella now occupying an intracortical position adjacent to several Haversian systems. These particular primary lamellae are laid in several formative phases. The white arrow marks consecutive, uninterrupted formation of the major phase, while the black arrow marks a cement line cutting across previous lamellae of the same major phase, splitting this local region into two separate minor formation phases due to a single, slight resorption focus. This presents stratigraphic evidence of a single phase of formation continuing in one region while at another, reversal occurs followed by formation, directing drift in a specific net direction. Subsequent phases to the bottom right of the image also bear evidence of targeted modeling resorption in the form of roughened cement lines that cross-cut previous lamellae. Also note the presence of an arrest line in a secondary osteon (black lined arrow) for comparison with cement lines demonstrating resorptive evidence. Thin-ground, undecalcified transection of archaeological, humeral mid-diaphysis, Dakhleh Oasis, Egypt. Micrograph taken with red quartz cross-polarized filter (hilfsobject). Scale bar indicates 100 μm.

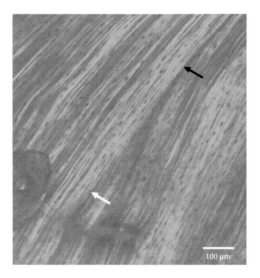

**Figure 3.13** Endosteal lamellae demonstrating complex phase activity. The white solid arrow marks continued uninterrupted formation through the entire field of view. Conversely, the black solid arrow denotes a modeling arrest line. Though subtle in appearance, the effect is significant, marking a pause in phase formation in the upper right region while formation continues for hundreds of micrometers (past the lower field of view boundary). Thin-ground, undecalcified transection of archaeological, humeral mid-diaphysis, Dakhleh Oasis, Egypt. Micrograph taken with red quartz cross-polarized filter (hilfsobject). Scale bar indicates 100 μm.

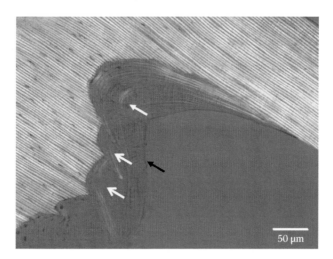

**Figure 3.16** A series of endocortical modeling formation phases present as adjustments to a much larger phase (past the lower field of view boundary). The white solid arrow marks the most recent phase, whereas the white lined arrows mark overlain fragments, indicating prior resorption took place before the final phase was formed. These phases are small enough to permit confusion with hemiosteons, although the latter are typically only reported in trabecular bone. Black solid arrow denotes medullary surface. Thin-ground, undecalcified transection of archaeological, humeral mid-diaphysis, Dakhleh Oasis, Egypt. Micrograph taken with red quartz cross-polarized filter (hilfsobject). Scale bar indicates 50 μm.

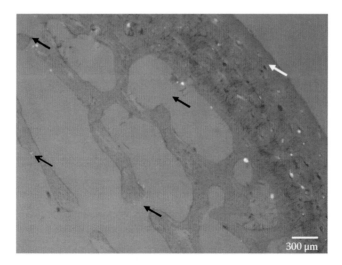

**Figure 3.20** Infant cortical woven expansion at the periosteum (white solid arrow) is countered by dramatic endocortical resorption (marked by Howship's lacunae roughening bone surfaces) both at the endosteal margin (black lined arrow) and in expanding, large, resorption bays (black solid arrows). Black solid arrows also denote loss of several "trabecularized" cortical connections. Thin-ground, undecalcified transection of archaeological, femoral mid-diaphysis, Dakhleh Oasis, Egypt. Micrograph taken with red quartz cross-polarized filter (hilfsobject). Scale bar indicates 300 μm.

A                                      B

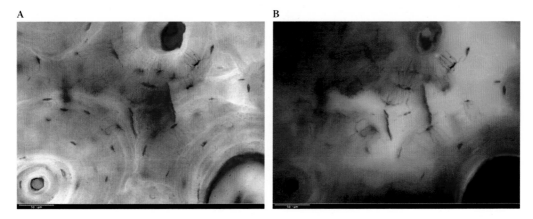

**Figure 8.4** Linear microcracks observed in human rib sections stained with basic fuchsin at 40× objective magnification under (A) bright field transmitted light compared to (B) epiflourescent reflected light. (Images by A. Agnew.)

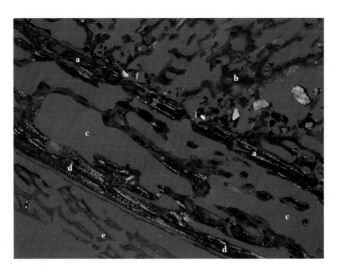

**Figure 10.8** Sundown Site, Arizona (USA), B-12/2, child: Infans I, pre-Columbian Sinagua. Parietal bone fragment. *Cribra cranii externa* due to osteomyelitis: a = *Lamina externa*, b = appositional bone on external lamina, c = *Diploë*, d = *Lamina interna*, e = appositional bone on internal lamina. Thin-ground section (70 μm) viewed in polarized transmission light using hilfsobject red 1st order (quartz) as compensator. Magnification 25×.

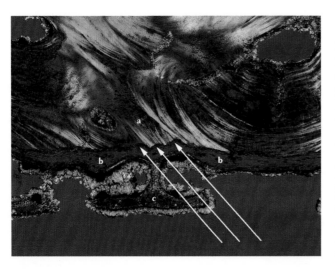

**Figure 10.10** İkiztepe (Turkey), IT-Türk-145, child: 2- to 3-year-old, 3rd millennium BC. Left parietal bone. *Cribra cranii interna* due to meningeal reactions (meningitis); detail out of Figure 10.9: a = lamellar bone, b = newly built woven bone, c = newly built woven bone plates, arrows = remodeled Howship's lacunae. Thin-ground section (70 μm) viewed in polarized transmission light using hilfsobject red 1st order (quartz) as compensator. Magnification 100×.

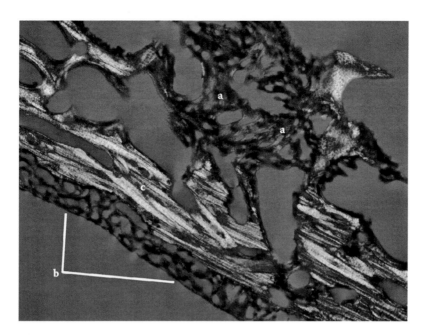

**Figure 10.11** Collection of the Department of Pathology, University of Göttingen (Germany), GP-1985901, senile individual, recent case, 20th century. Left frontal bone. *Cribra cranii interna* due to a pronounced nonspecific inflammatory process (osteomyelitis): a = newly built primitive woven bone trabeculae within the *Diploë*, b = new woven bone formation due to meningeal reaction induced by the osteomyelitic process, c = *Lamina interna*. Thin-ground section (70 μm) viewed in polarized transmission light using hilfsobject red 1st order (quartz) as compensator. Magnification 25×.

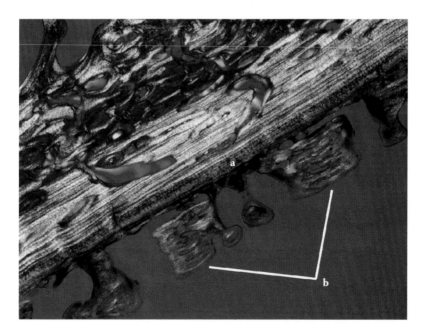

**Figure 10.12** Collection of the Department of Pathology, University of Göttingen (Germany), GP-1985616, adult individual, recent case, 20th century. Frontal bone. *Cribra cranii interna* due to a pronounced specific inflammatory process (tuberculosis): a = *Lamina interna*, b = newly built primitive woven bone on the internal lamina. Thin-ground section (70 μm) viewed in polarized transmission light using hilfsobject red 1st order (quartz) as compensator. Magnification 25×.

**Figure 10.13** Collection of the Department of Legal Medicine, University of Vienna (Austria), RMW-Sch5, adult individual, recent case, 20th century. Region of the external surface of the right frontal bone. Tertiary stage of venereal syphilis (small, developing gumma). Thin-ground section (70 µm) viewed in polarized transmission light using hilfsobject red 1st order (quartz) as compensator. Magnification 25×.

**Figure 10.14** Collection of the Department of Legal Medicine, University of Vienna (Austria), RMW-Sch4, adult individual, recent case, 20th century. Region of the external surface of the right parietal bone. Tertiary stage of venereal syphilis. Thin-ground section (70 µm) viewed in polarized transmission light using hilfsobject red 1st order (quartz) as compensator. Magnification 25×.

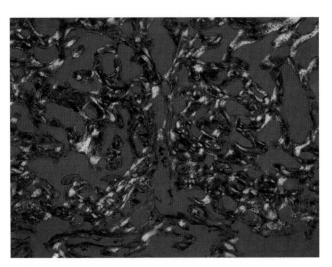

**Figure 10.15** Collection of the Department of Pathology, University of Göttingen (Germany), GP-1985688, adult individual, recent case, 20th century. *Diploë* of the frontal bone. Pronounced specific inflammatory process (venereal syphilis). Thin-ground section (70 µm) viewed in polarized transmission light using hilfsobject red 1st order (quartz) as compensator. Magnification 25×.

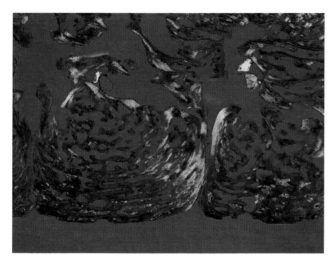

**Figure 10.16** Collection of the Department of Pathology, University of Göttingen (Germany), GP-1985688, adult individual, recent case, 20th century. Frontal bone. *Cribra cranii interna* due to a pronounced specific inflammatory process (venereal syphilis). Thin-ground section (70 μm) viewed in polarized transmission light using hilfsobject red 1st order (quartz) as compensator. Magnification 25×.

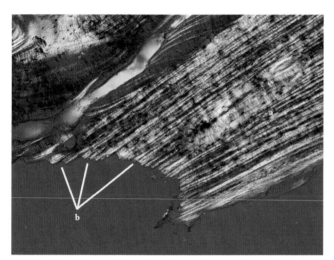

**Figure 10.18** Collection of the Department of Pathology, University of Göttingen (Germany), GP-1985616, adult individual, recent case, 20th century. Frontal bone. Internal lamina afflicted by osteolytic reaction due to a specific inflammatory process (tuberculosis): a = *Lamina interna*, b = Howship's lacunae. Thin-ground section (70 μm) viewed in polarized transmission light using hilfsobject red 1st order (quartz) as compensator. Magnification 25×.

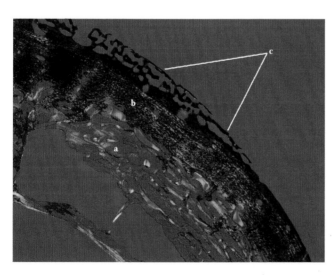

**Figure 10.19** Franzhausen-I (Austria), FH-338, child: 3- to 5-year-old child, 3rd–2nd millennium BC. Right humerus. Evidence of a subperiosteal hematoma due to scurvy: a = compact, osteonic bone substance of the shaft, b = compact, tangential lamellar bone substance of the shaft (resembling the later external circumferential lamellae), c = subperiosteal woven bone formation. Thin-ground section (70 μm) viewed in polarized transmission light using hilfsobject red 1st order (quartz) as compensator. Magnification 100×.

**Figure 10.20** Sindelsdorf (Germany), TIB-SK, adult individual, 5th–7th century AD. Tibia: Thickened bone shaft due to nonspecific hematogenous osteomyelitis. Thin-ground section (70 μm) stained with methylenblue viewed in plain transmission light. Magnification 1×.

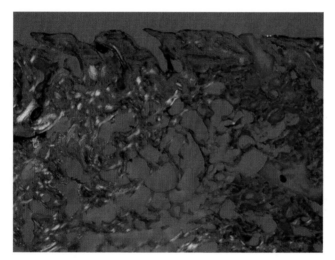

**Figure 10.26** San Diego Museum of Man, Alaska Inuit (USA), SDM-1915-2-787B, adult individual, Modern Times. Right tibia. Gummatous venereal syphilis. External surface of bone shaft: no original polsters, no grenzstreifen because of the relatively fast bone growth. Thin-ground section (50 μm) viewed in polarized transmission light using hilfsobject red 1st order (quartz) as compensator. Magnification 25×.

**Figure 10.28** Bajkara (Kazakhstan), Kurgan 1, pit 1, skeleton 1, mature male, Sarmatian Period (approx. 160–40 BC). Right tibia. Nongummatous venereal syphilis: well-developed polster formation on external surface of bone shaft. Thin-ground section (70 μm) viewed in polarized transmission light using hilfsobject red 1st order (quartz) as compensator. Magnification 25×.

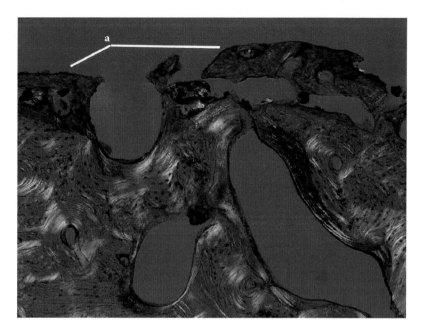

**Figure 10.32** Arzhan (Russia: Siberia), Kurgan 2, Burial 20, skeleton 1, young adult male, Scythian Period (700 BC). Right femur. Tuberculosis: a = newly built bone formation (osteoblastic) on the periosteal surface of the bone shaft. Thin-ground section (70 μm) viewed in polarized transmission light using hilfsobject red 1st order (quartz) as compensator. Magnification 100×.

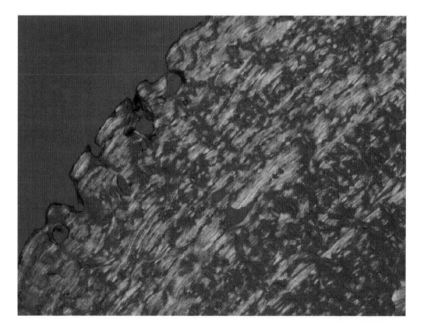

**Figure 10.33** Arzhan (Russia: Siberia), Kurgan 2, Burial 20, skeleton 1, young adult male, Scythian Period (700 BC). Right femur. Tuberculosis: newly built bone formation on the periosteal surface of the bone shaft, which shows in parts the morphology of agate bone. The external agate bone structures seem, at first sight, to be similar to small polsters or polster-like formations. Thin-ground section (70 μm) viewed in polarized transmission light using hilfsobject red 1st order (quartz) as compensator. Magnification 25×.

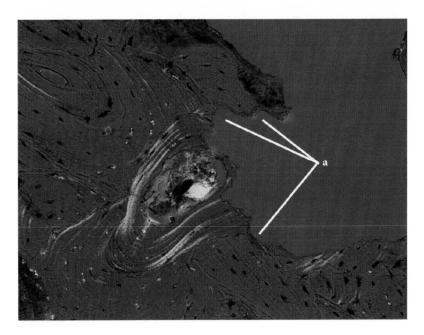

**Figure 10.35** Sayala (Egyptian Nubia), Burial K-68/2, 35- to 45-year-old female, Coptic Period (400–600 AD). Left clavicle. Metastasizing cancer: a = Howship's lacunae at the rim of a large resorption hole within the originally compact bone substance. Thin-ground section (50 μm) viewed in polarized transmission light using hilfsobject red 1st order (quartz) as compensator. Magnification 200×.

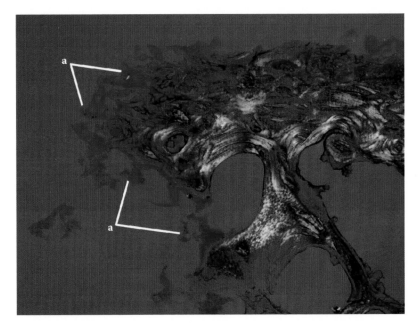

**Figure 10.36** Zwölfaxing (Austria), Burial 34, old adult female, Avarian Period (680–830 AD). Left frontal bone. Pseudopathology, a = glue (custodial activity), no pathologically changed bone matrix. Thin-ground section (50 μm) viewed in polarized transmission light using hilfsobject red 1st order (quartz) as compensator. Magnification 25×.

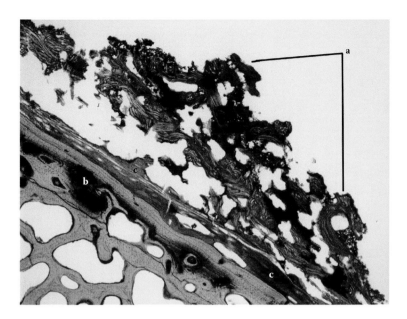

**Figure 10.37** Nimrud, NW-Palace (Iraq), Ind.-NIM-III, young adult female (queen?), Late Assyrian Period (700–612 BC). Fragment of Parietal bone. Pseudopathology, a = remains of textile resembling the product of an inflammatory process; b = external skull surface with *Lamina externa*; c = mummified remnants of scalp and periosteum. The green color is due to postmortem (diagenetic) staining by copper ions. Thin-ground section (70 μm) viewed in plain transmission light. Magnification 25×.

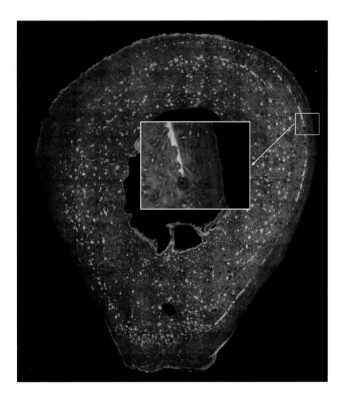

**Figure 13.2** Midshaft femoral cross-section from a 29-year-old male imaged by incident UV light shows adventitious labeling with tetracycline. Considerable remnants of earlier periosteal surfaces still persist from the teenage period (see inset). This underpins concerns about limitations imposed by sampling restricted regions near the periosteal surface.

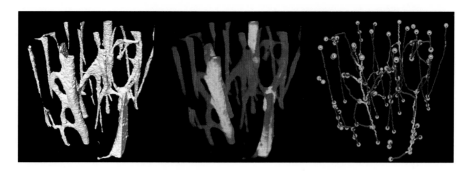

**Figure 15.3** Three-dimensional rendering of cortical canals within a 1 mm³ block of mid-femoral cortical bone (left); color-mapped 3D canal diameter with lighter colors denoting larger canals (middle); skeletonized canal structure with canal endpoints and branches highlighted (right). Nominal scan resolution of 3 microns.

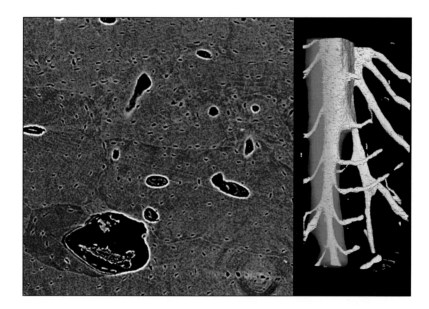

**Figure 15.5** SR micro-CT cross-sectional image (left) of cortical bone from the human femoral midshaft acquired with 1.4 micron nominal resolution and averaged through approximately 10 microns (seven slices). Phase contrast (white "halos") enhances the edges of the canals, lacunae, some cementing lines, and even enables visualization of soft tissue within the resorption space (bottom left). Three-dimensional rendering (right) of the region within the bottom half of the image depicts the newly forming osteon in transparency over the opaque canals. Data collected at the 2BM beamline of the Advanced Photon Source synchrotron. (The images on the left is of a block 0.72 mm square.)

# Histotaphonomy

LYNNE S. BELL

## Contents

## 9.1 Introduction

Histotaphonomy is taphonomy at the microstructural scale. In terms of human tissue, it may be applied to any body tissue, but for the purposes of discussion here, the skeletal and dental tissues are of interest. Histotaphonomy, or as it is also known, microstructural diagenesis, may be usefully thought of as a study of preservation and change. It includes notional preservation, not just of the original tissues, but of perimortem and postmortem changes included within the human tissues, which may themselves be preserved. Such changes are described as diagenetic, a term that has been borrowed from geology, and essentially includes all processes involved in the creation of sedimentary deposits prior to metamorphism. The co-option of this term introduced an awkward premise and has been problematic, since it suggests that all diagenetic change must occur postdepositionally. For both archaeology and forensic anthropology, this distinction has led interpretation, perhaps too far, in the direction of postskeletonization processes, without sufficient attention paid to death history and the role of whole body decomposition.

This chapter will briefly review nomenclature associated with histotaphonomy. It will outline the history of histotaphonomic enquiry and where we are now, and to some degree, where we are going. The chapter is not intended to be an exhaustive review and as such the presence or absence of citation implies no meaning beyond that of relevance to outlining this discussion.

## 9.2   Nomenclature

Taphonomy may be defined as the laws of burial. Weigelt published his classic treatise in 1927, describing how organisms die, decay, and become encased in sediment, and was the first to outline what is now known as taphonomy, calling it "biostratinomy." Weigelt's approach was heavily descriptive, and he would roam the countryside, meticulously recording mammals and reptiles in situ from recent death to skeletonization. For anyone interested in this field, his observations are both compelling and fascinating, and one cannot help reflect that he must have cut a somewhat macabre figure as he made his methodical sweeps through the landscape. It is to Efremov (1940), however, that the term *taphonomy* is first associated. Efremov, extended Weigelt's work, but outlined a more systematic approach to understanding and reconstructing past fossil assemblages, looking at the transitionary stages between death, entombment and lithification. Efremov wanted to establish predictive laws that could explain and help correct biases in the fossil record. Together, Weigelt's and Efremov's works provide us with the theoretical backstop upon which contemporary taphonomic research is based, namely, actualistic experiments, where animal proxies are observed in differing physiological and environmental scenarios in either a cross-sectional or longitudinal timeframe; or, to describe preexisting assemblages, be they forensic, archaeological, or palaeontological in nature.

## 9.3   Historical Background

The earliest description of postmortem alteration to bone and teeth was made by Wedl in 1864, and his initial observation was an accident. Wedl subsequently undertook a number of experiments where he submersed and buried defleshed bone and teeth, attempting to reproduce the changes he had observed initially. He was successful and described what would now be characterized as microstructural change associated with marine exposure and also bacterial change (Bell et al., 1996, 2008). From this date onward the literature is sparsely populated with studies that are driven, like Wedl, by curiosity (Roux, 1887; Schaffer, 1894, 1890, 1889) and even Tomes (1892) observed bacterial alteration to a single tooth: a tooth he had picked up in a cemetery.

The next extensive piece of research was reported by Sognnaes (1949, 1955, 1956, 1959). He collected historical human teeth from Palestine, Egypt, Iceland, Norway, and Guatemala and intended to screen them for postmortem change. The time periods were not contemporaneous, and clearly culturally distinct. He observed tunnels that had diameters of 2–10, 15–25, and 50–100 microns, which "corkscrewed" through the tissue; the commonest tunnels branched and had large ampulla-like widenings. All tissue, except enamel, was observed to have been affected. Sognnaes felt that no time relationship existed in terms of the severity of postmortem attack but remained puzzled as to the identity of the invading microorganism. He postulated that the observed postmortem tunneling may have occurred soon after death in the aerobic shallow layer of soil, prior to gaseous putrefaction.

A little quoted study by Syssoeva (1958) is mentioned here briefly to situate the idea that macroscopic change will be reflected microscopically. Syssoeva undertook a systematic study of 196 teeth from individuals aged between 6 months to 70 years, which had been buried for no longer than 10 years, in order to establish the earliest moment postmortem alteration might be observed. He made macroscopic, microscopic, and x-rayed derived observations and found that there were no obvious changes to the microstructure of teeth. Hence, it seemed that postmortem alteration was likely to be a postdepositional event that occurred some considerable time after death. Subsequent work by Clement (1958, 1963) and Falin (1961) looked at an array of material spread across a large cross-section of time and found evidence of Sognnaes's commonest type of postmortem tunneling. Falin felt that Syssoeva's work needed reappraisal, particularly the microscopic observations, since Falin considered there was no time relationship to the presence and distribution of postmortem alterations, and presumably felt something had been missed.

A set of three studies of human teeth from differing soil environments was made on a total of 372-plus human teeth aged to a maximum of 1000 years since death (Werelds, 1961, 1962, 1967). Werelds found similar tunneling, now associated with bacterial-like changes, in dentine and cementum. He also concluded that time was an irrelevant variable. Like Wedl, he conducted an immersion and a soil burial experiment of freshly extracted teeth. The immersion produced tunneling within a few months, and the soil burial exhibited postmortem alteration within the third year. This is an important study since it brought forward the timeframe for postmortem alteration to microstructure, and revalidated Wedl's much earlier observations. Poole and Tratman (1978) added an important observation to identify demineralization of tooth enamel over demineralization caused by antemortem carious activity in the mouth. The distribution of the demineralization is what is key, in that it will have a distribution unlike caries, and can therefore be ascribed as a postmortem event.

Marchiafara et al. (1974) reported that a Mucor fungus had created penetrating tunnels in human bone. The bone itself was harvested from cadavers, buried defleshed in flower pots in garden earth, and incubated wet at 20°C. Three fungal isolates were recovered and reseeded onto autoclaved bone. Of these, only Mucor grew and bone changes were observed within 15 to 20 days. Marchiafara et al. called the invasion "osteoclastic activity," which is a misnomer and a pity, since the work is fascinating, partly because two changes were observed: one penetrating tunnel that exhibited no decalcification right up to the free-edge, and another that did exhibit clear decalcification. This lack of demineralization, as we shall see, is one of the interesting and puzzling features of the marine change associated with marine exposure described by Bell et al. (1991, 1996), Bell and Elkerton (2008), and others (Arnaud et al., 1978; Ascenzi and Silverstrini, 1984).

## 9.4 Recent Work

This section is not intended to be a full review but instead flags some of the highlights of progress built upon earlier studies. What is important to remember, and the purpose of giving some detail on earlier work, is that most of what we have deduced about postmortem alteration to bone and teeth was documented almost completely by the mid 1970s and had caught the eye of the early microscopists in the late 1800s. This was all curiosity-driven research. What followed was a realization that this type of change was important for two main reasons: one, that it represented a serious form of contamination; and second, that such changes must be governable by biological and environmental processes, and could, by extension, provide important taphonomic information.

A great deal of work was focused during the 1980s and 1990s on diagenetic alteration. As mentioned earlier, this term has become synonymous with postmortem alteration and lodged the idea that all processes are postdepositional. Much of the literature asserts microstructural change occurs postskeletonization and, as a corollary, must be caused by soil-based microorganisms. This has been a fundamental premise and is repeated in the palaeontological, archaeological, and forensic anthropological (PAFA) literature. In terms of mapping the full extent of contamination a great deal of work has been usefully conducted on human and mammal material from many different environmental contexts. The idea that time is not the main driver to such changes has been repeatedly confirmed, and methods that extend our understanding of postmortem alteration at the microstructural level have been developed and extended from transmitted and cross-polar microscopy, to scanning electron microscopy (SEM)/backscattered electron (BSE), transmission electron microscopy (TEM), and confocal imaging. These techniques provided information that furthered our understanding of the skeletal and dental distribution of mineral-organic changes and to some extent, the three-dimensional relationship between normal and diagenetically altered tissues. What has been lost in this discourse, as an outcome of considering the main drivers as postdepositional, is the taphonomic usefulness of such changes. Little attention has been paid to the decomposition of the body at the point of death and immediately thereafter. There has been a serious disconnect between the archaeological and palaeontological literature concerning what is characterized as diagenetic change, to the forensic literature concerning whole body decomposition.

The need to understand perimortem history and what influences the body after death is very important in forensics. Perimortem interference and time-of-death estimates weigh heavily on investigations. In the longer term, the survival of skeletal elements and their postmortem dispersal are also an important area of taphonomic enquiry within forensics, and are playing a greater role in defining taphonomy for human remains. Decomposition is still poorly understood, but it has at least been at the forefront of forensic interest. Of importance here, is the role of the body's own indigenous (in vivo) gut bacteria in driving decomposition. It is known that the upper intestinal tract microflora will transmigrate into the postmortem vasculature within a 15-hour period after death, reaching all the major organs of the body (Kellerman et al., 1976). This means that intense bacterial activity is permeating the body via the vasculature and will quickly reach the internal osteonal microstructure of bone, that is, via the Haversian blood supply, and the pulpal aspect of teeth. This spread is used as a time-of-death indicator, where the superficial veins color up as a result of bacterial activity within a 3- to 5-day period and is known as "marbling." Anything that causes damage to the body perimortem, particularly the postmortem vasculature, can alter the manner and rate in which a body will decompose. Much attention has been paid to the entomological role in human decomposition because it can provide information on time since death (Anderson, 2005). The impact on the microstructure of skeletal tissues prior to skeletonization has not been investigated, largely because, in my opinion, this aspect has been informed by the discourse in archaeology and palaeontology. As a consequence, a kind of reinforcing circularity exists, where the skeleton is viewed as indestructible until it is entirely defleshed. Even though, we understand full well that the body's whole-body decomposition is promoted by its internal microflora and only latterly by external microflora.

## 9.4.1   Distribution of Bacterial Change

In the PAFA literature the idea that bacterial change (the main change seen in terrestrial archaeological skeletal material) was initially driven by in vivo overgrowth of gut bacteria into the postmortem vasculature, and thus on into the bone and teeth, was first suggested by Bell (1996) and Bell et al. (1991, 1996). This idea was latterly picked up by Trueman and Martill (2002) and given some real consideration by Jans et al. (2004). Jans et al. examined a large number of archaeological bony specimens (all skeletonized) from many different archaeological contexts and speculated that the distribution of bacterial changes was potentially driven by putrefactive bacteria accessing the bone via the Haversian system. In contradistinction, the external aspect of bone would be attacked by soil-originating bacteria, which Jans et al. the most likely distribution of such an attack. This view is problematic, since many bacteria in the gut and soil are common and ubiquitous, and furthermore one could argue, as other authors have, that the porous network acts as an easy gateway for soil bacteria and fungi to gain access to the internal aspect of bone once it is fully skeletonized (Hedges and Millard, 1995). The observed distribution described by so many authors in terrestrial contexts could then be created by soil microorganisms and thus create the very same postmortem lesions and changes. The question must become, which is it? The only way to answer this is to look not only at archaeological material, but to undertake actualistic and exclusionary experiments on whole bodies, with an upfront understanding of death history and body integrity.

## 9.4.2   Classification of Postmortem Microstructure

Microscopic observations of postmortem microstructural change to bone and teeth have been largely descriptive. Hackett (1981) usefully attempted a classification of postmortem alteration to microstructure. His classification provided four descriptive categories: Wedl, linear longitudinal, budded, and lamellate. The first category referred to the tunnel changes described originally by Wedl (1864) and later by Marchiafara et al. (1974). Hackett's Wedl tunnels fell well within their original descriptions, but the environmental history of Hackett's specimens was not well documented. The other three categories— linear longitudinal, budded and lamellate—are harder to apply and really are describing the same type of change, that is, bacterial change. The value of Hackett's work is that he attempted to bring together postmortem change into an interpretative framework, one that could be used to standardize two-dimensional observations. Other observations made by Hackett became somehow stuck in the literature. One in particular is that the origin of the invading bacteria, which Hackett considered the causal agent, gained access via the empty postskeletonized Haversian canal system from the surrounding soil, that is, external to the body. This idea was implicitly stated in previous literature and Hackett's work underscored this notion. Hackett's classification, however, is still current and has provided some useful baseline descriptive nomenclature. Beyond Hackett's classification, Hedges et al. (1995) created what has become known as the Oxford histological index (OHI). This classification is simple in that the amount of microstructurally recognizable bone in a transverse section surface or block face is scored, that is, it is given a numerical value. The simplicity of this index has had real success, and has been used in a number of studies to semiquantitate diagenetic alteration. Sometimes both classifications systems—Hackett's and the OHI— have been utilized together (Jans et al., 2004). The great gain of using an agreed form of classification is that we all know what we are talking about, and these two methods help deconstruct image-derived data.

### 9.4.3   Other Worlds

Outside of the dialogue that is ongoing in the PAFA literature concerning the microstructural alteration of skeletal tissues are other relevant but separate studies concerning emergent whale-fall ecosystems and coral and oyster fouling. These studies are methodologically similar to those in the PAFA literature, in that much of the data is observationally derived and actualistic, but use a different descriptive terminology. Whale-fall studies vary in their observational detail of such emergent specialized marine ecosystems created as a result of a long-lived nutritional locus suddenly appearing on the sea floor (whale carcasses can take decades to fully decompose), to the decomposition of the whale carcass itself, and of the movement and disintegration of its skeletal parts. A number of microfauna have been associated with actively tunneling whale bone, whereas sulfide-reducing bacteria and algal mats are thought to play a larger part in whole body decomposition (Goffredi et al., 2004). Recent work by Anderson and Bell (2010) documented the role of crabs and shrimp in the mechanical stripping of pig carcasses deliberately submerged in a deepwater marine context, with particular emphasis on element movement and survival, and the importance of dissolved oxygen to promote this type of marine activity.

There are a number of other marine organisms that create tunnels in calcareous substrates and these include snails (Symth, 1988), sea sponges (Young and Nelson, 1985), sea urchins (McClanahan and Kurtis, 1991) and octopi (Nixon and Macconachie, 1988). In terms of microborers, or endoliths (Golubic et al., 1975), this activity may be observed in a range of calcareous substrates in the marine environment and key environmental cofactors such as light, depth, and temperature are considered important. A large number of studies have been undertaken to characterize what is known as either "bioerosion" or "fouling" to oyster beds and coral reefs. This type of attack can occur as a perimortem event, leading to the eventual death of the substrate organism. Microtunneling was experimentally documented in a study by Wisshak et al. (2005), where a number of bivalves were exposed over a 2-year period in a deepwater fjord. A wide range of tunneling was documented and effort was put into identifying what microorganisms were creating these tunnels. From the point of view of the PAFA literature, it is apparent from the diversity of tunnel types and the different microorganisms that can create them that our current descriptive PAFA classifiers need expanding.

## 9.5   Can Postmortem Microstructural Change Be Used for Taphonomic Inquiry?

This is not a mischievous question. There is no doubt that postmortem change occurs, and we have many studies spread over a 100-year period detailing a good deal of them. That such change occurs is important to understanding contamination in order to perfect analytic protocols, and is clearly important and relevant. But do these changes really tell us anything that is useful taphonomically?

To answer this question I will give an example from my own work on the human remains recovered from the Mary Rose shipwreck (Bell and Elkerton, 2008). The Mary

Rose was the Vice Flagship of Henry VIII and she sank suddenly with virtually all hands lost on July 19, 1545. She was about to engage the French fleet in the Solent but sank before reaching the fleet, sinking in calm waters on a sunny day in 12–14 m of water.

From a taphonomic perspective, the Mary Rose represented a unique historical marine mass fatality where most died of drowning or severe trauma, were immediately deposited into a marine environment, decomposed within the ship itself, and the skeletal remains were subsequently exposed differentially to an enclosed and latterly a more open marine environment (Marsden, 2003). The depositional history of the wreck was not revealed until excavation and lifting. It was determined that after sinking, the ship came to rest on her starboard side, which resulted in a shifting of the internal ballast. The hull rapidly infilled with current-borne estuarine grey silts, which settled as a fine-grained sediment within the ship. This distinct layer was determined to have been deposited rapidly over a period of months and constituted what is referred to as the first Tudor layer (Marsden, 2003). During the slower formation of the second Tudor layer, formed over decades, seaweed lenses were included within a light gray, shelly clay mix, indicating a stable and partially exposed sea floor. During the formation of this second layer, the upper aspect of the hull collapsed and the interior of the ship became exposed to a much more open marine environment (Marsden, 2003). The ship itself was not considered encased by sediment until the third layer was deposited during the late 16th and 17th centuries, and consisted of a hard gray clay and broken shelly material (Marsden, 2003). A fourth layer, more mobile, being constantly reworked and redeposited, comprised the modern seafloor. Water temperature during excavation had a winter–summer variation of 12–13°C and 18–20°C, respectively (Rule, 1983). The human remains were found almost entirely in a disarticulated and commingled state with good representation of all elements of the skeleton (Stirland, 2000). Of the 415 men recorded as present, only 179 were accounted for by minimum number analysis (Stirland, 2000). A group of 17 mandibles were examined from the interior of the ship from both the first and second Tudor layers, and examined using SEM/BSE microscopy (which gave information on the microstructural arrangement and relative density of the tissue). What was evident was that a range of peripheral tunneling had affected mandibles recovered from the second Tudor layer, whereas those recovered from the first Tudor layer were unaffected. Most of the tunnels observed (84%) had diameters between 5 and 7 microns (Figure 9.1), with a smaller group having larger diameters. The tunnels themselves exhibited no remineralization at their tunnel boundaries and instead had a consistent free-edge. Confocal microscopy revealed that these tunnels bifurcate, something not evident from SEM/BSE imaging (Figure 9.2). It is important that this type of change had a different appearance and distribution to that associated with bacterial-driven terrestrial microstructural change (Figure 9.3), where characteristic remineralized "cuffing" at tunnel boundaries of small 1 micron postmortem lesions and large lamellate foci may be seen in bone and in dentine. These liquefaction foci have been observed as a form of dentinal caries in the living mouth (Jones and Boyde, 1987); only these in vivo lesions have a differing microanatomical distribution to those observed as a postmortem event.

From a strictly taphonomic standpoint, the Mary Rose skeletal material provides us with evidence of marine exposure on the one hand and differential preservation of tissue on the other, where rapid silting in the first Tudor layer seemingly prevented this tunneling from occurring. For me, this difference in site-formation processes is important, because what it demonstrates is even though we have human material with near-identical

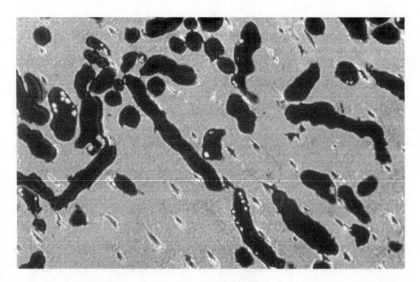

**Figure 9.1** A SEM/BSE image of dentine with invading tunnels penetrating. Note that no demineralization is evident at the border of these tunnels and tracks both along and at right angles to the dentine tubule direction.

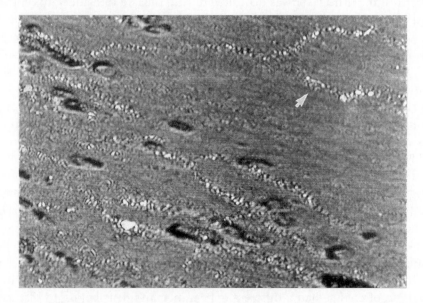

**Figure 9.2** Subsurface endolithic marine microboring seen as an internal reflection artifact. Note that the tunnels bifurcate (see arrow). Field width is 150 microns.

death history, the depositional sequence, or rather period of exposure on the sea floor, gives us information on differing taphonomic trajectories. In other words, such taphonomic information can be gained from microstructural change. There is then more to understand than straightforward evidence of marine exposure and a better understanding of what that means, particularly in terms of the period of exposure and, importantly, as demonstrated by Wisshak et al. (2005), what microorganisms are responsible and how they function in that environment. Plus, this type of postmortem change appears to be a genuine postskeletonization event. Something this author is uncomfortable with

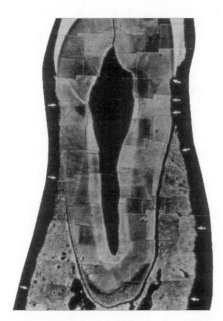

**Figure 9.3** Two SEM/BSE montages of terrestrial diagenetic change (right) and marine tunneling (left). Terrestrial change driven by bacterial ingress is via the pulp cavity into the open dentine tubules and branching network. In contrast, marine change is peripheral, affecting the external aspect of the tooth and tracking down the neck and tracking around the external aspect of the mandible. This is a typical example of the marine change and is representative of the postmortem changes observed within the Mary Rose sample. Left: Mary Rose specimen recovered from within the ship itself. Right: soil-buried archaeological medieval cemetery context.

assuming when dealing or understanding bacterially related terrestrial change to bone and teeth, since decomposition is known to be driven by intact gut microflora, or conversely, inhibited by interference with whole body integrity, that is, where whole body vasculature is damaged perimortem. Based on my experience with this unusually well-documented archaeological example, however, I contend that histotaphonomic enquiry is both valid and possible.

## 9.6 Conclusion

Although the Mary Rose is an unusually well-documented archaeological site, more work needs to be undertaken in a controlled and experimental form if we are to ascribe causal events as taphonomic statements. In forensic anthropology there is an increase in knowledge creation, particularly in understanding rates of decomposition and body disarticulation. Much more actualistic study of material from differing environments needs to be done alongside more experimental work, including attention to perimortem events and the early stages of decomposition, and not just postskeletonization outcomes. Overall, although interest in this field extends from the late 1800s to date, one has the feeling that histotaphonomy is still a young field, and one that is, as a result, an exciting field where much is still to be discovered.

# References

Anderson GS (2005) Forensic entomology. Minerva Medicolegale 125:45–60.

Anderson GS, Bell LS (2010) Deep coastal marine taphonomy: interim results from an ongoing investigation of decomposition in the Saanich Inlet, British Columbia. Proc Am Acad Foren Sci 16:381–382.

Arnaud G, Arnaud S, Ascenzi A, Bonucci E, Graziani G (1978) On the problem of preservation of human bone in sea water. J Human Evo 7:409–420.

Ascenzi A, Silverstrini G (1984) Bone-boring marine micro-organisms: an experimental investigation. J Human Evo 13:531–536.

Bell LS (1996) Post mortem microstructural change to the skeleton. Unpublished PhD thesis, University College London.

Bell LS, Boyde A, Jones SJ (1991) Diagenetic alteration to teeth in situ illustrated by backscattered electron imaging. Scanning 13:173–183.

Bell LS, Elkerton A (2008) Human remains recovered from a sixteenth century mass fatality: unique marine taphonomy in human skeletal material from the medieval warship the Mary Rose. Int J Osteoarch 18:523–535.

Bell LS, Skinner MF, Jones SJ (1996) The speed of post mortem change to the human skeleton and its taphonomic significance. Foren Sci Int 82:129–140.

Clement AJ (1958) The antiquity of caries. Brit Dent J 104:115–123.

Clement AJ (1963) Variations in the microstructure and biochemistry of human teeth. In: Brothwell DR (ed) Dental anthropology. Pergamon Press, London.

Efremov JA (1940) Taphonomy: a new branch of paleontology. Pan-Am Geol 74:81–93.

Falin LI (1961) Histological and histochemical studies of human teeth of the Bronze Age and Stone Ages. Arch Oral Biol 5:5–13.

Goffredi SK, Paull CK, Fulton-Bennett K, Hurtado LA, Vrijenhoek RC (2004) Unusual benthic fauna associated with whale fall in Monterey Canyon, California. Deep-sea Res I 51:1295–1306.

Golubic S, Perbius RD and Lukas KL (1975) Boring micro-organisms and microborings in carbonate substrates. In: Frey RW (Ed.) The study of trace fossils. Springer-Verlag, Berlin.

Hackett CJ (1981) Microscopical focal destruction (tunnels) in excavated human bones. Med Sci Law 21:243–265.

Hedges REM, Millard A (1995) Bones and ground water: towards the modeling of diagenetic processes. J Arch Sci 22:155–164.

Hedges REM, Millard A, Pike AWG (1995) Measurements and relationships of alteration of bone from three archaeological sites. J Arch Sci 22:201–209.

Jans MME, Neilsen-Marsh CM, Smith CI, Collins MJ, Kars H (2004) Characterization of microbial attack on archaeological bone. J Arch Sci 31:87–95.

Jones SJ, Boyde A (1987) Scanning microscopic observations on dental caries. Scan Micros 1:1991–2002.

Kellerman MS, Waterman NG, Scharfenberger LF (1976) Demonstration in-vitro of post mortem bacterial migration. Am J Clin Path 66:911–915.

Marchiafara V, Bonucci L, Ascenzi A (1974) Fungal osteoclasia: a model of dead bone resorption. Calc Tiss Res 14:195–210.

Marsden P (2003) Sealed by time: the loss and recovery of the Mary Rose. Mary Rose Trust, London.

McClanahan TR, Kurtis JD (1991) Population regulation of the rock-boring sea urchin Echinometra mathaei (de Blanville). J Exp Mar Biol Ecol 147:121–146.

Nixon M, Maconnachie E (1988) Drilling by Octopus Vulgaris (Mollusca: Cephalopoda) in the Mediterranean. J Zool Lond 216:687–716.

Poole DFG, Tratman EK (1978) Post-mortem changes on human teeth from late upper Palaeolithic/Mesolithic occupants of an English limestone cave. Arch Oral Biol 23:1115–1120.

Roux W (1887) Uber eine Knochenlebende Gruppe von Faderpilzen (Mycelites ossifragus). Z wiss Zool 45:227–254.

Rule MH (1983) The Mary Rose: the excavation and raising of Henry VIII's flagship. Conway Maratime Press, London.

Schaffer J (1889) Uber den feineren Bau Fossiler knocken. S B Akad Wiss Wien Math-nat III 98:319–382.

Schaffer J (1890) Uber Roux'sche Kanale in menschlichen Zahnen. S B Akad Wiss Wien Math-nat III 99:146–152.

Schaffer J (1894) Bermerkungen zur Geschichte der Bohrkanale in Knochen und Zahnen. Anat. Anz. 10:459–464.

Smyth MJ (1988) Penetrantia clionoides, sp. Nov. (Bryozoa), a boring bryozoan in gastropod shells from Guam. Biol Bull 174:276–286.

Sognnaes RF (1949) Studies on dental paleopathology. II. Differential diagnosis of post-mortem histopathology of teeth. J Dent Res 28:660.

Sognnaes RF (1955) Post-mortem microscopic defects in the teeth of ancient man. AMA Arch Path 59:559–570.

Sognnaes RF (1956) Histologic evidence of developmental lesions in teeth originating from Paleolithic, prehistoric and ancient man. Am J Path 32:547–578.

Sognnaes RF (1959) Microradiographic observations on demineralization gradients in the pathogensis of hard-tissue destruction. Arch Oral Biol 1:106–121.

Stirland AJ (2000) Raising the dead. John Wiley and Sons, New York.

Syssovena PR (1958) Post mortem changes to human teeth with time. Sudebnd-Medisthinskaya Ekspertiza I Kriminalistika na sluzhbe Sletsshviya 2:213–218 (Russian).

Tomes J (1892) Casual communication. Trans Odont Soc Brit 24:89–92.

Trueman CN, Martill DM (2002) The long-term survival of bone: the role of bioerosion. Archeometry 44:371–382.

Werelds RJ (1961) Observations macroscopiques et microscopiques sur certaines alterations post-mortem des dents. Bulletin du Groupement Interantional pour la Recherche Scientifique en Stomatologie 4:7–60.

Werelds RJ (1962) Nouvelles observations sur les degradations post-mortem de la dentine et du cement des dents inhumes. Bulletin du Groupement Interantional pour la Recherche Scientifique en Stomatologie 5:554–591.

Werelds RJ (1967) Du moment ou apparaiseent dan les dents humains les alterations post-mortem en forme d'evidements canaliculaires. Presence de lesions dentaires identiques in-vivo chez des poisons. Bulletin du Groupement Interantional pour la Recherche Scientifique en Stomatologie 10:419–447.

Wedl C (1864) Uber einen im Zahnbein und Knochen keimenden Pilz. Akademie der Wissenschaften in Wien. Sitzungsberichte Naturwissenschaftliche Klasse ABI. Mineralogie, Biologi Erdkunde, 50:171–193.

Weigelt J (1927) Recent vertebrate carcasses and their paleobiological implications. Verlag Von Max Weg, Leipzig. Trans. Edition J Schaefer (1989) University of Chicago, Chicago.

Wisshak M, Gettidis M, Freiwald A, Lundalv T (2005) Bioerosion along a bathymetric gradient in a cold-water temperate setting (Kosterfjord, SW Sweden): an experimental study. Facies, 51:93–117.

Young HR, Nelson CS (1985) Biodegradation of temperate-water skeletal carbonates by boring sponges on the Scott Shelf, British Columbia, Canada. Marine Geol 65:33–45.

# Light Microscopic Analysis of Macerated Pathologically Changed Bones

# 10

MICHAEL SCHULTZ

## Contents

## 10.1 Introduction

The history of paleohistology goes back to the 19th century (Garland 1993; Schultz in press; Stout 1978). The light microscopic investigation of bone samples taken from archaeological skeletal remains is routine in only a few paleopathological laboratories, although in the past, light microscopic techniques were frequently used to analyze the structure of subfossil and fossil bones (e.g., Ascenzi 1969; Hackett 1976; Kramar et al. 1983; Michaelis 1930; Moodie 1923, 1928; Pales 1939; Schaffer 1889; Weber 1927; Williams 1927). The reason for this exclusion is probably not based on lack of interest but rather on the fact that many users believe that (1) the preparation of thin-ground sections is very time consuming and technically highly demanding and that (2) the interpretation of morphological structures at the microlevel is difficult and requires experience. The first point is not correct. Nowadays, techniques are available (e.g., Frost 1958; Maat et al. 2006) that are less time consuming (e.g., Schultz 1988a, 2001; Schultz and Drommer 1983), although the quality of the thin-ground sections that results is not always equivalent to those produced with more time-consuming techniques. The second point is correct. Indeed, one does need a certain amount of experience to diagnose ground sections prepared from subfossil or fossil dry bone. Contributing to this is the presumption that morphological features (e.g., subperiosteal woven bone formation) selected to determine criteria (e.g., organized subperiosteal hematoma) that can help us to establish a disease diagnosis (e.g., scurvy) are frequently relatively manifold. Because this assumption is widespread, especially among paleopathologists just beginning to work in the field of paleohistology, it is frequently thought to be extremely difficult to define these criteria correctly thus hindering researchers from establishing reliable diagnoses. This reluctance to employ microscopic analysis in paleopathology has already been discussed (e.g., Ascenzi 1986; Ascenzi and Silvestrini, 1984; Bianco and Ascenzi 1993; Schultz 1986, 1997a, 2001). However, researchers should be encouraged to employ methods based upon light microscopy for several important reasons. There has been a growth in experience with diagnosing pathological conditions at the microlevel using thin-ground sections of macerated bone. This has led to a better understanding of histopathology, including the different growth behaviors of the newly built bony structure in the network of the primary bone, the differentiation of characteristic morphological features (e.g., dystrophic bone trabeculae vs. trabeculae originating physiologically), and an improved accuracy of allocation of these structures to special disease groups or diseases. Even though an immediate, reliable diagnosis is possible in only a few cases (e.g., anemic changes in the skull vault or the orbital roof), the inclusion of histological-based information can enhance our basic understanding of disease processes in the past.

During a paleopathological investigation, the situation sometimes arises that no reliable diagnoses can be established using only macroscopic, radiologic, or endoscopic techniques. In this case, it becomes necessary to investigate morphological features by microscopy if a more reliable diagnosis is desired. Unfortunately, taking samples for such a procedure is usually relatively destructive. However, as a rule, the advancement of our scientific knowledge can justify the destruction of a small part of the bone substance (the end justifies the means). Furthermore, the gross morphology of the sample taken can be virtually restored by a true-to-life cast or a plaster complement. Frequently, the findings of the microscopic analysis are of enormous value for the interpretation of pathological features and their significance for the etiology of a disease. Nevertheless, the size of a sample taken from a lesion should be carefully considered so that it allows the macroscopic character of the lesion to be conserved. In addition to vestiges of diseases, microscopic analysis can provide other kinds of information relating to taphonomy, age at death, and bone remodeling rates that can assist in diagnosis (cf. Großkopf 1989; Hackett 1981; Harsányi 1993; Herrmann 1977; Jans et al. 2004; Kerley and Ubelaker 1978; Moodie 1928; Nováček et al., 2008; Rose 2005; Schultz 1997b, 1999, in press; Smith et al. 2005; Stout and Lueck 1995; Stout and Paine 1992, 1994; Stout et al. 1996; Witzel et al. 2008). Macroscopic structures that look like the product of an inflammatory periosteal process, for example, can be unmasked as the product of a postmortem, that is, diagenetic, process (pseudopathology).

Because of the unavoidable bone damage due to removing samples from archaeological specimens, some researchers favor an investigation using micro-computed tomography (micro-CT; see Cooper et al. in this volume). As a rule, micro-CT is thought to be a non-invasive technique (e.g., Rühli et al. 2007). However, this assumption is not exactly correct. The piece of the sample examined will not be damaged at the virtual cutting plane; however, for most micro-CT equipment, analysis requires that the sample be deposited in the chamber of the micro-CT machine. For this procedure, the sample has to be cut from the bone because the chambers of modern micro-CT machines are too small to hold a bone longer than a few centimeters. Thus, the examination using the micro-CT technique is also an invasive procedure: bone has to be cut. In addition, micro-CT can alter the ultrastructure of bone, such as collagen structure and aDNA.

Today, paleopathologists are faced with new goals for their research that are beyond simple diagnosis. The study of the causes (etiology) and the origin (evolution) of ancient diseases as well as the spread and the frequencies of diseases in ancient peoples and places (epidemiology) have become important research objectives. As a result, paleopathology has become more interdisciplinary. For example, the cultural and social environment of past populations as well as their former geographic and climatic biotopes can be made accessible, within certain limits, by the knowledge of ancient stress markers and diseases from which these people suffered (Schultz 1982). It is well known that the environment influences the origin and the spread of many diseases. Thus, diseases and stress markers can be used to broadly reconstruct living conditions and external environments in the past. For any of these research goals, reliable diagnoses are indispensable. In many cases, reliable diagnoses can only be established using microscopic techniques. Thus, this chapter will demonstrate the use of light microscopic analyses in the field of paleopathology, illustrate and discuss the strengths of this procedure, and encourage researchers to use this technical tool in combination with the traditional techniques to establish reliable diagnoses.

## 10.2   Materials and Methods

### 10.2.1   Materials Examined in Paleohistology

As a rule, the reliability of the result of a microscopic analysis (diagnosis) of macerated, that is, dry bone, mummified soft tissues, and remains from bog bodies, depends primarily on the state of preservation. Occasionally, in archaeological specimens, the preservation of the bony tissue is so poor that it is not possible to render a diagnosis.

It is often extremely useful to compare the microstructure of archaeological specimens with the microstructure of recent tissue samples. Thin-ground section microscopy applied to recent dry bone materials from forensic cases, autopsies, and even to osteological museum collections offer examples of reliable diagnoses because the bony tissue is much better preserved than in archaeological specimens, and the features characteristic of various pathological processes are usually clearly observable (e.g., Schultz 1988b, 2003).

In general, most samples investigated in paleohistopathology are dry bone samples taken from subfossil human skeletal remains excavated at archaeological sites. On occasion, if protective circumstances occurred, remnants of mummified soft tissue can be detected in the paranasal sinuses and the middle ear region. This also holds true for animal skeletal material (e.g., Harsányi 1993). In archaeological bones, the state of preservation is highly variable, which can lead to variations in the informative value of analyses at the microlevel. Particularly in archaeological skeletal remains, pseudopathological features can frequently occur and must be recognized. Because fossilized bones are often rare and unique, microscopic analysis is rarely carried out (e.g., Schultz 1999, 2006; Teschler-Nicola 2006).

Light microscopic investigations of mummified human soft tissue remains, including bone, were undertaken at the beginning of the 20th century (Ruffer, 1910a, 1910b, 1911a, 1911b; Ruffer and Smith, 1910) and continued throughout the decade. The pathologist Andrew T. Sandison from Glasgow was one of the leading authorities of light microscopic research on mummified tissues. His innovative paleopathological work on ancient mummified tissues at the microscopic level (Sandison 1955a, 1955b, 1957, 1959, 1967a, 1967b, 1970, 1980) influenced numerous other researchers (e.g., Brothwell and co-workers 1969; Fornaciari 1999; Reyman 1977; Reyman et al. 1976; Tapp 1979, 1998; Zimmerman and Kelley 1982; Zimmerman and Tedford 1976) and is still useful today. As a rule, almost all soft tissues, such as tissues of the locomotor system (e.g., bone, muscles, tendons) and visceral organs (e.g., heart, lungs, stomach and intestine, liver, kidneys) can be examined after rehydration. The microscopic analysis of organs of the nervous system (e.g., brain) is, however, problematic.

Tissues of bog bodies have rarely been analyzed at the microlevel, although bone, skin, and dura mater of the brain as well as remnants of intestinal organs can be successfully studied (e.g., Mißbach-Güntner et al. 2010; Schultz et al. 2010).

## 10.2.2   Short Overview of the Methods and Techniques in Paleohistology

The most common technique applied to macerated, that is, dry bone, is light (optical) microscopy. This technique is not expensive and can be carried out in a relatively short time. Other techniques that are sometimes very useful with regard to special aims of research, for example, mineralization, include microradiography and scanning electron microscopy (cf. Schultz 2001) as well as atomic force microscopy, confocal laser scanning microscopy, and near-field scanning optical microscopy (cf. Maggiano et al. 2006). Techniques such as transmission electron microscopy and micro-CT are also applicable to histopathological analysis. However, these techniques are more elaborate than light microscopy, relatively expensive in their application, and often do not contribute as much to the subject as light microscopy using polarized light (e.g., Kuhn et al. 2007; Rühli et al; 2007, Schultz 2001).

As mentioned earlier, light microscopy is an invasive technique and the bone is damaged to obtain a sample for examination. Ideally, the bone must be cut by taking a sample in the region that represents the most characteristic morphological changes and includes (1) a healthy, nonaffected area, (2) an area with modestly developed changes, and (3) an area with severely pronounced changes.

Numerous suggestions have been made as to how to prepare macerated bone tissue for microscopy (e.g., Bell et al. 1996; Caropreso et al. 2000; Frost 1958; Maat et al. 2001, 2006; Schultz 2001; Schultz and Brandt 1987, cf. Schultz 1988a; Schultz and Drommer 1983), and the reader is referred to these publications for more detailed discussions of sample preparation. Principally, there are two ways to prepare recent macerated bone tissue for light microscopy. Samples can be (1) decalcified, cut with a microtome, stained, and viewed using transmitted light as they have been for more than a hundred years; or (2) examined as thin-ground sections using transmitted or reflected light. Harold M. Frost, an American orthopedic specialist, was a pioneer in the field of the investigation of macerated recent bone tissue. He developed a simple technique for the investigation of undecalcified recent bone that is still used today (Frost 1958).

Archaeological bone samples, which are naturally macerated, can be treated in a very similar way. However, because of the taphonomic processes to which they have been subjected, the bony structure might have changed radically at the microlevel (diagenesis). Therefore, such samples have to be handled with special care. As Cho (Chapter 14 of this volume) is already reporting on these techniques, only a few additional remarks are necessary. For the cleaning process of archaeological bone samples, brief exposure to ultrasonic cleaning is recommended; however, because the use of ultrasonic sound can affect the bone structure and introduce damage such as microfractures, its use may be contraindicated for especially friable bone. The staining of archaeological thin-ground sections is frequently problematic for histochemistry because the structures may not stain in their typical color. Furthermore, as a rule, it is of no significant use to stain thin-ground sections or decalcified sections prepared from archaeological specimens for light microscopy because frequently diagenetic changes will not allow a true stain (cf. Schultz 1988a). In general, biological tissues prepared for light microscopy are stained for better differentiation in a characteristic color using special aniline dyes, which bind to special substances in these tissues (chromotropes). However, these chromotropes might be affected in various ways by diagenetic processes. Thus, the characteristic color is frequently replaced by various colors that will not mark specific tissues but only the same structure changed by diagenesis (e.g., if the same stain produces different colorations of the same morphological structure, such as collagen fibers and mineralized bone substance).

There are principally two ways of analyzing macerated recent and archaeological bone samples by light microscopy: transmission (microtome sections and thin-ground sections) and reflected light (polished bone surfaces). In both techniques, plain and polarized light can be used. Additionally, investigation of polished surfaces with the backscattered mode of the scanning electron microscope (BSEM) is possible. Probably, the first investigator to successfully introduce BSEM in paleopathology was the British anthropologist L. S. Bell (Bell 1990).

Bones taken from mummies can be rehydrated, decalcified, and cut with a microtome, or can be treated as archaeological bone requiring no rehydration and no decalcification. Examination using undecalcified thin-ground sections prepared from mummified tissues can be extremely helpful, since during preparation the tissue sample is not rehydrated (see later), there is no risk that very small particles such as *microfilariae* (length approximately 13–280 μm) will be swept out during the rehydration process (Schultz 2001; Schultz and Gessler-Löhr 1992).

The microscopic examination of bone tissue taken from bog bodies includes two techniques that both provide relatively satisfying results: (1) decalcification, embedding in paraffin wax and cutting with a microtome, and staining with the usual dyes (sometimes, decalcification is not necessary because of the taphonomic decalcification already performed by the acids of the bog); and (2) preparation of undecalcified thin-ground sections. Principally, the light microscopic investigation of bone tissues of bog bodies involves the same procedures as described for macerated and archaeological samples (Schultz et al. 2010).

Bell and co-workers used methyl-methacrylate for the embedding of archaeological bone samples (Bell et al. 1996). Poly-methyl-methacrylates pervade tissues very well and are also able to interpenetrate large samples. However, there are also some disadvantages that people should be aware of when working with this resin (Schultz and Brandt 1987, cf. Schultz 1988a). For example, the sample to be embedded must be dehydrated completely, which is sometimes difficult in brittle, poorly preserved archaeological bone tissue. Furthermore, the procedure is laborious, sometimes unpredictable and relatively slow. Additionally, high temperatures might occur during polymerization that might affect the collagen fibers (e.g., Schultz 1997b, 2001), and cause shrinkage of the sample that can be as great as 20% (Schultz and Brandt 1987, cf. Schultz 1988a).

Lataster and co-workers used a polyester embedding procedure (Lataster et al. 1992). In thin-ground-section microscopy of archaeological bone, the use of polyester resins might introduce difficulties because there is some shrinking of the resin after embedding, which can affect the quality of the section (Schultz and Brandt 1987, cf. Schultz 1988a).

Epoxy resins are the most well-suited embedding plastics. Probably, the most well-known resins of this group are Araldit® (in the USA: Araldite®; e.g., Schultz 1988a) and Epon®, which are used successfully in transmission electron microscopy. Probably the best resin for application in paleohistology is Biodur® (type E12 and catalyst E1), which, due to its viscosity, has a very high permeation in undecalcified specimens and allows not only the preparation of small thin-ground sections (28 × 48 mm or 48 × 76 mm) but also of large ones (90 × 120 mm). Biodur® is used in the plastination procedure developed by Gunther von Hagens (1979) whose technique was modified for the embedding of archaeological specimens (Schultz and Brandt 1987). The procedure works with forced impregnation under relative vacuum on permanent exchange of the intermedium (dichloromethane), and guaranties best perfusion of the sample and excellent thin-ground sections in highest quality. The process includes drying, which takes at least 3 weeks. Dehydration of archaeological bone samples is not necessary because Biodur® is able to accept at least a small amount of moisture (Schultz 2001; Schultz and Brandt 1987, cf. Schultz 1988a; Schultz and Drommer 1983). When embedded using Biodur®, thin-ground sections of archaeological or recent bone are well preserved as far as collagen is concerned, and will not disengage from the glass slide on which it is mounted due to shrinking, twisting, or swelling, problems frequently observed in other embedding agents and resins. The most important feature of the whole embedding procedure is a complete penetration of the sample by the resins, which is easily achieved using Biodur® (modified plastination process primarily provided by Gunther von Hagens: Schultz 2001; Schultz and Brandt 1987, cf. Schultz 1988a; Schultz and Drommer 1983). The only disadvantage of this procedure in preparing thin-ground sections from brittle and poorly preserved bone samples is that it is relatively time consuming. The thickness of Biodur-embedded thin-ground sections ranges between 10 and 100 µm (10–50 µm for recent and archaeologically well-preserved samples; 70 µm for poorly preserved archaeological samples; 100 µm for microradiographs). A more detailed protocol dealing with the embedding procedure and the preparing of thin-ground sections has been published elsewhere (Schultz 1988a, 2001; see also the chapter by Cho in this volume).

## 10.3   Some Principles of Pathophysiology of Bony Tissue Observable in Dry Bones

One prevailing opinion is that the bony tissues principally act and react in the same or at least in a similar way during the influence of physical load and pathological conditions. There are two principle mechanisms that govern the development and the nature of bone, as well as the speed of the growth of the bony tissues, the change from spongy to compact bone substance, the remodeling of the microarchitecture including the creation of Haversian systems (osteons) and their fragments, interstitial lamellae, circumferential (general) lamellae, and tangential lamellae within the compact bone substance and the healing of pathological processes. These two principle mechanisms are (1) bone proliferation, which is a productive process caused by the osteoblasts; and (2) bone resorption, which is a lytic process caused by the osteoclasts. As a rule, under physiological conditions for the bone remodeling process, bone formation executed by the osteoblasts and bone resorption performed by the osteoclasts are in balance. It is important for the assessment of the vestiges of a pathological process to discern whether the process had occurred in the compact and spongy bone substance by the osteoclastic and osteoblastic reactions.

The speed of the growth of pathological newly built bone formations is of high diagnostic value for the differentiation between nonspecific (e.g., hematogenous osteomyelitis) and specific inflammatory bone diseases (e.g., treponematoses), and should not be underestimated in its usefulness. The speed of bone growth is expressed by the nature of the bone morphology observed in the microscopic image. Furthermore, it is helpful to know the sex and the biological age of the exhumed individual to correlate with the observed morphological features in order to better interpret the nature and the speed of the growth of the pathological structures. It should be noted that age consideration is only of minor importance in inflammatory diseases because the growth of pathological bone does not depend as much on the biological age, as is the case in tumorous bone diseases. As a rule, particularly in infants, children, juveniles, and young adults, physiological bone growth is more rapid than in old adults or seniles, that is, in young people the bony tissues grow relatively fast, in old people relatively slowly. Within certain limits, this is also the case in the growth of pathological bone. On the other hand, in adults the capacity of the immune system, as a rule, decreases with age, which influences the speed of pathological bone growth, secondarily.

Furthermore, the speed of pathological bone growth is different in nonspecific and specific infectious bone diseases. In general, in nonspecific infectious bone diseases, such as in hematogenous osteomyelitis, the newly built bone formations produced by the periosteum (proliferation process) grow relatively rapidly. This explains the irregular periosteal structure characteristic for this disease group (e.g., hematogenous osteomyelitis). In specific infectious bone diseases, such as in treponematoses and leprosy, pathological bone growth is relatively slow, and explains the development of microscopic features such as grenzstreifen and polster (Schultz 1994, 2001; Schultz and Roberts 2001; Schultz and Teschler-Nicola 1987).

In slowly growing periosteal processes, so-called agate bone ("Achatknochen") is produced (Lauche 1939; Schultz 1994; Schultz and Teschler-Nicola 1987). The term *agate bone* was used by Weidenreich (1930) to characterize newly built hard tissue structures, which show the morphological appearance of the stone agate in form of multiple bandings or microsediments. Using polarized light, similar morphological structures can be observed in thin-ground sections at the external surfaces of slowly grown bone caused by a periosteal affection, mainly an inflammatory process (Schultz 1994; Schultz and Teschler-Nicola 1987). In agate bone, which is frequently found in the peripheral (i.e., circumferential area of the shafts of affected long bones), the collagen fibers are oriented in a parallel pattern, tangentially to the external surface.

Woven bone is the first bone tissue to form the human skeleton during fetal and infant stages and is subsequently replaced by lamellar bone. However, woven bone might also be found in adults in regions of the skeleton under shearing stress, for example, near some of the muscle attachments, such as at the mandibular angle, or fracture callus. It also occurs in pathological states of high turnover, e.g., Paget's disease, hyperparathyroidism, and osteogenesis imperfecta.

## 10.4 The Light Microscopic Analysis of Dry Bone

To obtain useable information and to establish reliable diagnoses in paleohistopathology, relevant knowledge of the morphology, that is, the microarchitecture, and the pathophysiology of the bony tissue is desirable. As a rule, in macerated skeletal remains, no soft tissue or cells are present. Only very rarely might these structures be preserved in archaeological skeletal remains if protective surroundings in the ground were present, for example, as in the mastoid air cells or in the paranasal sinuses. Thus, important features, such as, granulocytes, osteoblasts, osteoclasts, and other macrophages as well as fibrous connective tissue, which all allow the pathologist to reliably diagnose pathological conditions in recent tissue samples, are not available for examination by the paleopathologist. Therefore, no cytological examination and only a limited histological examination can be carried out. Thus, the frequently postulated "biomedical clinical analogy, where it is assumed that the same pathologic changes and signs used to diagnose a clinical patient can be applied as diagnostic criteria in the interpretation of ancient material" (Weston 2009:188; cf. Klepinger 1983) is overly optimistic. Of course, these limitations make diagnosis difficult, sometimes frustrating and, additionally, frequently lead to the idea that it might not be at all possible to establish reliable diagnoses.

Currently, with the availability of new microscopic techniques, such as micro-CT, confocal laser scanning microscopy, and near-field scanning optical microscopy as well as atomic force microscopy, the capacity of the results provided by light microscopy is frequently underestimated. Some researchers believe that the results of an investigation might be more meaningful if the most novel technique is employed. Certainly, these techniques should not be ignored and sometimes they provide excellent results. However, light microscopy is a long-established technique in paleohistology, particularly using polarized light, and is the technique of choice because it is easy to employ; provides, as a rule, outstanding basic results; and is not an expensive application.

The backscattered mode of the scanning electron microscope, which is a very useful technique, cannot display the nature and the orientation of the collagen fibers and the associated crystals of the hydroxy-apatite. These are only convincingly observable in polarized transmission light. Particularly, using a hilfsobject red 1st order (quartz) as a compensator, the microarchitecture of the bony tissue can be studied in polarized transmission light. As in the backscattered mode of the scanning electron microscope, diagenetic products, such as sand and soil particles (e.g., silicate crystals) and products of degradation and transformation processes of the hydroxy-apatite (e.g., brushite), can be examined and differentiated.

### 10.4.1  What Can Light Microscopy Contribute to Paleopathology?

The reconstruction of the etiology and epidemiology of diseases in ancient populations is based on reliable diagnoses established from individual case studies. For this purpose, the light microscopic investigation is an indispensable method. Indeed, such results from archaeological skeletal or mummified remains enhance the reliability of a paleopathological diagnosis. However, as a rule, paleopathologists can only examine the vestiges of ancient diseases in dry bones, not the diseases themselves. Frequently, diagnoses established by macroscopy can be doubtful because macromorphological features are often similar in their external appearance. For example, it is not easy to differentiate macroscopically between bone appositions on external surfaces of long bones caused by various pathological conditions, such as metabolic diseases, infectious bone diseases, circulatory disorders, bone tumors and tumor-like conditions, and miscellaneous other conditions as well as bone healing after fracture (callus). Also radiologic techniques do not always provide satisfactory results because archaeological skeletal remains are frequently changed by diagenetic processes at the macrolevel, which might imitate the vestiges of osteolytic or osteoblastic processes. Diagenetic changes at the microlevel can be visible in a radiologic image (conventional x-rays or computerized tomography) if the diagenetic process had penetrated the bone in a diffuse way. However, even if bone samples are highly altered by diagenetic processes, light microscopy is particularly helpful and contributes diagnostically useful data. Of course, sometimes thin-ground sections tell us more about the diagenetic change the bone has passed through than about pathological conditions. However, lack of data on pathological changes might constitute an essential building block providing, in combination with the results of the macroscopic and radiological analyses, a reliable diagnosis.

Periosteal reactions on long bones are frequently seen in archaeological skeletal remains. If they are not caused postmortem as a result of a diagenetic process (pseudopathology, cf. Schultz 1986), these changes are frequently described as vestiges of *periostitis*. This term should be used carefully, because not all changes at the periosteal level are due to an inflammatory process caused by an infection which, indeed, must be described as periostitis (Schultz 1988a). Woven bone or lamellar bone formations beneath the periosteum might be caused (1) by an infection (periostitis); or (2) by circulatory disorders, hemorrhages, or tumorous processes, such as malign neoplasms (periostosis). Therefore, it is important to know that newly built bone formations, that is, bone appositions, beneath the periosteum are not always a response to an infection (Adler 1998, 2005; Jaffe 1972; Resnick and Niwayama 1981; Schultz 1988, 2001). An infection is caused by pathogenic organisms, such as bacteria. An inflammation, however, is the vascular response of the human organism to a defect or an injury of the tissues. Thus, an inflammation might also be induced by an infection. Finally, there are many conditions that are capable of provoking an inflammatory process. Mainly in the English written literature, all newly built bone formations are described as being due to "periostitis." Particularly, in articles dealing with physical anthropology and paleopathology, this term is frequently used to characterize subperiosteal bone formations. However, from the pathological point of view, these situations should be distinguished from each other more carefully. Paleopathological investigations show that hemorrhages of various origins (e.g., scurvy) frequently occurred in past populations. Due to their similar macromorphological appearance vestiges of hemorrhages cannot be differentiated reliably from each other. As a rule, it is not possible to assess the internal structure of bone appositions and the underlying compact or cortical bone tissue externally. In cases of hemorrhagic processes, such as in subperiosteal hematoma, as well as in cases of circulatory disorders or tumorous processes, processes actually emerge in the course of a noninfectious inflammation ("aseptic inflammation": periostosis), which might produce structures at the microlevel both similar to and dissimilar from those in infectious inflammation ("septic inflammation": periostitis). Therefore, it is difficult to differentiate between these two groups of processes: periostosis and periostitis. In hemorrhages, the newly built bone formations are situated on the external surfaces of nonaffected compact or cortical bone tissue, which is not the case in periosteal reactions caused by ostitic or osteomyelitic periostitis. In circulatory diseases, such as in hypertrophic osteoarthropathy (e.g., Bamberger-Marie diseases), the underlying compact or cortical bone tissue might only be affected in a relatively mild lytic way because of the relatively slow growth of the chronic process. However, as a rule, in circulatory disorders these changes are not as dramatically pronounced as in nonspecific hematogenous osteomyelitis. In tumorous diseases, the changes are, in general, similar in their intensity as mentioned before for the group of circulatory disorders. Only in rapidly growing tumors, such as metastatically spreading cancer, might periosteal changes be similar to or even more pronounced at the microlevel than those in nonspecific hematogenous osteomyelitis.

Additionally, we need to remember that paleopathologists usually do not have adequate amounts of material at their disposal for their investigations as do the pathologists working with recent tissue samples since soft tissues and cells are lacking in archaeological skeletal remains. The significance of the findings is limited in comparison to the interpretation of findings from recent, fresh pathology specimens, making paleopathology diagnosis extremely difficult. However, through the experience researchers gain by working intensively in the field of light microscopic investigation on archaeological specimens using thin-ground sections, a three-dimensional perspective of the morphological structures in the pathologically changed dry bone will develop.

## 10.4.2   Diagnosing Diseases in Macerated Bone

As a rule, in archaeological skeletal remains, vestiges of pathological conditions can be diagnosed. Frequently, disease groups or even diseases are diagnosable using the usual spectrum of methods and techniques (see earlier). Here, light microscopy plays an important role.

Over many years, there was the opinion that the results of a light microscopic investigation add little to what can be seen macroscopically or on x-ray films (Ortner and Putschar 1981). Thus, the well-known pathologist Walter G.J. Putschar* who contributed a great deal of knowledge and experience to paleopathology commented on this subject: "One should not, however, expect too much help from the microscopic examination of the macerated relic, since diagnostic microscopic bone patterns are rare. The most notable exception is probably the mosaic pattern of Paget's disease" (1966, pp. 58–59). Now, after intensive studies, we know today much more about the microarchitecture of macerated bone, for example, that mosaic pattern-like structures are also seen in the compact bone substance of long bone shafts affected by tertiary syphilis.

Principally, we can diagnose many morphological changes directly viewing the cut bone surface or the thin-ground section by the naked eye or by a magnifying glass. In these cases, we can allocate the pathologically changed structure to a disease group or even to a special disease, such as differentiating between anemia, scurvy, rickets, osteomyelitis, or

---

* Walter G. J. Putschar (1904–1987), born in Austria, worked as a pathologist before World War II at the Department of Pathology of the University of Göttingen (Germany), emigrated to the United States where he worked at the University of Charleston, West Virginia, and later at the Massachusetts General Hospital, Boston. After his retirement, he remained at the Smithsonian Institution at Washington where, together with Donald J. Ortner, in 1981 he published the handbook of paleopathology Identification of Pathological Conditions in Human Skeletal Remains (Ortner and Putschar 1981). Putschar was one of the leading paleopathologists of his time.

external periostitis (e.g., inflammation of the scalp) in cases of porotic hyperostosis of the skull vault (Cribra cranii externa) or the orbital roof (Cribra orbitalia) using the pathognomonic morphological features (Schultz 1986, 1993a, 2001, 2003).

By viewing thin-ground sections prepared from archaeological skeletal remains using polarized light, we can analyze the microarchitecture of bone relatively well, as long as the bone has not been too extensively destroyed by diagenesis. Particularly the course of the collagen fibers allows a morphological judgment as to whether the bone substance was pathologically changed during its lifetime. Not only the size, thickness, and orientation of bone trabeculae, but also the presence and the thickness of external and internal circumferential lamellae, the size and the number of Haversian systems and Haversian canals, the number of interstitial lamellae in the form of fragmented osteons, the presence and extension of tangential lamellae, the development of special cement lines, and the presence and number of Howship's lacunae might point to pathological conditions, according to the corresponding age groups. This last point is important because, as noted earlier, diseases frequently show a different behavior in the different age groups in terms of their course, exacerbation, and healing, and the occurrence and the development of a disease sometimes additionally depend also on the sex, the nutritional state, and other factors of the sociobiological biotope. To obtain the maximum information about a possible disease affecting an individual, it is necessary to extract all the microscopic information possible from a thin-ground section. The interpretation of the sum of all morphological microfeatures allows, as a rule, a reliable assertion about the nature of the changes and their relationship to a disease group or even to a special disease. In combination with the results of the macroscopic, endoscopic, and radiologic analyses, the results of the light microscopic investigation establish a reliable disease diagnosis. In many cases, the light microscopic examination presents the most convincing facts for the diagnosis.

### 10.4.2.1  *Subperiosteal Hemorrhages*

In some pathological processes, such as subperiosteal bleeding (e.g., hematoma caused by traumatic rupture of blood vessels or by increased permeability of blood through the vascular wall as in scurvy), but also frequently in circulatory diseases (e.g., primary and secondary hypertrophic osteoarthropathy, i.e., Bamberger-Marie disease) and tumorous diseases (e.g., malign neoplasm), the newly built bone formation is located on the external surface of the affected bone, which is, as a rule, not pathologically changed. In these cases, we should speak of periostosis and not periostitis (see earlier). Thus it is possible to differentiate, in paleopathology, between two different morphological patterns, which are, as a rule, associated with different pathological conditions or diseases.

In large, organized subperiosteal hematomas, which are healed in a bony stage and have a vertical extension of several millimeters, the newly built structures are, as a rule, spongy bone formations in which the trabeculae show a radial orientation (Van der Merwe et al. 2010). Frequently, the orientation of these trabeculae is not only caused by the size and the volume of the bleeding, but also by the physiological tone (tonus) and the tension of the muscles that might attach in the vicinity. These factors are together responsible for the radiating trabecular structure in the region of a formerly organized hematoma. However, in the region of small and flat subperiosteal hematomas caused by moderate bleeding from a slight hemorrhage, bulky bony trabeculae might be relatively short and frequently show an arcade-like appearance (Schultz 2001, 2003). Furthermore, if these structures become a little more voluminous and there are no muscle attachments in the vicinity, the main bone trabeculae are oriented approximately parallel to the original external bone surface. In this case, a characteristic framework might be observable, which slightly resembles the structure of a half-timbered building. Van der Merwe and co-workers suggest three stages of the further bony transformation in the region of a former hematoma, which explain the different morphological features seen in macerated bone specimens (Van der Merwe et al. 2010).

As an addition to subperiosteal hemorrhages, it should be mentioned that hematomas cannot ossify, as sometimes mistakenly reported in the paleopathological literature (Van der Merwe et al. 2010). The ossification of a hematoma is, from the pathological point of view, not possible. After the bleeding, a hematoma becomes organized, which means that connective-tissue cells migrate into the region of the hematoma and blood vessel proliferation takes place. The original hematoma is then changed to a formation of connective tissue. Subsequently, this connective tissue might be changed by osteoblastic activity into bone, although the change to a bony formation is not necessarily the case.

### 10.4.2.2   Specific and Nonspecific Bone Inflammations

The different structures occurring through specific and nonspecific bone inflammations, as well as the nature of bony tumors and tumorous lesions, can be observed microscopically (Schultz 2001), which can help to create standards for further microscopic investigations. However, at first sight, the microscopic differentiation in the groups of inflammatory and tumorous processes that affect compact and cortical as well as spongy bone substance is difficult (Hunnius et al. 2006; Schultz 1993b, 2001, 2003; Van der Merwe et al. 2010; Weston 2009). With knowledge of the age and the sex of the individual and information about the physiology of pathological processes, the characteristic morphological features observed in the light microscope can be interpreted relatively reliably. Very frequently, it is possible to connect the observed features to corresponding disease groups or establish a reliable disease diagnosis (examples are presented in the next paragraph).

Two major problems in the light microscopic examination of macerated bone samples are the diagnosis of treponemal diseases and the differentiation between nonspecific and specific inflammatory diseases (e.g., Hunnius et al. 2006; Van der Merwe et al. 2010; Weston 2009). These problems are compounded if we consider that various pathological conditions, and diseases, can coexist in the same organism.

The macroscopic morphology of the characteristic changes observed in nonspecific (e.g., hematogenous osteomyelitis) and specific inflammatory diseases (e.g., venereal syphilis) is well known and will not be mentioned here (e.g., Hackett 1976; Ortner 2003; Steinbock 1976). Light microscopic research on macerated syphilitic bones was done by several scholars (e.g., Blondiaux et al. 1994; Hershkovitz et al. 1994; Hunnius et al. 2006; Kozak 2005; Michaelis 1930; Schultz 1994, 2001, 2003; Schultz and Teschler-Nicola 1987; Van der Merwe et al. 2010; Weber 1927; Weston 2009; Williams 1927). One of the most characteristic features in venereal syphilis is gummatous periostitis of the diaphysis of long bones (Putschar 1966). However, gummatous syphilis, which is characterized by the gummata, is easy to diagnose at the microscopic level and, apparently, is rarely found in European archaeological remains. In recently macerated and archaeological bones suspicious of syphilis, Weber (1927), using light microscopy, clearly observed visible lines of varying thickness between the original bone surface and secondarily built bone formation, which he called *Grenzstreifen*. Weber (1927) found grenzstreifen only in bones suspicious for syphilis and thought that these structures are pathognomonic for this disease.

Grenzstreifen have to be regarded as the remnants of the external circumferential lamellae, which are still preserved over a longer time because of the relatively slow growth of the periosteal new bone. Thus, a grenzstreifen is a relatively reliable morphological criterion that characterizes slowly growing new bone formation frequently observed in treponematoses and situated subperiosteally on the original bone surface. After a further course of this disease, grenzstreifen might then be found within the compact bone because they are covered by newly built subperiosteal compact bone (Schultz 1994 2001, 2003; Schultz and Teschler-Nicola 1987; Weber 1927).

In treponematoses and leprosy, the speed of the growth of the pathological bone formations is relatively slow in comparison to the growth of pathological changes caused by nonspecific osteomyelitis, and the grenzstreifen is, therefore, as a rule, relatively frequently observable. In nonspecific osteomyelitis grenzstreifen is very rarely found, and if it is present, it is visible only over a very short distance.

While a well-visible grenzstreifen is presented by Hunnius et al. (2006; e.g., Figure 2, d and e, p. 563), Weston (2009) does not picture these structures convincingly. Apparently, Weston (2009) misunderstood the definition and the morphological structure of a grenzstreifen, which was well defined for the first time by Weber (1927). Elsewise it is difficult to understand why she described grenzstreifen in her figures where no grenzstreifen are observable (Figure 2, p. 189; Figure 3, p. 190; Figure 8, p. 192: here, only small external circumferential lamellae that are not packed between the primary compact and the secondary compact bone substance are visible; Figure 5, p. 190 and Figure 6, p. 191: here, the structure has the position, however, apparently does not show the design of a grenzstreifen). Furthermore, Weston (2009) criticizes Hunnius and co-workers (Hunnius et al. 2006) for their use of the term "Grenzstreifen and/or cement lines" (e.g., Hunnius et al 2006, p. 562). According to Weber (1927) and Schultz (2001, 2003) a grenzstreifen is not a cement line. However, because the grenzstreifen is a remnant of the external circumferential lamellae, it might terminate with a cement line.

Van der Merwe and co-workers (Van der Merwe et al. 2010) criticize that the grenzstreifen in the microphotograph presented by Schultz (2003, p. 86, Figure 6-19) "indicates the normal external circumferential lamellae of the cortex." That is, indeed, what it is. The grenzstreifen is the remnant of the external circumferential lamellae, which is embedded between the original compact and the secondary compact bone, and this is visible in the microphotograph (Schultz 2003, p. 86, Figure 6-19). Furthermore, it is clearly observable that these circumferential lamellae are reduced in their size and shape and are in a stage of replacement.

Polsters are only found at the periphery of a cross-section, and, if present, only within some parts of the circumference. According to Schultz and Teschler-Nicola (1987), well-developed polsters consist of mature lamellar bone and show the character of agate bone. It is useful to know that as any other morphological structure, polsters can change their micromorphology during the course of the disease. This means polsters are not permanently present in any specific inflammatory process. In general, in tertiary syphilis the periosteal lesions, such as polsters, are caused by relatively slowly growing processes in contrast to nonspecific hematogenous osteomyelitis. As already mentioned, as a rule, so-called agate bone is produced at the external surface of a bone shaft during slowly growing periosteal processes, mainly in stages of healing or partly healing (Lauche 1939). In cases of hypervascularization at the periosteal level, polsters will develop in place of the ribbon-like agate bone.

Weston (2009) suggests that there are also polsters in periosteally new bone formations caused by nonspecific inflammatory processes. This cannot be excluded, although this would be very rare in cases of nonspecific hematogenous osteomyelitis. However, what Weston (2009:192) is presenting in her Figure 10 is not a polster for the following reasons: (1) Polsters are found at the external surfaces of the shafts of long bones, not as Weston (2009:192, Figure 10) is showing within the layers of newly built bone formations. (2) It is well known that the nature and the orientation of the collagen fibers are necessary to diagnose polsters, and in the structure erroneously called a "polster" by Weston (2009, Figure 10) the collagen fiber bundles are not really visible. Because of these two facts, it is not possible to diagnose a polster as Weston has done. Furthermore, this case presented by Weston is a suitable example to clearly show the limits of the examination using the backscattered electron imaging, whereas in light microscopy using polarized light, collagen fibers are, as a rule, easily detectable. Van der Merwe and co-workers (2010) did not succeed in observing grenzstreifen and polsters. To detect a grenzstreifen and also polsters, it is essential to examine a complete long bone cross-section and not only a small sector of the transverse section. Furthermore, as a rule, it is a good idea to analyze at least two cross-sections of the same bone shaft. As a grenzstreifen is a remnant of the external circumferential lamellae, which is impacted within the compact bone mass consisting of the original compact bone substance (inside) and the newly built periosteal bone formation (outside) that was changed secondarily to compact bone substance (Schultz 1994, 2001; Schultz and Teschler-Nicola 1987; Weber 1927), it is only found at the periphery of a cross-section, and, if present, only within some parts of the circumference. Putschar (1966:60–61) also mentioned this phenomenon, which was familiar to the older generation of pathologists: "persistence of the external general lamellae beneath the periostial (periosteal) osteophyte is often seen in syphilis (Weber)." As a rule, a grenzstreifen is situated in the region of a thickened long bone shaft in which the thickening has not reached its maximum length. The most favorable region to find a grenzstreifen seems to be the area where the thickening had reached approximately a quarter or third of its length. This is easily understood because, in this area of the thickening, the pathological process was relatively fresh and the process had not changed the bony substance completely by the following remodeling. Thus, it is no surprise, that researchers do not always detect a grenzstreifen in a long bone cross-section at their first attempt using only a sector of one cross-section.

### 10.4.3  Selected Examples of Microscopic Diagnoses in Dry Bone

This section illustrates the useful application of light microscopy in paleopathology and explains how to establish reliable diagnoses in macerated bone specimens. The samples chosen should clearly reveal the differences between the various pathological conditions and diseases at the microlevel. Because of the given space in this book, only a couple of cases can be presented. However, for the purposes of differential diagnoses, similar topics and morphological conditions were selected.

#### 10.4.3.1  *Porotic Hyperostosis of the Orbital Roof* (Cribra orbitalia)

Porotic hyperostosis of the orbital roof is called *Cribra orbitalia* and is not regarded as a disease but rather as the morphological expression of various diseases (Schultz 2001). Thus, anemia (Figure 10.1), scurvy (Figure 10.2), rickets (Figure 10.3), and inflammatory conditions (Figure 10.4; e.g., ostitis/osteomyelitis of the bony orbital roof or an infection inside the orbit) originating, for example, from the paranasal sinuses, the nasal cavity or the endocranial cavity as well as tumorous lesions, can be the cause. As a rule, all of these

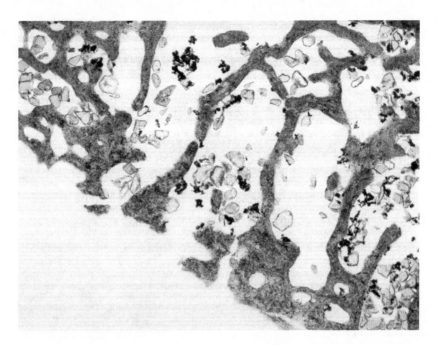

**Figure 10.1** St. Maria de Yamasee, Florida, Sk-106, 9- to 12-year-old child, Mission Period. Right orbital roof. *Cribra orbitalia* due to anemia. Thin-ground section (50 μm) viewed in plain transmission light. Magnification 25×.

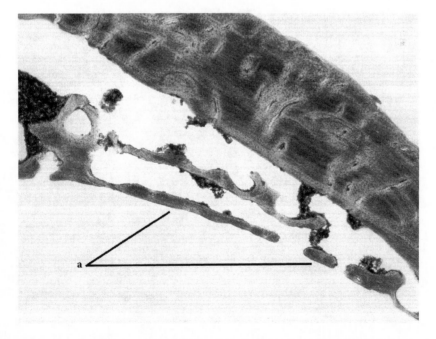

**Figure 10.2** Hailfingen (Germany), SK-2190, child: Infans II, 5th–7th century AD. Right orbital roof. *Cribra orbitalia* due to scurvy: a = newly built bone formation. Thin-ground section (70 μm) viewed in plain transmission light. Magnification 25×.

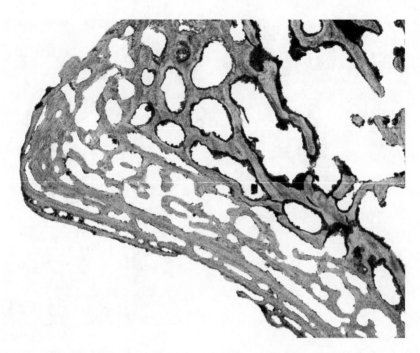

**Figure 10.3** İkiztepe (Turkey), IT-Türk-78e, child: 6- to 12-month-old, 3rd millennium BC. Right/left orbital roof. *Cribra orbitalia* due to rickets. Thin-ground section (70 μm) viewed in plain transmission light. Magnification 25×.

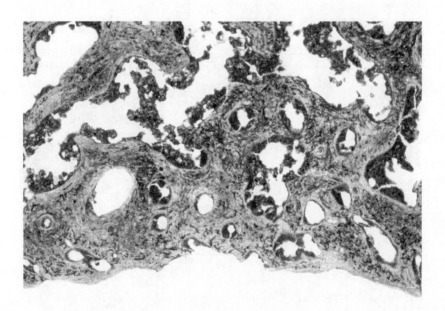

**Figure 10.4** Hailfingen (Germany), SK-1126, child: Infans II, 5th–7th century AD. Left orbital roof. *Cribra orbitalia* due to osteomyelitis. Thin-ground section (50 μm) viewed in plain transmission light. Magnification 25×.

can only be detected using microscopic techniques. Thus, from the study of the external appearance of the orbital roof alone, a reliable diagnosis is not possible and the lesions have to be assessed as stress markers.

Figures 10.1 through 10.4 clearly show the characteristic changes that are relatively easy to diagnose. In anemia (Figure 10.1), the bone trabeculae are oriented vertically (hair-on-end phenomenon), which can be explained by the enlargement of the cancellous bone (diploë) that leads to the radial growth of the bone trabeculae, accompanied by the thinning of the external lamina creating the characteristic porosity by pressure atrophy induced by the outgrowing diploë. In scurvy (Figure 10.2), the morphological changes that represent an organized hematoma (Figure 10.2, a) are, as a rule, only found on the external surface (orbital cortical bone lamina) below the periosteum (*Periorbita*), which means that the original bone, including the cortex, does not show pathological changes. The bone trabeculae are mainly oriented tangentially and the layer is relatively thin if the original hematoma was relatively flat. In rickets (Figure 10.3), the whole of the bony orbital roof is affected because chronic vitamin D deficiency is a systemic disease affecting the bone as a whole. Therefore, particularly the newly built bony trabeculae show, as a rule, a slightly dystrophic appearance. In an inflammatory process, such as periostitis or ostitis/osteomyelitis of the orbital roof (Figure 10.4), the characteristic physiological structure of the orbital roof (cortical and cancellous bone) might be completely lost due to osteoclastic and osteoblastic reactions, particularly, if stages of healing have taken place. In this context, it should not be forgotten that, in any changes due to the described diseases, episodes of healing might influence the characteristic structures described here.

### 10.4.3.2 Porotic Hyperostosis of the External Skull Vault (Cribra cranii externa)

The morphological changes observed in porotic hyperostosis of the external skull vault, which is called *Cribra cranii externa,* are highly similar to those described for *Cribra orbitalia* because they are due to the same pathological conditions. Figure 10.5 illustrates a well-pronounced case of anemia; Figure 10.6 shows an unusually large organized hematoma due to scurvy situated on the external skull lamina (Figure 10.6a) demonstrates an advanced case of chronic rickets; and Figure 10.8 represents a very aggressive, fast developing case of osteomyelitis in which the diploë was significantly destroyed by osteolysis (part c) and new bone formations were built up on the endocranial surface (part e), and, particularly, on the ectocranial surface (part b) of the skull vault (periostitis).

### 10.4.3.3 Porotic Hyperostosis of the Internal Skull Vault (Cribra cranii interna)

As we have seen before (Figure 10.8, e) in osteomyelitis of the skull vault, newly built bone formations might occur on the internal skull lamina. These changes would be macroscopically diagnosed because of their porotic character as *Cribra cranii interna*. However, also in inflammatory and hemorrhagic processes of the meninges, porotic changes on the endocranial skull lamina can be observed (Figure 10.9 and Figure 10.10). Thus, *Cribra cranii interna* are frequently due to nonspecific infectious diseases of the dura mater (e.g., bacterial meningitis, pachymeningitis). Occasionally, *Cribra cranii interna* can also be observed in nonspecific inflammations of the skull vault such as in nonspecific osteomyelitis (Figure 10.11, b) and, relatively rarely, due to specific infectious diseases, such as in tuberculosis (Figure 10.12, b) and venereal syphilis (Figure 10.16). Furthermore, survived

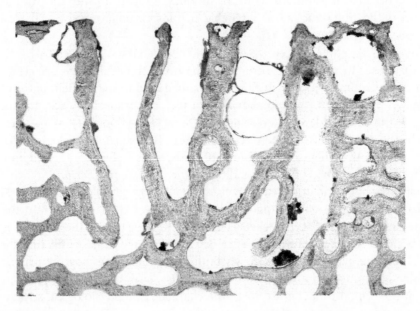

**Figure 10.5** Collection of the Department of Pathology, University of Göttingen (Germany), GP-1985495, child: Infans II, recent case, 20th century. Right parietal bone. *Cribra cranii externa* due to anemia. Thin-ground section (70 μm) viewed in plain transmission light. Magnification 25×.

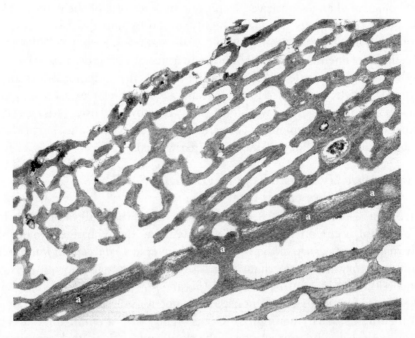

**Figure 10.6** Sundown Site, Arizona (USA), B-3/1, child: Infans I-II, pre-Columbian Sinagua. Frontal bone. *Cribra cranii externa* due to scurvy: a = *Lamina externa*. Thin-ground section (50 μm) viewed in plain transmission light. Magnification 25×.

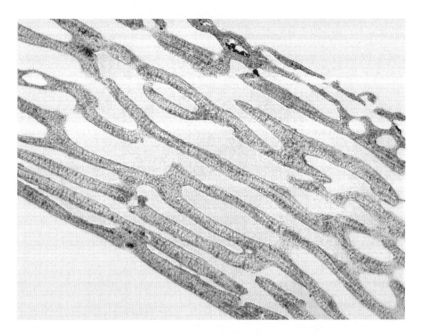

**Figure 10.7** Collection of the Department of Pathology, University of Göttingen (Germany), GP-1985903, child: Infans II, recent case, 20th century. Right or left parietal bone. *Cribra cranii externa* due to rickets. Thin-ground section (50 μm) viewed in plain transmission light. Magnification 25×.

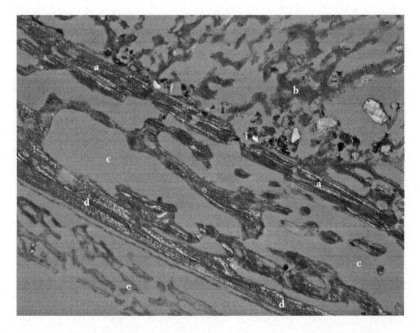

**Figure 10.8 (See color insert.)** Sundown Site, Arizona (USA), B-12/2, child: Infans I, pre-Columbian Sinagua. Parietal bone fragment. *Cribra cranii externa* due to osteomyelitis: a = *Lamina externa*, b = appositional bone on external lamina, c = *Diploë*, d = *Lamina interna*, e = appositional bone on internal lamina. Thin-ground section (70 μm) viewed in polarized transmission light using hilfsobject red 1st order (quartz) as compensator. Magnification 25×.

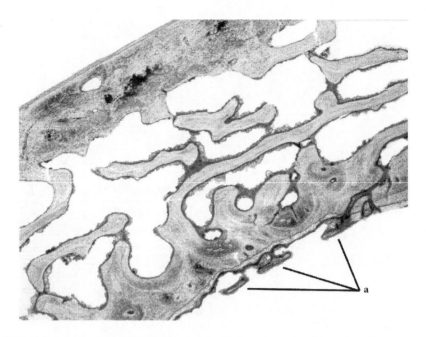

**Figure 10.9** İkiztepe (Turkey), IT-Türk-145, child: 2- to 3-year-old, 3rd millennium BC. Left parietal bone. *Cribra cranii interna* due to meningeal reactions (meningitis): a = newly built plates. Thin-ground section (50 µm) viewed in plain transmission light. Magnification 25×.

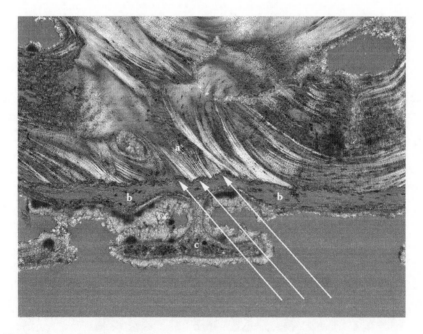

**Figure 10.10 (See color insert.)** İkiztepe (Turkey), IT-Türk-145, child: 2- to 3-year-old, 3rd millennium BC. Left parietal bone. *Cribra cranii interna* due to meningeal reactions (meningitis); detail out of Figure 10.9: a = lamellar bone, b = newly built woven bone, c = newly built woven bone plates, arrows = remodeled Howship's lacunae. Thin-ground section (70 µm) viewed in polarized transmission light using hilfsobject red 1st order (quartz) as compensator. Magnification 100×.

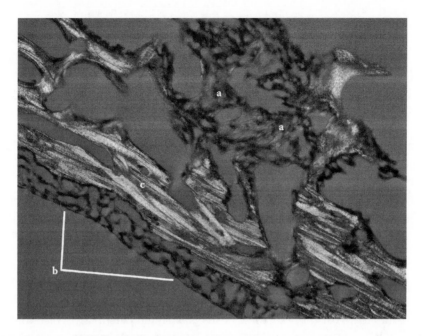

**Figure 10.11 (See color insert.)** Collection of the Department of Pathology, University of Göttingen (Germany), GP-1985901, senile individual, recent case, 20th century. Left frontal bone. *Cribra cranii interna* due to a pronounced nonspecific inflammatory process (osteomyelitis): a = newly built primitive woven bone trabeculae within the *Diploë*, b = new woven bone formation due to meningeal reaction induced by the osteomyelitic process, c = *Lamina interna*. Thin-ground section (70 μm) viewed in polarized transmission light using hilfsobject red 1st order (quartz) as compensator. Magnification 25×.

bleedings, for instance, due to scurvy or sometimes also to trauma or pathological processes of uncertain origin (e.g., *Pachymeningeosis hemorrhagica interna*) might be responsible for the occurrence of *Cribra cranii interna*.

The differential diagnoses of porotic hyperostosis of the internal skull vault called *Cribra cranii interna* is relatively difficult. This is to be expected in the anatomical situation of the endocranial cavity, which is filled with the brain and its meninges. As a rule, primarily, there is only little space for the development of the products of an inflammatory or hemorrhagic process. Therefore, in the case of slight bleeding, such as in scurvy, the newly built formations are relatively low in height. However, massive and permanent bleeding creates increased brain pressure causing displacement of the brain. Generally, this situation leads to, without an operation (trephination), death. Because such a pronounced hemorrhage cannot be survived we find only the vestiges of small hematomas on the internal lamina of macerated skulls. As a rule, in hemorrhagic processes, numerous, fine, and branched blood vessel impressions are predominantly observable on the internal skull lamina below small porotic plates (Schultz 1993a). According to the topographic situation, the same has to be taken into consideration with regard to inflammatory processes. As a rule, platelike structures (Figure 10.9, a) are suspicious of inflammatory processes (Schultz 1993a). In subadults, particularly in infants and young children, the skeletal system grows so rapidly that already after the short time of 10 to 14 days after the manifestation of bacterial meningitis bony structures have developed. In contrast to common opinion, also in ancient times, subadults were able to survive bacterial meningitis, although sometimes only for 2 weeks. In such cases, these bone formations consist of fresh woven bone (Figure 10.10, b,c), which might be preserved after death for many years (sometimes even for more than thousands of years) if the soil condition of the interred individual allows this. Rarely, the vestiges of osteoclastic reactions in the form of Howship's lacunae (Figure 10:10, arrows) within the original lamellar bone (Figure 10.10, a) are still visible and might be remodeled by woven bone.

### 10.4.3.4　Nonspecific Inflammatory Processes in the Skull Vault

Osteoclastic and osteoblastic bone reactions due to nonspecific inflammatory processes, such as hematogenous osteomyelitis, are relatively rare in archaeological human skeletal remains. In infants and young children bone grows very rapidly, thus vestiges of inflammatory processes of the skull vault show, as a rule, a more aggressive character in their morphology and, therefore, are more frequently observable than in skulls of adults (cf. Figure 10.8 and Figure 10.11). Because of the construction and the efficiency of the immune system of adult individuals, episodes of healing mainly in the region of the diploë (Figure 10.11, a) are more frequently observed than in subadults (cf. Figure 10.8, c). The nature of the newly built woven bone trabeculae is characteristic for hematogenous osteomyelitis of the skull vault. Hematogenous osteomyelitis is, as a rule, a fast growing process that spreads rapidly within the diploë by osteoclastic and osteoblastic reactions. Original bone that has been eaten away by the osteoclasts will be replaced after a short while by newly built very short, bulky trabeculae of primitive woven bone (Figure 10.11, a), which show a netlike connection filling the large, confluent resorption holes, characteristic for this disease. Additionally, woven bone formations are frequently observed on the external and the internal skull lamina (Figure 10.11, b).

### 10.4.3.5　Specific Inflammatory Processes in the Skull Vault

Specific inflammatory processes as found in venereal syphilis and tuberculosis of the skull vault show a completely different pattern in their physiology and, therefore, also in their morphology (Figures 10.12 to 10.18). As a rule, syphilis and tuberculosis are, in contrast to hematogenous osteomyelitis, relatively slowly developing diseases. Thus, the relatively slow course of the osteolytic destruction as well as the slow development of the osteoblastic reaction, which is responsible for the remodeling process in partial, or rather local healing, characterize these diseases. The famous Australian medical scientist and paleopathologist Cecil J. Hackett (1905–1995) described in his classic paper dealing with specific infectious diseases affecting the skeleton very distinctly the characteristic changes of venereal syphilis and tuberculosis at the macro- and the microlevel (Hackett 1976). However, using thin-ground section microscopy, it is not easy to find the characteristic features described in detail by Hackett (1976). In any case, the micromorphology of skull vaults affected, on the one hand, by hematogenous osteomyelitis (Figure 10.8 and Figure 10.11) and, on the other, by venereal syphilis (Figures 10.13 to 10.16) and tuberculosis (Figures 10.12, 10.17, and 10.18) apparently looks quite different.

In venereal syphilis, we might have gummata (Figure 10.13), which can sometimes partially heal so that the external skull surface, which is distinctly thickened, can become relatively smooth (Figure 10.14). In contrast to nonspecific osteomyelitis (cf. Figure 10.11), the diploë of the skull vault affected by venereal syphilis shows a monotonous morphology (Figure 10.15) that is represented by primitive woven bone and covers within the section the whole skull vault (Figures 10.14 to 10.16), whereas in nonspecific osteomyelitis, frequently island-like structures of original lamellar bone might be preserved within the

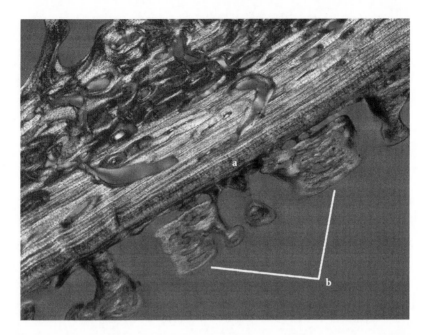

**Figure 10.12 (See color insert.)** Collection of the Department of Pathology, University of Göttingen (Germany), GP-1985616, adult individual, recent case, 20th century. Frontal bone. *Cribra cranii interna* due to a pronounced specific inflammatory process (tuberculosis): a = *Lamina interna*, b = newly built primitive woven bone on the internal lamina. Thin-ground section (70 μm) viewed in polarized transmission light using hilfsobject red 1st order (quartz) as compensator. Magnification 25×.

**Figure 10.13 (See color insert.)** Collection of the Department of Legal Medicine, University of Vienna (Austria), RMW-Sch5, adult individual, recent case, 20th century. Region of the external surface of the right frontal bone. Tertiary stage of venereal syphilis (small, developing gumma). Thin-ground section (70 μm) viewed in polarized transmission light using hilfsobject red 1st order (quartz) as compensator. Magnification 25×.

**Figure 10.14 (See color insert.)** Collection of the Department of Legal Medicine, University of Vienna (Austria), RMW-Sch4, adult individual, recent case, 20th century. Region of the external surface of the right parietal bone. Tertiary stage of venereal syphilis. Thin-ground section (70 µm) viewed in polarized transmission light using hilfsobject red 1st order (quartz) as compensator. Magnification 25×.

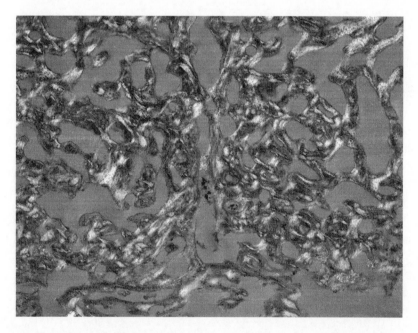

**Figure 10.15 (See color insert.)** Collection of the Department of Pathology, University of Göttingen (Germany), GP-1985688, adult individual, recent case, 20th century. *Diploë* of the frontal bone. Pronounced specific inflammatory process (venereal syphilis). Thin-ground section (70 µm) viewed in polarized transmission light using hilfsobject red 1st order (quartz) as compensator. Magnification 25×.

**Figure 10.16 (See color insert.)** Collection of the Department of Pathology, University of Göttingen (Germany), GP-1985688, adult individual, recent case, 20th century. Frontal bone. *Cribra cranii interna* due to a pronounced specific inflammatory process (venereal syphilis). Thin-ground section (70 μm) viewed in polarized transmission light using hilfsobject red 1st order (quartz) as compensator. Magnification 25×.

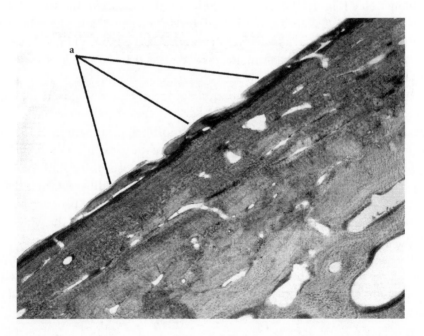

**Figure 10.17** Collection of the Department of Pathology, University of Göttingen (Germany), GP-1985616, adult individual, recent case, 20th century. Frontal bone. Vestiges of relatively slight periosteal reactions on the *Lamina externa* due to a pronounced specific inflammatory process (tuberculosis): a = newly built primitive woven bone. Thin-ground section (50 μm) viewed in plain transmission light. Magnification 25×.

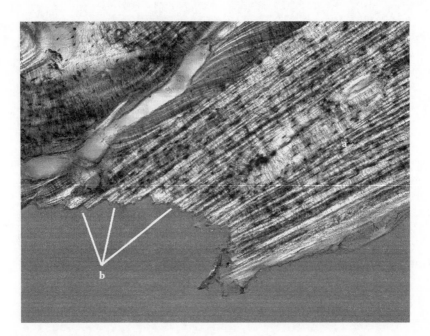

**Figure 10.18 (See color insert.)** Collection of the Department of Pathology, University of Göttingen (Germany), GP-1985616, adult individual, recent case, 20th century. Frontal bone. Internal lamina afflicted by osteolytic reaction due to a specific inflammatory process (tuberculosis): a = *Lamina interna*, b = Howship's lacunae. Thin-ground section (70 μm) viewed in polarized transmission light using hilfsobject red 1st order (quartz) as compensator. Magnification 25×.

affected bony tissue (Figure 10.11, c). Sometimes on the surface of the secondary internal lamina of the skull vault there are newly built formations (as a rule, the primary, i.e., the original external and internal lamellar laminae, are resorbed during the course of the disease) that document that the inflammatory process has reached the dura mater causing a meningeal reaction (Figure 10.16).

The tuberculous infection of the skull vault apparently leads to morphological features that look different from the microchanges described earlier in nonspecific osteomyelitis and venereal syphilis. The cause of this different morphological pattern at the microlevel probably has something to do with the variable speed of the growth of new bone formations and the development of bone resorption. Thus, in tuberculosis of the skull vault, the bony lesions develop relatively slowly (Figure 10.17, a), which is quite different from the situation in nonspecific osteomyelitis. Also, in venereal syphilis, the bony changes develop relatively slowly. However, whereas in venereal syphilis the bone changes cover the whole section of the skull vault, in tuberculosis the changes, for example, osteoclastic resorption expressed by a large number of Howship's lacunae, are only found in circumscribed places (Figure 10.18, b) close to a large resorption hole, which might penetrate the skull vault completely. Similar to venereal syphilis, the inflammatory process can affect the dura mater, which might lead to extensive new bone formations on the internal lamina (Figure 10.12, b).

### 10.4.3.6 Nonspecific Inflammatory Processes in the Shafts of Long Bones

As described before (Section 10.4.1), in cases of hemorrhagic processes, such as in a subperiosteal hematoma due to scurvy, the newly built bone formation (Figure 10.19, c), which represents a previous hematoma, sits directly on the original bone surface (Figure 10.19, b).

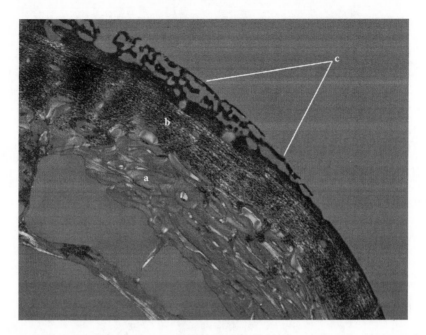

**Figure 10.19 (See color insert.)** Franzhausen-I (Austria), FH-338, child: 3- to 5-year-old child, 3rd–2nd millennium BC. Right humerus. Evidence of a subperiosteal hematoma due to scurvy: a = compact, osteonic bone substance of the shaft, b = compact, tangential lamellar bone substance of the shaft (resembling the later external circumferential lamellae), c = subperiosteal woven bone formation. Thin-ground section (70 µm) viewed in polarized transmission light using hilfsobject red 1st order (quartz) as compensator. Magnification 100×.

As a rule, the compact bone substance and the cortical bone beneath the periosteal layer (periostosis) are not affected by this pathological process.

In nonspecific hematogenous osteomyelitis (Figure 10.20), which typically is spread by the blood vessel system (hematogenous), characteristic morphological features are cloaca (Figure 10.21, a), fistula (Figure 10.22, a), sequestrum, and involucrum. All bones might be affected, however, as a rule, only one bone is diseased. A thickened bone shaft (Figures 10.20 to 10.22) is not characteristic because such a feature is also found in specific inflammatory diseases, for example, venereal syphilis. In this disease, the medullary cavity, the compact bone substance, and the periosteum are severely affected (Figures 10.20 to 10.22). Typical

**Figure 10.20 (See color insert.)** Sindelsdorf (Germany), TIB-SK, adult individual, 5th–7th century AD. Tibia: Thickened bone shaft due to nonspecific hematogenous osteomyelitis. Thin-ground section (70 µm) stained with methylenblue viewed in plain transmission light. Magnification 1×.

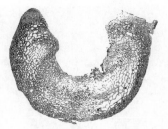

**Figure 10.21** Klosterneuburg, charnel house of St. Martin's church (Austria), Ind.-D4, adult individual, Early Modern Times. Right femur. Thickened bone shaft due to nonspecific hematogenous osteomyelitis: a = cloaca. Thin-ground section (70 μm) viewed in plain transmission light. Magnification 1×.

**Figure 10.22** Klosterneuburg, charnel house of St. Martin's church (Austria), Ind.-D7, adult individual, Early Modern Times. Left femur. Primary sclerotic occlusion of medullary cavity and secondary osteolytic focus with necrotic trabeculae, nonspecific hematogenous osteomyelitis: a = inactive, almost closed fistula. Thin-ground section (70 μm) viewed in plain transmission light. Magnification 1×.

for inflammatory diseases of the long bones, particularly for nonspecific osteomyelitis, are small foci of decayed bone matrix. These foci are situated within the region of the former original compact bone substance or in the area of the secondarily filled medullary cavity. Frequently, such foci contain necrotic materials and represent regions of local inflammations that may be the onset of a relapse, which might rapidly spread (Figure 10.23).

Principally, and in contrast to specific inflammatory diseases of the long bones, hematogenous osteomyelitis is characterized by the rapid growth of the pathologically changed structures that are found in a larger segment of the shaft (diaphysis, metaphyses) of the infected long bone (as a rule, unilocular). The changes due to this pathological process are frequently expressed by extensive osteolytic bone loss and enormous osteoblastic bone reaction (Figure 10.21). After a relatively short course of this disease, the complete original bone substance in the affected area might be changed by an intensive remodeling process (Figures 10.20 to 10.22). Only very rarely might structures, such as agate bone and grenzstreifen, be found, which are, however, relatively frequently observed in bones afflicted by treponematoses (e.g., venereal syphilis) and leprosy. Only occasionally, as an isolated structure, might polster-like features be visible that apparently never reach the frequency, the size, and the dimensions of those found in venereal syphilis.*

---

* In a series of eleven individuals from the Early Modern Times from the charnel house of Klosterneuburg, Austria, six individuals had suffered from hematogenous osteomyelitis in the lower extremity; five individuals had suffered from venereal syphilis (Schultz and Teschler-Nicola 1987). In the osteomyelitis examples, only in one case was an isolated polster-like structure visible (n = 1/6), whereas in the syphilis cases four of five individuals show polster (n = 4/5).

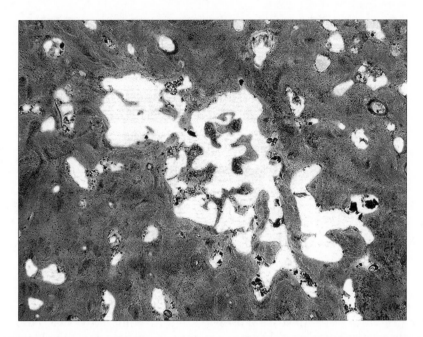

**Figure 10.23** Klosterneuburg, charnel house of St. Martin's church (Austria), Ind.-D5, adult individual, Early Modern Times. Left femur. Secondary osteolytic focus with necrotic trabeculae, nonspecific hematogenous osteomyelitis. Thin-ground section (70 μm) viewed in plain transmission light. Magnification 25×.

### 10.4.3.7 Specific Inflammatory Processes in the Shafts of Long Bones

In treponematoses, the shafts of long bone are also thickened; however, cloaca, fistula, sequestrum, and involucrum are missing and the lesions are found more frequently in the bones of the lower leg (tibia > fibula > femur) and the distal femurs in a symmetrical configuration (right and left bones). Generally, the bones that are sent for investigation to paleopathologists show the features of the tertiary stage of acquired venereal syphilis. We can differentiate between gummatous (Figure 10.24) and nongummatous syphilis (Figure 10.25), however, a combination of both is possible. As in nonspecific hematogenous osteomyelitis, the compact bone substance might be considerably destroyed, however, a partial healing or remodeling, particularly at the external circumference of the thickened bone shaft is possible (Figure 10.26). Similar to the situation in nonspecific osteomyelitis, the medullary cavity (osteomyelitis), the compact bone substance (ostitis), and the periosteum (periostitis) are afflicted. As the disease process develops relatively slowly, much slower than in nonspecific hematogenous osteomyelitis, the changes due to the osteosclerotic reaction are the main morphologic symptoms at the microlevel. Characteristic features might be visible, such as agate bone (Figure 10.27), polster (Figure 10.28) and grenzstreifen (Figure 10.29). Mature polsters are built of agate bone and are packed between primary periosteal blood vessels. They grow slowly and can frequently reach a height of more than 1 mm. The collagen fibers within the polsters show a parallel orientation to each other and, consequently, also have a tangential orientation to the external surface of the bone shaft (Figure 10.28). In contrast to other features, which are at first look very similar (cf. Figure 10.33), the collagen fibers run back to the original external surface of the bone shaft where the already mentioned blood

**Figure 10.24** San Diego Museum of Man, Alaska Inuit (USA), SDM-1915-2-787B, adult individual, Modern Times. Right tibia. Gummatous venereal syphilis: no polsters, no grenzstreifen because of the relatively fast bone growth, a = gumma. Thin-ground section (70 μm) viewed in plain transmission light. Magnification 1×.

**Figure 10.25** Klosterneuburg, charnel house of St. Martin's church (Austria), Ind.-E6/a, adult individual, Early Modern Times. Right tibia. Nongummatous venereal syphilis, a = anterior elongation of bone shaft (saber shin); b = region of polsters; c = region of grenzstreifen. Thin-ground section (70 μm) viewed in plain transmission light. Magnification 1×.

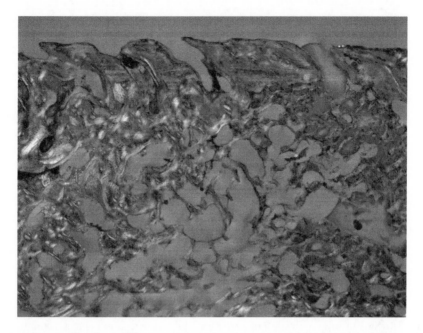

**Figure 10.26 (See color insert.)** San Diego Museum of Man, Alaska Inuit (USA), SDM-1915-2-787B, adult individual, Modern Times. Right tibia. Gummatous venereal syphilis. External surface of bone shaft: no original polsters, no grenzstreifen because of the relatively fast bone growth. Thin-ground section (50 μm) viewed in polarized transmission light using hilfsobject red 1st order (quartz) as compensator. Magnification 25×.

**Figure 10.27** Klosterneuburg, charnel house of St. Martin's church (Austria), Ind.-E3/a, adult individual, Early Modern Times. Left tibia. Nongummatous venereal syphilis: agate bone formation on external surface of bone shaft. Thin-ground section (70 μm) viewed in polarized transmission light. Magnification 25×.

**Figure 10.28 (See color insert.)** Bajkara (Kazakhstan), Kurgan 1, pit 1, skeleton 1, mature male, Sarmatian Period (approx. 160–40 BC). Right tibia. Nongummatous venereal syphilis: well-developed polster formation on external surface of bone shaft. Thin-ground section (70 μm) viewed in polarized transmission light using hilfsobject red 1st order (quartz) as compensator. Magnification 25×.

**Figure 10.29** Klosterneuburg, charnel house of St. Martin's church (Austria), Ind.-E4/b, adult individual, Early Modern Times. Left tibia. Nongummatous venereal syphilis: grenzstreifen within compact bone substance of bone shaft (between the original compact bone substance [right] and the newly grown compact bone substance [left]) mainly representing the remnant of the external circumferential lamellae. Thin-ground section (70 μm) viewed in polarized transmission light. Magnification 25×.

vessels are situated (Figure 10.28). Thus, at the external corners of the polsters, the collagen fibers change their direction at a 90° angle.

Sometimes, so-called sinuous lacunae are visible in long bones afflicted by treponematoses (Suzuki 1984). These relatively wide lacunae, which are situated in the demarcation line between the original compact bone substance and the newly built bone formation, are not surrounded by many circular lamellae as, for instance, Haversian systems. Their origin might have something to do with enlarged venae situated primarily on the original external surface of the bone shaft, which are, together with other factors, responsible for the pathological growth of new bone (passive hyperemia). However, very probably, sinuous lacunae are not pathognomonic for treponemal diseases because these structures are apparently also found in nonspecific inflammatory diseases.

Tuberculosis in long bones is rarely seen. Therefore, up to now, we do not know enough about the pathohistology of this disease in macerated long bones at the microlevel. In one such case the right femur of an individual who had suffered from bone tuberculosis demonstrated macroscopically slight vestiges of periosteal reaction.* In comparison with the changes in long bones caused by treponematoses and, particularly, nonspecific hematogenous osteomyelitis, the vestiges of tuberculous destruction are, as a rule, seemingly relatively mild. In the case presented here, we have, however, also vestiges of osteoclastic resorption that started from the medullary cavity (osteomyelitis, ostitis; Figure 10.30, a). Furthermore, we can observe slight periosteal changes on the external surfaces of the bone shaft (periostitis; Figures 10.31, a and 10.32, a). The periosteal reactions are responsible to a significant thickening of the shaft, however, in this case only at the microlevel (Figure 10.33).

### 10.4.3.8 Tumorous Bone Growth within Compact Bone of the Shafts of Long Bones

At the microlevel, the changes due to tumorous diseases, particularly to metastasizing cancer (Figure 10.34) are sometimes similar to those observed in nonspecific and specific infectious diseases (cf. Figure 10.30). However, osteoclastic changes in long bones caused by cancer metastases are frequently dominated by the large number of Howship's lacunae (Figure 10.35, a), which, unfortunately, might sometimes also be observed in aggressive inflammatory diseases. Therefore, further diagnostic criteria would be very useful, such as the detection of extracellular bone matrix proteins (Schultz et al. 2007).

### 10.4.3.9 Pseudopathology

Finally, it should be mentioned that, frequently, diagenetic changes or even custodial activities might simulate the vestiges of diseases (Schultz 1986, 1997b, 2001). This is referred to as pseudopathology and is demonstrated by the following two case examples.

In Figure 10.36 we see a thin-ground section of a sample taken from the skull vault of an early medieval Avar from Burgenland (Austria). The macroscopic diagnosis was venereal syphilis. However, the light microscopic investigation documented postmortem

---

* Male, 22–24 years old. Changes due to tuberculosis: 7th–10th thoracic vertebrae: characteristic tuberculous lesions, pronounced changes in the 8th thoracic vertebra (vertebral body with the exception of the superior plate, eaten away by a lytic process: tuberculous abscess caused marked kyphotic angulation); internal surfaces of the vertebral ends of the 4th–9th right and left ribs covered by bony appositions (left 7th rib with cavity in the region of the collum); right coxae, close to rim of acetabulum: cavity; right femur (left not present) slight periosteal reaction.

**Figure 10.30** Arzhan (Russia: Siberia), Kurgan 2, Burial 20, skeleton 1, young adult male, Scythian Period (700 BC). Right femur. Tuberculosis: a = large resorption hole (osteoclastic) in the region of the endosteal surface of the bone shaft. Thin-ground section (70 μm) viewed in polarized transmission light using hilfsobject red 1st order (quartz) as compensator. Magnification 25×.

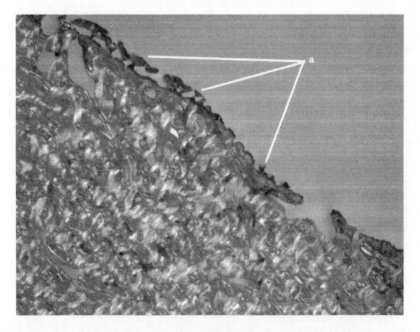

**Figure 10.31** Arzhan (Russia: Siberia), Kurgan 2, Burial 20, skeleton 1, young adult male, Scythian Period (700 BC). Right femur. Tuberculosis: a = newly built bone formation (osteoblastic) on the periosteal surface of the bone shaft. Thin-ground section (70 μm) viewed in polarized transmission light using hilfsobject red 1st order (quartz) as compensator. Magnification 25×.

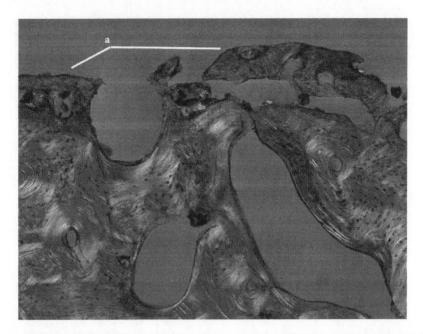

**Figure 10.32 (See color insert.)** Arzhan (Russia: Siberia), Kurgan 2, Burial 20, skeleton 1, young adult male, Scythian Period (700 BC). Right femur. Tuberculosis: a = newly built bone formation (osteoblastic) on the periosteal surface of the bone shaft. Thin-ground section (70 μm) viewed in polarized transmission light using hilfsobject red 1st order (quartz) as compensator. Magnification 100×.

**Figure 10.33 (See color insert.)** Arzhan (Russia: Siberia), Kurgan 2, Burial 20, skeleton 1, young adult male, Scythian Period (700 BC). Right femur. Tuberculosis: newly built bone formation on the periosteal surface of the bone shaft, which shows in parts the morphology of agate bone. The external agate bone structures seem, at first sight, to be similar to small polsters or polster-like formations. Thin-ground section (70 μm) viewed in polarized transmission light using hilfsobject red 1st order (quartz) as compensator. Magnification 25×.

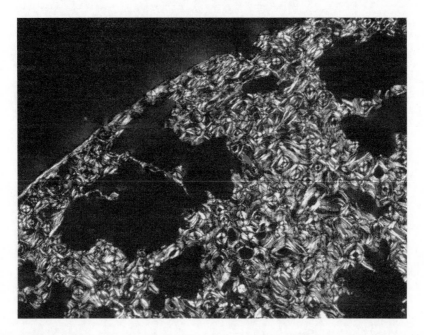

**Figure 10.34** Arzhan (Russia: Siberia), Kurgan 2, Burial 5, skeleton 1, young mature male (King of Arzhan), Scythian Period (700 BC). Right femur. Osteoclastic resorption in the external region of the compact bone substance due to carcinoma of the prostate. Thin-ground section (70 µm) viewed in polarized transmission light. Magnification 25×.

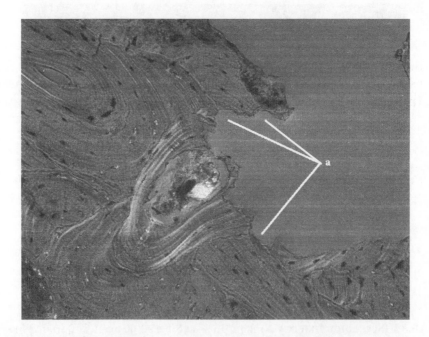

**Figure 10.35 (See color insert.)** Sayala (Egyptian Nubia), Burial K-68/2, 35- to 45-year-old female, Coptic Period (400–600 AD). Left clavicle. Metastasizing cancer: a = Howship's lacunae at the rim of a large resorption hole within the originally compact bone substance. Thin-ground section (50 µm) viewed in polarized transmission light using hilfsobject red 1st order (quartz) as compensator. Magnification 200×.

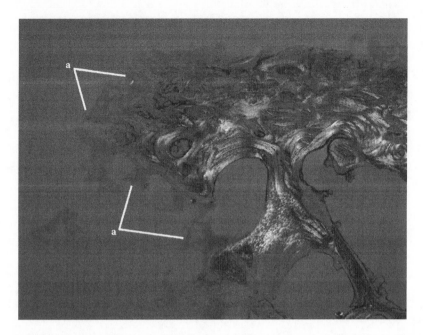

**Figure 10.36 (See color insert.)** Zwölfaxing (Austria), Burial 34, old adult female, Avarian Period (680–830 AD). Left frontal bone. Pseudopathology, a = glue (custodial activity), no pathologically changed bone matrix. Thin-ground section (50 μm) viewed in polarized transmission light using hilfsobject red 1st order (quartz) as compensator. Magnification 25×.

destruction due to diagenesis and some custodial activities: the brittle bone was covered with glue to protect the poorly preserved external surface (Figure 10.36, a).

The second case is also a thin-ground section of a sample taken from the skull vault of an Assyrian queen from Nimrud/Kalhu, Iraq (ca. 700–612 BC). Macroscopically, the layer (Figure 10.37, a) on the external surface of the skull vault (Figure 10.37, b) was diagnosed as the product of an inflammatory process of the scalp. However, the light microscopic examination revealed that the appositional structures were remnants of the periosteum and the scalp (Figure 10.37, c; green color due to copper staining) and fragments of textile (Figure 10.37, a), probably a burial cloth or a burial veil.

## 10.5 Final Perspectives

As a division of paleopathology, paleohistopathology has had an impact in this relatively new science by providing a number of different techniques to aid in establishing reliable disease diagnoses. However, the pathological conditions in archaeological skeletal remains are not directly comparable with the findings in recent bone samples at the microlevel because of the lack of soft tissues and cells. Thus, paleopathologists have to apply their own nomenclature to describe and characterize pathological conditions in archaeological skeletal remains also at the microlevel. To reach this goal, it will be necessary to increase the use of microscopic research in paleopathology and to develop new techniques to obtain more reliable data. Therefore, the methods and techniques of a paleohistopathological investigation of archaeological skeletal remains should be part of the arsenal of every paleopathologist. This means that if paleopathologists seek to obtain a reliable diagnosis and the

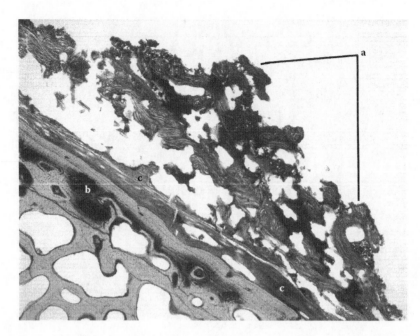

**Figure 10.37 (See color insert.)** Nimrud, NW-Palace (Iraq), Ind.-NIM-III, young adult female (queen?), Late Assyrian Period (700–612 BC). Fragment of Parietal bone. Pseudopathology, a = remains of textile resembling the product of an inflammatory process; b = external skull surface with *Lamina externa*; c = mummified remnants of scalp and periosteum. The green color is due to postmortem (diagenetic) staining by copper ions. Thin-ground section (70 μm) viewed in plain transmission light. Magnification 25×.

applied techniques, such as macroscopy, radiology, and endoscopy, cannot provide results that allow establishment of a scientifically acceptable diagnosis, microscopic analysis is the method of choice. There is no other possibility. However, if a researcher is convinced that a specific archaeological bone should indeed not be cut—perhaps for religious or other ideologically reasons—then such a researcher would be well advised to differentiate not between diseases but to report on stress markers (e.g., not syphilis, but periostitis).

What is the impact of microscopic research on paleopathology? This question is easily and quickly answered. Using light microscopic techniques, it is possible to establish general and differential diagnoses from dry bone samples. However, it should be kept in mind that, in paleohistopathology, the term *diagnoses* is sometimes not in accordance with this same term used in clinical medicine. Nevertheless, these diagnoses describe relatively precisely what had happened within the bone structure during the lifetime of the individual, although soft tissues and cells, which are the most important features in recent pathology, are not present. Thus, in combination with the results of the macroscopic, radiologic, and endoscopic examination, the findings of the light microscopic investigation, as a rule, allow reliable disease diagnoses. Only, if reliable diagnoses are available, can the etiology and epidemiology of ancient diseases be analyzed.

## 10.6  Acknowledgments

The author thanks Michael Brandt and Ingrid Hettwer-Steeger (Department of Anatomy, University Medical School of Göttingen, Germany) for preparing the thin-ground sections, and Cyrilla Maelicke (Göttingen, Germany) for reading the English text. Furthermore, for bone samples, the author wishes to thank Dr. Önder Bilgi (Istanbul, Turkey), Dr. Bernd Herrmann (Göttingen, Germany), Dr. Clark S. Larsen (Columbus, Ohio), Dr. Charles F. Merbs (Tempe, Arizona), Dr. Charlotte Roberts (Durham, England), Dr. Peter Schröter (München, Germany), Dr. Johann Szilvássy and Dr. Maria Teschler-Nicola (Wien, Austria), Dr. Rose Tyson (San Diego, USA), and Dr. Phillip L. Walker (Santa Barbara, California).

# References

Adler C-P (1998) Knochenkrankheiten—Diagnostik makroskopischer, histologischer und radiologische Strukturveränderungen des Skeletts. 2nd ed. Berlin: Springer-Verlag.

Adler C-P (2005) Knochenkrankheiten—Diagnostik makroskopischer, histologischer und radiologische Strukturveränderungen des Skeletts. 3rd ed. Berlin: Springer-Verlag.

Ascenzi A (1969) Microscopy and prehistoric bone. In: Brothwell DR, Higgs E, editors. Science in archaeology, London: Thames and Hudson, 526–538.

Ascenzi A (1986) Microscopy and ultramicroscopy in palaeopathology. In: Herrmann B, editor. Innovative trends in der prähistorischen anthropologie—Innovative trends in prehistoric anthropology. Mitt Berliner Ges Anthropol Ethnol Urgesch 7:531–536.

Ascenzi A, Silvestrini G (1984) Bone-boring marine microorganisms: An experimental investigation. J Human Evol 13:531–536.

Bell LS (1990) Palaeopathology and diagenesis: an SEM evaluation of structural changes using backscattered electron imaging. J Archaeol Sci 17:85–102.

Bell LS, Skinnere MF, Jones SJ (1996) The speed of post mortem change to the human skeleton and its taphonomic significance. Forensic Sci Int 82:129–140.

Bianco P, Ascenzi A (1993) Palaeohistology on human remains: a critical evaluation and an example of its use. In: Grupe G, Garland AN, editors. Histology of ancient human bone: Methods and diagnosis. Berlin: Springer Verlag, 157–170.

Blondiaux J, Boursier F, Dauchy P, Hanni C, Maure I, Soufflet L (1994) Deux tréponématoses osseuses antérieures a 1543. Etude anatomo-pathologique, élémentaire, sérologique et moléculaire (PCR). In: Dutour O, Palfí Gy, Berato J, Brun J-P, editors. L'origine de la syphilis en Europe. Avant ou après 1493? Toulon: Centre Archeologique du Var, 215–225.

Brothwell DR, Sandison AT, Gray PHK (1969) Human biological observations on a Guanche mummy with anthracosis. Am J Phys Anthropol 30:333–347.

Caropreso S, Bondioli L, Capannolo D, Cerroni L, Macchiarelli R, Condò SG (2000) Thin sections for hard tissue histology: A new procedure. J Microsc 199:244–247.

Fornaciari G (1999) Renaissance mummies in Italy. Medicina nei secoli 11:85–105.

Frost HM (1958) Preparation of thin undecalcified bone sections by rapid manual method. Stain Technol 33:273–276.

Garland AN (1993) An introduction to the histology of exhumed mineralized tissue. In: Grupe G, Garland A, editors. Histology of ancient bone: Methods and diagnosis. Berlin: Springer-Verlag, pp. 1–16.

Großkopf B (1989) Incremental lines in prehistoric cremated teeth: A technical note. Z Morphol Anthropol 77:309–311.

Hackett CJ (1976) Diagnostic criteria of syphilis, yaws and treponarid (treponematoses) and some other diseases in dry bones. Sitzungsberichte der Heidelberger Akademie der Wissenschaften 4:1–124.

Hackett CJ (1981) Microscopical focal destruction (tunnels) in exhumed human bones. Med Sci Law 21:234–265.

Hagens von G (1979) Impregnation of soft biological specimens with thermostetting resins and elastomers. Anat Rec 194:247–255.

Harsányi L (1993) Differential diagnosis of human and animal bone. In: Grupe G, Garland AN, editors. Histology of ancient human bone: Methods and diagnosis. Berlin: Springer Verlag, 79–94.

Herrmann B (1977) On histological investigation of cremated human remains. J Hum Evol 6:101–103.

Hershkovitz I, Rothschild BM, Wish-Baratz S, Rothschild C (1994) Natural variation and differential diagnosis of skeletal changes in bejel (endemic syphilis). In: Dutour O, Palfí Gy, Berato J, Brun J-P, editors. L'origine de la syphilis en Europe. Avant ou après 1493 Toulon: Centre Archeologique du Var, 81–87.

Hunnius v. TE, Roberts CA, Boylston A, Saunders SR (2006) Histological identification of syphilis in pre-Columbian England. Am J Phys Anthropol 129:559–566.

Jaffe HL (1972) Metabolic, degenerative, and inflammatory diseases of bones and joints. München: Urban & Schwarzenberg.

Jans MME, Nielsen-Marsh CM, Smith CI, Collins MJ, Kars H (2004) Characterisation of microbial attack on archaeological bone. J Archaeolog Sci 31:87–95.

Kerley ER, Ubelaker DH (1978) Revisions in the microscopic method of estimation age at death in human cortical bone. Am J Phys Anthropol 49:545–546.

Klepinger LL (1983) Differential diagnosis in paleopathology and the concept of disease evolution. Med Anthropol 7:73–77.

Kramar C, Baud CA, Largier R (1983) Presumed calcified Leiomyoma of the uterus. Arch Pathol Lab Med 107:91–93.

Kozak AD (2005) (The Populations of Kiev from the 10th–13th century AD with special interest to paleopathology)—Naselenia Kieva X-XIII ST. Za danimi paleopatologij (in Ukranian). PhD dissertation, Ukranian Academy of Science, Institute of Archaeology, Kiev.

Kuhn G, Schultz M, Müller R, Rühli FJ (2007) Diagnostic value of micro-CT in comparison with histology in the qualitative assessment of historical human postcranial bone pathologies. Homo–J Comp Hum Biol 58:97–115.

Lataster LMA, van Mameren H, Terwindt E (1992) Plastic embedding procedure for 15 μm sections of large undecalcified tissue blocks. Anat Rec 233:651–546.

Lauche A (1939) Die unspezifischen Entzündungen der Knochen. In: Lubarsch O, Henke F, Rössle R, editors: Handbuch der speziellen pathologischen Anatomie und Histologie IX, 4. Berlin: Verlag Julius Springer, 1–80.

Maat GJR, van den Bos RPM, Aarents MJ (2001) Manual preparation of ground sections for the microscopy of natural bone tissue: Update and modification of Frost's "rapid manual method." Int J Osteoarchaeol 11:366–374.

Maat GJR, van den Bos RPM, Aarents MJ (2006) Manual for the preparation of ground sections for the microscopy of bone tissue. Leiden: Barge's Anthropologica 7:1–18.

Maggiano C, Dupras T, Schultz M, Biggerstaff J (2006) Spectral and photobleaching analysis using confocal laser scanning microscopy: A comparison of modern and archaeological bone fluorescence. Mol Cell Probe 20:154–62.

Michaelis L (1930) Vergleichende mikroskopische Untersuchungen an rezenten, historischen und fossilen menschlichen Knochen. Veröffentlichungen zur Kriegs- und Konstitutionspathologie 6:1–92.

Mißbach-Güntner J, Dullin C, Alves F, Schultz M (2010) CT-Untersuchungen zur Analyse pathologisch bedeutsamer Alterationen der Knochenbinnenstruktur. In: Fansa M, Jopp E, Püschel K, editors. Das Kind aus der Esterweger Dose—Dokumentation einer außergewöhnlichen Skelett-Moorleiche. Oldenburg: Isensee-Verlag, 39–44.

Moodie RL (1923) Paleopathology: An introduction to the study of ancient evidences of diseases. Urbana, IL: University of Illinois Press.

Moodie RL (1928) The histological nature of ossified tendons found in dinosaurs. Am Museum Novitates 311:1–15.

Nováček J, Scheelen K, Drozdová E, Schultz M (2008) Ergebnisse der anthropologischen und paläopathologischen Untersuchungen an den Skelettresten der Leichenbrände vom Fundort Haiger "Kalteiche." In: Verse F, editor. Archäologie auf Waldeshöhen. Eisenzeit, Mittelalter und Neuzeit auf der "Kalteiche" bei Haiger, Lahn-Dill-Kreis. Münsterische Beitgräge zur ur- und frühgeschichtlichen Archäologie, Vol. 4, Jockenhövel A, editor. Rahden/Westfalen: Verlag Marie Leidorf, 137–163.

Ortner DJ (2003) Infectious diseases: Treponematosis and other bacterial infectious diseases. In: Ortner DJ, editor. Identification of pathological conditions in human skeletal remains. Amsterdam: Academic Press/Elsevier Science, 273–323.

Ortner DJ, Putschar WGJ (1981) Identification of pathological conditions in human skeletal remains. Smithsonian Contributions to Anthropology 28. Washington, DC: Smithsonian Institution Press.

Pales L (1930) Paléopathologie et pathologie comparative. Paris: Masson et Cie.

Putschar WGJ (1966) Problems in the pathology and palaeopathology of bone. In: Jarcho S, editor. Human palaeopathology. New Haven, CT: Yale University Press, 57–65.

Resnick D, Niwayama G (1981) Diagnosis of bone and joint disorders, Vol. I–III. Philadelphia: WB Saunders Company.

Reyman TA (1977) Schistosomal cirrhosis in an Egyptian mummy. Yrbk Phys Anthropol 20:356–358.

Reyman TA, Barraco RA, Cockburn TA (1976) Histopathological examination of an Egyptian mummy. Bull New York Acad Med 52:506–516.

Rose JC (2005) Defective enamel histology of prehistoric teeth from Illinois. Am J Phys Anthropol 46:439–446.

Rühli FJ, Kuhn G, Müller R, Schultz M (2007) Diagnostic value of micro-CT in comparison with histology in the qualitative assessment of historical human skull bone pathologies. Am J Phys Anthropol 133:1099–1111.

Ruffer MA (1910a) Remarks on the histology and pathological anatomy of Egyptian mummies. Cairo Sci J 4:1–12.

Ruffer MA (1910b) Note on the presence of "Bilharzia haematobia" in Egyptian mummies of the Twentieth Dynasty (1250-100 B.C.). Brit Med J 1:16–18.

Ruffer MA (1911a) Histological studies on Egyptian mummies. Mem Inst Égypt 6, Fasc. 3, iii, 39:11–54.

Ruffer MA (1911b) On arterial lesions found in Egyptian mummies (1580 B.C–525 A.D). J Pathol Bact 15:453–461.

Ruffer MA, Smith GE (1910) Pott'sche Krankheit an einer ägyptischen Mumie aus der Zeit der 21. Dynastie (um 1000 v. Chr.). In: Sudhoff K, Sticker M, editors. Zur historischen Biologie der Krankheitserreger 3. Giessen, 9–16.

Sandison AT (1955a) Reconstitution of dried-up tissue specimens for histological examination. J Clinic Pathol 19:522–523.

Sandison AT (1955b) The histological examination of mummified material. Stain Technol 30:277–283.

Sandison AT (1957) Preparation of large histological sections of mummified tissues. Nature 179:1309.

Sandison AT (1959) Persistence of sudanophilic lipid in sections of mummified tissues. Nature 183:196.

Sandison AT (1967a) Diseases of the skin. In: Sandison AT, Brothwell DR, editors. Diseases in antiquity. Springfield, IL: Charles C Thomas Publisher, 449–456.

Sandison AT (1967b) Degenerative vascular disease. In: Sandison AT, Brothwell DR, editors. Diseases in antiquity. Springfield, IL: Charles C Thomas Publisher, 474–488.

Sandison AT (1970) The study of mummified and dried human tissues. In: Brothwell DR, Higgs E, editors. Science in Archaeology. London: Thames & Hudson, 490–502.

Sandison AT (1980) Diseases in ancient Egypt. In: Cockburn TA, Cockburn E, editors. Mummies, disease, and ancient cultures. Cambridge: Cambridge University Press, 29–44.

Schaffer JR (1889) Über den feineren Bau fossiler Knochen. Sitzungsberichte der Kaiserlichen Akademie der Wissenschaften Wien, Mathematisch-Naturwissenschaftliche Klasse 3-7:319–382.

Schultz M (1982) Krankheit und Umwelt des vor- und frühgeschichtlichen Menschen. In: Wendt H, Loacker N, editors. Kindlers Enzyklopädie der Mensch 2. Zürich: Kindler Verlag, 259–312.

Schultz M (1986) Die mikroskopische Untersuchung prähistorischer Skeletfunde. Anwendung und Aussagemöglichkeiten der differentialdiagnostischen Untersuchung in der Paläopathologie. Archäologie und Museum 6. Liestal: Kanton Baselland.

Schultz M (1988) Paläopathologische Diagnostik. In: Knußmann R, editor. Anthropologie. Handbuch der vergleichenden Biologie des Menschen I, 1. Stuttgart: G. Fischer, pp. 480–496.

Schultz M (1993a) Spuren unspezifischer Entzündungen an prähistorischen und historischen Schädeln. Ein Beitrag zur Paläopathologie. Vestiges of nonspecific inflammations in pre-historic and historic skull. A contribution to palaeopathology. In: Kaufmann B, editor. Anthropologische Beiträge 4 A and 4 B. Aesch/Basel: Anthropologisches Forschungsinstitut Aesch and Anthropologische Gesellschaft Basel.

Schultz M (1993b) Initial stages of systemic bone disease. In: Gruppe G, Garland AN, editors. Histology of ancient human bone: Methods and diagnosis. Berlin: Springer Verlag, 185–203.

Schultz M (1994) Comparative histopathology of syphilitic lesions in prehistoric and historic human bones. In: Dutour O, Palfí Gy, Berato J, Brun J-P, editor. L'origine de la syphilis en Europe. Avant ou après 1493? Toulon: Centre Archeologique du Var, 63–67.

Schultz M (1997a) Microscopic structure of bone. In: Haglund WD, Sorg MH, editors. Forensic taphonomy. The postmortem fate of human remains. Boca Raton, FL: CRC Press, 187–199.

Schultz M (1997b) Microscopic investigation of excavated skeletal remains: A contribution to paleopathology and forensic medicine. In: Haglund WD, Sorg MH, editors. Forensic taphonomy. The postmortem fate of human remains. Boca Raton, FL: CRC Press, 201–222.

Schultz M (1999) Microscopic investigation in fossil hominoidea: a clue to taxonomy, functional anatomy, and the history of diseases. Anat Rec 257:225–232.

Schultz M (2001) Paleohistopathology of bone: A new approach to the study of ancient diseases. Yrbk Phys Anthropol 44:106–147.

Schultz M (2003) Light microscopic analysis in skeletal paleopathology. In: Ortner DJ, editor. Identification of pathological conditions in human skeletal remains. Amsterdam: Academic Press/Elsevier Science, 73–108.

Schultz M (2006) Results of the anatomical-paleopathological investigations on the Neanderthal skeleton from the Kleine Feldhofer Grotte (1856) including the new discoveries from 1997/2000. In: Kunow J, editor. Rheinische Ausgrabungen. Philipp von Zabern Verlag, Mainz, 277–318.

Schultz M (in press). Short history of paleohistology. In: Buikstra JE, Roberts CA, Schreiner SM, editors. The history of palaeopathology: Pioneers and prospects. New York: Oxford University Press.

Schultz M, Brandt M (1987) Neue Methoden zur Einbettung von Knochengewebe und zur Herstellung von Knochendünnschliffen, cf. In: Schultz M. 1988: Methoden der Licht- und Elektronenmikroskopie. In: Knußmann R, editor. Anthropologie. Handbuch der vergleichenden Biologie des Menschen I, 1. Stuttgart: G. Fischer, 698–730.

Schultz M, Drommer R (1983) Möglichkeiten der Präparateherstellung aus dem Gesichtsschädelbereich für die makroskopische und mikroskopische Untersuchung unter Verwendung neuer Kunststofftechniken. In: Hoppe WG, editor. Fortschritte der Kiefer- und Gesichts-Chirurgie 28. Experimentelle Mund-Kiefer-Gesichts-Chirurgie. Mikrochirurgische Eingriffe. Stuttgart: G. Thieme, 95–97.

Schultz M, Gessler-Löhr B (1992) Evidence of parasitosis in the mummy of a young Egyptian boy from the Graeco-Roman period. In: Organismo Autónomo de Museos y Centros, Cabildo de Tenerife, editor. Programa y Resumenes. Santa Cruz de Tenerife: Museo Arqueológico y Etnografico de Tenerife, 98.

Schultz M, Brandt M 1987, cf. Schultz 1988a. Methoden der Licht- und Elektronenmikroskopie. In: Knußmann R (ed): Anthropologie. Handbuch der vergleichenden Biologie des Menschen I, 1. Stuttgart: G. Fischer, 698–730.

Schultz M, Koel K, Jopp E, Püschel K, Gresky J (2010) Ergebnisse der paläopathologischen Untersuchung an dem Moorleichenskelett Esterweger Dose. In: Fansa M, Jopp E, Püschel K, editors. Das Kind aus der Esterweger Dose – Dokumentation einer außergewöhnlichen Skelett-Moorleiche. Oldenburg: Isensee-Verlag, 75–91.

Schultz M, Parzinger H, Posdnjakov DV, Chikisheva TA, Schmidt-Schultz TH (2007) Oldest known case of metastasizing prostate carcinoma diagnosed in the skeleton of a 2,700-year-old Scythian king from Arzhan (Siberia, Russia). Int J Cancer: 121: 2591–2595.

Schultz M, Roberts CA (2002) Diagnosis of leprosy in skeletons from an English later medieval hospital using histological analysis. In: Roberts CA, Lewis ME, Manchester K, editors. The past and the present of leprosy—Archaeological, historical, palaeopathological and clinical approaches. BAR International Series. Oxford: Hadrian Books, 89–104.

Schultz M, Teschler-Nicola M (1987) Krankhafte Veränderungen an den Skelettfunden aus dem Karner der St.Martinskirche in Klosterneuburg, Niederösterreich. III. Entzündliche Veränderungen an den langen Röhrenknochen. Ann Naturhist Mus Wien 89:252–296.

Smith CI, Craig OE, Prigodich RV, Nielsen-Marsh CM, Jans MME, Vermeer C, Collins MJ (2005) Diagenesis and survival of osteocalcin in archaeological bone. J Archaeol Sci 32:105–113.

Steinbock R. 1976. Paleopathological diagnosis and interpretation. Springfield, IL: CC Thomas.

Stout SD (1978) Histological structure and its preservation in ancient bone. Curr Anthropol 19:601–603.

Stout SD, Paine RR (1992) Histological age estimation using rib and clavicle. Am J Phys Anthropol 87:111–115.

Stout S, Paine RR (1994) Bone remodeling rates: A test on an algorithm for estimating missing osteons. Am J Phys Anthropol 93:123–129.

Stout S, Lueck R (1995) Bone remodeling rates and skeletal maturation in three archaeological skeletal populations. Am J Phys Anthropol 98:161–171.

Stout SD, Porro MA, Perotti B (1996) Brief communication: A test and correction of the clavicle method of Stout and Paine for histological age estimation of skeletal remains. Am J Phys Anthropol 100:139–142.

Suzuki T (1984) Palaeopathological and palaeoepidemiological study of osseous syphilis in skulls of the Edo Period. Tokyo: The University Museum/The University of Tokyo Press, Bulletin 23.

Tapp E (1979) Disease in the Manchester mummies. In: Davis AR, editor. Manchester Museum mummy project—Multidisciplinary research on ancient Egyptian mummified remains. Manchester: Manchester University Press, 95–102.

Tapp E (1998) The histological examination of an ovarian tumor. In: Harer WB, Taylor JH, editors. Irty Senu: Granville's Egyptian female mummy: The autopsies of 1824 and 1994. London: British Museum Press.

Teschler-Nicola M (2006) Taphonomic aspects of the human remains from the Mladeč Caves. In: Teschler-Nicola M, editor. Early modern humans at the Moravian Gate—The Mladeč Caves and their remains. Wien: Springer, 75–98.

Van der Merwe AE, Maat GJR, Steyn M (2010) Ossified haematomas and infectious bone changes on the anterior tibia: Histomorphological features as an aid for accurate diagnosis. Int J Osteoarchaeol 20:227–239.

Weber M (1927) Schliffe von mazerierten Röhrenknochen und ihre Bedeutung für die Unterscheidung der Syphilis und Osteomyelitis von der Osteodystrophia fibrosa sowie für die Untersuchung fraglich syphilitischer, prähistorischer Knochen. Beiträge zur pathologischen Anatomie und allgemeinen Pathologie 78:441–511.

Weidenreich F (1930) Das Knochengewebe. In: Möllendorf W von, editor. Handbuch der mikroskopischen Anatomie des Menschen, Vol. II Die Gewebe, 2nd Part Stützgewebe, Knochengewebe, Skeletsystem. Berlin: Verlag Julius Springer, 391–520.

Weston DA (2009) Brief Communication: Paleopathological analysis of pathology museum specimens: can periosteal reaction microstructure explain lesion etiology? Am J Phys Anthropol 140:186–193.

Williams HU (1927) Gross and microscopic anatomy of two Peruvian mummies. Arch Path Lab Med 4:26–33.

Witzel C, Kierdorf U, Schultz M, Kierdorf H (2008) Interpreting impairment of secretory ameloblast function in human teeth as revealed by hypoplasia and related microstructural defects of dental enamel. Am J Phys Anthropol 136:400–414.

Zimmerman MR, Kelley MA (1982) Atlas of human paleopathology. New York: Praeger Publishers.

Zimmerman MR, Tedford RH (1976) Histologic structures preserved for 21,300 years. Science 194:183–184.

# Histological Analyses of Human Bone from Archaeological Contexts

# 11

SUSAN PFEIFFER
DEBORRAH PINTO

## Contents

This chapter will focus on the histological study of bone tissue of archaeological origin, a topic that inevitably extends into the world of palaeoanthropology. Histological research of archaeologically derived bone tissue is part of a methodological continuum that includes various tissues other than bone (such as teeth and desiccated soft tissue) and applications that go beyond but are complementary to histomorphological characterization (such as microradiography and micro-computed tomography). The focus here will be on transmitted light microscopy as applied to bone. Given its long history and its relatively simple laboratory requirements, this approach holds considerable promise to become a normal part of analytical protocols. Guides regarding the methods of sample preparation for transmitted light microscopy are readily available (Robling and Stout 2008; Schultz 1997a, 1997b; Turner-Walker and Mays 2008; Ubelaker 1989). There is considerable variation in methodological approaches, so a newcomer to this field should read broadly. Nomenclature and symbols for many histomorphological structures are standardized and researchers are urged to follow established terminology for histomorphometry whenever possible (cf. Parfitt et al. 1987).

Bioarchaeology is the study of human remains from archaeological sites, understood and interpreted by considering the context from which they derive (Larsen 1997; Roberts 2009). In this context, bone histology can provide useful information. It can indicate whether small tissue fragments are human, indicate the age of a human at time of death, and sometimes provide information about the conditions compromising the person's health prior to death. A relatively new use for histological analysis is to assess bone sample quality, preliminary to ancient DNA (aDNA) work (Bell et al. 2008; Guarino et al. 2006; Roberts 2009). The preservation of histological structures is seen as a strong indicator of probable success in extracting aDNA from bone tissue. There is also interest in differentiating structures within human cortical bone tissue in the context of stable isotope analyses (Bell et al. 2001). These examples illustrate why all osteological education, even short courses, should include some introduction to the histomorphology (microscopic anatomy) of normal cortical and cancellous human bone.

Histological study of archaeologically derived material can contribute to research questions arising in forensic and biomedical fields. Archaeological sites, including historic cemeteries, can provide access to large numbers of skeletons, a higher proportion of nonadult skeletons than are found in modern settings, and instances of bone that has been modified by diseases that were untreated or were treated in inefficacious ways. There are challenges in applying histological methods to such samples, however. Even if there is cemetery information, we still have incomplete knowledge of each person in life. There can also be a range of tissue preservation problems, collectively known as diagenesis, which are the structural changes to tissues in the postburial environment (Pfeiffer 2000; Pfeiffer and Varney 2000; Stout 1978; Turner-Walker and Mays 2008). Whereas earlier publications tended to describe only those preparations that showed excellent bone preservation and failed to mention those preparations that yielded poor results, more recent literature explores the postmortem changes associated with physical and bacterial destruction. The acknowledgment and systematic exploration of methodological problems arising from diagenesis as a form of taphonomy are welcome (Grupe and Dreses-Werringloer 1993; Haglund and Sorg 1997; Jackes et al. 2001; Turner-Walker and Mays 2008). A dry, physically protected environment is best for structural preservation, whether the ambient temperature is cold or hot. Organically active environments lead to the most variable patterns of preservation.

The histological study of bone tissue is inevitably destructive, although the extent of alteration to a specimen may be rather slight, like the removal of less than a centimeter of bone from an already broken rib or the removal of a small core from an intact long bone. Guidelines for sampling have been developed by various institutions and research groups. Most current and future work in archaeologically derived bone histology will likely occur in contexts when human remains are being disinterred briefly (e.g., historic cemeteries) or when descendants have authorized specific research activities. A basic principle for all projects is found in the initial statement of a recently published set of guidelines: "The scientific question being addressed should be important enough to justify invasive sampling of hominid remains and should not be answerable by any other means" (Hublin et al. 2008:756–757).

Early studies of bone histology were exploratory, establishing the potential for this approach (Day and Molleson 1973; Dubois 1937; Graf 1949). Most histological research has been undertaken to answer questions in four categories, these being the differentiation of human from nonhuman, the estimation of age at death, the reconstruction of habitual activities in life, and the diagnosis of pathological conditions.

## 11.2    Areas of Application

### 11.2.1    Is the Bone Tissue from Homo Sapiens?

There is a substantial literature on the distinctions between adult human cortical bone and that of other species (Enlow and Brown 1956, 1957, 1958; Foote 1916). Basic information is readily found in texts (Byers 2008; Ubelaker 1989), but questions remain when the bone tissue is cancellous or diploic in structure, or when the tissue is from an infant or juvenile of various mammalian species (see also Mulhern and Ubelaker in this volume). The most commonly identified types of bone tissue are woven bone ("bundle bone"), primary bone that includes two types (plexiform bone, and primary lamellar bone with primary osteons), and secondary bone. Secondary bone includes structures known as secondary osteons (also called Haversian systems), as well as interstitial and circumferential lamellar bone. Nonhuman secondary osteons tend to be less circular, more regular in size within a cortical sample, and substantially smaller than those of humans, although with exceptions relating to body size (Hillier and Bell 2007). Some sources will assert that plexiform bone is not found in humans, yet there is lack of clarity regarding whether the bone tissue seen in human infants includes the plexiform type (Pfeiffer 2006). The human infant bone structures are probably primary woven bone or lamellar bone rather than plexiform, but diagenesis is especially common in the porous, small, partially mineralized bones of infants, so clarity is sometimes compromised. Nevertheless, through the histological study of autopsy specimens, the processes of bone modeling and remodeling are becoming more clearly understood (Streeter 2005; Streeter and Stout 2003).

Encouraging developments in this field are coming from the combined assessment of shape and size of structures. For example, although study samples remain small, secondary osteons in human juveniles appear to be of "adult size" from the first appearance (Pfeiffer 2006). Hence, the average area of human secondary structures at all ages appear to be larger than the average area of secondary osteons in deer, dog, or pig (Hillier and Bell 2007; Morris 2007); however, further research is necessary to address variations within and across species.

## 11.2.2    Age at Death

The methods of estimating adult age at death from cortical bone tissue are addressed elsewhere in this volume. The methods have been developed from known-age samples derived from medical school and autopsy dissections and forensic contexts, although research using historic cemetery samples has allowed researchers to refine their approaches (Cho et al. 2002). Archaeological samples can provide more genetic diversity and a different health regimen in life, as compared to modern samples. Crowder, examining femoral and rib samples from adult skeletons from Christ Church, Spitalfields, London, dating to the 18th–19th century (Molleson and Cox 1993), demonstrated that the most accurate histological age determination methods show the same bias as the results of aging methods based on gross morphology. There is a tendency for the youngest adults to be overaged and the oldest adults to be underaged. The error for the best histological methods is not greater than that associated with more established methods, like those based on pubic symphyses and sternal rib ends (Crowder 2005; Crowder and Pfeiffer 2010).

During the decades since Kerley's publications stimulated interest in histological methods (Kerley 1965, 1969, 1970; Kerley and Ubelaker 1978), there have been some attempts to use histological age estimates as a basis for palaeodemography of archaeologically derived cemeteries (cf. Pfeiffer 1980). However, researchers face a number of challenges. From burial environments that are frequently moist and organically active comes bone tissue that has been diagenetically altered, leading to relatively low research yields relative to the effort expended (Figure 11.1). The necessary permission for destructive testing must be based on a strong promise of definitive results and this is difficult to assess a priori. In addition, these same decades have marked ongoing dialogue about the relative value

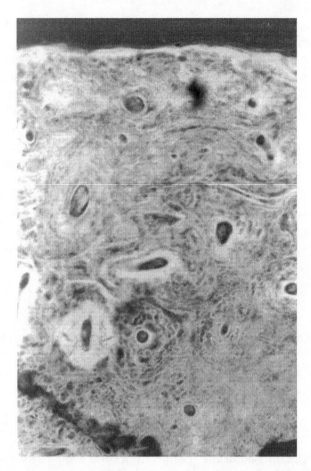

**Figure 11.1** A microradiograph of femoral cortex from an adult male whose body was buried in moist, sandy soil in a temperate climate from AD 1813 to 1987. The original secondary osteons and other structures have been greatly altered, probably through microbial activity. Elemental analysis shows a normal calcium to phosphorous ratio, but there is also a peak in silicon. The Canadian site where 28 soldiers were buried showed a wide array of tissue preservation patterns within a small area. (Sample from which the image was taken from Pfeiffer abd Varney 2000.)

of palaeodemographic reconstructions, as compared to other forms of bioarchaeological analyses (Bocquet-Appel and Masset 1982; Hoppa and Vaupel 2002; Wood et al. 1992). As histological age estimation methods become more precise and accurate, as diagenesis becomes more manageable and as interest in palaeodemography is renewed, the situation may change.

Histological methods may be most helpful when only an isolated bone or a unique burial is discovered and there is substantial interest in estimating age at death. Histomorphometric analyses were used to produce age estimates of Neanderthals from Shanidar (Thompson and Trinkaus 1981; Trinkaus and Thompson 1987) demonstrating some of the biologically oldest Neanderthals recovered. Streeter and colleagues (2001) were able to provide an age estimate for a Middle Pleistocene tibia from Boxgrove (UK) from a core of cortical bone. The estimate produced by microscopic techniques was higher than the macroscopic ones and showed that the Boxgrove1 individual was most likely in his or her fourth or fifth decade of life. Pfeiffer and Zehr (1996) estimated age at death around the fifth decade from a flake of bone that spalled off a broken surface of the humerus shaft from Border Cave (southern Africa, putatively late Pleistocene). Some studies have provided age estimates for archaeological samples in order to test the accuracy of methods developed on forensic or cadaveric populations. The most common method employed is that developed by Thompson (1979, 1981; Thompson and Galvin 1983) using small cores from the anterior mid-diaphysis of various major long bones. In 1981, Thompson and colleagues reported that histological analyses of femoral samples of Eskimo skeletons from St. Lawrence Island, Kodiak Island, Baffin Island, and Southampton Island using the Thompson method demonstrated consistently higher age estimates than morphological methods (Thompson and Gunness-Hey 1981; Thompson et al. 1981). This same analytical approach was tested on an archaeologically derived set of adults from historic burials from southern Ontario (ca. AD 1825–1920), with generally good results (Pfeiffer 1992). Pfeiffer notes that postmortem erosion of the periosteal surface led to a bias toward older ages, and cautions that tissue preservation influences both accuracy (including bias) and precision. The Thompson method is popular in bone histological analyses of archaeological material because it requires removal of only a small core or wedge of bone. In part to avoid even this amount of destruction to large bones, researchers were motivated to explore other possible sampling sites such as the (frequently broken) rib midshaft. An archaeologically derived sample, putatively the skeleton of Francisco Pizarro, was used to explore a new regression equation for estimating age from rib fragments (Stout 1986). He was able to acquire an age interval in the early 60s, which is consistent with Pizarro's known age at death.

Studies often use histology in archaeological settings to compare the efficacy of microscopic age estimation methods to macroscopic methods. Since true age at death cannot be known, demonstrated agreement between methods can increase confidence in the estimated ages. A test comparing the macroscopic age estimation techniques to the microscopic techniques was designed by Ericksen and Stix (1991) using skeletal remains from the 19th century First African Baptist Church cemetery in Philadelphia. A histomorphometric method assessing five fields along the periosteal surface of the anterior femoral cortex was developed by Ericksen (1991). Both types of techniques agreed with each other and the mean difference between the two methods for males was 1.4 years, while the difference for females was 4.7 years, thus demonstrating a relatively tight association between the two methods. Another study developed an approach using humeral and femoral specimens in order to provide age estimates for four Japanese archaeological samples, three from 14th–15th century graves and one from a 7th century tomb (Iwamoto and Konishi 1993). Development of new formulae was seen to be necessary because the prior equation using histomorphometric methods for a Japanese population was based on a relatively elderly sample. Because the macroscopic assessments of the archaeological sample indicated that these were young adults, a new equation based on a population with a better representation of younger individuals was developed. The histological age estimates for all but one of the archaeological samples were higher than the morphological estimates. Aiello and Molleson (1993) compared the accuracy of microscopically to macroscopically derived age estimates of the large Spitalfields crypt sample. The authors used two femoral shaft histological techniques: a modified version of Kerley's method (without access to the posterior location) and a method that uses two fields located in the middle intracortical region approximately anterio-medial and anterio-lateral on the femoral cross-section (Samson and Branigan 1987). The modified Kerley method performed better than the Samson and

Branigan method, from which they deduced that the periosteal surface is an important area for indication of age. When compared to various macroscopic methods using pubic symphyses, they found that the modified Kerley method was comparable. They concluded that their results did not warrant the use of microscopic methods over macroscopic ones.

Age at death in the archaeological context is an important piece of the biological profile; however, histological methods are rarely adopted. The reasons for this lack of use include the destructive nature of histological analyses, poor preservation of important microscopic structures, and the possibility of population-specific variation in bone microanatomy. In methods using the periosteal boundary such as those developed by Kerley (1965) and Thompson (1979), preservation of the outer surface is of utmost importance. Alterations to these areas can produce erroneous results, leading to a conclusion that these methods are not as useful as macroscopic methods. Nevertheless, in cases where macroscopic preservation of key features like the pelvis and skull is poor, yet tissue quality is good at histological sampling sites, histological analyses can provide an acceptable means of estimating age at death. In this sense, microscopic methods cannot be deemed better or worse than macroscopic methods; each complements the other in producing the biological profile of an unknown individual.

## 11.2.3   Habitual Activity and Diet

There is a rich and dynamic scholarly literature exploring the ways that bone tissue reflects a norm of reaction, responding to environmental factors within a genetically established range (Carter and Beaupré 2001; Garn 1970; Martin and Burr 1989). This literature forms the basis for reconstructions of past behavior based on the biomechanical properties of human long bones (Ruff 2008; Ruff et al. 1993, 2006; Stock and Pfeiffer 2001, 2004; Stock et al. 2005). A logical extrapolation from this line of investigation is that the structures that comprise the bone tissue should also be responsive, since it is through these structures that bone is gained or lost. Despite research approaches from various complementary perspectives, patterns are not yet clear.

The proposition that the relatively small secondary osteons of Late Pleistocene humans reflected their morphological robusticity (Abbott et al. 1996) provided the catalyst for various subsequent research approaches. Using the measure of osteon area (On.Ar, including both osteon and Haversian canal), the Pleistocene average of 27.7 $(mm^2)(10^{-3})$ is substantially smaller than the value from contemporary humans of around 40 $(mm^2)$ $(10^{-3})$ that was known at that time. Because cortical bone from ten adults that include both Neanderthals and early Homo sapiens shows the distinctly smaller secondary osteons, the pattern appears to be behavioral, rather than genetic. The pattern of smaller than modern secondary osteon areas has been found in other putatively ancient specimens (Pfeiffer and Zehr 1996) but not all of them (Sawada et al. 2004). Only very recently, a reexamination of osteon size and bone remodeling rates by Streeter and colleagues (2010) found the contrary, that is, the osteons of Neanderthals were not smaller than recent moderns nor were bone remodeling rates slower.

Based on the originally published values, combined with expectations regarding the norm of reaction of bone tissue, researchers have explored the question of whether variation in the size or shape of secondary osteons could be linked with the load history of bones. This would be helpful for interpreting the past in that the size and shape of osteons in archaeological populations may help indicate the intensity of their physical activities (see Skedros in this volume). One challenge has been to characterize the range of normal variability in human secondary osteon dimensions across a range of behavioral settings (Burr et al. 1990; Mulhern 2000; Mulhern and Van Gerven 1997; Pfeiffer 1998; Pfeiffer et al. 2006). It has been demonstrated that average secondary osteon size varies from one sample to another, and that quite consistently the secondary osteons from ribs are smaller than those from femoral midshafts (these are the two most commonly studied sampling sites). The difference in size between rib and femur suggests the influence of some biomechanical factor. Recent results from the study of a large, well-documented cadaveric sample indicate significant contributions to variance in femoral osteon size coming from age, weight, and sex, although not from stature (Britz et al. 2009). Using the earlier benchmarks for smaller osteons areas can illustrate the variability among recent human groups. Femoral midshafts show median On.Ar as low or lower than $27.7 \times 10^{-3}$ mm$^2$ in four of twenty 19th century Canadian settlers (St. Thomas' Anglican Church, three females and one male), and two of fourteen hunter-gatherers (South African Later Stone Age, both males), but none of twenty 18th century Hugenots (Spitalfields; data from Pfeiffer et al. 2006). None of the 87 femora studied by Britz et al. (2009) had median sizes this small. The challenge is to ascertain what behavioral features, if any, might distinguish individuals that have particularly large or small secondary osteons. Researchers are now introducing new variables to more clearly incorporate both osteon size and shape in their work (van Oers et al. 2008). As with all aspects of this research, clarity in the delimitations and definitions of each study, as well as demonstrations of the replicability of results, continue to be important.

Not only the size of osteons, but also structural features such as double zoning, drifting, and other variants have been quantified in experimental studies of various quadrupedal mammals. Research has demonstrated the absence of a consistent relationship between secondary osteon morphological characteristics and loading history (Skedros et al. 2007; see also Skedros chapter in this volume). On the other hand, examples from archaeologically derived contexts demonstrate the effect of habitual behaviors on secondary osteon density. Amputation is one such context, as illustrated by the cortical tissue of a young man from the turn of the 20th century. He had lived with a homemade below-the-knee prosthesis, a simple wooden peg, for several years. The femoral midshaft from his intact leg showed 28% remodeled bone, but the contralateral femur was 61% remodeled (Figure 11.2; Lazenby and Pfeiffer 1993). Thus, although age, weight, and sex may explain some portion of normal variability, there appear to be some behavioral factors that can affect remodeling rate.

Burr et al. (1996) found that even at high strain loads of 2000 microstrains remodeling rates were not increased. This study implies that in order for bone to display evidence of biomechanical loading resulting from physical activities, these loads would have to be of a substantial magnitude, that is, at least over 2000 microstrains, or, as in the earlier example, they would have had to substantially alter the direction of loading. Similarly, a study done by Peck and Stout (2009) demonstrated that in arthroplastic femora where the joint is replaced with a prosthesis, cross-sectional area increases while bone area decreases through increased endosteal resorption to accommodate biomechanical loading. These results demonstrate that not only can bone remodeling occur to manage loading strains, but its geometric properties can change. Therefore, the effects of strain on bone are varied and so are the resulting microanatomical changes. The exact mechanisms are still not clearly known and a well-substantiated framework for interpreting variation in secondary osteon structures remains to be developed.

**Figure 11.2** The grave (top) of a man in his mid-20s who used a homemade prosthesis to compensate for a below-knee amputation that occurred a considerable time prior to his death, AD 1899. Femoral midshafts show proportionally more remodeled bone (secondary osteons) on the leg that sustained the amputation (left) than on the intact leg (right). Note the presence of unremodeled bone in the intact leg. (Photo of grave courtesy of M. W. Spence; photos of histology courtesy of R. A. Lazenby.)

Histological exploration of archaeologically derived human bone can lead to novel discoveries, like the report of tetracycline-like fluorescence in bone from Sudanese Nubia (Bassett et al. 1980). It was argued that ingestion occurred through bacterially contaminated grain or ale, and therapeutic health effects were postulated (Keith and Armelagos 1983). Thereafter, similar fluorescence was reported from other sites in the region, signaling a continuance of this pattern for 1200 years (Cook et al. 1989). An alternate interpretation, that of postmortem diagenesis as a source of the fluorescence, was debated (Keith and Armelagos 1988; Piepenbrink 1986), but recent scrutiny with improved analytical methods appears to verify the original interpretation (Maggiano et al. 2006). To date, this phenomenon seems to be limited to one region and a relatively limited time period.

### 11.2.4 Pathological Conditions

Histological investigation can help to establish a probable etiology for abnormal bone conditions found in archaeological contexts. Schultz suggests that palaeohistology is centrally important to palaeopathological diagnoses (Schultz 2001, 2003). He argues that clinically established diagnostic features can be reinterpreted in the context of ancient remains in which many of the cells are absent and only their sequellae remain. A benefit from this interest in palaeohistology is that it necessitates a thorough understanding of tissue response among researchers. There are relatively few conditions in which histological structures are definitive, but histological characterization may contribute useful information in many contexts. Because it is destructive, it has not been considered a routine procedure (Ortner and Putschar 1981), although there is now more discussion of its justification. Imaging methods that provide cross-sectional images of cortical bone nondestructively, like CT scanning, can facilitate analysis when there is a need to differentiate between etiologies; for example, osteoporosis (osteopenia with thinned cortex) and hyperparathyroidism (osteopenia with porosity of the cortex).

The interpretation of slides from archaeological abnormal bone must be approached from a well-informed perspective, always attentive to the absent soft tissue. Changes to bone tissue arising from pathogens are often nonspecific, since skeletal metabolic response is limited to only resorption and deposition. The value of preparing a thin section or a surface for scanning electron microscopy (SEM) is often that of making the apparently simple distinction of whether bone deposition or resorption was occurring at the time of death. Smooth surfaces and edges comprised of well-mineralized bone, often lamellar in structure, suggest that deposition had been well underway at the site. Scalloped edges along the bone surfaces (such as Howship's lacunae) can indicate sites at which osteoclasts were active at the time of death, signaling resorption. However, the bone deposition process begins with a nonmineralized template that is only gradually mineralized. Hence, an apparently resorbing surface may have been in the early stages of deposition (Mosekilde 1990). SEM can be used to study bone surface topography of rare specimens that are not available for invasive procedures. These surfaces can demonstrate evidence of forming and resorbing bone surfaces. One limitation to SEM technique is that it does not provide information about intracortical activities.

There is a small number of pathological conditions that modify bone in ways that are distinctive enough that histological results can contribute to a definitive diagnosis. One of the liveliest areas of discussion focuses on treponemal infections, in part because of a sustained interest in the natural history of venereal diseases in the "Old" and "New" Worlds (Dutour et al. 1994; Powell and Cook 2005). In palaeopathology, a proposed etiology of syphilis is often based on changes to one or more long bones, especially the tibia. The tibia is often affected in treponemal diseases but is affected in ways that are grossly similar to hematogenous osteomyelitis. Schultz (2003) has identified two histological features that appear to be characteristic of the former but not of the latter. Polsters ("padding") and grenzstreifen ("border stripes") can be seen in thin sections because of the relatively slow progress of the treponemal diseases (venereal syphilis, endemic syphilis, yaws), whereas osteomyelitis and several other infectious diseases progress more quickly, leaving a very different histological signature (see the chapter by Schultz in this volume). A recent study of bone sections from individuals with documented venereal syphilis concluded that polsters and grenzstreifen are useful as a "rough guide for identifying syphilis in bone sections" (Von Hunnius et al. 2006:564). Interpretive complications arise from evidence that leprosy, too, can lead to polsters and perhaps to grenzstreifen (Blondiaux et al. 2002; Schultz and Roberts 2002).

Another example of a palaeopathological topic in which histology plays a role is that of Paget's disease, *osteitis deformans*. Its etiology is unclear, but it may arise from a low-grade viral infection. In modern times, it affects older Caucasians in all parts of the world, at frequencies of 10% to 15% by the ninth decade of life (Roberts and Manchester 1995). To better understand the disease, there is an interest in finding it among archaeological collections, especially those representing non-Caucasians. In the disruption of bone metabolism caused by Paget's disease, both deposition and resorption are heightened. This results in a mosaic of cortical bone structures, marked by numerous cement lines. It is this histological signature that distinguishes it from osteomalacia and hyperparathyroidism. Various instances of the disease have been documented from European contexts, although it appears to have been very rare. The diagnostic histological features have been well demonstrated in a case from medieval Ipswich, UK (Turner-Walker and Mays 2008). It has been argued that in the absence of characteristic histological features, a diagnosis of Paget's disease is unwarranted (Pinto and Stout 2009). A particular challenge arises because the high bone turnover and bone "softening" that characterizes this and other metabolic diseases of bone can exacerbate diagenetic deterioration of the bone tissue. This can make it more difficult to see the histological features.

Occasionally, fossils with pathological features are preserved sufficiently well for histological analysis. Pathological long bone fragments from Koobi Fora, Kenya, KNM-ER 1808, come from a partial female skeleton initially considered to be *Homo erectus* from ca. 1.6 million years ago (now more commonly considered as *Homo ergaster* or *Homo habilis* from 1.5 million years ago). Researchers suggest that she suffered from Vitamin A toxicity. Enveloping the normal cortex of the tibia is a substantial region of woven bone, causing an irregular and expanded bone surface. This is thought to have been caused by her eating the liver of a large predator, like a lion or leopard (Walker and Shipman 1996; Walker et al. 1982). The advanced nature of the condition suggests that these Homo sapiens precursors practiced compassion toward group members (Walker and Shipman 1996).

## 11.3   Conclusions

There is potential for considerable development in the field of histomorphology of cortical bone, as applied to tissue from archaeological contexts. A major limitation to the use of histomorphology is our lack of understanding of the complexities in bone biology. Researchers in this field have yet to identify all the biochemical regulators and pathways that control the formation and destruction of bone. Without this information, we are unable to explain age, sex, and population variations other than to say that they exist. These issues, however, are not necessarily limited to microscopic methods because what is seen at the histological level can manifest itself macroscopically. The amount of published work applying histological methods to archaeological samples has the potential to flourish as our understanding of the intricacies of bone biology expands.

Despite the challenges presented by variable tissue preservation and the reluctance to apply destructive methods, there are times when histological investigation can provide information that would be otherwise unavailable. This may pertain to the species represented by fragmentary remains, the age at death of deceased humans, distinctive behaviors. and some features of health during life. As discussed here, there are a number of areas where a clear understanding of histologically visible phenomena is just beyond reach. There is a symbiotic relationship between research undertaken on archaeologically derived material and on forensic material. Each can inform the other; future research questions will arise from both domains. Various aspects of the research reviewed here would benefit from tighter calibration. Research goals would be furthered if the international community of researchers were able to consult with one another more readily and were committed to defining variables and structural features in the same manner. For example, to fully understand the many manifestations of diagenetic alteration, we would do well to combine bioarchaeological and forensic inputs. Archaeology can provide numerous examples from diverse locales, and forensics can provide known contexts for time since death and treatment of the remains. With researchers working together using standardized descriptions and methods, the use of histological techniques may prove invaluable in bioarchaeological studies and in forensic contexts where ongoing investigations of criminal cases, mass disasters, and war crimes are always in need of accurate information for the identification of unknown decedents.

# References

Abbott S, Trinkaus E, Burr DB (1996) Dynamic bone remodeling in later Pleistocene fossil hominids. Am J Phys Anthropol 99:585–601.

Aiello LC, Molleson T (1993) Are microscopic ageing techniques more accurate than macroscopic ageing techniques? J Arch Sci 20:689–704.

Bassett E, Keith M, Armelagos G, Martin D, Villaneuva A (1980) Tetracycline-labeled human bone from ancient Sudanese Nubia (A.D. 350). Science 209:1532–1534.

Bell LS, Cox G, Sealy JC (2001) Determining life history trajectories using bone density fractionation and stable light isotope analysis: A new approach. Am J Phys Anthropol 166:66–79.

Bell LS, Kayser M, Jones C (2008) The mineralized osteocyte: A living fossil. Am J Phys Anthropol 137(4):449–456.

Blondiaux J, Durr J, Khouchaf L, Eisenberg LE (2002) Microscopic study and x-ray analysis of two 5th-century cases of leprosy. In: Roberts CA, Lewis ME, Manchester K (eds) The past and present of leprosy: Archaeological, historical, palaeopathological and clinical approaches proceedings of the international congress on the evolution and palaeoepidemiology of the infectious diseases 3 (ICEPID), University of Bradford, July 26–31, 1999. Archaeopress, Oxford.

Bocquet-Appel J, Masset C (1982) Farewell to paleodemography. J Hum Evol 11:321–333.

Britz HM, Thomas CDL, Clement JG, Cooper DML (2009) The relation of femoral osteon geometry to age, sex, height and weight. Bone 45:77–83.

Burr DB, Ruff C, Thompson DD (1990) Patterns of skeletal histologic change through time: Comparison of an archaic Native American population with modern populations. Anatomical Rec 226:613–616.

Byers S (2008) Introduction to forensic anthropology. Pearson/Allyn and Bacon, Boston.

Carter DR, Beaupré GS (2001) Skeletal function and form. Cambridge University Press, Cambridge.

Cho H, Stout SD, Madsen RW, Streeter M (2002) Population-specific histological age-estimating method: A model for known African-American and European-American skeletal remains. J Forensic Sci 47(1):12–18.

Cook M, Molto E, Anderson C (1989) Fluorochrome labeling in Roman period skeletons from Dakhleh Oasis, Egypt. Am J Phys Anthropol 80:137–143.

Crowder C (2005) Evaluating the use of quantitative bone histology to estimate adult age at death. PhD dissertation, University of Toronto.

Crowder C, Pfeiffer S (2010) The application of cortical bone histomorphometry to estimate age-at-death. In: Latham KE, Finnegan M (eds) Age estimation from the human skeleton. Charles C Thomas, Springfield, IL.

Day MH, Molleson TI (1973) The Trinil femora. In: Day MH (ed) Human evolution. Taylor & Francis, London.

Dubois E (1937) The osteone arrangement of the thigh-bone compacta of man identical with that, first found of Pithecanthropus. K Ned Akad Wet 40:864–870.

Dutour O, Palfi G, Berato J, Brun J-P (1994) L'origine de la syphilis en Europe: Avant ou apres 1493? Editions Errance, Toulon.

Enlow DH, Brown SO (1956) A comparative histological study of fossil and recent bone tissues, Part 1. Tex J Sci 8:405–443.

Enlow DH, Brown SO (1957) A comparative histological study of fossil and recent bone tissues, Part 2. Tex J Sci 9:186–214.

Enlow DH, Brown SO (1958) A comparative histological study of fossil and recent bone tissues, Part 3. Tex J Sci 10:187–230.

Ericksen MF (1991) Histological estimation of age at death using the anterior cortex of the femur. Am J Phys Anthropol 84:171–179.

Ericksen MF, Stix AI (1991) Histological examination of age of the First African Baptist Church adults. Am J Phys Anthropol 85:247–252.

Foote JS (1916) A contribution to the comparative histology of the femur. Hrdlicka A (ed) Smithsonian Institution, Washington D.C.

Garn SM (1970) The earlier gain and later loss of cortical bone, in nutritional perspective. Charles C Thomas, Springfield, IL.

Graf W (1949) Preserved histological structures in Egyptian mummy tissues and ancient Swedish skeletons. Acta Anat (Basel) 8(3):236–250.

Grupe G, Dreses-Werringloer U (1993) Decomposition phenomenon in thin sections of excavated human bones. In: Grupe G, Garland A (eds) Histology of ancient human bone: Methods and diagnosis. Springer-Verlag, New York.

Guarino FM, Angelini F, Vollono C, Orefice C (2006) Bone preservation in human remains from the Terme del Sarno at Pompeii using light microscopy and scanning electron microscopy. J Arch Sci 33:513–520.

Haglund AH, Sorg M (1997) Forensic taphonomy: The postmortem fate of human remains. CRC Press, Boca Raton, FL.

Hillier M, Bell LS (2007) Differentiating human bone from animal bone: A review of histological methods. J Forensic Sci 52(2):249–263.

Hoppa RD, Vaupel JW (2002) Paleodemography: Age distributions from skeletal samples. Cambridge University Press, Cambridge.

Hublin JJ, Paabo S, et al. (2008) Suggested guidelines for invasive sampling of hominid remains. J Hum Evol 55(4):756–757.

Iwamoto S, Konishi M (1993) Estimating the age at death in a group of historically unknown adults Okajimas Folia Anat Jpn 70(2–3):105–114.

Jackes M, Sherburne R, Lubell D, Barker C, Wayman M (2001) Destruction of microstructure in archaeological bone: A case study from Portugal. Int J Osteoarchaeol 11:415–432.

Keith M, Armelagos G (1983) Naturally occurring antibiotics and human health. In: Romanucci-Ross L, Moerman D, Tancredi L (eds) The anthropology of medicine: From culture to method. Praeger, New York.

Keith M, Armelagos G (1988) An example of in vivo tetracycline labeling: Reply to Piepenbrink. J Arch Sci 15:595–601.

Kerley ER (1965) The microscopic determination of age in human bone. Am J Phys Anthropol 23:149–164.

Kerley ER (1969) Age determination of bone fragments. J Forensic Sci 14(1):59–67.

Kerley ER (1970) Estimation of skeletal age: After about age 30. In: Stewart TD (ed) Personal identification in mass disasters. Smithsonian Institute, Washington D.C.

Kerley ER, Ubelaker DH (1978) Revisions in the microscopic method of estimating age at death in human cortical bone. Am J Phys Anthropol 49(4):545–546.

Larsen CS (1997) Bioarchaeology: Interpreting behavior from the human skeleton. Cambridge University Press, New York.

Lazenby RA, Pfeiffer S (1993) Effects of a nineteenth century below-knee amputation and prosthesis on femoral morphology. Int J Osteoarchaeol 3:19–28.

Maggiano C, Dupras T, Schultz M, Biggerstaff J (2006) Spectral and photobleaching analysis using confocal laser scanning microscopy: A comparison of modern and archaeological bone fluorescence. Mol Cell Probes 20:154–162.

Martin RB, Burr DB (1989) Structure, function, and adaptation of compact bone. Raven Press, New York.

Molleson T, Cox M (1993) The Spitalfields project, volume 2: The anthropology, the middling sort. Council for British Archaeology, York.

Morris H (2007) Quantitative and spatial analysis of the microscopic bone structures of deer, dog and pig. Master's thesis, Louisiana State University.

Mosekilde L (1990) Consequences of the remodelling process for vertebral trabecular bone structure: A scanning electron microscope study (uncoupling of unloaded structures). Bone Miner 10:13–35.

Mulhern DM (2000) Rib remodeling dynamics in a skeletal population from Kulubnarti, Nubia. Am J Phys Anthropol 111:519–530.

Mulhern DM, Van Gerven DP (1997) Patterns of femoral bone remodeling dynamics in a Medieval Nubian population. Am J Phys Anthropol 104:133–146.

Ortner DJ, Putschar WGJ (1981) Identification of pathological conditions in human skeletal remains. Academic Press, Washington, D.C.

Parfitt AM, Drezner MK, Glorieux FH, Kanis JA, Malluche H, Meunier PJ, Ott SM, Recker RR (1987) Bone histomorphometry: Standardization of nomenclature, symbols, and units. J Bone Miner Res 2(6):595–610.

Peck J, Stout S (2008) The effects of total hip arthroplasty on the structural and biomechanical properties of adult bone. Am J Phys Anthropol 138(2):221–230.

Pfeiffer S (1980) Bone remodeling age estimates compared with estimates obtained by other techniques. Curr Anthropol 21(6):793.

Pfeiffer S (1992) Cortical bone age estimates from historically known adults. Z Morph Anthrop 79:1–10.

Pfeiffer S (1998) Variability in osteon size in recent human populations. Am J Phys Anthropol 106(2):219–227.

Pfeiffer S (2000) Palaeohistology: Health and disease. In: Katzenberg MA, Saunders SR (eds) Biological anthropology of the human skeleton. Wiley-Liss, New York.

Pfeiffer S (2006) Cortical bone histology in juveniles. In: Grupe G, Peters J (eds) Microscopic examinations of bioarchaeological remains: Keeping a close eye on ancient tissues. Verlag Marie Leidorf GmbH, Rahden/Westf.

Pfeiffer S, Crowder C, Harrington L, Brown M (2006) Secondary osteon and Haversian canal dimensions as behavioral indicators. Am J Phys Anthropol 131:460–468.

Pfeiffer S, Varney T (2000) Quantifying histological and chemical preservation in archaeological bone. In: Ambrose SH, Katzenberg MA (eds) Biogeochemical approaches to paleodietary analysis. Kluwer Academic/Plenum, New York.

Pfeiffer S, Zehr M (1996) A morphological and histological study of the human humerus from Border Cave. J Hum Evol 31:49–59.

Piepenbrink H (1986) 2 examples of biogenous dead bone decomposition and their consequences for taphonomic interpretation. J Arch Sci 13(5):417–430.

Pinto DC, Stout SD (2009) Paget's disease in pre-contact Florida? Revisiting the Briarwoods site in Gulf Coast Florida. Int J Osteoarchaeol. doi: 10.1002/oa.1043.

Powell ML, Cook DC (2005) The myth of syphilis: The natural history of trepanematosis in North America. University Press of Florida, Gainesville.

Roberts C, Manchester K (1995) The archaeology of disease, 2nd ed.. Cornell University Press, Ithaca, NY.

Roberts CA (2009) Human remains in archaeology: A handbook. Council for British Archaeology, York.

Robling AG, Stout SD (2008) Histomorphometry of human cortical bone: Applications to age estimation In: Katzenberg MA, Saunders SR (eds) Biological anthropology of the human skeleton, 2nd ed.. Wiley-Liss, New York.

Ruff CB (2008) Biomechanical analyses of archaeological human skeletons. In: Katenberg MA, Saunders SR (eds) Biological anthropology of the human skeleton, 2nd ed. Wiley-Liss, New York.

Ruff CB, Holt B, Trinkaus E (2006) Who's afraid of the big bad Wolff? Wolff's law and functional adaptation. Am J Phys Anthropol 129(4):484–498.

Ruff CB, Trinkaus E, Walker A, Larsen CS (1993) Postcranial robusticity in Homo. I: Temporal trends and mechanical interpretation. Am J Phys Anthropol 91:21–53.

Samson C, Branigan K (1987) A new method of estimating age at death from fragmentary and weathered bone In: Boddington A, Garland AN, Janaway RC (eds) Death, decay and reconstruction approaches to archaeology and forensic science. Manchester University Press, Manchester.

Sawada J, Kondo O, Nara T, Dodo Y, Akazawa T (2004) Bone histomorphology of the Dederiyeh Neanderthal child. Anthropol Sci 112 (3):247–256.

Schultz M (1997a) Microscopic investigation of excavated skeletal remains: A contribution to paleopathology and forensic medicine. In: Haglund WD, Sorg MH (eds) Forensic taphonomy: the postmortem fate of human remains. CRC Press, Boca Raton, FL.

Schultz M (1997b) Microscopic structure of bone. In: Haglund WD, Sorg MH (eds) Forensic taphonomy: The postmortem fate of human remains. CRC Press, Boca Raton, FL.

Schultz M (2001) Paleohistology of bone: A new approach to the study of ancient diseases. Yrbk Phys Anthropol 44:106–147.

Schultz M (2003) Light microscopic analysis in skeletal palaeopathology. In: Ortner DJ (ed) Identification of pathological conditions in human skeletal remains, 2nd ed. Elsevier, New York.

Schultz M, Roberts CA (2002) Diagnosis of leprosy in skeletons from an English Later Medieval hospital using histological analysis. In: Roberts CA, Lewis ME, Manchester K (eds) The past and present of leprosy: Archaeological, historical, palaeopathological and clinical approaches proceedings of the international congress on the evolution and palaeoepidemiology of the infectious diseases 3 (ICEPID). University of Bradford, July 26–31, 1999. Archaeopress, Oxford.

Skedros JG, Sorenson SM, Jenson NH (2007) Are distributions of secondary osteon variants useful for interpreting load history in mammalian bones? Cells Tissues Organs 185(4):285–307.

Stock J, Pfeiffer S (2001) Linking structural variability in long bone diaphyses to habitual behaviors: Foragers from the Southern African Later Stone Age and the Andaman islands. Am J Phys Anthropol 115(4):337–348.

Stock J, Pfeiffer SK (2004) Long bone robusticity and subsistence behaviour among Later Stone Age foragers of the forest and fynbos biomes of South Africa. J Arch Sci 31:999–1013.

Stock JT, Pfeiffer SK, Chazan M, Janetski J (2005) F-81 skeleton from Wadi Mataha, Jordan, and its bearing on human variability in the Epipaleolithic of the Levant. Am J Phys Anthropol 128:453–465.

Stout SD (1978) Histological structure and its preservation in ancient bone. Curr Anthropol 19:601–603.

Stout SD (1986) The use of bone histomorphometry in skeletal identification: The case of Francisco Pizarro. J Forensic Sci 31:296–300.

Streeter M (2005) Histomorphometric characteristics of the subadult rib cortex: Normal patterns of dynamic bone modeling and remodeling during growth and development. PhD dissertation, University of Missouri, Columbia.

Streeter M, Stout S, Trinkaus E, Burr D (2010) Brief communication: Bone remodeling rates in Pleistocene humans are not slower than the rates observed in modern populations: A reexamination of Abbott et al. (1996). Am J Phys Anthropol 141(2):315–318.

Streeter M, Stout SD (2003) The histomorphometry of the subadult rib: Age associated changes in bone mass and the creation of peak bone mass. In: Agarwal SC, Stout SD (eds) Bone loss and osteoporosis: An anthropological perspective. Kluwer Academic/Plenum, New York.

Streeter M, Stout SD, Trinkaus E, Roberts MB, Parfitt SA (2001) Histomorphometric age assessment of the Boxgrove I tibial diaphysis. J Hum Evol 40:331–338.

Thompson DD (1979) The core technique in the determination of age at death in skeletons. J Forensic Sci 24(4):902–915.

Thompson DD (1981) Microscopic determination of age at death in an autopsy series. J Forensic Sci 26 (3):470–475.

Thompson DD, Galvin CA (1983) Estimation of age at death by tibial osteon remodeling in an autopsy series. Forensic Sci Int 22:203–211.

Thompson DD, Gunness-Hey M (1981) Bone mineral-osteon analysis of Yupik-Inupiaq skeletons. Am J Phys Anthropol 55:1–7.

Thompson DD, Salter EM, Laughlin WS (1981) Bone core analysis of Baffin Island skeletons. Arctic Anthropol 28(1):87–96.

Thompson DD, Trinkaus E (1981) Age determination for the Shanidar 3 Neanderthal. Science 212:575–577.

Trinkaus E, Thompson DD (1987) Femoral diaphyseal histomorphometric age determinations for the Shanidar 3, 4, 5, and 6 Neandertals and Neandertal longevity. Am J Phys Anthropol 72:123–129.

Turner-Walker G, Mays S (2008) Histological studies on ancient bone. In: Pinhasi R, Mays S (eds) Advances in human palaeopathology. John Wiley & Sons, Chichester.

Ubelaker DH (1989) Human skeletal remains: Excavation, analysis, interpretation. Taraxacum, Washington D.C.

Von Hunnius TE, Roberts CA, Saunders SR, Boylston A (2006) Histological identification of syphilis in Pre-Columbian England. Am J Phys Anthropol 129:559–566.

Van Oers RF, Ruimerman R, van Rietbergen B, Hilbers PA, Huiskes R (2008) Relating osteon diameter to strain. Bone 43:476–482.

Walker A, Shipman P (1996) The wisdom of the bones. Alfred Knopf, New York.

Walker A, Zimmerman MR, Leakey REF (1982) A possible case of Hypervitaminosis A in *Homo erectus*. Nature 296(18 March):248–250.

Wood JW, Milner GR, Harpending HC, Weiss KM (1992) The osteological paradox: Problems of inferring prehistoric health from skeletal samples. Curr Anthropol 33:343–370.

# Bone Histology Collections of the National Museum of Health and Medicine

# 12

BRIAN F. SPATOLA
FRANKLIN E. DAMANN
BRUCE D. RAGSDALE

## Contents

## 12.1 Bone Histology Collections at the NMHM

The Anatomical Division of the National Museum of Health and Medicine (NMHM) at the Armed Forces Institute of Pathology (AFIP) maintains a growing collection of histological slides of skeletal tissue that includes what is likely the most extensive collection of whole-mount orthopedic pathology slides in the world. Currently, the collections include more than 10,000 slides of stained and undecalcified bone and joint specimens ranging in size from standard 1-by-3 inch slides to 5-by-7 inch whole-mount slides. The slides illustrate human growth and development, normal musculoskeletal anatomy, bone and joint pathology, tumor pathology, histomorphometry, and comparative anatomy.

The pathological material consists primarily of whole-mount glass slides from the histology laboratory of the AFIP Orthopedic Pathology Department from over 4,500 diagnosed cases of bone disease.* Multiple cuts from each large tissue block are rendered in hematoxylin and eosin (H&E) and various special stains. Normal and comparative

---

* This chapter discusses only a select group of collections at the museum. Space considerations preclude a complete discussion of the museum's entire holdings on the subject of bone histology. For example, the museum also curates a vast collection of veterinary specimens, microscope slides, and associated records donated by James L. Shupe in 1992 from his many years of studying the effects of fluoride toxicity in animals.

zoological reference material is also well represented in a large format. Pathological material is supplemented by archival collections such as the Codman Registry of Bone Sarcoma (1920–1940) and the whole-mount collection of Dr. Dallas Phemister. The collections contain hundreds of slides from Dr. Ellis R. Kerley's research at AFIP, which includes the development of his histological method of age estimation for human bone and studies of primate growth and development. Recently donated slides originate from advanced graduate studies in histological age-estimation bone aging and the determination of human versus nonhuman bone.

## 12.2   Lent Clifton Johnson and AFIP Orthopedic Pathologists

Dr. Lent C. Johnson (1919–1998; Figure 12.1) began his career at the Armed Forces Institute of Pathology in 1942. As an Army major, he worked both at the Army Medical Museum and served as chief of the Fifth Service Command Tissue Center until 1944. After two years as chief of the Mayo General Hospital Laboratory, Johnson began 52 years of continuous service at the AFIP, 34 years as chief of orthopedic pathology (1946–1980) and 18 years as a senior investigator and consultant in that department.

During his lifetime, Johnson was one of the most respected orthopedic pathologists in the world. His numerous accomplishments include training thousands of military and civilian orthopedic pathologists; the establishment of the AFIP Registry of Orthopedic Pathology; and the creation of an orthopedic laboratory for the preparation of whole-mount bone sections, micro x-rays, and histochemical studies of metabolic bone disease. Owing to perfectionism, Johnson's publications were rare, but powerful synopses of bone biology (Johnson 1966) and bone pathology (Johnson 1953, 1964; Johnson et al.

**Figure 12.1**  Lent C. Johnson, MD, circa 1950s.

2000). He is considered one of the pioneers of the modern (post-1950s) paradigm of bone biology (Jee 2005).

Much of Johnson's research was facilitated by the ability to use the large format slide to demonstrate the full range of microscopic variation and appearance of adjacent normal and pathologic cellular morphology for a given case. For example, Johnson, Dr. Hans Vetter, and Dr. Walter Putschar (1962) examined a series of rare cases of "large, untreated simple bone cysts with a sarcoma arising from the wall of each cyst" using material from the collection. As bone cysts are typically considered benign, such rare instances were only poorly documented until this time. The contextualized transitional zones leading from bone cyst to tumor were not previously available for the type of systematic histological study made possible by large format slides.

For Johnson, the knowledge gained by studying the overall range of cellular response to disease augmented the pathologist's limited field of view when relying solely on the perspective of small amounts of biopsied material, fine-needle aspirates, and standard 1-by-3 inch slides. Since biopsied material may or may not include relevant diagnostic features, this broader perspective obviates the sampling error that otherwise can lead to wrong or overreaching diagnoses. In a single case, longitudinal sections display the zonal variation in intensity of the disease process and the resulting cellular responses. A series of large slides of the same disease process demonstrates progressive change and in some instances homeostasis. Large format slides are useful for clarifying puzzling details observed in corresponding clinical radiographs; and as a result, there is no better way to teach radiology than by correlating radiological images with histological details in large format slides.

## 12.3    Collections History and Composition

### 12.3.1    Johnson–Sweet Whole-Mount Collection of Orthopedic Pathology

The Johnson–Sweet Whole-Mount Collection began as the research archives of the AFIP Division of Orthopedic Pathology. The collection was developed from material drawn from the clinical, collaborative, and educational activities of the department following World War II. It was initiated by the singular influence of Johnson. Dr. Donald Sweet (Chief, 1980–2004) carried on the tradition of Johnson while the later remained on staff as an advisor and senior investigator until his death in 1998. Coauthor Dr. Bruce Ragsdale was on staff helping create and organize the collection from 1976 to 1986. The Johnson–Sweet Collection is composed of diagnosed case material that often includes substantial documentation of case history, radiologic correlations, treatment, and some follow-up. All categories of bone disease are well represented in the collections (Figures 12.2 and 12.3) and include rare conditions. Rare materials are available due to the fact that diagnostically difficult tumors and osseous infections from around the world were regularly sent to the department for expert opinion. The most common diagnoses in the Johnson–Sweet Collection, excluding Codman Registry material, are osteosarcoma ($n = 379$), chondrosarcoma ($n = 301$), giant cell tumor ($n = 240$), osteochondroma ($n = 184$), carcinoma ($n = 146$), fibrosarcoma ($n = 121$), enchondroma ($n = 119$), osteomyelitis ($n = 117$), fracture ($n = 115$), Ewing's sarcoma ($n = 86$), osteoarthritis ($n = 84$), Paget's disease ($n = 80$), fibrous dysplasia ($n = 79$), chondroma ($n = 68$), and myeloma ($n = 64$).

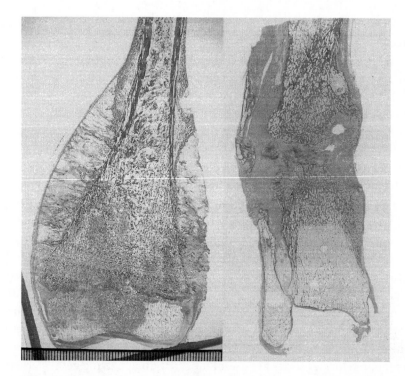

**Figure 12.2** Examples of whole-mount slides from the Johnson–Sweet Collection. (Left) A distal femoral osteosarcoma invading across the epiphyseal plate of an 8-year-old girl, with a classic "sunburst" periosteal reaction comprised of reactive and tumor bone and raising Codman angles proximally; (right) a pseudoarthrosis of distal tibia and fibula from an adult male following a fracture by a snapping cable on a boat deck.

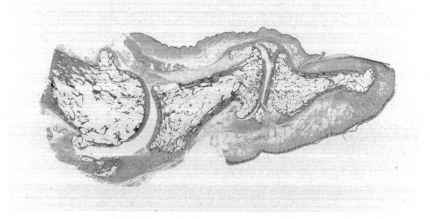

**Figure 12.3** 7 cm toe from a leprous foot. 3-by-4 inch whole-mount slide.

Many specimens have a detailed case history, clinical and specimen radiology images for comparison, micro x-rays, photomicrographs, and archived embedded gross tissue (Figure 12.4). Pathological material is supplemented by sections of developing human bone and normal adult bone as well as a substantial collection of comparative nonhuman material derived in part from material donated to the AFIP by the nearby Smithsonian National Zoological Park.

**Figure 12.4** Fibrocartilaginous dysplasia (fibrous dysplasia with massive cartilaginous differentiation) in fibula of an 8-year-old female with Albright's polyostotic fibrous dysplasia. The resected 15-cm long segment proximal fibula is (left to right) rendered as a band-saw-cut central slab, specimen radiograph and large format slide stained with aldehyde fuchsin (pH 1.0), which stains sulfated mucopolysaccharides purple, here rendered as black rims around centrally more collagenous cartilage lobules. Note intact growth plate. (From the Johnson–Sweet Collection.)

The Johnson–Sweet slides are derived from thousands of surgical and autopsy gross specimens and supporting material contributed by outside pathologists seeking consultative opinions from AFIP staff pathologists. Johnson began creating large format slides sometime after 1946 using a celloidin embedding technique originally developed for brain sections. Johnson learned the technique as a student at the University of Chicago from Dr. Dallas Phemister. This original process would take months to obtain a usable section. Soon after his arrival at AFIP, Johnson and the histology staff (Figure 12.5), of what was then the Army Medical Museum, developed a paraffin embedding technique that made it possible to get a usable specimen within four days (Dowding 1951; Johnson 1993).

The primary methods for creating whole-mount slides are outlined in the out-of-print 1968 *AFIP Histological Staining Methods Manual* (Luna 1968). Some details are summarized here for historical purposes. H&E stains predominate in the whole-mount collection, though Masson's trichrome and other special stains were commonly used. Undecalcified sections in a smaller format were also created as were hand-ground sections for demonstrating the structure of bone in microradiographs. All processing of large bone specimens was done by hand, whereas automatic processors handled the smaller pieces. A circa 1927 Sartorius microtome manufactured for cutting brains was being used to slice gross specimens of bone and joint as early as 1949 (AFIP 1949).

**Figure 12.5** AFIP staff histology technician Edward "Bud" Cunningham posing with a tour group behind a Sartorius microtome, 1950s. (Courtesy Dr. Bruce Ragsdale.)

Johnson's strong personality and influence shaped the department and the collection. In 1952 he presented a paper at the New York Academy of Medicine titled "A General Theory of Bone Tumors," in which he laid out the foundation of his approach to the interpretation of morphological and behavioral changes in pathological bone within the context of normal bone biochemistry and physiology. He emphasized how mechanical, circulatory, and metabolic influences, at particular locations and at certain developmental stages, help to explain observed histological and gross structural changes in diseased bone. In his teaching he emphasized the importance of correlating radiographic and clinical findings, a subject that would eventually get extensive treatment by others in the department.

In 1981, AFIP orthopedic pathologists Sweet and Ragsdale and radiologist Madewell standardized descriptive terminology for the macroscopic (gross and radiologic) features of bone lesions. Their three-part article series (Madewell et al. 1981; Ragsdale et al. 1981; Sweet et al. 1981) was directed at radiologists, pathologists, and orthopedic surgeons, and is most applicable to properly identifying neoplastic and inflammatory lesions. This work pointed out that the parameters of margins, periosteal reactions, and matrix patterns as disclosed in plain films permits a diagnostic accuracy in excess of 90% for bone tumors. Combinations of periosteal alterations, margins, and density changes help refine an "inflammatory category" diagnosis into one of the three types of skeletal inflammation: septic, granulomatous, or angiitic. Posttraumatic and some metabolic (e.g., hyperparathyroid bone disease) changes are also succinctly described with these terms. The authors emphasized that for accurate description and as a permanent record, specimen radiographs are indispensible since descriptive term choice in part relies on radiographic appearances. Together with gross photography, specimen x-ray should be a major priority. Since it is a nonhistological approach, the terminology defined in the three-article series can be advocated without alteration for use in paleopathologic descriptions. Ragsdale (1993) subsequently published an update of these concepts.

For Johnson and the staff pathologists, context was fundamental to understanding and diagnosing bone disease. Large format slides enabled the systematic study of tumors with a greater appreciation of the histological transition from normal regions to the pathological in an individual specimen, a perspective that could not be obtained with small format sections of biopsied tissue.

Countless collaborations and special studies carried out by Johnson and AFIP staff pathologists led to an accumulation of more than 4,500 cases over 50 years of study and diagnosis primarily between the late 1940s through the 1980s. In addition, sections were made from many of the museum's specimens of traumatic gunshot wounds and infections from the Civil War and World War I.

The Johnson–Sweet material was augmented by two series of archival non-AFIP research collections outlined next. These were the slides, radiologic studies and records of the Codman Registry of Bone Sarcoma of the 1920s and '30s and the Phemister Collection of orthopedic pathology ($n = 550$) created by Johnson's mentor Dr. Dallas Phemister. In total, the collection is, in effect, a longitudinal study of refinements and revisions of the categorization of bone tumors beginning with those made by the Committee on Bone Sarcoma in the early 1900s. Many diagnoses in the collection were made by the pathologists who first described and named tumors during their involvement with the work of the registry (e.g., Ewing's sarcoma, Codman's chondroblastoma, Phemister's chondrosarcoma). Johnson and the AFIP staff also reexamined cases in the original Codman Registry in light of their more up-to-date understanding of bone tumors.

## 12.3.2   Historic Collections (Codman and Phemister)

The Codman Registry of Bone Sarcoma is the oldest tumor registry in the country (Henry 1964). The registry began in 1920 prompted by hospital standardization pioneer Ernest. A. Codman's (1869–1940; Figure 12.6) interest in refining diagnostic criteria and classification of bone tumors. The material from the Codman collection was the basis for early classification nomenclature for bone tumors (Codman 1925) and subsequent revisions (Ewing 1939). At the time, depending on their education, pathologists employed a variety of terms for the same pathological conditions (Codman 1922), which caused significant confusion and hindered the systematic study of bone tumors. The committee took on the work of standardizing nomenclature and pathobiology of the various entities they encountered.

The registry was a longitudinal study of a large series of cases of bone tumors. The study was carried out between the years 1920 and 1940 and included long-term patient follow-up. The collection consists of over 2,300 bone tumors submitted by pathologists from across the United States. The slides were shuttled in trunks across the country to be evaluated by a committee of eminent surgeons and pathologists of the day along with all available histological, clinical, radiographic, and other case data. Among the prominent committee members were Joseph Bloodgood (1867–1935), William Coley (1862–1936), James Ewing (1866–1943), and Frank B. Mallory (1862–1941).

The Codman material was donated to the museum by the American College of Surgeons in 1953 and integrated into the Johnson–Sweet Collection. The digitally scanned case files include the original case files and handwritten diagnoses of participating doctors often with commentary (sometimes extensive) as well as photos of gross tissue and radiographs (Figure 12.7).

**Figure 12.6** Earnest A. Codman, MD, with trunks for shipping materials. (From the Registry of Bone Sarcoma.)

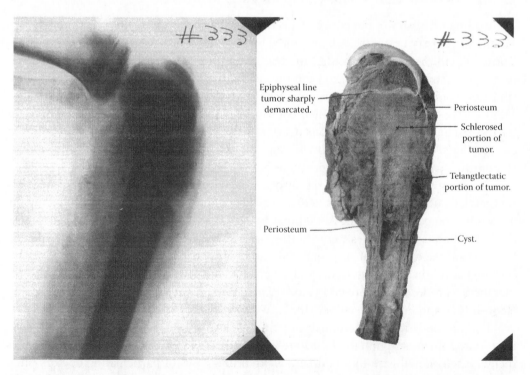

**Figure 12.7** Radiograph and labeled soft tissue photo of an osteosarcoma of a distal femur. Case 333, Codman Registry of Bone Sarcoma. Knee is at top.

Dr. Dallas B. Phemister was the second chair of the Registry of Bone Sarcoma (Codman being the first) and a participant from its inception. He was also a mentor of Johnson at the University of Chicago. The collection includes Phemister's collection of approximately 550 whole-mount orthopedic pathology slides produced from the late 1910s to the early 1930s. Johnson often cited Phemister as one of the people that influenced him the most. Phemister brought the large slide technique to the United States from Europe where he had learned the technique from pathologist Jakob Erdheim (Johnson 1993).

### 12.3.3   Kerley Collection

The museum's growing collection of nonpathological glass slides of decalcified (stained and unstained) and undecalcified human and nonhuman bone tissue originates from Dr. Ellis R. Kerley's research on microscopic age changes in bone structure of humans and chimpanzees conducted during his 8-year tenure with the AFIP. In 1957 Kerley took a position with the Veterans Administration as a physical anthropologist at the AFIP where he worked under the direction of Johnson (Sledzik 2001). At 33 years old, Kerley had gained professional experience as a staff anthropologist with the Bowman Gray School of Medicine (Ubelaker 2001) and as a specialist in human remains identification of the Korean War dead in Kokura, Japan (Hinkes 2001). At the time of his arrival with the AFIP, Kerley held a master's degree in anthropology.

In his early career, Kerley found himself among mentors such as Dr. Charles Snow as an undergraduate student in Kentucky; Drs. T. Dale Stewart and Thomas McKern in Japan; and Johnson while at the AFIP. Associations such as these no doubt solidified Kerley's academic foundation, while at the same time affected his professional development and future direction. Through his affiliation with the AFIP, and particularly Johnson, Kerley expanded his professional interests to include bone histology and pathology, amassing a collection of whole-mount human and nonhuman bone slides. Today, these slides along with accompanying documentation and original notes are curated by the Anatomical Division of the NMHM.

#### 12.3.3.1   *Human Bone Sections*

The human bone slide collection was created during the late 1950s and early 1960s, and is associated with Kerley's AFIP research on age-related changes of bone histomorphology. With these slides and associated data, Kerley explored normal human variation in four characteristics of bone microstructure: the frequency of osteons, osteon fragments, non-Haversian canals (primary vasculature canals), and the percentage of circumferential lamellar bone. This work resulted in his 1962 dissertation and subsequent publication of his research methods (Kerley 1965). A work that Ubelaker (2001) identifies as one of significance given the number of times the paper has been cited in subsequent publications on histomorphology.

The collection includes over 600 bone sections mounted on 1-by-3 inch and 2-by-3 inch glass slides, representing approximately 170 individuals. Slides from 126 of these individuals were used in Kerley's 1965 publication. Specimens originating from AFIP accessioned material are accompanied by antemortem clinical data. A small subsample of individuals is lacking detailed antemortem data owing to either an incomplete record or specimens originating from an archaeological context. The basic demographic profile for the specimens that have a recorded age at death ($n = 136$) is comprised of individuals from 0 to

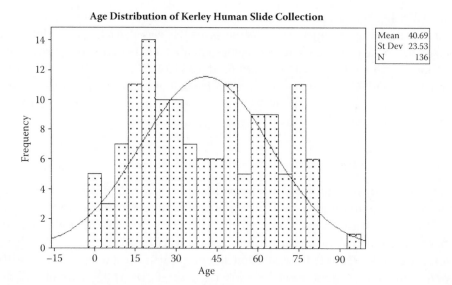

**Figure 12.8** Histogram showing the distribution of age at death for the Kerley histological collection of human skeletal material (n = 136).

95 years of age, and a mean and standard deviation of 41 ± 24 years (Figure 12.8). Both males (*n* = 91) and females (*n* = 37) are represented.

The slides are midshaft cross-sections of femur, tibia, and fibula. Some sections are decalcified and stained with H&E, while others are undecalcified hand-ground sections. Slide preparation followed AFIP standard operating procedures for histological slide preparation. We have found that over the last 50 years the mounting media on some slides has crystallized obscuring bone microstructure. The museum is currently working on a conservation project with AFIP Scientific Laboratories to restore affected slides so they can be available to researchers.

### 12.3.3.2  Nonhuman Bone Sections

The nonhuman primate bone sections were collected in the early 1960s and are related to research projects conducted at the AFIP by Johnson and Kerley on somatotype, skeletal biology, and comparative skeletal histomorphology. Kerley and Johnson initiated studies at the AFIP using the chimpanzee and other primates as research models of normal growth and development with the goal of equating primate skeletal age with human skeletal age and exploring the notion that skeletal type can predict body type. The nonhuman primates were obtained from two regional primate facilities: the Yerkes Laboratory of Primate Biology, Orange Park, Florida, and the Delta Regional Primate Research Center, Tulane University, Covington, Louisiana.

Kerley's baseline data would serve future studies addressing primate anatomical variation and changes in skeletal growth and development. In an unpublished AFIP internal document dated October 22, 1964, and titled "Constitutional and Skeletal Research in the Chimpanzee," Kerley wrote: "The increasing use of chimpanzees as human substitutes in aerospace and other investigative programs necessitates an understanding of age changes in the chimpanzee as well as a method of determining chimpanzee skeletal age for comparison with human data." His mention of space flight was related to the provisioning of anthropometric and skeletal data for the U.S. Air Force and NASA. Ultimately, Kerley published a subset of data from 35 chimpanzees, correlating normal variation in gross, radiographic, and microscopic changes of the skeleton with age (Kerley 1966).

Johnson's use of primate data, on the other hand, appeared to be related specifically to mechanisms of skeletal modeling and remodeling. In a April 20, 1966, letter to Dr. Riopelle, Director of the Yerkes Laboratory of Primate Biology, Johnson described the chimpanzee as a valuable model organism for studies on the relationship between muscle and bone and the mechanical control of bone remodeling. In the same letter, he later explains that although his publications (see Johnson 1964, 1966) were based on human material, "the courage to summarize this material was largely dependent upon the parallel studies of the chimpanzees which verified and supported the data from human material."

The nonhuman primate collection includes histological slides and associated records that document standard anthropometric data taken prior to exsanguination at the respective facilities. Necropsy data, such as radiographs and organ weights, were also recoded. By April 1966, 182 primates had been received by Johnson and Kerley though whole-mount histological slides were not prepared from every animal. Today, the histological slide collection of nonhuman primates includes 67 specimens. Major Primate genera represented include Pan, Hylobates, Erythrocebus, Saimiri, Papio, and Macaca. From each specimen, histological cross-sections and longitudinal sections were made. Midshaft cross-sections were taken from femur, tibia, fibula, humerus, radius, ulna, clavicle, third metacarpal, second metatarsal, and first lumbar vertebra. Metaphyseal and epiphyseal longitudinal sections were made from the proximal humerus, proximal and distal femur, proximal tibia, sternum, clavicle, second metatarsal, twelfth thoracic, seventh and third cervical, and the ninth costochondral rib. The slides are mostly large format, whole-mount glass slides of decalcified, H&E stained bone tissue.

## 12.3.4   Recent Acquisitions

Additional accessions of bone histology materials include samples of human and nonhuman specimens from recent research in bone biology (Benedix 2004; Tersigni 2005). The research specimens are stored with the larger Kerley human and nonhuman collections given the similarities in research design and methodological approaches that further evaluate age estimation and comparative nonhuman histomorphology.

A recent accession of nonhuman slides includes a small collection of commonly occurring mammals found in archaeological contexts. Species represented include deer (*Odocoileus virginianus*), cow (*Bos sp.*), pig (*Sus scrofa*), goat (*Capra hircus*), water buffalo (*Bubalus bubalus*), and Rhesus macaque (*Macaca mulatta*). Many of the specimens are from Southeast Asia. The bone samples are unstained calcified tissue mounted on 1-by-3 inch glass slides. This collection of slides was donated by the Joint POW/MIA Accounting Command Central Identification Laboratory (JPAC CIL) and was the product of dissertation research by Dr. Derek Benedix from the University of Tennessee (Benedix 2004). The project addressed the difficulty in differentiating fragmented human and nonhuman skeletal remains; material often encountered during JPAC CIL missions to recover and identify missing U.S. service members.

The second recent acquisition includes nearly 300 slides of long bones from five individuals. This set was created by Dr. Mariateresa Tersingi-Tarrant in fulfillment of her doctoral dissertation requirements from the University of Tennessee (Tersigni 2005). Slides include serial sections of human humerii, ulnae, radii, femora, tibiae, and fibulae. The bone samples are unstained calcified tissue mounted on 1-by-3 inch and 2-by-3 inch glass slides. The project evaluated within-bone variability of bone microstructure, and the utility of applying Kerley's (1965) age estimation formulas to fragmentary or incomplete long bones where identifying the location of midshaft may be problematic.

## 12.4   Collections Management and Access

The slide collections are organized by accession number and stored in steel cabinets at both the NMHM main museum building on the Campus of Walter Reed in Washington, DC, and at the museum annex facility in Gaithersburg, Maryland. Large format slide series are organized by accession number and stored upright in cardboard sleeves. A database of the Johnson–Sweet Collection and the Codman Collection allows searching of slides by diagnosis and accession number. A finding aid and inventory of the Kerley slide collection is underway. Inventory and collections management of x-rays, photomicrographs, associated records, and archived tissue materials is ongoing.

Case files, photos, and some radiographs from the Johnson–Sweet collection and the original Codman files have been digitally scanned at 300 dpi. These files include clinical data related to diagnosis, clinical test results, and treatment as well as physician correspondence.

The Anatomical Division is planning the development of an imaging laboratory at the future museum collections and research annex in Silver Spring, Maryland. All materials are available for research within established federal, Department of Defense, NMHM. and other relevant guidelines and policies. Collections will not be available during anticipated Department of Defense Base Realignment and Closure (BRAC) activities in 2010–2013 during which time the museum and its collections will be relocated to the Forest Glen Medical Center approximately 4 miles from its current location on the campus of Walter Reed Army Hospital in Washington, DC. Parties interested in research at the NMHM can make an appointment by contacting NMHM staff through the museum's Web page at http://nmhm.washingtondc.museum.

## 12.5   Conclusions

The NMHM Anatomical Division curates one of the largest bone slide collections in the world. The collections contain numerous subcollections of interest to the skeletal research community particularly in the areas of paleopathology, orthopedic pathology, physical anthropology, and forensic anthropology. The staff of the Anatomical Division anticipates growth in the amount of donated material and the development of a state-of-the-art facility for anthropological and medical histological research similar to the museum's other world-class anatomy collections, the Carnegie Human Embryo Collection and the Yakovlev Neuroanatomy Collection, both of which have substantially grown from their original size over the years. The Anatomical Division also maintains a large collection of anatomical and pathological specimens, which includes more than 5,600 dry bone skeletal specimens and 5,500 formalin fixed soft tissue specimens dating back to the Civil War.

# Disclaimer

The opinions and assertions contained herein are the expressed views of the authors and are not to be construed as official or reflecting the views of the Department of the Army, Navy, or Air Force; or of the Department of Defense.

# References

AFIP (1949) Armed Forces Institute of Pathology (AFIP) Washington DC Annual Report. AFIP Historical Archives, National Museum of Health and Medicine, Washington, DC.

Benedix DC (2004) Differentiation of fragmented bone from Southeast Asia: The histological evidence. The University of Tennessee, Knoxville.

Codman EA (1922) The registry of cases of bone sarcoma. Surg Gynecol Obstet 34:338.

Codman EA (1925) The nomenclature used by the Registry of Bone Sarcoma. Am J Roentgenol Radium Ther 13:105–126.

Dowding GL (1951) Rapid sectioning of whole bones. Bull Int Assoc Med Museums XXXII, July.

Ewing J (1939) A review of the classification of bone tumors. Surg Gynecol Obstet 68:971–976.

Henry RS (1964) The Armed Forces Institute of Pathology: Its first century, 1862–1962. Government Printing Office, Washington, DC.

Hinkes MJ (2001) Ellis Kerley's service to the military. J Forensic Sci 46:782–783.

Jee SSW (2005) The past, present and future of bone morphometry: Its contribution to an improved understanding of bone biology. J Bone Miner Metab 23:1–10.

Johnson LC (1953) A general theory of bone tumors. Bull NY Acad Med 29:164–171.

Johnson LC (1964) Morphologic analysis in pathology: The kinetics of disease and general biology of bone. In: Frost HM (ed) Bone biodynamics. Little Brown, Boston.

Johnson LC (1966) The kinetics of skeletal remodeling. Birth Defects Orig Artic Ser 2:66–141.

Johnson LC (1993) Transcript: Interview by Charles Stewart Kennedy, April 21 and June 2. AFIP Oral History Program. AFIP Historical Archives, National Museum of Health and Medicine, Washington, DC. Online: www.nmhm.washingtondc.museum/collections/archives/aproducts/aoralhistories/johnsnl.pdf.

Johnson LC, Vetter H, Putschar WGJ (1962) Sarcomas arising in bone cysts. Virchows Arch Anat Path 335:428–451.

Johnson LC, Vinh TN, Sweet DE (2000) Bone tumor dynamics: An orthopedic pathology perspective. Semin Musculoskelet Radiol 4(1):1–15.

Kerley ER (1965) The microscopic determination of age in human bone. Am J Phys Anthropol 23:149–163.

Kerley ER (1966) Skeletal age changes in the chimpanzee. Tulane Stud Zool 13:71–82.

Luna LG (1968) Manual of histologic staining methods of the Armed Forces Institute of Pathology, 3rd edn. McGraw-Hill, New York.

Madewell JE, Ragsdale BD, Sweet DE (1981) Radiologic and pathologic analysis of solitary bone lesions. Part I: Internal margins. Rad Clin North Am 19:715–748.

Ragsdale BD (1993) Morphologic analysis of skeletal lesions: Correlation of imaging studies and pathologic findings. In: Fenoglio-Preiser CM. (ed) Advances in Pathology and Laboratory Medicine, Vol. 6, Mosby, Chicago, 445–490.

Ragsdale BD, Madewell JE, Sweet DE (1981) Radiologic and pathologic analysis of solitary bone lesions. Part II: Periosteal reaction. Rad Clin North Am 19:749–783.

Sledzik PS (2001) A career takes form: Ellis Kerley's tenure at the Armed Forces Institute of Pathology (1957–1966). J Forensic Sci 46:777–779.

Sweet DE, Madewell JE, Ragsdale BD (1981) Radiologic and pathologic analysis of solitary bone lesions. Part III: Matrix patterns. Rad Clin North Am 19:785–814.

Tersigni MA (2005) Serial long bone histology: Inter- and intrabone age estimation. PhD dissertation, University of Tennessee, Knoxville.

Ubelaker DH (2001) Contributions of Ellis R. Kerley to forensic anthropology. J Forensic Sci 46:773–776.

# The Melbourne Femur Collection

## How a Forensic and Anthropological Collection Came to Have Broader Applications

# 13

C. DAVID L. THOMAS
JOHN G. CLEMENT

## Contents

## 13.1 Any Collection of Human Tissues: An Important Issue of Trust

The collection and study of human bone is vital for advancing medical knowledge, especially at a time when age-related bone diseases, such as osteoporosis, have the real capacity to impoverish everyone in society. One in ten people who suffer an osteoporotic hip fracture will die soon after the event, and at least a further 50% will suffer from chronic debility and deterioration in their quality of life. In 1995 the cost of hip fracture to the Australian community (a relatively small population of only 20 million people) was estimated at AUD$400 million and the situation continues to get rapidly worse as the population ages. Therefore, resourcing of bone research is essential for understanding normal aging and guiding future preventative measures. Additionally, the result of such research is continually improving techniques for interpreting skeletal remains in forensic, anthropological, and archaeological contexts.

High-quality research data can be obtained only from large bone collections that widely represent particular ages, sexes, and populations. For reference collections to be of use, it is also important that other information, such as age at death and sex, are known for each person from whom bone samples have originated. Surgically removed bone is one source of samples, however, there are inherent biases toward specimens both from older people and from those displaying pathological changes in their skeletons. There is also little opportunity to select the area from which bone is taken, which can impact study group sizes for research on specific skeletal areas. Similar problems arise from dissecting room collections because almost all the cadavers come from people who have indicated a willingness for their body to be donated for medical research upon their death. Invariably most of the cadavers arise from people who have died late in life. Conversely bone taken at medicolegal autopsy, although not exactly reflecting the true cross-section of any community, is nevertheless an almost ideal sample source because it does provide the widest cross-section of the community available to the scientist. Within limits (for example, the preservation of external appearance and the physical integrity of the body) it also provides the opportunity to choose specific sites from which to take samples. However, the formation of postmortem bone collections gives rise to numerous logistic complications and ethical responsibilities. These issues have no doubt contributed to the worldwide paucity of modern research collections of postmortem bone, thereby crippling some important fundamental research. Problems can be solved only when bone researchers work harmoniously with institutions that are able to provide large numbers of samples with known provenance, comprehensive biometric data and when the next of kin are willing to consent to donation because they trust both the collectors and recipients of research samples. The Melbourne Femur Collection (MFC) provides an excellent example of this three-way relationship.*

## 13.2    Establishing the Melbourne Femur Collection

Since 1991, a team of researchers at the Melbourne Dental School (University of Melbourne, Australia) has been collecting and analyzing postmortem specimens of human femora from the Victorian Institute of Forensic Medicine (VIFM) in Melbourne. The archive of bone and associated biometric and research data generated from almost 20 years of study is known as The Melbourne Femur Collection (MFC) and is augmented with a smaller proportion of material collected at surgery. A close working relationship between the Melbourne Dental School (MDS) and the VIFM had already been established via the provision of forensic odontological casework services, predominantly in the identification of the deceased. Odontological identification requires comparison between antemortem dental records and postmortem dental findings. However, one or more putative identities must first be established for the deceased in order to gather records as a basis to make a comparison. Anthropological assessment of remains can provide investigators with valuable starting points for establishing a positive identity: Population of origin, sex, stature, and age at death of adults can be estimated using the external shape and size of skeletal elements, such as the pelvis, femur, and skull. However, it is rarely possible to define these traits precisely, and estimates are usually given within fairly broad intervals. For age at death in adulthood, after tooth formation is complete (which is capable of giving quite accurate age assessments) these may vary by up to 10 or more years on either side of the true age. The estimation of age at death is therefore a significant forensic problem when unidentified skeletons, or individual bones, are found with no clues to indicate identity. In cases of commingled remains, such as those encountered upon exhumations of mass graves arising as a result of massacres occurring during wars or periods of serious civil unrest, the authors wish to emphasize that the right to an identity in death is an important

---

* Parts of this chapter have drawn upon the article "The Melbourne Femur Collection: The Gift of Human Tissue Underpins Important Medical and Forensic Research," which appeared in the VIFM Review, Volume 3, Issue 1, 2005, and have been used with permission.

human rights issue. Consequently the MFC was established to look at age-related changes in bone, with the expectation that many of these changes would be useful age indicators in the forensic context.

The MFC is now one of the world's most complete and best documented archives of contemporary human bone tissue specimens collected from people living in a highly economically developed Westernized society. Bone samples ranging from 1 cm transverse sections of the midshaft of the femur up to larger specimens, such as the proximal five-eighths of the femur, have been obtained through the services of the Donor Tissue Bank of the Victorian Institute of Forensic Medicine. The transplant coordinators, who normally approach the next of kin for permission to gather tissues, such as heart valves, bone, and corneas, for therapeutic purposes, specifically ask for permission to remove material for research. If this is granted (and about two-thirds of those approached agrees) then a questionnaire is administered that serves to filter donors who have had medical conditions or lifestyles that may have affected their bones. Thus far persons who have died suddenly and unexpectedly have been chosen for the donation of bone tissue because the researchers have wanted to study normal age-related changes to bone and avoid interpretive problems arising from the complications introduced by the impacts of disease, some medications, and prolonged immobility on the skeleton. For example, prolonged steroid use, known to predispose people to osteoporosis and immobility, can have similar effects causing bone loss and would, therefore, not reflect their true situation in life. In addition, age, sex, supine length, and weight are recorded along with the length (in centimeters) of the bone remaining in the body by mortuary technicians.

The present goal at the VIFM is to excise the proximal five-eighths of the right femur and to date (November 2009) 217 bones have been collected under this protocol. Recently a helical CT scanner was installed at the VIFM and all of the 4000 to 5000 bodies admitted for coronial examination per annum undergo head-to-toe scanning before proceeding to autopsy. Therefore clinical CT of the bone in situ in the body is available for about 40 of the femora in the MFC with many of the rest having either plain film or digital radiographs of the leg and hemi-pelvis. Such data would be invaluable for those interested in biomechanical modeling of gait, stance, and local loading of the hip joint. The addition of CT (or other radiographic images) to collections of skeletal material is now practical and recommended. This offers at least two major advantages; first, it provides a permanent 3D record of the bone as collected thus overcoming some of the reluctance of curators to allow samples to be studied using destructive methods; second, the digital data is easily archived and distributed thus broadening access to the collection.

Currently the MFC contains approximately 500 samples of postmortem femoral bone obtained from the VIFM (Table 13.1). The collection also contains 90 surgical samples (femoral heads removed during hip replacements) that were donated by patients of two local hospitals. For each VIFM bone sample, there is a small matching blood sample from the donor that can be (and has been) used in genetic studies of age-related changes such as putative markers for osteoporosis.

Each request for postmortem bone is subject to the most rigorous formal review in accordance with guidelines of the National Health and Medical Research Council in Australia. Furthermore, while Victorian state legislation did once permit removal of small autopsy tissue samples without family consent, the institute's staff and its associated researchers took the additional step of seeking next-of-kin permission well in advance of legislative changes that have now been passed into law. This means that all but the

**Table 13.1   Composition of the Melbourne Femur Collection**

| Number of Specimens | Nature of Material Stored and Associated Data | Documentation (All Samples Have Age, Sex, Height, and Weight Recorded) | Ages |
|---|---|---|---|
| 240 | 100 mm hard-ground sections most with contact microradiographs and digital montages | Pathologists reports from autopsy | 1 to 95 years |
| 120 | Osteoarthritic femoral heads—recovered following hemiarthroplasty—fixed in 70% ethanol/water | Patient questionnaire | 60 to 86 with a few younger ones |
| 217 | Proximal right femora | Next-of-kin questionnaire | 20 to 90 years |
| | 78 have pQCT scans with 300 micron voxels | | |
| | 150 have plane radiographs of the pelvis (the orientation and quality was determined by the condition of the cadavers) | | |
| | 82 have clinical CT with 1 mm voxels | | |

earliest bone samples included in the MFC have been obtained with family consent as well as in accordance with the law. This was a wise decision by the institute, which must constantly balance the feelings of the next of kin and the rights of the deceased with the needs of society for coronial information, and access to tissue for therapeutic purposes and research. The foresight of the VIFM was rewarded when tissue donation continued, even at a time when people were appalled by the insensitive and inappropriate retention of human remains in other institutions such as at Alder Hey Hospital and The Bristol Royal Infirmary in Britain (Hall 2001; Redfern 2001). The institute had clearly demonstrated to many Victorians that it was doing things correctly by implementing a transparent, fully documented, and accountable system that can be summarized as "doing it well by doing it right." Bone donation levels have always been high and the willingness to sanction tissue donation continues to this day, despite well-publicized problems that have occurred elsewhere with the retention of autopsy tissue for research. This public response implies a high level of trust in the procedures and practices of the VIFM, its associated ethics committee, and the researchers. At the time of donation, families are asked if they would like to be informed about future progress in research using tissue donated to the MFC. By doing so, the right to know (or not to know) is respected. For the few who have expressed a wish to be informed, a simple newsletter is distributed.

## 13.3   Age-Estimation Studies

The composition of specimens in the collection reflects some of the history and evolution of the thinking and research questions upon which it is based. The original context of the MFC was that of coronial investigations where findings are determined "on the balance of probability." However, a coronial investigation frequently leads to criminal prosecutions in a higher court where the standard of proof is much more rigorous "beyond reasonable doubt"; in this environment any errors can have serious adverse consequences. The samples collected in 1990–1993 reflected the desire to improve histological aging methods for forensic purposes and, based on the existing literature, we chose to acquire samples from the midshaft of the femur. The major differences from material in other collections in the world are that it is a contemporary, very well-documented assemblage of material from a single location in a single bone. It has been collected at autopsy (and thus subject to minimal taphonomic changes) and in many cases blood samples are also available; the bone specimens have not been embalmed using formalin, which is known to have significant effects on postmortem tissue mechanical properties but fixed using 70% ethanol/water that is not so deleterious for long-term storage as it has no breakdown products that demineralize tissue.

As mentioned, the MFC was established to expand the availability of methods for age estimation, especially for fragmentary and otherwise incomplete human remains. To increase both accuracy and precision of forensic age-at-death estimates, researchers in the latter half of the 20th century attempted to use information contained within the internal structure of bone tissue. The establishment of the MFC permitted the examination of age-related changes in bone tissue across the entire life span of the relationship between certain microscopic features of bone tissue, detectable in cross-sections of the femur midshaft, and the age at death of the person from whom the bone came being of particular forensic interest in the early days of the collection.

Several anthropologists (Amprino 1963; Kerley 1965; Simmons 1985; Singh and Gunberg 1970) demonstrated that the constant removal and replacement of bone tissue in the skeleton that takes place in life gives rise to progressive changes in the microstructure of bone that can be quantified, and which therefore can be correlated with the chronological age of the person. Techniques based upon this association have been used to estimate the age of unknown skeletal remains, both in forensic cases and in archaeological investigations of old burial sites. One consistent feature of adult human bone is the existence of osteons (Figure 13.1), also called Haversian systems after the histologist Clopton Havers who first

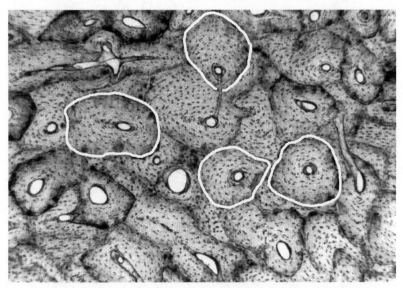

**Figure 13.1** A microscopic view of a cross-section of bone tissue from the dense cortex of the femur. The image is approximately 3.0 mm by 2.3 mm. The outlines of several osteons have been artificially emphasized to depict morphology. The bright ovoid region visible in each osteon is a central canal for a nutrient blood vessel, and the speckling on the image is caused by individual bone cell spaces.

described them. It has been claimed that over time, the number of osteons increase in spatial density along with a corresponding increase in fragments of osteons left over from ongoing internal bone remodeling. Early studies aimed at estimating the age at death of unknown remains by developing regression equations from studies of bones of known age. Frequently the origins of the bones and the nature of the ethical oversight of the projects were not stated (Kerley 1965; Kerley and Ubelaker 1978; Samson and Branigan 1987). However, such histomorphometric studies were seen as less subjective than other age-estimation methods such as the scoring of pubic symphysis, auricular surface, and sternal rib ends that were then available and so were consequently held to be of a higher standard. Nevertheless, those gross morphological methods can be notoriously inaccurate and the terms "higher standard" or "more accurate" need to be understood in this context.

Although the results of the histomorphometric studies published by others initially appeared promising, odontologists and osteologists at the VIFM experienced difficulties when using these techniques. One major concern related to the limitations associated with the need to choose sampling sites. Early studies had focused on counting osteons at a few sites around the femoral cortex and not across the entire cross-section of the organ, yet examination of bone cross-sections often reveals marked regional variation. We believed that this would undoubtedly introduce error into osteon counts because some regions within bones can be much more stable than others (Figure 13.2).

Between early 1990 and late 1993 the Melbourne research team, therefore, collected midshaft femoral samples from the whole life span, 1 to 100 years, for both sexes. This was

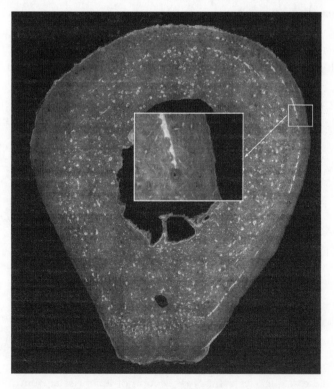

**Figure 13.2 (See color insert.)** Midshaft femoral cross-section from a 29-year-old male imaged by incident UV light shows adventitious labeling with tetracycline. Considerable remnants of earlier periosteal surfaces still persist from the teenage period (see inset). This underpins concerns about limitations imposed by sampling restricted regions near the periosteal surface.

so that not only age changes to bone microstructure in adulthood could be studied but so that the changes that occur in childhood that give rise to the mature pattern of vascularization in bone could be understood. This resulted in 240 short midshaft blocks collected under the authority of the coroner. These were removed at autopsy by the mortuary technicians. Each of these blocks was accompanied by a copy of the pathologist's report on the condition of the body and the cause of death. This report also recorded the age, sex, height (actually approximate supine length), and weight of the deceased.

The Melbourne research team then decided to build a semiautomated system to record and measure all features of interest from microradiographs made from sections of the entire cross-section of the femoral cortex (Figure 13.3). It became increasingly apparent as research progressed that the relationship between osteon density in the femur, assessed by our methods that utilized the counting of Haversian canals, and age at death was so poor as to be almost useless for forensic purposes in an Australian legal context. Nevertheless, analysis of the large amount of information gathered allowed us to develop a much deeper understanding of age-related changes in the femoral cortex (Thomas et al. 2000). However, this could only be determined with certainty because the Melbourne team had the opportunity to examine a greater area of bone tissue of known age than any previous researchers. The Melbourne group was the first to use information from the entire femur cross-section, rather than a few very small, fixed microscopic fields. This liberated us from sampling limitations imposed by the practicality of having to work from a few microscopic fixed fields and manual counting features that may or may not have been representative of the cortex as a whole. However, this analysis was still an approximation because we were only able to count those Haversian systems that were "complete" in the sense that there was a canal present. Of course in older bone that has experienced considerable turnover there may be

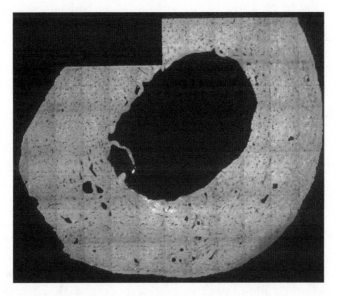

**Figure 13.3** This montage depicts a partially reconstructed cross-section of bone being examined sequentially using an automated computer-controlled image-acquisition system. This system collects contiguous "tiles" that can be reformatted to reconstruct the entire cross-section. The system recorded as many as 11,000 osteon canals for a single section, measured their size, and mapped their exact position. Each cross-section of bone can be examined in about 1 hour. This task would be impossible using manual methods.

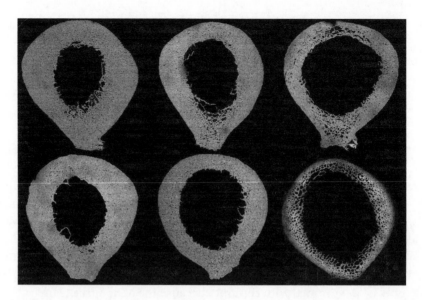

**Figure 13.4** Six contact microradiographs of cross-sections taken from the mid-shaft of the femur. Each one is taken from a different person, but all was either 78, 79, or 80 years old at their deaths. This illustrates the wide range of biological variation between people that suggests that "bone age" and chronological age may differ considerably.

large numbers of osteonal fragments that we were unable to quantify despite attempts to use computer vision methods at the time (Liu et al. 1996, 1999). Despite these shortcomings, taking cross-sectional morphometry and histomorphometry together we were clearly able to show that bones age at greatly different rates between individuals and this goes to the heart of the issue when trying to establish age at death from skeletal remains in the adult period. However, although our research methodology did not produce the favorable results that we had anticipated, it did generate copious high quality and detailed data (Figure 13.4).

## 13.4   Genetic Markers for Osteoporosis

Given that our ethical approval had stipulated that we study the samples for "age-related changes in skeletal tissues" in addition to its potential value as a forensic reference collection, the MFC has become a very important resource for our collaborators in the fields of mineral metabolism, clinical medicine, and osteoporosis research. The following paragraphs illustrate this.

Osteoporotic changes can affect both men and women; however, women are more likely to develop the condition earlier as they age (Figure 13.5A and Figure 13.5B). Researchers at the Garvan Institute in New South Wales (NSW), Australia, reported the finding of a genetic marker that would allow prediction of risk for developing osteoporosis in later life. A vitamin D receptor (VDR) allele was reported to account for about 75% of the inherited risk of osteoporosis (Morrison et al. 1994). If this had been the case it would have represented a tremendous scientific and medical advance that would have allowed the targeting of preventative therapies to those in the at-risk population. Therefore, in collaboration with the Department of Medicine at the Royal Melbourne Hospital, we initiated research

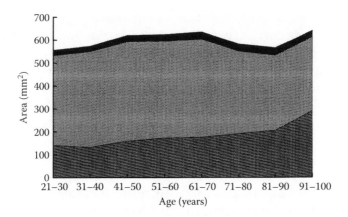

**Figure 13.5A** A partitioning of the cross-sectional area of the femora of males. The cortical bone area and the medullary area were measured macroscopically, the total intracortical void area was determined at much higher resolution from microradiographs. With age the intracortical void area changes very little; the predominant change is in the size of the medullary cavity in the center of the bone, which increases markedly at the expense of the cortex.

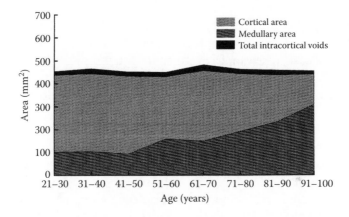

**Figure 13.5B** A partitioning of the cross-sectional area of the femora of females. As females age, the porosity of the bone "intracortical void area" also changes very little. However, the medullary area in the center of the bone increases dramatically in later life and consequently the surrounding cortical bone thins. The data is for the midshaft but in the neck of the femur a similar process leads to "osteoporotic fracture," which is probably a poor term to describe the real changes that occur as the change in porosity is probably less important than the thinning of the cortex.

to verify this using the MFC. We used matching blood and bone samples to search for a link between the degree of expression of the putative genetic "marker" and osteoporosis-related changes in the microstructure of bone. Specifically, organ size, shape of the cortical cross-section, cortex thickness, and its porosity were compared with levels of marker gene expression. This research took 3 years to complete.

Unfortunately, we found that the genetic marker identified in the NSW study only accounted for about 1% of an inherited tendency towards developing osteoporosis, rather than the 75% originally reported (Stein 1997). More recently the relationship between bone density and VDR alleles has been questioned (Ferrari 2008; Uitterlinden et al. 2006) and may only be a small part of a much more complex process. However, the MDS–Royal

Melbourne Hospital study did clearly demonstrate the serendipitous nature of research, since data originally collected for age-at-death estimates was invaluable in a study of potentially enormous significance to the future understanding of osteoporosis, a phenomenon that threatens to impoverish us all as the population continues to age. Furthermore, the retention of all morphological and histomorphological data gathered from several hundred persons, together with matching blood samples, will allow rapid investigation of the role of any further genes that might be identified as osteoporosis indicators or, for that matter, the ancestry of the donor.

## 13.5    The Significance of the MFC to Bone Research and Contributions to the Scientific Literature

The material collected, and the data derived from past and current studies has now become a research source of international significance and attracts many requests from high calibre scientists to access its resources for research on age-related bone changes.

For example, the Melbourne research team has collaborated with colleagues at

Drexel University, College of Medicine, Department of Neurobiology and Anatomy
New York University, College of Dentistry, Hard Tissue Unit
The University of Saskatchewan, Department of Anatomy and Cell Biology
Edinburgh University, Scotland, Department of Engineering
Cambridge University, Department of Medicine, and the Bone Research Unit, Addenbrooke's Hospital, Cambridge, England
Oxford University, Department of Archaeology
Cranfield University, England, Centre for Materials Science and Engineering
University of Auckland, New Zealand, Auckland Bioengineering Institute

These collaborations are in addition to more local collaborations with the Department of Physics at Latrobe University, Monash University Centre for Synchrotron Science, and the Commonwealth Scientific Industrial Research Organisation (CSIRO) of Australia.

The MFC has contributed to considerable advances of knowledge to date, and its potential future significance promises to be enormous and much more important normative data remains to be extracted from the collection. One current precondition to MFC access is that all research data generated by collaborators must be made available to the public via research publications. Each project approved is also studying a different set of age-related bone features in the same material, and in this way, every new discovery amplifies the value of those that preceded it.

Since the initial studies of age-at-death estimation, many other complementary projects have been completed on this theme, and others are continuing. From the first paper in 1995 up to late 2010, 27 scientific articles have been published in international peer-reviewed journals. These papers record work on many aspects of bone-aging research including the development of methods (Cooper et al. 2008; Liu et al. 1996, 1999; Myers et al. 2010), studies of femoral neck cortical geometry (Mayhew et al. 2005) and supporting trabecular bone (Thomas et al. 2008), the collagen fiber matrix (Goldman et al. 2003, 2009) and chemical composition (Hedges et al. 2007), as well as more direct study of age-at-death estimation methods (Thomas et al. 2000; Cooper et al. 2005). This ongoing journey may ultimately return to studying methods for estimating age at death, but this will be a by-product of a long series of studies of age-related changes in cortical bone.

## 13.6 Concluding Remarks

Professor John Clement at the Melbourne Dental School is currently responsible for curating the MFC and overseeing the ethical framework under which it exists and functions. He carries responsibility to make regular reports to the ethics committee of the VIFM. His responsibilities regarding the oversight of this collection illustrate the kinds of issues that obtain for the creation, conservation, and administration of research collections comprised of human tissues, including bone. Currently and in addition, any movement of tissue from Clement's laboratories can only be done with the knowledge and consent of the VIFM ethics committee. The committee has to be certain that the storage and security of the tissue will be equal to that in Clement's laboratory in Melbourne and that the local research team will work to the ethical standards imposed in Australia. The integrity of the collection is paramount and the families of donors retain the right to reclaim tissue from the archive at any time. No such requests have ever been made, but the audit and whereabouts of every piece of tissue has to be known and recorded at all times. Of course some investigations inevitably destroy tissue. For example, the preparation of typical 80-micron-thick plano-parallel ground sections destroys more tissue during sawing and grinding than is preserved to be examined microscopically. Similarly, one series of experiments to study carbon isotopic ratios of organic components within the bone required the complete destruction of a few milligrams of bone for examination in a mass spectrometer and so, by degrees, some samples are now very depleted. This loss of tissue has to be recorded and explained to the ethics committee of the VIFM to their satisfaction.

The MFC is a large and growing collection of human femoral bone tissue with accompanying radiographic images of the bones from which the samples were taken. There is also corresponding biometric data that permits biomechanical parameters to be calculated. Many samples also have a corresponding blood sample. This will permit genetic studies to be undertaken and genotype/phenotype comparisons to be made by reference to the enormous amount of histomorphometric data that has already been gleaned from the collection using a variety of methods in a hierarchical manner for the last two decades. The material has all been accumulated with rigorous ethical oversight and for the later part of the collection with the explicit informed consent of the next of kin to the deceased. Early work by other researchers made no mention of the ethics associated with acquisition of material, but recently attitudes have changed and current papers are clear about the source of samples and ethical oversight of the work (Chan et al. 2007; Martrille et al. 2009). The initial focus was a forensic one (with the understanding that it could also enhance anthropological knowledge) but there has been a progressive shift of emphasis toward understanding medical conditions such as osteoporosis. However, although the initial forensic anthropological focus has been broadened, the insights gained at every step of the journey of exploration of the collection has the potential to generate findings of important forensic significance.

What is the future for the MFC? Clement and his co-workers, who have worked on the collection since its inception, are becoming increasingly aware of the urgent need to fund the maintenance, development, and preservation costs of the MFC in perpetuity. Currently the transfer of responsibility for the collection from Clement's research team to the University of Melbourne Faculty of Medicine, Dentistry, and Health Sciences is being discussed as one solution to immortalize the collection. If the MFC continues to grow, then it will continue to reflect the changes in the composition of Melbourne society that are occurring now as the result of increasing migration from many parts of the world. Should the collection not grow but be retained as it currently exists, then it will provide a snapshot of Melbourne's predominantly Anglo-Celtic population who died in the 1990s. This will provide a reference for any subsequent secular trends in our society. Either way the collection will be an invaluable resource for future scholars. The MDS custodians of the collection do not, and ethically cannot, seek to commercialize it because the tissues were never donated with this understanding. In Australian law there is no property in a body and hence tissues cannot be sold. However, services associated with the harvesting of tissues can be reimbursed. Therefore, options are being explored for offsetting maintenance costs by developing a subscription fee system for scholars wishing to access the collection and associated archived data gathered by previous researchers. It is envisaged that this system would operate similarly to the VIFM Donor Tissue Bank's cost-recouping measures that support the provision of tissue for therapeutic use.

The authors wish to express their gratitude to the staff of the VIFM for their assistance in gathering the tissues that comprise the Melbourne Femur Collection. Special mention should be made of the staff of the donor tissue bank and the mortuary and members of the ethics committee for their support. Many families have, over a period of more than 15 years, generously and altruistically donated research tissue from their recently deceased family members in the hope that something good could be retrieved from their personal loss. It is hoped that this account will express the enormous appreciation the researchers feel for the privilege of access to such a unique collection of material. It must be acknowledged that the insight, trust, and generosity shown by the families of the deceased are really capable of enhancing the lives for many in society who will follow them. For that we, as researchers, express our gratitude and respect.

# References

Amprino R (1963) On growth of cortical bone and mechanism of osteon formation. Acta Anat 52:177.

Chan A H W, Crowder C M, and Rogers T L (2007) Variation in cortical bone histology within the human femur and its impact on estimating age at death. Am J Phys Anthrop 132:80–88.

Cooper D M L, Clement J G, Thomas C D L, Hallgrimsson B, Turinsky A L, Sensen C W, and Goldman H M (2008) Advances in high resolution imaging and the emerging application of 3D cortical bone histomorphometry in interpreting health. Am J Phys Anthrop Suppl 46:81.

Cooper D M L, Turinsky A L, Sensen C W, Clement J G, Thomas C D L, and Hallgrimsson B (2005) Prediction of age-at-death from 3D changes in the dimensions and structure of the cortical canal network at the anterior femoral midshaft. Am J Phys Anthrop Suppl 40:87–88.

Ferrari S (2008) Human genetics of osteoporosis. Clin Endocrinol Metab 22:723–735.

Goldman H M, Bromage, T G, Thomas, C D L, Clement, J G (2003) Preferred collagen fiber orientation in the human mid-shaft femur. Anat Rec 272A:434–445.

Goldman H M, McFarlin S C, Cooper D M L, Thomas C D L, and Clement J G (2009) Ontogenetic patterning of cortical bone microstructure and geometry at the human mid-shaft femur. Anat Rec 292A:48–64.

Hall D (2001) Reflecting on Redfern: What can we learn from the Alder Hey story? Arch Disease Child 84:455–456.

Hedges R E M, Clement J G, Thomas C D L, and O'Connell T C (2007) Collagen turnover in the adult femoral mid-shaft: Modeled from anthropogenic radiocarbon tracer measurements. Am J Phys Anthrop 133:808–816.

Kerley E R (1965) The microscopic determination of age in human bone. Am J Phys Anthrop 23:149–163.

Kerley E R and Ubelaker D H (1978) Revisions in the microscopic method of estimating age at death in human cortical bone. Am J Phys Anthrop 49:545–546.

Liu Z Q, Austin T, Thomas C D L, and Clement J G (1996) Bone feature analysis using image processing techniques. Comput Biol Med 26:65–76.

Liu Z Q, Liew H L, Clement J G, and Thomas C D L (1999) Bone image segmentation. IEEE Trans Biomed Eng 46:565–573.

Martrille L, Irinopoulou T, Bruneval P, Baccino E, and Fornes P (2009) Age at death estimation in adults by computer-assisted histomorphometry of decalcified femur cortex. J Forensic Sci 54:1231–1237.

Mayhew P M, Thomas C D, Clement J G, Loveridge N, Beck T J, Bonfield W, Burgoyne C J, and Reeve J (2005) Relation between age, femoral neck cortical stability, and hip fracture risk. Lancet. 366:129–135.

Morrison N A, Qi J C, Tokita A, Kelly P J, Crofts L, Nguyen T V, Sambrook P N, and Eisman J A (1994) Prediction of bone-density from vitamin-D receptor alleles. Nature 367:284–287.

Myers G R, Thomas C D L, Paganin D M, Gureyev T E, and Clement J G (2010) A general few-projection method for tomographic reconstruction of samples consisting of several distinct materials. Appl Phys Lett 96. doi:10.1063/1.3279150.

Redfern M (2001) The Royal Liverpool Children's Inquiry Report (The Redfern Report). The Stationary Office.

Samson C and Branigan K (1987) A new method of estimating age at death from fragmentary and weathered bone, in Death, decay and reconstruction, A Boddington, A N Garland, and R C Janaway, Editors. Manchester University Press.

Simmons D J (1985) Options for bone aging with the microscope. Yearb Phys Anthropol 28:249–263.

Singh I J and Gunberg D L (1970) Estimation of age at death in human males from quantitative histology of bone fragments. Am J Phys Anthrop 373–382.

Stein M S (1997) Determinants of bone fragility with age and in metabolic bone disease. PhD dissertation, University of Melbourne, Australia.

Thomas C D, Mayhew P M, Clement J G, Loveridge N, Burgoyne C J, and Reeve J (2008) Ageing effects on femoral neck trabecular bone: Role in hip fracture. Calcif Tissue Int 83:8.

Thomas C D L, Stein M S, Feik S A, Wark J D, and Clement J G (2000) Determination of age at death using combined morphology and histology of the femur. J Anat 196:463–471.

Uitterlinden A G, Ralston S H, Brandi M L, Carey A H, Grinberg D, and Langdahl B L (2006) The association between common vitamin D receptor gene variations and osteoporosis: A participant-level meta-analysis. Ann Intern Med 145:255–264.

# The Histology Laboratory and Principles of Microscope Instrumentation

# 14

HELEN CHO

## Contents

## 14.1 Introduction

As illustrated in earlier chapters, bone histology has many known applications in biological anthropology, forensic sciences, biomedicine, and biomechanics, to name a few. This chapter is geared toward the novice who has interests in studying skeletal tissue through histological means. Basic instrumentation and consumables necessary for a histology laboratory are addressed, followed by principles of light microscopy. It is essential for the practitioner to properly use and maintain the equipment for sample preparation and know how a microscope operates to correctly observe and collect histological data.

## 14.2 The Histology Laboratory

The physical space dedicated to bone histology must follow the specifications outlined by the Occupational Safety and Health Administration (OSHA), an agency under the U.S. Department of Labor, that was created in 1971 to reduce occupational deaths, injuries, and illnesses. Academic institutions and their laboratories must comply with OSHA regulations and standards, and eliminate dangers and hazards in research facilities by equipping laboratories with safety measures. Fume hoods are necessary to limit or to prevent exposure of researchers and other individuals to harmful chemical fumes. Flammable and toxic chemical liquids must be properly stored in chemical storage cabinets; many manufacturers offer a wide variety of designs and sizes that comply with OSHA regulations. Material Safety Data Sheets, or MSDS, that accompany every chemical liquid purchased will outline the procedures for proper storage, handling, and disposal; and contain important information on its physical properties, health effects, first aid procedures for accidents, and so forth. MSDS should be compiled and kept in the laboratory for reference. Personal protective gear, such as eye goggles, face shields, closed-toe chemical and slip resistant shoes, aprons, lab coats, and disposable gloves, prevent injury and direct contact with hazardous materials. An eyewash station or a faucet-mount eyewash should be installed and always functional. The latter is a convenient unit that attaches to existing faucets and delivers water upward upon activation. A sharps container, available in various sizes, is for the disposal of scalpel blades and broken glass microscope slides and coverslips, and biohazard bags and boxes to dispose of human and nonhuman tissue and other contaminated materials. As soft tissue will decompose, placing the biohazard bag inside a freezer will prevent decomposition and unpleasant odors. An upright or a chest freezer is needed if the study samples will include soft tissue. The institution's responsible personnel should schedule the pick up and proper disposal of both the sharps containers and biohazard bags. Last, hepatitis B immunization is necessary for the researcher due to contact with human tissue and sharp objects, particularly if the samples have soft tissue.

The bone histology laboratory should be a "wet" lab, or have water supply and drainage for histology instrumentation and hard tissue sample processing. Chemical-resistant work surfaces and stainless steel tables are ideal for ease in maintenance, cleaning, and decontaminating possible pathogens from human and nonhuman animal tissue. The work surfaces should be durable to safely support and accommodate the weight and size of various histology instruments. Aside from the space required for instruments, ample work surface to lay out bone samples in multiple stages of processing will create an efficient workflow, reduce clutter, and prevent mixing specimens with identification tags.

### 14.2.1  Preparing Bone Thin Sections for Microscopic Analysis

It is imperative that good quality thin sections are produced for microscopic analysis. Human skeletal samples are valuable and often difficult to obtain for invasive research, and familiarizing oneself with the histological procedures on nonhuman bone is recommended. The following procedures pertain to preparation of undecalcified cortical bone for histological analysis. Buehler equipment is most often used for producing undecalcified sections and at times described here. However, there are many alternative methods for preparing decalcified histological sections that employ different types of instrumentation and consumables.

### 14.2.2  Preparing Samples for Embedding

Bone samples procured by the anthropologist may be fleshed or devoid of soft tissue depending on the context in which the remains were recovered. Regardless, bone samples will require preparation before embedding. The histology samples, whether removed from small (e.g., rib, metacarpal) or large (e.g., femur) skeletal elements, should measure at least 2 to 3 cm in length to provide a sufficient sample. However, in some circumstances ideal sample lengths may not be available requiring the use of the entire sample to produce thin sections. In these situations one should determine if DNA analysis is requested before the entire sample is used for histological analysis. Depending on its size and cortical thickness, a band saw commonly used for construction, a Stryker® Autopsy Saw, or a small hand-held Dremel® tool can cut the longer bone samples to an appropriate or manageable size for further processing (e.g., embedding, sectioning, or grinding). Extra care should be taken with brittle and fragile samples as these tools will cause fragmentation; fragile samples may be cut into longer lengths to maintain structural integrity. It is advisable to include a reference mark on bone samples that will allow anterior, posterior, medial, and lateral surfaces to be identified on final cross-sections.

Archaeological samples can be embedded in plastic resin without much preparation. A soft-bristle brush is used to remove adhering soil on bone samples, while an ultrasonic cleaner will gently and safely remove the debris that has accumulated in the small pores and the medullary cavity via high frequency sound waves. Numerous models and sizes of ultrasonic cleaners, accessories, and cleaner solutions are available through companies such as Buehler (Lake Bluff, IL) and Fisher Scientific (Pittsburgh, PA). If multiple samples are simultaneously cleaned, the samples can be individually wrapped in cheesecloth and tied with a cotton string with an identification tag. At all stages of the thin-section preparation, each bone sample must be accompanied by an identification label.

Samples containing soft tissue should be defleshed and degreased before the embedding process. This is accomplished by employing a colony of dermestid beetles for defleshing, heating the samples under the fume hood in a pot with water and organic detergent, or simply soaking them in water to macerate soft tissue. Bleach and hydrogen peroxide will degrade bone and should never be used (Fenton et al. 2003). The water level is periodically checked and leaving the hotplate unattended for extended periods of time should be avoided. Depending on the condition of the samples, the heat treatment may last a few hours or longer until the soft tissue can be manually removed with hemostatic forceps and tweezers. The tissue, latex gloves, and other disposable contaminated materials are discarded in a biohazard bag. Although hot soapy water will remove most of the marrow fat, placing the bone samples on paper towels to air-dry will further degrease them. If the samples are still greasy, chemical degreasing methods include soaking the samples in a xyol solution of 60% industrial grade alcohol and 40% xylene (Nawrocki 1997). A solution of water, commercial powdered detergent, and household liquid ammonia will also deflesh and degrease bone (Fenton et al. 2003). The samples should be rinsed in clean water and air-dried completely before they are embedded. Tiesler and colleagues (2006) recommend a 7-day process of immersing the samples in different concentrations of alcohol and distilled water, acetone, and dichloromethane.

## 14.2.3   Embedding

The purpose of embedding the bone sample in plastic resin is to maintain its structural integrity during the cutting and grinding process. Although small, modern, "fresh" samples may not need to be embedded, archaeological samples that are dry and brittle must be embedded. An additional advantage of embedding, especially for samples of a forensic nature where chain of custody is of paramount concern, is that the sample is securely preserved along with a label. Appropriate molds should be chosen for the dimensions of the specimens. Suitable options include reusable rubber molds in various shapes and sizes, rectangular or square disposable peel-away plastic molds, and inexpensive hard plastic or rubber ice cube trays.

There are many types of resin for embedding samples, and several contributors to this volume have had success with EpoThin® manufactured by Buehler. EpoThin is a low viscosity epoxy resin that cures relatively quickly at room temperature into a clear plastic. The EpoThin hardener and resin are mixed according to product specifications and poured into molds that contain one bone sample in each. An incorrect ratio of resin to hardener or insufficiently stirred mixture will result in a sticky or extremely hard plastic and will pose a challenge during the cutting process. An alternative resin for researchers outside the United States is BIODUR® E 12 that requires the use of a heating cabinet or oven (Tiesler et al. 2006). As the molds will be removed after the resin has cured, each bone sample must include a paper label written in pencil or indelible ink so that the label is embedded with the bone (Figure 14.1). In many biomedical research labs, methyl methacrylate is used as the embedding medium. An advantage is that it can be removed with xylene, while a drawback is the expense and time involved in preparation. Details for its use and other aspects of the preparation of bone for histological examination, including staining, can be found in Anderson (1982).

To ensure impregnation of the resin throughout the bone sample, vacuum impregnation is highly recommended, though some bone histologists omit this step (Paine 2007). Proper impregnation will ensure success when producing thin sections. A fragile bone sample that is poorly infused with the plastic resin will break apart during the cutting, grinding, or polishing stages. Vacuum impregnation equipment is useful to remove air bubbles and to infuse the resin throughout the specimens (Figure 14.2). A simpler option is a vacuum bell jar available at science education and research supply companies. A significant number of bubbles may form on the surface of the resin during the minute or so of vacuuming, and vacuuming should continue until no bubbles are seen. Air must be allowed to enter the vacuum chamber very slowly after allowing the samples to rest for a

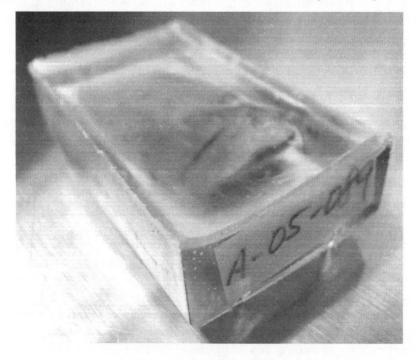

**Figure 14.1** A bone sample embedded with a label in epoxy resin.

**Figure 14.2** Example of a vacuum impregnation system.

minute; a quick return to atmospheric pressure will result in the molds tipping or resin splattering in the vacuum chamber. Generally, the samples remain submerged in resin as vacuum impregnation replaces the air in pores and medullary cavity with resin. If bone samples from small and light skeletal elements float, the bone can be gently pushed down with a wooden skewer to submerge it in the resin. When placing the specimen in its mold, the desired orientation of the thin section to be removed must be considered. For sectioning, sample orientation should be in accordance with the type of thin section required by the analytical method being applied.

The fumes produced by most embedding media are toxic. Therefore, the molds should be placed inside the fume hood with the blower on to cure according to specifications for the resin product. EpoThin cures within a day, BIODUR will take a few weeks (Tiesler et al. 2006), and the total embedding time for methyl methacrylate is 12 days (Anderson 1982). Once the resin has cured, the bone blocks are removed from the molds. Care should be taken when handling the blocks since the corners may be sharp enough to puncture skin. Tapping the corners against the work surface will blunt the hard plastic edges.

### 14.2.4   Cutting Thick Sections

A low speed, gravity, rotary saw fitted with a diamond embedded blade is commonly used for cutting thick wafers from bone blocks. Buehler, Leica, and INGRAM-WARD, MTI Corporation, and other companies manufacture various models of saws that range in capacity, price, and accessories that can be customized to include diverse types of metal chucks to accommodate bone blocks of various shapes and sizes, wafering blades varying in diameter, lubricating fluid, dressing stick, holding arm for the chuck, and so forth (Figure 14.3). Those employed within academia may check with their geology department for petrographic equipment that can be adapted to cut bone; geologists often employ the same equipment for cutting and grinding rock samples. In general, sledge microtomes are

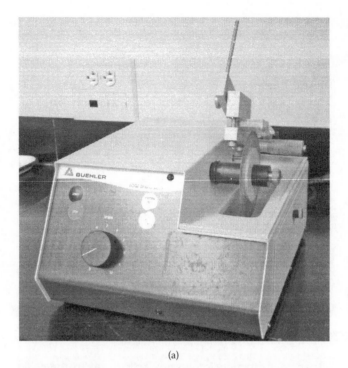

(a)

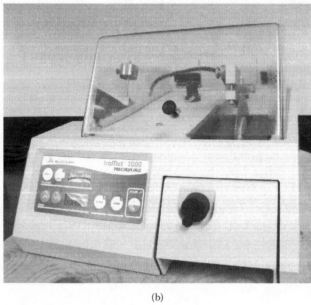

(b)

**Figure 14.3** Two IsoMet® models for cutting thick wafers.

not appropriate for histological analyses that require complete cross-sections of compact bone. Microtome knives can produce knife chatter on cortical bone, obscuring micro-structures, and curl or wrinkle the sections (Ries 2003).

There are several important details to consider regarding the cutting stage. Transverse sections of the femur midshaft, for example, require that wafers are cut perpendicular to the diaphysis, therefore, the block must be properly aligned in the holding arm via a chuck (Figure 14.4). The requisite method for histomorphometric age estimation, for instance, is

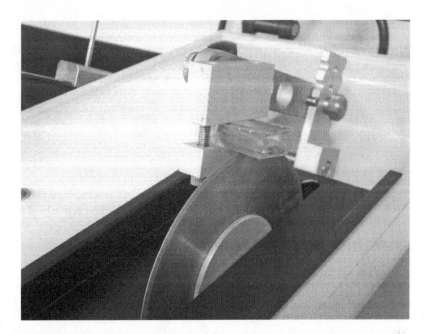

**Figure 14.4** Positioning of an embedded sample in the cutting chuck. Typical cross-sectional analysis requires that the thick wafers be perpendicular to their long axis.

a cross-section of the skeletal element, and an oblique cut will distort the morphology of longitudinal structures such as osteons (Haversian systems), making their measurement inaccurate. Too much weight and pressure on the bone block as the saw is rotating may result in breaking the wafer or the blade itself. The thickness of the wafer, about 100 to 150 µm, is controlled manually or digitally depending on the saw model. As a rule, the thinner the wafer removed, the less the grinding time and effort. Archaeological samples, even though embedded, will need to be cut slowly with adequate lubrication to avoid loss of bony material as the blade turns. If small amounts of bony material are lost during the cutting stage due to an imperfect infusion of plastic resin, a thin, even layer of Super Glue® on the exposed surface will maintain the structural integrity of cortical bone. Each time a block of embedded bone is mounted or remounted on the holding arm, a waste piece is cut to produce a parallel surface between the block and the cutting blade. To save time and usage of the saw, one should avoid trimming of the sample after remounting. Therefore, at least five to seven wafers should be cut before removing the block from the holding arm, even if only one or a few will be ground to produce thin sections. Extra wafers can be saved for future reanalysis. The diamond-embedded blade should be dressed occasionally using a dressing stick; some saw models have a built-in feature for the dressing stick so that the holding arm can be reserved for the specimen block. Hand-holding of dressing sticks should be avoided as this may result in broken blades.

### 14.2.5  Grinding, Polishing, and Mounting Thin Sections on Microscope Slides

The thick wafers are ground to a final thickness of 50–100 µm, thin enough to allow light to penetrate so that the microstructures can be viewed under the microscope. The grinding process may be accomplished in multiple ways to accommodate various budgets and

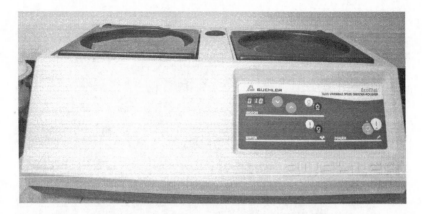

**Figure 14.5** EcoMet® grinder/polisher with two rotating plates.

sample quality. Some equipment, with an attachment to mount and hold thick sections, allows for automatic and simultaneous grinding of multiple samples to the desired thickness. Other models have one or two round metal plates that rotate at variable speeds, and round abrasive papers or grinding discs are affixed to the plate (Figure 14.5). With these grinders, the grinding is semimanual and more labor intensive but preferable for fragile samples. The wafer is held down on a rotating plate with a microscope slide or the Histolic Precision Grinding Fixture that will hold one standard microscope slide for precise and uniform removal of material (Figure 14.6). The round, heavy, palm-sized fixture is designed to prevent overgrinding and loss of bone. Crystalbond®, a temporary but strong adhesive that adheres well to glass, is heated to melt the adhesive onto the microscope slide and a thick wafer is affixed to the slide. After the adhesive cures, the slide is mounted on the grinding fixture, which is held down on a grinding plate as it rotates. HandiMet® is a type of grinder outfitted with four different abrasive rolls of paper and ideal for fragile samples that must be hand-ground (Figure 14.7). Four abrasive rolls of different grit value enable the researcher to switch from coarse to fine grinding without changing the rolls. The last option is to manually grind the thick wafer on abrasive paper placed on the work surface. The thick wafer is either affixed on a microscope slide with an adhesive or held between the slide and abrasive paper as the researcher grinds the wafer in a fast circular motion. Though it is more labor intensive than the use of specialized grinding and polishing equipment with a rotating plate, using a small suction cup on the slide to control its movement or wrapping a strip of abrasive paper around the slide and holding the loose ends will successfully produce thin sections (Figure 14.8). Lubricants used during the grinding process vary, but water is usually adequate. Regardless of the method, the thick wafer should be ground on low grit (coarser) paper initially and then switched to medium grit, to fine grit, and finally polished on polishing cloths or pads to remove scratches. Scratches on the cortical area can inhibit examination of microstructures, and once a thin section is set on the microscope slide and coverslipped, it is difficult to remove it for polishing. During the grinding process, the wafer is regularly viewed under a light microscope to check for thickness. Modern and well-preserved wafers that were cut thinner will require less grinding.

After the polishing step, the thin section is placed in an ultrasonic cleaner to remove debris from the abrasive paper that may be embedded in the cavities. The sample is cleared with a nontoxic and low odor compound such as Clear-Rite™ 3, a good substitute for xylene. Xylene is a popular chemical solution used in histology for tissue processing and

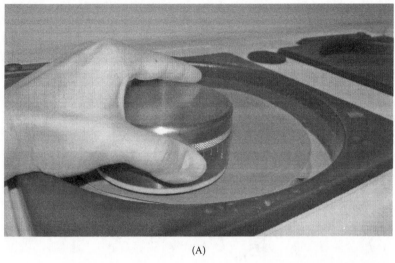

(A)

(B)

**Figure 14.6** Demonstration of two sample holding techniques during grinding: (A) Semi-manual grinding with the Histolic Precision Grinding Fixture and (B) a microscope slide wrapped with a piece of adhesive-backed sandpaper.

clearing, but it is a toxic compound that commonly causes headaches, nausea, dizziness, and more serious long-term effects. Therefore, discontinued use of xylene for histological tissue clearing is strongly recommended (Buesa and Peshkov 2009). The thin section should soak in the clearing agent in a glass jar with a lid for a few minutes and then dried or placed on a clean slide without drying if diagenetic changes are present in the cortex; not allowing the section to dry before coverslipping will reduce diagenetic inclusions such as mold and fungus. A generous amount of Permount® or other mounting medium is applied to the section and coverslipped. When coverslipping, one corner should touch the medium and the remaining corners are laid down, one at a time, allowing for the fluid to completely

**Figure 14.7** HandiMet® system for hand grinding.

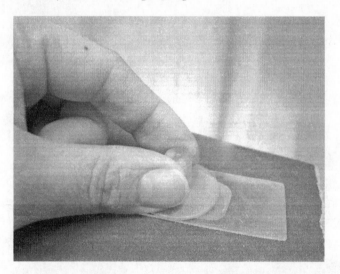

**Figure 14.8** Hand grinding on abrasive paper with a microscope slide and a suction cup.

make contact with the entire surface area of the coverslip. Gently pressing down will release air bubbles trapped in the bone section and squeeze out excess mounting medium. A piece of paper towel should be placed underneath the slide to absorb the excess fluid and a weight is placed on the coverslip so that the thin section will dry flat and will not curl up. Metal nuts or other inexpensive objects will perform the task and another piece of paper is placed between the weight and the coverslip to prevent the object from attaching to the coverslip. Once the mounting medium has set, it should be clear and transparent. Excess medium on the microscope slide may be cleaned with acetone or Clear-Rite 3 and the bone section is ready for histological analysis. A caveat about Permount is that over long periods of storage, it turns yellowish and cracks, often leaving the slides obscured with large air bubbles and an opaque specimen. Other mounting media exist in the industry but attention should be paid to their reaction with the clearing agent and the refractive index, which is addressed later within the discussion on microscopy. If the thin section is still affixed to the slide after grinding, it is unnecessary to remove the specimen for remounting on a different microscope slide. Removing the thin section mounted with Crystalbond will require that the slide be heated to melt the adhesive, and this procedure may result in damaging the specimen. Instead, clearing the thin section along with the microscope slide and applying the mounting medium and coverslip are recommended.

When the mounting medium has cured completely, the slides are stored in a microscope slide box. However, even slides that have been drying on a flat surface for days will result in the bone section drifting downward. It is recommended that the slides air-dry for a few weeks although the microscopic analysis could be carried out while the mounting medium is wet. Leftover bone blocks along with the unground thick wafers should be saved for future use. Damage to the ground thin section during storage or analysis will require the researcher to create a thin section de novo.

The process of cleaning, embedding, cutting, grinding, polishing, and mounting a bone sample can take several days to a week. Preparing numerous samples simultaneously will speed up the process. For example, embedding all the samples means that a batch of blocks will be curing and available at the same time. Once thick wafers are cut, grinding and polishing can take place while other bone blocks are being cut. It is imperative to be meticulous about keeping track of the identification code for each thin section, thick wafer, and block because each specimen moves through various steps before being mounted on a slide. User-friendly handheld labeling devices print out uniform and small adhesive labels for microscope slides. An indelible pen or a plain adhesive label will suffice as well.

The initial start-up cost to purchase instruments is the most significant and the instruments require little to no maintenance provided that they are used properly. The low-speed gravity saw blade, abrasive paper, chemicals, and other consumables are the only incurring costs in the histology lab. Over four decades ago, Harold Frost (1958) published a manual method for the preparation of undecalcified bone sections. More recently Maat et al. (2001) offered an updated and modified revision of Frost's original method, which Beauchesne and Saunders (2006) tested and further refined. This method remains an option, especially for anyone looking for one that requires minimal equipment, time, and expense. As with other research endeavors, discussions with those who conduct bone histology research will reveal novel techniques and products, and nuances and tips that will facilitate sample processing. Each bone histologist develops his or her own style in the sample preparation techniques. The final desired outcome for hard tissue histology is that each specimen is a transparent thin section with visible microstructures across the entire area of cortical bone for qualitative and quantitative analysis. The microscope is a versatile and powerful tool for hard tissue research, and as with sample preparation, it is necessary for practitioners to familiarize themselves with this instrument for observations and data collection.

## 14.3 Principles of Light Microscopy

Given the important role that microscopy plays in histological analysis it is imperative to understand the basic features and mechanics of the microscope and the physics of light. Because specific applications of microscopy are addressed in this volume, such as age estimation or assessing bone loss, the following sections are limited to general light microscopy and polarized light microscopy.

## 14.3.1   A Brief History of Light Microscopy

Histology could not be possible without the invention of the microscope. The purposes of the microscope are to magnify and to resolve a small object, in addition to measuring features and properties of a specimen. Resolution refers to revealing the fine details and closely spaced structures as separate and discrete entities. The unaided human eye can resolve objects that are separated by 0.1–0.2 mm, and this distance is the resolving power of our eyes (Croft 2006). Merely amplifying the small features is insufficient and resolution of the minute structures beyond the resolving power of our eyes must be achieved through a microscope (Slayter and Slayter 1992). Also of importance is sufficient contrast between the object and the surrounding material for the microstructures to be visible (Bradbury and Bracegirdle 1998). Because bone is yellowish to light brown with darker microstructures against the background of a translucent microscope slide and mounting medium, it is unnecessary to stain to enhance visibility for most histological methods typically employed in bioarchaeology, forensic anthropology, and paleontology.

The magnification system commonly employed in scientific research is similar to the original design constructed in the late 16th century by Hans and Zacharias Janssen, a Dutch father-and-son team who made eyeglasses. The first compound microscope was a hollow tube with a lens on either end, which differed from a simple microscope built with a single lens (e.g., magnifying glass; Slayter and Slayter 1992; Smith 1994). *Compound* refers to the two lenses that work together to produce the final magnified image and the basic concept of placing a lens close to the object and a second lens close to the eye has remained unchanged through the centuries. The Janssen microscope could magnify up to 10 times depending on the extent that the sliding tube was closed or extended, while contemporary models can magnify up to 2000 times.

Since its conception in the 16th century, the components of a compound microscope evolved considerably in the construction materials used to build the tube (e.g., wood, ivory, brass), a tripod stand to position the tube upright, a specimen stage at the base, a screwbarrel or draw tube focusing mechanism, and so forth. This basic monocular tripod design remained through the 18th century and was occasionally seen in the 19th and 20th century models. In the 18th century, the focusing mechanism was improved by clamping the tube to a vertical pillar to slide it up and down for coarse focus, and the microscopes encompassed a sturdier base, interchangeable objectives with multiple lenses, achromatic lenses to reduce the chromatic aberrations from white light that bent at varying degrees, and substage concave mirrors to illuminate and concentrate light from the sun or candle onto the specimen. By the late 18th century, some models incorporated a familiar inclined body tube on a tripod. Nineteenth century models assumed the modern microscope design, and general versatility in removing and replacing components was characteristic of the century. These models had adjustable circular or square specimen stages with spring clips, adjustable substage condenser lenses and mirrors to gather light, coarse and fine focus knobs or screws to move the stage or the tube up and down, sturdier arms rather than thinner pillars to mount the tube, and wider and sturdier bases. Importantly, achromat objectives to prevent optical aberrations were improved and binocular microscopes in which prisms split the light into separate eyepieces allowing for stereoscopic images were introduced in the

19th century. Early 20th century microscopes incorporated a rotating nosepiece to accommodate two to four higher magnification factor objectives, mechanical stage with scales, focusing knobs, fixed-length body tube or sliding focusing tube, immersion objectives, iris diaphragm, lamps and illumination system, and improved condenser to produce a cone of light (Davidson and Florida State University Research Foundation, 1995–2009).

## 14.3.2 Physics of Light

The microscope's magnification and resolution, color correction, and illumination of specimens were improved owing to the advancements in physics and a better understanding of light in the previous centuries. Light microscopy requires an understanding of the interaction between light, the object, and the observer's eye–brain complex. Light is a form of energy with continuous up and down motion and part of the electromagnetic spectrum of waves. Our eyes are sensitive to a specific wavelength that ranges from 750 to 400 nm, the part of the electromagnetic spectrum called visible light. Color in visible light is determined by the wavelength, the distance between two waves measured at the same points; whereas brightness or intensity of light is determined by amplitude, or the height of the waves (Murphy 2001). Apart from visible light, other types of light in the electromagnetic spectrum are arranged in order of wavelength frequency, the number of waves that pass through a given point in a second. Radio waves and microwaves have the longest wavelengths, the lowest frequencies, and the least amount of energy as wavelength is inversely related to frequency. Microwaves in our kitchens cause food molecules to spin and rub against each other, creating friction and heat. Infrared waves, the type of light used in television remotes, cause bonds between atoms in molecules to vibrate. Ultraviolet light is adjacent to the violet range of visible light and it is energy from the sun that penetrates the atmosphere and causes sunburns. X-rays and gamma rays are the highest frequency waves, contain more energy, and are widely applied in biomedicine to obtain images of dense bony tissue, kill cancerous cells, and so forth (Houck and Siegel 2006).

Much like the lens in eyeglasses, the microscope lenses are made of transparent materials and bend light in a predictable manner. The lens diameter is correlated with the magnification factor; as magnification increases, the lens diameter decreases to bend light more to create a larger image. Through geometry and controlling for the lens diameter, the size and position of the larger virtual image that the eye–brain complex perceives can be determined. Specifically, the focal length of the lens, or the distance between the two points of focus on both sides of the lens, is used to calculate the perceived size of a virtual image. A virtual image is one that can be seen only when looking through a lens and cannot be viewed directly like a real image projected onto a screen. There are limits to the size of the virtual image as magnifying the object produces a larger yet fuzzier image. Thus, resolution is limited due to light diffraction as it passes through a number of restricted openings in the microscope from the light source to the observer's eyes.

With a compound microscope, the total magnification occurs in two stages as a product of the first lens, or the objective lens, and the second lens, or the eyepiece lens. The observer looks through the first lens that is placed closer to the specimen and produces a real, inverted, enlarged image. The second lens, placed closer to the eyes and in line with the first lens in the hollow tube, acts like a magnifying glass and further enlarges the image, and the eye–brain complex perceives it as a virtual image in front of the eyes (Figure 14.9).

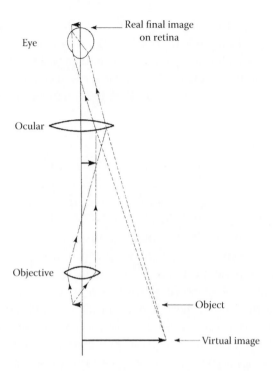

**Figure 14.9** Perception of a magnified virtual image by the eye–brain complex. (Modified from Murphy DB [2001] Fundamentals of light microscopy and electronic imaging. Wiley-Liss, New York, p. 3.)

### 14.3.3   Anatomy of a Light Microscope

Although modern microscopes bear little resemblance to the earlier models, many of the mechanical features existed centuries ago. The following description is limited to transmitted light microscopy, the type that is applicable to bone histomorphology (Figure 14.10). The base is the sturdy and wide support on which the instrument rests (1). The arm is the C-shaped upright portion attached to the base that supports the microscope (2). The stage is a circular or square horizontal plate on which the specimen rests, held in place by spring clips, and moves up and down to focus the specimen image (3). The stage has a central opening to allow visible light to pass through and into the lens system. The body tube is hollow with two lenses mounted at opposite ends and light passes through from one lens to another (4). The coarse adjustment knob is located on the arm that raises or lowers the specimen stage (5). The fine adjustment knob is located on the coarse adjustment knob that moves the stage in smaller magnitudes (6). The illuminator is a high-intensity artificial light source, either placed under the stage and built into the base for translucent specimens or placed above the stage for opaque specimens (7). Typically, bone histologists employ microscopes with the illuminator under the stage to examine thin translucent specimens. The condenser collects light rays from the illuminator and concentrates them uniformly on the specimen (8). Focusing light onto a specimen produces a bright even field of view and improves the image resolution but the condenser has to be adjusted and centered. The field of view refers to the specimen area that is seen when looking through the eyepieces. The condenser-centering screws on the side of the condenser are turned until the light

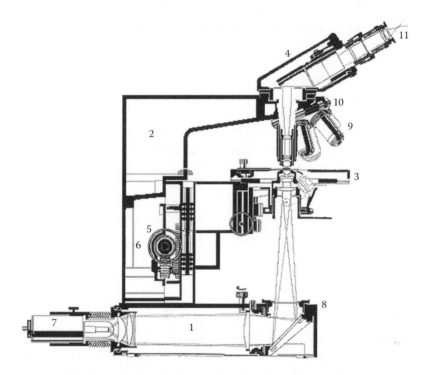

**Figure 14.10** Components of a modern light microscope. (Modified from Saferstein R [2007] Criminalistics: an introduction to forensic science, 9th edn. Prentice-Hall, Upper Saddle River, NJ, p. 183.)

beam is centered in the field. The iris diaphragm in the condenser is opened or closed to control the amount of light transmitted into the lens system and that is comfortable to view through the eyepieces. The objective lens is positioned closer to the stage and several objectives of different magnification (9) are mounted on a revolving nosepiece above the specimen (10) with the magnification, tube length, and numerical aperture information engraved on each. Typically, histomorphology requires 4×, 10×, 15×, 16×, or 20× objectives, and an objective is composed of several lenses that provide the resolution. In bone histomorphology, dry objectives, or those with air between the objective and the coverslip of the slide, are necessary. Immersion objectives that require the use of an immersion oil to function as a medium between the objective and the coverslip have greater magnification and resolving power (Bradbury and Bracegirdle 1998). The eyepiece lens is closer to the observer's eyes and modern microscopes are generally binocular (11). The oculars have a standard magnification of 10× and are focusable, enabling the researcher to adjust the eyepieces if one eye is stronger than the other. The eye cups, commonly found in the oculars, are rubber features that can be extended to keep the observer's eyes at a proper and consistent distance from the ocular. Unlike the earliest models, the eyepiece tube is inclined or tilted back for more comfort in viewing. Commonly, a trinocular microscope can accommodate a video or digital camera for capturing images and be interfaced with a computer analysis system.

Additional components that are relevant to quantitative bone histology (histomorphometry) include the eyepiece reticle, which fits inside one of the oculars. The round and transparent reticle is available with various geometric patterns of lines and crosshairs of known dimensions. The diameter of the reticle must match the inside diameter of the bottom of the eyepiece, which is removable and designed to accept a reticle. For histomorphometry, a stage micrometer and the grid, or the geometric pattern in a reticle, are required. The grid is superimposed over the image of the specimen and both the specimen and the grid are brought into sharp focus and viewed simultaneously for quantification.

An alternative method for histomorphometry is to employ an image analysis system, comprised of a video or digital camera mounted on the trinocular microscope to capture digital images, and a computer and image analysis software to record and view digitized images. Area and length measurements of microstructures (e.g., osteons, Haversian canals, resorptive bays) may be accomplished with its software program, and the practitioner will need a digitized image of a stage micrometer to calibrate the field areas seen on the computer screen. An important note about the image analysis system is that the digitized method should not replace the direct observation of the thin section for reasons addressed later, particularly for quantification of microstructures (e.g., counting the number of fragmentary osteons).

### 14.3.4   Polarizing Light Microscope

A polarizing light microscope is a compound microscope outfitted with two polarizers to allow the bone histologist to detect plane-polarized light. Ordinary light vibrates in all possible planes and polarized light is restricted to a single plane and vibrates in only one direction. A polarizer sits beneath the specimen stage and the preferred vibration direction is set left to right or east to west. A second polarizing filter called an analyzer is placed in the path of the polarized beam. The human eye is blind to the vibrational direction of light and polarized light appears no different to our eye from ordinary light, and an analyzer is required to see polarized light. The analyzer is aligned north to south, mounted on the body tube above the objectives, and manually slides in and out of the light path. When the polarizer and analyzer are aligned parallel to each other, the polarized light passes through and our eyes perceive the maximum intensity of transmitted light. If the analyzer is inserted with its orientation opposite that of the polarizer, that is, right angles or perpendicular, the filters are crossed, which results in total darkness or extinction. The analyzer and polarizer function as special filters by transmitting light in one direction and the orientation of the analyzer determines the intensity of transmitted light (Slayter and Slayter 1992; Wheeler and Wilson 2008). By allowing light to pass in a preferred direction, polarizers enhance the magnified image of anisotropic specimens like bone (Murphy 2001).

Some additional concepts are essential to the understanding and use of polarizing light microscopes. Refraction, or bending of light, occurs as light travels from one medium to another. Refractive index (RI) is a measure of the bending of light and dependent on the angle of the incident beam and internal composition of the material into which it enters. The refractive index of a vacuum is 1.0 and devoid of any material, and any transparent material has a RI greater than 1.0 (e.g., water RI = 1.33). When light passes from a less dense medium (e.g., air) to a denser medium (e.g., water), the speed of wave decreases. Conversely, when light passes from a denser medium to a less dense medium, the speed of wave increases. Isotropic materials such as gases and liquids are optically the same in all directions and have one RI, and light travels through them at the same speed with no directional restrictions. On the other hand, anisotropic materials have optical properties that vary with orientation of incoming light due to its internal structure, and light changes direction as it enters a different density medium (Croft 2006; Wheeler and Wilson 2008). That is, light entering two materials of different densities and RI values results in an artificial distortion of the object. Approximately 90% of solid materials including bone are anisotropic with varying refractive indices (Houck and Siegel 2006). The light interacts with the bone specimen before being collected by the objective, but because histological sections are translucent, much of the light is transmitted and passes through the bony matrix without being absorbed or diffracted. However, light will change directions and speed as it travels from air, to bone, and back to air due to the different RI of air and bone.

A specimen viewed in transmitted light must be in a mounting medium with a RI close to its own (Houck and Siegel 2006). If RI values of the bone sample and mounting medium are too different, an optical distortion will result, much like the appearance of a bent straw in a glass of water. Various mounting media with different refractive indices are available from scientific research suppliers. Permount, a popular medium among bone histologists, has a RI of 1.525 (Houck and Siegel 2006; Wheeler and Wilson 2008) and osteons have a RI of 1.5–1.6 (Ascenzi and Fabry 1959; Malvern Institution 1997). Applying a mounting medium with a similar RI to bone reduces refraction as light passes through the specimen and reaches the microscope lenses (Wheeler and Wilson 2008). An alternative mounting medium is Canada balsam with a RI of 1.525.

Cortical bone is composed of collagen fibers and hydroxyapatite crystals that vary in orientation but with a repeating pattern. This structural organization produces birefringence in bone, which is a common physical property of biological structures and crystals that results from division of light into at least two rays traveling at different speeds and directions in anisotropic materials. Birefringent specimens exhibit patterns of light and dark features that represent the structural organization of molecules. Polarizing light microscopes reveal this inhomogeneous internal structure in anisotropic bone and its varying orientation of collagen fibers that divides light into two beams (Slayter and Slayter 1992). A polarizing light microscope uses birefringence to cause light rays to interact in a way that yields information about the material.

Although the bone specimens are translucent at 50–100 μm, it is necessary to constantly adjust the fine focus to bring particular microstructures into sharp focus. Additionally, polarizers allow for maximum information to be gained from a specimen. Particularly if the quality of the thin section is less than ideal, switching back and forth from ordinary to polarized light by inserting or removing the analyzer enables the researcher to distinguish the microstructures of interest. For example, delineating cement lines and collagen fiber orientation is important to distinguish between intact and fragmentary osteons for histomorphometry. These osteon features are more evident under polarized light and by continuously focusing the specimen up and down with the fine focus knob.

## 14.4   Recommendations and Conclusions

This section addresses steps that need to be taken and some suggestions to consider prior to data collection through microscopy. Each ocular needs to be adjusted and brought into focus. The ocular with the eyepiece reticle can be removed from the body tube and the adjustment collar is turned until the grid is brought into sharp focus. The oculars are brought closer together or farther apart until a single field of view of the specimen is seen. Every researcher has different spacing between the eyes and the eyepieces are adjusted to suit the observer's eyes. Closing one eye and using the coarse and fine adjustment knobs for focusing with the open eye and repeating this step with the alternate eye should be carried out before both eyes are used to focus on a single field. Many individuals have a dominant eye that does not enable them to simultaneously view a single field with both eyes, which may strain the eyes.

A progressive increase in magnification from 1× to higher factors is the correct way to proceed to extract the maximum information from a specimen (Bradbury and Bracegirdle 1998). The researcher should begin by examining a prepared slide with the unaided eye, or magnification factor of 1×. Assessing the general quality of the thin section, missing tissue in the cross-section, width of the cortex, and signs of diagenesis can help determine the length of time that would be required to read a section and to anticipate areas of the section that will be challenging. At low magnification (e.g., 2×, 4×), the entire specimen can be scanned to evaluate the quality of the section before the requisite objective for quantification (e.g., 10×, 16×, 20×) is employed. The eyes will tire after viewing through the eyepieces and it is necessary to rest the eyes occasionally, even if it is to look up and focus on an object on a wall or elsewhere. Finding a quiet space without disruption for analysis is essential, particularly for the methodologies discussed in earlier chapters where microstructures are manually counted. Sitting on a comfortable chair to accommodate the researcher's sitting height to look into the oculars will affect efficiency.

Objectives, reticles, and other components are expensive and can easily break if dropped or mishandled, and thus, their maintenance is imperative. To change the objectives, the nosepiece should be held and rotated, and not the objectives, bearing in mind that the higher magnification objectives tend to be longer. The nosepiece is slowly rotated to ensure that the objective will clear the specimen and it may be necessary to lower the stage with the coarse adjustment knob before changing the objective. The proper way to carry the microscope, if necessary, is with both hands and supporting it from the base and the arm. When not in use, the microscope should be covered with a plastic cover, and the eyepieces and objectives should always be in place to prevent dust from accumulating inside the machinery. A dust cap may be used if an objective or an eyepiece must be removed for an extended time. Cleaning the lenses or ends of objectives should be carried out with great care since the glass can scratch easily. Lens paper and air blowers used for computer keyboards are appropriate. Academic institutions generally have a contract with a microscopy company or an instrumentation specialist who can routinely clean and check the components for mechanical maintenance. It is more cost effective to coordinate the routine maintenance with another academic department that utilizes microscopes.

Bone histology goes beyond looking at small microstructures. It requires the knowledge of bone's material properties, function, and development as well as microscopy. The researcher/practitioner should spend a significant amount of time reviewing slides before applying quantification techniques. If possible, individual training with an experienced bone histologist is strongly recommended as the training and skill from literature research is insufficient. As with the use of any instrument, familiarity and practice with a microscope is indispensable. If used properly, a microscope can be a powerful tool to obtain many types of quantitative and qualitative data from archaeological and modern bone tissue to estimate age at death, calculate bone remodeling rates, distinguish human from nonhuman animal bone, discern pathologies, and so forth.

# References

Anderson C (1982) Manual for the examination of bone. CRC Press, Boca Raton, FL.

Ascenzi A, Fabry C (1959) Technique for dissection and measurement of refractive index of osteones. J Biophys Biochem Cytol 6:139–142.

Bradbury S, Bracegirdle B (1998) Introduction to light microscopy. Springer-Verlag, New York.

Beauchesne P, Saunders S (2006) A test of the revised Frost's rapid manual method for the preparation of bone thin sections. Int J Osteoarchaeol 16:82–87.

Buesa RJ, Peshkov MV (2009) Histology without xylene. Ann Diagn Pathol 13:246–256.

Croft WJ (2006) Under the microscope: a brief history of microscopy. World Scientific, Hackensack, NJ.

Davidson MW, Florida State University Research Foundation (1995–2009) Museum of microscopy. Molecular expressions: expressing the world of optics and microscopy. http://micro.magnet.fsu.edu/primer/index.html. Accessed 3 November 3, 2009.

Fenton T, Birkby WH, Cornelison J (2003) A fast and safe non-bleaching method for forensic skeletal preparation. J Forensic Sci 48:274–276.

Frost H (1958) Preparation of thin undecalcified bone sections by rapid manual method. Stain Tech 33:273–277.

Houck M, Siegel J (2006) Fundamentals of forensic science. Academic Press, Amsterdam.

Maat GJR, Van Den Bos RPM, Aarents M (2001) Manual preparation of ground sections for the microscopy of natural bone tissue: update and modification of Frost's "rapid manual method." Int J Osteoarchaeol 11:366–374.

Malvern Institution (1997) Sample dispersion and refractive index guide. Malvern Instruments, Inc., Worcestershire, UK.

Murphy DB (2001) Fundamentals of light microscopy and electronic imaging. Wiley-Liss, New York.

Nawrocki S (1997) Cleaning bones. University of Indianapolis Archeology and Forensics Laboratory. http://archlab.uindy.edu. Accessed November 12, 2009.

Paine RR (2007) How to equip a basic histology lab for the anthropological assessment of human bone and teeth. J Anthr Sci 85:213–219.

Ries WL (2003) Techniques for sectioning undecalcified bone tissue using microtomes. In: An YH, Martin KL (eds) Handbook of histology methods for bone and cartilage. Humana Press, Totowa, NJ.

Saferstein R (2007) Criminalistics: an introduction to forensic science, 9th edn. Prentice Hall, Upper Saddle River, NJ.

Slayter EM, Slayter HS (1992) Light and electron microscopy. Cambridge University Press, Cambridge.

Smith RF (1994) Microscopy and photomicrography: a working manual, 2nd edn. CRC Press, Boca Raton, FL.

Tiesler V, Cucina A, Streeter M (2006) Manual de histomorfología en hueso no descalcificado. Universidad Autónoma de Yucatán, Mérida, Mexico.

Wheeler BP, Wilson LJ (2008) Practical forensic microscopy: a laboratory manual. Wiley-Blackwell, West Sussex, England.

# Technological Developments in the Analysis of Cortical Bone Histology

# 15

## The Third Dimension and Its Potential in Anthropology

DAVID M.L. COOPER
C. DAVID L. THOMAS
JOHN G. CLEMENT

## Contents

## 15.1 Introduction

Bone was among the first tissues to be studied with a microscope and research in the area of bone histology remains active to this day. As detailed in the previous chapters of this volume, much has been learned regarding the biology of bone and the application of this knowledge has been used to address a range of anthropologically relevant questions. That said, a common limitation of conventional histological techniques is that they are two-dimensional (2D) in nature. Bone tissue exists in three-dimensions (3D) and dynamically changes (remodels) over time introducing a fourth dimension. Two-dimensional methodologies therefore provide an inherently limited window on the inner workings of bone at the tissue level. For example, the superficially straightforward question of how long is the average secondary osteon in human bone has, in reality, proven very difficult to definitively address (Cooper et al. 2006). Visualization and analysis in 3D hold the potential to improve our understanding of bone biology and to hone related anthropological applications; however, the lack of efficient methodologies for achieving such analysis has represented a considerable hurdle. This chapter reviews the methodological approaches used historically to assess cortical bone histology in 3D and subsequently focuses on new technological developments in the area of high-resolution imaging, which are accelerating research in this area and making 3D histology of cortical bone a feasible and increasingly accessible reality.

## 15.2   Historical Perspectives

Although efficient methodologies for 3D analysis of cortical bone histomorphology have been lacking, 3D methods have not been absent entirely. Indeed, in what is likely the first published description of cortical bone histology, Anthony Van Leeuwenhoeck (1677–1678) included a hand-drawn 3D rendering (Figure 15.1). Van Leeuwenhoeck noted that a network of longitudinal and radial "pipes" permeates compact bone. Soon after, Clopton Havers (1691), the individual from whom the term *Haversian* has been derived, similarly described two types of pores that run parallel and perpendicular to the bone surface (1691/1977). Havers hypothesized that the function of the canal network was to convey medullary oils. While wrong in his interpretation of function, Havers's description of form has stood the test of time. In general, modern descriptions of the arrangement of cortical canals have changed little—essentially consisting of longitudinal (osteonal or Haversian) and transverse (Volkmann's) canals. As will be discussed, 3D methodologies have increasingly revealed a more complex, highly branched structure. Looking beyond the vascular canals, other histological features of bone were described by later pioneers of bone biology. In the mid 1800s, for example, Todd and Bowmann first described Haversian systems (1845) and Tomes and De Morgan (1853) described their formation within localized resorption (Haversian) spaces.

## 15.3   3D Histological Techniques

The early descriptions by Van Leeuwenhoeck and Havers were based upon relatively low-magnification observation of blocks of bone, which provided some appreciation of 3D structure. More detailed 3D assessment has required more sophisticated techniques. In general terms, three approaches have been employed to evaluate bone histology in 3D: (1) staining or casting the cortical canals; (2) serial sectioning/milling; and (3) confocal microscopy.

A variety of staining and casting approaches have been developed for different purposes. Superficial appreciation of the general alignment of cortical canals can be achieved by applying ink to abraded bone surfaces (Hert et al. 1994; Petrtýl et al. 1996). Visualization of canals below the surface requires the removal of the bone tissue after casting, an approach known as corrosion casting (Arsenault 1990), or the "clearing" of the bone tissue to render it transparent after the canals have been stained (Ruth 1947). Clearing techniques have enabled visualization of the overall pattern of vascular canals within bone (Albu and Georgia 1984; Dempster and Enlow 1959; Locke 2004; Ruth 1947), the observation of remodeling-related resorption spaces (Vasciaveo and Bartoli 1961), and comparisons of

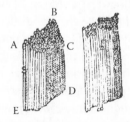

**Figure 15.1**  Van Leeuwenhoeck's rendering of cortical bone structure.

gross differences between the canal networks of different species (Georgia and Albu 1988; Georgia et al. 1982). As already noted, a core limitation of these approaches is that only the vascular canals are visualized and no other structural information is available (e.g., osteon boundaries, lamellae, etc.). An additional limitation is that there is no straightforward means of extracting quantitative 3D structural data and thus the results obtained are largely qualitative in nature.

In order to achieve more detailed 3D assessment of histological features—beyond porosity—serial analysis of 2D sections has been employed. Two of the most extensive applications of serial sectioning to cortical bone histology are the work of Cohen and Harris who traced the paths of secondary osteons in 3D (1958), and that of Tappen who examined the morphology of the resorption spaces, which create the templates for future osteons (1977). This approach was particularly difficult prior to the availability of computer technology and the limited scope of many past studies should be viewed in light of this fact. Three-dimensional reconstructions took the form of physical models, which were created from materials such as wires and cardboard (Amprino 1948; Cohen and Harris 1958; Kragstrup and Melsen 1983).

The use of computers has greatly simplified 3D rendering from serial sections, increasing automation (Odgaard et al. 1990) and enabling such advances as rapid manipulation of virtual models and transparent visualization of the relationship between internal structures (Schnapper et al. 2002). Stout and colleagues employed a combination of serial sectioning and computer rendering to study the 3D morphology of osteons in the dog. They reported a complex structure that is "dominated by branching" (Stout et al. 1999). Further, they revealed that 2D classification of some osteon types reflect artifacts of the plane of sectioning rather than meaningful biological differences. For example, dumbbell-shaped osteons are simply the result of sectioning an osteon near a branching point.

Serial sectioning offers the powerful advantage of potential visualization of all structures visible using light microscopy, including the enhancement of various structures through staining or labeling (Moshin et al. 2002). The most notable disadvantage of serial sectioning is its very tedious nature (DeHoff 1983), a factor that likely accounts for the limited number of studies that have utilized it. Additionally, this approach is highly destructive and not well suited for fragile anthropological specimens. Sequential ground sectioning (Robling and Stout 1999) represents a potential option but much information is lost between sections due to destruction by sawing and grinding.

Serial milling represents a variation on the serial sectioning approach where a series of surface images are captured as material is ground or cut away (Beck et al. 1997). The primary advantage of milling is the high degree of automation that is possible. Further, it can been combined with fluorescent labeling (Kazakia et al. 2007) to enhance visualization of histological features. This has, for example, enabled 3D assessment of microdamage in trabecular bone (Bigley et al. 2008), high-resolution assessment of trabecular bone surface texture (Slyfield et al. 2009), and even assessment of individual resorption cavities on trabeculae (Tkachenko et al. 2009). To our knowledge, this approach has never been applied to assess the 3D structure of cortical bone nor to anthropological bone in general.

Confocal microscopy refers to a collection of techniques that achieve "optical sectioning" of a target through the rejection of scattered and out-of-plane fluorescent light. The end result is a serial image dataset that is well suited for 3D rendering and quantitative analysis (Feng et al. 2007). Fluorescence in bone can be endogenous (Pilolli et al. 2008) or introduced to highlight target structures. A key strength of confocal microscopy is its high resolution, enabling 3D rendering of not only vascular canals and cellular spaces (osteocyte lacunae) but also the minute canaliculi extending between the lacunae (Sugawara et al. 2005). Examples of anthropological applications of this technology to bone include the assessment of hominid cranial bone structure (Bartsiokas 2002), comparison of fluorescence in modern and archaeological bone (Maggiano et al. 2006), and histo-mophometric analysis of archaeological bone (Papageorgopoulou et al. 2009). Confocal methods can be noninvasive, as demonstrated by the visualization of subsurface lacunae in an *Australopithecus afarensis* femur by Bromage and colleagues (2009). The primary draw-back of confocal microscropy is the limited penetration depth, which is generally less than 1 mm (Theer et al. 2003). Indeed, applications in bone frequently have depths on the order of a few tens of microns and are applied to prepared sections. Thus, confocal approaches are not well suited for 3D visualization of the complexity of osteon morphology or the cortical canal network.

In summary, conventional approaches for achieving 3D visualization of cortical bone histology have been applied in a relatively limited number of studies. These have tended to be small in scope and have yielded mostly qualitative information. Advances in automa-tion that have been realized through the use of computers have made 3D analysis more feasible and quantitative in nature; however, these approaches have, in many respects, been superseded by confocal microscopy and, where a greater penetration depth is needed, high-resolution x-ray-based imaging.

## 15.4   Micro-Computed Tomography

Computed tomography (CT) is an x-ray-based technique that generates serial cross-sectional images (tomograms) that can be utilized to noninvasively visualize internal structures in 3D. High resolution or micro-computed tomography (micro-CT) represents an extension of this technology down to the microscopic level. There are two variants of this technology based upon the x-ray source employed. Laboratory or desktop micro-CT systems are built around microfocus x-ray sources and are thus self-contained units. Synchrotron radiation (SR) micro-CT, as the name suggests, employs x-ray radiation created within a synchrotron facility. In the following discussion *micro-CT* will be used to refer to laboratory micro-CT, and *SR micro-CT* will refer to a synchrotron-based system.

### 15.4.1   Laboratory Micro-CT

Laboratory micro-CT was first described as a tool for 3D analysis of bone in 1989 (Feldkamp et al. 1989). From its beginning, the primary application of micro-CT has been the assess-ment of trabecular bone structure, focusing on changes associated with disease states such as osteoporosis (Borah et al. 2001). Just as radiography was rapidly integrated into anthropological inquiry (Lovell 2000), the potential of micro-CT was quickly recognized and this technology has already been employed within numerous anthropological studies. Micro-CT has, for example, been utilized to assess trabecular bone adaptation in nonhu-man primates (Fajardo et al. 2002, 2007; Maga et al. 2006; Ryan and Ketcham 2002a, 2002b, 2005), the ontogeny of trabecular bone morphology in humans (Ryan and Krovitz 2006), directional asymmetry and handedness (Lazenby et al. 2008a, 2008b), and paleopatho-logical assessment (Kuhn et al. 2007; Ruhli et al. 2007). Beyond bone, micro-CT has also seen application in the analysis of teeth (Gantt et al. 2006; McErlain et al. 2004; Olejniczak et al. 2007; Suwa and Kono 2005) and specialized technological developments have also been pursued, such as improved segmentation procedures for fossilized remains (Scherf and Tilgner 2009). The nondestructive nature of micro-CT combined with its capacity for quantitative 3D analysis of structure have been key factors driving its growing use in many areas of bone biology.

While the application of micro-CT to trabecular bone has become commonplace, its use for imaging cortical bone histology has been more limited. Cortical bone represents a greater challenge for micro-CT as the internal structures are much smaller than trabeculae. As such, it has been improvements in scan resolution that has enabled this emerging application for micro-CT. The first application of micro-CT to cortical bone was a study by Wachter and colleagues (2001), which compared percent cortical porosity measured from 2D micro-CT images against corresponding histological sections. Operating with the relatively coarse resolution of 30 microns, they found good agreement between the two techniques. These encouraging results were obtained in highly porous specimens and it is notable that no 3D renderings were presented. The use of higher resolution micro-CT to achieve 3D visualization of cortical porosity in human bone was first reported in 2003 (Cooper et al. 2003). Since that time a growing number of studies have employed micro-CT to visualize cortical canals in the midshaft of the human femur (Basillais et al. 2007; Cooper et al. 2004, 2006, 2007a, 2007b; Jones et al. 2004), femoral neck (Chen et al. 2009), and mandible (Renders et al. 2007).

Consistent visualization of cortical porosity in human bone requires resolutions on the order of 10 microns and higher (Basillais et al. 2007; Cooper et al. 2003, 2004) and even greater resolutions are needed for 3D reconstruction of the smallest vascular canals present (Cooper et al. 2007a; Figure 15.2). As with trabecular bone, a key advantage of micro-CT is the ability to not only visualize but also quantify structure in 3D (see Figure 15.3). Model-independent 3D measures developed for trabecular bone (see Borah et al. 2001 for a review), such as mean trabecular thickness and trabecular separation, can be directly transferred to the cortical canal network to assess parameters such as mean canal diameter and canal separation. Additional parameters related to the 3D connectivity and orientation of the canal network can also be readily extracted (Cooper et al. 2003).

The most significant limitation of laboratory micro-CT has been its inability to detect histological features beyond the porous canals (Cooper et al. 2004; Figure 15.2). Fine

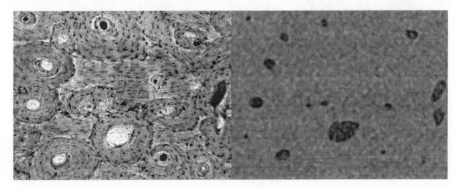

**Figure 15.2** Comparison between a micro-CT cross-sectional image acquired with a 3 micron nominal resolution (right) and a corresponding 100 micron thick ground section (left) of human mid-femur. No structural details beyond porosity are evident in the micro-CT image. (Each image is 1 mm wide.)

structures such as cement lines and lamellae are too small to be directly detected with 5–10 micron-scale resolutions and there is generally insufficient image contrast to accurately discern osteonal borders by density. Only in cases where newly formed bone has recently mineralized is there even diffuse evidence of osteonal dimensions from micro-CT (compare Figures 15.2 and 15.4). This limitation impedes conventional analysis of remodeling-related parameters such as osteon population density and osteon dimensions. That said, resorption spaces and canals are integral components of the remodeling process and the

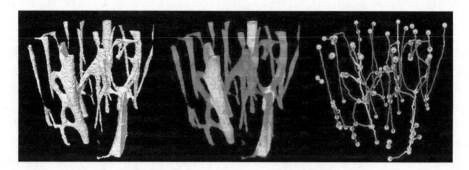

**Figure 15.3 (See color insert.)** Three-dimensional rendering of cortical canals within a 1 mm³ block of mid femoral cortical bone (left); color-mapped 3D canal diameter with lighter colors denoting larger canals (middle); skeletonized canal structure with canal endpoints and branches highlighted (right). Nominal scan resolution of 3 microns.

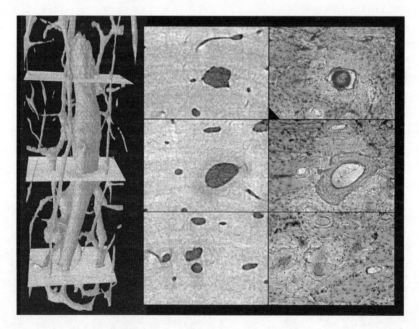

**Figure 15.4** Three-dimensional rendering of a remodeling event (newly forming osteon) active at the time of death within a human femoral sample (left). Corresponding 2D micro-CT images (middle) and ground histological sections (right) matching the planes superimposed on the 3D rendering. The osteoclastic cutting cone is advancing toward the top of the image and evidence of a closing cone is seen in the middle set of images where new lamellae of bone are evident in the ground section and some diffuse evidence of reduced density (darker gray) is evident in the micro-CT image. Each 2D image is approximately 0.7 mm wide. Nominal scan resolution of 1.4 microns.

osteons it produces. As such, remodeling progressively alters the canal network and 3D analysis of canals provides a window, albeit limited, into the 3D nature of osteons themselves. For example, new osteons are superimposed on the existing cortical structures and thus remodeling increases the complexity of the canal network with respect to the number of branching points (Cooper et al. 2007b). Another window into the remodeling process provided by micro-CT is the direct visualization of the resorption spaces associated with the basic multicellular units (BMUs; Cooper et al. 2006), which create new secondary osteons (Figure 15.4).

Consistent detection of secondary osteons themselves and other detailed features (e.g., lamellae) have thus far eluded laboratory micro-CT. The use of more advanced x-ray sources, such as synchrotron facilities, are beginning to yield amazing images that are further bridging the gap between conventional histology and imaging for a number of tissues.

## 15.4.2 Synchrotron Micro-CT

A synchrotron is a specialized form of particle accelerator that generates light (radiation) spanning the spectrum from infrared to x-rays. This radiation is generated when the path of electrons traveling near the speed of light is altered by magnetic fields. The advantage of using synchrotron radiation for micro-CT is the brilliance of the radiation, which is orders of magnitude greater than conventional x-ray sources. This improves image quality, reduces scan time, enables higher resolution, and facilitates the use of monochromatic (single energy) x-rays (Peyrin 2009). As with laboratory micro-CT, SR micro-CT has been more extensively applied to trabecular bone; however, the higher resolution of these systems has opened the door to a range of analytical possibilities spanning the various hierarchical levels of bone structure from macro to nano (Muller 2009; Peyrin 2009). Indeed, submicron imaging, or nano-CT, is possible. The cortical canal network in human (Bousson et al. 2004), rat (Matsumoto et al. 2006, 2007), and even mouse (Schneider et al. 2007, 2009) bone can been assessed with SR micro-CT. Operating with resolutions on the order of 1–2 microns, the mouse studies just noted were able to assess the distribution of osteocyte lacunae, and similar resolution has revealed these same structures in human bone (Peyrin et al. 1998; Hannah et al. 2010; see also Figures 15.5 and 15.6). The improved image quality of SR micro-CT has also resulted in some limited success in 2D segmentation of low-contrast features of cortical bone such as individual osteons (Peter et al. 2007).

Beyond advances associated with improvements in x-ray absorption (attenuation) contrast imaging (the conventional form of contrast used in most x-ray based imaging), SR micro-CT is capable of using the interaction (refraction) of x-rays within a target sample as a means of generating edge-enhancing contrast known as phase contrast (Betz et al. 2007; Meuli et al. 2004; Rustichelli et al. 2004). Phase contrast is particularly powerful for imaging soft tissues such as cartilage (Zehbe et al. 2009) and these techniques are even enabling improved visualization of fossils encased in amber, where nonmineralized tissues can survive (Sutton 2008). Phase contrast can, however, also be employed to improve visualization of structures within mineralized tissues such as bone and teeth. One of the most dramatic examples of this has been the noninvasive visualization of Striae of Retzius within an australopithecine tooth conducted by Tafforeau and Smith (2008). Visualization of these structures, which are of comparable scale to features in bone such as cement lines and individual lamellae, suggests that 3D analysis of osteons is indeed possible using SR micro-CT. Our own preliminary investigations support this very conclusion (Figure 15.5),

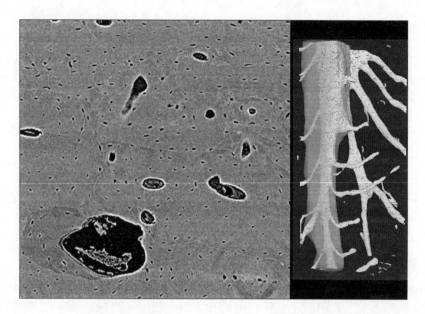

**Figure 15.5 (See color insert.)** SR micro-CT cross-sectional image (left) of cortical bone from the human femoral midshaft acquired with 1.4 micron nominal resolution and averaged through approximately 10 microns (seven slices). Phase contrast (white "halos") enhances the edges of the canals, lacunae, some cement lines, and even enables visualization of soft tissue within the resorption space (bottom left). Three-dimensional rendering (right) of the region within the bottom half of the image depicts the newly forming osteon in transparency over the opaque canals. Data collected at the 2BM beamline of the Advanced Photon Source synchrotron. (The images on the left is of a block 0.72 mm square.)

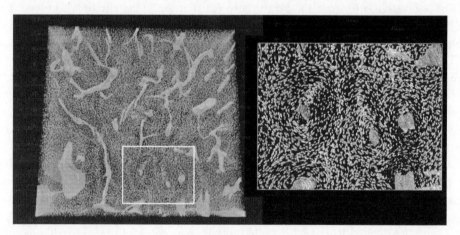

**Figure 15.6** SR micro-CT based 3D rendering of cortical canals and osteocyte lacunae within a human femoral midshaft specimen (region demarcated by white rectangle is magnified on the right) scanned at 1.4 μm nominal resolution. Data collected at the 2BM beamline of the Advanced Photon Source synchrotron.

yielding improved delineation of osteon borders and even simultaneous visualization of soft tissue within cortical canals. The limitations of SR micro-CT include access (e.g., there are a limited number of synchrotron facilities in the world) and the small field of view (e.g., a few millimeters) associated with the highest imaging resolutions.

## 15.5    Anthropological Potentials

Following soon after the discovery of x-rays, anthropologists recognized the potential of imaging and integrated this tool into various lines of inquiry. The application of computed tomography and its increasingly high-resolution permutations represents a continuation of this trend. The development of nondestructive 3D cortical bone histology represents an exciting new step in this progression with wide-ranging potential. Looking over the chapters within this volume, one could envision an impact in each of the topics covered. On the most basic level, the ability to achieve comparable 2D analysis of cortical bone histology nondestructively would represent a profound advance. Beyond this, 3D analysis of remodeling-related change promises to expand our understanding of bone biology in the present, generating novel insights into the past. The same can be said of dental biology, and, as already discussed, some of the most dramatic advances achieved in synchrotron imaging have been in the area of anthropological dental imaging. Our understanding of the growth, development, and aging of the skeleton will be refined and, in turn, applied analytical techniques will be improved. Age estimation, for example, is an area where 3D analysis of the cortical canal network has already demonstrated some potential (Cooper 2005). Functional interpretation may be improved through 3D analysis. Osteon orientation, for example, is believed to reflect predominant loads (Hert et al. 1994; Petrtýl et al. 1996) and thus 3D analysis of canal orientation (Renders et al. 2007) may ultimately improve our interpretation of function from skeletal remains. Similarly, analysis of the scale and arrangement of the cortical canal network may prove useful for identification of different taxa.

A key area for further exploration is paleopathology. The study of bone loss in the past will be enhanced through the capacity to directly visualize the porosity within cortical bone. This will enable direct and meaningful comparisons between past populations and modern reference samples. Low-resolution clinical densitometry techniques, such as dual energy x-ray absorptiometry (DXA), cannot differentiate between biologically induced changes in density versus diagenetic alterations. For example, while photon absorptiometry (a precursor to DXA) was applied to archaeological remains (Perzigian 1973), Stout and Simmons (1979) cautioned that without correlative microscopic evidence it is unclear whether bone density detected with this method reflects preservation rather than biologically related processes such as aging and disease. Kneissel and colleagues (1994) examined bone loss in an archaeological population using a collection of techniques and found that histological techniques (light microscopy and scanning electron microscopy) yielded better correlation between results than those from DXA. These differences were attributed to diagenetic changes, which were apparent in the electron microscopy images. Ultimately, they concluded that DXA should not be applied to the analysis of archaeological bone (Kneissel et al. 1994). Despite such findings, the application of densitometric techniques to archaeological samples has continued, operating under the assumption that diagenetic change is relatively equal across specimens (Ekenman et al. 1995; Gonzalez-Reimers et al. 2002; Lynnerup and Von Wovern 1997) or that diagenesis has an insignificant impact on the *patterns* of bone density found either within or between populations (McEwan et al. 2004; Poulsen et al. 2001; Turner-Walker et al. 2001). The ability to directly assess cortical bone porosity represents a significant advance that effectively eliminates concerns about diffuse diagenetic density changes. Provided the porous and solid phases of bone tissue can be differentiated, the degree of change in mineral concentration is irrelevant.

Only physical destruction of cortical microstructure would preclude micro-CT analysis (in addition to all other forms of microscopic investigation). Notably, the preservation of cortical canals, despite extensive diagenetic alteration, was the impetus for the age estimation method developed by Samson and Branigan (1987). Being nondestructive, micro-CT analysis will preserve samples for subsequent testing such as stable isotope analysis, DNA extraction, and radiocarbon dating. In the case of the most important of specimens, the nondestructive nature of micro-CT ensures valuable insight can be obtained while preserving materials for future study.

## 15.6   Conclusions

The early pioneers of bone histology first detected the porosity within cortical bone and more detailed appreciation of the complex morphology of osteons surrounding the canal network came later. The development of noninvasive x-ray-based imaging techniques has progressed along a similar path. Laboratory micro-CT has quickly been established as a validated, efficient, and increasingly accessible means of achieving 3D analysis of human cortical bone porosity. The detection of additional histological features—including osteons themselves—is just beginning to be realized through the use of synchrotron-based micro-CT systems. Three-dimensional perspectives are revealing a more complex and varied structure within cortical bone, which will undoubtedly lead to advances in our understating of bone's dynamic biology. The potential to integrate these established and emerging methodologies into the study of bone and specifically into anthropological inquiry is tremendous.

## Acknowledgments

We thank Professor Stephen Cordner, director of the Victorian Institute of Forensic Medicine, and the staff of the mortuary and the Donor Tissue Bank for their assistance in the collection of the bone specimens used in the SR micro-CT images and many of the micro-CT studies cited. We are also particularly grateful to the next-of-kin of the donors for permission to remove bone for research purposes. The authors additionally acknowledge the Australian Synchrotron Research Program, which is funded by the Commonwealth of Australia under the Major National Research Facilities Program. Use of the Advanced Photon Source was supported by the U.S. Department of Energy, Basic Energy Sciences, Office of Science under Contract No. W-31-109-Eng-38. Data was collected at the APS with the help of Dr. Andrew Peele, LaTrobe University, his student Mr. Kevin Hannah, and the beamline scientist for 2BM Dr. Francesco DeCarlo whose assistance is gratefully acknowledged. Finally, thanks also go to Bree Erickson for her hard work generating many of the figures for this chapter.

## References

Albu I, Georgia R (1984) Some aspects of the system of Haversian canals in the diaphysary compact bone in man. Morphol Embryol (Bucur) 30(1):17–20.

Amprino R (1948) A contribution to the functional meaning of the substitution of primary by secondary bone tissue. Acta Anat 5:291–300.

Arsenault AL (1990) Vascular canals in bovine cortical bone studied by corrosion casting. Calcif Tissue Int 47:320–325.

Bartsiokas A (2002) Hominid cranial bone structure: a histological study of Omo 1 specimens from Ethiopia using different microscopic techniques. Anat Rec 267(1):52–59.

Basillais A, Bensamoun S, Chappard C et al (2007) Three-dimensional characterization of cortical bone microstructure by microcomputed tomography: validation with ultrasonic and microscopic measurements. J Orthop Sci 12(2):141–148.

Beck JD, Canfield BL, Haddock SM et al. (1997) Three-dimensional imaging of trabecular bone using the computer numerically controlled milling technique. Bone 21(3):281–287.

Betz O, Wegst U, Weide D et al. (2007) Imaging applications of synchrotron X-ray phase-contrast microtomography in biological morphology and biomaterials science. I. General aspects of the technique and its advantages in the analysis of millimetre-sized arthropod structure. J Microsc 227(Pt 1):51–71.

Bigley RF, Singh M, Hernandez CJ et al (2008) Validity of serial milling-based imaging system for microdamage quantification. Bone 42(1):212–215.

Borah B, Gross GJ, Dufresne TE et al. (2001) Three-dimensional microimaging (MRmicroI and microCT), finite element modeling, and rapid prototyping provide unique insights into bone architecture in osteoporosis. Anat Rec 265(2):101–110.

Bousson V, Peyrin F, Bergot C et al. (2004) Cortical bone in the human femoral neck: three-dimensional appearance and porosity using synchrotron radiation. J Bone Miner Res 19(5):794–801.

Bromage TG, Goldman HM, McFarlin SC et al (2009) Confocal scanning optical microscopy of a 3-million-year-old Australopithecus afarensis femur. Scanning 31(1):1–10.

Chen H, Zhou X, Shoumura S et al. (2009) Age- and gender-dependent changes in three-dimensional microstructure of cortical and trabecular bone at the human femoral neck. Osteoporos Int 21(4):627–636.

Cohen J, Harris W (1958) The three-dimensional anatomy of Haversian systems. J Bone Joint Surg Am 40A(2):419–434.

Cooper D, Turinsky A, Sensen C et al. (2007a) Effect of voxel size on 3D micro-CT analysis of cortical bone porosity. Calcif Tissue Int 80(3):211–219.

Cooper DM, Matyas JR, Katzenberg MA et al. (2004) Comparison of microcomputed tomographic and microradiographic measurements of cortical bone porosity. Calcif Tissue Int 74(5):437–447.

Cooper DM, Thomas CD, Clement JG et al (2006) Three-dimensional microcomputed tomography imaging of basic multicellular unit-related resorption spaces in human cortical bone. Anat Rec A Discov Mol Cell Evol Biol 288(7):806–816.

Cooper DM, Thomas CD, Clement JG et al. (2007b) Age-dependent change in the 3D structure of cortical porosity at the human femoral midshaft. Bone 40(4):957–965.

Cooper DM, Turinsky AL, Sensen CW et al. (2003) Quantitative 3D analysis of the canal network in cortical bone by micro-computed tomography. Anat Rec B New Anat 274(1):169–179.

Cooper DML (2005) 3D micro-ct imaging of human cortical bone porosity: a novel method for estimating age at death. PhD thesis. University of Calgary, Canada.

DeHoff RT (1983) Quantitative Serial Sectioning analysis: preview. J Microsc 131(3):259–263

Dempster WT, Enlow DH (1959) Patterns of vascular channels in the cortex of the human mandible. Anat Rec 135(3):189–205.

Ekenman I, Eriksson SA, Lindgren JU (1995) Bone density in medieval skeletons. Calcif Tissue Int 56(5):355–358.

Fajardo RJ, Muller R, Ketcham RA et al. (2007) Nonhuman anthropoid primate femoral neck trabecular architecture and its relationship to locomotor mode. Anat Rec (Hoboken) 290(4):422–436.

Fajardo RJ, Ryan TM, Kappelman J (2002) Assessing the accuracy of high-resolution X-ray computed tomography of primate trabecular bone by comparisons with histological sections. Am J Phys Anthropol 118(1):1–10.

Feldkamp LA, Goldstein SA, Parfitt AM et al. (1989) The direct examination of three-dimensional bone architecture in vitro by computed tomography. J Bone Miner Res 4(1):3–11.

Feng D, Marshburn D, Jen D et al. (2007) Stepping into the third dimension. J Neurosci 27(47):12757–12760.

Gantt DG, Kappleman J, Ketcham RA et al. (2006) Three-dimensional reconstruction of enamel thickness and volume in humans and hominoids. Eur J Oral Sci 114 Suppl 1:360–364; discussion 375–366, 382–363.

Georgia R, Albu I (1988) The Haversian canal network in the femoral compact bone in some vertebrates. Morphol Embryol (Bucur) 34(3):155–159.

Georgia R, Albu I, Sicoe M et al. (1982) Comparative aspects of the density and diameter of Haversian canals in the diaphyseal compact bone of man and dog. Morphol Embryol (Bucur) 28(1):11–14.

Gonzalez-Reimers E, Velasco-Vazquez J, Arnay-de-la-Rosa M et al. (2002) Double-energy X-ray absorptiometry in the diagnosis of osteopenia in ancient skeletal remains. Am J Phys Anthropol 118(2):134–145.

Hannah KM, Thomas CDL, Clement JG et al. (2010) Bimodal distribution of osteocyte lacunar size in the human femoral cortex as revealed by micro-CT. Bone 47:866–871.

Havers C (1691/1977) Osteologia nova, or, Some new observations of the bones and the parts belonging to them, with the manner of their accretion, and nutrition, communicated to the Royal Society in several discourses. University Microfilms International, Ann Arbor, MI.

Hert J, Fiala P, Petrtýl M (1994) Osteon orientation of the diaphysis of the long bones in man. Bone 15(3):269–277.

Jones AC, Milthorpe B, Averdunk H et al. (2004) Analysis of 3D bone ingrowth into polymer scaffolds via micro-computed tomography imaging. Biomaterials 25(20):4947–4954.

Kazakia GJ, Lee JJ, Singh M et al. (2007) Automated high-resolution three-dimensional fluorescence imaging of large biological specimens. J Microsc 225(Pt 2):109–117.

Kneissel M, Boyde A, Hahn M et al. (1994) Age- and sex-dependent cancellous bone changes in a 4000y BP population. Bone 15(5):539–545.

Kragstrup J, Melsen F (1983) Three-dimensional morphology of trabecular bone osteons reconstructed from serial sections. Metab Bone Dis Relat Res 5(3):127–130.

Kuhn G, Schultz M, Muller R et al. (2007) Diagnostic value of micro-CT in comparison with histology in the qualitative assessment of historical human postcranial bone pathologies. Homo 58(2):97–115.

Lazenby RA, Angus S, Cooper DM et al. (2008a) A three-dimensional microcomputed tomographic study of site-specific variation in trabecular microarchitecture in the human second metacarpal. J Anat 213(6):698–705.

Lazenby RA, Cooper DM, Angus S et al (2008b) Articular constraint, handedness, and directional asymmetry in the human second metacarpal. J Hum Evol 54(6):875–885.

Leeuwenhoeck A (1677–1678) Microscopical observations of the structure of teeth and other bones: made and communicated, in a letter by Mr. Anthony Leeuwenhoeck. Philos Trans R Soc Lond, B, Biol Sci 12:1002–1003.

Locke M (2004) Structure of long bones in mammals. J Morphol 262(2):546–565.

Lovell NC (2000) Paleopathological description and diagnosis. In: Katzenberg MA, Saunders SR (eds) Biological anthropology of the human skeleton. Willey-Liss, Toronto.

Lynnerup N, Von Wovern N (1997) Mineral content in medieval Greenland Norse. Int J Osteoarchaeol 7:235–240.

Maga M, Kappelman J, Ryan TM et al. (2006) Preliminary observations on the calcaneal trabecular microarchitecture of extant large-bodied hominoids. Am J Phys Anthropol 129(3):410–417.

Maggiano C, Dupras T, Schultz M et al. (2006) Spectral and photobleaching analysis using confocal laser scanning microscopy: a comparison of modern and archaeological bone fluorescence. Mol Cell Probes 20(3–4):154–162.

Matsumoto T, Yoshino M, Asano T et al. (2006) Monochromatic synchrotron radiation muCT reveals disuse-mediated canal network rarefaction in cortical bone of growing rat tibiae. J Appl Physiol 100(1):274–280.

Matsumoto T, Yoshino M, Uesugi K et al. (2007) Biphasic change and disuse-mediated regression of canal network structure in cortical bone of growing rats. Bone 41(2):239–246.

McErlain DD, Chhem RK, Bohay RN et al. (2004) Micro-computed tomography of a 500-year-old tooth: technical note. Can Assoc Radiol J 55(4):242–245.

McEwan JM, Mays S, Blake GM (2004) Measurements of bone mineral density of the radius in a medieval population. Calcif Tissue Int 74(2):157–161.

Meuli R, Hwu Y, Je JH et al. (2004) Synchrotron radiation in radiology: radiology techniques based on synchrotron sources. Eur Radiol 14(9):1550–1560.

Moshin S, Taylor D, Lee TC (2002) Three-dimensional reconstruction of Haversian systems in ovine compact bone. Eur J Morphol 40(5):309–315.

Muller R (2009) Hierarchical microimaging of bone structure and function. Nat Rev Rheumatol 5(7):373–381.

Odgaard A, Andersen K, Melsen F et al. (1990) A direct method for fast three-dimensional serial reconstruction. J Microsc 159(3):335–342.

Olejniczak AJ, Tafforeau P, Smith TM et al. (2007) Technical note: compatibility of microtomographic imaging systems for dental measurements. Am J Phys Anthropol 134(1):130–134.

Papageorgopoulou C, Kuhn G, Ziegler U et al. (2009) Diagnostic morphometric applicability of confocal laser scanning microscopy in osteoarchaeology. Int J Osteoarchaeol, Epublished.

Perzigian AJ (1973) The antiquity of age-associated bone demineralization in man. J Am Geriatr Soc 21(3):100–105.

Peter Z, Bousson V, Bergot C et al. (2007) Segmentation of low contrast features in bone micro-CT images by a constrained region growing approach based on watershed. Proceedings of the 4th IEEE Symposium on Biomedical Imaging: From Nano to Macro. ISBI. pp. 968–971.

Petrtýl M, Hert J, Fiala P (1996) Spatial organization of the Haversian bone in man. J Biomech 29(2):161–169.

Peyrin F (2009) Investigation of bone with synchrotron radiation imaging: from micro to nano. Osteoporos Int 20(6):1057–1063.

Peyrin F, Salome M, Cloetens P et al. (1998) Micro-CT examinations of trabecular bone samples at different resolutions: 14, 7 and 2 micron level. Technol Health Care 6(5–6):391–401.

Pilolli GP, Lucchese A, Maiorano E et al. (2008) New approach for static bone histomorphometry: confocal laser scanning microscopy of maxillo-facial normal bone. Ultrastruct Pathol 32(5):189–192.

Poulsen LW, Qvesel D, Brixen K et al. (2001) Low bone mineral density in the femoral neck of medieval women: a result of multiparity? Bone 28(4):454–458.

Renders GA, Mulder L, van Ruijven LJ et al. (2007) Porosity of human mandibular condylar bone. J Anat 210(3):239–248.

Robling AG, Stout SD (1999) Morphology of the drifting osteon. Cells Tissues Organs 164(4):192–204.

Ruhli FJ, Kuhn G, Evison R et al. (2007) Diagnostic value of micro-CT in comparison with histology in the qualitative assessment of historical human skull bone pathologies. Am J Phys Anthropol 133(4):1099–1111.

Rustichelli F, Romanzetti S, Dubini B et al. (2004) Phase-contrast microtomography of thin biomaterials. J Mater Sci Mater Med 15(9):1053–1057.

Ruth EB (1947) Gross demonstration of the vascular channels in bone. Anat Rec 98:59–66.

Ryan TM, Ketcham RA (2002a) Femoral head trabecular bone structure in two omomyid primates. J Hum Evol 43(2):241–263.

Ryan TM, Ketcham RA (2002b) The three-dimensional structure of trabecular bone in the femoral head of strepsirrhine primates. J Hum Evol 43(1):1–26.

Ryan TM, Ketcham RA (2005) Angular orientation of trabecular bone in the femoral head and its relationship to hip joint loads in leaping primates. J Morphol 265(3):249–263.

Ryan TM, Krovitz GE (2006) Trabecular bone ontogeny in the human proximal femur. J Hum Evol 51(6):591–602.

Samson C, Branigan K (1987) A new method of estimating age at death from fragmentary and weathered bone. In: Boddington A, Garland AN, Janaway RC (eds) Death, decay and reconstruction approaches to archaeology and forensic science. Manchester University Press, Manchester.

Scherf H, Tilgner R (2009) A new high-resolution computed tomography (CT) segmentation method for trabecular bone architectural analysis. Am J Phys Anthropol 140(1):39–51.

Schnapper A, Reumann K, Meyer W (2002) The architecture of growing compact bone in the dog: visualization by 3D-reconstruction of histological sections. Ann Anat 184:229–233.

Schneider P, Krucker T, Meyer E et al. (2009) Simultaneous 3D visualization and quantification of murine bone and bone vasculature using micro-computed tomography and vascular replica. Microsc Res Tech 72(9):690–701.

Schneider P, Stauber M, Voide R et al. (2007) Ultrastructural properties in cortical bone vary greatly in two inbred strains of mice as assessed by synchrotron light based micro- and nano-CT. J Bone Miner Res 22(10):1557–1570.

Slyfield CR, Jr., Niemeyer KE, Tkachenko EV et al. (2009) Three-dimensional surface texture visualization of bone tissue through epifluorescence-based serial block face imaging. J Microsc 236(1):52–59.

Stout SD, and Simmons, DJ (1979) Use of histology in ancient bone research. Yearbook of Physical Anthropology 22:228–249.

Stout SD, Brunsden BS, Hildebolt CF et al. (1999) Computer-assisted 3D reconstruction of serial sections of cortical bone to determine the 3D structure of osteons. Calcif Tissue Int 65(4):280–284.

Sugawara Y, Kamioka H, Honjo T et al. (2005) Three-dimensional reconstruction of chick calvarial osteocytes and their cell processes using confocal microscopy. Bone 36(5):877–883.

Sutton MD (2008) Tomographic techniques for the study of exceptionally preserved fossils. Proc Biol Sci 275(1643):1587–1593.

Suwa G, Kono RT (2005) A micro-CT based study of linear enamel thickness in the mesial cusp section of human molars: reevaluation of methodology and assessment of within-tooth, serial, and individual variation. Anthropolog Sci 113:273–289.

Tafforeau P, Smith TM (2008) Nondestructive imaging of hominoid dental microstructure using phase contrast X-ray synchrotron microtomography. J Hum Evol 54(2):272–278.

Tappen NC (1977) Three-dimensional studies of resorption spaces and developing osteons. Am J Anat 149:301–332.

Theer P, Hasan MT, Denk W (2003) Two-photon imaging to a depth of 1000 micron in living brains by use of a Ti:Al2O3 regenerative amplifier. Opt Lett 28(12):1022–1024.

Tkachenko EV, Slyfield CR, Tomlinson RE et al. (2009) Voxel size and measures of individual resorption cavities in three-dimensional images of cancellous bone. Bone 45(3):487–492.

Todd RB, Bowmann W (1845) The Physiological Anatomy and Physiology of Man. Blanchard and Lea, Philadelphia.

Tomes J, de Morgan C (1853) Observations on the structure and development of bone. Philos Trans R Soc Lond, B, Biol Sci 143:109–139.

Turner-Walker G, Syversen U, Mays S (2001) The archaeology of osteoporosis. Eur J Archaeol 4(2):263–269.

Vasciaveo F, Bartoli E (1961) Vascular channels and resorption cavities in the long bone cortex the bovine bone. Acta Anat 47:1–33.

Wachter NJ, Augat P, Krischak GD et al. (2001) Prediction of cortical bone porosity in vitro by microcomputed tomography. Calcif Tissue Int 68(1):38–42.

Zehbe R, Haibel A, Riesemeier H et al. (2009) Going beyond histology. Synchrotron micro-computed tomography as a methodology for biological tissue characterization: from tissue morphology to individual cells. J R Soc Interface. doi: 10.1098/rsif.2008.0539.

# Index